A 7

W9-BML-430

AMERICAN EPOCH
A History of the
UNITED STATES
Since 1900

VOLUME I

AMERICAN EPOCH

Volume I: An Era of Economic Change, Reform,
and World Wars 1900–1945
Volume II: An Era of Total War and
Uncertain Peace 1938–1980

AMERICAN EPOCH

A History of the

UNITED STATES

Since 1900

Volume I: An Era of Economic Change,
Reform, and World Wars   1900–1945

Arthur S. Link

George Henry Davis '86 Professor of American History and
Editor and Director of The Papers of Woodrow Wilson
Princeton University

William B. Catton

Professor Emeritus and Historian in Residence
Middlebury College

Fifth Edition

Alfred A. Knopf • New York

To David Wayne Hirst,
Friend and Colleague

THIS IS A BORZOI BOOK
PUBLISHED BY ALFRED A. KNOPF, INC.

Fifth Edition
987654321

All inquiries should be addressed to Alfred A. Knopf, Inc., 201 East 50th Street,
New York, N.Y. 10022.

Published in the United States by Alfred Knopf, Inc., New York, and
simultaneously in Canada by Random House of Canada Limited, Toronto.
Distributed by Random House, Inc., New York.

Library of Congress Cataloging in Publication Data
Link, Arthur Stanley.
An era of economic change, reform, and world wars, 1900-1945
(Their American epoch, a history of the United States since 1900; v. 1)
Includes bibliography and index.
1. United States—History—1901-1953. I. Catton,
William Bruce, 1926- joint author. II. Title.
E741.L56 1980 vol. 1 973.9s [973.91]
ISBN 0-394-38357-2 (Random House) 80-12331

Book design by Lorraine Hohman
Cover design by Sol Schurman
Maps and charts by Theodore R. Miller

Manufactured in the United States of America

Published 1955; Second Edition 1963; Third Edition 1967; Fourth Edition 1973;
Fifth Edition 1980

Preface

The decision of the editors at Alfred A. Knopf to reset this fifth edition of *American Epoch* and publish it in a new format gave us an opportunity to review the fourth edition. The result is, we think, no routine revision. We have scrutinized the existing text in order to bring it into accord with the most recent interpretations and research. We have also updated the bibliography to mid-1979. The major revisions and additions, of course, involve events of the 1970s. Even though we are still close to these events, it is possible, on account of the available amount of documentary materials and relevant secondary works, to see them in something like historical perspective. Persons may well differ over details of the Vietnam war, but surely the present consensus concerning our involvement in that tragic conflict is not likely to change. We think that the lessons of the Watergate affair and the crisis of the presidency that culminated in Richard Nixon's resignation are also clear.

As we write this Preface, the American people are involved in an energy crisis, and they confront decisions that will affect their future for generations to come. We are not pessimistic about the future, although our conclusions and predictions about the merits of present policies must necessarily be tentative. *American Epoch* is fundamentally the story of a people who, for all their faults and mistakes, have faced dire problems of war, domestic conflict, and depression—and have overcome them. We are confident that after a difficult period of adjustment and reappraisal the nation will also come to satisfactory terms with the dire problems of today.

We are pleased to present this book anew and to note that it has now reached its twenty-fifth anniversary. We hope that it will prove as instructive to students in the future as it has been in the past.

We are grateful to David Follmer, Executive Editor of the College Department of Random House/Alfred A. Knopf, for his constant support and encouragement; to John Sturman of the College Department for seeing this volume through to publication; and to Lawrence Haas, a graduate student at Princeton University, for his help in updating the bibliography. The dedication is an attempt to express some small measure of our appreciation for a friendship and a professional association that has greatly enriched both of our lives for over a quarter of a century.

ARTHUR S. LINK
WILLIAM B. CATTON

Princeton, New Jersey
Middlebury, Vermont
October 23, 1979

Contents

Maps

Charts

AN ERA OF ECONOMIC CHANGE, REFORM, AND WORLD WARS 1900–1945

In which the American people experience both the benefits and the disadvantages of rapid industrial growth, attempt substantial political and economic reform, and contribute decisively to Allied victory in two world wars.

1

The American People

During

the Progressive Era

The years from 1900 to 1920 were a golden period of American development. They were usually prosperous years, marked by solid progress in living standards for all classes. They were, moreover, hopeful years. Americans, confident that they had the ability to set aright the social and economic injustices inherited from the nineteenth century, launched a virtual crusade on all levels of government to revitalize democracy, bring economic institutions under public control, and find an answer to the twin evils of special privilege and poverty.

The progressive generation was, finally, a period when Christian moralism subdued the crass materialism of the Gilded Age, and morality and righteousness became the keynotes of politics.[1] The YMCA movement swept through colleges and universities, and social Christianity triumphed over Calvinism, as man's first duty became love of man instead of God. Drunkenness, prostitution, the exploitation of women and children, stock watering—these and other evils were bound to fall before the reformer's

---

[1] For a general definition of progressivism and a description of the various progressive movements, see pp. 52-54.

3

trumpet blast. It did not even seem rash during this heady season to think that Americans, by participating in a world war and reconstruction, might help to usher in a new age of democracy, peace, and progress everywhere.

1. *The American People, 1900-1920: A Demographic View*

From 1900 to 1920 the population of the United States increased nearly 40 percent, from 75,994,575 to 105,710,620. Although 70 percent of the people still lived east of the Mississippi River in 1920, the most spectacular growth had occurred in the West. The Pacific states, for example, more than doubled in numbers over the two decades, as contrasted with a growth of 43 percent among the Middle Atlantic states.

The most striking trend in American population from 1900 to 1920 was the steadily increasing migration of people from the countryside to cities. Urban population grew nearly 80 percent, a rate of increase six and a half times that of the rural areas. More than 40 percent of the people lived in towns and cities over 2,500 in 1900. The percentage of town and city dwellers was 51.4 two decades later; if we include persons in towns under 2,500, the percentage of urban population in 1920 was actually 60. As cities grew larger they began to acquire a different character, more and more becoming centers of commerce and industry, where people from outlying areas went to work and then returned to suburban homes. This trend was evidenced in the 26.5 percent growth between 1910 and 1920 of the so-called metropolitan districts, that is, cities of 200,000 or over with a number of outlying suburbs. By 1920 there were thirty-two such metropolitan districts in which 30,188,543 people, or more than 28 percent of the total population, resided.

Most Americans—88 percent, to be exact—were white in 1920. There were over 400,000 Indians and Orientals and 10,463,131 Negroes in the United States, but blacks were a smaller proportion of the population in 1920 than they had been in 1900. Most Americans in 1920 were also native-born. But the numbers of the foreign-born had increased, under the impact of the tremendous immigration of the past two decades, from 10,341,276, or 13.6 percent of the total population in 1900, to 13,920,692, or 13.2 percent of the total in 1920. Nearly 83 percent of the foreign-born lived either in the North or Middle West, but 85 percent of the Negroes lived in the South, with the highest concentration in South Carolina, Georgia, Florida, Alabama, Mississippi, and Louisiana.

As medical knowledge expanded through experience and research, Americans grew healthier every year during this period. Indeed, the progress of medicine was spectacular in overcoming the ancient ravagers of

POPULATION CHANGE, 1900–1920

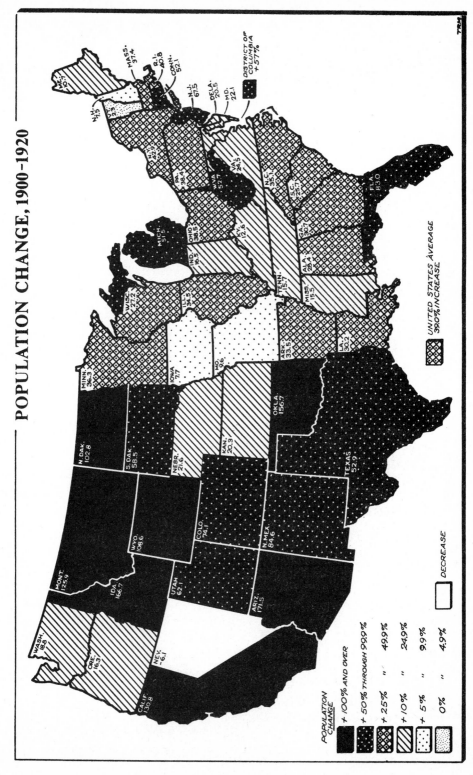

MASS. 37.4
R.I. 40.8
CONN. 52.1
ME. 10.7
N.J. 67.5
DELA. 20.5
MD. 22.1
DISTRICT OF COLUMBIA + 57%
N.H. 7.5
VT. 2.3
PA. 28.4
W.VA. 52.7
VA. 24.5
N.C. 35.1
S.C. 25.7
FLA. 83.0
MICH. 51.5
OHIO 38.5
IND. 16.5
KY. 12.6
GA. 30.7
ALA. 22.4
WIS. 27.5
TENN. 15.7
MISS. 15.5
LA. 30.2
MINN. 36.3
IOWA 7.7
MO. 9.6
ARK. 33.5
OKLA. 156.7
N.DAK. 102.8
S.DAK. 58.5
NEBR. 21.6
KAN. 20.3
TEXAS 52.9
MONT. 125.9
WYO. 108.6
COLO. 74.1
N.MEX. 84.6
IDA. 166.7
UTAH 62.1
ARIZ. 171.5
WASH. 18.8
ORE. 16.3
NEV. -6.1
CALIF. 130.8

UNITED STATES AVERAGE
39.0% INCREASE

DECREASE

POPULATION CHANGE
+ 100% AND OVER
+ 50% THROUGH 99.9%
+ 25%   "   "   49.9%
+ 10%   "   "   24.9%
+ 5%   "   "   9.9%
0%   "   "   4.9%

TRM

5

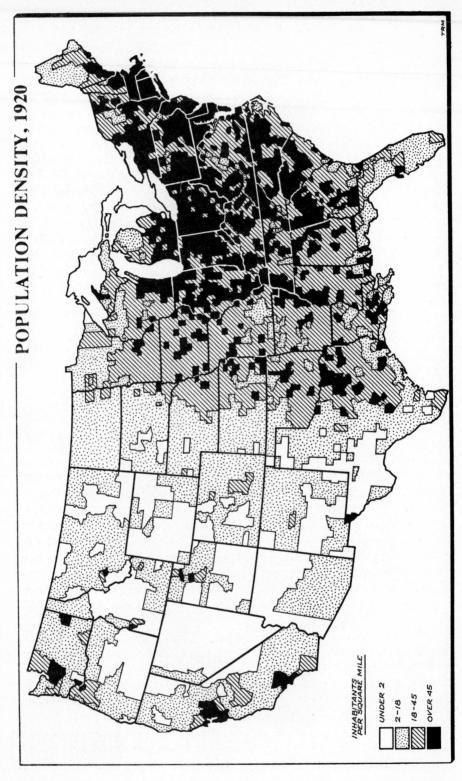

INHABITANTS
PER SQUARE MILE

UNDER 2
2-18
18-45
OVER 45

mankind. The death rate in areas where reliable statistics were kept declined between 1900 and 1920 from 17 to 12.6 per thousand for whites and from 25 to 17.7 per thousand for nonwhites. This progress was made possible in part by a sharp decline in deaths from typhoid fever and tuberculosis, and in part by the practical elimination of smallpox and malaria.

In spite of great progress accomplished through utilization of new techniques, drugs, and a broadening knowledge of the causes of disease, much remained to be done in this field by the end of the First World War. For example, one authority concluded in 1909 that the death rate could be reduced one-fourth by the partial elimination of preventable diseases. Hundreds of thousands of workers were needlessly killed, maimed, or disabled each year. At the same time, a committee on the physical welfare of New York City's school children found that 66 percent of these children needed medical care or better nourishment, 40 percent needed dental care, 31 percent had defective vision, and 6 percent suffered from malnutrition.

2. The American People: Income, Wealth, and Industry

The most striking economic phenomenon of the first years of the twentieth century was the steady increase in the wealth and income of the people of the United States. Adjusted to fluctuations in the cost of living, the total national income increased from $36,557,000,000, or $480 per capita, at the turn of the century, to $60,401,000,000, or $567 per capita, in 1920. The economic progress of the period can also be read in the steadily increasing volume of industrial production. To state the matter briefly, while population increased by about 40 percent during the decades between 1899 and 1919, the number of manufacturing establishments increased 32 percent; capital invested, more than 250 percent; average number of wage earners, nearly 100 percent; and value of products, 222 percent.

The major manufacturing industries at the turn of the century were still the enterprises that furnished the basic necessities—meat packing, iron and steel, foundries and machine shops, lumbering, milling, clothing, textiles, and tobacco. By the time the Census of Manufactures of 1919 was taken, however, there were abundant signs that a new technology, with all its implications for social life, was in process of coming into being. Industries that were either small or in their infancy in 1900—paper and printing, chemicals, and petroleum products—had burgeoned into lusty giants by 1919. The automobile industry, which had scarcely existed in 1900,

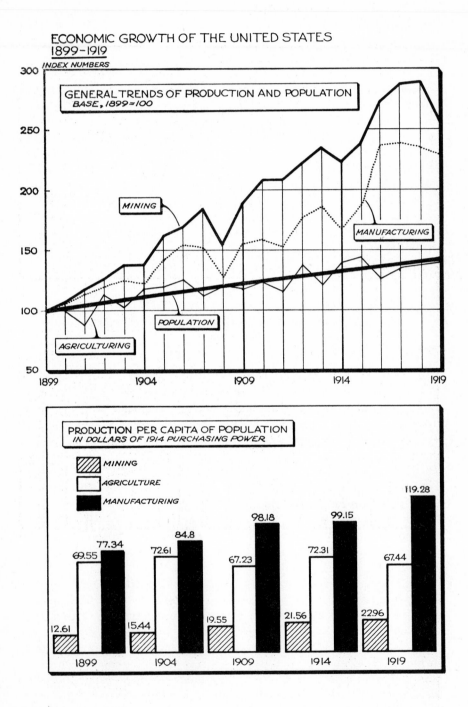

ECONOMIC GROWTH OF THE UNITED STATES
1899–1919

INDEX NUMBERS

GENERAL TRENDS OF PRODUCTION AND POPULATION
BASE, 1899=100

MINING

MANUFACTURING

POPULATION

AGRICULTURING

300
250
200
150
100
50

1899   1904   1909   1914   1919

PRODUCTION PER CAPITA OF POPULATION
IN DOLLARS OF 1914 PURCHASING POWER

MINING
AGRICULTURE
MANUFACTURING

1899   1904   1909   1914   1919

12.61   15.44   19.55   21.56   22.96
69.55   72.61   67.23   72.31   67.44
77.34   84.8   98.18   99.15   119.28

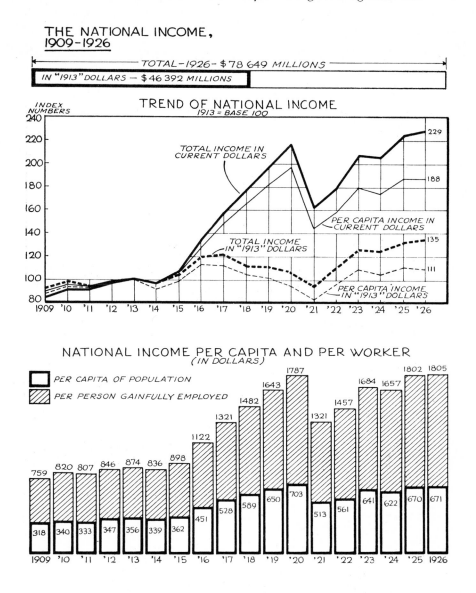

THE NATIONAL INCOME, 1909-1926

TOTAL—1926—$78 649 MILLIONS

IN "1913" DOLLARS — $46 392 MILLIONS

TREND OF NATIONAL INCOME
1913 = BASE 100

INDEX NUMBERS

TOTAL INCOME IN CURRENT DOLLARS

PER CAPITA INCOME IN CURRENT DOLLARS

TOTAL INCOME IN "1913" DOLLARS

PER CAPITA INCOME IN "1913" DOLLARS

NATIONAL INCOME PER CAPITA AND PER WORKER
(IN DOLLARS)

☐ PER CAPITA OF POPULATION

▨ PER PERSON GAINFULLY EMPLOYED

THE GROWTH OF AMERICAN MANUFACTURES
1899–1921

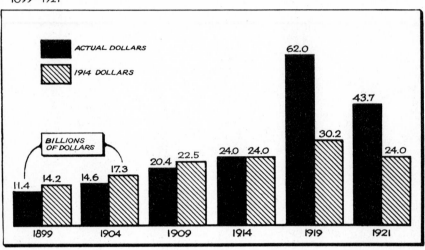

now ranked second only to steel among the manufacturing industries and turned out a product valued at nearly $4 billion.

Slightly less than 33,800,000 men and an additional 8,637,000 women, or a total of about 42,437,000 persons, were gainfully employed in the United States in 1920. Generally speaking, the prewar years were marked by full employment and a rising material standard of living for all classes. Yet the benefits of prosperity were not always distributed evenly, and the share of the national income received by the wealthy few was only slightly diminished on account of the high tax policies of the second administration of Woodrow Wilson. According to the best but still unreliable estimates, the richest families, constituting 1.6 percent of the population, received 10.8 percent of the national income in 1896. More accurate figures taken from income tax returns reveal that the wealthiest 5 percent received 14.98 percent of the national income in 1913 and 12.34 percent in 1920.

3. American Agriculture Finds Stability

American agriculture enjoyed such stability and prosperity during this period of industrial expansion as it had not known since 1865. As a result of the technological revolution, which was already beginning to make its impact felt, farm population decreased from 32,077,000 in 1910 to 31,556,000 in 1920. During the same decade, however, land under cultivation increased from 878,792,000 acres to 955,878,000 acres, and gross

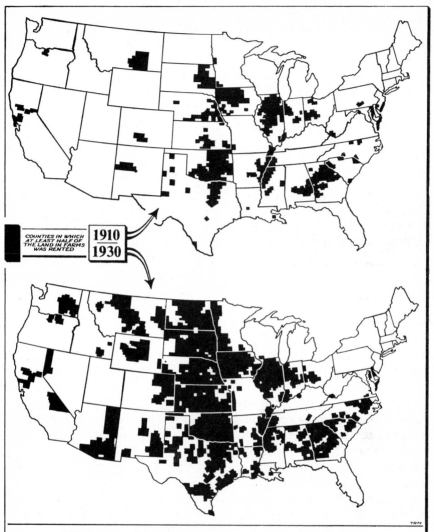

COUNTIES IN WHICH AT LEAST HALF OF THE LAND IN FARMS WAS RENTED

1910
1930

SPREAD OF FARM TENANCY, 1910 AND 1930

farm income rose from $7,477,000,000 to $15,907,000,000. One result of this phenomenal increase was not only unparalleled prosperity for farmers, but also a general increase of nearly 400 percent in the value of farm property.

This spectacular increase in the value of farm property made the acquisition of land more difficult at the very time when the supply of free arable land was being exhausted. Thus, while the number of farm owners increased only slightly (from 3,201,947 to 3,366,510) from 1900 to 1920, the number of tenants increased by 21 percent. More than 38 percent of all farms were operated by tenants in 1920, as contrasted with 35.3 in 1900 and 25.6 percent in 1880. Farm tenancy, especially sharecropping, was so common in the South that its prevalence in that region evoked little comment. But the spread of tenancy through the heartland of the Middle West during the first two decades of the twentieth century was so inexorable as to raise the question of whether a large minority of midwestern farmers were not rapidly approaching a condition of peasantry. One authority concluded in 1914 that 40 percent of the farms in the corn belt were operated by tenants. In 1920 tenants worked between 42 and 43 percent of all farms in the immensely rich states of Illinois and Iowa.

4. The Changing Tide of Immigration

Immigration was not only the most persistent but also one of the most important forces in American history down to the outbreak of the First World War, for the development of the United States was governed in large measure by the ebbing and onrushing tide of alien peoples to the Atlantic shores. Almost 14 million immigrants came to the United States between 1860 and 1900, and over 14.5 million followed from 1900 to 1915. The majority of immigrants after 1860 came from England, Ireland, Germany, and Scandinavia and were akin culturally and historically to older American stock. However, an immigration of peoples heretofore unfamiliar to most Americans—Italians, Slavs, Magyars, and Jews from southern and eastern Europe—began around 1880. This so-called new immigration accounted for only 18.3 percent of the total in the decade from 1881 to 1890, but it soon became a rushing stream. Almost 52 percent of the immigrants were from southern and eastern Europe from 1891 to 1900, and the proportion grew to 72 percent from 1901 to 1910. Let us examine the three major groups of new immigrants and see the causes of their coming to a country with a civilization so different from their own.

THE ITALIANS.   Italian emigration to the United States began slowly in the 1880s and reached important proportions about 1900. More than 2

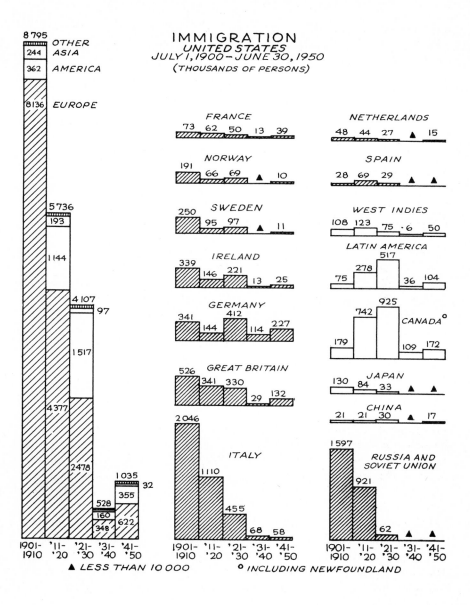

IMMIGRATION
UNITED STATES
JULY 1, 1900 – JUNE 30, 1950
(THOUSANDS OF PERSONS)

8 795 — OTHER
244 — ASIA
362 — AMERICA
8136 — EUROPE

FRANCE
73 62 50 13 39

NETHERLANDS
48 44 27 ▲ 15

NORWAY
191 66 69 ▲ 10

SPAIN
28 69 29 ▲ ▲

SWEDEN
250 95 97 ▲ 11

WEST INDIES
108 123 75 ·6 50

IRELAND
339 146 221 13 25

LATIN AMERICA
75 278 517 36 104

GERMANY
341 144 412 114 227

742 925 CANADA°
179 109 172

GREAT BRITAIN
526 341 330 29 132

JAPAN
130 84 33 ▲ ▲

CHINA
21 21 30 ▲ 17

ITALY
2046 1110 455 68 58

RUSSIA AND SOVIET UNION
1597 921 62 ▲ ▲

5 736
193
1144
4 107
97
1517
4377
2478
1035
32
355
528
160
622
348

1901–1910 '11–'20 '21–'30 '31–'40 '41–'50
▲ LESS THAN 10 000   ° INCLUDING NEWFOUNDLAND

million Italians came to the United States from 1901 to 1910, and an additional 889,000 entered during the four years before the war. The high mark was reached in 1907, when 286,000 passed through the gates at Ellis Island.

Italy alone among the western nations deliberately encouraged emigration and used it as an instrument of national policy to rid herself of surplus population and increase the supply of gold from abroad. The great majority of Italian immigrants came from Sicily and the southern provinces, where estates were largest and living standards were lowest. The Italian peasant, moreover, faced the unpleasant prospect of serving two years in the army as a conscript. Finally, the Italian birth rate was one of the highest in Europe, so that only an extraordinary death rate kept population from increasing to the point of disaster. To escape starvation and the lash of the landlord and the army officer, millions of Italians fled to the United States, Argentina, Brazil, and Uruguay.

THE SLAVS.   The migration of the Slavic peoples of eastern Europe to the United States exceeded even the outpouring of the Italians and constituted the major element in the new immigration. From Austria-Hungary and Russia, which governed most of the Slavic peoples before the First World War, there came 619,000 immigrants from 1881 to 1890, 1,191,000 from 1891 to 1900, and over 5.5 million from 1900 to 1914. As these figures include about 1.5 million Jews, we must reckon the total Slavic immigration to the United States from 1881 to 1914 at about 6 million. Ranked in order of numerical importance, they were Poles, Slovaks, Croatians, Ruthenes, Czechs, Bulgarians, Serbians, Russians, and Dalmatians. Except for the Russians, they were all oppressed subjects of a dominant nationality; 95 percent of them were peasants only a generation or two removed from serfdom. Exploited by landlords, they were poor, ignorant, and, like the Italians, were one-fourth to one-half illiterate.

THE JEWS.   Nearly 2 million Jews entered the United States from 1881 to 1915. The great bulk of them came from Russian Poland or Russia, about one-fourth from Austria-Hungary, and a few from Rumania. The reasons for this great exodus, paralleled only by the movement of the Jewish people at the time of the destruction of Jerusalem and the great dispersion, are not hard to find.

Most of the Jews had congregated in Poland during the Middle Ages because tolerant Polish kings welcomed them. Russia acquired the provinces in which the Jews were concentrated when Poland was partitioned in the eighteenth century, and the czarist government embarked upon a long and deliberate policy of persecution after 1881. Jews were forbidden to live beyond the "pale of settlement," that is to say, their original area of domicile in the western provinces. Exceptions were made in favor of those in certain occupations, but educational and other forms of discrimination reduced the numbers who could avail themselves of this privilege. Although forced to serve in the army, they could not become officers. Subjected to numerous and heavy taxes, they could never aspire to political office.

Thus the four scourges—poverty, militarism, religious persecution, and political tyranny—were in varying degrees responsible for the willingness of Italians, Slavs, and Jews to embark upon the long journey to the New World. All authorities agree, however, that the forces drawing immigrants to America—the lure of new opportunities, propaganda of steamship companies, and tall tales of recruiting agents—were more powerful than the forces driving them from their homelands. Moreover, most of the new immigration was made in direct response to the need for unskilled labor in the United States and was stimulated by agents of employment bureaus working closely with railroad and industrial employers.

Irish immigrants had supplied a large proportion of the unskilled laborers from 1846 to about 1890. As the Irish gradually moved up the economic and social ladder and the numbers of Irish immigrants declined, the Slavs and Italians followed in their footsteps and did the work that they had previously done. Only 16 to 17 percent of the Italians, 3 to 5 percent of the Ruthenes, Croatians, Rumanians, and Slovaks, and 8 to 10 percent of the Magyars and Poles were skilled workers when they came to the United States. Invariably they went to the industrial areas of the East and Middle West and found employment on railroads, in textile factories in New England, steel mills in Pittsburgh and Chicago, midwestern stockyards, and coal mines from Pennsylvania to Colorado. By 1914 they constituted the bulk of the working force in the basic industries. The Jews were as poor as other eastern European immigrants, but they brought with them a high degree of skill and experience in the trades. They congregated in the garment sweatshops of New York, Chicago, and other large cities mainly because they found Jewish employers in the clothing industry.

5. The Social Impact of the New Immigration

The fact that the American society absorbed this transfusion of different national strains without violent reactions was testimony to its growing maturity and adaptability. Yet it was everywhere evident that the processes of social assimilation, which had on the whole worked admirably among the Germans, Irish, and Scandinavians, practically ceased to operate among the new immigrants. Older Americans viewed them suspiciously and thought that they were an inferior people, incapable of understanding American ideals.

This hostility was evidenced in the formation in 1887 of the American Protective Association, an anti-Catholic organization much like the Know-Nothing party of the 1850s, and in the spreading fear that the new immigration would undermine Anglo-American institutions and eventually dilute the old American racial stock. It was reflected, also, in the absence of any governmental effort to protect the immigrant from exploitation and thievery. But the worst aspect of the record was the exploitation of these immigrants by the railroads and industries. Surveying the American scene in 1915, the Commission on Industrial Relations noted that two-thirds of immigrant families lived at a subsistence level or below.

All foreigners, regardless of race, nationality, or physical and moral condition, could enter the United States before 1882. In that year the first general federal immigration act was passed, and the process of restriction was begun when, at the insistence of Californians, Chinese were excluded for ten years. The Chinese Exclusion Act was reenacted from time to time and made permanent in 1902. No sooner had the fears of Californians been quieted regarding the prospect of a Chinese inundation than another and more alarming prospect arose—the specter of an invasion of the state by Japanese workers and farmers. There were only 2,000 Japanese subjects in the United States in 1890, but two decades later their number had increased to 110,000. A powerful and well-organized agitation for exclusion of the Japanese led in 1907-1908 to the negotiation of an agreement between the American and Japanese government that virtually ended Japanese immigration to the continental United States (see pp. 144-145).

Thus almost complete exclusion of Orientals had been accomplished by 1908. Moreover, the doors had been shut against paupers, the sick and diseased, polygamists, prostitutes, contract laborers, anarchists, and convicts. By this time, however, the demand for a severe restriction, if not outright exclusion, of most European immigrants was mounting on all sides. The weapon that the exclusionists advocated at this time was a literacy test. President Cleveland had vetoed a bill imposing such a test in 1897. Such a measure passed Congress in 1913 and again in 1915 only to be nullified by the vetoes of President Taft and President Wilson. The exclusionists in Congress finally mustered sufficient strength in January 1917 to pass an immigration bill imposing the literacy test over Wilson's veto. Thus the open door to America—for centuries the gateway of opportunity for countless millions—was partially closed.

6. American Negroes During the Progressive Era

The gloomiest aspect of the American social scene during the first two decades of the twentieth century was the condition of Negroes. Foreign observers could never cease to wonder how Americans could boast of democracy while denying essential democratic privileges to one-tenth of the population. The great paradox was not resolved during the progressive period. In fact, the social and political status of blacks worsened by and large, while their economic status only slightly improved.

Optimists, to be sure, could point to a few signs of progress since 1865. Demonstrating a passion for education in the face of incredible obstacles, Negroes had reduced their illiteracy rate from 95 percent in 1865 to 44.5 percent in 1900. And even greater progress was made during the decades between 1900 and 1920. The illiteracy rate among Negroes ten years of age and over declined from 30.4 percent in 1910 to 22.9 percent in 1920.

The Negro's progress toward education had been accomplished before 1900 with the help of northern philanthropists and churches and only slightly with the aid of the southern states. After 1900, however, there was an increasing awareness throughout the white South, especially in the border states, of the need for greater public aid to Negro education. Even so, no southern state by the end of the First World War was making a serious effort to provide anywhere near equal or even adequate educational opportunities for its Negro youth. In 1910, for example, there were only 141 Negro high schools, with a total of 8,251 pupils, in all the states from Maryland to Texas.

Meanwhile, social and political forces had been at work in the South to make the progressive era a time of profound discouragement for Negroes. For one thing, the Civil War and Reconstruction had not altered southern racial concepts or southern determination to keep blacks in a subordinate status. For another, slavery had given way to sharecropping, so that the vast majority of Negroes found not economic freedom, but merely another form of bondage after 1865. As a substitute for the social controls of slavery, which went by the board in 1865, the southern whites after Reconstruction had substituted a legal caste system that prohibited intermarriage and established a severe pattern of segregation for schools, public places, and transportation facilities. Informal race controls were tightened, and many a Negro suffered the extreme penalty for violating the rules of racial etiquette. Finally, many southern states in the late 1870s and early 1880s began gradually to make voting by Negroes difficult. The southern legislatures acted cautiously in this regard, however, and large numbers of Negroes voted in many southern states as late as the 1890s.

A genuine political division among southern white voters occurred for the first time since 1860 during the Populist revolt, and both Democrats and Populists bid for Negro votes. This resurgence of Negro political activity frightened both agrarian and conservative southerners and led them to conclude that the Negro must be removed forever as a participant in southern political life. Mississippi had shown the way to disfranchise the great mass of Negro voters in 1890—by use of a literacy test, poll tax, provisions requiring an understanding of the Constitution, and long residence requirements for registration—without openly violating the Fifteenth Amendment. Then, as an aftermath of the revival of Negro political activity during the Populist upsurge, all southern states except Maryland, Tennessee, and Kentucky disfranchised Negro voters from 1895 to 1907.

The one man who, more than any other person, brought peace between the races in the South after this bloody decade of conflict was Booker T. Washington. His rise to leadership of the Negro people was one of the most dramatic episodes in the history of the United States. Born a slave in Franklin County, Virginia, in 1856 and educated at Hampton Institute in his native state, Washington founded Tuskegee Institute in Alabama in 1881 as a school where Negro boys and girls might learn to become useful members of southern communities as teachers, farmers, and tradesmen. Washington was recognized as the preeminent spokesman of American blacks by 1895. Therefore, it came as something of an official pronouncement when, at the height of the disfranchisement movement, he counseled southern Negroes to eschew politics and learn to become good citizens. Whites all over the country quickly seized upon his program of vocational education and political quiescence for southern blacks as a formula for racial peace.

This so-called Washington Compromise found favor especially among conservative southerners and won their limited support for Negro education. But it did not operate to diminish the anti-Negro passions of the southern masses. The Populist revolt brought to the fore a new leadership of violent men. Some, like Cole L. Blease of South Carolina, were sheer demagogues; others, like James K. Vardaman of Mississippi, had many qualities of statesmanship. All these new leaders, however, rose to power on a wave of racism that found expression in violence in many forms. The last sixteen years of the nineteenth century had witnessed more than 2,500 lynchings, and the century had ended with a race riot in Wilmington, North Carolina, the climax of the disfranchisement campaign in that state. This was followed in the twentieth century by other riots, the worst of which occurred in Atlanta in September 1906. Moreover, lynching continued in the twentieth century to be an important aspect of race control, as more than 1,100 blacks fell victims, from 1900 to 1914, to mobs that often discarded the rope for the faggot.

To Negroes, however, the most frightening development of this period was the spread of southern racial concepts and techniques of violence to the North and Middle West. Southern orators like Benjamin R. Tillman of South Carolina carried the message of white supremacy to northern audiences and stimulated latent prejudices. The most effective southern propagandist was Thomas Dixon, an erstwhile Baptist minister of North Carolina, whose novels, *The Leopard's Spots* (1902) and *The Clansman* (1905), were calculated to arouse the basest racial prejudices of white readers and sold by the hundreds of thousands. *The Clansman* was made into a motion picture, *The Birth of a Nation*, in 1915, which was a powerful factor in stimulating race riots in the North and Middle West during and after the First World War. These will be related in a later chapter.

It is small wonder, then, that the progressive era was a dreary period for

Negroes ambitious for the advancement of their race. There was, however, one ray of hope: the development of an aggressive and advanced leadership among both races. Foremost among the militant Negroes was a young scholar, William E. B. Du Bois, a native of Massachusetts with a doctor's degree in history from Harvard University. Du Bois and a small group of Negro intellectuals met at Niagara Falls, Canada, in June 1905, adopted a platform demanding political and economic equality for black men, and announced their determination to begin a new war for emancipation. Meeting the following year at Harpers Ferry, West Virginia, the site of John Brown's raid, the Niagara movement, as the Du Bois group was called, reiterated its resolves and renewed its courage.

Progressives and champions of social justice in the North at first paid scant attention to the Niagara rebels. Then, an anti-Negro riot occurred in Springfield, Illinois, in August 1908, within half a mile of Lincoln's home, and humanitarians in the North at last awoke to the imminent threat of the southernizing of their section. The young black rebels and a distinguished group of white educators, clergymen, editors, and social workers met in New York City on Lincoln's birthday in 1909 to consider the crisis in race relations. A year later they organized the National Association for the Advancement of Colored People. It was pledged to work for the abolition of all forced segregation, equal justice for Negroes, and enlarged educational opportunities for Negro children. The only black official of the NAACP during its formative period was Du Bois, who was director of publicity and research and editor of the association's monthly magazine, *The Crisis*. But the selection of Du Bois as official spokesman signified that the revolt against the Washington Compromise had at last found powerful support among the progressives in the North and held promise for the day when the northern people would rediscover their equalitarian heritage.

7. The Growth of American Education

The federal commissioner of education could boast at the turn of the century of the steady development of educational institutions since 1890 and of an increase of 19.2 percent in the number of children enrolled in public and private schools and institutions of higher learning. These general national statistics, however, obscure the details of the educational picture in the various regions. Progress in the North and Midwest, for example, had been even more substantial than they would indicate. On the other hand, the situation in the South in 1900 was so gloomy that leaders of the regions wondered if there were any hope at all. Southern children on an average received three years of public schooling, as compared with the average of nearly seven years for children in the North. Southern states spent an average of $9.72 per pupil in 1900, as compared with an expenditure of $20.85 per pupil in the north central states.

The general educational picture had improved perceptibly by the end of the First World War, but the most significant advances are not revealed by general statistics. To begin with, the growth of kindergartens since 1900 had evidenced the expanding influence in America of the champions of the child of preschool age. Only about 250 cities had established kindergartens in 1900. By 1920, on the other hand, there were almost 8,000 separate kindergartens, with 511,000 children enrolled. Even more important was the remarkable expansion of public high schools from 1900 to 1920. There were about 6,000 public high schools in the United States, with 500,000 pupils, in 1900. Twenty years later there were over 14,000, with some 2 million students enrolled.

The most important educational revolution in this period occurred in the South. Under the spur of publicists like Walter H. Page and philanthropic agencies like the Southern Education Board, political leaders launched virtual crusades for education in the southern states. The result was a mass awakening from 1902 to about 1910, comparable to the educational revival that swept through the North and Middle West before the Civil War. In the short span of a decade, appropriations for school purposes by the southern states doubled, enrollment of white children increased almost a third, and the average length of the school term lengthened from five to six months. Southern illiteracy, moreover, declined from 11.8 percent of the native whites in 1900 to about 5.5 percent in 1920 and from 44.5 percent of the Negroes ten years of age or older to about 22.9 percent.

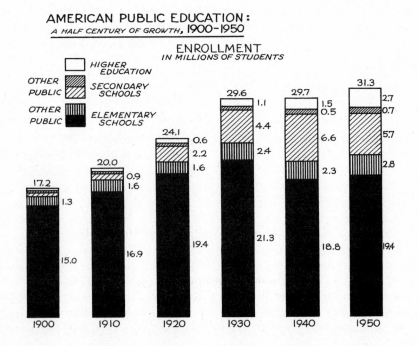

AMERICAN PUBLIC EDUCATION:
A HALF CENTURY OF GROWTH, 1900–1950

ENROLLMENT
IN MILLIONS OF STUDENTS

A revolution in the theory and practice of education was also getting under way at this same time. Educational psychologists and experimentalists were already beginning to undermine older pedagogical theories and were stimulating a new scientific attitude toward children even as the twentieth century opened. The new so-called progressive theories gained wider acceptance in the years before the war, especially after the philosopher John Dewey, a Vermonter teaching first at the University of Chicago and afterward at Columbia University, assumed leadership of the movement.

Dewey set out to fulfill the American dream of a public school system that was the chief training ground for democracy. Repudiating the classical tradition that emphasized formal and polite learning, he advocated a curriculum that had meaning for an urban age and prepared the child to live in a democratic society. He taught, moreover, that curriculum and subject matter should be adapted to the needs and capabilities of children, not of adults; that the learning process should be centered around the child's own experiences; and that "learning by doing" should supplant memorization of data that had no meaning to the child. His theories were assailed by traditionalists and sometimes violently abused by his own disciples. Even so, Dewey left such a deep imprint on American educational theory and practice that he can be said to have accomplished, almost single-handed, one of the significant cultural revolutions of his time.

Important developments were also taking place in higher education in the United States. For one thing, the formation of the Association of American Universities in 1900 and of regional associations soon afterward marked the beginning of a concerted campaign to raise academic standards all over the country. As a result, the number of colleges and universities increased only slightly between 1900 and 1920, from 977 to 1,041; at the same time, their enrollment more than doubled from 238,000 to 598,000. Other important changes were taking place in this field: enormous improvement in facilities for graduate and specialized training; a significant development of technical education and growth of private institutions, like the Massachusetts Institute of Technology, and state engineering and agricultural colleges; new methods of teaching; expansion of state aid to public universities, colleges, and junior colleges; and the beginning of an important adult education movement.

8. Religious Institutions and Movements

The most important social phenomenon of the prewar period was the survival of religion after the violent storms of the last quarter of the nineteenth century. The growth of skepticism, the war between Darwinists and fundamentalists, and the spread of philosophies like Marxian scientific materialism and social Darwinism had so promoted the growth of secularism that probably a large majority of American intellectuals by 1920 would have disavowed Christian faith. Yet Christian ethics not only survived but found wider acceptance and fuller meaning. American Protestantism largely abandoned fundamentalism and rediscovered the ancient Christian message of social justice, while the Roman Catholic church expanded its ministry to the poor.

The years before the taking of the religious census in 1916 were a period of substantial growth in numbers, influence, and wealth for all religious groups. All told, Protestant bodies enrolled 26,205,039 members in 1916, as compared with 20,857,303 in 1906; and among Protestant denominations the Baptist and Methodist bodies were easily the most numerous and powerful. But the most spectacular religious development during the period 1890-1916 was the tremendous growth of the Roman Catholic church in the United States, the result chiefly of the new immigration. This church grew from 7,343,186 members in 1890 to 15,721,815 in 1916, a gain of 114.1 percent. During its period of rapid growth the Roman Catholic church was neither torn by internal dissensions nor concerned with theological disputes. There was a movement in the late nineteenth century to "Americanize" the Catholic church in the United States by bringing it into close cooperation with other religious groups. This effort was ended by Pope Leo XIII's firm stand in 1899 in behalf of traditional practice. Any trend toward modernism in the church, moreover, was firmly suppressed by Pope Pius X in 1907. Thereafter, modernism simply did not exist in American Catholicism.

The decision to adhere to traditional Catholic doctrines and practices did not, however, signify any diminution of the social conscience of the Catholic church. Catholic bishops and priests were shepherds of most of the new immigrants and a large portion of the submerged urban masses; they well knew what poverty and suffering were. James Cardinal Gibbons of Baltimore had been one of the leading champions of the Knights of Labor during the 1880s. His attitude was probably decisive in the issuance in 1891 of Pope Leo XIII's encyclical *Rerum Novarum,* one of the most important assertions of the rights of labor. Catholic laymen and priests like Father John A. Ryan of the Catholic University of America figured prominently in the twentieth-century movement for adoption of social and economic legislation.

For American Protestantism, on the other hand, the progressive era was a time of change on all sides. The old divisive forces that had kept Protestant groups separated were still at work, evidenced by the steady offshooting of new sects from parent bodies. The most notable of these new movements was Christian Science, founded around the turn of the century by a remarkable Bostonian, Mrs. Mary Baker Eddy. She denied the existence of death, evil, or the material world and worked out a new science from the Scriptures by asserting that disease did not exist. Christian Science had gained almost 100,000 adherents by the First World War and was growing rapidly. The most numerous of the new sects, however, were the various holiness, or pentecostal, bodies, most of which came out of Methodism and taught a primitive fundamentalism.

Furthermore, Protestantism was still suffering the effects of the profound division in its ranks between traditionalists, who adhered steadfastly to ancient creeds and confessions, and modernists, who ranged theologically all the way from liberal orthodoxy to outright humanism, but who usually emphasized the social mission of the church at the expense of doctrine. There could be no doubt that modernists were in the ascendancy from 1900 to 1920. The northern Presbyterian church preserved the purity of its doctrines at the cost of expelling several of its most distinguished ministers and of losing control of its leading school, Union Seminary in New York City. The Lutherans generally remained impervious to the new intellectual currents. But northern Methodists, northern Baptists, and Congregationalists were by and large captured by the modernist clergy.

In spite of these divisive forces, there were numerous signs during the first years of the twentieth century that forces drawing Protestant bodies together were at last beginning to prevail. Even the great division between traditionalists and modernists was a cohesive force, since it cut across denominational barriers and drew persons together on one side or the other. Within the denominations, too, unifying forces gathered strength. The union of the northern Presbyterian and Cumberland Presbyterian bodies in 1906, for example, healed an old wound in the ecclesiastical body. Northern Baptist groups gradually came together in close cooperation, while the three principal Methodist bodies set under way a movement for unification that would come to fruition years later.

Among the denominations, morever, subordination of minor theological differences and cooperation on various levels of church activity became the prime objective of Protestant leaders after 1900. Unity came first on the local level, in the formation of city, county, and state federations of churches, and in older organizations like the Young Men's Christian Association, the Young Women's Christian Association, the International Sunday School Association, and the American Bible Society. The dream of the champions of Protestant unity was finally realized in 1908 with the formation of the Federal Council of Churches of Christ in America. Spokesmen of thirty-three evangelical bodies and 17 million members sharing common beliefs and purposes united to proclaim their faith in the ecumenical church.

The launching of the Federal Council of Churches in 1908 also signified the triumph in American Protestantism of the social gospel, a movement to revitalize the church and proclaim Christianity's message to an industrial society. There had always been a strong socially minded left wing of Protestantism in America, at least since the advent of Methodism in the eigheenth century. By 1865 the church had tamed the older frontier areas and overcome slavery, only to be confronted afterward by a host of new and less obvious challenges—social Darwinism, aggressive materialism, and new forms of bondage.

Perhaps a majority of urban Protestant churches during the Gilded Age fell under the control of businessmen concerned mainly with laying up treasures on earth. Perhaps their ministers glorified the captains of industry as fervently as did the college professors and editors of the day. Yet the years from 1870 to 1890 were a time also of the awakening of the social consciousness of Protestantism. An increasing number of clergymen began to measure the competitive, exploitative *Zeitgeist* by the Christian standard and found the new values wanting. Some of these pioneers found an answer in Christian Socialism; others rejected socialism but sought to resurrect the old Christian doctrine of brotherhood. In any event, a significant articulation of social Christianity emerged out of the widespread discussion of the 1870s and 1880s. It was evident by 1890 that Protestantism was changing, that it was becoming less otherworldly in outlook and beginning to view salvation in social and ethical, as well as in theological, terms.

The years from 1890 to 1920 saw the social gospel come of age. The 1890s witnessed wholesale acceptance of the theory of evolution by liberal theologians. The consequent accommodation of religion to Darwinism was accompanied by the elevation of the three ancient Christian beliefs to new prominence in American religious thought. They were, first, the conviction that God is everywhere present and works through human institutions; second, belief in the fatherhood of God and the brotherhood of man; third, the view that the Kingdom of God is here now and that the chief duty of the church is the extension of that Kingdom. Together, these beliefs constituted a frame of reference and a point of departure for the proponents of social Christianity.

The host of social gospel preachers increased, and their good works multiplied from 1890 to the end of the First World War until it seemed that urban Protestantism had truly been transformed. At the same time, Christian Socialism became respectable and commanded the sympathy, if not the allegiance, of an increasing number of clergymen. The Salvation Army, founded by William Booth in London in 1878, spread to the United States in 1880 and, after 1890, expanded its relief and rehabilitation work among the outcasts of society. So-called institutional churches, which sponsored hospitals, missions, social and relief agencies, and boys' and girls' clubs, spread through the great cities. Finally, most of the major denominations officially recognized their social mission around 1900 by establishing commissions of social service.

Among the champions of the social gospel one man emerged as leader and spokesman—Walter Rauschenbusch, for many years professor of church history at Rochester Theological Seminary. A socialist, Rauschenbusch reserved his severest criticism for industrial capitalism, a "mammonistic organization with which Christianity can never be content." For the law of competition he proposed to substitute cooperation, collectivism, and democracy, and thus to hasten the consummation of the Kingdom of God on earth. The publication of Rauschenbusch's eloquent *Christianity and the Social Crisis* in 1907 immediately established him as the major prophet of the social gospel movement.

A year after the publication of *Christianity and the Social Crisis* the social gospel achieved fulfillment in the formation of the Federal Council of Churches, for the movement for Protestant unity had from the beginning stemmed more from social action impulses than from any desire to achieve doctrinal accord. At its first meeting in Philadelphia the council adopted a ringing manifesto, "The Church and Modern Industry," placing official Protestantism squarely behind the movement to end exploitative capitalism through social welfare legislation and the strengthening of labor unions.

For all its power and commanding influence, the social gospel movement was a development in urban Protestantism. It was in the campaign to end the liquor traffic that urban and rural Protestants found a common outlet for mutual social energies and impulses. The later excesses of the prohibitionists and their failure to change the habits of a nation should not obscure the fact that in the beginning, at least, the temperance and prohibition movements were responses to one of the major social challenges of the time. The liquor problem grew to menacing proportions between 1860 and 1880, as investment in the liquor business increased 700 percent, saloons multiplied in the cities, and intemperance increased everywhere. Moreover, liquor interests cooperated with vice rings and corrupt politicians, so that saloons were often fronts for houses of prostitution, and liquor dealers' associations and brewers worked hand in glove with city bosses.

The answer of the aroused church membership to this, as they thought, dire threat to home and family was immediate and emphatic. The Protestant churches, containing most of the nondrinking population, went directly into politics in the 1880s and 1890s. On the local level they smashed saloons and elected city councils opposed to the liquor dealers. On the county and state levels they organized alliances and leagues to work for local option and statewide prohibition. Leadership in the temperance agitation in the North and Middle West was taken by the Methodists, often more socially alert than other Protestant groups. In the South, Methodists and Baptists joined hands in the movement.

The Women's Christian Temperance Union, founded by Frances Willard in 1874, was the first successful attempt to marshal the ranks of Protestantism against the liquor traffic. But effective organization of church forces on a national scale came only in 1895 with the formation of the Anti-Saloon League at Washington, D.C. Methodist, Baptist, Presbyterian, and Congregational churches went into politics under the league's aegis with such determination that the division between church and state almost ceased to exist in many southern and midwestern states. The leagues—with their general superintendents, organizers, and hosts of speakers—became the most powerful factors in politics in many states.

The goal of Anti-Saloon leaders was at first local option or statewide prohibition. Three-fourths of the American people lived in dry counties by 1917, while two-thirds of the states had adopted prohibition. As the movement gained power, however, it assumed more and more the character of a religious crusade. The Anti-Saloon leaders lost sight of their original objective after 1913 and began to agitate for national prohibition by constitutional amendment. The powerful Anti-Saloon lobby in Washington obtained passage in 1913 of the Webb-Kenyon Act, which prohibited transportation of alcoholic beverages into dry states. Three years later a prohibition amendment received a majority vote, though not the necessary two-thirds, in both houses of Congress. When Congress imposed prohibition on the District of Columbia in 1917, it was evident that the day was not far distant when Protestantism's crusade would culminate in nationwide prohibition by federal amendment.

9. Main Trends in Literature

Regenerative forces combined between 1900 and the First World War to produce a literary flowering in the United States and to lay foundations for new trends in American creative writing. It was a productive and fertile period. Traditionalism survived under new forms; a new literary genre, naturalism, reached its apogee; and literary preeminence passed from the East to the Middle West and, to a lesser degree, to the South.

The Victorian giants were either dead or dying by the turn of the century. Henry James, who had discovered reality in the drawing room, had escaped to the more congenial British milieu. His creative energies were almost spent by 1900. William Dean Howells lived on until 1920, but while he remained a friend of many young authors his great work was also done. Mark Twain, the novelist of American boyhood, survived like a ghost from the nineteenth-century past until 1910. His only significant work after 1900 was *The Mysterious Stranger*, published posthumously.

For all their realism, authors like James and Howells lived in a moral universe. Realism to them meant probing into human character and mirroring life as they found it. Their subjects may have been drab or driven by greed, but they were above all else human beings with will, spirit, and purpose. Their work was taken up in the early twentieth century by a goodly company—Ellen Glasgow of Virginia, Willa Cather of Nebraska, Dorothy Canfield of Kansas and Vermont, Ole Rölvaag of Minnesota, and

Edith Wharton of New York. They depicted life in the new South, the Middle West, or New York drawing-room society in all its stark drabness, irony, and tragedy. As realists, however, they also knew the other side of the picture. And in the end they glorified the human spirit, magnified the struggle against evil, and thus carried on the humane tradition.

Meanwhile, a new literary movement, naturalism, was beginning in the 1890s to make its first impression on American writers. The leading French naturalist, Emile Zola, enunciated the philosophy of the new school. The writer, he said, must study human nature as the biologist studies the animal world and describe sheerly natural phenomena without compassion and without applying moral criteria. It was a discipline too strong for most Americans, and early so-called naturalists like Jack London, Frank Norris, Hamlin Garland, Ambrose Bierce, and Stephen Crane were more harsh realists than true disciples of Zola.

The publication in 1900 of Theodore Dreiser's *Sister Carrie*, however, marked a real turning point in American literary history. Here was a genuine effort to discover a new view of humanity based upon the findings of science and to discern a theory of existence divorced from religious beliefs. Dreiser found an answer to the search for truth in biology. Man is an animal driven by instincts to struggle for survival in an impersonal universe. In his striving for wealth, power, or sexual satisfaction, he reverts to his true animal nature, and the façade of civilization falls away. Social forces, moreover, are impersonal and drive the weak, who cannot outwardly defy social conventions, to crime and violence.

The American public was not yet ready for such strong literary fare, and Dreiser bided his time without compromising his integrity. When he published *Jennie Gerhardt* in 1911 he won not popular acclaim, but acceptance by a wide circle of intellectuals. Dreiser's leadership of the naturalistic school was firmly secured with his publication of *The Financier* in 1912 and *The Titan* in 1914. Although naturalism had not become an obsession among American writers by 1914, it clearly commanded the allegiance of a majority of serious young writers. The day could not be far distant when it would dominate the ethos of American literature.

The years before the First World War witnessed, too, a remarkable outburst of poetic creativity. As the Victorian era gave way to the modern age, the genteel tradition survived in a simpler form; new poetic forms emerged, and poetic themes varied from the very abstruse to the homely and common aspect of life. But, withal, a real renaissance occurred, and America recovered her poetic voice.

The two poetic giants of the early years of the twentieth century, William Vaughn Moody and Edwin Arlington Robinson, were both traditionalists who wrote in the genteel manner. Moody, a professor at the University of Chicago, was an idealist outraged by the social and economic injustices of his time and by his country's venture into imperialism. His "Ode in Time of Hesitation" (1900) and "Gloucester Moors" and "On a

Soldier Fallen in the Philippines," both published in 1901, were prophetic expressions of America's social consciousness. Robinson, however, dealt with a simpler and more abiding theme—the individual's search for God and truth in darkness and suffering. Life and human destiny remained mysterious to Robinson; he could not fathom their secrets. Yet in the "black and awful chaos of the night," he felt "the coming glory of the Light." His first collected works, *The Children of the Night*, appeared in 1897. *The Town Down the River* (1910) and *The Man Against the Sky* (1916) established him as the preeminent man of letters among a remarkable generation of poets and novelists.

Robinson was in some respects a latter-day Puritan, in others a transcendentalist. Such could not, however, be said of a new school of poets of the people. They came upon the literary horizon in 1912 with the publication in Chicago of *The Lyric Years*, an anthology of contemporary verse, and the printing of the first issue of *Poetry: A Magazine of Verse*. The editor of *Poetry*, Harriet Monroe, was certain that traditionalism was passing, and so she urged poets to write about contemporary life. The Chicago poets, Vachel Lindsay, Edgar Lee Masters, and Carl Sandburg, replied enthusiastically. Lindsay's "General William Booth Enters into Heaven," published in the first issue of *Poetry*, marked the beginning of his ecstatic glorification of the common people and their destiny. Masters, a Chicago lawyer who wrote poetry as an avocation, laid bare the alleged sham and moral shabbiness of small-town America in *Spoon River Anthology* (1915). On the other hand, Sandburg, whose first volume appeared in 1916, magnified Chicago: the roaring, brawling hog butcher and steelmaker of the world. Another poet of the common people, Robert Frost, was not a Chicagoan. He was the bard of the farmers and workers of New England, and his quiet verse mirrored the staid New Hampshire countryside. The publication of his *A Boy's Will* in 1913 and *North of Boston* a year later immediately established his eminence among the new poets.

At the same time another revolt against the genteel tradition was brewing far to the east, among a group of American and English poets in London. These were so-called imagists, led by Ezra Pound, Amy Lowell, and later T. S. Eliot. They were striving toward a new verse form and new artistic standards. Asserting that the poet's purpose was to re-create impressions caught in the fleeting image, they rejected metrical form and rhyming as artificial devices that posed obstacles to the creation of the pure image. Rejecting also romanticism as being the literary expression of a decadent humanistic culture, the imagists sought merely to re-create the impressions of everyday life.

These novelists and poets raised American literature to new eminence and gave it such standing in the western world as it had not enjoyed since the 1840s and 1850s. But none of the truly creative writers of the early twentieth century enjoyed material success or popular acclaim. Except for the few who had independent incomes or other professions, they lived in obscure poverty, like Edwin Arlington Robinson, who was rescued by Theodore Roosevelt and given a sinecure in the New York Customs House, or Vachel Lindsay, who earned his bread by touring the country as a vagabond minstrel. Americans were actually reading and buying more books than ever before by the First World War; but the reading public rewarded sentimentalists and romanticists who amused and entertained them without questioning their virtue.

2

Aspects of
Economic Development,
1900–1920

Pride in the nation's economic growth since the end of the depression of the 1890s had in large measure given way by the end of the progressive period to foreboding among many thoughtful Americans. Along with growth had come a steady movement toward concentration of economic power in fewer and fewer hands. This movement in industry, finance, and transportation was one of the most powerful and significant forces in recent American history. For one thing, it completely transformed an economy of relatively small competitive producers into one dominated, and to a degree controlled, by an oligarchy of giant corporations. For another, many of the domestic problems of this century, at least before 1917, arose from the obvious necessity either of halting the movement toward monopoly or oligopoly—that is, domination of an industry by a few large producers—or else of bringing the great corporations, banks, railroads, and public service monopolies under effective public control.

No other question received as much attention or stimulated as many investigations and proposals for amelioration. Journalists, publicists, and politicians described the changes taking place: big business was becoming monopolistic, or nearly so, while the few men who dominated Wall Street were also extending their control into industry and transportation. As the statistics were plain enough for all to read, the people reluctantly agreed that the old promise of American life—the promise of equality of opportunity and a fair field for all comers—was rapidly becoming an anachronism. How to revitalize this promise—in brief, how to bring the great new aggregations of economic power under social control—constituted progressivism's greatest challenge and dilemma.

This question, which perplexed the progressive mind and agitated the American people, is beyond the scope of the present chapter. Here we are concerned only with the development and progress of the concentration movement—how it came about and where it seemed to be heading.

1. The Emergence of the Modern Corporation

The most obvious and the most important development in American industry after the Civil War was the rise of the corporation as the dominant type of industrial organization. The corporate form was used extensively before 1865 only in transportation, insurance, banking, and, to a lesser degree, in textiles. However, with the enlargement of industrial units, the spread of mass-production techniques, and the growth of the trust movement after 1865 (see below), the corporation rapidly displaced the proprietorship and partnership as the chief agency for combining capital and labor. Corporations turned out 66 percent of all manufactured products by 1899. Ten years later the proportion had increased to 79 percent.

The men who managed American corporations and made important decisions during the latter part of the nineteenth century usually owned the properties that they controlled. However, the domination of corporations by the men who owned them gradually gave way from 1900 to 1920 in the face of a new trend: the emergence of the giant supercorporation, ownership of which was so widely dispersed that there could be no real correlation between ownership and management. In other words, one consequence of the emergence of the large corporation was the establishment in power of a professional managerial class who were only theoretically accountable to stockholders.

The most important factor stimulating the growth of the supercorporation was the movement of bankers into the transportation and industrial fields. The process first began on a large scale during and after the Panic of 1893, when J. P. Morgan & Company and Kuhn, Loeb & Company, the two leading Wall Street investment firms, set about reorganizing and consolidating bankrupt railroad properties. Morgan was so successful in rehabilitating insolvent railroads that he began to seek an opportunity to extend his control into industry. His chance came when a bitter rivalry between Andrew Carnegie and certain producers of finished steel products, with whom Morgan was associated, threatened to plunge the entire steel industry into a chaotic price war. Morgan came forward at this juncture with a plan to combine 60 percent of the iron and steel producers into one giant corporation. This resulted in the creation in 1901 of the United States Steel Corporation, the retirement of Carnegie, the great freewheeling entrepreneur, and the establishment of the House of Morgan as the dominant power in the industry. This event was a turning point in modern American history, but it was only a beginning. As Morgan combined more and more industries and railroads after 1901, his power grew almost by geometric ratio. He was not merely the organizer and consolidator. He also underwrote the floating of securities that launched the new corporations on their way. And through his representatives on boards of directors, and because he controlled the sources of credit, he was able to exercise a decisive voice in the corporations' policies.

The process of banker consolidation and control did not culminate until the 1920s, but the effects of this revolution in the character, ownership, and control of large corporations was already apparent by the outbreak of the First World War. By this date supercorporations dominated many fields of American enterprise: steel and iron, railroads, anthracite coal, agricultural machinery, copper, the telephone and telegraph, and public utilities. Hundreds of thousands of shareholders now owned these properties, but control had passed from owners to a managerial class responsible to a board of directors, who in turn were often beholden to investment bankers.

2. The Consolidation Movement in Industry, 1879-1903

The movement toward concentration of control in industry went through two major phases before the First World War: first, the trust movement, which began in 1879 and ended about 1890; second, the consolidation movement from 1897 to 1903, in which combinations were mainly constructed by using the holding-company form, under which a parent company owned the stock of its subsidiaries.

Most of the trusts of the first period of combination were organized by the manufacturers and businessmen directly involved, without the intervention of professional promoters or underwriting bankers. The trust was simply an extralegal arrangement by which competing manufacturers pooled properties to achieve monopoly. The Standard Oil Trust of 1879, superseded by the Trust Agreement of 1882, engineered by the dominant refiner, John D. Rockefeller, affords a good example of how this was done. First, the Trust Agreement was approved by the stockholders and owners of forty-odd oil companies, which together controlled over 90 percent of the refining industry and an almost equal proportion of the pipe lines. Second, a valuation of the properties and assets of the member corporations was made, and trust certificates with a par value of $100 each were issued in exchange for the property on the basis of this valuation. Finally, the combined properties were managed by nine trustees elected on a basis of stock ownership. Following Standard Oil's lead, similar trusts were organized in other important branches of industry; other combinations, organized by purchase or as holding companies, were also launched in the late 1880s and early 1890s.

The use of the trust form to achieve monopoly was abandoned in the 1890s, and the combination movement came almost to a standstill for a time. The Panic of 1893 was in part responsible, but even more important were the sweeping laws against conspiracies in restraint of trade that were enacted by Congress and many state legislatures. Few manufacturers were willing to risk heavy damages and dissolution by federal and state courts. The situation changed drastically in 1895, however, when the Supreme Court decreed that the federal antitrust law, the Sherman Antitrust Act of 1890, did not apply to combinations in the field of manufacturing.

The apparent removal of the formidable federal barrier to industrial combinations, the election of McKinley in 1896, and the return of prosperity in 1897 all combined to clear the way for a second consolidation movement that lasted until 1903. So great was this movement that in comparison the consolidations of the earlier period pale into insignificance. All told, not more than twelve important combinations, with a total capitalization of under $1 billion, had been organized from 1879 to 1897. Yet the Census of Manufactures in 1899 reported some 185 combinations with a total capital of over $3 billion. They accounted for nearly one-third of the entire capitalization of all manufacturing industries in the country. A comprehensive survey of American corporations in 1904 listed 305 industrial combinations, with an aggregate capital of nearly $7 billion, in operation. In addition, thirteen important combinations, with a capital of $500 million, were in process of reorganization; and combinations controlled fully two-fifths of the manufacturing capital of the United States. With 95 percent of the nation's mileage under the control of six groups, concentration in railroads had reached an even more spectacular level than had been achieved in industry. Moreover, some 1,330 public service corporations had been consolidated into a few holding companies that had a combined capitalization of $3.75 billion.

The reasons for this tremendous number of consolidations are not hard to find. Having acquired an understandable dislike of severe competition during the depression of the 1890s, manufacturers were easily persuaded that combination offered a sure means of controlling the price of their products and maintaining an orderly market. The fact that the three most important monopolies—Standard Oil, American Sugar, and American Tobacco—had prospered and paid dividends while the rest of industry struggled through destructive price wars was not lost upon the business community. Manufacturers, moreover, anticipated increased profits through the vertical integration of plants to achieve a continuous industrial process, large-scale production, the exploitation of the national market, and the utilization of by-products. In other words, large-scale enterprises would have capital to invest in labor-saving machinery and research, and they could assure control of raw materials and engage in nationwide marketing.

The consolidation movement came to a halt in 1904, chiefly because almost every branch of industry susceptible to combination had already been combined. But the activation of the federal antitrust law by Theodore Roosevelt and his successor, William H. Taft, was also an important factor in bringing the movement to an end. In fact, from 1904 to 1914 the federal government on the whole succeeded in compelling the great corporations to comply with the antitrust law. Most of the genuine monopolies were dissolved. Other combinations, like the International Harvester Company, the New Haven Railroad, and American Telephone and Telegraph, voluntarily acquiesced in reorganization plans approved by the attorney general. By 1914 the era of monopoly in American industry had passed, and a new economic structure was emerging. It was an oligopolistic structure, in which a few giant corporations dominated their branches of industry and usually determined price and wage policies. We will examine this development in greater detail in a future chapter.

3. *The Emergence of Financial Empires*

The savings of the middle and upper classes began to flow into banks and insurance companies as the wealth of the United States increased during the two decades before American intervention in the First World War. All American financial institutions combined had assets and resources of only $9 billion in 1899. Only twelve years later the country could boast of savings and liquid capital of nearly $28 billion. As a result, the entrepreneurs of the money market, the investment bankers, assumed leadership after 1897 in marshaling and allocating capital for industrial, railroad, public utility, and other forms of expansion. As we have seen, they were also the chief agents in promoting and financing the new consolidations. But the portentous fact was not the growth of American wealth, for that reflected an expanding and healthy economy; it was the startling concentration of control that took place among banks and insurance companies and the transformation of leading investment bankers from entrepreneurs of capital into dominant forces in the American economy.

So swift were these processes of concentration that there were by 1904 two financial empires in Wall Street: the House of Morgan and the Rockefeller group. Using its profits from railroad reorganization and promotion of large corporations, the Morgan firm bought control of the National Bank of Commerce and partial ownership of the great First National Bank of New York City. From this vantage point Morgan rapidly extended his control or influence over other banks and trust companies in New York, Philadelphia, and Chicago. Moreover, the House of Morgan was represented in the councils of United States Steel, International Mercantile Marine, International Harvester, General Electric, and other large corporations. By 1904 it controlled, besides, the Southern, Reading, Northern Pacific, Great Northern, New Haven, Erie, and other railroads, whose total mileage was over 47,000 and whose combined capital amounted to nearly one-fourth of the group railroad capital in the United States. Such an empire might have satisfied a man of modest ambition. However, Morgan set out around 1900 to win the richest prize of all—the large New York insurance companies. Control of their huge resources would open an almost unlimited market for securities. Morgan won the New York Life and Mutual Life by interlocking their directors into his own system. Finally, he bought a controlling interest in the Equitable Life in 1910. These three companies had assets of nearly $2 billion by 1913 and some $70 million of new money every year for investment.

On the other side of Wall Street was the far-flung Rockefeller group with its allies: the National City Bank, Hanover National Bank, Farmers Loan and Trust Company, and lesser banks; the Standard Oil Company; the Union Pacific, Southern Pacific, and nine other major railroads; and Morgan's rival in the investment and promotion fields, Kuhn, Loeb & Company, headed by Jacob H. Schiff. The normal process of concentration had been reversed to construct this financial imperium. Industrialists in the Standard Oil monopoly had channeled their excess profits into investment and promotion.

Around the Morgan and Rockefeller empires clustered a number of smaller kingdoms. "These two mammoth groups jointly . . . constitute the heart of the business and commercial life of the nation," one financial expert wrote in 1904, "the others all being the arteries which permeate in a thousand ways our whole national life, making their influence felt in every home and hamlet, yet all connected and dependent on this great central source, the influence and policy of which dominates them all."

The two groups did not always live in peace before 1907. Their rivalry for control of railroads, corporations, and insurance companies was sometimes bitter and on one memorable occasion reached the point of open war. The stakes of this battle were nothing less than control of most of the western transcontinental railroads. Morgan and his ally, James J. Hill, controlled the two northern transcontinental systems, the Northern Pacific and the Great Northern, in 1901. On the other hand, Edward H. Harriman and Kuhn, Loeb & Company controlled the central and southern systems, the Union Pacific and Southern Pacific. Neither group controlled the Burlington, the outlet to Chicago used by the Hill lines. Hill persuaded the owners of the Burlington to sell their railroad to the Northern Pacific and Great Northern in 1901, and Harriman and Schiff executed a daring flank attack by attempting to buy control of the Northern Pacific. The ensuing battle in the New York Stock Exchange drove the price of Northern Pacific common from $100 to over $1,000 a share. When the smoke had cleared it was discovered that Harriman and Schiff owned a majority of the shares of Northern Pacific, but that Hill and Morgan still controlled a majority of the voting stock. The rivals agreed to terms of peace to avert further conflict. They formed the Northern Securities Company, a holding company to control the Northern Pacific and Great Northern lines, and Harriman and Schiff were given minority representation on the board of directors. In addition, Harriman was awarded a seat on the board of the Burlington.

Morgan's preeminence was spectacularly revealed during the Panic of 1907, when he dramatically marshaled Wall Street's resources to prevent total demoralization of the securities markets. After this demonstration of personal power, the Rockefeller-Kuhn, Loeb group concluded that further opposition to the Morgan combination was futile. Thus, the Morgan and Rockefeller groups were merged from 1907 to 1913 into one confederated association by interlocking directorates and purchases of one another's stocks.

This confederation's power was dramatically highlighted by the careful investigation of a House subcommittee—the Pujo Committee—in the early months of 1913. This committee found that the Morgan-Rockefeller community of interest had achieved a very considerable control of the credit resources of the nation by consolidating bank and trust companies, gaining control over insurance companies, and interlocking their directorates among the boards of railroads and industrial and public utility corporations. How widely this influence extended was illustrated by the fact that the Morgan-Rockefeller group had 118 directorships in 34 banks and trust companies, with total resources of over $2.5 billion; 30 directorships in 10 insurance companies, with total assets of over $2 billion; 105 directorships in 32 transportation systems, with a total capitalization of more than $11 billion; 63 directorships in 24 producing and trading corporations, with a total capitalization of over $3 billion; and 25 directorships in

12 public utility corporations, with a combined capitalization of over $2 billion. In brief, the House of Morgan and its allies on January 1, 1913, had 341 directorships in 112 banks, railroads, industries, and other corporations with aggregate resources or capitalization of more than $20 billion.

The question whether a "money trust" existed as a result of the aggrandizement of power by the Wall Street bankers was hotly debated before the Pujo Committee. The committee did not claim that the Morgan empire had established an absolute monopoly of credit. It revealed beyond cavil, however, the vast and growing concentration of control of money and credit in the hands of a few men. The significance of the committee's findings was not lost upon the American people. How could genuine economic freedom and equality of opportunity exist in such circumstances? "This is the greatest question of all," Woodrow Wilson observed, "and to this statesmen must address themselves with an earnest determination to serve the long future and the true liberties of men."

4. *The United States and the World Economy, 1897-1914*

Foreign trade had been the lifeblood of the American economy since colonial times. Reflecting the profound changes taking place in the domestic economy, the volume and character of foreign trade underwent important changes from 1897 to 1914. First, foreign trade expanded at a faster pace during this period than at any time since the Civil War. Exports increased from almost $1.4 billion in 1900 to nearly $2.5 billion by 1914, while imports rose from $850 million to $1.8 billion during the same period. Second, an important shift in the character of exports and imports took place. In 1900 agricultural products constituted 60 percent of the nation's exports, manufactured products only 35 percent. By 1914 manufactured products accounted for nearly 49 percent of American exports. At the same time, development of new industries at home lessened American demand for manufactured goods from abroad and stimulated increased demand for raw materials like rubber, tin, and manganese.

The rapid growth of American exports of manufactured goods and capital before 1914 foretold the coming of the day when the United States would occupy a commanding position in the world economy. However, London was still the center of international exchange before 1915, and the United States continued to occupy its traditional status as debtor to Europe. In 1897 Europeans held American securities, over half of them in railroads, valued at nearly $3.5 billion. By the eve of the First World War, European investments in the United States, direct and indirect, had more

U.S. FOREIGN TRADE
1900 - 1948

BILLIONS OF DOLLARS

15.0

12.5

10.0

U.S. ENTERS
WORLD WAR I

U.S. ENTERS
WORLD WAR II

7.5

SURPLUS OF
EXPORTS

1929
STOCK MARKET
CRASH

5.0

DOMESTIC
EXPORTS

SURPLUS OF
IMPORTS

2.5

IMPORTS FOR
CONSUMPTION

1900   1908   1916   1924   1932   1940   1948

than doubled. In part this was offset by American investments abroad, but the balance of payments still ran heavily against the United States.

Nonetheless, the two most significant trends during the period 1897-1914 were the growth of American exports of manufactured goods and the rapid increase in the export of American capital abroad. The first was achieved in spite of the lack of a sizable American merchant marine, experience in doing business in foreign countries, or a well-organized governmental program to support foreign trade. The growth of American investments abroad, on the other hand, took place under the guidance of experienced bankers and often with the support of the State Department.

The United States was the richest and industrially the most powerful nation in the world when it went to war with Spain in 1898. But up to this time practically every available dollar had gone into building railroads, opening the West, and constructing industries at home. American investments abroad totaled only $684,500,000 on the eve of the Spanish-American War. Yet this figure stood at $3,513,800,000 in 1914. Except for $692,000,000 invested in Europe and $246,000,000 in the Far East, American capital had not ventured far from home. American capitalists had invested $867,200,000 in Canadian mines, industries, and railroads. The encouragement given foreign investors by the seemingly stable Díaz government of Mexico from 1877 to 1911 had attracted $854,000,000 from the United States, most of which went into railroads, mines, ranches, and oil. American investments in Cuba, which was a quasi-protectorate of the United States after 1898, grew from $50,000,000 in 1897 to $200,000,000 by 1914. By the latter date Americans had also invested $136,000,000 in the other Caribbean islands, $93,000,000 in Central America, and $366,000,000 in the more stable countries of South America.

5. The Conditions and Hazards of Labor, 1897-1914

The period 1897-1914, generally speaking, was a time of relative stability and steady economic progress for labor. Except for a brief interlude in 1908, full employment prevailed during most of the period. Real earnings of all workers in manufacturing, the only group for whom we have reliable statistics, increased at the rate of 1.3 percent annually from 1890 to 1914, for a total increase of 37 percent for this entire period. It would have increased more had there not been a rise of 39 percent in the cost of living for workers during the period 1897-1914.

This picture of increasing and steadier employment accompanied by a substantial increase in real wages did not encourage the friends of labor. Surveying the industrial scene in 1915, the majority members of the Commission on Industrial Relations, appointed by President Wilson to ascertain the causes of industrial unrest, observed that "a large part of our industrial population are . . . living in a condition of actual poverty. How large this proportion is can not be exactly determined, but it is certain that at least one-third and possibly one-half of the families of wage earners employed in manufacturing and mining earn in the course of the year less than enough to support them in anything like a comfortable and decent condition." The social consequences of this state of affairs were ominous: children of the poor died at three times the rate of children of the middle classes; 12 to 20 percent of the children in six large cities were underfed and undernourished; only one-third of all children enrolled finished elementary schools; less than 10 percent of the children in public schools were graduated from high schools.

There were, even so, encouraging developments that offered hope for the future. To begin with, some progress had been made since 1897 toward reducing the hours of labor in industry and transportation. Average hours in industry fell from 59.1 a week in 1897 to 55.2 in 1914. These general averages, however, obscure the important differential in hours worked between organized and unorganized labor. The movement for shorter hours had begun in the building, printing, and other skilled and organized trades and was most successful among them. One survey, for example, revealed that in six unionized industries average weekly hours declined from 53.4 in 1897 to 48.8 in 1914. In contrast, average weekly hours in eight unorganized industries declined from 61.9 to 58.2 during the same period.

Secondly, the first real progress was made during the years from 1907 to 1914 toward reducing the hazards of labor. Statistics of industrial accidents are unreliable for this period, but an incomplete survey in 1907 revealed that at least 500,000 American workers were either killed, crippled, or seriously injured while at work. As late as 1913, according to a more reliable survey, 25,000 workers were killed on their jobs, and another 700,000 were seriously injured.

The sporadic efforts made by several states to reduce the industrial accident rate had been unproductive before 1907. Between 1907 and 1914, however, the public awakened to the great wastage of human resources by industrial deaths and accidents. The safety movement began in 1907, when the United States Steel Corporation inaugurated a comprehensive campaign to reduce the accident toll. So successful was this program that a few other leading corporations and railroads, notably the International Harvester Company and the Chicago & North Western Railroad, instituted safety campaigns before 1914.

Thirdly, the reports of social workers and factory inspectors in many states also focused public attention on the social necessity of healthful working conditions in industry. The problem was most acute in textile mills and garment sweatshops where large numbers of women and children were employed. In fact, nowhere in the country were working conditions so incredibly bad as in the garment sweatshops of New York City, most of which were located in tenements that were literally firetraps. The Triangle Shirtwaist Factory fire on the East Side in 1911, in which 148 women lost their lives, led to the appointment of a Factory Investigating Commission and a thorough revision of New York's factory code between 1912 and 1914.

Finally, the urgency of eliminating occupational diseases like phosphorus and lead poisoning was brought home to employers and the public in a number of ways from 1900 to 1914. Medical research provided the essential knowledge, while state and national reform groups, like the American Association for Labor Legislation, carried on the necessary propaganda work. A campaign against phosphorus matches, for example, resulted in the enactment in 1912 of a federal statute forbidding their manufacture. Lead poisoning in its various forms was partially eliminated. But the greatest progress came when the American Medical Association joined hands with the American Association for Labor Legislation to begin a comprehensive campaign against industrial diseases.

6. The Rise of the American Federation of Labor

Nothing better illustrates the precarious position that workers occupied in American society during the half century between the Civil War and the First World War than the story of labor's attempts to achieve some measure of protection through organization. Organized labor passed through several phases during this long period and was confronted at times with almost insurmountable obstacles. Nonetheless, labor organizations won a larger degree of recognition than ever before in American history. And although labor's great goal—unionization of all workers—was unrealized by 1914, the foundations of a strong labor movement had been well laid.

There were two initial attempts at labor organization on a national scale between 1865 and the late 1880s before the dominant pattern of unionization was established. The first, the National Labor Union, founded in 1866, was a loose aggregation of trade unions and assorted reform groups. It was practically defunct by 1872. More important was the Knights of Labor, organized in Philadelphia in 1869. It attempted to organize workers along industrial rather than craft lines, without regard to sex or race. The union won a few spectacular strike victories and attained a membership of over 700,000 by early 1886, but it rapidly disintegrated after newspapers and employers charged it with responsibility for a serious riot in Chicago in May 1886.

While the Knights of Labor was enjoying momentary success, the leaders of the Cigar Makers' Union, Samuel Gompers and Adolph Strasser, were building the first powerful trade union in American history. Other unions federated with the cigar makers in a Federation of Organized Trades in 1881, and the union was reorganized as the American Federation of Labor in 1886. The AF of L under Samuel Gompers, who dominated the organization until his death in 1924, for the most part spurned industrial unionism (that is, unionism that groups all workers in a single industry into a single organization) and built upon the foundation of craft and trade unions. From its beginning, moreover, the AF of L eschewed utopianism and was avowedly opportunistic and practical in its objectives.

The AF of L's lasting power was demonstrated when it weathered the defeat of the steelworkers' and miners' unions in major strikes in 1892 and 1894 and came out of the depression in 1897 with 265,000 members. From this point it soon fought its way to dominance in the American labor movement. Its membership had climbed to 548,000 by 1900. There were spectacular gains until 1904, when membership reached 1,676,000. Then membership declined under the hammer blows of an organized employer campaign until 1911, when it began slowly to mount again. It stood at a little over 2,000,000 in 1914.

Standing apart from the AF of L were the four railroad brotherhoods—the conductors, engineers, trainmen, and firemen—who since the 1880s had been the best-paid workers in the country, a labor aristocracy conscious of their power and privileged position. They had won the ten-hour day throughout the country by 1910. Then in 1916 the four unions, 400,000 strong, combined to do battle for their next objective, the eight-hour day. This they won with the adoption by Congress of the Adamson Act, establishing the eight-hour day as the standard for all workers engaged in interstate railway transportation.

7. *The Progress of Unionization in the Coal Industry*

The period from the end of the Panic of 1893 to the First World War was a time of labor's first concerted striving toward the goal of industrial democracy. Many factors combined to give the AF of L opportunities and advantages that its predecessors had not enjoyed: superb esprit de corps accompanied by a feeling of solidarity, wise leadership, and a public opinion that was growing less hostile to the labor movement. Building largely on foundations already laid, Gompers and his colleagues from 1897 to 1914 succeeded in expanding membership and winning collective bargaining, higher wages, and shorter hours in most of the building trades and the skilled crafts. On the other hand, labor's new militancy was matched by an equally aggressive determination on management's side to prevent unionization in the mass industries. This, therefore, was the crucial question. Could the AF of L carry the fight into the basic industries and triumph over great aggregations of power?

The first test came in the effort of the United Mine Workers of America, an industrial union affiliated with the AF of L, to organize the coal industry. Decisively beaten in a general coal strike in 1894, the UMW had only 10,000 members and seemed dead by 1897. Leaders of the union nonetheless demanded increased wages and recognition, and the operators' refusal set off a general strike in the bituminous fields that began on July 4, 1897. The strikers were well organized and magnificently led, and operators in western Pennsylvania, Ohio, Indiana, and Illinois surrendered in the following September. It was a notable victory, not merely because the miners won recognition, higher wages, and other demands, but also because it was a spur and inspiration to the entire labor movement.

Emerging from this strike well organized and over 100,000 strong, the UMW now turned its sights on the anthracite coal industry centered in five counties of northeastern Pennsylvania and controlled by nine railroad companies. The president of the UMW, John Mitchell, authorized a strike on September 12, 1900, and 150,000 anthracite miners walked out of the pits. The union had demanded recognition, establishment of labor-management committees to settle petty disputes, a wage increase, and the right to employ checkweighmen. Before the strike was over, Mitchell waived the demand for recognition and suggested that the remaining issues be arbitrated. And when the operators granted a 10 percent wage increase and made other concessions in October 1900, Mitchell gladly called off the strike. Although the UMW won only part of its demands, it had succeeded in accomplishing its major objective—thorough organization of the anthracite industry.

The anthracite operators refused even to discuss wage rates with UMW officials in 1902, and Mitchell called a second strike that began on May 14. Public opinion strongly favored the miners and veered even more sharply in their favor as the result of an incident that occurred in August. A citizen of Wilkes-Barre appealed in the name of Christianity to George F. Baer, president of the Reading Railroad, to end the strike by giving in to the union. Baer replied in a letter, which was subsequently published, that the interests of the miners would be protected, "not by the labor agitators, but by the Christian men to whom God, in His infinite wisdom, has given control of the property interests of the country."

As the strike dragged on into the autumn of 1902 coal prices skyrocketed, and people in the eastern cities thought they faced a serious coal famine. President Roosevelt summoned Mitchell and leading operators to a White House conference on October 3, 1902. While Mitchell agreed to submit the issues to arbitration and to end the strike, the operators denounced the UMW as a lawless body and declared that they would never arbitrate. This was too much for Roosevelt. He issued secret orders to the army to move 10,000 troops into the anthracite region, seize the mines, and operate them as receiver for the government. Next he sent Secretary of War Elihu Root to New York City to warn J. P. Morgan, who had close financial ties with the operators, of the impending seizure. Morgan and Root at once sketched out a plan of mediation, and the operators accepted it with the reservation that no labor official should be appointed to the arbitration commission. Mitchell approved the plan, insisting only that the president be given complete freedom in naming arbiters. Roosevelt added a humorous touch, which he greatly enjoyed, by appointing the former grand chief of the Railway Conductors' Brotherhood to the commission in the capacity of "sociologist."

Roosevelt's intervention and the subsequent arbitration of the dispute was a landmark in American labor history. For the first time the federal government had looked at an industrial dispute on its merits, without automatically taking management's side. From the commission's award the miners won the nine-hour day, a 10 percent wage increase, the right to select checkweighmen, and a permanent board of conciliation. Not until

1916 did the UMW finally win recognition from the anthracite operators. Even so, the gains from the victory of 1902 were significant indeed.

Thus, the UMW had organized the eastern and midwestern bituminous areas and the entire anthracite industry by 1903. On the troubled frontiers of coal, however, they met fierce resistance and defeat that spelled eventual disaster. West Virginia was the key to long-range success or failure; for so long as the West Virginia fields were unorganized, the UMW and northern operators could never be protected from the competition of this low-wage and low-cost area. The UMW executed full-scale campaigns in 1900 and again in 1902 to organize the state, but all their efforts failed. Meanwhile, the task of organizing the southern area became increasingly important and difficult as new coal fields were opened in Virginia, Kentucky, Tennessee, and Alabama. The UMW launched a third great strike in West Virginia in 1912 and 1913 but was only partially successful. So long as West Virginia and other southern fields remained unorganized there could be neither stability in the coal industry nor security for the UMW.

In the meantime, the miners suffered bloodier defeats on another frontier, Colorado. A UMW strike against John D. Rockefeller's Colorado Fuel and Iron Company and other operators in 1903-1904 ended in rout for the union and deportation of many of the strikers. Ten years later, in September 1913, the UMW again attempted to overcome the Colorado coal companies. This time the state was torn by violent civil war, set off when National Guard troops attacked and burned a strikers' tent colony at Ludlow on April 20, 1914, killing eleven women and two children.

The Ludlow Massacre and civil war in Colorado horrified the nation, provoked investigations by a congressional committee and the Industrial Relations Commission, and set off a wave of sympathy for the strikers. But John D. Rockefeller, Jr., who now controlled the Colorado Fuel and Iron Company, refused to surrender to the UMW. Rejecting President Wilson's plan of settlement, he instituted a labor relations program, the chief feature of which was the formation of a company union, which retained for management full power over policies affecting the workers. Nonetheless, the American people (and young Rockefeller as well) had been taught a tragic lesson in the consequences of industrial despotism and absentee capitalism.

8. "As Steel Goes"

Socialists and other left wing elements in the labor movement often charged that Gompers and the AF of L represented only the aristocracy of labor and that they were indifferent to the necessity of organizing the basic industries that employed the mass of workers. These critics ignored some important facts. This was a period when organized labor progressed from impotence to a position of considerable power, in spite of the absence of any favorable legislation or any effective public support in behalf of the labor movement. To say that Gompers and his leaders did not recognize the importance of unionizing the basic industries, like iron and steel, textiles, and lumber, is simply not true. But Gompers knew the AF of L's weakness as well as its strength, and he knew that the time had not yet come for an all-out campaign against mass industries.

The wisdom of Gompers's view was confirmed many times during the progressive period. The AF of L's most discouraging and significant reversal was its failure to organize the steel industry. All during the period under discussion steel stood as an antiunion bastion, setting an open-shop pattern for other mass industries and providing antiunion leadership for thousands of small manufacturers.

Carnegie had defeated the Amalgamated Iron, Steel and Tin workers, which then included only skilled workers, during the violent Homestead strike of 1892. When the Carnegie plants were merged into the United States Steel Corporation in 1901, union officials decided that they now had no alternative but to attempt to organize all steelworkers, skilled and unskilled. First, however, the Amalgamated demanded that the union scale of wages be paid in all plants of the American Sheet Steel, American Steel Hoop, and American Tin Plate companies, all subsidiaries of United States Steel. The directors of the corporation offered a compromise that would have halted the progress of unionization. The union officials refused and then, on August 10, 1901, called a general strike against all plants of the steel corporation. A majority of workers walked out, but the strike for a number of reasons was doomed from the beginning. In the end the Amalgamated surrendered unconditionally. The corporation agreed to pay union wages, but the wage rate was no longer an important issue. In return, the union withdrew from fourteen mills, agreed neither to seek to extend its influence nor even to welcome new members, and conceded the corporation's right to discharge workers for union activities.

Officials of United States Steel made no direct assaults upon the carcass of the Amalgamated for a time after their victory of 1901. Instead, they instituted measures to win the loyalty of the workers: profit sharing was begun in December 1902; an employee-safety program was launched in 1906–1907; and finally a workmen's compensation and old-age pension program was inaugurated in 1910. Meanwhile, the American Sheet and Tin Plate Company, the last of the unionized subsidiaries of the corporation, posted notices in June 1909 announcing that it would begin an open-shop policy on July 1. The protests of the Amalgamated were not even acknowledged, and the union called a second general strike against the corporation. Although the workers responded en masse throughout the far-flung steel empire and the AF of L joined the struggle with financial support, the strikers never had a chance. After holding out for fourteen months they surrendered on August 23, 1910.

Thus, after 1909 the United States Steel Corporation boasted an open shop throughout its vast domain. Moreover, the Lake Carriers' Association, an ally of United States Steel, destroyed the Lake Seamen's Union during a long and bitter strike from 1909 to 1912. The establishment of management's absolute authority in all branches of the steel corporation had been accomplished by relentless warfare against the union, use of spies and blacklisting of strike leaders, domination of local governments, and a welfare program that undermined the union's appeal. United States Steel remained the citadel of antiunionism in the mass industries until 1937.

9. *Left Wing Unionism and the Rise of Socialism*

Left wing unionism first developed on an important scale not in the teeming cities of the East, but in the mining regions of the western slope of the Rockies. Here raw industrial absolutism provoked brutal retaliation by frontier miners. The result was class warfare on a grand and violent scale without ideological overtones. Out of this morass of class conflict an organization emerged in 1905. It was the Industrial Workers of the World, a coalition of the Western Federation of Miners, the socialistic American Labor Union, and the Socialist Trade and Labor Alliance. Organized along industrial lines, the IWW was frankly revolutionary. Its weapons were revolutionary rhetoric, organization of the mass of workers, and strikes; its objectives were abolition of the wage system and establishment of a proletarian commonwealth.

The IWW showed signs of coming apart at the seams within a year after its formation. The basic difficulty was dissension between leaders of the Western Federation of Miners, who were more interested in promoting labor's immediate goals than in building the socialistic state, and the head of the Socialist Trade and Labor Alliance, Daniel De Leon, a dogmatic Marxian theorist. De Leon was unceremoniously expelled in 1908, and from this time on the IWW was a champion of lower-class workers without concern for pure revolutionary dogma. In the West it fought the battles of the lumbermen, migratory workers, and frontier miners. Its emphasis on the militant strike brought it into collision with employers, the police, and the courts, and prevented any systematic organizational campaigns. In the East the IWW provided leadership for unskilled workers whom the AF of L had ignored. It led a strike in Lawrence, Massachusetts, against the American Woolen Company in 1912 and won a wage increase. It took command of rebellious silk workers in Paterson and Passaic, New Jersey, and led them in a successful strike in 1912 and 1913.

While the IWW was careening from one bloody conflict to another, the political counterpart of left wing unionism, socialism, was struggling for a program and a means of expression. The Socialists were united during the 1890s in the Socialist Labor party, which De Leon ruled until his inflexible Marxist dogma provoked a rebellion by a moderate element in 1899-1900. Meanwhile, in 1897 the midwestern labor leader, Eugene V. Debs, had founded a potential rival, the Social Democratic party, dedicated to advancing public ownership of railroads, utilities, and industrial monopolies. The anti-De Leon faction in the Socialist Labor party, headed by Morris Hillquit of New York and Victor Berger of Milwaukee, joined the Debs group in Indianapolis in 1901 to launch the Socialist Party of America.

The Socialist party included visionaries and dogmatic Marxians, but it was so completely dominated by the moderates—Debs, Hillquit, and Berger—that it was more the left wing of progressivism than a revolutionary workers' party. The party had a membership of over 58,000 by 1908; four years later the figure stood at nearly 126,000. The party's influence during this period, however, was far greater than its small membership would indicate. Socialist administrations by 1912 governed Berkeley, California, Milwaukee, and Schenectady. One of the party's leaders, Victor Berger, sat in the House of Representatives and was soon joined by another Socialist from New York City's East Side, Meyer London. And the Socialist presidential candidate, Debs, polled over 897,000 votes in the election of 1912.

10. The Counteroffensive of the Employers, Injunctions, and the AF of L in Politics

For a time at the turn of the century it seemed that the lion and the lamb might lie down together. The sign of impending industrial peace was the organization in 1900 of the National Civic Federation, founded to prove that "organized labor cannot be destroyed without debasement of the masses." The federation's leaders included industrialists like Mark Hanna and George W. Perkins, bankers like J. P. Morgan, and labor spokesmen like Samuel Gompers and John Mitchell. For a few years the federation rendered service to the labor movement by lending a sort of respectability to the AF of L.

That the federation represented only a minority of employers, however, was demonstrated by a significant movement that was already on foot when the federation was organized. It was a mass offensive of employers to destroy unionism altogether and to establish an open-shop pattern throughout American industry. This counterattack began in 1900 in Dayton, Ohio, where the union movement had made considerable progress.

Within two years the local employers' association had driven the unions out of town. Flushed with victory, propagandists went from Dayton to arouse employers in other cities to the defense of what they called "the American Plan"—that is, the open shop. So successful were responding employers' associations in Beloit, Wisconsin, Sedalia, Missouri, and Chicago, that the leaders of the open-shop crusade received appeals for assistance from employers' groups all over the country.

Obviously, what most industrialists and businessmen wanted was destruction of the labor movement. The National Association of Manufacturers took command of the open-shop campaign in 1903 and formed the Citizens' Industrial Association for the purpose of forming employers' associations throughout the country. The Citizens' Industrial Association also executed a broad campaign to rally public opinion behind the American Plan. Appealing to the average citizen's individualism and prejudices, this propaganda defended the right of Americans to work when and where they pleased, depicted labor organizers as agitators and Socialists, and portrayed employers as champions of free enterprise and ancient American liberties. This counteroffensive did not destroy unionism, but it struck such a heavy blow that the AF of L not only failed to grow but actually lost membership between 1904 and 1910.

Gompers had managed to fight off those idealists who advocated aligning the AF of L with the Socialist Labor party, the Populists in 1892, and the Democrats during the great battle of 1896. It would have been difficult for Gompers to maintain this policy of nonpartisanship in any event, given the momentum and attraction of the progressive movement. But one event, more than any other, was responsible for the AF of L going into the political arena. It was the entrance of the federal courts into labor disputes in a decisive way. It began during the Chicago railroad strike of 1894, when the attorney general of the United States obtained an injunction against Eugene V. Debs and other leaders of the American Railway Union for conspiring to restrain trade and obstruct the movement of mail. The theory upon which this and later injunctions were issued was that the prohibitions against restraint of trade embodied in the Sherman Antitrust Act of 1890 applied as much to labor and farm unions as to corporations. The effect of this doctrine, which was confirmed by the Supreme Court in 1895, was not to outlaw unions, per se, as illegal conspiracies, but to forbid union practices that might be construed to be unreasonable, or illegal, restraints upon trade.

The Sherman Act was used before 1901 less against illegal industrial combinations than against labor's allegedly illegal weapons—mass picketing, the sympathetic strike, the secondary boycott, and blacklisting of goods manufactured by antiunion employers. It was the continued intervention of the federal courts after 1901 that finally compelled Gompers and the AF of L to take an active role in national politics. The immediate provocation arose out of two cases involving the boycott of nonunion products—the *Danbury Hatters'* case and the *Buck's Stove and Range Company* case.

The United Hatters of North America in 1902 called a strike against a hatmaker of Danbury, Connecticut, D. E. Loewe and Company, and declared a nationwide boycott of Loewe's products. Officials of the company struck back by organizing the American Anti-Boycott Association and by suing the United Hatters in 1903 for triple damages of $240,000 under the Sherman Act. The Supreme Court five years later confirmed the judgment of the lower courts that the boycott was a conspiracy in restraint of trade. The district court thereupon awarded the company full damages and made members of the union personally responsible for payment of the claim. In the second case, the Buck's Stove and Range Company in 1907 obtained an injunction in a federal court ordering officials of the AF of L to end a boycott against the company's products. Gompers and the executive committee of the AF of L ignored the injunction, and a federal court sentenced them all to jail for terms ranging from six months to one year. The Supreme Court in 1914 upheld the injunction but removed the penalties on a technicality.

The effect of the rulings in these two test cases was to confirm that all of labor's strike activities fell within the purview of the federal courts, and that union leaders and members were liable to jail terms and loss of property if they defied injunctions. In short, labor might wage industrial warfare only if the federal courts approved. Obviously, the AF of L's surest means of protection against such judicial interference was to obtain amendment of the Sherman law to give labor unions immunity from its prohibitions.

The leaders of the AF of L tried in various indirect ways from 1900 to 1906 to force the desired changes in the Sherman Act, but their pressure, as contrasted with the growing political power of the NAM, was pitifully weak. Gompers and his associates decided in 1906 that the time had come to begin an all-out political campaign. First they presented to President Roosevelt and Congress a bill of grievances, demanding, among other things, amendment of the Sherman law and relief from judicial interference. Next, they entered the congressional campaign of 1906 and helped to elect six union members to the House of Representatives. Two years later Gompers presented the AF of L's demands to the platform committees of the Republican and Democratic national conventions. The Republicans refused to make any concessions or promises, while the Democrats adopted a disingenuous platform plank that seemed to promise substantial relief. Taking what they could get, Gompers and his colleagues openly campaigned in behalf of the Democratic ticket headed by William Jennings Bryan.

The Republican victory in 1908 was only a momentary reversal, for the political situation from 1910 to 1912 seemed to offer the AF of L an opportunity finally to achieve its goal. Internal warfare split the Republican party and made certain a Democratic victory in 1912. And when the Democrats nominated a progressive, Woodrow Wilson, and reaffirmed the promises that they had made to labor four years before, Gompers and his executive committee campaigned openly and effectively for the Democratic ticket. Wilson won a sweeping victory in the electoral college, the Democrats won control of both houses of Congress, and it seemed that labor's friends were finally in control of the federal government.

In large measure labor's hopes were realized during the period of Wilson's first administration, from 1913 to 1917. The new secretary of labor, William B. Wilson, was a former secretary-treasurer of the UMW; some fifteen union members sat in the House of Representatives; and the new president was considerably more susceptible to labor pressure than Roosevelt or Taft had been. The changed climate was everywhere evident in Washington—in the exposure of an NAM lobby by a congressional committee in 1913; in the forthright investigation of the Colorado coal strike in 1914 by the House labor committee and the Industrial Relations Commission; in the adoption in 1915 of the Seaman's Act, sponsored by Gompers and Andrew Furuseth of the International Seamen's Union, which freed sailors from bondage to their labor contracts; in passage of the Smith-Hughes Act in 1916 (approved in 1917), providing for federal aid to state vocational education; and in the passage of the Burnett immigration bill, which established a literacy test for immigrants, over Wilson's veto in 1917.

Even so, the AF of L's chief objective was still amendment of the Sherman Act to give unions immunity from prosecution for using illegal strike weapons. In this campaign Gompers and the AF of L lobby ran head on into the stubborn opposition of President Wilson and the Democratic majority in Congress. The issue first arose decisively during the preparation of new antitrust legislation, the Clayton bill, in 1914. This measure as it emerged from the House judiciary committee included no provisions for labor's benefit. Gompers and his now powerful lobby at once descended upon Congress and the White House. Labor spokesmen in the House threatened to oppose the Clayton bill, and there were many stormy conferences between the labor leaders and administration spokesmen. So firmly did the administration maintain its stand, however, that Gompers had to accept a compromise that denied the AF of L its supreme objective. The House committee added sections to the Clayton bill providing for jury trials in criminal contempt cases and circumscribing the issuance of injunctions in labor disputes. Another provision declared that neither farm nor labor unions should be construed to be illegal combinations, per se, in restraint of trade. But since the courts had repeatedly declared that labor unions were not unlawful combinations, this declaration by Congress conferred no new benefits. A final provision legalized strike activities that the courts had heretofore approved.

President Wilson and the chairman of the House committee that framed the labor sections of the Clayton bill frankly declared that the bill did not give labor unions immunity from prosecution for violating the antitrust law. But Gompers hailed the Clayton Act as labor's "Magna Charta" and announced that the AF of L had finally won freedom from judicial interference under the Sherman law. As we shall see in a later chapter, the Supreme Court thought otherwise.

3

A Variety of

Progressive Movements

When an assassin's bullet catapulted Theodore Roosevelt into the presidency in 1901, the United States was already in the first stages of the political convulsion that historians, perhaps somewhat loosely, call the progressive movement. Basically, progressivism was the response of the great majority of Americans to the problems generated by recent industrialization and urbanization. Most disturbing were the breakdown of responsible government in city, state, and nation; the spread of slums, crime, and poverty in the large cities; the exploitation of labor, particularly women and children; the growth of industrial and financial concentration; and, above all, the emergence of great economic concentrations—railroads, large corporations, and banking empires—that could profoundly affect the destinies of the people while remaining beyond their control.

In actual fact, there was no such thing as a progressive movement. That is, there was no organized campaign uniting all diverse efforts at political, social, and economic reform. On the contrary, there were numerous progressive movements operating in different areas simultaneously. For example, there was the effort of social workers and students of the labor question to bring state and national governments to the side of women, children, and other unprotected groups. This movement for social justice was often, but not always, independent of the movement for political reform. There was the far-reaching campaign, getting under way in the 1890s, to end the reign of corruption in, and to restore representative government to, the cities. Next came a movement to bring state governments out of their subservience to railroads and corporations and to make them instruments for advancing social welfare. Finally, there was a progressive movement on the national level, the main thrust of which was the attempt to subject railroads, industrial corporations, and banks to effective public control.

There were two broad currents in progressivism during its early years—reform and reconstruction. Many Americans were reformers because they worked for honest and efficient government, but some of them had no desire for any important reconstruction to take place in the areas of political or economic life. They might, for example, believe strongly in the businesslike administration of government while at the same time they regarded the income tax or plans to aid farmers as pernicious class measures. Other Americans believed in both reform and reconstruction. To achieve the latter, they came to rely more and more upon concerted, purposeful, and democratic governmental action. The political and economic reconstructionists were the growing, dominant element among progressives after the Panic of 1893. It is these champions of the expansion of governmental power that will hereafter be referred to as "progressives."

It is important to be very clear about one central fact: progressives were not Socialists. To be sure, progressives generally desired expansion of governmental power in order to substitute collective for individual decisions in broad matters of social and economic policy. However, they sought the reform and reconstruction of capitalism, not its destruction; their great goal was not the establishment of a socialistic commonwealth, but rather the achievement of a humane and democratic capitalistic system that would benefit all people.

It was inevitable that this should have been true because progressivism, particularly in its political manifestations, was primarily a revolt of the middle classes—small businessmen and bankers, the more prosperous farmers, and editors, professors, clergymen, and other professional groups—against a state of affairs that seemed to guarantee perpetual control to the privileged few who owned the wealth of the United States. Although progressives from time to time worked creatively and effectively with the leaders of organized labor on all levels of government, progressivism had no solid basis of popular support among the masses of workers and cannot be said to have been truly labor oriented. Moreover, while leadership in the reform movements of the 1890s was to a significant extent agrarian, extreme farm unrest subsided after the return of prosperity in

1897. Leadership in the revolt against the status quo passed, therefore, to the cities and towns.

It does no gross harm to historical truth to say that something like a general progressive reform movement was beginning to take shape by the early 1900s. To a significant degree, progressives were united by a common ideology. Social justice reformers were organized in state and national associations and united behind common programs. City reformers united in the National Municipal League in 1894. In the arena of national politics, moreover, progressives in both the Republican and Democratic parties sought the same objectives and often worked together to achieve them.

1. The Dynamics of Progressivism

Progressivism's major components had their origins as recognizable movements in the 1890s. They were among the immediate responses to the economic distress caused by both the agrarian depression of that period and the Panic of 1893. It is more difficult to explain why the movement gained its greatest momentum and achieved its most important triumphs between 1897 and 1917, a time of expanding prosperity and national contentment. Some recent writers have suggested that the prime dynamic forces were the resentment that older established classes felt toward the *nouveaux riches* and the general fear of the middle classes that they were being ground between the rising upper and lower classes. This is what is called the "status revolution" theory of progressivism's causation. The theory has been tested in particular situations many times, but in no instance have scholars been able to substantiate it. Invariably, they have found that progressives and their conservative opponents came from the same classes and ethnic and religious backgrounds. The moving forces in progressivism were as complex and varied as the movement itself, and they are to be found only in the details of historical record.

Progressivism's roots lay deep in American evangelical Christian and democratic traditions, but it had its immediate origins in a series of disconnected movements for reform and reconstruction during the 1890s. The first of these was the agrarian revolt, which culminated in populism and a Populist-Democratic fusion in 1896. The Populists and then the Democratic-Populist candidate in 1896, William Jennings Bryan, failed to win national power because they remained essentially agrarian spokesmen and never won the support of either industrial labor or the urban middle classes. However, populism and Bryanism did shake the political foundations and cause a certain realignment of the two major parties. More important, the propaganda spread by the Populists publicized widespread distress and at the same time revived the concept of governmental action to ensure economic well-being. In addition, the Populists' emphasis upon greater popular participation in, and control of, political and financial institutions paved the way for sweeping reforms in the near future.

The sharp intensification of human distress during the Panic of 1893 dramatized for increasing numbers of urban Americans the wide contrast between the privileged position of the well-to-do and the plight of the poor. The impact was heaviest on ministers, priests, and social workers in the slums of the great cities. As Walter Rauschenbusch, the social gospel leader, said about the poor whom he saw in New York during the depression of the 1890s: "They wore down our threshold, and they wore away our hearts. . . . One could hear human virtue cracking and crumbling all around." The suffering that resulted from the depression stimulated enormously the two movements that furnished much of the moral zeal for progressivism—the social gospel and the movement for social justice.

Americans in the 1890s, already convulsed by the indictments of the Populists and Bryan, were further agitated by a burgeoning literature of exposure. It started with Henry George's *Progress and Poverty* (1879); gained momentum with the publication of Edward Bellamy's utopian socialist novel, *Looking Backward* (1888); and came to fully developed form in Henry Demarest Lloyd's scathing indictment of the Standard Oil Trust, *Wealth Against Commonwealth* (1894). From this time onward, arraignment and exposure were the order of the day in American journalism. Moreover, by the 1890s economists, political scientists, sociologists, and other publicists were beginning to challenge successfully the philosophical foundations of the laissez-faire state—social Darwinism and classical economics—and the whole cluster of ideals associated with rugged individualism. Leading this revolt were young economists like Richard T. Ely, sociologists like Lester F. Ward, political scientists like Woodrow Wilson, and iconoclasts like Thorstein Veblen. Their ranks would swell mightily in the early 1900s.

A final generative force was the rapid growth of the urban middle classes in the United States between the Civil War and the First World War. Three profoundly important things happened to these classes in the 1890s and early 1900s. First, they grew so rapidly in numbers because of business expansion that they were able to wield the balance of political power in many sections of the country by 1900. Second, influential segments of these groups, molded by their specialized training and professional standards and affiliations, joined in insisting upon rationality and efficient administration in public affairs. Finally, because they were the best educated and most idealistic segment of the population, they were deeply affected by the exposures of corruption and the accounts of economic and social distress. By the late 1890s they were building up a full head of steam of moral indignation. The boiler would soon explode with very significant political repercussions.

With these observations by way of introduction, let us examine one of the most significant and fruitful reform movements in American history.

2. *The Social Justice Movement*

The social justice movement was the first large-scale attempt to palliate the grosser aspects of American life—the miserable living conditions of city masses, the exploitation of women and children in industry, and the degradation of submerged, unprotected workers. The vanguard in the movement were priests and ministers who worked in the slums. However, a separate class of social workers, usually employed by charity organizations and settlement houses—community centers that began to spring up in the late 1880s—emerged in the 1890s. They constituted a growing and vociferous element in American society after 1900. They made intensive surveys of labor conditions, causes of poverty, and means of alleviating social distress. As time passed, moreover, they became departmentalized, some concerned with care of immigrants, some with problems of labor, some with juvenile delinquency. As one authority has said, "By the latter part of the 1890s a start had been made toward the accumulation of social facts; after the turn of the century the study of mankind was to be carried forward with a vigor and zest that imparted a characteristic tone to the intellectual climate of the Progressive era."[1]

The leaders of the social justice movement by 1900 had gone far beyond the concept of private amelioration and were beginning to evolve ambitious new schemes of social salvation. What they now envisaged was nothing less than the systematic use of state police power to accomplish rearrangement of economic relationships. In other words, state governments, and later the federal government, should enter the battle to protect the weak—first by legislation based upon investigations of social workers, next by employing social workers as agents of enforcement.

First to come under the concerted attack of the social justice forces was the old problem of child labor. It posed the most poignant challenge, for by 1900 probably 1.7 million children under sixteen were employed in the cotton mills of New England and the South, in the berry fields of New Jersey, and on farms. The problem grew even worse as the textile industry advanced in the South during the early years of the twentieth century.

[1] Robert H. Bremner, *From the Depths: The Discovery of Poverty in the United States* (New York, 1956), p. 85.

The attack on child labor opened simultaneously on two fronts—in the Southeast in 1901, with the introduction of child labor bills in the legislatures of the Carolinas, Georgia, and Alabama; in the North, with adoption of pioneer legislation by New Jersey, New York, and Illinois in 1903–1904. The southern and northern wings of the movements came together in 1904 in the National Child Labor Committee, which had twenty-five branch committees in twenty-two states by 1910.

The accomplishments of this dedicated band constituted perhaps the greatest single triumph of the social justice movement before the First World War. In 1900 twenty-four states and the District of Columbia made no provision for a minimum age for workers. But by 1914 every state but one had established a minimum age limit, usually fourteen, while many states had prohibited children between fourteen and sixteen from working at night and in dangerous occupations.

The movement for a federal child labor law did not reach serious proportions until near the end of the progressive period. Senator Albert J. Beveridge of Indiana introduced the first federal bill in 1906, but the National Child Labor Committee refused to endorse it on the ground that it was best to work for a while longer in the states. However, conditions seemed ripe for federal action in 1914, and the committee sponsored the introduction of a bill in Congress that year. It prohibited the shipment in interstate commerce of goods manufactured in whole or in part by children under fourteen and of products of mines or quarries where children under sixteen were employed. The measure passed the House of Representatives in 1914 but languished in the Senate while spokesmen of the NAM and southern textile interests denounced it as an unconstitutional invasion of the police power of the states. Then President Wilson pushed the bill, now called the Keating-Owen bill, through the Senate in the summer of 1916. It was the most significant victory of the social justice movement before the New Deal.

A second major objective of the social justice crusade was protection of women in industry by limiting the number of hours they might work. Illinois enacted the first enforceable eight-hour law for women in 1893— the result of the labors of Florence Kelley of Chicago's Hull House, the settlement house founded by Jane Addams. However, the state supreme court nullified the Ilinois statute two years later, and leadership in this campaign passed to the East. There the standard was carried by consumers' leagues, which were organizations of socially minded women. Beginning with the enactment of statutes by New York in 1896 and Massachusetts in 1900 limiting women's hours to sixty a week, the movement spread slowly to Nebraska, Michigan, Colorado, Oregon, Washington, and Tennessee. Once the United States Supreme Court ended doubt about the constitutionality of women's hours legislation, the movement gained enormous momentum. Thirty-nine states enacted hours legislation for the first time or strengthened existing laws between 1909 and 1917.

A third, and perhaps the most ambitious, social justice objective was minimum wage legislation for women workers. By enacting the first statutes of this kind from 1896 to 1909, Australia and Great Britain provided inspiration to American reformers. An even more important impetus came from governmental and private investigation in the United States from 1911 to 1914. They revealed that large numbers of women received wages entirely inadequate to maintain a decent standard of living. The National Consumers' League made minimum wage legislation part of its long-range program in 1910, and the Women's Trade Union League joined the fight in the following year. The campaign had begun.

This feminine coalition scored its first victory in 1912, when the Massachusetts legislature established a wage commission empowered to recommend minimum wages for women and to expose employers who refused to conform. The following year saw the adoption by eight midwestern and western states of statutes that went the whole way and empowered wage commissions to establish binding minimum wage rates. However, the movement lost most of its strength after 1913. During the following decade only six additional states, the District of Columbia, and Puerto Rico joined the states that sought to protect the living standard, health, and morality of women workers.

The last major objective of the champions of social welfare was establishment of public systems of industrial accident insurance. Western European nations had long since demonstrated the excellence and feasibility of such systems. In the United States, however, the common law rules relating to industrial accidents still governed the payment of damages.[2] The obvious injustice of throwing practically the entire financial burden of industrial accidents and deaths on workers and their families—for that was usually the result of the application of the common law rules—led to an early movement to abrogate or modify these doctrines. Most states by 1910 had modified the common law rules in favor of the injured worker; even so, he was little better off than before because he still had to sue to recover damages. Maryland, Montana, and the federal government experimented from 1902 to 1909 with crude and limited systems of accident insurance, but this represented all that had been accomplished to this date. A brief period of intense official investigation into the entire subject ensued between 1909 and 1913. All commissions concluded that the prevailing compensation system had collapsed and recommended enactment of accident insurance laws. A wave of protest and legislation swept over

---

[2] Briefly stated, under these common law rules the injured employee was not entitled to compensation if he had willingly assumed the risks of his job, if he was himself negligent, or if his injury had been caused by a fellow worker's negligence. Moreover, in most cases the injured employee had to sue for damages and prove that he had suffered as a direct result of his employer's negligence.

the country as the people learned the facts. Ten states established insurance systems in 1911, and twenty states, three territories, and the federal government followed suit from 1912 to 1916.

Thus it was that professional social workers, students of the labor problem, and leaders of advanced social opinion grew strong during the progressive era, emerged as a redemptive element in the American democracy, and banded together in crusades to transform an individualistic and competitive society into something approximating the welfare state. There were dozens of organizations and more campaigns for social reforms than we have space to relate. Some social justice advocates, going far beyond the objectives we have described, set on foot discussions of social security, unemployment relief, and laws designed to advance the interests of organized labor. These pioneers on the advanced social frontier failed to obtain the legislation that they advocated. They were, however, blazing trails for a new social justice movement that would come to fruition in the 1930s. The line of descent from the social justice movement of the early 1900s to the New Deal is clear and straight.

3. The Supreme Court and Social Legislation

Social justice reformers were not only beset by the opposition of employers and other representatives of selfish economic interests, but they also faced even more formidable opposition from yet another source—the bench and bar of the United States. The great majority of American lawyers and judges at the turn of the century had been reared in the Anglo-American legal tradition, which often valued liberty above justice and the rights of property above humanity. They believed firmly in the automatic operation of economic laws, cultivated strong hostility to the concept of public control, and were usually ranged on the side of railroads and large corporations.

The implications of this fact for the social justice movement become at once apparent when one recalls the peculiar power of judges in the American constitutional system. Unlike their counterparts elsewhere in the western world, American judges had established the privilege of determining whether legislation violated the provisions of written state and federal constitutions. As judges nowhere rendered decisions in an intellectual vacuum, their own preconceived notions of the proper functions of government invariably affected their legal judgments. In rendering decisions in cases involving social legislation, therefore, judges often unconsciously permitted inherited prejudices, instead of sound legal precepts, to control decisions that they made.

Proponents of social welfare legislation occasionally ran afoul of the verdicts of state judges, but federal courts, and eventually the United States Supreme Court, posed the greatest threat. This was true during the progressive period, not because federal courts always nullified state efforts at social amelioration, but because the Supreme Court in the 1880s had established the doctrine that corporations were persons within the meaning of the Fourteenth Amendment. (For this development, see pp. 106–107.) Corporations were therefore at liberty to appeal to federal courts for protection; and federal judges insisted upon reviewing state regulatory legislation to determine whether it violated the Fourteenth Amendment's dictum that no state should deprive a person of life, liberty, or property without due process of law.

It was not, however, until 1898 that the Supreme Court rendered its first important decision involving state labor legislation. In *Holden v. Hardy* the court upheld a Utah statute establishing the eight-hour day for miners. The decision also expounded in forceful language the legal theories underlying all social legislation by the states, namely, that it was the duty of the state to protect the health and morals of its citizens; that this protection could be afforded by proper use of police power; and, finally, that such use of police power did not unlawfully infringe the freedom of contract guaranteed by the Fourteenth Amendment. While this decision clearly established the right of the states to limit the hours of labor in dangerous occupations, it did not affirm the constitutionality of hours legislation for any and all occupations. In fact, no one was quite sure how far the states might go in this respect until the Supreme Court set one limitation in its decision in *Lochner v. New York* in 1905.

The *Lochner* case involved the constitutionality of a New York statute that limited the hours bakers could work to ten a day and sixty a week. Counsel for the state argued that the bakers' law protected the public's food supply. Lochner's counsel, on the other hand, replied that the law unduly violated the freedom of employer and employee to make a labor contract. A bare majority of the court decided that the time had come to call a halt to improper use of state police power. Asserting that the bakers' trade was not particularly unhealthy, the majority concluded that "Statutes of the nature of that under review, limiting the hours in which grown and intelligent men may labor to earn their living, are mere meddlesome interferences with the rights of the individual." In other words, a state could not contravene the freedom of contract unless there were obvious and compelling reasons for exercising police power.

Worse still for the social justice reformers, the *Lochner* decision created grave doubt about the constitutionality of legislation restricting hours of labor merely on the basis of sex. This issue arose in 1907, when an employer challenged an Oregon ten-hour law for women. Perceiving that this was a supreme crisis in the life of the social justice movement, Florence Kelley, chief factory inspector of Illinois, and Josephine Goldmark, the driving spirit in the National Consumers' League, turned to Louis D. Brandeis of Boston, nationally known as "the people's attorney," to defend the law; Brandeis gladly agreed.

Brandeis had long argued that the law had not been altered to fit the new conditions of American economic and social life. The trouble was, he said, that neither lawyers nor judges knew anything about the economic and social conditions out of which cases arose. He proposed to substitute a sociological jurisprudence in the place of a myopic legal traditionalism. As Brandeis put it, "A lawyer who has not studied economics and sociology is very apt to become a public enemy." The Oregon case gave Brandeis an opportunity to put his sociological jurisprudence to practical use and, even better, to demonstrate it before the whole legal profession. In preparing his brief he gave only two pages to conventional legal reasoning and citation of precedents. In contrast, he used more than one hundred pages to demonstrate the economic and social consequences of long hours of work by women. By citing evidence drawn from hundreds of sources he proved that long hours were dangerous to women's health and morals and that reasonable hours produced tangible social benefits.

The case, *Muller* v. *Oregon*, was argued before the Supreme Court in January 1908. Plaintiff's counsel asserted that women, equally with men, were endowed with a freedom of contract that no legislature could impair. To this Brandeis again responded with a masterful array of facts. Brandeis's argument won the day even though the court was dominated by traditionalists. In upholding the constitutionality of the Oregon ten-hour law, the court for the first time admitted the need for facts to establish the reasonableness or unreasonableness of social legislation.

It was an epochal victory for the social justice movement; even more important was the fact that Brandeis's technique of marshaling economic and social data in defense of social legislation soon became ordinary legal practice. Four additional cases involving women's hours legislation reached the Supreme Court from 1908 to 1915. In each case the court adhered to the principle set forth in *Muller* v. *Oregon*, approving even a comprehensive California eight-hour law for women.

The Supreme Court during the period 1898–1915 also reviewed a number of state child labor laws. In no field of social legislation were reformers on surer constitutional ground, and the court consistently affirmed the right of the states to protect their children by prohibiting them from working in hazardous occupations or at an age that was prejudicial to their health and morals. However, it was still a moot question before 1918 whether Congress could use its control over commerce to regulate the labor of children.

Obviously, the court had been profoundly influenced by the progressive upheaval. The extent of that influence was demonstrated in 1917, when the court passed on almost all forms of labor legislation. In *Bunting* v. *Oregon*, the justices tacitly reversed their decision in *Lochner* v. *New York* by approving an Oregon ten-hour law for men in industry. In *Wilson* v. *New* the court narrowly sustained the Adamson Act, which established the eight-hour day for railway workers engaged in interstate commerce. In *Stettler* v. *O'Hara* an evenly divided court upheld an Oregon statute establishing minimum wages for women. Finally, the court upheld the constitutionality of the three systems of industrial accident insurance then in effect in various states. Indeed, it seemed beyond doubt that sociological jurisprudence had at last found acceptance by the highest court in the land.

4. *The Struggle for Women's Rights*

As the reader has undoubtedly inferred, much of the forward thrust of the social justice, temperance, and other reform movements of the late nineteenth and early twentieth centuries came from women. The same great social and economic developments that generated progressivism were also at work to produce what was perhaps the most remarkable generation of women in American history. Urban middle-class women, freed from age-old slavery to household routine by the introduction of various domestic conveniences and especially by the abundance of cheap servants, began to go to college and professional schools in significant numbers in the 1880s. In 1890 some 2,500 women graduated from college; their number increased to nearly 8,500 in 1910. They were too well educated and imbued with a desire to be socially useful to be content to be mere adornments or sheerly homemakers. Several hundred thousand of them went to work, principally as teachers and office workers. Others moved into the mainstream of social reform, founding and staffing settlement houses, leading the fight against the saloon, working for child labor legislation and the regulation of the hours and wages for women, and helping to organize female workers in the garment sweatshops. To mention only a few among a multitude, there was Jane Addams, who founded Hull House in 1889 and became in the eyes of many the greatest woman of her generation; Lillian D. Wald, who opened the Henry Street Settlement in New York in 1895; Margaret Dreier Robins and Mary McDowell, who were driving forces in the National Women's Trade Union League, founded in 1903; Josephine Shaw Lowell, Florence Kelley, and Josephine Goldmark, who were leaders in the National Consumers' League, organized in 1899; and Julia Lathrop, who was appointed first head of the United States Children's Bureau in 1912.

It was inevitable that such a generation of women would not be content to be second-class citizens, wards of fathers and husbands and deprived of the ballot. Women argued that the United States could never be a true democracy so long as it denied the vote to half its citizens. They pointed to the increase in the number of women in the labor force from 4 million in 1890 to nearly 7.5 million in 1910 as proof that women desperately needed the ballot in order to protect their economic interests. However, they wanted suffrage above all because, as one authority has written, it would be "a vital step toward winning human dignity, and the recognition that they too were endowed with the faculty of reason, the power of judgment, the capacity for social responsibility."

The movement for woman suffrage had in fact begun in 1848 and did not lack devoted leaders during the following half century in Lucretia Mott, Elizabeth Cady Stanton, and Susan B. Anthony. However, the real power and momentum of the movement awaited the emergence of the new middle-class generation and the awakening of a large group among the male population to the indignity and injustice of denying the vote on account of sex. In fact, by 1900 only the territory of Wyoming in 1869 and the state of Wyoming in 1890, Colorado in 1893, and Idaho and Utah in 1896 had granted suffrage to women.

What had been a somewhat desultory campaign turned into a crusade in 1900 with the election of Carrie Chapman Catt as president of the National American Woman Suffrage Association, which had been founded in 1890 by the merger of two hitherto rival organizations. The fight for women's rights now spread from the West to the East and became a significant part of the general progressive upheaval of the time. Women not only spoke and organized indefatigably, but they also mounted suffrage parades in all the large cities. More militant groups—like the Equality League (later the Women's Political Union), the Congressional Union for Woman

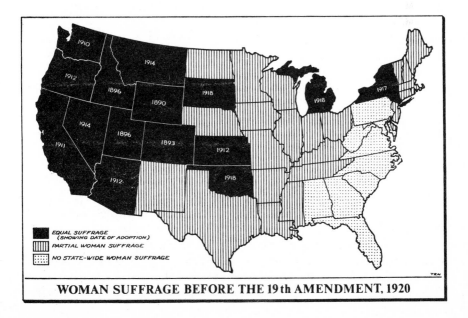

WOMAN SUFFRAGE BEFORE THE 19th AMENDMENT, 1920

Suffrage, and the National Woman's Party—demonstrated, picketed, heckled political candidates, and occasionally went to jail, where they carried on hunger strikes in imitation of their British counterparts.

It was evident by 1910–1911, when the states of Washington and California adopted woman suffrage, that the movement was becoming irresistible. Arizona, Kansas, and Oregon fell in line in 1912. In 1913 Illinois granted women the right to vote in presidential elections; Montana and Nevada joined the suffrage ranks in 1914; and the key state of New York fell to women crusaders in 1917. By this date pressure for a federal suffrage amendment was also virtually irresistible. Under the prodding of President Woodrow Wilson, the House of Representatives, on January 10, 1918, approved an amendment forbidding the states to deny suffrage on account of sex; and the Senate, in response to a personal appeal from Wilson, concurred on June 4, 1919. The suffrage amendment, the Nineteenth Amendment, became a part of the Constitution on August 26, 1920, after Tennessee completed the thirty-sixth ratification.

Meanwhile, along with political equality had come a comprehensive revision of state laws permitting women to own, inherit, and bequeath property and a revision of divorce statutes protecting women's economic rights and their right to custody of children.

The millennium had not come for American women by 1920. They were still grossly discriminated against in employment and wages, particularly in the professions. Many of them still lived in semislavery to fathers and husbands. However, the first great goal of general political equality had been won, and that must be counted as one of the most important milestones in the progress of American democracy toward equality for all persons.

5. *The Muckrakers*

While social workers were beginning their investigations and formulating their programs, a revolution in the field of journalism was also slowly taking form. Its principal aspect was the emergence of a group of reporters, called muckrakers, who trumpeted dire warnings of changes portentous for the future of democracy. These publicists who probed all the dark corners of American life did not make the progressive movement. The social justice movement and the campaign to clean up the cities and states, for example, were well on foot when they entered the battle. However, by exposing the shame and corruption of American public life the muckrakers fired the righteous indignation of the middle classes. In so doing, they helped to make the progressive movement a national uprising instead of a series of sporadic campaigns.

A medium for the muckrakers came in the 1890s with the cheap magazine. *Cosmopolitan, Munsey's,* and *McClure's* were already in the field by 1900, catering to the reading habits of the middle classes. The leader of the three, *McClure's,* was the creature of S. S. McClure, an ebullient but erratic Irishman who was evolving a novel concept of the cheap magazine as the nineteenth century ended. Understanding the public excitement over the growth of railroad and industrial combinations, he decided to publish articles of contemporary economic and social significance. Giving complete freedom and generous financial support to his writers, McClure imposed only two standards—accuracy and readability.

To Ida M. Tarbell, a young writer on his staff, McClure in 1896 assigned the task of writing a history of the Standard Oil Company. He expected that her series would begin the following February. Miss Tarbell, however, spent five years in hard research and writing before her work was completed. Her *History of the Standard Oil Company,* which began in *McClure's* in November 1902 and ran for the following fifteen months, virtually took the country by storm. Although she was coldly objective and a master of the evidence, Miss Tarbell fully revealed the methods that Rockefeller and his partners had used to build the oil monopoly.

At about the time that Miss Tarbell was completing her study, a courageous circuit attorney in St. Louis, Joseph W. Folk, was exposing the corruption of the local Democratic boss. *McClure's* managing editor, Lincoln Steffens, went to investigate, and that was how one of the best reporters of the twentieth century began his remarkable career as a muckraker. From the Missouri city Steffens went on to investigate political conditions in Minneapolis, Cleveland, New York, Chicago, Philadelphia, and Pittsburgh. He found everywhere essentially the same government by corrupt alliances of politicians and businessmen. He returned to write about them in *McClure's,* and to publish his articles in book form in 1904 as *The Shame of the Cities.* Steffens next studied political affairs in several states, and his findings were embodied in a second series in *McClure's* in 1905 and 1906, published in book form in the latter year under the title *The Struggle for Self-Government.*

The third of the trinity of *McClure's* great muckrakers was Ray Stannard Baker, a young journalist from the Middle West, who investigated social and economic problems. He explored the labor situation, for example, and wrote for *McClure's* a revealing account of the Colorado coal strike of 1903-1904. His scholarly and convincing indictment of railroad malpractices, *The Railroads on Trial,* strengthened President Roosevelt's hand in the battle to enlarge the powers of the Interstate Commerce Commission. His *Following the Colour Line* was a pioneer study of prevailing white racist attitudes in the North and South.

Among other writers on the staff of *McClure's,* two were notable. Burton J. Hendrick in 1906 publicized the revelations of corruption and mismanagement among the New York insurance companies, which a commission headed by Charles Evans Hughes had brought to light the year before. George Kibbe Turner's articles in 1909 on the alliance between the Chicago police and organized prostitution led to a famous vice commission's report on the midwestern city in 1911.

McClure's experiment soon proved that the public would buy a magazine devoted to serious discussions of contemporary problems, and other publishers were not long in following his example. *Collier's*, under the editorship of Norman Hapgood, led crusades against twin evils: the patent medicine fraud and the fraud of William Randolph Hearst, the yellow journalist who owned *Cosmopolitan* and a string of daily newspapers. Charles Edward Russell's exposure of the Beef Trust, published in *Everybody's* in 1905, was another notable contribution.

It was inevitable, however, that the muckraking technique would be adopted by publishers and writers of dubious integrity and exploited merely for financial gain. The first of the yellow muckrakers was Thomas W. Lawson, a stock market gambler and former president of the Amalgamated Copper Company, whose series, "Frenzied Finance," in *Everybody's* in 1905, allegedly exposed the insides of the monster, high finance. His revelations of financial corruption were lurid and highly exaggerated, but they had a tremendous impact. The circulation of *Everybody's* jumped in one year from 150,000 to over 750,000; and there can be no doubt that Lawson contributed to the public demand for control of the stock market that culminated in the Pujo Committee's investigation of 1913.

It was a sure sign that muckraking was heading for the gutter when William Randolph Hearst announced in 1906 that his *Cosmopolitan* would soon publish exposures that would be "the most vascular and virile" of them all. What Hearst had in mind was a series entitled "The Treason of the Senate," which the novelist David Graham Phillips was then writing. As it turned out, Phillips combined truth, fiction, and outright prevarication. But his indictment of the Senate added a powerful impetus to the movement for direct election of senators.

6. The Literature of Revolt

Contemporaneous with muckraking in magazine journalism was the proliferation of a fictional literature dedicated to the cause of democracy. Social and economic criticism ran the gamut from harsh exposés to frank appeals for a proletarian revolution. Frank Norris's *The Octopus* (1901) and *The Pit* (1903) told of the Southern Pacific Railroad's domination of the politics of California and the grain speculators' control of the wheat market. The naturalist Theodore Dreiser contributed two powerful socioeconomic studies, *The Financier* (1912) and *The Titan* (1914), based on the career of

Charles T. Yerkes, a traction magnate of Chicago in the 1890s. David Graham Phillips exploited the theme of the corrupting power of money in *The Great God Success* (1901) and *The Second Generation* (1907), while his *Susan Lenox, Her Fall and Rise*, (1917) analyzed the social forces that drove a country girl in the city to prostitution. Robert Herrick's *The Memoirs of an American Citizen* (1905) and *Clark's Field* (1914) were impressive portrayals of the rise of men of wealth in an acquisitive society.

Socialist literary critiques of the shortcomings of American democracy were, if anything, even harsher than the works already cited. Robert Hunter's *Poverty* (1904) and Ben B. Lindsey's *The Beast* (1910), for example, indicted capitalism for making greed, exploitation, poverty, and corruption inevitable. In *The Bitter Cry of the Children* (1906) John Spargo offered a moving plea for child labor reform and a damning indictment of a system that consumed its young. Jack London, like Spargo, a leader in the Socialist party, was easily the most violent literary radical of his time. His *The Iron Heel* (1907) portrayed the capitalistic system at its alleged worst. In *The War of the Classes* (1905) and *Revolution* (1910) London affirmed his faith in the ultimate triumph of the workers.

Foremost in influence among the Socialist critics was Upton Sinclair, whose most important work during the progressive period was *The Jungle* (1906). It was a story of a Lithuanian immigrant working in the Chicago packing houses. Intended as a plea for socialism, *The Jungle* was a moving indictment of an economic system that allegedly brought hunger and misery to great masses of people. As Sinclair later lamented, *The Jungle* appealed to the stomachs rather than the hearts of the American people. They ignored what he said about socialism but were revolted by his descriptions of the filthy conditions of the slaughtering houses. The novel was, therefore, a powerful factor in compelling passage of the Meat Inspection Act in 1906.

The political novelists of the first decade of the twentieth century were more prolific, if less critical of American institutions, than the socioeconomic writers. Alfred Henry Lewis's *The Boss* (1903), based upon the career of Richard Croker of Tammany Hall, and Elliott Flower's *The Spoilsman* (1903) portrayed in fictional form the political corruption that Lincoln Steffens knew so well. Brand Whitlock, from his experiences in the government of Toledo, Ohio, added two powerful novels to the literature of exposure—*The Thirteenth District* (1902) and *The Turn of the Balance* (1907). Booth Tarkington, in *The Gentleman from Indiana* (1899), *In the Arena* (1905), and other novels, exploited the theme of corruption of the political life of a state by railroad and business interests.

The most popular of these political novelists was Winston Churchill of New Hampshire, whose *Coniston* (1906) and *Mr. Crewe's Career* (1908) sold by the hundreds of thousands. Churchill seemed to think that a regeneration of American politics would occur if only the sturdy, plain people turned the rascals out and elected honest men. Equally naive was William

Allen White's *A Certain Rich Man* (1909), a collection of platitudes with an incredible ending. If Churchill and White illustrated the shallowness of many of the political writers, David Graham Phillips exemplified in fictional form the strenuosity of this literary movement. In *The Plum Tree* (1905) he attempted to expose the system of corruption and special privilege everywhere in the United States.

Whether profound or shallow, these leaders of the literary revolt against the status quo made a considerable contribution to the progressive movement. They wrote on subjects ranging from child labor to the use of state troops to break strikes. Their achievement in highlighting corruption in politics and in revealing the darker phases of American society furnished a basis in conviction for the national effort to achieve government representative of the people and responsive to their social and economic needs.

7. Intellectual Progressivism

Every movement of vitality eventually reaches a point where it spawns philosophers who attempt to systematize its thought and formulate a philosophy to justify its practical program. Although the progressive movement was no exception to this rule, its intellectuals had to do more than merely construct a new philosophy. They first had to overturn the whole structure of ideas upon which the defenders of the status quo rested their arguments: social Darwinism and individualism; the cult of hostility to government; the belief that the Constitution was an inspired document and that the Supreme Court was the interpreter of divine judgment; and, finally, the idea that railroad builders, financiers, and captains of industry had contributed to the nation's economic progress. These concepts had become so firmly embedded in the popular mind by 1900 that together they constituted the American creed. They had to be destroyed before progressive concepts could find wholesale acceptance.

Inherent in practically every aspect of the progressive offensive, furthermore, was the ultimate objective of planting faith in the efficacy of public measures of amelioration and control. Students of labor legislation, champions of social justice measures, and expounders of the new sociological jurisprudence, for example, were all trying to build a basis in economic and social fact for the necessity of positive government. So also were social gospel leaders, when they preached doctrines of social salvation, and sociologists, when they urged the necessity of thinking of wrongdoing in social as well as individual terms.

The most significant formulation of progressive political theory came from the pen of Herbert Croly, a New York journalist, whose major works, *The Promise of American Life* (1909) and *Progressive Democracy* (1914), at once established him as the chief philosopher of progressivism. Moreover, as editor of *The New Republic*, which he founded in 1914, Croly gathered around him most of the leading young social and economic thinkers of the time. Croly's writings provided progressives with their cogent arguments in behalf of positive legislation.

He began by arguing that the most widely accepted American political tradition was the Jeffersonian tradition of distrust of government and extreme individualism in economic affairs. This tradition, Croly said, had become identified with democracy because Jefferson was in fact the first American democratic philosopher and leader. In contrast, the Hamiltonian tradition of strong government had been closely identified in the popular mind with special privileges for the upper classes, because Hamilton was an ardent champion of these classes. Most Americans still believed that the promise of American life could be realized only if the golden age of competition could be restored by withdrawing all special privileges to the business classes. The fact was, Croly warned, that such a policy of laissez faire and drift in an age of inevitable big industry and big finance could only carry the nation to an equally inevitable ruin—to aggrandizement of power by the special interests and the degradation of the masses.

Who could save the nation from such peril? How could the American dream of democracy and equality of opportunity be fulfilled? The answer, Croly said, was clear. Progressives must abandon their romantic Jeffersonian concepts and support a program of positive and comprehensive state and federal intervention on all economic fronts. This would mean, for one thing, that progressives would have to abandon opposition to class or special-interest legislation. Such a program had perhaps served a useful purpose at one time, but it was now the chief intellectual stumbling block.

The important task ahead, Croly declared, was first to define the national interest and then to achieve its fulfillment by careful planning and legislation. The important question, of course, was who would define the national interest? Croly answered by calling for a new nationalism that would attract the leadership of the "best minds" in the task of reconciling planning and positive government with the democratic tradition.

The year 1912 saw the publication of a second significant plea for a new political positivism—Walter Weyl's *The New Democracy*. Weyl did not share Croly's mystical faith in the "national interest" and the "best minds." He was much more concerned with facts and figures, and he made self-interest the motivation for his program of social and industrial democracy. In brief, he said, a democracy could not allow large groups to be degraded and exploited because these same groups would in the end resort to violence and perhaps destroy society. Walter Lippmann's *Preface to Politics* (1913), and *Drift and Mastery* (1914), supplemented Croly's and particularly Weyl's arguments. Lippmann, then a young socialist in process of shedding his parlor radicalism, assumed the necessity of democratic collectivism. His major argument was for a pragmatic approach to politics, one based on science and unencumbered by so-called moral criteria.

Another important component of the intellectual attack on the conservative ideology was the discrediting of the divine-origin theory of the Constitution, which was often invoked by opponents of the direct election of senators and other neodemocratic proposals. Discontent over the undemocratic features of the Constitution was as old as the document itself, but not until the progressive period did scholars and politicians evolve the thesis that the Constitution had been written deliberately to frustrate the democratic movement.

This thesis was first systematically developed by Walter Clark, chief justice of North Carolina, in an address at the University of Pennsylvania Law School in 1906. The following year, in *The Spirit of American Government*, Professor J. Allen Smith of the University of Washington repeated Clark's assertion that a minority had conceived the Constitution in class interest and imposed it upon the majority in order to thwart their aspirations. Charles A. Beard, a young historian at Columbia University who had discovered Marx and Engels in England around the turn of the century, went to work to prove that the Constitution had been written to protect merchants, great landowners, moneylenders, and speculators. His findings were embodied in 1913 in *An Economic Interpretation of the Constitution*. Progressives could now say that the Constitution, which had so often stood in the way of their reforms, was no more sacrosanct than any other part of the American past.

As a final blow, intellectual progressives applied the full weight of scholarship and sarcasm toward discrediting the belief that railroad builders, financiers, and captains of industry were heroes and contributors to American progress. The most trenchant of the critics of the moneyed classes was Thorstein Veblen, a strange quondam economics professor, whose economic theory had much greater impact in the 1930s than during his own day. His most widely read work, *The Theory of the Leisure Class* (1899), was a biting attack against the standards and practices of contemporary American business civilization. The most prolific of the debunkers of the plutocracy was Gustavus Myers, a socialist, who grimly set to work to discover how great fortunes in the United States had been accumulated. His *History of the Great American Fortunes*, published in three volumes in 1909-1910, confirmed the old charge that large American fortunes had been made through plunder and preemption of natural resources.

There were, of course, many other leaders equally prominent in this extraordinary and far-reaching revolt of the intellectuals. While we cannot measure their contribution precisely, we can surely say that their part in making the progressive movement a permanent force in American life was not small. Their great contribution lay in discrediting a conservative ideology that had strongly buttressed the status quo and in formulating a philosophy for the social-welfare state. In this respect and for this reason, therefore, the intellectuals were the true leaveners of progressivism.

8. *The Shame of the Cities*

Through the agitation of political leaders and the exposures of muckrakers, the American people, from the 1890s to about 1910, discovered that representative political institutions in their cities had broken down almost completely. Instead of being governed by representatives impartially chosen, most American cities were ruled by political machines that resembled the modern corporation in their hierarchical structure. The head of the machine was known as the "boss," "big man," or "leader." Because of his generally unsavory reputation, he usually held no office. Almost invariably he had risen from the ranks after years of service. The boss operated like a general in charge of field forces. His orders were commands, passed down from the "ring" to its hundreds or thousands of workers. Machines, usually superbly organized and smoothly run, were the invisible governments of great cities, affecting the well-being of millions of people.

Woodrow Wilson once declared that the prevailing form of American city government had been constructed as if to make the usurpation of power by an extraconstitutional organization inevitable. Wilson's statement was essentially correct. When city charters were granted or rewritten during the high tide of Jacksonian Democracy, their framers deliberately dispersed power and responsibility among numerous agencies—the mayor, a two-house council, and sometimes independent boards and commissions. The result was not democratic government. It was a form under which responsible government was nearly impossible because the agencies for achieving it did not exist. Into the power vacuum created by this system of checks and balances and division of authority moved the kind of political machine just described. For all its sins, it did have enough cohesion and concentration of authority to govern.

The machine survived even when forms of government were changed. A more important reason for its existence and power, therefore, was the fact that it rendered service to large numbers of people. The majority of voters in 1900 did not ask whether the organization was corrupt but whether it did something for them. The machine made it a point to do things for them. Its agents met the friendless immigrant at the dock and helped him to find shelter and work. Precinct captains provided coal and food for Widow Flanagan or Mrs. Moskowitz when they were in need. There was nothing scientific about the machine's charity, to be sure. But the submerged third of the people cared little about honesty and efficiency so long as they lived in poverty and slums. They wanted social services that the machines knew how to give and that progressives had not yet developed.

The machine survived also because it was held together by the twin codes of patronage and loyalty. The chief source of livelihood of lesser dignitaries was petty office and graft, and the boss could command a host of willing workers so long as he had favors to bestow. Loyalty and friendship also played an important role in keeping the organization intact. Organization politics, moreover, afforded social and political opportunities for immigrant and minority groups such as they could never find in "respectable" society. In fact, the machine was one of the few cohesive and unifying forces in the social chaos of metropolitan life.

The oil best calculated to lubricate the political machine was the loot that it received. On the lower levels, bribery—in the form of money paid to politicians and policemen by criminals, prostitutes, saloon keepers, and others—was extremely widespread, highly organized, and fabulously profitable. The Chicago Vice Commission reported in 1911, for example, that the annual profit from vice in that city was $15 million, and that one-fifth of this sum was paid to police in the form of graft.

The most dangerous kind of bribery was the money paid by businessmen for protection, special privileges, and public rights. To begin with, the great economic interests in the cities turned "their dollars into votes and their property into political power" by buying control of the political machines. Corruption was inevitable so long as businessmen wanted exemption from equitable taxation. In addition, there were numerous opportunities in large and rapidly growing cities for bribery of another kind—purchase of franchises and contracts. New city railway lines had to be constructed; sewerage, gas, electrical, and water lines had to follow new areas of development. The boss usually had franchises and contracts at his disposal; even perpetual franchises could be bought. It was top-level bribery of this kind that was most dangerous to the public interest and most profitable to the machine.

This, therefore, was the "System," as Lincoln Steffens called it. This was the pattern of corruption that characterized American municipal politics at the turn of the century. Some cities, to be sure, outshone the others in refining the art of misgovernment. In St. Louis, for example, the Democratic boss systematically sold franchises, licenses, and exemptions to the respectable leaders of the business community. The boss of Minneapolis operated the most spectacular system of police graft in the country. In Pittsburgh two Republican leaders owned the city council and grew rich on contracts and utilities. Philadelphia presented the sorriest sight of all— a place where the citizens cheerfully acquiesced in the total subversion of representative government.

9. *The Municipal Reform Movement*

The general prevalence of municipal corruption and misrule stimulated the first important *political* development in the progressive movement— the crusade for municipal reform. It began in a sporadic way in the 1890s, with the emergence of Hazen S. Pingree, mayor of Detroit, as the first significant progressive municipal reformer. The widespread breakdown of city social services during the Panic of 1893 led to the formation of the National Municipal League, the temporary overthrow of Tammany Hall in New York in 1894, and the triumph of a reform coalition in Baltimore a year later.

The years 1896–1897, however, seem to mark a dividing line between spasmodic uprisings and widespread revolt. The first of these insurrections occurred in Chicago, where the city council was busily selling the public's most valuable rights to Charles T. Yerkes, a utilities magnate. As protests against the corrupt selling of franchises began to swell, some 232 civic leaders met in 1895, organized the Municipal Voter's League, and launched a nonpartisan campaign to clean up the city government. By pitilessly exposing the records of corrupt aldermen, the league won control of the city council in the aldermanic elections of 1896 and 1897. In the latter year, moreover, the league helped elect a progressive mayor, Carter Harrison, and Chicago was saved from the grafters, at least momentarily.

The reform movement in Chicago illustrated what could be accomplished by an aroused citizenry without an outstanding single leader. Elsewhere the municipal reform movement followed a similar pattern. Various nonpartisan good government leagues combined in New York City in 1913 to overthrow Tammany rule and elect a young reform mayor, John Purroy Mitchel. In Minneapolis an energetic citizens' committee and a fearless grand jury exposed the system of police graft operated by Mayor A. A. Ames and put Ames and his henchmen in prison.

The dominant pattern of municipal reform, however, was redemption through leadership of some dynamic and often colorful popular tribune. The most famous and influential member of this group was Tom L. Johnson of Cleveland. Elected mayor in 1901 on a platform demanding equal taxation and the three-cent fare on trolley lines, Johnson gathered some of the ablest young municipal administrators in the country and moved first against the inequalities of the tax lists. He next opened fire on railroads and utilities, which owned extensive property in Cleveland but paid hardly any taxes. The state legislature doubled railroad taxes in 1903–1904, while the utilities consented to a doubling of their assessments.

All these battles were mere skirmishes compared to the great campaign that Johnson waged for the three-cent fare. The climax came when Johnson and his council established competing trolley routes and invited outside capitalists to bid for them. The local traction interests appealed to the state Republican ring for protection. The state ring, in turn, appealed to the supreme court of Ohio; it declared that all charters of Ohio cities were void because they had been created by special legislation. With all city governments of Ohio thus destroyed, the ring called the legislature into special session to adopt a uniform municipal code. It replaced the old system of concentrated power that had prevailed in Cleveland with government by divided authorities and independent boards.

Such tactics did not daunt Tom Johnson. He kept on appealing to the people and winning mayoralty campaigns. Eventually he concluded that public ownership of utilities and traction properties was the only way to eliminate the worst source of municipal corruption. Johnson was finally beaten in 1909, less than a year before his death. But his program was saved by the election of his chief lieutenant, Newton D. Baker, as mayor in 1911.

Such was the kind of persons who led the progressive movement in the cities. All municipal reformers fought common enemies: entrenched and corrupt politicians allied with privileged business and criminal elements. They all sought the same goals: impartial government, fair taxation, regulation of public service companies, and expanded social services for the lower classes. These remained always the chief objectives. But progressives soon learned that it was not enough to throw the rascals out and inaugurate a program of economic and social reform. Politics remained; and reformers could never rest secure so long as bosses controlled the party structure. Thus, inevitably, progressives turned also to the task of changing the political mechanisms in the hope that greater popular participation and control would lay a secure basis for economic and social reforms that were already begun.

Progressives in the cities, therefore, joined hands with other reform groups in a frontal assault on bosses and machines by establishing the direct primary for nominating candidates and adopting the short ballot, initiative, referendum, and recall. As these campaigns were part of the progressive movement on the statewide level, we will discuss them later in this chapter.

Municipal reformers also fought hard to obtain home rule and an end to legislative interference in municipal administration. As Tom Johnson and other progressives soon discovered, city machines were invariably components of state rings. After smashing the local machine, it profited progressives little if the state ring, acting through the legislature, could nullify all their gains. This often happened because in most states city governments were creatures of the legislature and completely under its control. Municipal reformers were not notably successful in their struggle to be free from legislative interference, because rural and small-town legislators were loath to yield control over metropolitan revenues. Four states, Missouri, California, Washington, and Minnesota, had granted home rule to cities by the turn of the century. Eight other states granted this coveted privilege from 1900 to 1914, but only two of them, Michigan and Ohio, had any large cities of consequence.

The most far-reaching progressive proposal for institutional change struck at the heart of the problem of municipal government and seemed to offer the greatest hope of saving the cities. This was the plan to abolish the old mayor-council system entirely and to substitute government by a commission of nonpartisan administrators. The commission form, much discussed in the 1890s, was first put to use when a hurricane and tidal wave devastated Galveston, Texas, on September 8, 1900. With a corrupt city council utterly incapable of facing the tasks of reconstruction, leading property owners of Galveston appealed to the state legislature to assume the government of the city. The legislature responded by establishing a government by five commissioners, elected, after 1903, by the people.

The commission plan first won nationwide prominence when the Iowa legislature in 1907 adopted a more elaborate version of the Texas model. The Iowa statute allowed cities over 25,000 to adopt the commission form. More important, it incorporated the initiative, referendum, and recall as part of the machinery of city politics and provided for nomination of commissioners in nonpartisan elections. At once Des Moines adopted the commission form, and thereafter it was known as the "Des Moines Idea." More than one hundred cities had adopted commission government by 1910; by the eve of the First World War the number had exceeded four hundred—chiefly medium-sized cities in the Middle West, New England, and the Pacific states.

Experience soon demonstrated that the commission form had inherent weaknesses that were not evident at the outset. It failed really to concentrate responsibility for administration, since there was no guarantee that the commissioners would be expert managers. Progressives slowly evolved a refinement of the commission form. The final product was the city manager plan, first adopted in its complete form by Dayton, Ohio, in 1913, after a great flood had inundated the city and the mayor and council could not cope with the emergency. This innovation preserved the best features of the commission plan and eliminated most of its weaknesses. All authority was vested in a board of commissioners, elected on a nonpartisan basis, who made laws and policies for the city. The commissioners appointed a city manager, usually a trained expert, to administer the various departments of the government, and the city manager, in turn, was responsible in all matters to the commissioners.

The new form seemed such a logical way to achieve responsible and expert administration without sacrificing the principle of democratic control that it spread rapidly and soon displaced the commission form in many cities. More than three hundred cities had adopted the city manager plan by 1923.

Thus the progressive movement in the cities stimulated the rise of a host of new leaders and the development of political institutions calculated to facilitate popular rule and responsible government. To charge, as certain critics have done, that city reformers did not abolish all evils and bring the millennium is at best naive. For the most part they were tough-minded men, who well knew that venality and corruption would survive, regardless of the form of government, so long as men profited thereby. They must be judged on a basis of the obstacles that they faced and what they accomplished rather than condemned for failing to change human nature or reconstruct society. Surveying the American scene at the end of the progressive period, competent authorities concluded that the municipal reformers had in large measure succeeded. The era of flagrant corruption had by and large passed. Cities were governed more efficiently than they had been a decade before, and a new class of professional municipal administrators were in training throughout the country. In short, if the city was not yet the hope of American democracy, it was no longer its nemesis.

10. The Shame of the States

Corruption and special privilege held sway in many states around the turn of the century in the same manner and for the same purpose that they reigned in the cities. Just as the city machine was the medium through which corrupt businessmen obtained contracts, franchises, and immunities from the city government, so also was the state machine, or ring, the medium through which such favors were bought on the state level.

The boss system in the states varied greatly from state to state and from party to party. City organizations usually formed the basis for the state machine, although in rural states the county courthouse rings were the important components. In states with a tremendous concentration of population in one metropolis, the boss of the great city machine was often head of the state organization. In other states politicial power was more widely dispersed. In any event, party authority was concentrated in the state committee, headed by a state chairman who represented the dominant leader or leaders in the state. It was the state chairman who usually organized the legislature, controlled legislation, and made deals with railroad and corporation lobbyists.

Two states, Missouri and New Jersey, afford exaggerated but vivid illustrations of how the so-called system operated in most states of the Union at the turn of the century. In Missouri the bribery or "boodle" system worked at peak efficiency to govern the state in the interest of railroads and corporations. The corrupting agency was the lobby at the state capital, representing important railroad and business interests. The medium through which the lobby worked in this case was the party caucus in the legislature. Because the lobby bought control of the caucus, even honest legislators were caught in its net and forced to do its bidding. In Missouri, as in many other states, the lobby was the real, the living government that operated behind the façade of constitutional forms.

The control of state politics by a corporation-machine alliance reached its apogee in New Jersey. The leaders of the business and financial communities were in fact often the leaders of the dominant Republican party, and it was usually unnecessary for businessmen to corrupt legislators and state officials. The railroad lobby in 1903, for example, furnished the chief justice of the state, the attorney general, the state comptroller, the commissioner of banking and insurance, and one of the members of the state board of taxation. It was probably no coincidence that railroads at the time paid only one-third of their just share of the tax burden. Moreover, both United States senators from New Jersey were interested in public utilities, while the retiring attorney general was on the boards of three public service corporations. It was not surprising that public utilities in the state enjoyed immunity from equitable taxation and public regulation.

11. *The Progressive Movement in the States*

Like the municipal reform movement, the great revolt against the system in the states was a culmination rather than a beginning. In the South and West, agrarian radicalism was supplanted by progressivism from 1896 to 1900, as urban spokesmen assumed leadership in the struggle against railroad and corporation dominance. The Middle West, where the dominant GOP was firmly controlled by the vested interests at the turn of the century, was convulsed by a series of spectacular revolts from 1900 to 1908. Under insurgent leaders like Robert M. La Follette of Wisconsin, Albert B. Cummins of Iowa, and Albert J. Beveridge of Indiana, the midwestern states were transformed from bastions of conservative Republicanism into strongholds of progressivism. In the East the progressive revolt had a more decidedly urban complexion, as it often grew out of earlier campaigns in the cities. But progressivism was no less spectacular in the East than in the Middle West. The following developments, among others, signified the power and strength of eastern progressivism: Charles Evans Hughes's election as governor of New York in 1906 and 1908 and his courageous battles for the direct primary and public regulation of utilities and railroads; the New Idea movement in New Jersey, which began in 1906 as a rebellion within the Republican party and culminated in the election of a

Democrat, Woodrow Wilson, as governor in 1910; and the sweeping triumph of progressivism in Ohio, with the adoption of a new constitution and the election of a Democratic progressive, James M. Cox, as governor in 1912. The politics of the Pacific coast states, too, were transformed by the triumph of such reformers as Hiram W. Johnson of California and William S. U'Ren of Oregon.

What we are dealing with here was obviously no minor phenomenon but a political revolt of national proportions and momentous consequences for the future of American politics. So successful were progressive leaders in the several states by 1912 that all observers agreed that a thoroughgoing revolution had been accomplished since 1900. In most states the power of the bipartisan machines had been shattered or at least curtailed, and an older generation of conservative leaders had been supplanted by younger newcomers. State governments were representative of the rank and file and more responsive to their economic and social needs.

"Give the government back to the people!"—the battle cry of progressivism in the states—not only reflected the conviction that state government had ceased to be representative but also pointed up the major objective of the movement. But how could the system be destroyed? What were the processes and techniques of this counterrevolution against privilege?

The first, indeed the absolutely essential, ingredient was leadership. In every state in which progressivism triumphed there was some aggressive leader who carried the fight to the people and, after winning, provided responsible and effective government. Indeed, it is now evident that the progressives' most lasting contribution to American political practice was not the mechanical changes that they instituted, but rather the fact that they awakened the American people to the necessity for responsible leadership in a democracy.

Progressive leaders in the states, moreover, made a concerted campaign to overhaul the existing structure of political institutions. If representative government had broken down under the old forms, progressives argued, then new institutions had to be devised to facilitate popular control of parties and governments. Invariably, the first objective of reform leaders was the inauguration of the direct primary system of nominating candidates and party officials. This objective took priority because the old system of nomination by conventions seemed to afford the bosses an easy means of perpetuating their control. Practically all city and state elective officials before 1900 were nominated at party conventions on district, county, and statewide levels. Normally such conventions were easily bought or controlled; usually they were well-oiled cogs in the machine. Reform forces might capture the conventions and momentarily subdue the bosses, but it was an extraordinarily difficult undertaking.

The progressive remedy was simple and direct: make it easier for voters and more difficult for bosses to control the party by instituting a system of nominating candidates directly by the people. The direct primary apparently originated in Pennsylvania in the 1840s, but it was not used extensively on the local level until the 1890s, and then it was to be found mainly in the South. Mississippi in 1902 was the first state to adopt a compulsory, statewide primary law. Wisconsin enacted similar legislation the following year as the first major item in Governor La Follette's reform program. From this time on the system spread rapidly through all sections, so that by 1916 only Rhode Island, Connecticut, and New Mexico had failed to enact primary legislation of some kind.

State progressives usually campaigned next for a variety of institutional reforms: the short ballot, to reduce the number of elective officials and concentrate responsibility in government; corrupt practices legislation, to control and limit campaign contributions and expenditures; and the direct election of United States senators by the people instead of by the state legislatures. Progress in the field of short ballot reform was notable only in the area of municipal government with the rapid spread of the commission and city manager forms. Practically every state adopted stringent corrupt practices laws, while Congress in 1907 and 1909 prohibited corporations, insurance companies, banks, and railroads from contributing to campaign funds in federal election contests. For many years, however, reactionary forces in the Senate would not allow a constitutional amendment for direct election of senators to pass. Many states, therefore, turned to an indirect method of electing senators directly. This was accomplished by requiring senatorial candidates to be nominated in primary elections and candidates for the state legislature to swear that they would vote for the senatorial candidate thus nominated by the people. The United States Senate, after a scandal involving the election of William Lorimer, Republican boss of Illinois, to that body in 1909, approved the Seventeenth Amendment for direct election in 1912. It became a part of the Constitution on May 31, 1913.

Many skeptical progressives refused to agree that the foregoing reforms sufficed. Convinced that representative government might become subverted by the forces of privilege even under the new and more democratic forms, they proposed to give the people an alternative and a last resort— the initiative and referendum.[3] The initiative and referendum were used most widely in the West, where South Dakota first adopted them in 1898. During the next ten years only Utah, Oregon, Nevada, Montana, and Oklahoma joined the experiment in direct legislation. But fifteen other states, including several in the East and South, adopted the measures from 1908 to 1915. The movement came to a virtual standstill in 1915, however, as

[3] The initiative is a device whereby the electorate may enact legislation against the will of the legislature. Upon petition of a stipulated percentage of the voters, the legislature must consider the measure that the petitioners propose. If the legislature refuses to approve the bill it must call a special election in which the voters may enact or reject the measure. The referendum, on the other hand, is a device by which voters may nullify a measure already approved by the legislature.

conservatives launched a vigorous counterattack, and experience soon proved that the mass of voters were not competent to deal with technical matters of legislation.

As a further safeguard of the popular interest, progressives championed the recall, a device that afforded the voters a handy means of removing unsatisfactory elective officials. First used in Los Angeles in 1903, the recall found widest acceptance in cities that adopted the commission and city manager forms. Oregon made the recall applicable to elective state and local officials in 1908, and nine other states, most of them in the West, followed suit from 1911 to 1915. This form of recall provoked strenuous opposition from conservatives, but defenders of the status quo saved their choicest invectives for the recall of judges. If the people could remove judges for making unpopular decisions, then what minority and property rights would be safe from the assaults of an irrational majority? Seven states—Oregon, California, Arizona, Nevada, Colorado, Kansas, and North Dakota—adopted the recall of judges. The violent controversies over the measure at the time now seem rather pointless; not a single judge of a superior or state supreme court has been removed since the recall of judges was first proposed. As an alternative means of protecting the right of the states to use police power for social and economic ends, Theodore Roosevelt in 1912 proposed the recall of decisions by state courts that nullified such legislation. Only Colorado, in 1913, adopted this measure, and the Colorado supreme court in 1921 declared the statute unconstitutional.

Critics have accused progressive leaders of naively believing that representative and truly democratic government could be restored by mere alterations in the mechanics of politics. The charge reveals a profound ignorance of the progressive era. There were undoubtedly fools among the leaders of the reform movement in the states. But the great majority were realistic politicians who well knew that the changes they proposed were merely instruments to facilitate the capture of political machinery. They used these instruments, therefore, to gain and hold power. And they must be judged for what they accomplished or failed to accomplish on the higher level of substantive reform.

Their achievements in the realm of social and economic legislation were imposing indeed. We have already related the progress of the movement in the states for social justice legislation, so-called moral reform through prohibition, and the development of public education. In the realm of strictly economic legislation, progressive leaders in the states made substantial progress toward subjecting railroads and public service corporations to effective public control. Beginning with the Georgia Railroad Commission of 1879 and culminating in the adoption by the Wisconsin legislature of Governor La Follette's bill for a railroad commission in 1905, the movement for state regulation advanced steadily. Indeed, so effective had it become by 1914 that the railroad managers were then begging

Congress to save them from harassment by state commissions. It was during the progressive era, too, that the movement for expert regulation by state commissions of rates and services of public service corporations and of insurance and investment companies began and reached its first culmination.

These were all important substantive reforms and together constitute an imposing record. But in assessing progressivism's achievement we should not dismiss lightly the political changes that it effected. By their emphasis on simplified forms of government, greater popular participation in, and control over, the electoral process, and responsible leadership, the progressive leaders transformed the theory and practice of politics in the United States. Looking back in 1913 upon his hard battles for the people as governor of Wisconsin, Robert M. La Follette penned a fitting epilogue, not only for the progressive movement in Wisconsin, but for progressivism in many other states as well: "This closes the account of my services in Wisconsin—a time full of struggle, and yet a time that I like to look back upon. It has been a fight supremely worth making, and I want it to be judged, as it will be ultimately, by results actually attained. If it can be shown that Wisconsin is a happier and better state to live in, that its institutions are more democratic, that the opportunities of all its people are more equal, that social justice more nearly prevails, that human life is safer and sweeter—then I shall rest content in the feeling that the Progressive movement has been successful."[4]

[4]*Autobiography of Robert M. La Follette* (Madison, Wis., 1913), pp. 368–369; see also Belle Case La Follette and Fola La Follette, *Robert M. La Follette*, 2 vols. (New York, 1953), I, p. 192.

4

✦✦✦❋✦✦✦

Politics and Problems

of the Republican Era,

1901–1910

It was inevitable that the progressive revolt should soon spread from the cities and states into the larger arena of national politics. This was true because there is no real dividing line between state and federal politics in the American system. It was true even more because the spread of the railroad, financial, and industrial networks across state boundaries created important problems with which the federal government alone could constitutionally cope.

This and following chapters relate the impact of the progressive upheaval upon national politics and policies. At the beginning of the twentieth century the dominant Republican party was controlled by men who frankly urged a program of generous assistance to the business interests and who abhorred the very concept of public regulation. Under William Jennings Bryan, some of the minority Democrats were cautiously moving toward a more progressive position, but they had mounted no comprehensive and rational attack on the system of privilege. Within less than a decade, however, the progressive ferment had wrought mighty changes in the American political scene. Advanced progressives, who sought to make the federal government a positive, regenerative force, were a large element in the Republican party by 1910. Moreover, the Democrats were united and confident under new leadership. In brief, the progressive movement, which had already brought important changes in federal policies, stood on the verge of culmination and fulfillment.

1. *Theodore Roosevelt and the Progressive Movement[1]*

No account of national progressivism would be complete without some note of its most extraordinary leader during its early period. Theodore Roosevelt, who came to the presidency by a tragic circumstance, presided over the nation's destinies during a time of agitation for, and development of, a national reform program. He opportunely adapted his policies to meet the changing configurations of political power. He was, however, no mere creature of circumstance, but rather a prime moving force in history.

Born on October 27, 1858, the scion of a well-to-do mercantile and banking family, he was reared in the genteel Knickerbocker traditions of New York City. Afflicted with a frail body and weak eyes, while still young he determined to make himself physically strong. He overcame his weakness by dint of exhausting labors and ever after gloried in the strenuous life and manly virtues. Whether as cowboy and gunfighter, Rough Rider during the Spanish-American War, or big game hunter in Africa, Roosevelt proved that physically he was as good as the best and that he did not know the meaning of fear.

From his social environment and especially from his father, Roosevelt acquired a compulsion to do good for people less fortunate than himself. While most persons of his class gave money to settlement houses or home missions, Roosevelt went into politics after graduating from Harvard in 1880. Part of his motivation must have been the strong moral sense he acquired from his Dutch Reformed religion and its Calvinistic emphasis upon righteousness. In any event, Roosevelt usually viewed political contests as struggles between the forces of good and evil and, like Wilson and Bryan, he became a preacher-at-large to the American people.

Background, training, temperament, and personal associations all combined in Roosevelt to produce a fundamentally cautious and conservative, rather than doctrinaire, approach to politics. Justice to all classes, and therefore legislation in the general interest, became his guiding principle. A patrician, he viewed with righteous anger the vulgarity and materialism

---

[1]Parts of the following section first appeared in Arthur S. Link, "Theodore Roosevelt in His Letters," *Yale Review*, 43 (Summer 1954), pp. 589–598; reproduced by permission of the editors of the *Yale Review*.

of the newly rich captains of industry, financiers, and railroad speculators. Yet experience and a sense of justice prevented him from condemning whole classes or accepting the socialist dictum that it was the economic system that was alone responsible for social wrongdoing. Roosevelt's conservatism, moreover, was manifested in his insistence upon continuity and his abhorrence of men who advocated unnatural change. Believing that progressive adaptation to new circumstances could not occur unless order and social stability first existed, he feared a mob as much as he feared the malefactors of great wealth.

It is proof of his complexity that Theodore Roosevelt must be reckoned a progressive in spite of his basically conservative approach to politics. On a bedrock of democratic idealism he built a structure of legislative policies the shape of which was usually determined by the pragmatic need of the hour. Experience, whether as governor of New York or president of the United States, led him to the conclusion that only organized political power, that is, government, could meet the manifold challenges that industrialism raised in city, state, and nation. For this reason he was primarily a progressive, even though he refused to be doctrinaire about his progressivism.

In the practice of politics Roosevelt was as hardheaded a realist as ever sat in the presidential chair. He was a realist because he recognized and respected power. Thus, while he was governor of New York, he worked with the Republican boss of that state as long as he could do so honorably. When he assumed the presidency in 1901 he found political power in the Republican party concentrated in the state organizations and exercised by their representatives in Congress. He did not attempt to destroy the party hierarchy; indeed, he worked with and through it. The important point is that Roosevelt not only accepted existing power structures as he found them in New York and Washington but that he also became a master politician, able to use his party for his own and the country's interests.

Indeed, in the way in which he conceded the smaller points in order to win the important objectives and mastered the political game without yielding his own integrity, Roosevelt symbolized the moral man confronted by the dilemmas of an immoral society. Doctrinaire reformers demanded the whole loaf of reform and denounced Roosevelt when he accepted half or two-thirds of the loaf. Roosevelt knew that he could not transform society and politics by one bugle blast. He knew that men are usually governed by selfish motives and that politics is fundamentally not a moral profession. Knowing these things, he tried to use selfishness to achieve a moral end—the advancement of human welfare. He also tried to strengthen altruistic tendencies whenever he found them.

These, then, were some of the features of Roosevelt's personality and philosophy. There was, however, another trait that to a varying degree dominated all the rest—his love of power, which mounted as the years passed and at times verged on egomania. Love of his own opinions often obscured the truth in Roosevelt's mind and caused him to think that he was above the law and ordinary conventions. Yet his confidence was as much a source of strength as of danger, giving him the self-confidence essential to leadership. Combined with intelligence and energy, it made him a superb administrator, precisely because he was bold enough to do unprecedented things.

Personal judgments of Roosevelt will vary, but no one should make the mistake of not taking him seriously. Because he was a leader of men it was given to him to make a large contribution to the progressive movement, to the art of government in the United States, and to the diplomacy of his country. In fact, since Lincoln, only two other presidents, Wilson and Franklin Roosevelt, have made comparable contributions.

Theodore Roosevelt's most lasting contribution to American political practice was his exercise of leadership and revitalization of the presidency. A long line of second-rate politicians had occupied the White House from 1865 to 1901. With the exception perhaps of Cleveland they were not even leaders of their own party, much less of the country. Because of the entrenched position of the Old Guard professionals in Congress, Roosevelt was never able to dominate the veterans on Capitol Hill. But he was able to bend a stubborn Congress to his will by making himself the one great popular spokesman in the country. By exploiting some of the powers inherent in the presidency, he proved that effective national leadership was possible in the American constitutional system.

Roosevelt's contributions to the science of administration alone would entitle him to distinction among the presidents. Perceiving that the only alternative to rule by private wealth was the development of a strong, efficient administrative state, democratically controlled but powerful enough to make important economic decisions, he advanced the science of administration as no president before him had done. He and his able associates strengthened the Civil Service, put the consular service on a professional basis, modernized the army's command structure, brought the navy to an unprecedented peak of efficiency, and carried forward a specific program of conservation of natural resources. Moreover, he helped to broaden the powers of an old agency, the Interstate Commerce Commission, and created a new one, the Bureau of Corporations. In brief, during the Roosevelt era democracy learned to become efficient.

A third contribution is almost as important as Roosevelt's development of the presidential power. It was his vindication of the national, or public, interest over all private aggregations of economic power. The open contempt that bankers, monopolists, and railroad managers displayed toward the law and the highhanded manner in which they dealt with the people filled him with loathing and anger. He retaliated by asserting the supremacy of the people over private interests in three far-reaching ways. First, he withdrew more than 200 million acres of public lands to curb the plunder of a great national heritage. Second, he activated the Sherman

Antitrust Act and began a movement that succeeded in curbing industrial monopoly in the United States. Third, he forced adoption of the Hepburn Act of 1906, which deprived the railroads of ultimate sovereignty in the rate-making process. In the anthracite coal strike of 1902, he was preparing to go the full limit in asserting the public interest—by seizing and operating the coal mines if the operators should refuse to mediate the controversy. Such actions marked the momentous beginnings of legislation and administration that culminated in the New Deal and the democratic welfare state.

2. Roosevelt and the Republican Party, 1900-1904

The leaders of the Republican party laid their plans carefully for the election of 1900. President William McKinley was of course the inevitable presidential choice of the GOP. The death in 1899 of Vice-President Garret A. Hobart left the second place on the ticket open and created an unusual opportunity for Thomas C. Platt, Republican boss of New York State. Platt had nominated Theodore Roosevelt, the hero of the Spanish-American War, for governor of New York in 1898 in order to win. Elected easily, Roosevelt attacked corruption with vigor, championed social legislation, and was consequently soon at odds with Platt. Hobart's death offered a dignified yet final method of getting Roosevelt out of New York. The Republican Old Guard could silence Roosevelt by elevating him to the vice-presidency, and Platt would be saved the embarrassment of having to nominate him again for governor in 1900.

McKinley and his adviser, Mark Hanna, responded coldly when Platt first presented his plan. "Don't any of you realize," Hanna is later alleged to have remarked, "that there's only one life between this madman and the White House?" But Platt was so persistent that Hanna finally gave in. Roosevelt, with his usual perception, at once saw through Platt's scheme. He had grave misgivings about accepting his consignment to oblivion. His friends, however, suggested that he would be the logical presidential candidate in 1904, and when the nomination was offered to him, he could think of no alternative but to accept.

The Democrats nominated Bryan for a second time, and the Nebraskan made his campaign chiefly on the issues of imperialism and trust control. Bryan soft-pedaled the silver issue and tried to make the election a solemn referendum on imperialism. As one diplomatic historian has shown, the election was more a repudiation of Bryanism and a thumping endorsement of prosperity than a popular expression on colonial policy. McKinley was elected by an even greater majority than in 1896.

Therefore, McKinley and Roosevelt were inaugurated on March 4, 1901. Platt said a pleasant good-by; Hanna stood at McKinley's right hand; and businessmen thanked God that all was right with the world. But the point of Platt's joke was lost in September 1901 when an assassin mortally wounded McKinley at Buffalo. "That damned cowboy," as Hanna called Roosevelt, was now president of the United States!

Those impatient reformers who expected Theodore Roosevelt to reorganize the Republican party and assume control of Congress at once understood neither the political situation nor the new president. The great industrial and financial interests since the Civil War had constructed an organization within the Republican party that could not be overthrown by direct assault.The preeminent leader of the party was Mark Hanna of Ohio, McKinley's adviser and a member of the Senate. Nearly equal in power was Senator Nelson W. Aldrich of Rhode Island, the avowed spokesman of Wall Street. Allied with Hanna and Aldrich in the upper house were John C. Spooner of Wisconsin, William B. Allison of Iowa, and Orville H. Platt of Connecticut. They and other Old Guardsmen controlled the Senate and protected the industrial, financial, and railroad interests. Furthermore, the Old Guard were firmly entrenched in the House of Representatives. The Speaker after 1902 was Joseph G. Cannon of Illinois, a thoroughgoing reactionary, who ruled the House with rural wit and an iron hand. Cannon not only appointed all committees but was also chairman of the rules committee that determined the priority of bills. It was not difficult for him to block "dangerous" legislation.

Advice came to Roosevelt from all sides in the autumn of 1901 to move slowly. It was unnecessary. Since he was in no position to challenge the Old Guard, Roosevelt determined to work with them for a time. He announced immediately after his accession that he would continue McKinley's policies and retain his cabinet. Obviously, Roosevelt was feeling his way and assuring his nomination in 1904. Not yet ready to make war on the Old Guard, he came to terms with them. He went to Aldrich's home in Rhode Island in August 1902 and a short time later conferred at Oyster Bay, Long Island, with leading Republican senators. The upshot of these negotiations was Roosevelt's promise to leave the protective tariff system and monetary structure essentially undisturbed. The senators, in return, gave Roosevelt freedom of action in other matters.

The enormous agitation for railroad regulation and destruction of so-called trusts was beginning to have a significant impact on the Middle West, where a popular revolt against the policies of Hanna and Aldrich was getting under way. The first signs of this upheaval were the election of Robert M. La Follette as governor of Wisconsin in 1900, on a platform demanding the direct primary and effective railroad regulation, and the rise of Albert Baird Cummins as the dominant political leader in Iowa in 1901. Roosevelt realized far better than Aldrich and his friends the neces-

sity of appeasing midwestern opinion. His first move was to instruct the
attorney general in February 1902 to announce that he would soon institute proceedings to dissolve the Northern Securities Company, the gigantic railroad combination that J. P. Morgan had recently formed (see pp.
35–36).

The midwestern progressives could not be propitiated by this one act
alone. They demanded drastic tariff reductions, federal regulation of railroad rates, and more vigorous action against the large corporations. Roosevelt made a tour through the Middle West in August 1902; the following
year, in April, he returned to the region. The more he said the more it was
clear that he understood and sympathized with the midwestern antagonism to Hanna and the Wall Street crowd.

This became drastically clear in Roosevelt's first hard fight in Congress
for reform legislation. It occurred in the early months of 1903 as a consequence of Roosevelt's demand for a provision, in a bill creating a Department of Commerce and Labor, for establishment of a Bureau of
Corporations with full power to investigate business practices. Opposition
from the big business interests was immense, but Roosevelt won his measure by stirring public opinion.

3. *The Election of 1904 and the Emergence of a Progressive Leader*

As the time for the national conventions of 1904 drew near, Roosevelt laid
careful plans for winning his chief objective, the chance to be president in
his own right. Quietly but surely he retired Hanna as chief dispenser of
patronage and made his own alliances with dominant state organizations,
especially in the South. Hanna was Roosevelt's only serious rival, but the
Ohioan died on February 15, 1904, and no one stood in Roosevelt's way.
He therefore received the nomination at the Republican convention on
June 23, 1904, without even a show of opposition.

Having twice failed with Bryan, the Democrats decided to try a con-
servative to offset the impulsive Roosevelt. They nominated Judge Alton
B. Parker of New York, an obscure and ineffectual third-rate politician.
On the whole, the campaign was a drab affair. Near the end, however,
Parker enlivened the contest by charging that Roosevelt was blackmailing
Wall Street into supporting the Republican ticket. The charge was false,
but somehow Roosevelt became badly frightened by rumors that certain
Wall Street interests were pouring huge sums into the Democratic war
chest. Rejecting the suggestion that he appeal directly to the people for
small contributions, Roosevelt allowed his manager to raise money in the

usual way.[2] The voters could not have taken Parker's blackmail charge seriously, for they elected Roosevelt by the largest popular majority that had ever been given a presidential candidate. He received 7,628,500 votes to 5,084,000 for Parker and 421,000 for Eugene V. Debs, the Socialist candidate.

Events soon proved that Roosevelt had given no hostage to Wall Street by accepting its lavish contributions. On the contrary, he had won more real power with the people by 1904 than any president since Lincoln. The wine of victory exhilarated him and strengthened his determination to be the real leader of the country, the spokesman of the majority. His Annual Message of 1904 gave hints of an advanced position, but it was his address before the Union League Club of Philadelphia, delivered in January 1905, that blazoned his new progressivism. Great industries and wealth, he warned, must submit to public control; specifically, the public interest demanded effective regulation of railroad rates.

Pressure on Roosevelt from the Middle and Far West to support such causes as railroad regulation, the direct election of senators, and control of corporations mounted incessantly from this time forward. Moreover, Bryan and progressive Democrats were charging that the president talked loudly but was essentially a straddler. Roosevelt, however, did not merely give in to these pressures. Haunted by the fear that failure to appease popular demand would provoke revolution, he took personal control of the reform movement in the summer and fall of 1905. He launched an attack on the meat packers, beginning with a thorough investigation of the industry. And when Congress assembled in December 1905, he demanded a stringent railroad-regulation law, a pure food and drug law, publicity for campaign contributions, and additional conservation legislation.

The more vigorously Roosevelt asserted leadership, the more successes he won. He succeeded in pushing through a pure food and drug law and a meat inspection act; he forced the passage of a railroad-regulation bill in 1906; and he advanced the cause of conservation through executive action. Moreover, he attacked the so-called trust problem with renewed vigor, not only by many dissolution suits, but perhaps even more effectively through a number of searching exposures by federal agencies. He recognized the intensity of the midwestern demand for tariff reduction, but he never thought that the tariff was an important factor in preserving the system of privilege. He knew, also, that the country needed currency reform and more effective regulation of the banking system, but he never pressed these issues before Congress and the country.

[2] Edward H. Harriman, the railroad magnate, contributed $50,000 personally and collected $200,000 more from other sources. J. P. Morgan gave $150,000, and the three life insurance companies that he controlled added another $148,000. Two Standard Oil partners, H. H. Rogers and John D. Archbold, gave $100,000; and although Roosevelt demanded that this gift be returned, his managers quietly ignored his request. In all, corporations contributed nearly three-fourths of the $2,195,000 collected by the Republican National Committee.

Day in and day out during 1906 and most of 1907, however, Roosevelt gave eloquent voice to the demand for extension of public authority over great aggregations of wealth. It is easy to condemn Roosevelt for not doing more than he did—for not fighting hard for tariff and banking reform, for example. It is also easy to forget that the national progressive movement was only yet in the making, that conservative Republicans controlled Congress (in fact, there were few if any progressives in the Senate until Roosevelt's second administration), and that his leadership of the reform cause was courageous and effective.

Roosevelt was forced to restrain his reform energies during the last months of 1907 in the wake of a severe panic in Wall Street. Bankers and railroad men blamed the administration for loss of public confidence, but the panic was brought on by a worldwide credit stringency and by the very speculative excesses that Roosevelt had condemned.

Depressed economic conditions only momentarily paralyzed Roosevelt's reform impulses. He knew that the popular desire for progressive change was as strong as ever and bound to grow. Thus, while congressional leaders awaited his abdication in pleasant anticipation, Roosevelt intensified his propaganda for reform. A special message to Congress on January 31, 1908, sounded the keynote of a campaign for advanced national legislation that would culminate in a political revolt in 1912 and other consequences. Roosevelt was outraged by the Supreme Court's nullification of the federal Employers' Liability Act of 1906 and demanded new legislation; he also urged the states to adopt accident compensation systems. Moreover, he condemned the courts for using injunctions merely to protect property in labor disputes and urged Congress to empower the Interstate Commerce Commission to make a physical valuation of railroad property and supervise the financial operations of the railroads. Finally, he suggested closer supervision of corporations, either through federal licensing "or in some other way equally efficacious"; and denounced speculators and dishonest businessmen. "The Nation," he warned, "will not tolerate an utter lack of control over very wealthy men of enormous power in the industrial, and therefore in the social, lives of all our people. . . . We strive to bring nearer the day when greed and trickery and cunning shall be trampled under feet by those who fight for the righteousness that exalteth a nation."

4. The Election of 1908

Roosevelt by the end of 1907 was the spokesman for the masses of Republican voters and the real leader of his party. Even the special interests who could delay or defeat his program in Congress could not have prevented his renomination in 1908. He enjoyed being president and delighted in the thought of another four years at the helm. But he had given a pledge after the election of 1904 that he would not run again, and an inner compulsion urged him to stand by his promise.

It was the most fateful decision of Roosevelt's career and perhaps the unwisest. By refusing to heed the popular call in 1908 he denied himself the opportunity to render his greatest service to the Republican party. A Roosevelt in the White House from 1909 to 1913 might well have averted the disastrous rupture that occured in 1912. In any event, he had the power to name his successor and was determined to use it.

The ablest member of the constellation around the president was Elihu Root, who had served as secretary of war from 1899 to 1904 and as secretary of state since 1905. Roosevelt was sorely tempted to make this able corporation lawyer his successor, but he knew that the Middle West would never accept Root because of his Wall Street connections. Finally Roosevelt turned to William Howard Taft of Ohio, his secretary of war, who was one of his staunchest supporters in the Cabinet. Taft had a distinguished record as a federal judge, governor general of the Philippines, and secretary of war. He had good family connections, an eastern education, an excellent mind, and unquestioned integrity. Most important, he seemed eager to carry forward the Roosevelt policies.

Roosevelt, in January 1908, began to set all the machinery of the party organization in motion to assure Taft's nomination. Asserting publicly that the Republican convention should be free to choose its candidate, Roosevelt by the end of May was privately boasting that he had prevented his own renomination and could dictate the naming of Taft. At the Republican convention that met in Chicago in June, therefore, the Ohioan was nominated on the first ballot on a platform that promised, among other things, tariff revision and a federal system of postal savings banks.

The Democrats, meeting in Denver, turned again to Bryan in this year of Rooseveltian supremacy. Although he was by now something of a perennial candidate, the Nebraskan at least seemed able to save his party from another such disaster as it had suffered in 1904. Bryan had come a long way toward progressivism since 1896. He was not a great intellect, but he had a keen ear for the voice of the people and was free from any connection with special privilege. He made his campaign largely on the tariff and trust questions and, promising relief from indiscriminate injunctions, made a frank appeal for labor support. Taft, on the other hand, attacked Bryan as a demagogue, pledged himself to continue the Roosevelt policy of substantial justice to all classes, and promised tariff revision.

As all observers predicted, Taft won easily (he received 7,675,000 votes to 6,412,000 for Bryan); but it was significant that Bryan increased the Democratic vote by a million and a third over 1904 and carried the South, Oklahoma, Colorado, Nevada, and Nebraska. More significant for the future was the marked rise of Republican insurgency, or advanced progressivism, in the Middle West. Heretofore the midwestern progressive Republican bloc in Congress had been a small minority. In the Sixty-first Congress, which would meet in 1909, they would be a powerful force in both houses.

5. Republican Troubles Under Taft

Roosevelt left the United States soon after Taft's inaugural to hunt big game in Africa and then to go on an extended tour of Europe. His departure was applauded in financial circles, where many wished luck to the lions. Conservatives, generally, were sure that Taft would align himself with the Old Guard in Congress. Progressives, on the other hand, were certain that he would come to their support. As it turned out, neither group was entirely right—or wrong.

It would be unkind to say that Taft took the presidency under false pretenses. On the eve of his magistracy he thought that he was a progressive. He shared Roosevelt's belief in the supremacy of the public over the private interest. He believed in railroad regulation, was ruthlessly opposed to monopolies, and honestly wanted to continue Roosevelt's policy of preserving the nation's heritage of natural resources. In a normal period of political quietude he would have been a beloved president.

The years of Taft's reign, however, were highly abnormal. It was a time of agitation and revolt. Civil war within the Republican party impended, and open party warfare could have been averted only by bold presidential leadership. Unhappily, Taft was temperamentally unfit to play the role that history demanded. He could not lead in a time of trouble because leadership in such circumstances required wholehearted commitment and abandonment of the judicial quality that was dominant in his character. Taft was a philosophical progressive, but he could not get on with progressive leaders in Congress because they were too harsh in their denunciations, too impatient, too willing to experiment with untried measures.

The new president was forced to choose between the Old Guard leaders in Congress and the insurgent Republican bloc at the very outset—that is, at the beginning of the special session that convened in March 1909 to consider tariff revision. As the Republicans now had a majority of only forty-seven in the House of Representatives, insurgent leaders concluded that the time had come to combine with Democrats to unhorse the tyrannical Speaker, Joe Cannon. When it seemed that the insurgents were bound to succeed, the Speaker appealed to Taft for help, promising to support the president's legislative program in return. Taft was in a perplexing dilemma because he did not like Cannon and yet he needed his cooperation. He made his first mistake: he endorsed Cannon and hinted that the insurgents should give up their campaign if they wanted a share in the patronage. In the end it was the defection of a group of southern and Tammany Democrats, not Taft's opposition, that frustrated the insurgents' coup d'état. Yet many progressives suspected that the president had betrayed them.

This incident only marked the beginning of the alienation of the progressives from the president. Effective White House leadership in the future could easily have repaired the damage done during the fight over the speakership. Instead of leading boldly, however, Taft soon blundered again, this time in a battle over tariff revision that split the Republican party in the spring of 1909. (For details of this epochal conflict, see pp. 97–98.)

There is no doubt that Taft sincerely desired substantial tariff reductions. But he erred in the beginning by refusing to interfere in the fight in Congress and by failing to rally public opinion behind the cause of tariff reform. When he finally did intervene, moreover, he acted in such a manner as to cause midwestern insurgents, who were leading the fight for tariff reduction, to believe that he had deserted them and surrendered to special privilege. Although the president won a few noteworthy concessions, the bill that was signed—the Payne-Aldrich Act—represented a substantial victory for the eastern manufacturers. By this time—the late summer of 1909—the Middle West was seething with rebellion. Although few men realized the fact, the doom of the Taft administration had been sealed.

Taft embarked in September 1909 upon a 13,000-mile speaking tour from Boston to the West Coast to assuage popular discontent. Instead of calming the storm, he arrayed the insurgent masses decisively against himself by a series of indiscreet speeches. He publicly eulogized Nelson W. Aldrich of Rhode Island, leader of the Old Guard in the Senate. He rebuked midwestern senators who had voted against the tariff bill. And he climaxed his blunders by declaring at Winona, Minnesota, that the measure was the best tariff act that the Republican party had ever passed. After the Winona address, midwesterners were certain that Taft had deserted to the Old Guard.

No sooner had public agitation over the Payne-Aldrich debacle quieted than a worse catastrophe completed the alienation of the progressives. This was the Ballinger affair, which grew out of a feud between the secretary of the interior, Richard A. Ballinger, and the chief of the Forestry Service in the Department of Agriculture, Gifford Pinchot. The root of the trouble was the fact that Pinchot was a conservationist and Ballinger was not. An investigator in the Interior Department, Louis R. Glavis, told Pinchot that Ballinger had connived with the Morgan-Guggenheim syndicate to validate certain withdrawals of Alaskan coal lands. Pinchot believed the accusation, urged Glavis to present his evidence to the president, and publicly denounced Ballinger as a traitor to conservation.

Glavis presented his indictment to the president, who accepted Ballinger's rebuttal and authorized the secretary to dismiss Glavis for insubordination. Pinchot, however, refused to halt his attack and virtually forced Taft to remove him from the Forestry Service in January 1910. Meanwhile, the controversy had developed into a national cause célèbre, with conservatives defending the administration and progressives charging treachery and fraud.

The climax came when Democrats and insurgent Republicans in Congress forced an investigation of the Interior Department. A packed committee voted Ballinger a clean bill of health. But the trenchant questions asked by Louis D. Brandeis, who represented Glavis, exposed Ballinger, not as a corrupt public official, but as an opponent of conservation and a champion of the far western demand for rapid distribution of the remaining public domain. Instead of dismissing Ballinger and appointing a genuine conservationist in his stead, Taft continued stubbornly to defend him and thus exacerbated popular discontent.

Progressive Republicans in the House of Representatives were ready in the early months of 1910 to try again to shear Speaker Cannon of his dictatorial control over legislation. Aware of the impending attack, the Speaker struck back by declaring that he would fight to the end. An insurgent Democratic coalition, led by George W. Norris of Nebraska, deposed the Speaker from the rules committee in March 1910 and deprived him of power to appoint members of standing committees. Certainly Taft secretly approved, for he well knew what a liability Cannon was. Yet because he did nothing by word or deed to encourage the insurgents, the country concluded that Taft was on Cannon's side.

The misunderstanding about Taft's position in the fight against Cannon caused a final and complete break between the administration and the insurgents. They quarreled with Taft over the terms of a bill to strengthen the powers of the Interstate Commerce Commission. They accused him of conspiring with Wall Street when he proposed establishment of a postal savings system. Convinced that the insurgents were maneuvering in every possible way to destroy him politically and goaded by incessant and often unfair attacks, Taft turned fiercely against the progressives and joined the Old Guard in a powerful campaign to destroy insurgency. Taft, Aldrich, and Cannon conferred in March 1910 and formulated a plan of attack. It involved using money and patronage, first to build up strong conservative organizations in the Middle West and then to defeat insurgents for renomination in the impending spring primary elections. The plan was quickly carried out. Patronage in the midwestern states was given to supporters of the president, while Old Guard spokesmen invaded the region and exhorted voters to support administration candidates.

In fighting bitterly for their political lives, the insurgents virtually declared their independence of the party dominated by Taft, Aldrich, and

Cannon. It was a momentous battle, for its outcome would determine the fate of the GOP, not only in the Middle West but in the nation as well. The railroad, industrial, and financial interests of the Midwest supported the administration almost solidly, but the people in every state supported their rebel leaders. Nothing was more indicative of the inevitable doom of the Taft administration than the failure of its anti-insurgent campaign. The flames of midwestern progressivism had grown into a raging prairie fire of insurgency. Already insurgents were talking about organizing a new party if Taft were renominated; already midwestern eyes were turning to Theodore Roosevelt for leadership in the impending battle. Before we discuss these events, however, let us turn back and see how political leadership confronted issues that agitated the American people during the Republican era.

6. Struggles for Tariff and Tax Reform, 1894-1913

No public questions were more potentially explosive and at the same time more perpetually discussed after the Civil War than tariff and tax policies. By the turn of the century the elaborate system of tariff protection and the virtually complete immunity from taxation that wealth enjoyed had become to progressives the very symbol of control of the federal government by allied industrial and banking interests.

The Democrats had made a fumbling effort at tariff and tax reform during the second Cleveland administration. The outcome, the Wilson-Gorman Tariff Act of 1894, represented at best a feeble effort at downward revision and left the protective structure essentially unimpaired. But a coalition of western and southern representatives forced into the tariff bill an amendment levying a 2 percent tax on all net incomes of individuals and corporations over $4,000.

By a strained and obviously class-conscious opinion, a bare majority of the Supreme Court ruled the income tax unconstitutional in 1895. It would be many years before progressives were strong enough to overcome the Old Guard's opposition to an income tax amendment. Meanwhile, Republicans would have spared themselves much future trouble if they had left well enough alone in tariff legislation. However, McKinley was eager to propitiate the agrarian Middle West after his close victory over Bryan in 1896, and so he called a special session of Congress in March 1897 to consider tariff revision. The president desired only a moderate revision of the Wilson-Gorman rates. But senators from western states held the balance of power and forced a substantial increase in duties on agricultural raw materials like wool and hides. Eastern senators, in turn, obtained increased duties on woolens, silks, and other manufactured products. The upshot of this log-rolling was the Dingley tariff, the highest tariff in American history to that time.[3]

Manufacturing interests and western agricultural producers were able to forestall any attempt at general revision for twelve years after the adoption of the Dingley Act. At the same time conservatives kept an equally firm hand on tax policy. Congress imposed a moderate estate tax during the Spanish-American War. But this impost was repealed in 1902, and the federal government reverted to its usual practice of obtaining revenue almost entirely from consumption taxes—customs duties and excise taxes on tobacco and alcoholic beverages—that fell most heavily on the lower and middle classes.

Nevertheless, strong forces were at work during the first years of the twentieth century to culminate eventually in an irresistible movement for tariff and tax reform. First, the passage of the Dingley Act at the beginning of the period of frantic industrial combination lent apparent proof to the charge, often pressed by Bryan and other Democrats, that the high protective system stimulated the growth of monopolies and supercorporations at home. Second, the cost of living increased nearly one-fourth between 1897 and 1907, and the average consumer saw a close relation between high tariffs and high prices, although there was often no connection between the two. Third, widespread discussion of the increasing concentration of incomes and wealth alarmed the middle class and stimulated the conviction that only income and inheritance taxes could reverse a process that seemed to threaten the future of American democracy.

The most significant factor in the beginning of a powerful movement for tariff and tax reform was the awakening of the Middle West. After an epochal struggle in 1901, Iowa Republicans nominated the progressive Albert B. Cummins for governor and wrote into their platform his proposal to remove all duties on articles manufactured by so-called trusts. Thereafter the "Iowa Idea," as Cummins's suggestion was called, became a stock feature of most midwestern state Republican platforms. Although the movement for downward revision soon became nationwide and included many small businessmen, the midwestern insurgents remained the most consistent advocates of tariff reform in the GOP.

Roosevelt recognized the potential danger of popular discontent and was often tempted to take leadership of the movement for tariff revision. He failed to act for three reasons. First, he agreed with his Old Guard

---

[3]The Dingley Act, however, authorized the president to negotiate reciprocal agreements on certain enumerated articles, principally in the French and Latin American trade. Such agreements were later made with France, Italy, Brazil, and other nations. Section 4 of the Dingley Act, moreover, authorized the president to negotiate commercial treaties under which the American tariff might be reduced up to 20 percent in return for reciprocal benefits. These treaties had to be approved by both houses of Congress and could not run for more than five years. The State Department subsequently negotiated eleven such treaties, none of which Congress approved.

friends that such a move would disrupt the GOP. Second, he shrewdly struck a bargain with Speaker Cannon in late 1904 by which he agreed to jettison tariff revision in return for Cannon's promise to clear the road for a railroad regulation bill in the House of Representatives. Third, and most important, Roosevelt thought that the tariff was a question of expediency, not of principle. In this belief he revealed progressivism's divided mind on the issue. On the other hand, both Roosevelt and Taft agreed in 1908 that the tariff question could no longer be evaded. At their insistence, a plank declaring "unequivocally for the revision of the tariff" was written in the Republican platform. Moreover, by 1908 both Roosevelt and Taft had come out squarely for graduated federal estate, gift, and income taxes.

Thus it seemed that the movement for genuine tariff and tax reform had reached a point of culmination when President Taft called Congress into special session in March 1909 to consider tariff revision. The administration's bill, sponsored by Sereno E. Payne of New York, chairman of the House ways and means committee, put a number of important raw materials on the list and substantially reduced rates on iron and steel products, agricultural implements, sugar, and lumber. The measure included a federal inheritance tax ranging from 1 to 5 percent. Although the Democrats made an unsuccessful effort to add an income tax amendment and then voted against the Payne bill for party reasons, they, like midwestern insurgents, were pleasantly surprised when the House approved the bill.

It was an altogether different story in the Senate. There Senator Aldrich and his finance committee took the Payne bill in hand and reported it on April 12, 1909, without the provision for an inheritance tax and with 847 amendments, the majority of which effected increases. Instead of lowering the Dingley rates, as the Rhode Island senator claimed, the Aldrich bill actually increased the ad valorem duties from 40.21 to 41.77 percent. In all fairness, it should be added that Aldrich and his committee were under almost unbearable pressure for rate increases and that the Rhode Islander usually acted under this goad and not on his own initiative.

A wave of indignation swept over the country, and especially the Middle West, as the implications of Aldrich's surrender to the special interests became clear. In the Senate a group of insurgent Republicans waged an open fight against the finance committee's amendments. They also joined Democrats to include an income tax as a substitute for the discarded inheritance tax. So effective was their campaign that Aldrich headed it off only by accepting Taft's proposal for a 2 percent tax on the net incomes of corporations and by agreeing to the passage of an income tax amendment to the Constitution.

With strong administration support in the violent intraparty battle in the Senate, Aldrich put his bill across on July 8, 1909. It included the corporation income tax, restored the duties on hides, iron ore, and lumber, and greatly increased the Payne rates on a number of manufactured products. The final struggle came when the conference committee met shortly afterward. At last bestirring himself on behalf of lower rates, Taft persuaded the committee to accept free hides and reductions in prevailing duties on shoes, lumber, coal, and iron ore. Nonetheless, the bill that the committee approved and Taft signed was a victory for the manufacturing East and an affront to the insurgent Middle West.[4]

The Payne-Aldrich debacle had profound and almost immediate repercussions. For one thing, it widened to an even greater extent the gulf between insurgents and the Taft administration. For another, it enabled the Democrats to capture the House of Representatives in the congressional elections of November 1910. Following hard on the heels of disaster for the GOP, Taft proceeded further to alienate midwestern opinion by driving for reciprocity with Canada.

Confronted with an impending trade war between the United States and her northern neighbor, the State Department concluded a reciprocal trade agreement with the Canadian government in January 1911 that promised to draw the two nations into an economic union. The agreement placed all important agricultural products, industrial raw materials, and raw lumber and wood pulp on the free list. Moreover, it substantially reduced prevailing rates on many manufactured products. The president presented the agreement to Congress on January 26, 1911, for approval by joint resolution; and when the Senate refused to act before the regular session ended, Taft called Congress into special session for the first week in April.

In the subsequent battle over reciprocity that raged from April nearly to August, the recently formed alignment of progressive Republicans was totally destroyed. The Democrats joined Taft's friends in Congress in supporting the agreement because it represented a tremendous victory for free trade. For the same reason the Old Guard fought the measure. The midwestern insurgents, on the other hand, accused the administration of sacrificing midwestern farm interests in order to widen the foreign market for eastern manufactured products. They fought the treaty, therefore, even more bitterly than did the Old Guard. For once Taft exerted himself strenuously and won the fight in Congress with the nearly solid support of the Democrats. The House approved the agreement on April 21, the Senate on July 22, 1911. But it seemed that Taft could not succeed, even when he did the statesmanlike thing. Aroused by talk in the United States of annexation, Canadian voters on September 21, 1911, repudiated the Liberal government that had negotiated the reciprocity agreement.

The antireciprocity coalition of insurgents and the Old Guard was short-lived. In fact, insurgents combined with Democrats even while the battle over reciprocity was raging to pass three tariff bills—a farmers' free list

---

[4] As the matter of tariff rates is infinitely complicated, it is almost impossible to specify the average rates of the Payne-Aldrich bill. The figure usually given by authorities is 37 percent. The measure also established a tariff board to make scientific studies of various phases of the tariff question and to advise Congress and the president.

bill, which removed duties from about one hundred articles that the farmer bought; a wool and woolens bill; and a bill reducing duties on iron and steel products, cotton goods, and chemicals. Taft vetoed these measures on the ground that they were not "scientific." Moreover, progressive Democrats and Republicans joined hands throughout the country during 1911 and 1912 to obtain ratification of the Sixteenth, or income tax, Amendment, which Congress had submitted to the states in 1909. The first chapter in the history of twentieth-century tax reform was completed on February 25, 1913, when the amendment became a part of the Constitution.

7. The Railroad Problem

Agitation for effective public control of railroad rates and services antedated the progressive revolt by several decades. First came efforts by midwestern and southern legislatures during the 1870s and 1880s to institute regulation, either by statute or commission. Some of these attempts succeeded partially; others failed completely. In any event, during the 1880s the conviction grew that only Congress could deal effectively with rebating, stock watering, pools that destroyed competition, and exorbitant rates for goods and passengers in interstate commerce. Experience, and the Supreme Court's decision in the *Wabash* case of 1886, forbidding the states to regulate *interstate* rates, demonstrated that the really important railroad evils were beyond the jurisdiction of the states.

As a result the American people by 1886 had firmly determined to institute federal regulation and end the reign of unbridled freedom in the field of transportation. The legislative response to this overwhelming demand, the Interstate Commerce Act of 1887, was avowedly tentative in character. It specifically forbade pooling, discrimination, rebating, and higher charges for a short haul than a long one. As for rates, it declared that all charges should be reasonable and just and required railroads to publish rate schedules. Finally, the measure established the Interstate Commerce Commission, the first federal regulatory agency, to administer the law. Adoption of the Interstate Commerce Act, unenforceable though it turned out to be, marked a turning point in the exercise of federal power in the United States. For the first time the federal authority had been extended into an important area of private economic activity.

Railroad managers seemed eager to abide by the law for a brief time after the adoption of the act of 1887. But the ICC ran head on into the refusal of railroad managers to testify when it tried to stamp out rebating, and it required years of adjudication to establish the commission's authority to compel testimony. However, it was the Supreme Court's narrow interpretation of the commerce act that deprived the ICC of any real power. In the maximum freight rate cases of 1896 and 1897, the court ruled that the commission did not have the power to fix rates. Moreover, in the *Alabama Midlands* case of 1897 the Supreme Court practically emasculated the prohibition against discrimination in charges for long and short hauls. Indeed, after these decisions the ICC became nothing more than a fact-finding body and openly confessed its inability to cope seriously with the problem of regulation.

Thus by 1900 the whole problem of federal railroad regulation had to be fought out all over again in Congress and the country. The first amendment to the Interstate Commerce Act, the Elkins Act of 1903, was adopted, ironically enough, in response to the pleas of the railroad managers themselves. The rebating evil, they warned, had grown to such monstrous proportions that it threatened to bankrupt the railroads. Congress responded at once with the Elkins Act, which outlawed any deviation from published rates.

The "railroad senators" who framed the Elkins Act carefully avoided giving the ICC any authority over the rate-making process. Yet it was obvious on all sides that this was what the great majority of farmers and businessmen wanted most. At this high point of public agitation, Theodore Roosevelt took leadership of public opinion. In his Annual Message of December 1904 he recommended that the ICC be empowered, upon complaint of shippers, to fix maximum rates, subject to review by the courts. The House of Representatives in response passed the Esch-Townshend bill, implementing the president's suggestion, by the impressive majority of 326 to 17. Seeking to delay or postpone further action, Republican leaders in the upper house instructed the commerce committee to investigate the railroad problem during the spring and summer of 1905. As it turned out, the committee's investigation was no whitewash but rather uncovered a far-flung propaganda campaign by the railroads against federal regulation.

Armed with this new evidence of railroad misdoing, Roosevelt pressed his campaign for legislation all during the summer and fall of 1905. So enthusiastic was the popular response that even the railroad senators began to tremble. The House of Representatives quickly passed the administration's measure, the Hepburn bill, in February 1906. Although it fell short of what advanced progressives wanted, the bill went straight to the core of the railroad problem by empowering the ICC, upon complaint by shippers, to lower rates already established.

The Hepburn bill was referred in the Senate to the commerce committee, the chairman of which was the multimillionaire Stephen B. Elkins of West Virginia, who, along with Aldrich, led the railroad senators. Realizing that he could not control the administration majority on the committee, Aldrich allowed it to report the Hepburn bill unamended. In order to outflank the committee, Aldrich arranged to have the fiery Democrat, Ben

Tillman of South Carolina, report the bill and defend it on the Senate floor. At this stage, the astute Rhode Islander proposed amendments to cripple the bill. The most important of these endowed the courts with sweeping authority to review and nullify the ICC's rate decisions.

Debate raged for two months in the Senate over Aldrich's amendment. Roosevelt contended that judicial review should be limited solely to determining whether the ICC had exercised due process in fixing rates. He fought with unusual resourcefulness for a time. Then, when it seemed that a coalition of Democrats and administration Republicans could put the measure across without Aldrich's consent, several Democrats deserted the coalition. At this point—that is, early May 1906—Roosevelt executed a brilliant maneuver. Instead of going down to defeat with progressives who still demanded narrow court review, Roosevelt maneuvered Aldrich into accepting a compromise amendment. Framed by Aldrich, sponsored by William B. Allison of Iowa, and approved by the president, it was accepted; and the Hepburn bill became law on June 29, 1906.

Some progressives charged that Roosevelt had betrayed the cause of railroad regulation, but the verdict in this historic dispute must go to Roosevelt. The Allison amendment authorized district courts to issue interlocutory, or suspensive, injunctions against the ICC's decisions, it is true; but it also provided for speedy appeals to the circuit courts and the Supreme Court. Moreover, only these courts could reverse the commission's rulings, and they were instructed to pass upon such rulings with the same seriousness that they would exercise in passing upon acts of Congress, with the presumption always in favor of the ICC. Thus so-called broad court review was hedged about with such effective limitations that judicial nullification of the Hepburn Act was well-nigh impossible.

Furthermore, an examination of the general provisions of the Hepburn Act emphasizes the dimensions of Roosevelt's victory. To begin with, the ICC was empowered, upon complaint, to investigate and lower rates. In other words, ultimate control over rates was taken from private hands and given to an agency of the people. The commission, in addition, gained jurisdiction over express and sleeping car companies, switches and spurs, and pipe lines. Finally, the act required a uniform system of cost accounting by the railroads, eliminated the old free-pass evil, and required railroads to divest themselves of outside properties after 1908. The latter provision was aimed chiefly at the anthracite coal monopoly controlled by nine eastern railroads.

The effect of the broadening of the ICC's power was at once apparent. Shippers made more than 9,000 appeals to the commission within two years, while railroad managers seemed almost in a chastened mood. Then railroad managers began suddenly to challenge the ICC in 1908, and their action in turn caused a crowding of the dockets of the circuit courts. In addition, the railroads made general rate increases in 1909, and the masses of people realized for the first time that the commission could deal only with specific increases, upon complaint, and lacked power to suspend or revoke general rate advances.

The railroads' resistance to regulation and the general rate increases of 1909 at once stimulated increased agitation for a further strengthening of the ICC's power. In response, President Taft, in the summer of 1909, requested Attorney General George W. Wickersham to prepare a new railroad bill. The measure that Wickersham drafted greatly enlarged the commission's rate-making power and established a commerce court, which should have original jurisdiction in appeals from the rulings of the ICC. The midwestern insurgent senators were disappointed because the Wickersham draft made no provision for valuation of railroad property by the commission, and they strongly disapproved the proposal for a commerce court, with power of broad review. Even so, the insurgents' opposition to the president's bill might have been less violent had it not seemed that Taft was willing to change the measure to satisfy the demands of railroad spokesmen. Taft conferred with six railroad presidents early in January 1910, even before the measure was introduced in the House, and he changed the bill to allow railroads to acquire competing lines. To progressives, this looked suspiciously like collusion. And when Senator Aldrich announced that he would support the bill, they were certain that some evil scheme was being plotted.

The president's measure, introduced in the House of Representatives in January 1910 as the Mann bill, at once fell into the hands of a progressive Republican-Democratic coalition. It struck out the provision permitting mergers of competing lines, added amendments for physical valuation and equality in charges for long and short hauls, and brought telephone and telegraph companies under the jurisdiction of the Interstate Commerce Commission. Meanwhile, insurgents in the Senate had launched a violent attack on the president's bill, which the commerce committee reported without amendments. Taft made the measure a test of party loyalty, and insurgents joined Democrats and threatened to rewrite the bill altogether. After the progressive coalition struck out the provisions contrary to the Sherman Antitrust Act, Aldrich turned to the Democrats. If they would support the administration's railroad bill, Aldrich said, the administration would agree to approve statehood acts for New Mexico and Arizona. As the Democrats were eager for the admission of the two territories, they sealed the bargain. Thus the progressive Republican-Democratic coalition changed into a Democratic-Regular Republican majority, and the administration's railroad bill passed the Senate essentially intact.

Nonetheless, the bill that emerged from the conference committee, which Taft approved as the Mann-Elkins Act, represented more a victory for the progressives than for the administration. The new legislation empowered the ICC to suspend general rate increases and revise rates on its own initiative. It also established a commerce court to hear appeals directly from the commission. These provisions had been originally parts of the president's bill. On the other hand, all important progressive amendments, except the provision for physical valuation, were retained by the conference committee. Railroads were not allowed to acquire competing lines. Telephone, telegraph, cable, and wireless companies were defined as common carriers. The prohibition in the act of 1887 against discriminations in charges for long and short hauls was strengthened. As a result of the hard fight that progressives made in support of these amendments, the Mann-Elkins Act of 1910 had become legislation comprehensive in character, not merely supplementary.

Progressives in Congress now redoubled their efforts to obtain physical valuation as the basis for rate making by the ICC. Valuation of railroad property would enable the commission to fix rates on a basis of the true value of railroad property, rather than on a basis of watered capitalization. This was the chief reason why progressives supported and railroad spokesmen opposed the proposal. To conservatives, moreover, physical valuation seemed to be the first step in eventual nationalization. Nonetheless, the insurgent-Democratic congressional coalition won this last objective in the closing months of the Taft regime. The Physical Valuation Act of 1913 required the Interstate Commerce Commission to report the value of all property owned by every common carrier subject to its jurisdiction, including the original cost, the cost of reproduction new, and the cost of reproduction less depreciation. When completed, the act declared, such valuations were to be accepted as prima facie evidence of the worth of the property in all actions by the commission.

8. The Federal Antitrust Policy, 1890–1913

Almost simultaneous with the beginning of the agitation for railroad regulation was a widespread movement to destroy the infant industrial combinations of that day, the trusts. (For a discussion of the origins and progress of the trust movement in the United States, see pp. 32–34.) At least fourteen states and territories had written antitrust provisions into their constitutions by 1890, while thirteen others had adopted antitrust laws. Almost without exception, these were western and southern states—a reflection of the impact of the agrarian crusade against railroads and monopolies. The state antitrust crusade gained new momentum from 1890 to 1900. By the latter date forty-two states and territories attempted to outlaw monopolies, either by constitutional provision or by statute.[5]

[5]Practically all these states and territories prohibited restraint of trade that was contrary to the public interest. Some twenty-nine states prohibited suppression of competition through pools, agreements to limit quantity or divide sales territories, price-fixing agreements, and so on. A number of states, moreover, attempted to outlaw cutthroat practices, such as price cutting to destroy competition, so-called tying contracts, and discriminations in prices made for the purpose of destroying competition.

It became increasingly obvious that sporadic and uncoordinated action by the states could neither destroy monopoly nor restore competition, especially when New Jersey in 1888 permitted the legal incorporation of trusts as holding companies. By this date the popular agitation had reached such a high pitch that both major parties incorporated antitrust planks in their platforms. And when President Benjamin Harrison endorsed the demand for a federal antitrust law in his Annual Message of December 1889, Congress did not dare refuse to act.

Its response, the Sherman Antitrust Act of 1890, was brief and to the point. The core was embodied in Section 1. It prohibited "every contract, combination in the form of trust or otherwise, or conspiracy, in restraint of trade or commerce among the several States, or with foreign nations," and provided punishment for such misdoing. Section 7, moreover, stipulated that any person injured by illegal combinations or conspiracies might sue and recover threefold damages and the cost of the suit.

No statute ever enacted by Congress reflected more accurately an overwhelming popular demand. Yet the Sherman law, after several prosecutions by the Harrison administration, fell into neglect and general contempt until 1902. Effective enforcement of the law depended largely upon the Justice Department. But attorneys general during the Cleveland and McKinley administrations did little to carry out the popular mandate to destroy the trusts because neither Cleveland nor McKinley had any sympathy for the objectives of the Sherman Act—except insofar as the provisions of the law might be applied against labor unions.

A case in point was *E. C. Knight* v. *United States*, 1895, in which the government challenged the monopoly recently acquired by the American Sugar Refining Company of Philadelphia. Instead of vindicating the Sherman law, Cleveland's attorney general, Richard Olney, presented the government's case in such a manner that the Supreme Court thought that it had to declare that the Sherman Antitrust Act did not apply to combinations in manufacturing. The consequences of Olney's calculated subversion were far-reaching, but we should not fall into the common error of thinking that the Supreme Court entirely emasculated the antitrust law. As we shall see later, on every opportunity afforded by the government, that tribunal evidenced its willingness to carry out the mandate embodied in the statute.

It was obvious as the new century opened that only a president's determination to give teeth to the measure was needed to make the Sherman law really effective. Theodore Roosevelt understood the dimensions of the popular fear of trusts, abhorred monopoly, and personally resented the power that uncontrolled wealth exercised over the nation's destiny. He therefore resolved to vindicate national sovereignty by bringing great combinations to book. His chief weapons were publicity and the Sherman law. He made investigations and publicity of mergers and so-called trusts possible on a systematic scale by his victory in the fight in 1903 for establishment of the Bureau of Corporations in the Department of Commerce and Labor.

In the form of direct attack, the Justice Department under Roosevelt instituted eighteen proceedings in equity, obtained twenty-five indictments, and participated in one forfeiture proceeding. Beginning with his first prosecution, the suit to dissolve the Northern Securities Company in 1902, Roosevelt pressed relentlessly forward against combinations. The president, later in 1902, ordered prosecution of the Swift, Armour, and Nelson Morris companies—the so-called Beef Trust—for organizing the National Packing Company to acquire control of independent packing firms in the Middle West. The Supreme Court rendered a unanimous verdict for the government in 1905. But the packers continued to defy the government, and it was not until 1920 and 1921 that competition was effectively restored to the meat industry. The climax of Roosevelt's campaign came with sweeping indictments by the Justice Department of the Standard Oil Company in 1907 and of the American Tobacco Company in 1908. These two cases, the most important in the history of the antitrust movement before 1945, did not reach final settlement until 1911.

Roosevelt's contribution to the antitrust cause has been derided by most historians in spite of this effort and achievement. Their failure to understand his contribution stems, among other things, from a faulty appreciation of his objectives. Unlike some progressives, who would have limited the size of corporations, Roosevelt never feared bigness in industry—unless bigness was accompanied by monopolistic control and a disposition on the part of management to defy the public interest. Thus, he never moved against two prominent combinations, United States Steel and International Harvester, because he never had good evidence to prove they were monopolies or were illegally suppressing competition. The Taft administration later instituted dissolution proceedings against these two corporations, but the Supreme Court confirmed Roosevelt's judgment in both cases.

Roosevelt's aggressive program of publicity and prosecution was carried forward at an even more intensive pace by President Taft and his attorney general, George W. Wickersham. When Congress refused to enact Taft's proposal for federal incorporation, a corporation commission, and legislation against stock watering, the Taft administration moved in a wholesale way against combinations. All told, Taft instituted forty-six proceedings for dissolution, brought forty-three indictments, and instituted one contempt proceeding. His two most important cases, those against United States Steel and International Harvester, ended in failure. His two most important victories, over Standard Oil and American Tobacco, were scored in proceedings that Roosevelt had instituted. The government, after five years of legal warfare, won complete victory in 1911 with the Supreme Court's order for dissolution of the gigantic oil and tobacco monopolies. The Court implicitly repudiated the *Knight* decision and made it plain that the holding-company form could not be used to evade the Sherman law. The primary objectives of the antitrust movement had been fairly accomplished by the end of the Taft administration. There was no longer any constitutional doubt that the federal government possessed ample power to prevent monopoly and suppress unfair trade practices in the day-to-day operations of businessmen. Because of Roosevelt's and Taft's vigorous prosecutions, moreover, the age of monopoly was over. Great corporations remained and dominated certain industries, but these oligopolies existed by the sufferance of public opinion and a government that jealously guarded their smaller competitors.

9. *The Supreme Court and Economic Policy Before the First World War*

In the American constitutional system Congress proposes and the Supreme Court disposes. The phrase is of course a hyperbole, but it points up a problem that continually perplexed progressives who were struggling to extend the boundaries of governmental power. Unlike their counterparts in other countries, American reformers in state and nation were never free to develop at will a system of administrative regulation. For one thing, they were bound by a written constitution capable of being construed as the bulwark of a laissez-faire policy. For another, they were restrained by the fear that a conservative Supreme Court, which insisted upon having the final word, would not tolerate the extension of governmental power that they sought to accomplish.

To begin with, the Supreme Court by 1900 had established the right to review all state attempts to regulate railroads and corporations. This power the court had assumed as a result of one of the most important revolutions in judicial theory in American history. It began when Roscoe Conkling, while arguing the case of *San Mateo County* v. *Southern Pacific Railroad* before the Supreme Court in 1882, asserted that the congressional committee that framed the Fourteenth Amendment had intended to confer federal citizenship upon corporations. As Conkling had been a member of the committee and produced its secret journal, the court listened carefully to his argument, although it did not take judicial cognizance of it. In *Santa Clara County* v. *Southern Pacific Railroad*, 1886, and in the *Minnesota Rate* case, 1889, however, the court accepted Conkling's reasoning and declared that corporations were federal citizens, entitled to protection by the Fourteenth Amendment against action of the states that would deprive them of property, or income, without due process of law. Finally, in *Smyth* v. *Ames*, 1898, the Supreme Court reached the last stage in its judicial revolution. Nebraska had established maximum charges on freight carried entirely within the state. Overturning the Nebraska statute, the court reaffirmed the federal citizenship of corporations, declared that rates must be high enough to guarantee a fair return to railroads, and warned state legislatures that the courts existed, among other reasons, for the purpose of protecting property against unreasonable legislation.

In none of these cases did the Supreme Court deny the right of the states to regulate railroads and other corporations. It only insisted that state regulation be reasonable and fair and not invade the jurisdiction of Congress. Until a body of doctrine defining due process regarding state regulation had been built, however, the effect of the court's new departure was to create a twilight zone of authority. Judges of the numerous federal district courts could prevent the states from acting; and the states had no recourse but to await the verdict of the high tribunal.

Progressives, therefore, charged that the Supreme Court had usurped the administrative function of the states and imposed its own notion of due process and reasonableness on state commissions. They resented even more bitterly the systematic manner in which the court narrowed the authority of the ICC under the act of 1887 and even reduced that great statute to an unenforceable platitude. In view of the absence of any specific delegation of the rate-making authority to the commission by the Interstate Commerce Act, the court could probably not have ruled otherwise. Impatient progressives, however, found the court a more vulnerable scapegoat than Congress.

Progressives were on more solid ground when they denounced the Supreme Court's nullification of the income tax provision of the Wilson-Gorman Tariff Act of 1894. By a five-to-four decision in *Pollock* v. *Farmers' Loan and Trust Company*, 1895, the court reversed precedent by declaring that the income tax was in part indirectly a tax on land and would therefore have to be apportioned among the states according to population. It was easily the most unpopular judicial ruling since the *Dred Scott* decision of 1857. For one thing, the income tax decision effectively blocked the movement for a more democratic tax policy until a constitutional amendment could be adopted. For another, the court's majority had obviously made a political rather than a judicial judgment. Coming as it did in the same year in which the court upheld the conviction of Debs and other officials of the American Railway Union for violating the Sherman law, the income tax decision only deepened the popular conviction that the highest tribunal in the land had become the tool of railroads, corporations, and millionaires.

Popular distrust was further intensified in 1895 when the Supreme Court, in the case of *E. C. Knight* v. *United States*, seemingly emasculated the Sherman Antitrust Act's prohibition against industrial monopoly. That the court was actually willing to interpret the Sherman law liberally was demonstrated, however, in a series of important antitrust cases from 1897 to 1899. In the *Trans-Missouri Freight Association* case of 1897, the justices affirmed that the Sherman law applied to railroads and outlawed a pool operating south and west of the Missouri River. The court reaffirmed this judgment in the *Joint Traffic Association* case of the following year. And in the *Addyston Pipe Company* case, 1899, the justices made it clear that the Sherman law applied also to manufacturers who combined in pools to eliminate price competition.

Thus by the turn of the century the Supreme Court had firmly established the rule that combinations formed directly to suppress competition in the transportation and distribution of products were illegal. Promoters of industrial combinations and their lawyers, however, continued to assume on account of the *Knight* decision, discussed earlier, that manufacturing consolidations did not fall under the prohibitions of the antitrust act. This illusion the court finally and completely shattered in its decisions in the *Standard Oil* and *American Tobacco* cases rendered in 1911.

The *Standard Oil* and *American Tobacco* decisions represented, therefore, a complete accommodation of legal doctrine to prevailing antitrust sentiment. But even more important was the fact that they marked the end of a long struggle within the court itself over the basic meaning of the Sherman Antitrust Act. Did that statute forbid all restraints of trade, or did it prohibit only unreasonable, that is, direct and calculated, restraints? The Supreme Court's majority had consistently ruled before 1911 that the Sherman law proscribed all restraints, reasonable and unreasonable.[6] However, Justice Edward Douglass White had vigorously dissented in the *Trans-Missouri Freight Association* case of 1897, declaring that the framers of the antitrust law had intended to outlaw only unreasonable restraints. He reiterated his position over the years and won converts to it. He finally won a majority to his side in the *Standard Oil* and *American Tobacco* cases and, as chief justice, he wrote the "rule of reason" into American legal doctrine. The Sherman law, he declared, prohibited only unreasonable restraints of trade. Actually, the rule of reason was the only standard by which the antitrust law could be enforced, as the court had tacitly admitted years before. Hence the promulgation of the rule of reason represented the greatest victory thus far accomplished in the long fight to destroy monopoly in the United States.

[6]In common law doctrine a reasonable restraint of trade is any restraint that is ancillary to an otherwise legal contract. Almost any form of contract involves such reasonable restraint of trade. By agreeing to sell his product to one person, for example, a manufacturer restrains trade to the extent that he cannot sell the same goods to another person. An unreasonable restraint of trade, on the other hand, occurs when businessmen enter into agreements, the objectives of which are to restrain trade. Thus conspiracies to control prices, restrict production, divide markets, and so on are unreasonable restraints of trade.

5

Woodrow Wilson
and the Flowering of
the Progressive Movement,
1910–1916

The years from 1910 to 1916 were a time of fulfillment for American progressivism. We have seen how various reform movements in the cities and states came to fruition during this period. In addition, a virtual revolution took place in the more important area of national politics. The Republican party was convulsed by internal schisms and suffered a violent rupture from 1910 to 1912; and Theodore Roosevelt attempted in the latter year to rally progressives of all parties under the banner of a third party. As the Democrats now had a reform leader of their own in Woodrow Wilson, Roosevelt failed to build either a solid progressive phalanx or a permanent party. Instead, he split the Republican majority and enabled the Democrats to capture control of the presidency and of Congress.

But Roosevelt did more than make possible a Democratic victory in 1912. By championing an advanced program of federal economic and social regulation, he also pointed up the major dilemma confronting American progressives. Could national regeneration be achieved, as most Democratic progressives thought, merely by destroying special privilege and applying the rule of equity to all classes? Or could the promise of

American life be fulfilled only through a program of federal intervention and participation in economic and social affairs, as Roosevelt and Herbert Croly contended?

Advocates of these two concepts of progressivism battled all during the first Wilson administration to shape the form and character of federal legislation. As the new president exercised an extraordinary control over Congress, the outcome of the conflict—in fact, the future destiny of the progressive movement—was largely in his hands. Let us now see how progressivism came to flood tide, how Wilson guided it from one channel into another, and how the basis for a later and bolder program of federal action was laid by the time the United States entered the First World War.

1. The Disruption of the Republican Party and the Reorganization of the Democratic Party

There were numerous warnings in all parts of the country during the spring and summer of 1910 that a violent storm impended in the Republican party. The most portentous was the near hurricane velocity of the insurgent revolt in the Middle West. President William Howard Taft hastily sought to make peace with his enemies and save his party from disaster after the failure of his concerted attempts to purge midwestern progressives in the primary campaigns of 1910. The insurgents, now determined to seize control of the GOP and prevent Taft's renomination in 1912, rebuffed the president's overtures and began a search for a leader of their own.

A second signal of Republican distress was the estrangement between Roosevelt and Taft, which was fully evident by the time the former president returned from Europe in June 1910. The coolness that Roosevelt felt toward his former friend was the outgrowth partly of incidents like the Ballinger affair, but above all it was the result of Roosevelt's growing conviction that Taft had allowed the Old Guard to maneuver him into a position that made the revolt of the insurgents inevitable. Roosevelt was firmly committed to the progressive cause, but he tried hard to bring the warring factions together. Feeling rebuffed by the administration when he endeavored to mediate between conservatives and progressives in New York State, the former president set out upon a speaking tour in the summer of 1910 to kindle the flames of progressivism. So enthusiastic was the popular response that he was catapulted into leadership of the rebellion against Taft and the Old Guard.

Democrats harvested the fruits of Republican dissension and popular protest against the Payne-Aldrich tariff and the Ballinger affair in the congressional and gubernatorial elections of Novermber 1910. The House of Representatives went Democratic for the first time since 1892, and Democratic governors were elected in many normally Republican states in the East and Middle West. There could be no doubt that progressive agitation was rising to flood tide or that a Republican party dominated by Taft, Aldrich, and Cannon faced almost certain defeat in 1912.

The Republican insurgents, on the other hand, were determined to win in 1912, but to win with their own ticket and platform. Many signs in 1910 and early 1911 pointed to Senator Robert M. La Follette of Wisconsin as the leader of the rebels, especially after prominent insurgents formed the National Progressive Republican League in January 1911 to fight for the senator's nomination. La Follette had the support of a small and dedicated band of idealists, but the great mass of Republican progressives wanted Roosevelt. Convinced that his party faced certain defeat if Taft was renominated and persuaded that La Follette could never be nominated, Roosevelt at last gave in to the pleas of his friends and announced his candidacy for the Republican nomination on February 24, 1912.

The battle for control of the GOP that occurred from March through May 1912 was bitter and violent. In the thirteen states that held presidential primaries, Roosevelt won 278 delegates, as compared to 48 for Taft and 36 for La Follette. On the other hand, Taft controlled the southern states, had the support of Old Guard strongholds like New York, and dominated the Republican National Committee. Consequently the Taft forces organized the national convention that met in Chicago on June 18, awarded themselves 235 of the crucial 254 contested seats, and proceeded ruthlessly to renominate the president on the first ballot on June 21.

Meanwhile, over three hundred Roosevelt delegates had stormed out of the convention and, in consultation with Roosevelt, had decided to return to Chicago and form a new party dedicated to advancing the cause of progressivism. The outgrowth of the insurgents' anger and dedication was the Progressive party, organized in Chicago on August 5 and 6, 1912. Roosevelt, saying that he felt like a bull moose, came in person on August 6 and delivered his acceptance speech, "A Confession of Faith."

The high excitement of these events at Chicago should not be allowed to obscure their significance or the importance of the platform, the "Contract with the People," that the convention of the new Progressive party adopted. It erected mileposts that the American progressive movement would follow for the next fifty years. It was, in fact, the most important American political document between the Populist platform of 1892 and the Democratic platform of 1936. The Progressive party platform of 1912 approved all objectives of the social justice reformers—minimum wages for women, child labor legislation, workmen's compensation, and social insurance. It endorsed neodemocratic demands for the initiative, referendum, and recall, the recall of state judicial decisions, nomination of presidential candidates by preferential primaries, and woman suffrage. Finally, it demanded establishment of powerful new agencies—a federal trade commission and a federal tariff commission—to regulate business and industry. In brief, it proposed to transform state and federal governments into positive, dynamic agencies of social and economic regeneration.

A crucial struggle had also been occurring in the meantime for control of the Democratic party. Bryan remained titular head, but he announced soon after the elections of November 1910 that he would not be a candidate for a fourth nomination, and a host of new leaders rose to claim his mantle. Woodrow Wilson, who had made a brilliant and successful campaign for the governorship of New Jersey, quickly emerged as the most formidable Democratic claimant. In a spectacular display of leadership, Wilson forced through an unwilling legislature a series of measures that implemented the program for which New Jersey progressives had been fighting for almost a decade. As a consequence of these triumphs, many progressive Democrats throughout the country by the summer of 1911 were thanking God that they had a new leader and spokesman. For his part, Wilson threw himself into the movement for his nomination for the presidency with such vigor that it seemed at the beginning of 1912 that he would easily win leadership of the Democrats.

Wilson's apparent success made the meteoric rise of his chief rival, Champ Clark of Missouri, Speaker of the House of Representatives, all the more surprising. In contrast to the New Jersey governor, who represented the newcomer and the nonprofessional in politics, Clark was an old-line politician who had served without distinction in the House since the 1890s. Temperamentally and intellectually unfit to be president, Clark nonetheless inherited most of Bryan's following in the West, made alliances with a number of eastern and southern state organizations, and won the support of William Randolph Hearst and his chain of newspapers.

Thus, while Wilson campaigned fervently and won not quite one-fourth the delegates to the Democratic national convention, Clark negotiated shrewdly and harvested a crop nearly twice as large. To make matters worse for Wilson, Oscar W. Underwood of Alabama, chairman of the House ways and means committee, had entered the contest and won more than one hundred southern delegates who probably would have otherwise gone to Wilson.

It was a critical moment in the life of the Democratic party and, indeed, in the history of the country, when the delegates assembled for the national convention in Baltimore on June 25, 1912. Since nothing less than control of the federal government was at stake, the convention was a bitter affair from the beginning. The outcome of preliminary contests over organization, in which Bryan and the Wilson forces were defeated by the conservative leaders with the help of the Clark delegates, seemed to forecast Clark's impending victory. Clark took a commanding lead in the early balloting. Then the ninety Tammany-controlled New York delegates went to the Speaker on the tenth ballot, giving him a majority—but not the then necessary two-thirds. Yet the expected and seemingly inevitable Clark landslide did not materialize; in fact, Clark lost votes on the next few ballots. A long and grueling battle followed in which the Wilson managers gradually undermined Clark's strength and finally won a two-thirds majority for the New Jersey governor on the forty-sixth ballot.

It has long been mistakenly assumed that Bryan's action in changing his vote from Clark to Wilson on the fourteenth ballot was the decisive factor in this miraculous conclusion. Actually, a number of other circumstances were more responsible for Wilson's victory. However, Bryan did at least dominate the writing of the historic Democratic platform of 1912. It denounced the Payne-Aldrich tariff, promised honest downward revision, and demanded legislation to destroy so-called trusts and establish a decentralized banking system free from Wall Street control. It held out hope for early independence to the Filipinos. Finally, it approved the amendments for the income tax and direct election of senators and favored exempting labor unions from prosecution under the Sherman law. Although it was neither as advanced nor as nationalistic as the Progressive party's "Contract with the People," the Democratic platform did promise at least the destruction of the system of special privileges for business that Republicans had carefully erected since 1861.

2. *The Campaign and Election of 1912*

A meaningful division in American politics occurred for the first time since 1896 during the presidential campaign of 1912. The four parties and tickets in the field offered programs that well reflected the existing divisions of political sentiment. Although the Republican platform contained concessions to the dominant progressive sentiment, voters understood that Taft's reelection would mean a continuation of Old Guard leadership and policies. In extreme contrast stood Eugene V. Debs, the Socialist candidate, and his party. Offering a program envisaging the gradual nationalization of resources and major industries, Debs campaigned as if he thought he had a chance to win.

The campaign, however, soon turned into a verbal duel between Roosevelt and Wilson. Both men were progressives, yet they reflected in their respective programs and philosophies a significant ideological divergence in national progressivism. Roosevelt's program, the New Nationalism, represented the consummation of a philosophy that had been maturing in his mind at least since 1908, if not since 1905. Like Herbert Croly, Roosevelt urged progressives to examine their basic political assumptions and to see that the historic American democratic creed, which was intensely individualistic, was no longer adequate for an urbanized and industrialized soci-

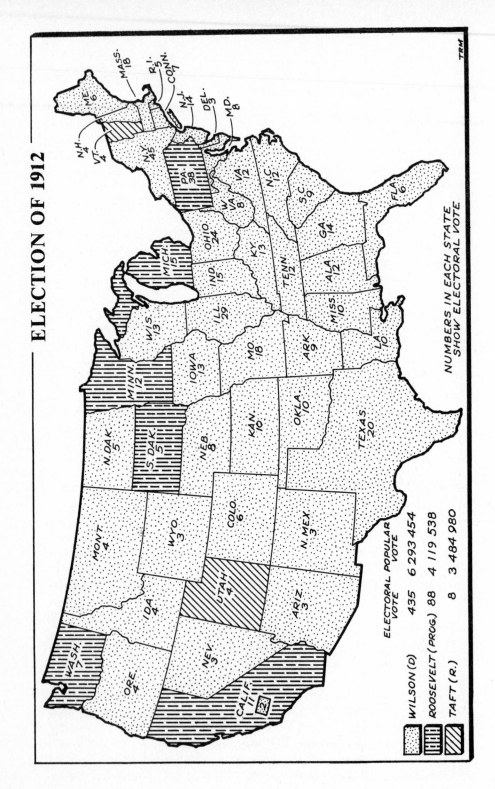

ELECTION OF 1912

	ELECTORAL VOTE	POPULAR VOTE
WILSON (D)	435	6 293 454
ROOSEVELT (PROG.)	88	4 119 538
TAFT (R.)	8	3 484 980

NUMBERS IN EACH STATE
SHOW ELECTORAL VOTE

WASH. 7
ORE. 4
CALIF. 11 [2]
NEV. 3
IDA. 4
MONT. 4
WYO. 3
UTAH 4
ARIZ. 3
N. MEX. 3
COLO. 6
N. DAK. 5
S. DAK. 5
NEB. 8
KAN. 10
OKLA. 10
TEXAS 20
MINN. 12
IOWA 13
MO. 18
ARK. 9
LA. 10
WIS. 13
MICH. 15
ILL. 29
IND. 15
OHIO 24
KY. 13
TENN. 12
MISS. 10
ALA. 12
GA. 14
FLA. 6
S.C. 9
N.C. 12
VA. 12
W. VA. 8
PA. 38
N.Y. 45
N.H. 4
VT. 4
ME. 6
MASS. 18
R.I. 5
CONN. 7
N.J. 14
DEL. 3
MD. 8

TRM

ety. Practically, Roosevelt declared, this meant that progressives must abandon laissez faire for democratic collectivism and be willing to use the federal government as a regulator and protector of business, industry, and workers. It meant, in brief, that progressives must surrender their hostility to strong government and espouse instead a New Nationalism that would achieve democratic ends through Hamiltonian, or nationalistic, means.

In expounding this philosophy in the campaign of 1912, Roosevelt advocated a policy toward big business that was entirely at variance with the individualistic tradition. Let us recognize, he said, that concentration and bigness in industry are inevitable in many fields. At the same time, let us subject the large corporations to comprehensive public control through a powerful federal trade commission. Let us also recognize that the great mass of American workers, especially women and children, are powerless to protect themselves, hence let us use the state and federal governments to improve their lot—among other things by minimum wages for women, workmen's compensation, federal prohibition of child labor, and expanded public health services.

Wilson, a recent convert to progressivism, had no such well-constructed program in mind. Still imbued with a strong residue of laissez-faire concepts, he believed that the federal authority should be used only to destroy artificial barriers to the full development of individual energies, not to rearrange social and economic relationships or to give protection to special classes. He was also a state-rights Democrat, fundamentally suspicious of bold use of federal power. Acting like a traditional Democrat, Wilson began his campaign by promising to destroy the Republican system of tariff protection as the first step in restoring competition. When this issue failed to catch fire, he followed the suggestion of Louis D. Brandeis and moved to what he made the fundamental issue of his campaign— emancipation of business and labor from monopolistic control. Lashing out at Roosevelt's proposals for social legislation and control of corporations, he warned that the New Nationalism could end only with big businessmen controlling the federal government and enslaving workers. In contrast, he promised to destroy monopoly and unleash the potential energies of businessmen by restoring conditions under which competition could flourish. This he would do, specifically, by instituting tariff reform, freeing credit from Wall Street control, and strengthening the Sherman Antitrust Act so as to outlaw unfair trade practices and break up interlocking directorates. This program Wilson called the New Freedom. In brief, it envisaged the destruction of special privileges, restoration of the reign of competition, and reliance for future progress on individual enterprise. On social and economic justice, Wilson was somewhat ambiguous. Since his own ideas were in flux, it is difficult to know precisely where he stood. In any event, he offered no definite program like Roosevelt's.

The most striking fact of the campaign was Roosevelt's failure to split the Democratic ranks and create a solid progressive coalition. The results, therefore, were obvious long before election day. Wilson polled 6,286,214 popular votes; Roosevelt, 4,126,020; Taft, 3,483,922; and Debs, 897,011. Although Wilson received slightly less than 42 percent of the popular votes, his victory in the electoral college was overwhelming because of the multiple division of popular votes. The disruption of the GOP, moreover, gave the Democrats a large majority in the House and a small but workable majority in the Senate.

The election of 1912 seems to have demonstrated that the American people were in an overwhelmingly progressive, if not rebellious, mood. Had progressive Republicans and progressive Democrats been able to unite behind a single ticket and platform, progressivism's triumph would have been even more spectacular. As it was, the Democrats would control the federal government chiefly because of the disunion among their opponents. The future of the progressive movement in the United States would depend upon Wilson's ability to bring the reform program to fulfillment and unite the two divergent wings.

3. *Woodrow Wilson and the Progressive Movement*

No man in American history before 1910 had such a meteoric rise to political preeminence as Woodrow Wilson. Born in a Presbyterian manse in Staunton, Virginia, on December 29, 1856, he grew to boyhood in a South convulsed by Civil War and Reconstruction. After graduating from Princeton University in 1879, Wilson studied law at the University of Virginia and tried unsuccessfully, in 1882 and 1883, to practice law in Atlanta. Disillusioned by the sharp practices of lawyers in Atlanta at that time, he entered the new Johns Hopkins University in Baltimore and won a doctor's degree in political science and history in 1886. He taught successively at Bryn Mawr College, Wesleyan University, and Princeton University from 1885 to 1902. He found an outlet for his political energies in lecturing and writing, and above all in analyzing the weaknesses inherent in the structure of the national government. The basic cause of the failure of leadership in the American political system, he asserted in his most famous work, *Congressional Government* (1885), lay in the separation of executive from legislative responsibility and leadership.

Wilson's election as president of Princeton University in 1902 gave him his first opportunity to practice the principles of leadership that had been maturing in his mind. Visualizing himself as a prime minister, he put into operation a reorganized curriculum and a new method of undergraduate instruction, the preceptorial system of discussion in small groups. As he emerged as an educational leader of national prominence, he also became increasingly articulate as a spokesman of Democratic conservatism.

Wilson probably would not have allowed his suppressed political ambitions to revive had events continued to go well for him at Princeton. He attempted in 1906 and 1907 to reorganize the social life of undergraduates by abolishing their eating clubs and substituting quadrangles, or residential colleges, in their stead. Students and alumni were so bitterly opposed that the trustees felt compelled to withdraw their approval of the quadrangle plan. This first reversal was so humiliating that Princeton's prime minister nearly resigned. But the really crushing blow, the event that made Wilson willing to embark upon an uncertain political career when the opportunity arose in 1910, was his defeat in a personal controversy in 1909 and 1910 with the trustees and dean of the graduate school over the establishment and control of a graduate college.

While the graduate college controversy was at its height in the spring of 1910, George Harvey, editor of *Harper's Weekly*, persuaded the leading Democratic boss of New Jersey, James Smith, Jr., to nominate Wilson for the governorship. Wilson accepted the nomination chiefly because the situation at Princeton had become personally intolerable to him. Once in politics, however, he refused to play the role that Harvey and Smith had cut out for him. Sensing that the progressive movement in his state was at flood tide, he came out squarely behind the progressive program and, with the support of insurgent Republicans, won a startling victory in November 1910. As we have mentioned, he boldly seized control of the Democratic party in New Jersey, pushed a comprehensive reform program through an assembly heretofore dominated by bosses and lobbyists, and then undertook a nationwide campaign that carried him into leadership of the Democratic party in 1912 and the White House in 1913.

For the next four years Wilson occupied the same position with regard to national progressivism that Theodore Roosevelt had occupied from 1905 to 1909. However, changed circumstances and differences in personality made Wilson's role in the development of the movement considerably different from Roosevelt's. Unlike Roosevelt, Wilson had not participated in any early progressive movement. In Trenton, and later in Washington, he was given leadership of state and national movements ripe for fulfillment. The chief thing required of him was to act as the catalytic agent of his time—to rally and strengthen his forces, to synthesize ideas and proposals, and then to use his incomparable powers of articulation and leadership to translate these ideas into statutory realities.

Roosevelt had never really mastered the powerful and entrenched Old Guard machine in Congress. By appealing to the country he had forced Congress to act, but he never actually led the legislative branch of the government. In contrast, Wilson found a congressional situation in 1913 that afforded a unique opportunity for a strong executive. For one thing, there was no Democratic machine in Congress. For another, Democratic leaders, after wandering in the wilderness for twenty years, were determined to make good and cooperate for the success of their program and party. Wilson was thus privileged to be the best and most effective kind of leader in the American system—the parliamentary leader of a cooperative congressional majority. A strong believer in party government and responsibility, Wilson prepared a legislative program, personally guided congressmen in drafting measures, and mediated between various factions when disputes inevitably arose over principles and details.

Wilson's first and most important contribution to the national progressive movement, therefore, was his strengthening and extension of the power of the presidency. By his own example he demonstrated that the president has it in his power not only to represent the majority opinion, as Roosevelt had done, but also to destroy the wall between the executive and legislative branches. His second great contribution was a more immediate one—the manner in which he used this leadership to bring the national progressive movement to legislative consummation.

Men followed Wilson because he was determined to fulfill party pledges and to act for the good of the country, and above all because he nobly articulated their own highest ideals and aspirations. Among friends and associates Wilson was usually warm and intimate. He was in most circumstances an excellent administrator who gave the greatest possible rein to subordinates. But he commanded loyalty by superior intelligence and by appealing to principles and moral purposes more than to personal friendship. Wilson's leadership succeeded so long as his massive intelligence and moving eloquence survived the hazards of an increasingly demanding presidential career. Even so, his leadership was impaired by certain defects even during the heyday of his powers. The most striking of these was a tendency to value his own intuitive and moralistic judgments over conclusions deduced from an analysis of sometimes unpleasant facts. Moreover, he too often assumed that others were as high-minded as he; consequently, he was sometimes a poor judge of men. Finally, his strong activism and urge to achieve his own solutions sometimes, although not always, prevented him from making necessary compromises.

Most historians agree that these were usually minor flaws. Wilson brought to the presidency new life and vigor informed by an almost intuitive ability to probe and understand public opinion. Perhaps better than any other president he was adept at the alchemy of transforming broad principles and traditions into statutory realities. He gave leadership in nobility of character and eloquence of language unrivaled since Lincoln, indeed, unexcelled by any president in our history.

4. The New Freedom

The first item on Wilson's legislative schedule was tariff revision, for Democratic promises would be hollow so long as the Payne-Aldrich Act— that symbol of business privilege—remained in force. On the day of his inauguration, March 4, 1913, therefore, Wilson called a special session of Congress; and he went in person before the two houses on April 8. By breaking the precedent established by Jefferson, Wilson asserted his personal leadership in legislation and focused the attention of the country on Congress. Even more, he conferred frequently with Chairman Oscar W. Underwood while the House ways and means committee prepared the new tariff bill.

The measure that Underwood presented to the House on April 22, 1913, honestly fulfilled Democratic promises of tariff reform. It was not a free trade bill, but rather an attempt to place American industries in a genuinely competitive position with regard to European producers. All products manufactured by so-called trusts, such as iron and steel products and agricultural machinery, were placed on the free list, while most raw materials, clothing, food, shoes, and other such items were either put on the free list or given only incidental protection. The general average of the Underwood duties was about 29 percent, as contrasted with the 37 to 40 percent level of the Payne-Aldrich Act. Finally, to compensate for the anticipated loss of revenue, the ways and means committee added a provision levying a graduated but slight tax on incomes.[1]

The Underwood bill passed the House by a thumping majority on May 8, but the battle for tariff reform had only just begun. By insisting on free sugar and free wool, Wilson had antagonized Democratic senators from Louisiana, Montana, and Colorado, the states that produced these raw materials, and a change of three Democratic votes in the upper house could change a Democratic majority into a minority. It was a dangerous situation, but the president took unprecedented steps. First he applied heavy personal and political pressure on wavering Democrats. Then on May 26 he issued a statement to the country denouncing the swarms of lobbyists who infested Washington and were hard at work to defeat tariff reform.

This bold strategy succeeded far beyond the president's expectations. In response to Wilson's indictment of the lobbyists, La Follette and other progressives in the Senate instituted a searching inquiry into lobbying and compelled senators to reveal personal property holdings that might be affected by tariff legislation. Under such penetrating publicity the opposition of Democratic senators, except for the two Louisianians, vanished, and the road ahead was clear for honest reform. In fact, by putting food and other farm products on the free list, the Senate finance committee, headed by Furnifold Simmons of North Carolina, actually reduced the Underwood rates by 4 percent. Moreover, a threatened rebellion of progressive senators of both parties forced the finance committee to increase the levy on incomes from a maximum of 4 percent to a maximum of 7

[1] It levied a flat tax of 1 percent on all personal and corporate incomes over $4,000 and an additional surtax of 1 percent on incomes from $20,000 to $50,000, 2 percent on incomes from $50,000 to $100,000, and 3 percent on incomes over $100,000.

percent.[2] The Senate approved the tariff bill on September 9, 1913; the House conferees accepted the Senate amendments; and Wilson signed the revised and strengthened Underwood-Simmons bill on October 3.

It was fortunate for Wilson that he emerged from this first and crucial test stronger than before, for at the moment he signed the Underwood-Simmons Act a controversy provoked by his attempt to reorganize the national banking and currency systems was brewing furiously. Practically every authority recognized the imperative need for speedy reform, lest the entire awkward banking structure collapse in another depression.[3] The trouble was that different interests and groups demanded different kinds of legislation. The banking community and conservative Republicans almost unanimously supported the plan proposed by the Aldrich Commission, appointed in 1908 to study banking reform, to establish a great central bank, with branches, controlled by the dominant banking interests. The Democrats had condemned the Aldrich plan in their platform of 1912, but they were well-nigh fatally divided. The progressive faction demanded a reserve system and currency supply owned and controlled by the government. They pointed to the revelations of the Pujo Committee, which investigated the so-called Money Trust in early 1913, to prove that only decisive public control could destroy the existing concentration of credit resources in Wall Street. On the other hand, conservative Democrats, still fearful of Bryan's monetary heresies, proposed a decentralized reserve system, free from Wall Street domination, but owned and controlled by private interests.

It was amid such confusing and divided counsels that Wilson tried to steer a middle course and evolve a policy that would be acceptable to all factions. He commissioned Carter Glass of Virginia, chairman of the House banking committee, to prepare a preliminary bill. As Glass was a leader of the conservative Democratic faction, he drafted a measure that would have established a system consisting of as many as twenty reserve banks, under private control and without central direction. At Wilson's insistence, Glass added a provision for a central governing board, on which bankers would have minority representation, to coordinate the far-flung reserve system.

The publication of the original Glass bill set off a controversy in administration circles that threatened for a time to disrupt the Democratic party.

---

[2]The Senate bill, to which the House agreed, levied an income tax of 1 percent on income over $4,000 and an additional surtax ranging to 6 percent.

[3]The banking and currency systems established by the Civil War legislation were totally unfit for the needs of a great industrial and commercial nation. For one thing, the currency was based upon the bonded indebtedness of the United States and was therefore inflexible; worse still, the national banking structure was without any effective central control or workable machinery for mobilizing banking reserves. The Panic of 1907 had prompted Congress to enact the Aldrich-Vreeland Act of 1908, which allowed banks to issue emergency currency against securities and bonds, but this measure was never meant to be a long-run solution and was devised only to meet emergencies.

Bryan, Secretary of the Treasury William G. McAdoo, and Robert L. Owen, chairman of the Senate banking committee, led progressive Democrats in demanding a reserve and currency system owned and controlled entirely by the government. In addition, agrarian spokesmen in the House denounced the Glass bill because it made no provision for destroying the Money Trust or furnishing credit to farmers. Confronted by a seemingly impossible situation, Wilson moved serenely but decisively. Upon the advice of Louis D. Brandeis, the president decided that the bankers should be denied representation on the proposed Federal Reserve Board and that Federal Reserve currency should be the obligation of the United States. At Bryan's urging, he allowed the agrarian faction to amend the Glass bill to provide short-term credit facilities for farmers. On the other hand, private banking interests would own and largely control the Federal Reserve banks and have a voice in an advisory commission that would counsel the Federal Reserve Board. Thus Wilson's mediating leadership in this first great crisis in banking reform enabled the progressive, agrarian, and conservative Democratic factions to find an acceptable compromise.

No sooner had the controversy within the administration been settled than another more violent storm burst over the country. Bankers and their spokesmen were up in arms, denouncing the revised Glass bill as harebrained, socialistic, and confiscatory. Organized banking groups and banking journals raged all during the late summer and autumn of 1913, but gradually preponderant general opinion turned in the administration's favor. The Glass bill passed the House in September by a large majority; considerably revised, it passed the Senate on December 19, and the president signed it four days later.

The Federal Reserve Act established twelve Federal Reserve banks owned by member banks[4] and controlled by boards of directors, the majority of whom were chosen by member banks. As the central banks of their various districts, reserve banks held a portion of member banks' reserves and performed other central banking functions. The Glass measure also created a new currency, Federal Reserve notes, issued by the reserve banks to member banks on the basis of collateral consisting of commercial and agricultural paper and a 40 percent gold reserve. This Federal Reserve currency was flexible, that is, it would expand or contract in volume in direct relation to the needs of the business community. Uniting and controlling in a limited fashion the entire system was a Federal Reserve Board of seven members, appointed for long terms by the president with the consent of the Senate.

It was the great merit of the Federal Reserve Act that it provided means to mobilize the major part of the banking reserves of a region, indeed of the entire country; created a new and flexible, yet absolutely

[4]All national banks were required to join the Federal Reserve system. State banks were free to join the system but were not compelled to do so.

sound, currency; effectively destroyed the concentration of credit resources in a few financial centers; and reinforced private control on the
local level, tempered by a degree of public supervision and national coor-
dination. Doctrinaire progressives like La Follette denounced the Federal
Reserve Act because it did not provide for comprehensive federal control
or ownership and operation of the national banking system. Yet the framers of the measure never intended to implement such far-reaching policy.
In the spirit of Wilson's New Freedom they conceived a banking and
currency system in which the private and the public interests would work
in harmony and be reconciled by the Federal Reserve Board.

5. *The Turning Point in Wilsonian Progressivism*

The Federal Reserve Act marked the high tide of the New Freedom
doctrines. Wilson gave numerous evidences throughout 1913 and the early
months of 1914 of his determination to adhere strictly to his limited reform program and his resolution not to surrender to the movements then
on foot to commit the federal government to advanced social and economic legislation. The root of the disagreement between the president and
the agrarian, labor, and social justice reformers stemmed from divergent
conceptions of the proper role that the federal government should play.
Like Theodore Roosevelt, advanced progressives championed measures
aimed at using federal authority to benefit special, if underprivileged,
classes. Thus controversy inevitably arose when Wilson invoked New
Freedom concepts to thwart the demands of these powerful pressure
groups.

So resolutely did the president stand in defense of the New Freedom, in
fact, that for a time he obstructed or refused to encourage the fulfillment
of a large part of the progressive program. We have already seen how he
blocked the AF of L's campaign to obtain immunity for labor unions from
application of antitrust law to their illegal strike activities (see pp. 50–51).
In the same manner, Wilson in the spring of 1914 prevented passage of a
bill that would have established a system of long-term rural credits financed and operated by the federal government. Or, again, when the
National Child Labor Committee's child labor bill passed the House in
1914, Wilson refused to fight for its approval by the Senate because he
thought it unconstitutional. He also refused to support a woman suffrage
amendment because he thought that suffrage qualifications should be determined by the states.

Three other incidents revealed the extent to which the president opposed or refused to encourage advanced progressive legislation. The first
was his momentary obstruction of the movement to reduce the number of

immigrants coming to American shores. Restriction, or outright exclusion, of immigration had long been an objective of the AF of L, many sociologists, and many social workers. The instrument proposed by these groups, the literacy test, was embodied in the Burnett immigration bill that passed Congress on January 2, 1915. Wilson vetoed this measure, and his veto held. Two years later, in January 1917, Congress overrode his veto of a similar bill.

The second incident was Wilson's near veto of the La Follette seamen's bill in March 1915. Initiated by Andrew Furuseth, president of the International Seamen's Union, this measure imposed rigorous safety requirements on all vessels in the American maritime trade. More important, it freed American and foreign sailors on vessels coming to American ports of their bondage to labor contracts. Wilson at first supported the seamen's bill, as it conferred no special privileges and did no more than place maritime workers on an equal footing with other workers. The State Department, however, strongly opposed the measure because it unilaterally abrogated some thirty treaties with the maritime powers. After much soul-searching and after Senator La Follette, the measure's chief sponsor, agreed to give the State Department ample time to renegotiate the treaties, Wilson approved the seamen's bill on March 4, 1915. Obviously, it was not an administration measure.

The third incident was perhaps the most revealing. It came early in the New Freedom dispensation, when Wilson permitted his secretary of the treasury and postmaster general to segregate certain black and white workers in their departments. This provoked such a storm of protest from Negroes and from white progressives in the North that the administration reversed what was in fact a very limited segregation policy late in 1914. The incident, nonetheless, revealed the absence in administration circles of any strong concern for social justice, at least for Negroes.

The first important movement toward more advanced progressivism occurred in the early months of 1914 as Wilson and congressional leaders set about to prepare antitrust legislation. Advanced progressives demanded establishment of an independent trade commission armed with a kind of freewheeling authority to oversee business activities and suppress unfair trade practices. At the outset Wilson insisted upon a solution more in accord with the New Freedom doctrine of limited intervention. His original antitrust program was embodied in two measures, the Clayton bill and the Covington interstate trade commission bill. The former enumerated and prohibited a series of unfair trade practices, outlawed interlocking directorates, and gave private parties benefit of decisions in antitrust suits originated by the government. The Covington bill created an interstate trade commission to supplant the Bureau of Corporations. The new commission would have no independent regulatory authority but, like the Bureau of Corporations, would act merely as a fact-finding agency for the executive and legislative branches.

The publication of the administration's bills provoked such an outbreak of confusing dissent that it seemed for a time that there might be no legislation at all. Because the Clayton bill failed to provide immunity from antitrust prosecution for labor unions, spokesmen of the AF of L were up in arms. Because the measure attempted to enumerate every conceivable restraint of trade, advanced progressives in both parties denounced it as futile. Because it did not attempt to destroy outright the oligarchical financial and industrial structure, agrarian radicals from the South and West claimed that the Clayton bill was a betrayal of Democratic pledges. Wilson was visibly shaken by these attacks, but in the confusion of voices he did not know where to turn.

When the president seemed most uncertain, his informal adviser, Louis D. Brandeis, came forward in April 1914 with an alternative that involved virtually abandoning the effort to prohibit unfair trade practices by the statutory method. Instead Brandeis proposed outlawing unfair trade practices in general terms and then establishing a federal trade commission endowed with ample authority to suppress restraints of trade whenever they occurred. Brandeis's solution had been embodied in a trade commission bill, introduced earlier by Representative Raymond B. Stevens of New Hampshire.

Although Brandeis's proposal envisaged at least something like the kind of regulation of business that Roosevelt had advocated and Wilson had at least implicitly condemned in 1912, it seemed to be the only practical answer to an otherwise insoluble problem. Thus Wilson at once made the Stevens bill the cornerstone of his new antitrust policy, and administration leaders in Congress sidetracked the Covington bill and pressed the Stevens measure instead. His faith in the efficacy of a strong commission complete, Wilson now acquiesced in and presided over the weakening of the rigorous provisions of the Clayton bill; he signed the measure on October 15, 1914.[5]

Meanwhile, the president had bent all his energies toward obtaining congressional approval of the Stevens trade commission bill. After a hard battle he won a decisive victory because the Federal Trade Commission Act that he approved on September 26 committed the federal government to a policy of vigorous regulation of all business activities. In sweeping terms it outlawed, but did not attempt to define, unfair trade practices. Moreover, it established a Federal Trade Commission to supersede the Bureau of Corporations, armed with authority to move swiftly and directly against corporations accused of suppressing competition—first by issuing cease and desist orders and then, if that recourse failed, by bringing the accused corporations to trial.

[5]The Clayton Act forbade contracts requiring purchasers to buy from only one producer or seller; forbade corporations to purchase the stock of other corporations when the result would be to lessen competition substantially; outlawed interlocking directorates, when their existence operated substantially to lessen competition; and made court decisions in antitrust suits initiated by the government prima facie evidence in private damage suits.

Wilson's acceptance of what might roughly be called a Rooseveltian legislative solution was matched to a considerable degree on the level of direct antitrust activity. Rejecting agrarian radical demands for a relentless campaign against bigness, per se, Wilson and his attorneys general instead continued the Roosevelt-Taft policy of moving only against combinations that seemed obviously to have been in restraint of trade. For example, they continued Taft's case against United States Steel, in spite of that corporation's offer to settle out of court. What was new in the antitrust story under Wilson was the eagerness of officials of several important combinations to accept government-dictated reorganizations in order to avoid prosecution. The American Telephone & Telegraph Company, the New Haven Railroad, and the Southern Pacific Railroad, among others, accepted consent decrees proposed by the Justice Department in 1913 and 1914. The Federal Trade Commission never seemed able to fulfill the hopes of its founders during the balance of the Wilson era. It was hobbled first by incompetence and internal dissension. It had little to do during the period of American belligerence, 1917–1918, as antitrust prosecutions were then generally suspended. It finally came to life in 1919–1920 in a victorious campaign to destroy the old Beef Trust.

Wilson's acceptance of the Federal Trade Commission bill during the congressional discussions of 1914 was also an important turning point in the history of the national progressive movement. It was the first important sign that the president might be willing to abandon his doctrinaire New Freedom concepts and surrender to the rising progressive demands for bold social and economic legislation in other fields. Any such surrender, however, would have to come in the future, for adoption of the Clayton and Federal Trade Commission acts in the autumn of 1914 seemed to signal the completion of the president's reform program. In a public letter to Secretary of the Treasury McAdoo on November 17, Wilson asserted that the legislation of the past eighteen months had destroyed the Republican system of special privilege and ended the antagonism between business and the public. The future, he added, would be a time in which businessmen would adapt themselves to changed conditions and the nation would enter a new era "of cooperation, of new understanding, of common purpose." In brief, the reconstructive phase of the national progressive movement was over; reform would now give way to readjustment.

6. The Triumph of the New Nationalism

As it turned out, Wilson's forecast of future political developments was somewhat naive. By the time that the president wrote his letter to McAdoo a profound upheaval in American politics—the virtual disappearance of the Progressive party—had occurred during the congressional elections of November 3, 1914. The outbreak of war in Europe a few months before had diverted American attention from the campaign and evoked a general disposition to stand by the president. Even so, the Democratic majority in the House of Representatives was reduced from seventy-three to twenty-five, and Republicans swept back into power in key states like New York, Pennsylvania, Illinois, and New Jersey. So powerful was the tide that a general Republican victory in 1916 seemed probable.

The months passed, and the nation was convulsed by alarms of war with Germany and a great debate over preparedness. It was obvious by January 1916 that Theodore Roosevelt would abandon his third party and join with his erstwhile enemies to drive the Democrats from power. Democratic defeat in the impending presidential campaign was virtually inevitable if he succeeded in leading most Progressives back into the Republican camp. The urgent necessity facing Wilson and his party at the beginning of 1916, therefore, was to find some means of luring at least a large minority of the former Progressives into the Democratic ranks. This strategy offered the only possible hope of converting a normal Democratic minority into a majority in November 1916. To execute the strategy, however, Wilson and the Democratic party had to cast off the shackles of state rights and laissez-faire doctrines and convince still suspicious Progressives that they offered the best hope of positive economic and social reform.

Although adopting advanced progressive concepts and legislation required abandoning some of the ideological foundations upon which the New Freedom rested, Wilson did not shrink from the necessity. Moreover, it is probably accurate to say that changed convictions, growing out of his own experience during the past two years, were as much responsible for Wilson's change of course as was political expediency. Beginning in January 1916, he embarked upon a new course of action; and because his new departure seemed to offer the only hope of staying in power, most Democrats in Congress followed him willingly.

The first sign of this metamorphosis was Wilson's appointment of Louis D. Brandeis to the Supreme Court on January 28, 1916. Progressives of both parties were delighted, for Brandeis was one of the leading exponents of social and economic reform in the country. The president called the sponsors of the much controverted rural credits bill to the White House shortly afterward and told them that he would support their measure. He was as good as his word, and the Federal Farm Loan Act passed Congress in May.[6] A few months later, after the presidential campaign had begun, spokesmen of the social justice forces informed Wilson that they regarded the pending child labor and federal workmen's compensation bills as the

---

[6]This measure established twelve Federal Farm Loan banks capitalized at $750,000 each, which should extend long-term credit to farmers on a basis of land and improvements. It also created a Federal Farm Loan Board to supervise the new system.

acid tests of his progressivism. Wilson had said not a word to this point in advocacy of these measures. Now he applied heavy pressure on Democratic leaders in the Senate and obtained their passage in August.[7]

The extent of Wilson's commitment to advanced progressivism can best be understood when we perceive the long-run significance of the Child Labor Act of 1916. By this measure, Congress for the first time used its power over interstate commerce in an important way to control conditions under which employers might operate their industries. Did this signify the beginning of a new and enlarged federal regulation under the commerce clause, as the NAM spokesman declared, "of any commodity produced in whole or in part by the labor of men or women who work more than eight hours, receive less than a minimum wage, or have not certain educational qualifications"? Progressives hoped and conservatives feared that it did. In any event, it seemed that a constitutional way had been found to extend federal control over all phases of the manufacturing process.

Nor did the foregoing measures alone represent the full extent of Wilson's espousal of the program embodied in the Progressive platform of 1912. Echoing a proposal Roosevelt had made in 1912, Wilson in 1916 sponsored and obtained passage of a bill to establish an independent tariff commission, allegedly to remove the tariff issue from politics. Moreover, in language that Roosevelt might have used, Wilson publicly reversed historic Democratic policy and approved the principle of rational protection for certain infant industries. He supported and won passage of a series of measures launching the federal government upon a new program of aid to the states for education and highway construction.[8] Finally, he sponsored but did not obtain adoption until January 1918 of the Webb-Pomerene bill to permit American manufacturers to combine for the purpose of carrying on export trade.

Thus it was that political necessity and changed political convictions compelled a president and party who had taken office in 1913 for the purpose of effectuating a limited reform program to sponsor and enact the most far-reaching and significant economic and social legislation in American history before 1933. Looking back in 1916 upon the development of the progressive movement since 1912, observers might well have been

[7]Drafted by the American Association for Labor Legislation, the Kern-McGillicuddy Compensation Act established a model workmen's compensation system for federal employees. The Keating-Owen child labor bill, sponsored by the National Child Labor Committee, which became the Child Labor Act of 1916, forbade the shipment in interstate commerce of goods manufactured in whole or in part by children under fourteen, and of any products manufactured by children under sixteen employed more than eight hours a day.

[8]These were the Bankhead Good Roads Act of 1916, which provided federal funds to match state appropriations for interstate highways, and the Smith-Hughes Act of 1917, providing federal funds on a matching basis for vocational education in public high schools. An earlier measure, the Smith-Lever Act of 1914, provided federal money on a matching basis for agricultural extension work.

puzzled by the revolution that had occurred. On the one hand, Wilson and his party had tacitly abandoned the New Freedom, and the president could justly claim that Democrats were also progressives and boast that his party had enacted practically all the Progressive platform of 1912. On the other hand, Theodore Roosevelt, the great expounder of the New Nationalism in 1912, had by 1916 abandoned his platform to the Democrats and was striving mightily to defeat the party that had carried out his proposals.

6

The Growth of
the United States
as a World Power,
1898–1917

Between the end of the Napoleonic Wars in 1815 and the outbreak of the Spanish-American War in 1898, the American people enjoyed such freedom from foreign vexations as they had never known before 1815 and would not experience in the twentieth century. The United States was not normally active in world politics before 1898, for the American people did not want to sit in the councils of the mighty, engage in the scramble for colonies and concessions, or play the game of power politics. They only desired to be let alone. They were determined to defend the Monroe Doctrine, that cornerstone of their foreign policy. But defense of the Western Hemisphere was defense of America's splendid isolation.

Yet a nation is not isolated merely by wishing to be. In fact, forces were at work during the high tide of American insularity, 1865–1898, to make continued isolation soon impossible. First, the United States during this period was emerging as the dominant industrial power in the world. American financiers and manufacturers were beginning to export capital and goods and to acquire markets and interests abroad that their government could not ignore. Moreover, because of their strategic economic position, the American people would find it difficult to avoid involvement in a future European war. Thus, although few Americans realized the fact in 1900, the United States had a vital stake in the peace of Europe. Second, swift technological advances were drawing the world closely together and diminishing the strategic value of America's oceanic defensive barriers. Finally, the rise of Germany as the dominant military power in Europe and Japan as an aspiring power in Asia during the last quarter of the nineteenth century upset the old balance of power upon which American security had in some measure depended.

1. The Acquisition and Administration of the American Colonial Empire, 1898-1917

The American people entered blithely upon the war with Spain in 1898 for the sole purpose of freeing Cuba from Spanish tyranny. Even so, a few thoughtful leaders of the war movement like Theodore Roosevelt and Henry Cabot Lodge welcomed the war for the opportunity it offered to acquire bases in the Caribbean and Pacific. Looking toward the day when the United States would construct an isthmian canal and need naval bases to guard its approaches, they urged annexation of Puerto Rico, Spain's other Caribbean possession, and retention of naval bases in Cuba. As for the Pacific, they urged and won annexation of Hawaii a few months after the war with Spain began. As assistant secretary of the navy, Roosevelt, on February 25, 1898, had instructed Commodore George Dewey, commanding the Asiatic squadron then at Hong Kong, to prepare to attack the Spanish fleet in Manila Bay in the event of war. But neither Roosevelt nor any other responsible spokesman of the administration contemplated taking the Philippine Islands.

Yet the American commissioners at the peace conference that met in Paris from October 1 through December 10, 1898, demanded and won not only Cuba's freedom and the transfer of Puerto Rico to the United States, but also the cession of Guam and the entire Philippine archipelago. The United States by this act extended its frontiers far out into the Pacific and assumed the burden of pacifying the Philippines and then defending them against future aggression.

The immediate issue of imperialism was settled for a time after the ratification of the Treaty of Paris in 1899 and McKinley's second victory over Bryan in 1900. The United States would continue to hold and administer the Philippines, at least until the Filipinos were ready for self-government. But the American people soon discovered that it is far easier to acquire a colonial empire than to govern it. On the outbreak of the war with Spain, Commodore Dewey and the American consul at Singapore had helped a Philippine leader, Emilio Aguinaldo, return to Luzon to lead a revolt against Spanish authority. Aguinaldo succeeded so well that he and his forces were besieging Manila when American troops occupied the city.

The Filipinos wanted independence, not merely a transfer of sovereignty to a new foreign master. When it became obvious that the United States intended to impose its own authority, Aguinaldo and his rebel forces raised anew the standards of revolt on February 4, 1899. So stubbornly did the Filipinos fight that McKinley eventually had to send some 70,000 troops to the islands; and before pacification was completed American commanders had resorted to the same primitive tactics that the Spaniards had unsuccessfully employed in Cuba; and about 10,000 Americans and 100,000 Filipinos had lost their lives. Aguinaldo's capture on March 23, 1901, signaled the end of resistance and the beginning of a long era of peaceful development of the islands.

The McKinley administration began—even before the rebellion was suppressed—to work out plans for a permanent government. A civilian administration, headed by William Howard Taft as civil governor, supplanted military rule on July 4, 1901. A year later Congress passed an Organic Act for the Philippines and established a government for the islands that survived until 1916. While the act reflected the conviction that the Filipinos were not yet ready for autonomy, it also bespoke an intention to give them the opportunity to learn the difficult art of self-government.[1]

The results of superb administration, generous appropriations by Congress, and the determination of American leaders to lay a solid foundation for self-government in the Philippines were spectacularly evident by 1913. By this date, Filipinos constituted four out of the nine members of the commission, 71 percent of the classified employees in the civil service, 92 percent of the teachers, and all governors of the Christian provinces. In addition, the Philippine government had established a splendid system of schools and other public services, dispensed impartial justice, and carried out important land reforms.

It is not surprising, therefore, that Roosevelt and Taft shuddered when the Democrats came to power in 1913, for the Democrats had advocated early independence for the Filipinos during every presidential campaign since 1900. Woodrow Wilson was elected in 1912 on a platform that reiterated this position, and the new Organic Act for the Philippines that Congress passed on August 29, 1916, the Jones Act, fell little short of giving the Filipinos dominion status. This measure created an elective senate to supplant the commission as the upper house of the Philippine legislature, lowered suffrage requirements, and provided that the governor-general should appoint heads of executive departments, except the

---

[1] The Organic Act made Filipinos citizens of the Philippine Islands; created an executive branch consisting of the governor-general and a commission, to be appointed by the president with the consent of the United States Senate; established an Anglo-American system of courts; and provided for establishment of a two-house legislature, the lower house to be elected by the Christian tribes and the upper house to consist of the commission.

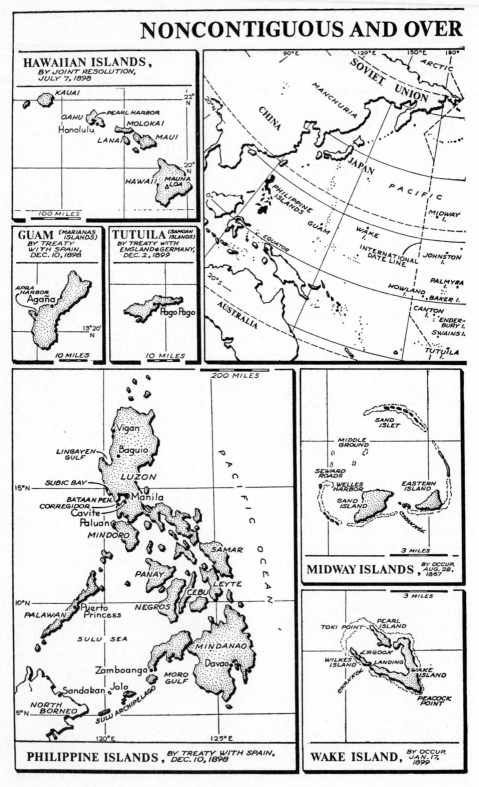

NONCONTIGUOUS AND OVER

HAWAIIAN ISLANDS,
BY JOINT RESOLUTION, JULY 7, 1898

KAUAI
OAHU PEARL HARBOR
Honolulu MOLOKAI
LANAI MAUI
HAWAII MAUNA LOA
22° N
20° N
100 MILES

GUAM (MARIANAS ISLANDS)
BY TREATY WITH SPAIN, DEC. 10, 1898

APRA HARBOR
Agaña
13°20' N
10 MILES

TUTUILA (SAMOAN ISLANDS)
BY TREATY WITH ENGLAND & GERMANY, DEC. 2, 1899

Pago Pago
10 MILES

SOVIET UNION
ARCTIC
90°E 120°E 150°E 180°
CHINA
MANCHURIA
JAPAN
PHILIPPINE ISLANDS
GUAM
PACIFIC
MIDWAY I.
WAKE I.
INTERNATIONAL DATE LINE
JOHNSTON I.
EQUATOR
PALMYRA
HOWLAND BAKER I.
AUSTRALIA
CANTON
ENDERBURY I.
SWAINS I.
TUTUILA
20° N
0°
20° S

PHILIPPINE ISLANDS, BY TREATY WITH SPAIN, DEC. 10, 1898

200 MILES
Vigan
LINGAYEN GULF
Baguio
LUZON
SUBIC BAY
15° N
BATAAN PEN.
CORREGIDOR
Cavite Manila
Paluan
MINDORO
SAMAR
PANAY
LEYTE
CEBU
10° N
NEGROS
PALAWAN Puerto Princess
SULU SEA
MINDANAO
Davao
Zamboanga MORO GULF
Sandakan Jolo
NORTH BORNEO
SULU ARCHIPELAGO
5° N
120° E 125° E
PACIFIC OCEAN

MIDWAY ISLANDS, BY OCCUP. AUG. 28, 1867

SAND ISLET
MIDDLE GROUND
SEWARD ROADS
WELLES HARBOR
SAND ISLAND
EASTERN ISLAND
3 MILES

WAKE ISLAND, BY OCCUP. JAN. 17, 1899

3 MILES
TOKI POINT
PEARL ISLAND
LAGOON
WILKES ISLAND LANDING
WAKE ISLAND
PEACOCK POINT

SEAS EXPANSION, 1867-1914

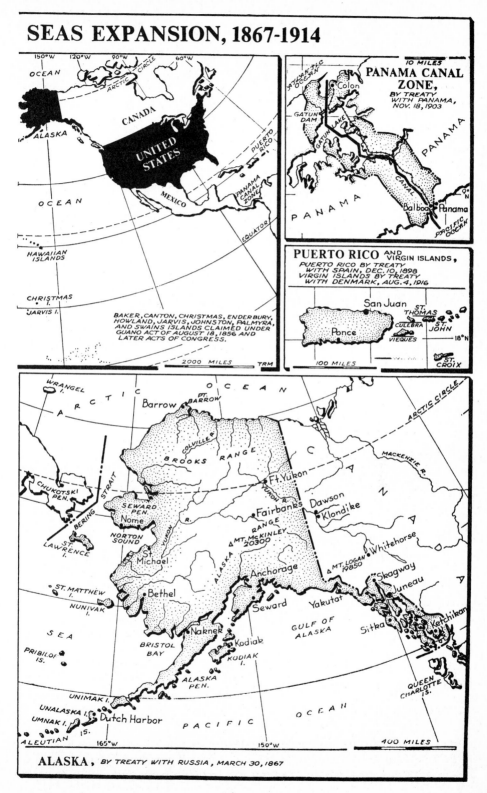

PANAMA CANAL ZONE, BY TREATY WITH PANAMA, NOV. 18, 1903

PUERTO RICO AND VIRGIN ISLANDS, PUERTO RICO BY TREATY WITH SPAIN, DEC. 10, 1898 VIRGIN ISLANDS BY TREATY WITH DENMARK, AUG. 4, 1916

BAKER, CANTON, CHRISTMAS, ENDERBURY, HOWLAND, JARVIS, JOHNSTON, PALMYRA, AND SWAINS ISLANDS CLAIMED UNDER GUANO ACT OF AUGUST 18, 1856 AND LATER ACTS OF CONGRESS.

ALASKA, BY TREATY WITH RUSSIA, MARCH 30, 1867

head of the Department of Public Instruction, with the consent of the Philippine senate. The Jones Act, however, reserved ultimate sovereignty to the United States.

With a view toward hastening independence, Wilson's governor-general, Francis Burton Harrison, cooperated with the native nationalist leaders, Sergio Osmeña and Manuel Quezon, in transferring power to native departmental heads and to leaders of the assembly and senate. Filipinos were running their own affairs so well by the end of the Wilson era that Governor Harrison and the president urged Congress to grant independence at once. The Republicans, who now controlled Congress, refused and attempted in 1921 to restore a larger measure of American control. Even so, it was evident by this date that the logic and application of American policy since 1901 could culminate in only one solution—independence.

Pacifying Cuba and establishing a stable government in the island were considerably less difficult than the task that Americans confronted in the Philippines. An American military government did heroic work from 1898 to 1902 in repairing the damage of the civil war, building roads and schools, cleaning up cities, and establishing order in rural districts. Meanwhile, in 1900 the military governor, General Leonard Wood, had arranged the election of a constituent convention, which in 1902 adopted a frame of government for the new republic.

The American government was now ready to withdraw its forces and leave the Cubans to manage their own affairs. But President McKinley and Secretary of War Elihu Root agreed that the United States bore a special responsibility for Cuba's future behavior. Therefore, the administration resolved to draw the Cuban republic into a special relationship with the United States. The Platt Amendment to the army appropriations bill of 1901 spelled out this relationship. It stipulated that Cuba should make no treaties with other powers that might impair its independence, assume no debts it could not pay, carry on the sanitation program begun by the military government, and lease certain naval bases to the United States. Most important was a provision authorizing the United States to intervene in Cuba, if that was necessary to maintain orderly government and discharge Cuba's international obligations.

The Cubans under duress wrote the Platt Amendment into their constitution in 1902 and signed a treaty with the United States in 1903 that embodied its provisions. Peace and prosperity reigned in the island for a brief time, especially after the Cuban-American reciprocity treaty of 1903 opened the American market to Cuban sugar. After the second national elections in December 1905, however, widespread rioting against the government broke out, and President Tomás Estrada Palma appealed for American intervention.

Roosevelt was reluctant to undertake the thankless task. He finally sent troops into the island in 1906 and established a provisional government under Charles E. Magoon, governor of the Canal Zone. There was some talk in administration circles at this time of making Cuba a permanent protectorate, but Roosevelt repudiated it angrily. New Cuban elections were held; a government was formed; and the Americans withdrew in January 1909. The State Department afterward intervened frequently on a diplomatic level, but American troops were sent into the republic to preserve order only in 1911 and 1917. On each occasion their stay was brief.

Governing America's other island dependencies[2] proved a relatively simple task. Hawaii, annexed by joint resolution of Congress on July 7, 1898, was made an incorporated territory on April 30, 1900, and thereafter enjoyed all territorial rights of self-government. Puerto Rico, occupied by the American army in July 1898, was given civil government by the Foraker Act in 1900 and a large measure of self-government by the Jones Act of 1917, which also granted American citizenship to Puerto Ricans.

The chief diplomatic objective of the American government after 1900 became, as we shall see more fully in later sections, the building of an isthmian canal and the establishment of naval supremacy in the Caribbean. After the British withdrew the larger units of their West Indian squadron in 1904–1905, the United States was in fact the dominant power in the Caribbean. But there was always the danger, often more illusory than real, that Germany would attempt to establish naval bases in the area, possibly by acquiring the Danish West Indies. Secretary of State John Hay negotiated a treaty with Denmark in 1902 for purchase of the Danish West Indies, or Virgin Islands; but the Danish Parliament, acting, Americans suspected, under pressure from Germany, refused to ratify the treaty. When the Danish government in 1916 offered to sell the islands at the inflated price of $25 million, the American government concluded the deal without haggling. The islands were transferred on March 31, 1917, and were governed by the Navy Department until 1931.

2. The Panama Incident and Two Hemispheric Disputes

The dramatic voyage of the battleship *Oregon* from Puget Sound around Cape Horn to Cuban waters in 1898 to participate in the war with Spain underscored the absolute strategic necessity of a canal linking the Atlantic

[2]The United States by 1900 had also acquired a string of coaling stations in the Pacific beyond Hawaii: Midway Island, acquired in 1867; the Samoan Islands, occupied jointly with Germany and Great Britain from 1889 to 1899 and divided between Germany and the United States in the latter year; Guam, ceded by Spain in the Treaty of Paris of 1898; and Wake, acquired formally in 1899. All these islands were governed by naval officers under orders from the Navy Department.

and Pacific oceans, while the development of the West Coast and anticipation of a great American trade with the Far East highlighted the economic need. A diplomatic obstacle, however, stood athwart the achievement of what was by 1900 a great national objective. That obstacle was the Clayton-Bulwer Treaty of 1850, in which the United States and Great Britain had each agreed not to construct a canal without the other's participation. The British government was now eager to win American friendship and gave up its right to participate in building the canal in the first Hay-Pauncefote Treaty, negotiated at Washington in 1900. This treaty, however, forbade the United States to fortify the canal. The Senate refused to ratify the treaty without amendments providing for fortification. The British then went all the way, and the second Hay-Pauncefote Treaty, concluded on November 18, 1901, acknowledged the right of the United States exclusively to build and fortify the canal.

Discussion in Washington now centered on the proper route. President Roosevelt and a large majority of Congress favored the Nicaraguan route, and the Isthmian Canal Commission, which McKinley had appointed, officially concurred in November 1901. The House of Representatives approved the commission's recommendation on January 9, 1902. In the meantime, however, Philippe Bunau-Varilla and William Nelson Cromwell, agents of the French New Panama Canal Company, had been working assiduously to sell their company's rights to the route across the Isthmus of Panama.[3] Faced with the possibility of losing everything, the directors of the French company hastily cut their price from $109 million to $40 million. Their bargain offer, the advantages of the Panamanian route, and the providential eruption of a volcano in Nicaragua caused Roosevelt, the commission, and Congress to change their minds. The Spooner Act, approved by Roosevelt in June 1902, stipulated that the Panamanian route should be used, provided that a satisfactory treaty could be concluded with Colombia, which owned the Isthmus, within a reasonable time. Otherwise, the act declared, the Nicaraguan route should be chosen.

The State Department during the following months applied extraordinary pressure on the Colombian government to sign a treaty authorizing the construction of a Panamanian canal. The Colombian minister left for home in disgust. Secretary Hay then concluded a treaty with the Colombian chargé, Tomás Herrán, on January 22, 1903. It authorized the United States to build a canal across the Isthmus of Panama in return for payment

---

[3] The builder of the Suez Canal, Ferdinand de Lesseps, organized a French company in 1879 for the construction of a Panamanian canal. Over $250 million had been wasted by 1889 in a vain attempt to conquer tropical diseases and the jungle, and the French company went into bankruptcy. The New Panama Canal Company was organized in 1894 to take over the assets of the bankrupt corporation. Bunau-Varilla, formerly chief engineer of the old company, was a large stockholder in the new concern. Cromwell was a prominent New York attorney with considerable influence in Republican circles.

of $10 million and an annual rental of $250,000. The American Senate approved the Hay-Herrán Treaty on March 17, 1903. The Colombian government, however, balked. Public opinion in Colombia opposed the treaty because it impaired the nation's sovereignty in the proposed Canal Zone, but Colombia's leaders had an additional reason for refusing to ratify the treaty. The French company's concession would expire in 1904; all its rights and property would then revert to Colombia. By delaying action for only one year, the Colombian government would be in position to demand the $40 million that would otherwise be paid to the French company.

The fact that the Colombian government was acting well within its rights did not seem significant to President Roosevelt. It was, he said, as if "a road agent had tried to hold up a man," and Colombians were "entitled to precisely the amount of sympathy we extend to other inefficient bandits." He made plans, therefore, to seize the Isthmus and to justify such action by the Treaty of 1846 between the United States and New Granada (Colombia), under which the former guaranteed the neutrality and free transit of the Isthmus.

Meanwhile, Bunau-Varilla was setting plans on foot that would obviate the need for violent American action. Working through his agents in Panama, this astute Frenchman organized a Panamanian "revolution" against Colombia. The State Department took no part in these intrigues, but Bunau-Varilla informed the president and secretary of state of the plot, and he could deduce from what they said that Colombia would not be allowed to suppress a revolution. Roosevelt, moreover, dispatched *U.S.S. Nashville* to Colón, on the Atlantic side of the Isthmus. *Nashville* arrived at Colón on November 2, 1903; on the following day the army of patriots rebelled at Panama City, on the Pacific side. Thereupon the commander of *Nashville* landed troops at Colón and forbade Colombian troops in the city to cross the Isthmus and suppress the rebellion. In fact, the Colombian commander agreed to take his troops back to Colombia in return for a generous gift from Bunau-Varilla's agent.

At 11:35 in the morning of November 6 the American consul at Panama City informed the State Department that the revolution had succeeded. At 12:51 P.M. Secretary Hay instructed the consul to extend de facto recognition to the new government of Panama. Fearing that the Panamanians would now demand a share of the $40 million, Bunau-Varilla persuaded Roosevelt to receive him as the minister from Panama. He signed a treaty with Secretary Hay on November 18 that conveyed to the United States, in perpetuity, a zone ten miles wide across the Isthmus. In return the United States agreed to pay $10 million in cash and an annual rental of $250,000. The leaders of the new republic had no choice but to ratify this treaty.

The American government took possession of the Canal Zone on May 4, 1904, and set about preparing to excavate the great ditch. Before work could proceed, Colonel William C. Gorgas, one of the conquerors of yellow fever, had to clean up the region and subdue the fever-carrying mosquitoes. Congress approved a plan for a lock canal in 1906; Roosevelt gave responsibility to the army engineers in the following year. The first ship passed through the canal on January 7, 1914. Seven months later, on August 15, 1914, the canal was opened to the commerce of the world.

Many thoughtful Americans regretted the means that Roosevelt had employed to accomplish the objective even while they agreed that construction of the Panama Canal was a great boon to mankind. Criticism of Roosevelt's Big Stick diplomacy in Panama was bitter in 1903 and 1904, and the American public began to suffer from acute pangs of conscience as more details were revealed, especially by a congressional committee in 1912. On the other hand, never once did Roosevelt admit that he had perhaps acted unwisely or wrongly. Every action of his administration in the Panamanian affair, he once wrote, had been "in accordance with the highest, finest, and nicest standards of public and governmental ethics." Roosevelt grew bolder in his own defense as the years passed, until in 1911 he finally spoke the truth: "I am interested in the Panama Canal because I started it. . . . I took the Canal Zone and let Congress debate; and while the debate goes on the Canal does also."

Two other diplomatic incidents, the Venezuelan blockade and Canadian-American boundary disputes, revealed the arrogance, strident nationalism, and growing concern for American supremacy in the Western Hemisphere that characterized Roosevelt's diplomacy during the first years of his presidency. The Venezuelan trouble began when the dictator of that republic, Cipriano Castro, refused even to acknowledge his country's indebtedness to European creditors. Great Britain and Germany, later joined by Italy, instituted a blockade of Venezuela in December 1902 after obtaining the State Department's approval. American public opinion viewed the intervention suspiciously from the beginning. It became greatly agitated when the Germans bombarded Fort San Carlos and destroyed a Venezuelan town in January 1903. Meanwhile, Castro had signified his readiness to submit the debt question to the Hague Court.

The German bombardment also caused Roosevelt to suspect German intentions. For a moment it seemed that the Berlin government would refuse Castro's offer of mediation. Then Roosevelt, in February 1903, called in the German ambassador and told him that he had put Admiral George Dewey in charge of the Atlantic fleet for its annual maneuvers in West Indian waters. Public opinion was so aroused, Roosevelt went on, that he would regretfully be obliged to use force if the Germans took any steps toward acquiring territory in Venezuela or elsewhere in the Caribbean. Roosevelt's warning was probably unnecessary, for the Germans certainly had no desire to risk a serious incident with the United States. They and the British gladly accepted arbitration to escape from a potentially dangerous situation.

The boundary dispute with Canada involved the long finger of Alaska that runs from Alaska proper down the Pacific Coast to the latitude 54° 40′. It first became acute when gold was discovered in the Canadian Klondike region in 1896. Because it seemed clear that the United States had an airtight case, the State Department refused for several years to arbitrate the conflicting claims.[4] Roosevelt was at first inclined to let the matter rest; then he studied the case and concluded that the Canadians had completely fabricated their claim. Secretary of State John Hay, therefore, negotiated a convention with the British government in 1903 providing that six "impartial jurists of repute"—three appointed by the president of the United States and three by the king of England—meet in London and settle the question by majority vote.[5] The tribunal convened in London in September 1903. It soon became evident that the Americans would vote as a bloc, that the two Canadian members would support their country's claims, and that the decision would rest with the British commissioner, Lord Chief Justice Alverstone. Meanwhile, Roosevelt had already decided to ask Congress for authority to run the boundary line himself if the tribunal did not endorse the American claims. After the tribunal convened, Roosevelt carefully repeated this threat in conversations and letters for the benefit of the British foreign office. Whether Lord Alverstone was more influenced by the president's threat than by the merits of the American case, we do not know. In either event, to the disgust of the Canadians he voted consistently with the American commissioners and thus helped to cement Anglo-American friendship.

3. The Roosevelt Corollary to the Monroe Doctrine

On the day before the Senate ratified the Hay–Bunau-Varilla Treaty the Hague Court rendered a verdict that held significant implications for the United States. That tribunal ruled that Germany, Great Britain, and Italy, the very powers that used force against Venezuela, were entitled to first claim on payments by Venezuela to European creditors. In brief, the Hague Court's decision put a premium on intervention at a time when American security interests in the Caribbean were being multiplied by the decision to construct the Panama Canal.

Roosevelt knew after the Venezuelan blockade affair that the United

---

[4]The Canadians claimed that the line should run thirty miles inland in a straight line from the sea and should not be adjusted to the heads of the bays and inlets. The Americans argued that the boundary should run along a line thirty miles inland from the heads of these bays and inlets.
[5]The American representatives were Secretary of War Elihu Root, Senator Henry Cabot Lodge of Massachusetts, and former Senator George Turner of Wisconsin, none of whom was either impartial or a jurist of any great repute.

States could not thereafter tolerate European armed intervention on a major scale in the Caribbean. On the other hand, he knew also that he could not command sufficient naval power to stand off Europe by announcing a policy of nonintervention by outside powers in the Western Hemisphere. Some other way of reconciling American security needs with European economic interests in the Caribbean had to be found. The British prime minister, Arthur Balfour, had suggested one solution in 1902: Britain would support the Monroe Doctrine and abstain from intervention in the New World if the United States would take responsibility for seeing that the necessity for such intervention did not arise.

A situation developed only two years later in the Dominican Republic that compelled Roosevelt to work out some kind of policy. That Caribbean republic defaulted on its foreign debt of $32 million after prolonged civil war. As there was a strong probability that European powers would intervene if he did not, Roosevelt sent Admiral Dewey and the assistant secretary of state to the troubled republic to investigate. The latter recommended establishment of an American receivership to collect and disburse the Dominican customs. This course was soon agreed upon, and American representatives in Santo Domingo signed a protocol with Dominican officials on January 20, 1905. It stipulated that the United States should collect the Dominican customs, turn over 45 percent of the receipts to the local government, and apply the balance for liquidation of the Dominican Republic's foreign debt.

Roosevelt and Root put the new arrangement into operation so smoothly that neither Dominican pride nor Latin American sensitivity was offended. The American receiver general persuaded the Dominican Republic's creditors to scale down their claims from $32 million to $17 million, and the new debt was refunded at a lower rate of interest. More important was the fact that the little republic enjoyed peace and prosperity as it had never known before, since customs houses were no longer prizes to be won by successful revolutionists.

The Dominican incident was most important in the long run because Roosevelt seized the opportunity it afforded to announce a new Latin American policy—the Roosevelt Corollary to the Monroe Doctrine. Roosevelt forecast his corollary in a public letter to Secretary Root on May 20, 1904, and articulated it more fully in his Annual Message in the following December. Chronic wrongdoing by an American republic might require intervention by some civilized nation, he said on the latter occasion, and "the adherence of the United States to the Monroe Doctrine may force the United States, however reluctantly, in flagrant cases of such wrongdoing or impotence, to the exercise of an international police power." In other words, the president declared that the United States owed it to the European powers to guarantee that no cause for intervention should arise since the Monroe Doctrine prohibited European use of force in the Western Hemisphere.

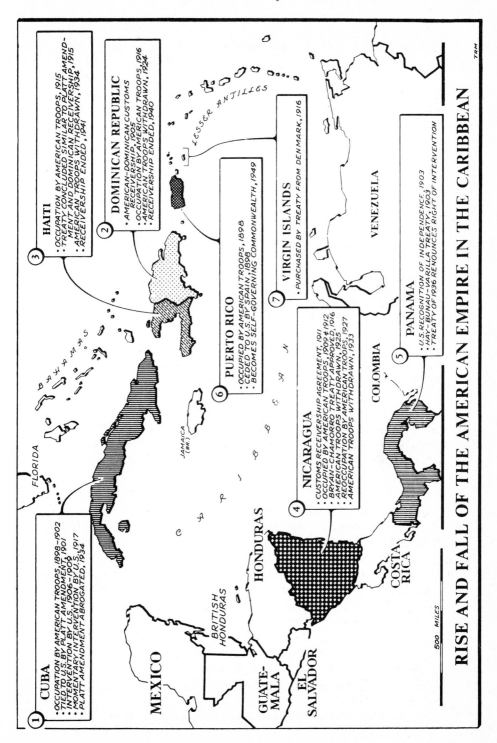

RISE AND FALL OF THE AMERICAN EMPIRE IN THE CARIBBEAN

① **CUBA**
- OCCUPATION BY AMERICAN TROOPS, 1898-1902
- TIED TO U.S. BY PLATT AMENDMENT, 1901
- INTERVENTION BY U.S., 1906-1909
- MOMENTARY INTERVENTION BY U.S., 1917
- PLATT AMENDMENT ABROGATED, 1934

② **DOMINICAN REPUBLIC**
- AMERICAN-DOMINICAN CUSTOMS RECEIVERSHIP, 1905
- OCCUPATION BY AMERICAN TROOPS, 1916
- AMERICAN TROOPS WITHDRAWN, 1924
- RECEIVERSHIP ENDED, 1940

③ **HAITI**
- OCCUPATION BY AMERICAN TROOPS, 1915
- TREATY CONCLUDED SIMILAR TO PLATT AMENDMENT AND DOMINICAN RECEIVERSHIP, 1915
- AMERICAN TROOPS WITHDRAWN, 1934
- RECEIVERSHIP ENDED, 1941

④ **NICARAGUA**
- CUSTOMS RECEIVERSHIP AGREEMENT, 1911
- OCCUPIED BY AMERICAN TROOPS, 1909 & 1912
- BRYAN-CHAMORRO TREATY APPROVED, 1916
- AMERICAN TROOPS WITHDRAWN, 1925
- REOCCUPATION BY AMERICAN TROOPS, 1927
- AMERICAN TROOPS WITHDRAWN, 1933

⑤ **PANAMA**
- U.S. RECOGNITION OF INDEPENDENCE, 1903
- HAY-BUNAU-VARILLA TREATY, 1903
- TREATY OF 1936 RENOUNCES RIGHT OF INTERVENTION

⑥ **PUERTO RICO**
- OCCUPIED BY AMERICAN TROOPS, 1898
- CEDED TO U.S. BY SPAIN, 1898
- BECOMES SELF-GOVERNING COMMONWEALTH, 1949

⑦ **VIRGIN ISLANDS**
- PURCHASED BY TREATY FROM DENMARK, 1916

LESSER ANTILLES

FLORIDA

BAHAMAS

JAMAICA (BR.)

CARIBBEAN

MEXICO

GUATEMALA

EL SALVADOR

BRITISH HONDURAS

HONDURAS

COSTA RICA

COLOMBIA

VENEZUELA

500 MILES

TRM

The Roosevelt Corollary was based upon false assumptions and bad history, for no American statesman, not even Roosevelt, had ever before interpreted the Monroe Doctrine as forbidding temporary European interventions to compel Latin American states to pay debts or discharge international obligations. Roosevelt was simply invoking the sanction of a historic doctrine to justify a major change in American foreign policy: hereafter the United States would tolerate no further European interventions in the Caribbean region.

4. *Theodore Roosevelt and the New Diplomacy in Europe and Asia*

The years from 1901 to 1909 saw a perilous growth of international tension in Europe and the Far East. Germany's simultaneous determination to dominate the Continent and challenge Britain's naval supremacy brought about a diplomatic revolution in Europe by forcing Britain to seek rapprochement, first with France and then, in 1907, with Russia as well. In the Far East the old balance of power was upset by the rise of Japan and Russia's determination to control Korea and Manchuria. Theodore Roosevelt boldly grasped the nettle danger to help maintain the balance of power in the Far East and to avert a general European war into which the United States might be drawn. That attainment of these objectives required abandonment of the traditional posture did not deter Roosevelt. He played the game of power politics as if he were a divine-right monarch, but he played it well and for the peace of the world.

Roosevelt's chief objective in European affairs was to be an impartial friend in order to help to relieve the growing tension between the Entente powers and Germany. Friction between France and Germany centered during the early years of the twentieth century on Morocco, where France was closing the doors to German and other foreign merchants. France's ally, Russia, became embroiled in war with Japan in 1904, and the kaiser and his foreign office saw an opportunity to call France's hand and perhaps also to break the newly formed Anglo-French entente. The kaiser in 1905 thereupon demanded an international conference to define the status of Morocco. The French refused, and the kaiser appealed to Roosevelt for support. Although he was extremely reluctant to intervene, Roosevelt knew that war might break out unless the French gave in. Therefore, he brought such pressure to bear on England and France that they consented to attend a conference.

The kaiser had won the first round. But the Germans faced a solid

Anglo-French bloc, which usually had the support of the American delegates, when the conference met at Algeciras in southern Spain in early
1906. The General Act of Algeciras, signed on April 7, 1906, represented
superficially a victory for commercial freedom in Morocco. However, it
gave the French such control over the sultanate that they were able quietly to close the door to non-French trade. But that was in the future. At
the moment, when a general war seemed probable, Roosevelt had intervened decisively and helped Europeans to find a peaceful alternative.

Working out a viable Far Eastern policy posed an even greater challenge to Roosevelt's skill. The basic American objectives in the Far East
had been defined by Secretary of State John Hay in the Open Door notes
of 1899 and 1900—to preserve the commercial Open Door to, and the
territorial integrity of, China, and to protect the vulnerable Philippines
from Japanese attack. Moreover, the American emotional investment in
China by 1905 was considerable as a result of a tremendous growth of
American missionary, medical, and educational work. Indeed, most
Americans now regarded their government as China's sole defender
against allegedly rapacious European and Japanese imperialism.

The chief threat to the peace of the Far East in the late 1890s and early
1900s was Russian expansion into Manchuria and Korea. In order to halt
Russian expansion, the British concluded an alliance with Japan in 1902.
And, when war broke out between Japan and Russia in 1904, American
sympathy went to the Nipponese. Convinced that Japan was playing
America's game by curbing and offsetting a growing Russian preponderance in the Far East, Roosevelt supported the Japanese, even to the extent
of warning Germany and France that he would not countenance their
going to the support of Russia.

The Japanese had won a series of spectacular victories on land and sea
by the spring of 1905, but the empire was so exhausted that it could not
maintain a major effort much longer. The Japanese cabinet, therefore,
appealed secretly to President Roosevelt on April 18 to offer mediatory
services. The American president was reluctant to undertake what was
bound to be a thankless task, yet he believed that a Japanese victory was
essential to maintenance of the existing power balance. Thus he invited
the belligerents on June 8 to come to a peace conference to end the
"terrible and lamentable conflict."

The conference opened at the Portsmouth, New Hampshire, Navy Yard
on August 9, 1905. The Japanese commissioners, not satisfied with winning
control of southern Manchuria, Korea, and the southern half of Sakhalin
from Russia, also demanded a huge monetary indemnity. The latter demand caused American opinion to turn sharply against Japan, and the
Japanese leaders, realizing that they had gone too far, yielded this point
rather than risk resumption of hostilities.

The Treaty of Portsmouth of 1905 in effect preserved the balance of power that Russian expansion had threatened to destroy. Russia remained an important Pacific power, but Japan now stood as an effective counterpoise. Whether this configuration would protect American interests in the Far East depended upon many factors, the most important of which was the Japanese government's future conduct. Roosevelt could not control Japanese policy; he could only try to channel it in a direction advantageous to the United States. Even before the Portsmouth Conference opened, he sent Secretary of War Taft, then in Manila, to Tokyo to come to an immediate understanding with the Japanese cabinet. Taft concluded an executive agreement with the prime minister, Taro Katsura, on July 25, 1905. By its terms the United States recognized Japan's suzerainty over Korea, and Japan disavowed any designs on the Philippines.

The Japanese welcomed Roosevelt's recognition of their new status in the Far East, but events were developing in the United States that threatened to impair good relations between the two countries. The most dangerous trouble was brewing in California on account of Japanese immigration into that state.[6] It seemed following the Russo-Japanese War that the relatively small stream of Japanese immigrants would become a rushing tide. With Congress indifferent to the problem, Californians organized to take matters into their own hands. As the first step in an anti-Japanese campaign, the San Francisco board of education adopted an order on October 11, 1906, requiring the segregation of all Oriental school children.

The Japanese people, still flushed with their victory over the largest power in Europe, were in no mood to let this insult pass. The Japanese ambassador lodged a formal protest with the secretary of state on October 25, 1906, while irresponsible newspapers in both countries tried to stir war passions. It was a dangerous situation, but Roosevelt acted with superb caution and good sense. He did not ignore the fact that war was a possibility, but he was certain that the segregation order violated the Japanese-American Treaty of 1894, which guaranteed most-favored treatment to Japanese subjects in the United States. He was determined if necessary to use the army to protect the rights of the Japanese in California; at the same time he understood that Japanese immigration was the root of the trouble and resolved to bring it to an end.

Roosevelt solved the difficulty by a judicious mixture of courtesy and sternness. At his invitation the mayor and board of education of San Francisco came to the White House in February 1907. Roosevelt promised to use diplomacy to stop Japanese immigration; in return, the school board

[6]There were 12,000 Japanese in California in 1900. In that year the Japanese government announced that it would cease issuing passports to laborers who wished to go to the continental United States. Japanese kept coming to California, however, at the rate of 500 to 1,000 a year until 1905.

revoked the segregation order. Then the president negotiated, in 1907 and 1908, the so-called Gentlemen's Agreement with the Japanese. In this document the imperial government promised to issue no more passports to peasants or workers coming directly to the continental United States.

In order to disabuse the Japanese of any notion that he had acted out of fear of them, Roosevelt decided in the summer of 1907 to send an American fleet of sixteen battleships on a cruise around the world—by way of the Pacific. While the fleet was on its epochal voyage the Japanese foreign minister instructed his emperor's ambassador in Washington, Baron Takahira, to open negotiations for a comprehensive understanding with the American government on all phases of the Far Eastern question. The outcome was the Root-Takahira Agreement of November 30, 1908, by which Japan and the United States agreed to help maintain the status quo in the Pacific, to respect each other's territorial possessions, and to support jointly the Open Door in China and the independence and territorial integrity of that country. Here indeed was a program of cooperation which, if faithfully adhered to, might provide a modus vivendi for Japanese-American peace for all time to come.

The United States was a world power in fact as well as in name when Roosevelt left the White House in 1909. By blunt and sometimes questionable diplomacy Roosevelt had established undisputed American supremacy in the Caribbean area. By abandoning old traditions against interference in non-American affairs, he had helped to preserve the peace of Europe. And by a policy of realism, he had supported the rise of Japan and come to friendly understanding with that power. This was no mean record for a man who has often been described as an amateur diplomatist.

5. *Taft and "Dollar Diplomacy" in the Caribbean and the Far East*

William Howard Taft, who was unfit and unwilling to be a strong leader in world affairs, deliberately abandoned Roosevelt's policy of participation in European politics and blundered into partial reversal of Roosevelt's policy of maintaining Japanese good will. But the new president and his secretary of state, Philander C. Knox, could not reverse Roosevelt's policy of protecting American supremacy in the Caribbean area without endangering national security. In fact, they went far beyond the limited kind of intervention that Roosevelt and Root had practiced and devised a new policy, "dollar diplomacy," to strengthen American power in the approaches to the canal. It involved using private American banking resources to displace European concessionaires and creditors, and hence to strengthen

American influence in the Caribbean region, where, as Knox said, "the malady of revolutions and financial collapse is most acute precisely . . . where it is most dangerous to us."

Soon after taking office in 1909, Knox tried to persuade American bankers to take over the debt owed British investors by Honduras. The secretary signed a treaty with the Honduran minister in 1911 for refunding of that country's foreign debt by American bankers and establishment of an American customs receivership. The government of Honduras, however, refused to ratify the convention. Again, in 1910, Knox persuaded four New York banking firms to invest in the National Bank of the Republic of Haiti in order to help the black republic to stabilize its currency.

These activities were merely a prelude to Knox's most important action in the Caribbean area, his intervention in Nicaragua. That country at the beginning of the Taft administration was ruled by a dictator, José Zelaya, who was nursing an old grudge against the United States. He vented his spleen on the United States–Nicaragua Concession, a mining company owned by Pittsburgh capitalists, and even went so far as to make plans to offer an option on the Nicaraguan canal route to the Japanese government. Officials of the United States–Nicaragua Concession helped to engineer a revolution against Zelaya in 1909, and the State Department sent marines to the Nicaraguan city of Bluefields to protect foreign nationals and property. As a consequence of Knox's interference, Zelaya was overthrown and Adolfo Díaz, former secretary of the United States–Nicaragua Concession, was installed as president in 1911 with the State Department's blessing.

Knox now moved swiftly to bring Nicaragua completely under American control. He signed a treaty with the Nicaraguan minister on June 6, 1911, for refunding of the Nicaraguan foreign debt by two New York banking firms and establishment of an American customs receivership. Democrats in the Senate blocked ratification of this, the Knox-Castrillo Treaty. At the request of the State Department, however, the New York bankers advanced $1,500,000 to Nicaragua and received in return majority control of the state railways and the National Bank of Nicaragua. An American receiver-general of Nicaraguan customs was appointed by the banking houses and approved by the two governments later in the same year.

As it turned out, the new Díaz government did not have the support of a majority of Nicaraguans. In defiance of the State Department they continued to look to Zelaya and his Liberal party for leadership. The Liberals raised the standards of revolt in 1912, and Díaz would have fallen had not Taft rushed 2,700 marines to Nicaragua to suppress the uprising. So bitter was anti-Díaz and anti-American sentiment that the marines continued to occupy the country for many years.

The American intervention and occupation did not solve Nicaragua's most pressing requirement—her need for financial assistance in refunding her foreign debt and paying claims arising from the revolutions of 1909 and 1912. Chiefly to satisfy the national treasury's need for ready cash, Secretary Knox signed a treaty in 1913 with the Nicaraguan minister for payment of $3 million to Nicaragua by the United States. In return Nicaragua granted to the United States an exclusive option on its canal route, the privilege of establishing a naval base on the Gulf of Fonseca, on the Pacific side, and a ninety-nine-year lease on the Great Corn and Little Corn islands in the Caribbean. The treaty was negotiated too late to be ratified before the Sixty-second Congress expired on March 4, 1913, and the Wilson administration inherited the unpleasant task of persuading the Senate to ratify the convention.

The objectives of dollar diplomacy in the Far East were nearly as ambitious as in the Caribbean. Toward the end of the Roosevelt administration a clique in the State Department headed by a young career diplomat, Willard Straight, began to lay plans to sponsor American investment in Manchuria in order to offset Japanese influence in that province. Restrained by Secretary Root's firm hand, Straight and his colleagues came into control of Far Eastern policy when Knox took the helm at the State Department. Their opportunity to press for a more aggressive policy came in 1909, when a consortium of British, French, and German bankers signed a contract with the Chinese government to build a network of railways in central and southern China.

Straight and his friends in the Far Eastern Division of the State Department easily won Knox to their side by arguing that American participation in the consortium was necessary to enable the United States to defend the Open Door and the territorial integrity of China. Accordingly, the State Department in 1909 demanded that American bankers be permitted to participate in the loan. An American banking syndicate formed by J. P. Morgan & Company was admitted to the consortium, along with Japanese and Russian bankers, in May 1911. But for various reasons the project never prospered, and President Wilson, in March 1913, announced the withdrawal of the American group.

Meanwhile, Secretary Knox pressed forward in a more reckless move— that is, with his ill-fated proposal, made in late 1909, for internationalization of Manchurian railways in order to offset growing Japanese and Russian influence in the province. The British, who were at this very time encouraging Japanese expansion in Manchuria in order to keep them at safe distance from the British sphere of influence, promptly rebuffed Knox's suggestion. The Japanese, on the other hand, regarded the proposal as an attempt to undermine their influence in an area that Roosevelt had tacitly recognized as being within the Japanese orbit. In short, Knox's proposal was ill conceived and naively made. It angered the British, drove the Japanese and Russians into an anti-American bloc, and even alienated the American banking group.

The historian must conclude that, on the whole, Taft's record in foreign affairs was even more barren than in domestic politics. The most important outcome of dollar diplomacy in Latin America was an armed intervention in Nicaragua that lacked strategic necessity, failed to bring peace to Nicaragua, and intensified anti-American feeling. The result of dollar diplomacy in the Far East was an embittering of Japanese-American relations without any benefit to the United States. For the failure of his foreign policy Taft had only himself and his secretary of state to blame. Where Roosevelt had been wise and farsighted, Taft was indolently ineffectual; where Root had been suave, Knox was often offensive. The contrast goes far toward explaining the unsatisfactory state of American foreign relations when Woodrow Wilson took office on March 4, 1913.

6. *The New Freedom Abroad*

Humanitarians hailed Wilson's inauguration in 1913 as beginning a more idealistic era in American foreign relations. Most Democrats since 1901 had consistently condemned Roosevelt's and Taft's policies of military intervention, quasi-protectorates, and dollar diplomacy. They stood for early independence for the Filipinos and fought for a moderate naval building program designed only to implement a diplomacy of defense. The character and convictions of the new makers of American foreign policy also seemed to promise a new era in diplomacy. No public leader of his generation was more eloquent in articulating the liberal, idealistic international program than Woodrow Wilson. Long before he became the prime exponent of international organization and collective security, Wilson had championed a diplomacy that sought the good of mankind above the selfish interests of the United States. Moreover, Wilson's secretary of state, William Jennings Bryan, was easily the leading opponent of imperialism and navalism and a pioneer in the movement to advance peace through arbitration and conciliation.

The first sign of a New Freedom in foreign policy was Bryan's ambitious peace plan, launched only a few months after Wilson's inauguration. In its practical aspects, Bryan's plan was based soundly upon the experience of his predecessors in trying to steer arbitration treaties through the Senate. Secretary of State John Hay had negotiated a series of arbitration treaties that excluded all disputes involving vital interest and national honor. But the Senate in 1905 amended these treaties to make its consent to each arbitration necessary, and Roosevelt withdrew them. Secretary Root three years later persuaded Roosevelt to yield to the Senate's demand; he then negotiated twenty-five limited arbitration agreements in 1908 and 1909. However, the Senate rebelled again when President Taft and Secretary Knox signed new treaties with Britain and France in 1911 providing for arbitration of all "justiciable" questions, including disputes affecting national interest and honor. The upper house consented to ratification of these treaties in 1912 but exempted all important questions from possible arbitration. Taft in disgust refused to promulgate the mutilated treaties.

Bryan found a solution that he thought would achieve unlimited arbitration without arousing the Senate's suspicions. Bryan's treaties provided not for arbitration, but for submission of all disputes to permanent commissions for investigation for a period of one year. Neither party would resort to war or increase its armaments during this interval of "cooling off." After the investigation was completed, the parties might accept or reject the commission's findings. Both countries would then be free to go to war, but Bryan was confident that hostilities could not occur in such circumstances. Bryan signed the first conciliation treaty with El Salvador on August 7, 1913, and negotiated twenty-nine other such agreements during the following year with Great Britain, France, Italy, and lesser powers.

Further evidence of New Freedom idealism was the administration's withdrawal of the American banking group from the six-power consortium that had been formed in 1911 to finance construction of the Hukuang Railway in China. The United States, Wilson said on March 18, 1913, could not approve the loan agreement because it would lead to intolerable interference in Chinese affairs. A few weeks later, as if to emphasize his determination to cut loose from all such imperialistic conspiracies, Wilson recognized the new Republic of China without first consulting other powers.

A third example of idealistic diplomacy was Wilson's settlement of the Anglo-American dispute provoked when Congress, in August 1912, exempted American ships engaged in coastwise trade from payment of Panama Canal tolls. The British foreign office objected soon afterward that the exemption violated the Hay-Pauncefote Treaty's promise of equal rates for ships of all nations. Wilson could not run the risk of splitting his party so long as the tariff and banking bills hung in the fire; but after these measures were safely passed, he met the Senate foreign relations committee, on January 28, 1914, reviewed the critical state of American foreign relations, and urged repeal of the exemption provision in order to restore fully cordial relations with the British government. The president reiterated his plea before a joint session of Congress on March 5, 1914. The Hearst press roared, and some Democrats in Congress threatened rebellion. But the House of Representatives approved a repeal bill on March 31, which the Senate then passed on June 11, 1914.

Wilson's and Bryan's determination to do the moral if unpleasant thing in foreign affairs was evidenced, finally, in the treaty of reparation that they negotiated with Colombia to make amends for Rooseveltian sins. In a treaty signed at Bogotá on April 6, 1914, the United States expressed "sincere regret" for anything that had occurred to impair good relations between the two countries, agreed to pay $25 million to Colombia for the loss of Panama, gave the government of Colombia free use of the canal, and assured Colombian citizens equality of treatment with Americans in the Canal Zone. Roosevelt's friends in the Senate blocked ratification in 1914 and again in 1917, but the Wilson administration's intentions had been clearly demonstrated. The sight of the great government of the United States apologizing to a helpless neighbor stirred a wave of warm and cordial feeling toward the United States throughout Latin America.[7]

7. New Troubles with Japan, 1913–1917

The record of the Wilson administration's relations with Japan from 1913 to 1917 demonstrates that good intentions alone do not always suffice to settle delicate international disputes. The possibility of new difficulties was raised during the campaign of 1912, when Democrats and Progressives launched a campaign in California for a law prohibiting Japanese ownership of land. Instead of perceiving the dangers, Wilson conferred with California leaders and even volunteered a method to exclude Japanese from land ownership without violating the Japanese-American commercial treaty of 1911. Acting upon the president's suggestion, the California Assembly, on April 15, 1913, passed an alien bill prohibiting, in an indirect manner, Japanese ownership of land.

A crisis suddenly developed when news of the California Assembly's action was published in Japan. Then the California Senate exacerbated the tension on April 21 by adopting an alien land bill that was openly anti-Japanese. A rising war fever in Japan brought Wilson to his senses and compelled him to act. He first addressed a public appeal to the Californians, urging them not to make their alien land bill openly discriminatory. Next he sent Bryan to Sacramento to plead for caution. Wilson's and Bryan's supplications did not budge the California leaders from their determination to humiliate the Japanese people. The legislature on May 9, 1913, approved a bill excluding from land ownership persons "ineligible to citizenship"—words hateful to the Japanese. Governor Hiram W. Johnson signed the measure in spite of last-minute appeals from Wilson and Bryan.

For a brief moment it now seemed possible that Japan and the United States might be heading for war. The Japanese ambassador lodged a strong protest with the State Department on May 9; Japanese public opinion was at a dangerous point of anger. So explosive was the situation that the joint board of the army and navy warned Wilson on May 13 and 14 that war with Japan was "not only possible, but even probable." The joint board urged the president to transfer American warships in Chinese waters to the Philippines to help avert a surprise Japanese attack.

---

[7]The Harding administration negotiated a new treaty in 1921 that awarded the Colombian government $25 million but omitted the specific apology.

It was a dangerous situation, but Wilson and Bryan kept their heads. Correctly assuming that the Japanese government did not want war, they rejected the joint board's advice and relied exclusively on diplomacy. Many notes passed between Tokyo and Washington during the remainder of 1913 and the first months of 1914. The Japanese proposed a treaty guaranteeing the mutual right of land ownership. In reply, Wilson and Bryan promised to negotiate such a treaty when it was politically possible to obtain ratification. But that time did not come soon enough, and the new Japanese foreign minister, Baron Kato, abruptly terminated the negotiations in June 1914. Thus relations between the governments were gravely unsettled when the war in Europe spread to the Far East and raised new difficulties for the United States.

As Wilson and Bryan perceived, there was now the grave danger that Japan would take advantage of Europe's adversity to extend her influence in China. When Japan entered the war on the side of the Allies and seized the German naval base and concession in Shantung Province of China, the American leaders were disturbed but helpless to prevent such action. When the Japanese government proceeded in the early weeks of 1915 to attempt to impose a treaty embodying twenty-one demands on China, adherence to which would have made China virtually a satellite of Japan, Wilson and Bryan entered the ensuing controversy as defenders of China, voicing their opposition to the more extreme Japanese demands in a series of statements to the press and in notes to the Japanese and Chinese governments during April and May 1915. The most important of these was a caveat that Robert Lansing, counselor of the State Department, had drafted and that Bryan sent to Tokyo and Peking on May 11. It declared that the United States would not recognize any Sino-Japanese agreement violating the political and territorial integrity of China and the Open Door policy. The British foreign office had meanwhile become aroused and applied heavy pressure on the Tokyo cabinet in favor of a policy of moderation. The upshot of these Anglo-American protests was the Japanese government's abandonment for the time being of its plan to bring China under its control.

Following this crisis the Japanese pressed forward to enhance their economic position in China by offering capital that European bankers could no longer supply. Wilson responded by reversing his position on an international bankers' loan to China. Through the State Department he announced on November 9, 1917, that the American government was contemplating creation of a new four-power consortium of American, British, French, and Japanese bankers to supply desperately needed capital to China. Actually, the American determination to offset Japanese economic expansion in China had been evident months before this announcement and had prompted the Japanese government to ask Washington for a frank avowal of its policy. When correspondence failed to yield satisfactory understanding, the Tokyo foreign office sent a special envoy, Viscount Kikujiro Ishii, to Washington. Intense if intermittent discussions between Ishii and Robert Lansing, now secretary of state, ensued between September 6 and November 2, 1917. The extent of their divergence became clear when Ishii insisted that the United States recognize Japan's paramount interest in China, in the same way that Japan had recognized the paramount American interest in Mexico. Lansing replied that Japan should reaffirm her allegiance to the Open Door and help maintain Chinese independence.

The two men were unable to come to clear and firm agreement and, as diplomats often do, used ambiguous language to make a show of accord. In an agreement signed on November 2, 1917, the United States recognized that Japan had special interests in China, especially in provinces contiguous to Japanese possessions—presumably Manchuria and Shantung. In return, Japan reaffirmed her support of the Open Door and the territorial and administrative independence of China. Moreover, Japan promised in a secret protocol not to take advantage of the war situation to seek special rights in China that would abridge the interests of citizens of friendly powers. Ambiguous though it was, the Lansing-Ishii Agreement served to stabilize Japanese-American relations until a more comprehensive understanding could be achieved after the war ended.

8. *Further Penetration of Central America and the Caribbean*

In contrast to Wilson's and Bryan's promises of a new policy of nonintervention toward Latin America stands a record of wholesale diplomatic and military interference in the affairs of neighboring states unparalleled at any time in the annals of American diplomacy. How can this contradiction between promise and performance be explained?

To begin with, the Wilson administration inherited a foreign policy aimed primarily at protecting the future Panamanian lifeline. This policy could not be reversed without abandoning what seemed to be the cornerstone of the American security system. Actually, the Democratic leaders believed implicitly in the necessity of preserving American supremacy in the Caribbean and Central American areas, and they were willing to undertake even bolder programs than their Republican predecessors had envisaged.

In the second place, although Bryan and the Democratic party had solemnly condemned so-called dollar diplomacy as insidious financial imperialism, circumstances compelled the new secretary of state to use the very instrument that he had denounced. In the beginning, however, Bryan had other plans. To free Latin America from the snares of foreign concessionaires and bankers, he proposed a farsighted plan. It envisaged the assumption and refunding by the United States government of the external debts of the small Latin American states. But Wilson rejected this proposal as being too "radical," and Bryan concluded that he had no alternative but to continue to use private capital to consolidate American influence in a vital area.

These two points help to explain why there was no essential change in the Latin American policies of the United States in 1913. But the motives behind Wilson's and Bryan's extension of the Roosevelt-Taft policy lay deeper than simply a desire to protect American security interests. Wilson and Bryan were missionaries of democracy and freedom. They sincerely wanted to help less fortunate neighboring peoples to find peace and develop democratic institutions. Thus they intervened, not to subjugate and enslave, but to enlighten, instruct, and liberate.

The formulation of their program in Nicaragua shows how all these factors combined to shape and control policy. Bryan could not withdraw American troops from Nicaragua without inviting civil war and the inauguration of a bitterly anti-American regime in an area close to the canal. He continued, therefore, to support the Knox-sponsored Díaz government, which the Nicaraguan people would almost certainly have overthrown had they been free to do so.

Having concluded that it was necessary to control the government of Nicaragua, Bryan was also willing to go the whole way and regularize Nicaragua's special relation to the United States in treaty form. Counsel for the Nicaraguan government in June 1913 presented to the State Department the draft of a document that was later known as the Bryan-Chamorro Treaty. Like the agreement that Secretary Knox had negotiated and the Senate had refused to ratify a few months before, the Bryan-Chamorro Treaty provided for an American option on the Nicaraguan canal route for $3 million and also for other privileges. Unlike Knox's instrument, the Bryan-Chamorro Treaty also permitted the United States to intervene in Nicaragua to preserve order, protect property, and maintain Nicaraguan independence. The Senate approved the treaty on February 18, 1916, but only after the provision authorizing American intervention in Nicaragua's internal affairs had been removed. Actually, the deletion made no difference in State Department policy, which continued to be one of active interference in all phases of Nicaraguan politics.

The conclusion of this treaty marked only the beginning of a further penetration of the Caribbean area that culminated in the occupation of the Dominican Republic and Haiti. This final penetration occurred not because the Wilson administration sought imperialistic advantage or feared immediate European intervention, but rather because intervention and American control seemed the only way to save the Dominican and Haitian peoples from anarchy and starvation.

The Dominican Republic by the summer of 1914 was approaching a condition of anarchy as a result of recent revolutions. Officials in the Latin American Affairs Division of the State Department argued that only full-scale military occupation would save the Dominican people from chaos. Wilson intervened, first, by trying to persuade the warring chieftains to lay down their arms, agree upon a provisional president, and allow the United States to assume control of the Dominican finances and police force. The Dominican leaders consented to the first two proposals but would not sign a treaty making their country a virtual protectorate of the United States. Wilson decided that the time for drastic action had come when the leader of the strongest rebel band launched a new revolution in 1916. Wilson gave the orders and American marine and naval forces seized Santo Domingo on May 15, 1916, and took control of the government. And when the Dominican chieftains still refused to ratify the proposed treaty, the American naval commander established a military government on November 29, 1916.

Haitians had also indulged frequently in the revolutionary habit, but they had contrived before 1915 to pay their external debts and escape foreign intervention and control. However, the political situation in the black republic grew so anarchic during 1914 and 1915 that the State Department concluded that American control of Haitian customhouses was the only possible way to remove the incentive to revolution. An excuse for intervention presented itself when a new revolution exploded in June 1915. American marines and bluejackets seized Port-au-Prince on July 28, and the commanding American naval officer took control of the Haitian government on August 9 and compelled the national assembly to elect a pro-American, Sudre Dartiguenave, as president of Haiti. The State Department, moreover, now imposed a treaty—revised to provide not only American supervision of Haitian finances but also establishment of a native constabulary under American control—upon the puppet regime.[8]

To such extremes was the administration of Woodrow Wilson carried by the desire to protect American interests and end the reign of tyranny and anarchy in the Caribbean and Central American regions. The one feature of this policy that prevented it from becoming imperialistic was the idealism that prompted Wilson and especially Bryan to adopt it. Instead of using American diplomatic and military power to promote the exclusive material interests of American citizens, Bryan guarded the interests of the people of Nicaragua, Haiti, or Cuba as vigilantly as he guarded the welfare of the American people. On numerous occasions, for example, he prevented corrupt Latin American politicians from selling special rights and resources to American bankers.

[8] When Dartiguenave balked at signing away his country's independence, Secretary of State Lansing threatened either to find a new president of Haiti or else to establish complete military government. Dartiguenave signed the treaty on September 16, 1915. It was ratified by the Haitian senate on November 12, 1915, and approved by the United States Senate on February 28, 1916.

Wilson and Bryan climaxed their hemispheric policy by attempting to unite American republics in a Pan-American Alliance, binding them to respect one another's territorial integrity, guarantee one another's political independence, and settle all disputes by peaceful methods. Practically all the small states approved the proposed pact, and Brazil enthusiastically supported it. Argentina, on the other hand, was not pleased, while Chile was positively opposed to any treaty that would bind her hands in her old border dispute with Peru. As American diplomats were never able to overcome Chile's opposition, Wilson's plans for a hemispheric League of Nations collapsed.

9. Wilson and the Mexican Revolution

The crucial test of New Freedom diplomacy came when Wilson sought to apply a policy of helpfulness through interference in Mexico from 1913 to 1917. The background of the story can be told briefly. The old regime of Porfirio Díaz had been overthrown in 1911 by the reformer Francisco I. Madero. Madero tried to destroy the special privileges of the upper classes and provoked the inevitable counterrevolution. The head of the army, Victoriano Huerta, seized control of the Mexican government on February 18, 1913, and arranged the murder of the deposed president five days later. The Taft administration did not recognize Huerta as provisional president, but Britain, France, Germany, and other powers followed conventional practice in according recognition to the new regime.

This was the situation when Wilson was inaugurated in March 1913. There were appeals from representatives of American investors in Mexico to accord immediate de facto recognition to Huerta's government, but Wilson hesitated because of personal revulsion against Huerta and his "government of butchers." Another development caused him to hesitate further. It was the beginning of an anti-Huerta movement in the northern states of Mexico, led by the governor of Coahuila, Venustiano Carranza. Wilson, therefore, waited to see whether Huerta could consolidate his power.

The American president had decided on a policy by the middle of June 1913. The secretary of state informed Huerta on June 14 that the United States would attempt to mediate between Huerta's government and the followers of Carranza, called Constitutionalists, if Huerta would hold early constitutional elections and agree not to be a candidate for the presidency. President Wilson a short time later recalled the American ambassador from Mexico City and sent John Lind, former governor of Minnesota, to confer with the Mexican leaders. Lind's objectives, in brief, were to obtain

Huerta's elimination and the establishment through Wilson's mediation of a constitutional government that the United States could recognize and support.

Wilson of course assumed that the Mexicans would welcome his assistance. The fact was, however, that all factions, Constitutionalists as well as Huertistas, bitterly resented the president's interference and applauded when Huerta rejected Wilson's offer of mediation. Thus rebuffed, Wilson went before a joint session of Congress on August 27, 1913, explained his mediation proposal and Huerta's rebuff, and declared that the United States would adopt a policy of "watchful waiting."

During the next four or five weeks the situation in Mexico seemed to improve. Then Sir Lionel Carden, the new British minister, arrived in Mexico City. Carden was an intimate of S. Weetman Pearson, Lord Cowdray, who had large oil interests in Mexico. As Mexico was then practically the sole source of oil for the Royal Navy, one major objective of British foreign policy was to keep oil flowing from Mexican wells. Wilson suspected that Cowdray controlled Huerta and that Carden was sent to Mexico City to keep Huerta in power. In any event, on October 10, 1913, the day before Carden officially presented his credentials at the presidential palace, Huerta arrested most of the members of the chamber of deputies and inaugurated a full-fledged military dictatorship.

Wilson was so angered by Huerta's usurpation that he abandoned his policy of watchful waiting at once. First, he informed the powers that he would proceed to employ "such means as may be necessary" to depose Huerta. Next, he prepared an angry note to the British foreign office, accusing the British leaders of keeping Huerta in power against his wishes. The note was never sent, but in subsequent correspondence the president make it clear that Britain would have to choose between the friendship of Huerta and that of the United States. In view of the then perilous state of European affairs, the British foreign secretary, Sir Edward Grey, had no alternative but to withdraw support from Huerta.

Wilson now proceeded to his second step. This move involved nothing less than the cooperation of the United States and the Constitutionalists in a war against Huerta, to be followed by the establishment of a new government in Mexico. The president in November 1913 sent an agent to Carranza's camp at Nogales, Mexico, with an offer of cooperation and support. Wilson was surprised and indignant when Carranza replied that the Constitutionalists did not want American support, would oppose with arms the entry of American troops into Mexico, and would proceed to establish their own government in their own way. All that the Constitutionalists desired from the American government, Carranza said, was the privilege of buying arms and ammunition in the United States.

Wounded by Carranza's reply, Wilson withheld aid from the Constitutionalists for two months after the Nogales conference. But as it became increasingly apparent that the revolutionists could never overthrow Huerta without a larger supply of war matériel, Wilson, on February 3, 1914, revoked the arms embargo that Taft had applied. Nonetheless, the speedy triumph of the Constitutionalists that Wilson confidently expected did not occur. In fact, by the beginning of April 1914 Huerta was stronger than he had been before the arms embargo was lifted.

For Wilson this was a catastrophic development. For one thing, he had by this time become emotionally deeply committed to the revolutionary cause. For another thing, he was determined to destroy the entire imperialist system in Mexico and make it possible for the Mexican people not only to govern themselves, but also to control their own resources. Yet how could this be done without provoking war also with the Constitutionalists? There seemed no way out of the dilemma until a trivial incident at Tampico on April 10, 1914, offered an excuse for drastic action. A Huertista colonel arrested the paymaster and several of the crew of *U.S.S. Dolphin* when they landed their whaleboat behind the lines at Tampico, then under attack by the Constitutionalists. When the Huertista commander in Tampico heard of the incident he at once ordered the release of the American sailors and sent an apology to Admiral Henry T. Mayo, commander of the American fleet off Veracruz.

That would have been the end of the matter had not Mayo rejected the apology and demanded a twenty-one-gun salute to the American flag and had not the president backed up Mayo's demand. Huerta agreed to render the salute, but only provided an American warship returned a simultaneous volley. In response, Wilson went before a joint session of Congress on April 20 and asked for authority to compel Huerta to respect the honor of the United States. Before Congress could act on the president's request, news arrived in Washington of the impending arrival at Veracruz of a German merchant ship, *Ypiranga*, with a load of ammunition for the Huerta government. Without waiting for congressional sanction, Wilson on April 21 ordered the fleet to occupy Veracruz and prevent *Ypiranga* from unloading her cargo. He did this, however, only after Huerta's commander in Veracruz had promised to withdraw his troops to Mexico City. Fighting, which Wilson definitely did not expect, broke out when students from the Mexican naval academy fired upon the American bluejackets. Veracruz was in American hands by April 22 after sharp fighting and heavy casualties.

Wilson was appalled by the news of the bloodshed and moved quickly to contain the fighting and prevent a general war. Such a conflict seemed possible when Carranza denounced the Veracruz occupation as wanton aggression and threatened to resist the Americans if they attempted any forward movement.

Wilson had blundered into his predicament, but he had no intention of going to war with Mexico, and certainly not against the Constitutionalists, who he believed offered the only hope for the lasting reform and reconstruction of Mexico. Then the Argentine, Brazilian, and Chilean envoys in Washington, on April 25, offered to mediate the dispute. In mutual relief Wilson and Huerta accepted the offer. The American and Mexican dele-

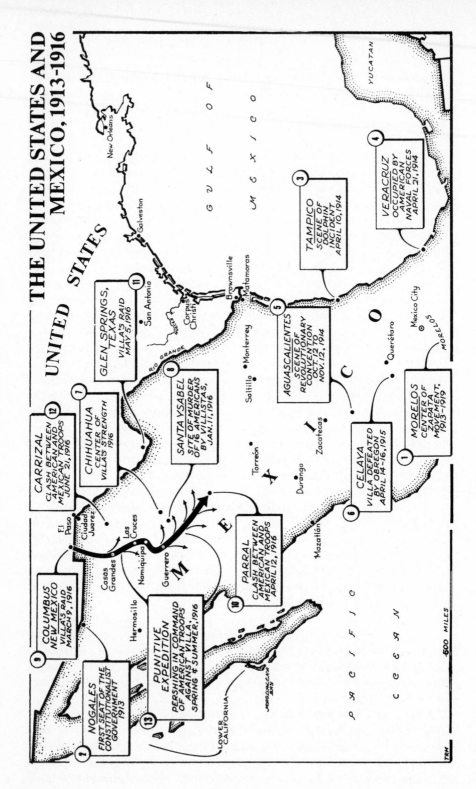

THE UNITED STATES AND MEXICO, 1913-1916

UNITED STATES

UNITED STATES

GULF OF MEXICO

MEXICO

PACIFIC OCEAN

LOWER CALIFORNIA

YUCATAN

New Orleans

Galveston

San Antonio

Corpus Christi

Brownsville

Matamoras

Monterrey

Saltillo

Zacatecas

Torreón

Durango

Mazatlán

Hermosillo

El Paso

Ciudad Juarez

Las Cruces

Namiquipa

Casas Grandes

Guerrero

Querétaro

Mexico City

MORELOS

RIO GRANDE

MEXICO

3 TAMPICO SCENE OF DOLPHIN INCIDENT APRIL 10, 1914

4 VERACRUZ OCCUPIED BY AMERICAN NAVAL FORCES APRIL 21, 1914

11 GLEN SPRINGS, TEXAS VILLA'S RAID MAY 5, 1916

5 AGUASCALIENTES SCENE OF REVOLUTIONARY CONVENTION OCT. 12 TO NOV. 12, 1914

8 SANTA YSABEL SITE OF MURDER OF 16 AMERICANS BY VILLISTAS, JAN. 11, 1916

12 CARRIZAL CLASH BETWEEN AMERICAN AND MEXICAN TROOPS JUNE 21, 1916

7 CHIHUAHUA CENTER OF VILLA'S STRENGTH 1916

1 MORELOS CENTER OF ZAPATA MOVEMENT, 1913-1919

6 CELAYA VILLA DEFEATED BY OBREGON APRIL 14-16, 1915

9 COLUMBUS NEW MEXICO VILLA'S RAID MARCH 9, 1916

10 PARRAL CLASH BETWEEN AMERICAN AND MEXICAN TROOPS APRIL 12, 1916

13 PUNITIVE EXPEDITION PERSHING IN COMMAND OF AMERICAN TROOPS AGAINST VILLA, SPRING & SUMMER, 1916

2 NOGALES FIRST SEAT OF THE CONSTITUTIONALIST GOVERNMENT 1913

500 MILES

JAMES MAC DONALD 1955

TRM

gates met at Niagara Falls, Canada, from May 20 until July 2, 1914. As the days passed Huerta's power waned, and the Constitutionalists drove closer to Mexico City. Huerta abdicated on July 15, 1914, after taking one parting shot at the "puritan" in the White House; Carranza and his armies entered Mexico City on August 20.

Huerta's retirement, however, did not signal the beginning of peace in Mexico, for a rupture in the Constitutionalist ranks soon plunged Mexico anew into civil war. The chief cause of the schism was the rivalry between the first chief of the revolution, Carranza, and his most successful general, Francisco, or "Pancho," Villa, who, though ignorant and politically untrained, seemed to offer the best hope for revolutionary land reform. Into this critical and delicate situation the American government moved with alacrity. The president sent an agent to Mexico in August 1914 to propose a convention of revolutionary leaders and subsequent establishment of a new provisional government. Carranza and his generals approved the American plan, and Carranza agreed to retire, provided Villa also gave up his command. That Villa had no intention of withdrawing, however, was evidenced when he declared war on Carranza three weeks before the convention was to meet.

In spite of this evidence of Villa's bad faith, the convention did assemble at Aguascalientes from October 12 through November 12, 1914. Villa controlled a majority and established a provisional government in Mexico City that enjoyed the limited support of the United States for a time. However, Carranza's leading generals, Alvaro Obregón and Pablo Gonzáles, withdrew and joined Carranza in his new headquarters at Veracruz, recently evacuated by the American forces.

Thus the civil war began again between the constructive wing of the revolution headed by Carranza and the plundering elements under Villa's control. While Villa waited for the Carrancistas to collapse, Carranza broadened his reform program, strengthened his armies, and began a military campaign in January 1915 that drove Villa and his forces northward from the capital. Then Obregón destroyed Villa's offensive power in one great battle at Celaya in April 1915, and the bandit chieftain sought refuge in his native stronghold of Chihuahua.

The swift destruction of Villa's government compelled the Wilson administration to revert to a policy of neutrality in the Mexican conflict. At the same time, the renewal of the civil war set off a vociferous demand in the United States for intervention. For a time Wilson rebuffed these counsels and insisted that Mexicans be allowed to settle their problems in their own way. Gradually, however, his resistance weakened, and, on June 2, 1915, he warned the rival factions to compose their differences or else expect corrective measures by the United States. Two months later, furthermore, Wilson and his new secretary of state, Robert Lansing, called in leading Latin American envoys in Washington to help formulate a plan to eliminate Carranza and create a new provisional government in Mexico.

Events over which Wilson had no control, however, again took over direction of his Mexican policy. First, while Wilson and Lansing talked, Carranza acted. By August 1915 it was evident that Carranza's power was growing daily and that intervention by the United States would provoke a general war with the Mexican people. Second, the United States became embroiled during the summer of 1915 in a serious diplomatic controversy with Germany over the use of submarines against Allied merchant ships. As the possibility of war with Germany increased, Wilson's and Lansing's willingness to risk military involvement in Mexico diminished. Finally, the two American leaders learned that the German government was trying to encourage a war between Mexico and its neighbor in order to lessen American pressure against the unrestricted use of submarines. This revelation caused the Washington government to take a hard second look at plans for intervention.

The only alternative to intervention seemed to be recognition and support of Carranza. Hence Wilson swiftly reversed American policy, persuaded the Latin American envoys to cooperate, and extended de facto recognition to Carranza's provisional government on October 19, 1915. During the next three months relations between the United States and the de facto regime were friendly, and Wilson's troubles would have been at an end had no untoward events occurred. As it turned out, perplexities were just beginning.

The chief troublemaker was Villa. He had somehow got word of an alleged agreement between Carranza and Wilson by which Carranza, in return for a large loan from the United States, would make Mexico a virtual protectorate of the United States. The rumor, incidentally, was utterly without foundation. Villa may also have wanted to provoke war between the two countries. A band of Villistas stopped a train at Santa Ysabel, fifty miles west of Chihuahua City, on January 11, 1916, removed seventeen Americans, and shot sixteen of them on the spot. When this massacre failed to cause American reprisal, Villa made a bold raid on Columbus, New Mexico, on March 9, 1916, burning the town and killing nineteen inhabitants.

At once President Wilson ordered army commanders in Texas to assemble an expedition for the pursuit of Villa. At the same time he sought, and thought that he had obtained, the consent of the leaders of the de facto government for the entry of an American force into Mexican territory. Finally, he sent a punitive expedition, under command of Brigadier General John J. Pershing, across the border on March 18. The dispatch of the punitive expedition would have provoked no crisis if Villa had been quickly apprehended. However, Villa cunningly led his pursuers deep into Mexico. The punitive expedition had penetrated more than 300 miles into northern Mexico by April 8, 1916, but Villa was still defiantly at large. At this point the expedition halted and gave all appearances of becoming an army of occupation.

The president refused, contrary to the advice of his military counselors, to withdraw Pershing's command. He made this fateful decision chiefly because the State Department was not convinced that Carranza was either able or willing to control the bandit gangs that menaced the American border. On the other hand, the Mexican leaders were beginning to suspect that Wilson intended to occupy northern Mexico permanently. As this suspicion grew they gave less attention to pursuing Villa and more to preparing for an inevitable showdown with the United States.

Neither government wanted war, yet a situation was developing that could lead only to hostilities. A skirmish between American and Mexican troops occurred at Parral on April 12 in which forty Mexicans were killed. Such a wave of anger swept over Mexico that Carranza could do nothing less than demand prompt withdrawal of the expedition. The Washington government refused, and Carranza took two steps preparatory to a final reckoning. First, on May 22 he addressed a bitter note to the United States government, accusing it of warlike intentions; second, he ordered his field commanders to resist the American forces if they moved in any direction other than toward the border. Wilson replied by calling practically the entire National Guard to the border on June 18 and by sending a stinging rebuke to Carranza on June 20, declaring that the United States would not withdraw the expedition and warning that any attacks on American soldiers would lead to "the gravest consequences."

The *casus' belli* occurred only a few hours after the American note of June 20 was delivered in the Mexican capital. An American patrol tried to force its way through a Mexican garrison at Carrizal in northern Chihuahua. The Mexicans lost thirty men but killed twelve and captured twenty-three Americans. As first reports to Washington told of a treacherous ambush, Wilson demanded the immediate release of the prisoners and prepared a message to Congress asking for authority to occupy northern Mexico, action that could have resulted only in full-scale war. He did not deliver the message because newspapers on June 26 published an account of the Carrizal incident written by an American officer on the spot. It revealed that the Americans had been guilty of an aggressive attack. A wave of revulsion immediately swept through the American people; Wilson was bombarded with appeals for peace from leaders in all walks of life; and war fever passed from Washington almost at once.

The upshot of the Carrizal affair was the eventual settlement of the most troubling phase of the Mexican-American problem. Wilson agreed when on July 4 Carranza suggested the appointment of a Joint High Commission to investigate and recommend. American and Mexican commissioners met from September 6, 1916, through January 15, 1917, and pondered all aspects of the Mexican problem. The Joint High Commission broke up without agreement on January 15, 1917. Now Wilson had to choose between surrendering to Carranza's renewed demand for withdrawal or accepting the possibility of war with Mexico. As events were now inexorably drawing the United States into the European war, the president had no alternative but to yield. The withdrawal was begun on January 27, and a nearly tragic chapter in the history of American foreign relations was happily ended.

The recalling of the punitive expedition and Wilson's de jure recognition of Carranza's new constitutional regime on March 13, 1917, marked a momentous turning point in modern Mexican history. Henceforward the Mexican people could pursue their difficult progress toward democratic institutions free from outside control. Wilson in large measure had made this great opportunity possible. Single-handed he had prevented the European powers from coming to Huerta's aid, assisted the Constitutionalists in deposing the usurper, and stood off powerful forces in the United States that sought the downfall of the revolution.

7

The Road
to War,

1914–1917

A mericans, on the eve of the most frightful war in history
up to that time, thought that they were still living in a secure international
community, in which a benevolent British sea dominion and a fine world
balance of power would operate almost automatically to protect the Monroe Doctrine without a huge American naval and military establishment.
Then things suddenly went awry in 1914. German armies destroyed the
balance on the Continent; German submarines threatened to destroy British control of the seas. The established international community had collapsed, and Americans found themselves at a crossroads in their history.
Upon their reactions to the First World War depended not only the fate of
Europe but the destiny of the United States as well.

1. American Neutrality, 1914–1915

To Americans who believed that a general war was virtually impossible,
the outbreak of the First World War came, as one North Carolinian wrote
in November 1914, "as lightning out of a clear sky." The dominant Ameri-

can reaction in August 1914 was relief that America was far removed from the scene of conflict, coupled with conviction that the United States had no vital stake in the outcome. Even ardent champions of the Allies approved when President Wilson issued an official proclamation of neutrality on August 4 and, two weeks later, urged Americans to be impartial in thought as well as in deed. To be sure, many Americans were unable to follow the president's injunction all the way. The United States was deluged from 1914 to 1917 with propaganda in behalf of the opposing alliances. Probably a majority of thoughtful Americans, concluding that Germany and Austria were primarily responsible for the war's outbreak, desired an Anglo-French victory. However, until 1917, that same majority continued to hope and pray that this country could avoid participation.

The sudden threat and then the outbreak of war in Europe in late July and early August of 1914 set off an economic panic in the United States and compelled the Wilson administration to take drastic steps to protect the domestic economy. To protect the nation's gold reserve, Washington adopted a policy of discouraging loans by American bankers to the belligerents. The president, however, permitted Secretary Bryan to say that the administration disapproved of private loans to belligerent governments because such loans violated the spirit of neutrality.

Wilson had also begun negotiations to protect American neutral trade. Since the British soon swept German raiders from the seas and began slowly but inexorably to extend far-reaching controls to prevent neutral trade with the Central Powers, the American government's early difficulties were all with Great Britain. By the end of February 1915, when the British system of maritime controls was severely tightened, the British admiralty had mined the North Sea, laid down a long-range naval blockade of Germany and neutral Europe, and seized American ships carrying certain noncontraband,[1] particularly food, to Italy, Holland, and other European neutrals for transshipment to Germany.

The crucial question during this early period of the war was whether the United States would accept the British maritime system, some aspects of which probably exceeded the bounds of international law (or what neutrals had traditionally considered to be the laws governing war at sea), or whether the United States would insist to the point of war upon freedom of trade with Germany in all noncontraband materials. The reaction of the United States as the principal neutral power was complicated by the inapplicability of many traditional rules to new weapons such as the mine and the submarine. Wilson's first impulse was to insist sternly upon full respect for American commercial rights. However, his options were

---

[1] Under traditional international law, goods during wartime fall into three categories: (1) absolute contraband, that is, materials destined directly for the use of military forces; (2) conditional contraband, that is, goods susceptible of being used by military forces; and (3) noncontraband, that is, food, raw materials, and goods destined only for use by civilians. Under traditional law, a belligerent could seize and confiscate absolute contraband, had to prove that conditional contraband was destined for military forces in order to confiscate it, and was required to allow noncontraband to pass to its enemy.

severely limited, and on second thought he decided not to push the British to the wall. He acquiesced and allowed the State Department to lodge firm but friendly protests that reserved American rights for future adjudication.

This decision was virtually inevitable. The British did control the seas, and their maritime measures were essentially grounded in the beginning on traditional law and custom. Under British control of the Atlantic, American direct trade with Germany and Austria declined from $169,289,775 in 1914 to $1,159,653 in 1916. At the same time American trade with the Allies rose from $824,800,237 to $3,214,480,547. In short, the United States became virtually an Allied warehouse, from which munitions, food, and other vital raw materials flowed in an increasing stream. This outcome, it should be emphasized, derived from British control of the seas, not from any official American favoritism. Indeed, the United States would have been altogether unneutral had it challenged legitimate use of British sea power.

The Allied-American war trade was not the only consequence of American acquiescence in the British sea measures. The system of international exchange began to collapse as Allied, and particularly British, purchases began to assume enormous proportions in the spring and summer of 1915. As it became evident that continued adherence to Bryan's ban against loans would destroy the only important foreign trade in which Americans could then engage, the administration, including Bryan himself, began gradually to retreat. Bryan opened the door to large-scale loans on March 31, 1915, by declaring that the State Department would not oppose a $50 million "commercial credit" by the House of Morgan to the French government.

Bryan's approval of the French commercial credit partially reversed the State Department's ban on loans. The issue was raised even more squarely when an Anglo-French commission came to the United States in September 1915 to negotiate an unsecured public loan of $500 million. The State Department announced that it had no objections to the loan, thus specifically lifting the Bryan ban, and the United States soon became the arsenal of credit as well as of war materials for the Allies. American bankers advanced an additional $1.8 billion to the Allied governments to finance the war trade during the next eighteen months. Unlike the first Anglo-French public loan, all later loans were secured 100 percent by high-grade American and South American securities, and none was sold by public campaign.

These were some of the ties of trade and credit that bound the United States to the Allies by the autumn of 1915. It is important that we understand why the president approved policies that operated so powerfully to the advantage of one alliance. Perhaps one decisive factor in Wilson's decision to acquiesce in the British maritime system was his conviction, shared by many Americans in 1914 and 1915, that German methods and objectives were morally reprehensible and that the triumph in Europe of imperial Germany, militaristic and expansive, would constitute a potential threat to the security of the United States. We can only surmise that this conviction played a vital role in policy.

We can be more certain that another factor decisively shaped Wilson's neutral policies. It was the fact that he had virtually no choice but to accept British sea measures and allow the United States to become an arsenal of the Allies. The president, roughly speaking, faced the following situation in 1914 and early 1915: on one side, the Germans had used superior land power to overrun Belgium and the industrial areas of France; on the other side, Great Britain had used superior naval power to control the Atlantic and keep open her indispensable sources of supply. In accomplishing these objectives both Germany and Great Britain violated traditional international law to varying degrees but operated within a traditional framework. Because the United States was not prepared to halt the German invasion of Belgium, the president withheld any condemnation of this violation of the European treaty system. Because he had no desire to insure a German victory, the president acquiesced in the British maritime system. Only if Great Britain had been fighting for objectives that imperiled American security would Wilson have been justified in attempting to deny to the British advantages flowing from their control of the seas.

2. The German Submarine Challenge, 1915

When Germany used a new weapon, the submarine, to challenge British control of the seas, Wilson was compelled to reexamine his whole plan of neutrality. This was necessary because the British and French governments responded to the submarine challenge with a total interdiction of all trade with the Central Powers. Hereafter the United States could no longer acquiesce in the British blockade without impairing friendly relations with Germany, nor acquiesce in the German submarine blockade without impairing friendly relations with the Allies and perhaps also guaranteeing a German victory. In other words, the United States could not be absolutely impartial in these new circumstances; it was bound to give an advantage and impose a disadvantage either way it turned.

The submarine issue arose in such a way, however, as to confuse the American people and their leaders. The German admiralty on February 4, 1915, announced the inauguration of a submarine blockade of the British Isles. All enemy vessels in a broad war zone would be destroyed without warning; even neutral vessels would not be safe because of British misuse of neutral flags. The imperial government, German spokesmen explained, had adopted this extreme measure in retaliation against the British food

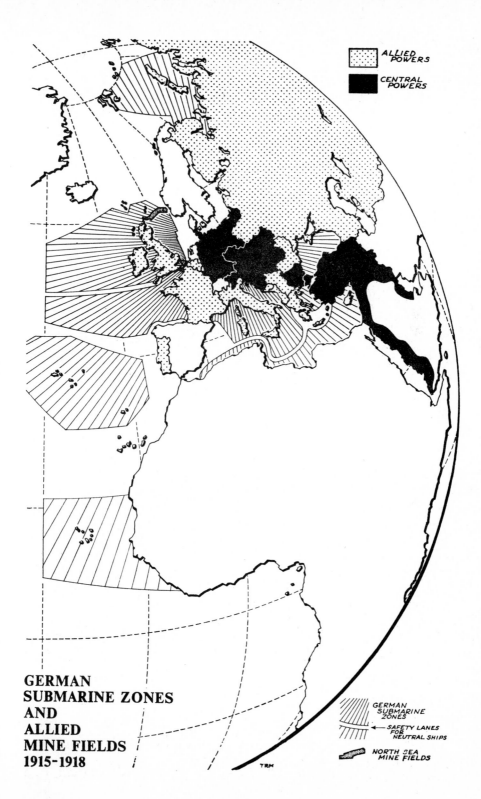

ALLIED
POWERS

CENTRAL
POWERS

GERMAN
SUBMARINE ZONES
AND
ALLIED
MINE FIELDS
1915-1918

GERMAN
SUBMARINE
ZONES

← SAFETY LANES
FOR
NEUTRAL SHIPS

NORTH SEA
MINE FIELDS

blockade. Germany would abandon her submarine blockade, they added, if the British abandoned their campaign to starve women and children.

Wilson addressed a note of reply to Berlin on February 10, 1915, warning that the United States would hold Germany to a "strict accountability" for illegal destruction of American ships and lives. At the same time, Wilson endeavored to persuade the British to lift their blockade against food. Even though the submarine blockade was 90 percent bluff at this time, the British agreed to allow foodstuffs to enter Germany, provided that the Germans would give up use of U-boats against merchant shipping. Actually, the German food supply was adequate at this time. The German government insisted, therefore, that the British permit free entry into Germany of raw materials as well as food. The British of course refused.

When the submarine bluff failed to frighten the British, the German government began a general terror campaign of sinking, without warning, unarmed British passenger vessels in the North Atlantic. The great German-American crisis of 1915 revolved entirely around the alleged right of Americans to travel in safety on these British liners. This issue was raised when a submarine sank without warning the British liner *Falaba* on March 28, 1915, and one American was drowned. The president and his advisers during the next five weeks tried to formulate a policy that would protect American rights without provoking a serious crisis with Germany. Bryan argued that the American government should warn its citizens against traveling on belligerent merchantmen and give Germany the same freedom to violate international law that it had granted Britain. Different advice came from Robert Lansing, then counselor of the State Department, and the Joint Neutrality Board, an agency established to advise the State, War, and Navy departments on matters of international law. They contended that the sinking of the unarmed *Falaba* was such a flagrant violation of international law that the United States could not avoid taking a firm stand, even if it provoked a diplomatic crisis.

In essence, the president had to decide whether to yield to the German threat and abandon certain American technical rights on the seas. It was a decision he did not want to make, and there is good evidence that he had decided not to press the *Falaba* case. However, an event occurred on May 7 that forced him to meet the German challenge to freedom of the seas— the sinking without warning of the British liner *Lusitania* off the coast of Ireland, with the death of more than 1,200 noncombatants, including 128 Americans.

Americans were horrified, but few of them wanted to go to war, and Wilson shared their disinclination to fight. His first *Lusitania* note of May 13, 1915, invoked the rights of humanity in appealing to the imperial German government to halt its campaign against unarmed merchantmen. The German foreign office replied evasively, and Wilson renewed his plea. And when the German government replied equivocally for a second time, Wilson was both conciliatory and stern in his third *Lusitania* note. He admitted that submarine operations might be conducted within traditional rules, provided that U-boat commanders warned their victims and provided for the safety of passengers and crews. On the other hand, he warned that the United States would regard a repetition of ruthless sinkings as "deliberately unfriendly." This was the language of ultimate diplomacy.

So eager was Bryan to avoid doing anything that might conceivably lead to war that he resigned on June 8, 1915, rather than sign the second *Lusitania* note. In contrast, Wilson was willing to risk war rather than yield what he thought was a deeply moral principle—respect for human life even during wartime. When a submarine sank the White Star liner *Arabic* on August 19, with the loss of two American lives, the president and his new secretary of state, Lansing, resolved to force a showdown. This new crisis forced the German government to reveal that it had issued secret orders to U-boat commanders on June 6 to spare large passenger liners. It also prompted the German emperor on August 26 to order total abandonment of unrestricted submarine operations against all passenger ships. Therefore, the German ambassador in Washington informed Lansing on September 1 that unresisting liners would not be sunk without warning and without provision being made for the safety of passengers and crew.

The *Arabic* pledge preserved the peace and was a major diplomatic triumph for the president. Nonetheless, he could not have been encouraged by the perilous state of American foreign relations and the signs of disunity and confusion at home during the summer of 1915. There were numerous revelations of German conspiracies against American neutrality and of German intrigues to provoke conflict between the United States and Mexico. Such exposures naturally intensified the anti-German sentiment that had grown by leaps and bounds since the sinking of *Lusitania*. On the other hand, the great mass of Americans were still stubbornly opposed to a belligerent policy.

Meanwhile, the Washington government, after seeming to acquiesce in the British blockade instituted in March 1915, had made it clear in a note to the London foreign office on July 14, 1915, that the United States meant to defend the rights of neutral trade. This was followed by a long and stinging note to London on October 21. Denouncing the British blockade as "ineffective, illegal, and indefensible," it seemed to signal the beginning of a firm American defense of freedom of the seas against all comers.

3. The Diplomacy of Mediation, 1915-1916

It was not easy to know what to do in the face of strong demands at home both for stern defense of American rights on the seas and preservation of peace almost at any price. Obviously, the surest way out of this dilemma was to end the war by mediation. Hope for peace ebbed and flowed all during the period of neutrality. At Wilson's request, Colonel Edward M. House, his most trusted adviser on foreign affairs, went to Europe in January 1915 to explore the possibility of American mediation. He found British officials willing to discuss peace terms, provided that the Germans consented to evacuate Belgium, disarm after the war was over, and give definite guarantees of a future peaceful policy in Europe. But the Germans would make no promises, for they were not yet prepared to face the issue of Belgium's future. House's first peace mission ended in failure.

The German refusal to cooperate for peace and the subsequent submarine controversy and revelations of German intrigues in the United States convinced House that German triumph in Europe would gravely imperil future American security. He had no desire to destroy German power in Europe, for he regarded Germany as a bulwark against Russia. He concluded during the autumn of 1915 that circumstances demanded nothing less than positive action by the United States to end the war and create a new international structure that would safeguard American security. He thought that these goals could be accomplished through cooperation between the United States and the Allied governments in a drive for a reasonable peace.

House first revealed his plan to Wilson on October 1915 and with Wilson's consent broached the matter to Sir Edward Grey, British foreign secretary, soon afterward. Grey replied that the Allies might indeed be willing to consider a negotiated peace if the United States was prepared to join a postwar League of Nations, and Wilson decided to send House to Europe for new talks. In brief, Wilson and House envisaged close Allied and American cooperation in forcing Germany to the peace table. If the Germans refused even to negotiate, the United States would probably enter the war on the side of the Allies. On the other hand, if the German government agreed to negotiate, the United States would cooperate with the Allies at the peace conference in attempting to compel Germany to accept a reasonable settlement. Finally, if Germany withdrew from the conference and renewed hostilities, the United States would probably join the war on the Allied side.

Certainly Wilson and probably House thought of armed intervention only as a last, desperate resort. They knew that there was grave danger of war if they continued to allow the German admiralty indirectly to determine American foreign policy. They thought that the chances of obtaining a reasonable settlement through the president's mediation were good. But, they reasoned, even should the United States have to enter the war under House's plan, the nation would at least be acting on its own volition and in behalf of a cause worth fighting for—a just settlement and an effective postwar international organization. At least Americans would not be fighting merely to vindicate technical rights on the seas.

To carry forward this peace project, House arrived in London on January 6, 1916. After preliminary conferences with Grey and other British leaders, he went to Berlin and Paris, where conversations convinced him that mediation was impossible until the summer campaigns had ended. He was back in London in February and moved to bring the British to definite accord. House and Grey initialed a memorandum embodying their understanding on February 22, 1916. The president, it said, was ready to move for peace when the Allied governments gave the signal, and—although this was implied by what Grey said and was not included in the document—the Allies presumably would welcome Wilson's mediation according to the plan worked out by Colonel House.

Meanwhile, Wilson and Lansing on the other side of the water had embarked upon a separate diplomatic campaign that nearly wrecked House's negotiation, threatened to draw Germany and the United States into accord, and caused such a controversy in Congress that Wilson almost lost control of American foreign policy. The immediate background was the nearly successful conclusion in January and early February 1916 of Lansing's negotiations with the German government for settlement of the *Lusitania* affair. Even though the Germans were unwilling to admit the outright illegality of the sinking of the liner, they assumed liability for loss of American lives and offered a suitable indemnity.

The issue that set off a diplomatic and political explosion was a larger controversy over armed merchant ships. Months before the submarine challenge was raised, the State Department had issued regulations classifying defensively armed merchant ships as peaceful vessels. But the British not only armed merchant ships during 1915 but also ordered them to attack submarines, and Wilson and Lansing began to wonder whether it was fair to require submarines to surface before they attacked. Convinced that the American people did not want to go to war over the submarine issue, Lansing—with the president's approval—decided to try to find comprehensive understanding with the German government. On January 18, 1916, he sent the Allied governments a proposal for a new modus vivendi to govern maritime warfare. Repeating the German argument that any armed merchant ship was offensively armed in relation to the submarine, it suggested that the Allies disarm their merchant ships. More important, it warned that the American government was considering classifying armed merchantmen as auxiliary cruisers.[2]

Coming at the time when House was in London promoting intimate Anglo-American cooperation for peace, Lansing's modus vivendi struck like a bolt from a clear sky in the British capital. Sir Edward Grey remarked bitterly that the United States was proposing nothing less than

---

[2]Such action by the United States government would in effect have excluded armed merchantmen from American ports, for under international law belligerent warships could stay only twenty-four hours in a neutral port and could purchase only enough fuel to reach their nearest home port.

destruction of the entire British merchant marine. Colonel House at once perceived the incongruity of his government's proposing a close entente with Great Britain at the very time that it was threatening to adopt a policy that might lead to Britain's defeat. House therefore urged Lansing to hold his proposal in abeyance. Before the secretary of state could withdraw his modus vivendi, however, the German government, on February 10, 1916, announced that its submarines would sink all armed merchant ships without warning beginning on February 29.

Instead of acquiescing, Lansing declared on February 15 that the United States would *not* warn its citizens against traveling on ships armed for limited defense. Democratic leaders in Congress, baffled by this seeming reversal and alarmed by the thought of going to war to protect Americans traveling on armed belligerent merchantmen, went to the White House on February 21 to protest. But Wilson stood firm and declared that he would hold Germany to strict account. News of the president's response provoked panic in the House of Representatives. Democratic members of the foreign affairs committee agreed unanimously to demand prompt action on a resolution offered by Representative Jeff McLemore of Texas, warning Americans against traveling on armed ships, while Democratic leaders in the House visited the president again in the morning of February 25 to warn that the McLemore Resolution would pass by a two-to-one margin. Moreover, Senator Thomas P. Gore of Oklahoma introduced an identical resolution in the upper house soon after Democratic House leaders returned from their conference at the White House.

Wilson acted with customary boldness in this great challenge to his leadership, and he won the tabling of the Gore and McLemore resolutions after a bitter parlimentary struggle. But because he refused for reasons of security to explain his stand, many Democratic leaders began to suspect that he meant to take the country into war. Actually, Wilson had repudiated Lansing's proposed modus vivendi because he realized that he would destroy completely his standing as a mediator among the Allies and give tremendous military advantage to Germany if he insisted upon its adoption.

Events soon gave Wilson an opportunity to force a final reckoning with Germany without raising the issue of armed ships. A submarine torpedoed without warning an unarmed channel packet, *Sussex*, with eighty casualties on March 24, 1916. After agonizing deliberation, Wilson went before a joint session of Congress on April 18 and read the terms of an ultimatum that he had just sent to Berlin: the United States would sever relations if the German government did not abandon its unrestricted submarine operations against all shipping, belligerent and neutral.

Wilson's ultimatum brought to a head a controversy over submarine policy then going on in Germany between the military and civilian branches of the government. Discussion convinced the emperor that the

admiralty did not have enough submarines to conduct a successful blockade or to justify bringing the United States into the war. He announced
submission to the president's demands on May 1. The German foreign
office informed the State Department three days later that henceforth
submarine commanders would observe the rules of visit and search before
sinking merchant vessels. But the note ended with a warning that Germany reserved freedom of action and might again resort to intensified
submarine warfare if the United States did not compel the British to observe international law concerning neutral trade. So complete was the
German surrender in this so-called *Sussex* pledge that the tension between
the two governments diminished almost at once.

4. The Preparedness Controversy, 1914-1916

The great German-American crisis of 1915-1916 had an impact on the
American people that was more powerful than the shock caused by the
war's outbreak. Among a small minority it stimulated the conviction that
the United States could not safely permit the triumph of German militarism in Europe and the destruction of British sea power. Much more important was the fact that the submarine crisis caused many Americans for
the first time to realize that they lived in a chaotic international community; that force, not reason, was the final arbiter in disputes between nations; and that the United States because of its military weakness was
practically powerless to affect the outcome of the war in Europe or even
to protect its own security. Preparedness advocates were quick to seize
the opportunity afforded by the submarine controversy. Beginning in the
spring of 1915, they poured out articles and books in a virtual flood.
    Wilson knew that he could not continue to oppose preparedness with-
out giving the Republicans a formidable issue for the presidential campaign of 1916. However, it would be inaccurate to say that only political
considerations shaped his thinking on the subject after the *Lusitania* crisis.
He knew the weaknesses of the American military establishment better
than most other men. He knew the disadvantage of dealing from weakness
in diplomacy. On July 21, 1915, therefore, he requested his secretaries of
war and of the navy to recommend programs that would satisfy the needs
of national security.
    The general board of the navy proposed adoption of a long-range naval
construction program to give the United States equality with Great Britain
by 1925. The Army War College proposed a substantial increase in the
regular army, scrapping the National Guard, and creation of a volunteer
national reserve—a so-called Continental Army—of 400,000 men as the
first line of defense. The president presented this as the administration's

program in an address on November 4, 1915, and in so doing set off one of the most violent political controversies of the decade.

The issues went deeper than any mere difference of opinion over military policy. The great majority of American progressives were obsessed with a passion for domestic social and economic reform. They believed that wars were always caused by bankers, industrialists, and scheming diplomats. Inevitably they reacted with startled indignation to the president's proposals. To them Wilson was at best a dupe, at worst, a turncoat willing to betray the cause of progressivism and convert the country into an armed camp. Led by Bryan and numerous peace organizations, antipreparedness spokesmen launched a campaign with a powerful appeal to workingmen and farmers.

A group of some thirty to fifty Democrats in Congress, most of them Southerners and Westerners, formed an antipreparedness bloc to wrest control of policy from the president. Through a member of their group, Claude Kitchin of North Carolina, House majority leader, Democratic antipreparedness congressmen were able to pack the key House military affairs committee when Congress met in December 1915. They were immovable when Secretary of War Lindley M. Garrison urged the most important feature of the army's reorganization plan—abandonment of the National Guard and creation of the new Continental Army. The administration and the House Democratic leaders were in hopeless deadlock by the middle of January 1916. Wilson decided to carry the issue to the people. In an extended speaking tour in late January and early February he urged preparedness as a national cause and pleaded for the Continental Army plan. He returned to Washington on February 4, however, to find his Democratic opponents more inflexible than before. Consequently Wilson yielded to the House leaders in order to obtain any legislation, and this provoked Secretary Garrison to resign on February 10. He was succeeded by the less intransigent Newton D. Baker of Cleveland, a progressive opponent of preparedness.

Garrison's resignation cleared the road, and the House adopted an army reorganization bill on March 23, 1916. It merely increased the regular army from 100,000 to 140,000 men and enlarged and brought the National Guard under control of the War Department. Then came the *Sussex* crisis. As the nation waited for word of peace or war from Berlin, preparedness champions in the Senate pushed through a measure that embodied most of the Army War College's proposals, including a Continental Army. But the *Sussex* crisis had passed by the time the House and Senate conferees resolved their differences in mid-May, and the measure that they had approved embodied mutual concessions. The Army Reorganization bill, which Wilson signed on June 3, 1916, increased the regular army to 11,327 officers and 208,338 men; integrated the National Guard into the national defense structure and increased its authorized strength; and permitted the War Department to establish a number of volunteer summer training camps.

Meanwhile, the naval affairs committees of the two houses had been biding their time. Although most progressives in principle opposed unusual naval expansion, they concentrated their main energies on the army bill. The House on June 2, 1916, approved a bill that ignored the administration's request for a five-year building program but actually provided more tonnage than Secretary of the Navy Josephus Daniels had requested for the first year. The Senate went even further and adopted a bill on July 21 that provided for completion of the five-year building program in three years. Up to this time the president had not interfered in the course of naval legislation. Now he used all his influence to persuade the House leaders to accept the Senate bill. The House capitulated on August 15, 1916, by accepting the important provisions of the Senate measure without altering a word.

The last victory belonged to the antipreparedness radicals in finding new revenues to pay for military and naval expansion. Conservatives proposed to meet the entire cost by a bond issue and increased consumption taxes. Spokesmen of progressive, farm, and labor groups were up in arms, demanding that the wealthy classes, whom they blamed for forcing preparedness on the country, pay the full bill. This ground swell had an immediate impact on the southern and western Democrats who controlled the House ways and means committee. Their measure, adopted by the House on July 10, doubled the normal income tax without lowering exemptions; raised the maximum surtax from 6 to 10 percent; levied a tax of from 1 to 8 percent on gross receipts of munitions manufacturers; imposed a new federal estate tax ranging from 1 to 5 percent; and repealed special consumption taxes that had been imposed in 1914. In the Senate, midwestern progressives like George W. Norris of Nebraska and Robert M. La Follette forced even further changes,[3] so that the Revenue Act of 1916 represented a frank effort to "soak the rich." It was populism and Bryanism finally triumphant—the first important victory in the equalitarian attack on privileged wealth in the United States.

5. *The Campaign and Election of 1916*

Not since 1910 had the American political scene seemed so confused as during the early months of 1916. The president's preparedness program and his stand on armed ships had nearly disrupted the Democratic party. On the other hand, Republicans were even more divided than their opponents. The eastern wing of the GOP was demanding tremendous military

[3]The Senate increased the surtax to a maximum of 13 percent; levied a new tax on corporation capital, surplus, and undivided profits; increased the estate tax to a maximum of 10 percent; and increased to 12½ percent the maximum tax on munitions manufacturers. All these amendments were accepted by the House.

and naval increases, and the eastern leaders, Roosevelt, Elihu Root, and Henry Cabot Lodge, were beginning a fierce denunciation of the president for his allegedly cowardly refusal to defend American rights on the seas and in Mexico. In contrast, the great majority of midwestern Republican voters and leaders bitterly opposed further preparedness and wanted peace even at the price of abandoning rights on the seas.

Democrats closed ranks after Wilson's surrender during the battle over the army bill and after the peaceful settlement of the *Sussex* crisis. It was obvious by the middle of May that there would be no Democratic rupture, although it was not yet clear what position that party would take on foreign policy during the coming campaign. The key to the future was the alignment of former Progressives—whether they would follow Roosevelt back into the Republican party or would be won to the Democratic party by Wilson's espousal of advanced progressive measures (pp. 125–128).

The chief task before the Republicans was to find a candidate and write a platform that would hold the conservative East without alienating the progressive, pacifistic Midwest and West. At the Republican National Convention that opened in Chicago on June 8, 1916, the party managers rejected Roosevelt, who had made a hard fight for the nomination, and chose instead Charles Evans Hughes, former governor of New York and now an associate justice of the Supreme Court. Adoption of a platform demanding "a straight and honest neutrality" and only "adequate" preparedness was, in the circumstances, an outright repudiation of Roosevelt's demands for a strong policy toward Germany and an effort to appease both the Middle West and the important German-American element. Roosevelt was disgruntled and disappointed, but he was so eager to avoid another four years of what he called Wilson's cowardly infamy that he disbanded his Progressive party and took to the field for Hughes.

The Democrats assembled in national convention in St. Louis on June 14. They dutifully approved the platform that Wilson and his advisers had prepared;[4] and they cheerfully renominated the president on June 15. Otherwise Wilson's plans for the convention went awry. He had planned that the convention should make "Americanism" and patriotism the keynotes of the coming campaign. Instead, the convention gave one long and tremendous ovation for peace, as delegates stormed and demonstrated when speakers extolled Wilson's success in keeping the country out of war.

The campaign that followed was full of strange surprises, but soon a clear pattern of issues emerged. Hughes tried to avoid a straightforward discussion of neutrality and was unable to attack the Democratic reforms of the past three years without seeming reactionary. He finally concen-

---

[4]The Democratic platform made an open bid for Progressive support by promising adoption of an advanced program of federal social legislation, endorsed a neutral foreign policy, and commended the administration's program of "reasonable" preparedness. It also endorsed the proposal then being put forward by various groups for the establishment of a postwar league of nations.

trated his main fire on Wilson's Mexican policy and alleged Democratic inefficiency. Everywhere that he spoke he made votes for Wilson by petty criticisms and failure to offer any constructive alternatives.

Wilson was unable to enter the campaign until September because of a threatened nationwide strike for the eight-hour day by the railroad brotherhoods. He averted this catastrophe by forcing through Congress the Adamson Act, which established the eight-hour day as the standard for all interstate railroad workers. Once this crisis was over, Wilson, on September 23, began a series of speeches that left Republicans dazed. Hughes, thinking that he had finally discovered an issue, denounced the Adamson Act as a craven surrender to the railroad workers. Wilson replied that the eight-hour day was the goal for which all workers should strive. Hughes denounced the Democrats for lacking a constructive program. Wilson replied by pointing to the most sweeping reform program in the history of the country.

Hughes's straddling and Wilson's bold defense of progressivism caused such a division on domestic issues as the country had not seen since 1896. The left wing of the progressive movement, including many Socialists, single taxers, sociologists, social workers, and intellectuals and their journals, moved en masse into the Wilson ranks. Most of the leaders of the Progressive party repudiated Roosevelt and came out for the president. The railroad brotherhoods, the AF of L, and several powerful farm organizations worked hard for the Democratic ticket. Finally, virtually all important independent newspapers and magazines came to Wilson's support. Thus a new political coalition that included practically all independent progressives came into being during the campaign of 1916 as a result of Wilson's and the Democratic party's straightforward espousal of reform legislation.

To interpret this campaign solely in terms of domestic issues, however, would be to miss its chief development: the fusion of progressivism with the peace cause that the president and his campaigners accomplished. Wilson was profoundly impressed by the peace demonstrations at St. Louis at the very time that he was growing suspicious of the Allies. Unhesitatingly, he took personal command of the peace movement. He charged that the Republicans were a war party and that Hughes's election would mean almost certain war with Mexico and Germany. By implication he promised to keep the country out of war. So overwhelming was the response in the Middle West to the peace appeal that Democratic orators took up the battle cry. "He kept us out of war" became the constant refrain of campaign speeches and the chief theme of Democratic campaign literature.

Early returns on election night, November 7, revealed that Hughes had made nearly a clean sweep of the East and the eastern Middle West. But the tide turned suddenly in Wilson's favor as returns from the trans-Mississippi West came in. To the core of the Solid South, Wilson added New

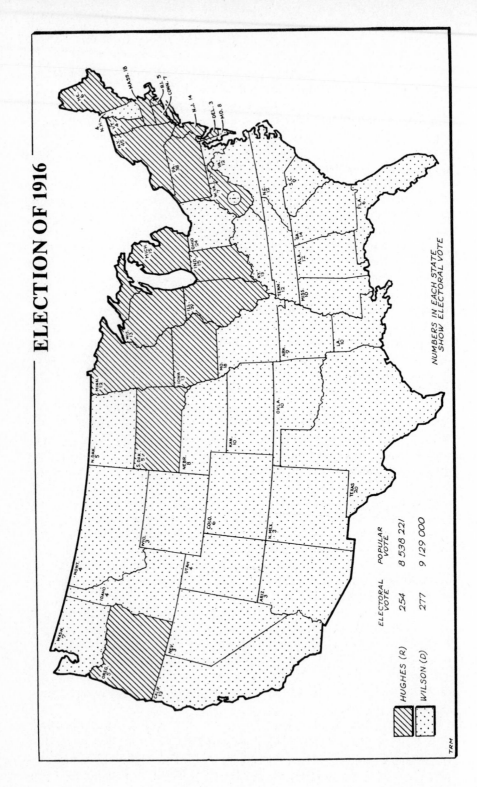

ELECTION OF 1916

NUMBERS IN EACH STATE
SHOW ELECTORAL VOTE

	ELECTORAL VOTE	POPULAR VOTE
HUGHES (R)	254	8 538 221
WILSON (D)	277	9 129 000

TRM

Hampshire, Ohio, Kansas, Nebraska, North Dakota, Montana, Wyoming, Colorado, New Mexico, Arizona, Utah, Nevada, Idaho, Washington, and California—for a total of 277 electoral votes and a majority of 23. He received 9,129,000 popular votes, as against 8,538,221 for Hughes. It was a gain for the president of nearly 3,000,000 votes over 1912.

The causes of Wilson's breath-taking victory became apparent soon after the returns were in. Democratic promises of continued peace, prosperity, and progressive policies won most independents, a large minority of former Progressives, women voters in the suffrage states, and the left wing element that usually voted the Socialist ticket. The defection to Wilson of some 400,000 persons who had voted Socialist in 1912 was alone sufficient to give the president a majority in key states like California. These advanced progressives when added to the normal Democratic minority gave Wilson a bare majority and enabled the Democrats narrowly to control Congress for another two years.

6. The United States Enters the War

Let us now go back to the story of American relations with the belligerents where we left it at the end of the *Sussex* crisis. The *Sussex* pledge greatly relieved the tension in German-American relations, and events soon afterward cast a dark shadow over relations between the United States and Great Britain. To begin with, Sir Edward Grey made it plain during the spring and summer that the Allies would not welcome the president's mediation so long as they had any hope of military victory. To Wilson and House this was a crushing blow, almost a betrayal; they began to suspect that the Allies desired a vindictive peace, not a righteous settlement. Secondly, American opinion was profoundly shocked by the British army's ruthless suppression of the abortive Irish Easter Rebellion of April 24, 1916. "The Dublin executions," observed *The New Republic*, "have done more to drive America back to isolation than any other event since the war began." Really dangerous Anglo-American tension rose during the summer and autumn as the British intensified their economic warfare in a supreme effort to bring all neutral commerce, even shipping, under their control. Against these new infringements of American neutral rights the State Department protested in menacing language, while the president obtained power from Congress in September to use the armed forces against any nation that discriminated against American commerce.

Wilson could neither take steps to bring the British to book nor launch a peace campaign of his own so long as the nation was in the throes of a presidential campaign. Once the election was over, however, he faced a situation that demanded speedy and decisive action. Both sides were now resolved to use their most desperate weapons to break a deadlock that was consuming manpower and resources at a prodigious rate. For Great Britain this meant further intensification of economic warfare. For Germany it meant revoking the *Sussex* pledge and launching a wholesale campaign against maritime commerce.

To preserve American neutrality in the face of an all-out struggle on the seas would be virtually impossible, and yet that was what the American people wanted Wilson to do. The only way to peace and safety, the president knew, was to bring the war to an end. Yet this would be difficult to achieve in view of continued British hostility to peace negotiations. Wilson obviously had no alternative but to seek peace through cooperation with the German government, which, since the end of the *Sussex* crisis, had been urging him to take leadership in a drive for peace. The president informed House and Lansing on November 14 and 15, 1916, that he had decided to try to end the war. But what would happen, House and Lansing asked, if the Germans agreed to a reasonable settlement and the Allies refused? In that event would not the United States be driven into sympathetic alliance with Germany against the Allies? Wilson replied that he was willing to run this risk. He obviously did not think that it was very great.

While Wilson continued these discussions, civilian and military leaders in Berlin concluded that the success of their recent campaign in Rumania had created a situation favorable to a peace move. They drafted terms that would have assured German mastery of Europe; agreed that Wilson should be used only to force the Allies to the peace table and then ignored during the actual conference discussions; and resolved to begin an all-out submarine campaign if their peace move failed. When Wilson did not move quickly enough, the German government, on December 12, invited its enemies to a peace conference.

Wilson backed up the German overture on December 18 by calling upon the belligerents to define the objectives for which they were fighting. He next undertook highly secret negotiations with the German and British governments looking toward peace. The British cabinet sent word that it was willing to negotiate on liberal terms, but the German foreign office was evasive and finally informed the president that it did not desire his presence at the peace table. Meanwhile, Wilson went before the Senate on January 22, 1917, to clarify the American position and to explain what kind of a peace settlement the United States would be willing to help enforce. It had to be a peace among equals, he said, a "peace without victory," without indemnities and annexations.

The tragic irony was that the kind of settlement Wilson outlined was possible only if the German leaders were willing to accept a draw and cooperate with him in forcing the Allies to abandon their own equally extreme objectives. Unfortunately, the men in control of the German government did not trust the American president and had abandoned all hope of peace through negotiation. They gave their answer to Wilson's appeal on January 31, 1917: after February 1 submarines would sink without warning all ships, belligerent and neutral, in a broad zone around Great Britain, France, and Italy, and in the eastern Mediterranean. The German admiralty would allow one American ship to sail weekly between New York and Falmouth, England, provided that the ship was suitably marked.

Wilson in response broke diplomatic relations with Germany on February 3, 1917, but he was still hopeful that the Germans would not carry out their threats against American commerce. He continued to pray during the remainder of February that events would not force the nation into war. Meanwhile, demand for protective arming of American ships grew on all sides as more and more ships stayed at their berths and goods began to pile up in warehouses and on wharves. At first Wilson stubbornly refused, saying that the country was not willing to run the risk of war. However, he received a message from Ambassador Walter Page in London on February 25 that removed all his doubts as to German intentions. It was a dispatch transmitting a message, intercepted and deciphered by the British, from the German foreign secretary, Arthur Zimmermann, to the German minister in Mexico City. In the event that Germany and the United States went to war, Zimmermann's message read, the minister should propose to the Mexican govenment an alliance by which Mexico would join the war against the United States and receive as reward "the lost territory in Texas, New Mexico, and Arizona." Moreover, the minister should request President Carranza to invite Japan to join the new anti-American coalition. Further indication of German intentions came on the same day that Wilson received the Zimmermann telegram, February 25. A submarine sank the British liner *Laconia* without warning off the Irish coast with the loss of American lives.

Wilson on the following day asked Congress for authority, first, to arm American ships for defense and, second, to employ other measures to protect American commerce on the high seas. There was little objection in either house to giving the president authority simply to arm merchantmen. But there was overwhelming opposition to empowering him to wage an undeclared naval war. Wilson tried to force Congress's hand by giving the Zimmermann message to the Associated Press, which published it on March 1. A tremendous surge of anger swept over the country, but a small group of western and southern radicals in the Senate stood firm. Refusing to abdicate the war-making power to the president, this "little group of willful men," as Wilson labeled them, insisted on talking the armed ship bill to death in the closing hours of the Sixty-fourth Congress.

Events from this point on led straight to war. The president announced on March 9 that he would put guns and naval crews on merchant vessels, and then he called Congress into special session for April 16. German submarines on March 18 sank three American merchant vessels with great loss of life. The demand for war, which had heretofore been largely confined to the East, now spread to the South and West. And at this moment of excitement came the first Russian Revolution, which overthrew the autocratic government and established a liberal constitutional regime. To many Americans who had feared Russian anti-Semitism and despotism more than German militarism, the news from Petrograd ended all doubts as to the issues of the war.

The country tottered on the brink of war, but Wilson brooded in hesitation and despair. Yet he finally did accept the decision for war that his advisers were urging upon him. Having moved up the date for the convening of Congress, he went before the joint session on April 2 and asked for a resolution recognizing that a state of war existed as a result of actions of the German government. After recounting the German aggressions against American neutrality, he tried to find moral justification for leading the American people into this "most terrible and disastrous of all wars." The world, he declared, must be made safe for democracy and led to a universal dominion of righteousness through a concert of free peoples. There was opposition in both houses from antiwar progressives, but the Senate approved the war resolution on April 4, and the House concurred two days later.

Who willed American participation? Radicals and Socialists gave an answer in 1917 that was reiterated many times in the 1930s: the United States had been driven to war by businessmen, bankers, and munitions manufacturers. These enemies of the people had worked in devious ways to protect their profitable trade and enormous investments in an Allied victory. Moreover, this argument went on, Americans had been deceived by cunning propagandists into believing that the Allies were fighting for righteous objectives. The basic trouble, professors of international law added, was that the American government had not been truly neutral.

Obviously no such simple generalizations explain the complex causes for the decision for war in 1917. There is no evidence that bankers and businessmen affected that decision in any important way, and the effect of propaganda has been vastly overrated. In the final analysis it was Wilson, influenced by public opinion and his own conception of right and duty, who made the important decisions that shaped American policy. In the beginning he pursued a course of more or less strict neutrality that favored the Allies because the British controlled the seas. Then, as the British rejected his leadership in his drive for peace in the spring and summer of 1916, the president moved toward a policy of independent mediation. The Germans would have found a friend in the White House eager to join hands with them in 1916–1917 if they had wanted a reasonable settlement and evinced a readiness to cooperate in building a peaceful and secure postwar world.

In view of the pacific state of American public opinion and Wilson's own convictions at the beginning of 1917, it is reasonable to assume that there would have been no war between Germany and the United States had the German government stayed at least technically within the bounds of the *Sussex* pledge. The German leaders knew this, just as they knew that their plan for all-out warfare against commerce would inevitably drive the United States to war. But after much doubt and conflict among themselves, they rejected American friendship and cooperation and chose to run the risks of American belligerency because they did not trust Wilson and had concluded that their only hope lay in a desperate bid for all-out victory. In German hands, in the final analysis, lay the decision for war or peace with America.

8

The American
Democracy at War

The American people entered the First World War on a Wilsonian note of idealism, not really knowing what the struggle was about or the objectives for which their new friends and enemies were fighting. A recognition of this fact caused President Wilson to attempt to give a moral and altruistic meaning to American participation, to depict intervention in terms of the strong and pure democracy putting on the breastplate of righteousness to do battle for the Lord.

For their earlier refusal to heed all warnings that they had a vital stake in the outcome of the war, the American people paid a fearful price in divisions and doubts and organized efforts to sell the war to them. Nearly fatal was the almost utter lack of readiness for a great military and industrial effort. American unpreparedness and inability to retaliate had been the key factor in the German decision to launch unrestricted submarine warfare in 1917. More important still, the inability of the United States to throw a powerful army without delay into the battle in France prolonged the war and increased the danger of German victory.

In an astonishing manner, however, the American democracy organized for war. The industrial and military mobilization thus hastily accomplished produced the food, materials, ships, and manpower that tipped the balance and broke the deadlock on the western front in 1918. Let us now see how this was done and at what price.

1. An Army to Save the Allies

Neither Wilson nor his military advisers understood the weakness of the Allied military situation in the spring of 1917. Americans had assumed as a matter of course since 1914 that the Allies would win. Most Americans visualized their contribution in terms only of shipping, naval support, credit, and materials even after it was evident that the United States would enter the war. Allied war missions to Washington soon gave different advice.

Wilson and his advisers were shocked when British and French generals revealed that their governments were beginning to draw upon their last reserves. Fortunately, the Army War College had made plans for raising a large American army. The question of how this army should be raised had been hotly debated in Congress during the months preceding the adoption of the war resolution. And administration and army officials, as well as a large segment of thoughtful opinion, had agreed that conscription offered the only rational and democratic method. Even so, the selective service bill, presented to Congress soon after the adoption of the war resolution, set off a bitter struggle in the House of Representatives. Wilson insisted that conscription was essential to victory. In the end he had his way, although there was a hard struggle over age limits and sale of alcoholic beverages at or near army camps. In the measure that Wilson signed on May 18, 1917, the House won its fight to set the minimum age at twenty-one instead of nineteen, as the army demanded, and the Anti-Saloon League won another victory over Demon Rum.

Secretary of War Newton D. Baker enlisted state and local officials in making the first registration on June 5, 1917, a nationwide demonstration of patriotism. On that date 9,586,508 men between the ages of twenty-one and thirty-one registered without commotion, riot, or organized resistance. Congress on August 31, 1918, expanded the age limits to include all men between eighteen and forty-five. Draft boards registered 24,234,021 men, of whom 6,300,000 were found to be available and 2,810,296 were inducted into the army. In addition, volunteer enlistments in the army, navy, and marine corps brought the total number of men and women under arms by November 1918 to 4,800,000.

For commander of the projected American Expeditionary Force the president and secretary of war turned to Major General John J. Pershing, who had recently commanded the punitive expedition in Mexico. Arriving in Paris on June 14, 1917, to establish the headquarters of the AEF, Pershing quickly realized that the Allies were militarily almost bankrupt and obsessed by a passion for defense. He looked forward to the day when he would command a great fresh army that would lead the British and French out of their trenches. Allied military leaders argued that available American troops should be integrated into the existing defensive structure and subordinated to Allied field commanders. However, Pershing stubbornly insisted on preserving the identity and integrity of his command and even demanded a share of the front. The French command gave him the small and quiet Toul sector east of Verdun to defend with his initial force of 14,500 men.

The Germans began a series of heavy blows in October 1917 that pointed up the urgent need of large American reinforcements and forced the Allied governments to unite effectively for the first time. Following a near rout of the Italian armies by the Germans and Austrians came the triumph of the Bolsheviks in Russia, which raised the possibility that Russia would soon withdraw from the war. The Allied prime ministers assembled in extraordinary conference at Rapallo, Italy, in November 1917 and created a Supreme War Council to sit at Versailles and coordinate and direct military operations. During the next few months Pershing and President Wilson were subjected to heavy pressure by British and French leaders to permit American troops, even troops inadequately trained, to be amalgamated into their armies. Pershing refused, promising that he would have an army of a million men in France by the end of 1918.

It seemed, however, that the Germans would win the war before Pershing's reinforcements could arrive. The imperial army hit hard at the British Fifth Army in the valley of the Somme on March 21, 1918, and rolled it back. The Allied leaders and President Wilson hastily elevated Marshal Ferdinand Foch to the post of supreme commander five days later, and

THE UNITED STATES ARMY
IN WORLD WAR I

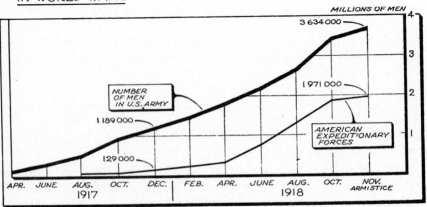

Pershing offered his four divisions for use anywhere on the front. The Germans renewed their offensive against the British on April 9, captured enormous quantities of booty and 60,000 prisoners, but failed to break the British lines. The German forces then turned hard against the French on May 27 and pushed to Château-Thierry on the Marne, only fifty miles from Paris. Foch on May 31 sent the American Second Division and several regiments of marines to bolster French colonial troops in this sector, and American troops for the first time participated in an important way. They pushed the Germans back across the Marne at Château-Thierry and cleared the enemy out of Belleau Wood from June 6 to 25.

The German general staff began its last great drive—to break through the Marne pocket between Rheims and Soissons and reach Paris—on July 15. Some 85,000 Americans were engaged in this battle. The German thrust was quickly parried, and the force of the German drive was spent by July 18. Foch then began a counteroffensive against the weak western flank of the German line from the Aisne to the Marne, between Rheims and Soissons. In this engagement, which lasted until August 6, eight American divisions and French troops wiped out the German salient. British and French armies, reinforced by new American divisions, shortly afterward began offensives that did not end until they neared the Belgian frontier in November.

American soldiers began to pour into France in large numbers while Foch was mounting his offensive mainly with British and French troops. The American First Army, 550,000 strong and under Pershing's personal command, was placed in front of the St. Mihiel salient at the southern end of the front on August 10. The Americans pressed forward in the morning of September 12; within three days they had wiped out the German salient and captured 16,000 prisoners and 443 guns. It was the first independent American operation of the war.

The tide was turning rapidly. Pershing had 1,200,000 men, 2,417 guns, and 324 tanks by September 26 and was eager, as he afterward said, "to draw the best German divisions to our front and to consume them." He now hurled his force against the German defenses between Verdun and Sedan. His goal was the Sedan-Mézières railroad, the main supply line for the German forces in this sector. Both sides threw every available man into the battle that raged all during October. The German lines began to crumble on November 1; Americans reached the outskirts of Sedan and cut the Sedan-Mézières railroad on November 7. The American victory in this so-called Meuse-Argonne offensive destroyed a major portion of the German defenses and, coupled with British and French successes in the central and northern sectors, brought the war to an end.

An American tempted to exaggerate his country's contribution to the victory is less inclined to boast when he recalls that only 112,432 Americans died while in service, as compared with 1,700,000 Russians, 1,385,300 Frenchmen, and 900,000 Britons. Belated though it was, the

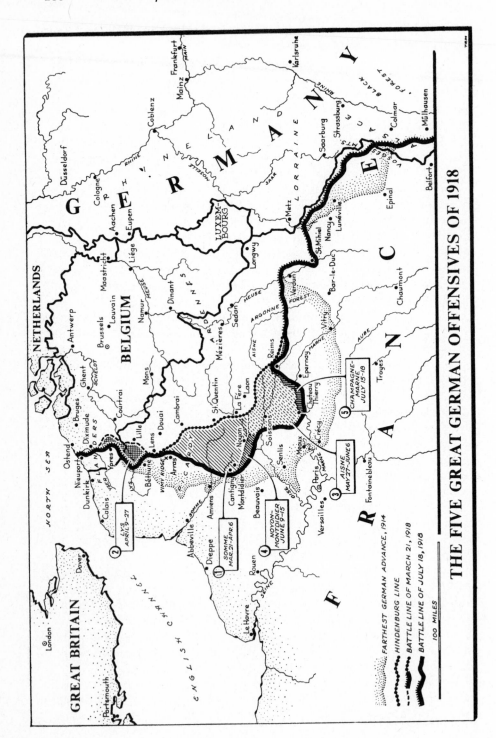

THE FIVE GREAT GERMAN OFFENSIVES OF 1918

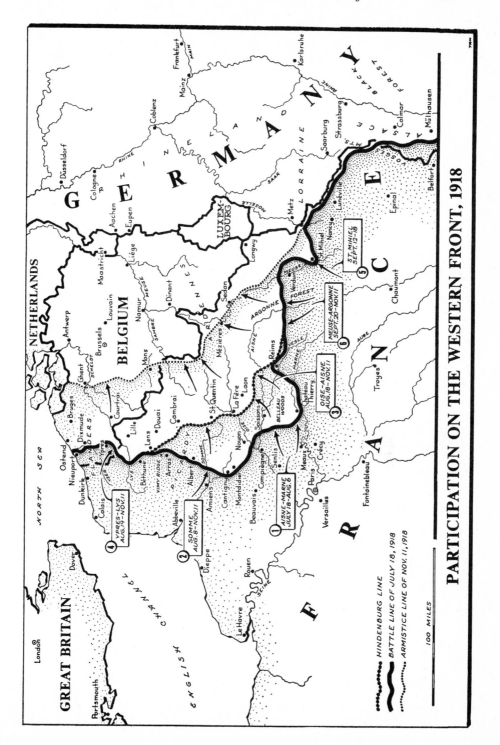

PARTICIPATION ON THE WESTERN FRONT, 1918

American contribution came perhaps in the nick of time to enable the Allies to withstand the last great German assault. On April 1, 1918, at the beginning of the German drive and before the American build-up in France, the Germans had a superiority of 324,000 infantrymen on the western front. By June American reinforcements gave the Allies a majority in manpower. By November the Allied preponderance was more than 600,000 men, enough to overwhelm the German defenses. Americans could rightly say, therefore, that their contribution had at least been decisive.

2. *The United States Navy and the War*

As U-boats set out in February 1917 to destroy all seaborne commerce, the most dangerous threat to the Allied cause came first not on land but on the seas. The German admiralty had calculated that sinkings at the rate of 600,000 tons a month would bring England to her knees within six months, and it seemed for a time that the promise of the U-boat champions would be fulfilled. All told, submarines destroyed more than 6.5 million tons of shipping during 1917, while all American, Allied, and neutral shipyards combined built only 2.7 million tons. "They will win, unless we can stop these losses—and stop them soon," Admiral Jellicoe, first sea lord of the admiralty, told the American liaison admiral in London, William S. Sims, in mid-April 1917.

The adoption of the war resolution found the American navy ready and eager to join the battle. Secretary Daniels and his staff conferred with British and French admirals on April 10 and 11, 1917, and mapped out a preliminary division of duty. The American navy would defend and patrol the Western Hemisphere, while the British fleet would carry the brunt of the antisubmarine campaign in waters around the British Isles with what help the American navy could spare. American assistance was not long in coming. The first six destroyers reached Queenstown, Ireland, on May 4; there were thirty-five American destroyers stationed at that base by July 5; and 383 American craft were overseas by the end of the war.[1]

The British system of defense against submarines in April 1917 consisted of dispersing sea traffic widely and then channeling merchant ships through heavily patrolled waters around the British Isles. The system created a positive deathtrap for merchantmen, as there simply were not enough ships to patrol the area. To the obvious alternative—the convoy system—British naval planners and masters of merchant ships objected, arguing that convoys were slow and merchant ships could not stay in

---

[1] The administration immediately suspended the large building program authorized by the legislation of 1916 and adopted plans in May 1917 for the construction of 250 destroyers and 400 subchasers.

formation. But as the submarine toll mounted a minority in the British admiralty joined Secretary Daniels and Admiral Sims in virtually demanding the use of convoys. Even after the feasibility of the plan had been demonstrated in the latter part of May 1917, the British admiralty contended that it did not have enough warships to use the system generally. However, the American reinforcement of destroyers turned the tide in July, and convoys for merchant ships were begun. The intensified antisubmarine campaign and inauguration of the convoy system were the two decisive factors that brought the U-boats under control. Shipping losses fell from 881,027 tons in April to half that figure in December 1917; and British losses never ran above 200,000 tons a month after April 1918.

The American navy's next task was to transport and supply the AEF. The Navy Department had seven troop and six cargo ships, totaling 94,000 tons, on hand on July 1, 1917. By November 1918 it had created a Cruiser and Transport Force of 143 vessels, aggregating 3,250,000 tons, which carried 911,047 soldiers to France. In addition, every available British transport was pressed into service in the Atlantic Ferry when the need for American manpower grew acute in 1918. Slightly more than 1,000,000 soldiers were carried by British vessels. The troop carriers were so fast and closely guarded by naval escorts that only two of them, both British vessels, were sunk on the eastbound voyage.

The American navy, with more than 2,000 vessels and 533,000 officers and men in service at the end of the war, had attained unparalleled size and fighting effectiveness. By November 1918 American ships were patrolling the far reaches of the Western Hemisphere and cooperating with Japanese and British forces in the Far East, while 834 vessels and 200,000 men were either serving in European waters or else transporting troops and supplies to France. By insisting on the adoption of the convoy system, American naval strategists had made a significant contribution to operations that assured an Allied-American victory at sea. By throwing its destroyers into the campaign against the submarines, the American navy perhaps turned the tide against the U-boats in the first Battle of the Atlantic. And by transporting nearly half the AEF and almost all the army's cargo to France, the navy made possible the defeat of Germany in 1918 instead of 1920, as the Allied leaders had originally planned.

3. The Triumph of a Democratic Tax Policy During Wartime

Americans entered the First World War without the slightest conception of the costs of participation. Although predictions as to long-run costs were impossible, two facts became apparent almost at once. First, the structure of international exchange would collapse and the European Allies would be in desperate straits unless Britain and France received huge credits, not a piddling few hundred million dollars. Second, the Revenue Act of March 3, 1917, which had increased taxes only slightly, was grossly inadequate to meet war needs.

Without opposition a somewhat dazed Congress approved the first War Loan Act on April 23, 1917. It authorized the Treasury to issue $2 billion in short-term notes and $5 billion in bonds, $3 billion of which should be lent to the Allies. Congress added subsequent authorizations as the needs of the American and Allied governments grew, so that the government had borrowed $23 billion on a long-term basis by 1920.

Out of the $33.5 billion that is reckoned as the cost of the war to the American people by 1920, therefore, some $23 billion was charged to future generations, and about $10.5 billion was raised by taxes. Determining how much should be borrowed and how much should be raised by taxes set off protracted struggles in Congress. Conservatives of both parties advocated recourse to consumption taxes, borrowing, and perhaps slight increases in income taxes. Progressives and radicals, on the other hand, believed that the wealthy classes, who had allegedly driven the country to war, should be forced to bear practically the entire cost through extraordinary income, inheritance, and excess profits taxes.

Between these two extremes stood the president, the secretary of the treasury, and a large majority of Congress. Secretary McAdoo at first thought that half the costs could be met by taxation; but he revised his figure downward to 35 percent as expenditures skyrocketed. Congressional leaders finally agreed upon a new War Revenue bill, which Wilson signed on October 3, 1917. It imposed a graduated excess profits tax ranging from 20 to 60 percent; increased the normal income tax to 4 percent for individuals and 6 percent for corporations; and increased the maximum surtax to 63 percent. The measure, moreover, increased excise taxes and imposed new ones on luxuries, services, and facilities. Finally, it increased the estate tax to a maximum of 25 percent.

The War Revenue Act of 1917 imposed 74 percent of the financial burden of the war on large individual and corporate incomes alone. Even so, radicals in the Senate denounced the bill as a betrayal of the people because it failed to confiscate all incomes over $100,000. The appalling way in which expenditures mounted during the early months of 1918 convinced Wilson and McAdoo that their radical critics had at least been partially right. The president appeared before a joint session on May 27, 1918, and urged the imposition of additional levies on incomes, profits, and luxuries. Congress's response, the Revenue Act of 1918, approved by the president on February 24, 1919, increased the prevailing tax burden by almost 250 percent and put four-fifths of the load on large incomes, profits, and estates. The normal tax on individual net incomes up to $4,000 was increased to 6 percent, while all net incomes above $4,000 had to pay a normal tax of 12 percent.[2] An additional surtax ranging up to 65 percent brought the total tax on the largest incomes to 77 percent. In addition, the excess profits tax was increased to a maximum of 65 percent.

The effect of the war revenue legislation can best be seen by comparing the fortunes of the wealthy classes with those of other groups during the war period. The average annual real earnings of workers in manufacturing, transportation, and coal mining were 14 percent higher in 1917 than in 1914 and 20 percent higher in 1918 than in 1914. A rapid increase in agricultural prices also brought new prosperity to farmers. The real income, after taxes, of all persons engaged in farming was 25 percent higher in 1918 than in 1915.

It is instructive to contrast these spectacular economic gains by the large majority of low-income receivers with the fortunes of the upper classes during the war period. To be sure, there were notable cases of "swollen" profits among certain industries, particularly munitions, shipbuilding, and steel; and the number of persons reporting incomes—before taxes—of between $50,000 and $100,000 increased from 5,000 in 1914 to 13,000 in 1918. But the gains of the wealthy classes as a whole were far less important than a few sensational figures would indicate. Total disbursements to owners in manufacturing, measured in terms of real income, increased hardly at all from 1913 to 1916. Real income from property increased about 30 percent in 1917 and then fell back in 1918 almost to the level of 1916. But since the recipients of this income from property paid about seven-eighths of the total personal income taxes in 1917 and 1918, it is evident that they suffered a sizable economic loss as a result of the war.

The old picture of the American upper classes fattening on the nation's misery during wartime is, to say the least, overdrawn. The effect of the tax policies shaped by a progressive administration and majority in Congress was greatly to lighten the relative share of the tax burden carried by the overwhelming majority of Americans, and sharply to increase the burdens of that small minority who had paid only slight taxes before 1916. Thus progressives could boast in 1918 that their leaders were putting democracy to work at home with a vengeance, while American soldiers were fighting to save democracy in Europe.

4. The Mobilization of Industry and Agriculture

Preliminary groundwork for a mobilization of industry had been laid before the United States entered the war. Congress in the preparedness legislation of 1916 had established a Council of National Defense, com-

[2]This rate applied only for the balance of 1918. For subsequent years the normal rate would be 4 percent on net incomes up to $4,000 and 8 percent on all incomes above that figure.

posed of six Cabinet members, and the council's working body, the Advisory Commission, made up of business, industrial, railroad, and labor representatives. The council was armed only with limited authority, but it proceeded to take a complete inventory of America's industrial plant and then to establish, on March 31, 1917, a Munitions Standards Board.

This board was soon reorganized as the General Munitions Board and given control over the purchase and supply of ammunition for the armed forces. But the new agency never established its authority over the armed services and the Allied purchasing commissions, and it was evident by the early summer of 1917 that only a central authority, with far-reaching controls, could bring order out of the prevailing chaos. The Council of National Defense abolished the General Munitions Board on July 28, 1917, and created in its place the War Industries Board (WIB) to serve as a clearing house for purchases, allocate raw materials and control production, and supervise labor relations.

The WIB made rapid progress in many fields of industrial mobilization, but it failed to coordinate military purchases because it lacked direct authority over the War and Navy departments. It seemed that the war effort at home was collapsing. The winter of 1917–1918 was terribly severe. Heavy snows blocked the railroads so frequently that there were fuel shortages in the East and a decline in steel production. Rumors of inefficiency led the Senate military affairs committee to begin a searching investigation in December 1917 of the mobilization effort. It revealed a near breakdown in railroad transportation, confusion in the War Department, and failure to provide adequate shelter and clothing for soldiers in cantonments.

The exposures of the Senate military affairs committee led Republicans to demand establishment of a coalition War Cabinet to take direction of the war effort out of the president's hands. Wilson's answer to this challenge to his leadership was as usual bold. He wrote out a measure—the so-called Overman bill—conferring on himself practically unlimited power to organize and direct the nation's resources. As Congress did not adopt the Overman bill until May, the president summoned Bernard M. Baruch, a Wall Street broker with much experience in the WIB, to the White House on March 4, 1918, and made him chairman. Acting under his emergency war powers, the president also granted sweeping new authority to the agency to conserve resources, advise purchasing agencies as to prices, make purchases for the Allies, and, most important, determine priorities of production and distribution in industry.

Gathering about him one hundred of the ablest businessmen in the country, Baruch soon established the WIB as the most powerful agency in the government, with himself as economic dictator of the United States and, to a large extent, of the Allied countries as well. And before many months had passed the board had harnessed the gigantic American industrial machine, mainly by instituting severe controls over the use of scarce materials, particularly steel, and brought such order into the mobilization effort that criticism almost vanished.

An urgent need in the spring of 1917 was an increased flow of food from the United States to provide the margin between life and death for the British, French, and Italian armies and peoples. The president on May 19, 1917, announced inauguration of a food control program under Herbert Hoover, recently director of the Belgian Relief Commission. Hoover's agency at first acted without legal authority as a subcommittee of the Council of National Defense. However, after a lengthy and bitter debate, Congress on August 10, 1917, adopted the Lever Act, giving the president sweeping authority over production, manufacture, and distribution of foodstuffs, fuel, fertilizers, and farm implements. The measure also empowered the president to institute a limited price control over certain scarce commodities. Wilson created the Food Administration on the day that the Lever bill became law and delegated full authority to Hoover.

The most urgent task in the summer of 1917 was production and control of wheat. Bad weather and an epidemic of black stem rust had caused a sharp decline in the American crop in 1916. The domestic supply was nearly exhausted by January 1917, and the price of wheat was skyrocketing. The Lever Act fixed a minimum price of $2.00 a bushel in order to stimulate production; and the Food Administration, on August 30, 1917, offered to buy the 1917 crop at $2.20 a bushel and established the United States Grain Corporation to purchase and distribute wheat. But 1917 was another poor wheat season, and stocks of bread grains abroad fell below the danger point in early 1918. Only by loyal cooperation from American housewives and the severest economies and controls was Hoover able to find enough wheat to carry Britain and France through the winter. Nature was more bountiful in 1918, and the bumper wheat crop of that year assured a plentiful supply of bread. The Food Administration's second major objective was increased production of hogs, as pork was another important staple in the Allied diet. When Hoover's agency began its work in the spring of 1917, the slaughtering of hogs was running 7 to 10 percent below the figure for the corresponding period in 1916. The Food Administration solved the problem in November 1917 by setting hog prices so high—at $15.50 per hundredweight—that farmers (and hogs) outdid themselves and nearly doubled production in 1918 and 1919.

For over-all accomplishment with a minimum of confusion and direct controls the Food Administration rivaled the reorganized WIB under Baruch's direction. By appealing to American pride and patriotism Hoover persuaded people to tighten their belts on meatless and breadless days. Consequently, the United States was able to export 12,326,914 tons of food in 1917-1918 and 18,667,378 tons in 1918-1919, as compared with an average for the three prewar years of 6,959,055 tons.

5. *Shipping and Railroads*

The British prime minister, David Lloyd George, told a group of Americans in London a few days after the United States entered the war: "The absolute assurance of victory has to be found in one word, ships, in a second word, ships, and a third word, ships." And so it seemed, as submarines took a fearful toll, nearly 900,000 tons of shipping, in that gloomy April of 1917. The Washington administration, however, promised "a bridge of ships" and chartered the Emergency Fleet Corporation, a subsidiary of the United States Shipping Board, on April 16 to build ships faster than submarines could sink them.

The government's shipbuilding program began with great fanfare but soon ran afoul of adversities. In the end it was the most important failure of the American war effort. The heads of the Shipping Board and the Emergency Fleet Corporation quarreled so violently that small progress had been accomplished by July 1917. The president removed them both and gave full power to Edward N. Hurley, energetic chairman of the Federal Trade Commission. Moving with great speed, Hurley began construction of new shipyards along the Atlantic coast; they contained ninety-four shipways and were supposed to produce 15 million tons of shipping. But the Emergency Fleet Corporation had delivered only 465,454 tons of new shipping by September 1918, while the first ship from the corporation's largest shipyard—at Hog Island, near Philadelphia—was not delivered until December 3, 1918.

Meanwhile, the Shipping Board had moved in more fruitful directions to marshal an American merchant marine. First, it seized and put into service ninety-seven German ships in American harbors, totaling more

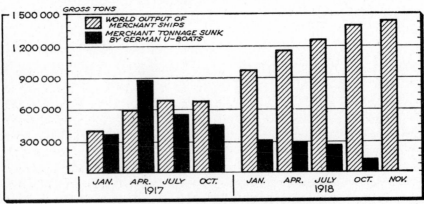

SUBMARINE SINKINGS AND SHIPBUILDING
JANUARY, 1917 TO NOVEMBER, 1918

than 500,000 tons. Second, Hurley on August 3, 1917, commandeered for the Shipping Board the 431 ships, totaling 3 million tons, then under construction in private shipyards. Finally, in March 1918, he seized over half a million tons of Dutch shipping then in American ports. Through purchase, seizure, and requisition, the Shipping Board by September 1, 1918, had acquired the large fleet without which the AEF could never have been transported and supplied.

Organization of American railroads was assumed during most of 1917 by a voluntary Railroads War Board. It worked in cooperation with the Council of National Defense to divide traffic and move troops and army supplies. Struggling under an extraordinary burden and lacking any unified control, the railroads seemed near collapse in December 1917, when snows blocked lines and cold weather froze switches and impeded the operation of terminals. Conditions in the eastern freight yards and ports were nearly chaotic by Christmas. Therefore, the president on December 28, 1917, put all railroad transportation under the control of a United States Railroad Administration headed by William G. McAdoo. By controlling traffic on a rational, nationwide scale, spending more than $500 million for long-needed improvements and equipment, and subordinating passenger traffic to war needs, the Railroad Administration created an efficient national transportation system that met fully the demands of the great military effort of 1918.

6. Government and Labor During Wartime

In no area of public policy was the Wilson administration's determination to reinforce democracy at home during wartime better illustrated than in the field of labor policy. The president and his advisers rejected proposals to conscript labor and refused to allow the machinery of the labor market to regulate wages and hours. Instead, they embarked upon what soon became a comprehensive program designed to guarantee full utilization of manpower without depriving labor of rights and living standards that it had already won.

Like most other wartime policies, the labor program evolved slowly in response to need, experience, and the administration's maturing social conscience. The War and Navy departments had the most immediate and the largest interest in uninterrupted production and could wield direct power over manufacturers and contractors. They moved quickly into the field of labor relations during the first months of the war. There was still a need for unified policies and national direction of the labor administration. Hence the president established the National War Labor Board (WLB) on April 8, 1918, as a supreme court for labor controversies. Under the joint chairmanship of Frank P. Walsh, a distinguished labor lawyer, and former President William H. Taft, the WLB heard 1,251 cases affecting 711,500 workers. Lacking any statutory authority, the board enforced its rulings through the president's war powers. For example, when the Smith & Wesson Arms factory at Springfield, Massachusetts, refused to accept the WLB's decision, the War Department simply commandeered the plant. On the other hand, when workers in the munitions factories in Bridgeport, Connecticut, threatened to strike rather than accept the board's award, the president wrote a sharp letter to the Machinists' union at Bridgeport, telling members that they could either work or fight.

The members of the WLB soon discovered that they were actually more a policy-making than an arbitral body; yet they often had to decide labor policies on a basis of insufficient information and without knowing the needs of the country as a whole. To fill the need for a scientific agency to determine general policies, President Wilson created the War Labor Policies Board in May 1918. Under the direction of Felix Frankfurter the new agency undertook the gigantic task of surveying the whole labor field, standardizing wages and hours, and giving a central direction to the flow of labor. One result was the establishment in the Department of Labor of a United States Employment Service that registered over 5 million workers and placed 3.7 million of them in vital industries.

This, then, was the administrative machinery that mobilized American manpower and inaugurated the most significant and far-reaching social experiment in the history of the United States to that time. In general, the government threw its war power to labor's side and accomplished such sweeping social gains as to warrant the conclusion that a virtual revolution was effected during wartime. A few particulars will illustrate the generalization. All the various administrative boards, for example, recognized and protected the right of workers to organize and bargain collectively. As a result, total membership of the AF of L grew from 2,072,702 in 1916 to 3,260,168 in 1920. Secondly, the administration compelled the adoption of the eight-hour day when it was possible to do so without disrupting industrial operations. The result was a sharp decline in the hours of labor, from an average of 53.5 per week in 1914 to 50.4 in 1920, while the proportion of wage earners in manufacturing who worked 48 hours or less a week rose from 11.8 percent in 1914 to 48.6 percent in 1919. Thirdly, the War and Navy departments and various labor boards worked diligently to improve conditions of labor and prevent exploitation of women and children by manufacturers with government contracts. Moreover, when the Supreme Court in 1918 invalidated the Child Labor Act of 1916, Congress responded immediately by levying a prohibitive 10 percent tax on products manufactured in whole or in part by children under fourteen. Fourthly, the federal administrators attempted to guarantee all workers under their jurisdiction a living wage, that is, an income sufficient to provide a minimum of health and decency. In the face of a 50 percent increase in the cost of living from 1914 to 1918, such a program involved heroic efforts to keep wages abreast of the rising level of prices. Because of full employment and the vigilance of the war labor agencies, however, the average annual real income of labor increased 14 percent above the pre-war level in 1917 and 20 percent above that level in 1918.

These efforts involved such federal intervention as few progressives had dreamed of before 1917. Under the spur of war necessity, an advanced element in the administration had demonstrated that public control of hours, wages, and working conditions could be effected without enslaving workers or causing undue hardship on management. The experiment was abandoned after the war, to be sure, but a precedent for future action in another dire emergency had been established.

7. Public Opinion and the War

At the outset there was a profound division in public sentiment over American participation in the war. It is impossible to estimate the extent of opposition to the war resolution soon after its adoption. Probably a majority reluctantly accepted it as the only solution, but there were millions of Americans—Socialists, extreme radicals, many progressives, and tens of thousands of German- and Irish-Americans—who still believed that American intervention was the work of an unneutral president and great evil forces that abetted him.[3]

To convert this hostile opinion and educate all citizens to an understanding of American objectives, Wilson, only a week after the adoption of the war resolution, created the Committee on Public Information with George Creel, a progressive journalist from Denver, as head. One of Creel's first official acts was the establishment of a voluntary press censorship that worked remarkably well. He next turned to the more difficult task of making Americans war-conscious; before the war had ended he had mobilized 150,000 lecturers, writers, artists, actors, and scholars in the most gigantic propaganda campaign in American history.

As a consequence an official line was sold to the American people. One side of the propaganda glorified American participation in terms of an idealistic crusade to advance the cause of freedom and democracy throughout the world—a concept that the president reiterated in 1917 and 1918. The other side portrayed the German menace in striking colors, in terms of the Hun attempting to despoil Europe and extend his dominion to

---

[3] The Socialist party before its suppression was the only important organization that opposed the war effort. Socialist mayoralty candidates in 1917 polled 22 percent of the popular vote in New York City, nearly 34 percent in Chicago, 44 percent in Dayton, Ohio, and 25 percent in Buffalo—an impressive indication of the extent of popular feeling against participation.

the Western Hemisphere. Although the Creel committee rejected the cruder atrocity stories, it appropriated and spread many of the official Allied atrocity charges.

The Creel committee's efforts to make Americans war- and security-conscious came at a time when they were already distraught by rumors of disloyalty, espionage, and sabotage. The result of Creel's propaganda, and even more of the agitation of volunteer organizations like the National Security League and the American Protective League, was to stimulate such an outbreak of war madness as the country had never before witnessed. Most of the hysteria was turned against German-Americans, all things German, and the antiwar radicals and progressives. Each state had a committee of public safety, with branches in every county and city; and in many areas these committees were not much better than vigilante groups. It was they who conducted reigns of terror against German-Americans, especially in Montana, Minnesota, and Wisconsin. La Follette, as the leader of the progressives who voted against the war resolution, was burned in effigy in Madison, expelled from the Madison Club, and publicly censured by most of the faculty of his beloved University of Wisconsin. The climax came when the Minnesota Public Safety Committee demanded his expulsion from the Senate.

As one historian has shrewdly observed, the majority of Americans in their hatred of things German lost not only their tolerance but their sense of humor as well. Statues of heroes like Von Steuben and Frederick the Great were taken from their pedestals. Many states forbade the teaching of German or church services conducted in German. Sauerkraut was renamed "liberty cabbage," German measles, "liberty measles." The crowning blow came when Cincinnati ruled pretzels off free lunch counters in saloons.

8. *Civil Liberties During Wartime*

All governments try to protect themselves against enemies from within as well as from without during extreme crises. To Wilson and other administration leaders it was an absurd situation when the federal government could force men to fight and give their lives for their country and yet could not punish persons who attempted to obstruct the war effort or gave aid and comfort to the enemy without violating the law of treason.[4] The president's answer to opponents of the war was the Espionage Act of June

---

[4]Several Civil War statutes, still on the books in 1917, prohibited conspiracies to resist recruiting and persuade men to resist the draft; but these laws did not affect individuals. The only statute applying to individuals was the treason law, which applied only to treasonable acts, not utterances, and was extremely difficult to enforce.

15, 1917. It provided imprisonment up to twenty years and/or a fine up to $10,000 for persons who willfully made false reports to help the enemy, incited rebellion among the armed forces, or attempted to obstruct recruiting or the operation of the draft. An equivalent of censorship appeared in a section empowering the postmaster general to deny the use of the mails to any matter which, in his opinion, advocated treason, insurrection, or forcible resistance to the laws of the United States. Postmaster General Albert S. Burleson of Texas had been a staunch supporter of Wilson's policies, but he was neither tolerant nor discriminating in judgment, and he used his vast new power to establish a capricious censorship. For example, he banned the *American Socialist* from the mails soon after the passage of the Espionage Act. Two other leading Socialist publications, *The Masses* and Victor Berger's daily *Milwaukee Leader*, fell under the Texan's ban in August and October 1917.

In effect the Espionage Act became a tool to stamp out dissent and radical, but never conservative, criticism. As one authority has observed, "It became criminal to advocate heavier taxation instead of bond issues, to state that conscription was unconstitutional though the Supreme Court had not yet held it valid, to say that the sinking of merchant ships was legal, to urge that a referendum should have preceded our declaration of war, to say that war was contrary to the teachings of Christ. Men have been punished for criticising the Red Cross and the Y.M.C.A."[5] A movie producer, Robert Goldstein, was sentenced to prison for ten years for displaying a movie about the American Revolution that allegedly incited hostility against an associate of the United States. The most famous case involved Eugene V. Debs, the leader of the Socialist party. Debs expressed his frank revulsion at the war in a speech before a Socialist convention in Canton, Ohio, on June 16, 1918. He was speedily brought to trial and sentenced to a term of ten years in federal prison.

In all fairness it should be said that the administration was not responsible for the excesses of this legal witch hunt. Indeed, President Wilson courageously headed off a movement to have so-called traitors tried and punished by military courts. The excesses were the outcome largely of the hysteria and maelstrom of hatred that converted district attorneys, judges, and juries into persecutors of a dissenting minority. Federal judges in the North had stood forthrightly, although usually vainly, during the Civil War in defense of civil liberties against encroachments by the military commanders. However, the federal courts provided no effective defense during the First World War against the momentary madness of the majority. None of the sedition cases reached the Supreme Court until after the war was over. But in *Schenck* v. *United States*, 1919, Justice Oliver Wendell Holmes, speaking for a unanimous court, upheld the Espionage Act. Schenck had admittedly counseled resistance to the draft. In ordinary

[5]Zechariah Chafee, Jr., *Freedom of Speech in the United States* (Cambridge, Mass., 1941), p. 51.

times, Holmes said, such action would have been legal. In wartime, however, Congress had power to prevent utterances that might constitute a "clear and present danger" and provoke evils that Congress had a right to prevent.

The government's power over thought and utterance was inevitably gradually enlarged, not diminished, as the war progressed. The Trading-with-the-Enemy Act of October 6, 1917, empowered the president to censor all international communications and gave the postmaster general sweeping powers of censorship over the foreign-language press in the United States. Still the attorney general claimed that he lacked a means to check disloyalty and asked Congress for broader authority. Congress moved again in April and May 1918, but not so much in response to the attorney general's request as in reaction to two developments that had shaken the country during preceding months.

The first of these was the government's suppression of the Industrial Workers of the World, a left wing union which, as we have seen, functioned mainly among western lumbermen, miners, and agricultural workers. The IWW conducted a violent campaign during the first eight months of 1917 against the copper companies, especially the Anaconda in Montana and Arizona. The production of vital copper began to decline precipitously, and the Justice Department moved swiftly. Federal agents raided IWW offices throughout the West on September 5, 1917, and arrested the union's leaders. Nearly one hundred of them were subsequently tried, convicted, and imprisoned.

The second development was the mounting of war hysteria during the preceding winter, especially in states like Montana and Minnesota, where the IWW and German-Americans were an important element. The Montana legislature met in special session February 1918 to consider the crisis; and Governor Samuel V. Stewart signed a criminal syndicalism act on February 21. It prohibited any language calculated to bring the American Constitution, form of government, flag, or armed forces into disrespect or contempt.

Spurred by appeals from the West, Congress succumbed to the clamor for legislation against sabotage and sedition. The Sabotage Act, approved April 20, 1918, was aimed at the IWW and made willful sabotage of war materials, utilities, and transportation facilities federal crimes. The Sedition Act, signed by the president on May 16, 1918, was modeled after the Montana statute and supported chiefly by senators from the Rocky Mountain states. The Espionage Act had empowered the government to punish seditious utterances only if it could prove that injurious consequences would result directly from such utterances. The Sedition Act, in contrast, extended the power of the United States over speech and printed opinion, regardless of consequence. It forbade disloyal, profane, scurrilous, or abusive remarks about the form of government, flag, or uniform of the United States, or any language intended to obstruct the war effort in any way. In addition, the postmaster general was empowered to deny the use of the mails to any person who, in his opinion, used the mail service to violate the Sedition Act.

All told, 2,168 persons were prosecuted and 1,055 were convicted under the Espionage and Sedition acts, sixty-five for threats against the president, and only ten for actual sabotage. But this reckoning gives little indication of the extent to which suppression of dissent was carried out by organized groups who lynched, whipped, tarred and feathered, or otherwise wreaked vengeance on labor radicals, German-Americans, or any persons suspected of disloyalty. In retrospect, the war hysteria seems the most fearful price that the American people paid for participation in the First World War.

9

The Great Crusade

Ends in a Separate Peace

We can see in retrospect that the participation of the United
States in the First World War restored a preponderance of strength to the
Atlantic powers, but that Britain and France were more severely weakened by the war than was Germany. We can also see that a future preponderance of the Atlantic community depended upon the continued active
participation of the United States in the western coalition. In other words,
the future peace of the world depended upon the willingness of the
American people to maintain a new Anglo-French preponderance of
power, at least until a genuine world concert could come into being.

Wilson and perhaps a majority of thoughtful Americans realized this
fact in 1919 and 1920. Many Americans, however, were unprepared to
assume the duties of leadership that circumstances seemed to demand.
When the Paris Peace Conference gave birth not to a Wilsonian millennium, but to a settlement that seemed to embody many of the old evils
that they had fought to destroy, American crusaders by the thousands
turned into cynics and wished only to abandon Europe to an inevitable
self-destruction. But this disillusionment over the Treaty of Versailles was
not the only factor in the rejection by the American people of leadership

in world affairs. Historic and powerful isolationist sentiments revived in full force once the war was over and provided an ideological frame of reference to which opponents of the treaty could appeal. Old anti-British animosities found a more virulent expression for having been suppressed during the war, while various national groups rebelled against aspects of the treaty. But the most fatal and decisive development was the manner in which the question of a peace settlement was subordinated, by Democrats and Republicans alike, to partisan ambitions. This was the factor chiefly responsible for the failure of the treaty in the United States.

The story we are about to relate has about it many elements of high tragedy. A concert of free peoples and the greatest aggregation of military power the world had yet seen ended in bitter and inglorious rupture, and a chain of events was set in motion that led to the Second World War.

1. The Formulation of the Liberal Peace Program

The formulation of the liberal peace program illustrates the way in which thoughtful minorities affect the course of history. Groups of intellectuals and humanitarians in all western European nations not long after the out-break of the war began to study prevention of future wars. Their remedy called for open diplomacy, an end to antagonistic balances of power, no postwar indemnities or annexations, self-determination for subject nation-alities, democratic control of foreign policies, freedom of the seas, and disarmament on land. Their suggestions were causing a tremendous fer-ment by the spring of 1916. An American counterpart was the League to Enforce Peace, organized in June 1915. It numbered among its leaders former President Taft, President A. Lawrence Lowell of Harvard, and Hamilton Holt, editor of *The Independent*, and it proposed a powerful international organization to preserve peace.

The most important moment in the peace movement came when Wil-son espoused the league idea and the liberal peace program. The president had refused before 1916 to make any public comment on the causes of the war or proposals for a settlement. But in a speech before the League to Enforce Peace in Washington on May 27, 1916, he came out boldly in support of American participation in a postwar association to maintain freedom of the seas and the territorial integrity of its members. When this momentous declaration evoked much favorable comment and little criti-cism, Wilson incorporated the league concept in the Democratic platform and made it a leading issue in the ensuing presidential campaign of 1916.

Encouraged by a favorable popular response, Wilson next conjoined the league concept to the liberal peace program in his "Peace without Vic-tory" speech to the Senate on January 22, 1917. He reaffirmed his belief that the American people were prepared to join a postwar League of Nations and help maintain peace. He went further, however, and for the first time outlined in general terms the kind of peace that the American people would be willing to help enforce. It was a settlement giving independence to the Poles and autonomy to oppressed nationalities, guaranteeing freedom of the seas, and substituting a world community of power for the old system of a divided Europe. This would be a peace without great indemnities and annexations, except—and this could only be inferred from the address—perhaps to return Alsace-Lorraine to France and give Russia access to the Mediterranean.

There can be no doubt that Wilson believed that this was the only kind of peace worth fighting for because it was the only kind of peace that would endure. Yet he let the opportunity pass to obtain such a settlement when he might have won it most easily—during the anxious two months before the American war resolution. Failing to use American intervention as a bargaining weapon for peace objectives that the United States could approve, he permitted the country to drift into war merely to defend highly questionable maritime rights.

His second mistake was nearly as damaging. Wilson from the beginning of American belligerency insisted on maintaining the fiction that the United States was carrying on a private war with Germany, as an associate but not an ally of the Entente, presumably free to withdraw when it had won its objectives. This thinking was unrealistic, for after April 6, 1917, the United States and the Allied countries had to make war together, win together, and make peace together.

This became apparent soon after the American declaration of war, when the president and Allied leaders first discussed a possible settlement. Certainly after his talks with the British foreign secretary, Arthur Balfour, in late April 1917, Wilson knew the terms of some of the secret treaties that the Allied governments had concluded for the division of German and Austro-Hungarian territory and colonies. He knew also that he faced an inevitable showdown on the whole subject of peace terms. On several occasions he attempted to broach the subject with the British and French and was diverted from his efforts by warnings that such talk would cause a fatal division in the face of the impending German onslaught on the western front. Wilson comforted himself with the thought that he could *force* Britain and France to accept his terms after the war was over. "By that time," he predicted, "they will among other things be financially in our hands."

Unable, as he thought, to come to definite agreement with the Allied governments and acting in response to demands at home and abroad for a clear statement of war aims, Wilson launched his own campaign for a liberal and just peace settlement. The opening note of this campaign, the Fourteen Points address, came in response to the direst catastrophe that had befallen the Allies since the beginning of the war. The Bolsheviks overthrew the socialistic Kerensky government in November 1917, appealed to war-weary peoples to put an end to the fighting, and announced their intention to expose the Allied governments by publishing their secret agreements on war aims. Failing to receive any response to these moves, the Bolsheviks opened separate peace negotiations with Germany.

Some answer had to be made. The American people, Wilson said, would not fight for "any selfish aim on the part of any belligerent." After trying vainly to persuade the Interallied Conference in Paris to formulate a reply, Wilson set himself independently to the task on January 5, 1918. Three days later he went before a joint session of Congress to announce the peace program for which the United States and the Allies were fighting. It was enumerated in fourteen points. The first five were general and called for open diplomacy, freedom of the seas "alike in peace and in war," removal of artificial trade barriers, reduction of armaments, and an "absolutely impartial adjustment of all colonial claims." Point 6 demanded the evacuation of Russia by German forces and self-determination for the Russian peoples. Points 7 and 8 called for German evacuation of Belgium and France and proposed the return of Alsace-Lorraine to France. Point 9 called for the readjustment of Italy's boundary along the clear line of nationality. Point 10 called for autonomy for the subject nationalities of Austria-Hungary. Point 11 called for the evacuation and restoration of Rumania, Serbia, and Montenegro. Point 12 called for autonomy for the subject peoples of the Ottoman empire. Point 13 called for the creation of a free and independent Poland with access to the sea. For the end the president saved the capstone, Point 14: "A general association of nations . . . affording mutual guarantees of political independence and territorial integrity to great and small states alike."

The Fourteen Points at once became the great manifesto of the war. Enthusiastically received by liberal and labor groups in the United States and the Allied countries, the outlined peace program also had a powerful appeal to the German people. Wilson had promised not the destruction of Germany but the welcoming of a democratized Reich into the new concert of power. Although the Allied leaders used the Fourteen Points as a weapon of war, they gave no indication that they were willing to adopt them, verbatim, as a basis for peace. Nonetheless, Wilson intensified his campaign for a liberal peace all during the spring and summer of 1918.

2. Armistice: 1918

Wilson's opportunity to take command of armistice negotiations arose as a result of the weight of the Allied-American offensive on the western front that began in July 1918. General Ludendorff, one of the German supreme commanders, demanded on September 29 and October 1 that the imperial civil authorities obtain an armistice immediately. A new chancellor, Prince Max of Baden, a liberal antimilitarist, was at this moment in process of forming a new government. When the high command warned that the army could not hold long enough to permit protracted negotiations, Prince Max appealed to President Wilson on October 3 for an armistice based on the Fourteen Points and subsequent Wilsonian pronouncements.

There were demands for driving straight to the Rhine, but Wilson resolved to end the fighting, provided an effective German surrender could be obtained. Actually, Ludendorff and the other German leaders hoped to use the supposedly simple Wilson to win the respite that they needed in order to prepare defense of the Fatherland. Wilson's reply to Prince Max's appeal revealed that the president understood German purposes. The United States was ready to consider peace negotiations, Wilson wrote on October 8, but only if the Central Powers would evacuate Belgium and France and give adequate guarantees that they would not resume hostilities—in other words, if Germany was prepared to admit defeat. Furthermore, Wilson added, he would negotiate only with a responsible, legitimate civilian government, not with the military masters of Germany.

Prince Max replied on October 12, assuring Wilson that he spoke in the name of the German people, accepting the Fourteen Points, and suggesting that a mixed commission be established to supervise the evacuation of France and Belgium. The president responded on October 14. Rejecting the suggestion of a mixed commission, he made it clear that the only kind of armistice that he would approve was one that guaranteed the present supremacy of the American and Allied armies. This note fell like a bolt in Berlin. The German commanders were now all for fighting to the last man. At the same time, it was evident that the morale of the German people was destroyed beyond repair, and the civilian government finally took control. Prince Max informed Wilson on October 20 that Germany accepted the president's conditions.

Convinced that the German peace appeal was sincere, Wilson replied on October 23 that he would transmit that appeal to the Allied governments and discuss with them the question of an armistice. Agreement on the military and naval terms had been reached by the evening of November 4 by the Supreme War Council, the Interallied Naval Council, Colonel House, representing President Wilson, and the British, French, and Italian premiers. In the meantime, events were transpiring within Germany that made acceptance of almost any terms by the German authorities inevitable. Wilson's message of October 23 to Prince Max had contained the hint that a German republic would fare better at the peace conference than an imperial Germany. Feeling in civilian and military circles reached such a point that the emperor abdicated and fled to Holland on November 8. The lowering of the imperial standards so shattered the army's morale that Germany was afterward incapable of waging even a purely defensive war.

Meanwhile, discussions in the Allied camp had brought Allied and American differences over peace terms sharply into the open. Believing that he had now or never to win Allied approval of his peace program, Wilson sent Colonel House to Paris to enforce a showdown with the Allied premiers. At the first conference on October 29 the Allied spokesmen claimed that they did not know what the Fourteen Points were. House read them. David Lloyd George, the British prime minister, refused point blank to accept Point 2 regarding freedom of the seas; the French and Italian leaders concurred. House replied that the president might feel compelled to lay the matter before the American people and make a separate peace if his colleagues refused to accept the Fourteen Points. He reiterated this warning on the following day and headed off a whole host of French and Italian objections.

The Allied leaders surrendered for the moment in the face of this threat, but not until the president had agreed that the British might reserve freedom of action on Point 2, and that the Germans should be told that they would be required to pay reparations for all civilian damages caused by their aggression. The Supreme War Council approved the compromise on November 4. On the following day Wilson informed the German government that Marshal Foch was ready to receive its representatives. German delegates met the French marshal and a British naval representative in Foch's headquarters in a railroad car in Compiègne Forest on November 8. At 5:15 on the morning of November 11 they signed articles providing for a rapid withdrawal of the German armies beyond the right bank of the Rhine, surrender of a huge quantity of matériel and 150 submarines, and withdrawal of the German surface fleet to the Baltic.

3. Preliminaries to the Peace Conference

The president would need the full support of the American people in the months following the armistice if he was to win the peace settlement that he had set his heart upon. But he could have overwhelming support at home only if he continued to be the spokesman of the entire country, of Republican moderates as well as Democrats of good will. In this situation, which demanded adroit and national leadership, Wilson so failed to unite the country that it was doubtful whether he spoke for a majority of his people when the peace conference opened.

He made his first mistake even before the guns were silenced on the western front, at the close of the hotly contested off-year congressional campaign. Importuned on all sides by Democratic congressional and senatorial nominees for individual endorsements such as he had given many times before, Wilson decided to issue a blanket appeal to the country. Instead of asking voters to elect candidates who would support him regardless of party affiliation, he made a frankly partisan appeal for a Democratic Congress on October 25, 1918. "The return of a Republican majority to either House of the Congress," he said, "would . . . certainly be interpreted on the other side of the water as a repudiation of my leadership." It was an invitation to disaster. By attempting to make political capital out of foreign policy, Wilson outraged the numerous Republicans whose support had made his war measures possible and threw the question of the peace settlement into the arena of partisan discussion. Even worse, Wilson had declared that he would stand repudiated in the eyes of the world if the people did not vote the Democratic ticket. He had asked for a vote of confidence when he should have known that such a vote is impossible in the American constitutional system.

It is ironical that Wilson's appeal probably had little effect on the outcome of the elections on November 6. Other factors—business resentment against high taxes, disaffection of western wheat farmers because the administration had put ceilings on wheat prices and allowed cotton prices to rise uncontrolled, all the large and petty irritations that stemmed from the war, and the normal inclination of a majority to vote Republican—these, rather than Wilson's ill-timed and futile appeal, accounted for the Republican victory.[1]

Whether or not he stood repudiated by his own people, President Wilson had to proceed. He went ahead unperturbed, sustained by the conviction that he was the representative not only of the great majority of Americans, but of forward-looking people everywhere. Wilson announced on November 18, 1918, that he would go to the peace conference in Paris as head of the American delegation. Believing as he did that only he could prevail against the forces of greed at Paris, and that the fate of the liberal international program depended upon his presence at the peace conference, Wilson thought that he had no choice in the matter. He went to Paris because stern duty called him there, and whether his decision was a mistake is at least debatable.

Wilson's choice of the peace commissioners was, as things turned out, more obviously a blunder. The commissioners, in addition to the president, were Colonel House, Secretary of State Lansing, General Tasker H. Bliss, a member of the Supreme War Council, and Henry White, an experienced Republican diplomat. They were all able men, but circumstances demanded more than mere ability. Other considerations aside, political necessity demanded appointment of a peace commission that was broadly

---

[1] In the next, or Sixty-sixth, Congress, the Republicans would outnumber the Democrats in the House of Representatives 237 to 190 and have a majority of 2 in the Senate.

representative, for Wilson would fail in the critical period after the peace conference if he could not command the support of the Senate and a large minority of Republicans. Wilson understandably ignored the Senate, because he knew that he would have to include Henry Cabot Lodge of Massachusetts, who would be the new chairman of the foreign relations committee, if he appointed any senators at all. Personal relations between the president and Senator Lodge were already so bad that Lodge's appointment was out of the question. On the other hand, it is difficult to understand why Wilson ignored certain other prominent Republicans, notably William H. Taft, who might have worked loyally with him in Paris. The answer lies perhaps in Wilson's growing realization that the important work would, perforce, have to be done by the heads of government at the conference, and in his belief that he would need a group of advisers whom he could trust absolutely. But by refusing to take prominent Republicans to Paris, Wilson offended the great body of moderate Republicans and lent credibility to the charge then current that he intended to maintain an exclusive Democratic monopoly on peacemaking.

4. The Versailles Compromise

Wilson, the peace commissioners, and a large body of technical experts sailed from New York aboard the *George Washington* on the morning of December 4, 1918. The American delegation, Wilson told the experts assembled on board, would be the only disinterested spokesman at the conference; the Allied leaders did not even represent their own people. "Tell me what's right and I'll fight for it," he promised. The situation in Europe did not, however, portend easy sailing for one who wished merely to fight for the right. England was in the throes of a parliamentary campaign that found Lloyd George and his Conservative-dominated coalition obliged to give hostages to the aroused passions of the electorate. The French were in a state of postwar shock and clamoring for fearful retribution. Italians expected compensation for their losses in the form of large accretions of Austrian territory. Germany was torn by revolt, and the old Austro-Hungarian Empire had already crumbled. Moreover, the meeting place of the conference, Paris, was a hotbed of anti-German hatred. The crippling terms that the Germans had imposed on the Russians in the Treaty of Brest-Litovsk in March 1918 could be used to put aside arguments in favor of greater leniency. At the same time, consideration of long-term issues was handicapped by the immediate fears of the spread of Bolshevism into central and even western Europe. As has often been said, Bolshevism was the ghost that stalked the peace conference. As for Russia, the situation in that country was in so much flux on account of a civil war raging between the Bolsheviks and their enemies, called Whites, that it would be difficult if not impossible for Wilson and Allied leaders to try to vindicate Wilson's earlier demand in his Fourteen Points address for absolute self-determination for the Russian people. All through the early months of 1918, Wilson had sternly vetoed fantastic Anglo-French proposals for intervention in Russia to reestablish the eastern front. Under intense Allied pressure, Wilson, in August 1918, had reluctantly dispatched about 5,000 troops to join British forces at Murmansk to guard military supplies there against possible capture by the Germans. He had also sent a force of some 10,000 men under General William S. Graves to Vladivostok to keep the door of escape open for a sizable Czech army fleeing eastward from the Bolsheviks. More important, this force was also to keep an eye on the Japanese, who sent some 73,000 troops into Siberia.

The British and French later sent large forces into Russia to bolster the Whites—action that proved in the end to be totally futile. But beyond this limited action, which we have already described, Wilson would not go. Throughout the peace conference he stoutly rejected all proposals for cooperative military Allied-American intervention in Russia. The Russian people, he insisted, should be given the right to settle their own problems in their own way. Moreover, while avowing his hostility to revolutionary communism, he also said that the Russian Revolution was an authentic social and economic revolt against centuries-old oppression and injustice, and that it would be impossible to turn it back by military force.

Wilson first made triumphal tours of Paris, London, and Rome. He then returned to Paris on January 12, 1919, for discussions with the Allied leaders, who made plans for the first plenary session that met six days later. So unwieldy was the conference that important questions were referred to a Council of Ten representing Great Britain, France, Italy, the United States, and Japan, while the detail work was divided among sixty commissions on which the small nations were represented. In order to hasten the conference's work, the Council of Ten was abolished on March 24, and the so-called Big Four—Wilson, Lloyd George, Premier Georges Clemenceau of France, and Prime Minister Vittorio Orlando of Italy—began a long series of private discussions. At the same time, the Council of Five, consisting of the foreign ministers of the five great powers, was established to discuss matters of subordinate importance.

A treaty for Germany had been hammered out and presented to the government of the new German republic by the end of April. The German foreign secretary appeared before a plenary session to receive the treaty on May 7; the German delegates presented a comprehensive reply on May 29; the German National Assembly at Weimar approved the treaty on June 23. The formal ceremony of signing was held on June 28, 1919, in the Hall of Mirrors of the Versailles Palace, where the German empire had been proclaimed forty-eight years before.

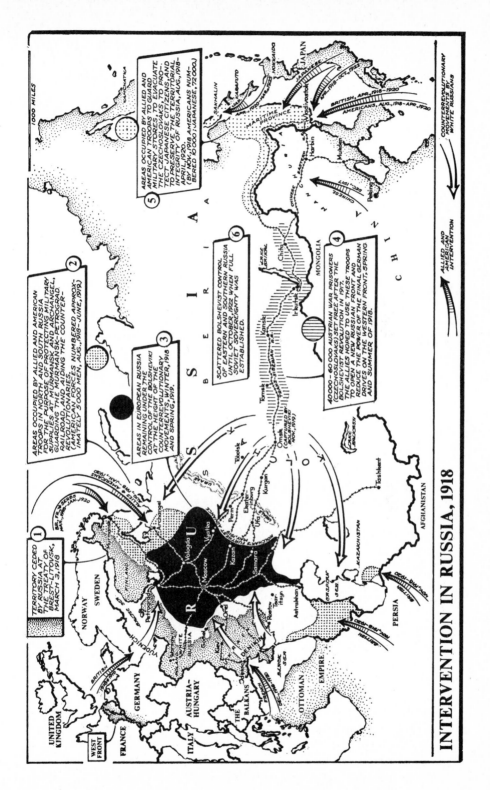

INTERVENTION IN RUSSIA, 1918

1. TERRITORY CEDED BY RUSSIA BY THE TREATY OF BREST-LITOVSK, MARCH 3, 1918

2. AREAS OCCUPIED BY ALLIED AND AMERICAN TROOPS IN NORTH AND SOUTH RUSSIA FOR THE PURPOSE OF PROTECTING MILITARY SUPPLIES AT MURMANSK AND ARCHANGEL, GUARDING THE MURMANSK-PETROGRAD RAILROAD, AND AIDING THE COUNTER-REVOLUTIONARIES. (AMERICAN FORCES NUMBERED APPROX-IMATELY 5,000 MEN, AUG., 1918–JUNE, 1919.)

3. AREAS IN EUROPEAN RUSSIA REMAINING UNDER THE CONTROL OF THE BOLSHEVIKI AT THE HEIGHT OF THE COUNTERREVOLUTIONARY MOVEMENTS, WINTER, 1918 AND SPRING, 1919.

4. 40,000–60,000 AUSTRIAN WAR PRISONERS (CZECHOSLOVAKS) SET FREE AFTER THE BOLSHEVIST REVOLUTION IN 1917. THE ALLIES HOPED TO USE THESE TROOPS TO OPEN A NEW RUSSIAN FRONT AND REDUCE THE POWER OF THE FINAL GERMAN DRIVES ON THE WESTERN FRONT, SPRING AND SUMMER OF 1918.

5. AREAS OCCUPIED BY ALLIED AND AMERICAN TROOPS TO GUARD MILITARY STORES, TO EVACUATE THE CZECHOSLOVAKS, TO PRO-TECT THE JAPANESE CITIZENS, AND TO PRESERVE THE TERRITORIAL INTEGRITY OF RUSSIA, AUG., 1918–APRIL, 1920. (BY NOV., 1918 AMERICANS NUM-BERED 10,000 (JAPANESE, 72,000))

6. SCATTERED BOLSHEVIST CONTROL OF EASTERN AND SOUTHERN RUSSIA UNTIL OCTOBER, 1922 WHEN FULL SOVIET SOVEREIGNTY WAS ESTABLISHED.

ALLIED AND AMERICAN INTERVENTION

COUNTERREVOLUTIONARY MOVEMENTS BY WHITE RUSSIANS

1000 MILES

213

This chronology ignores the thousand small details and the writing of treaties with other Central Powers. What concerns us most at this point, however, is what Wilson accomplished at Paris. How did his liberal peace program fare, in spite of the high passions that pervaded the deliberations? The answer is that Wilson accomplished less than he fought for and a great deal more than his critics later admitted. The Versailles treaty was a compromise between the Fourteen Points and what the Allied, and especially the French, peoples demanded.

The foremost problem was security against future German aggression in the west. Foch and Clemenceau proposed to tear the west bank of the Rhine from Germany and create buffer states under French control. Wilson resisted this demand with Lloyd George's assistance. Instead, France had to be satisfied with the return of Alsace-Lorraine, which was in accord with the principle of self-determination and the Fourteen Points; the permanent demilitarization and a fifteen-year occupation by Allied forces of the west bank of the Rhine; and an Anglo-French-American treaty of mutual defense against Germany. It was this promise of a triple defensive security treaty that persuaded Clemenceau to abandon his demand for the creation of buffer states in the Rhineland. Finally, the German army and navy were so severely limited in size that a future German war of aggression was to be impossible. On the whole, Wilson, Lloyd George, and Clemenceau succeeded in erecting an intelligent defensive structure that, if maintained in full vigor, might have preserved the peace of Europe. Certainly it did not violate the Fourteen Points in any important way.

Secondly, Wilson found the spokesmen of Britain, the British Dominions, Japan, and Italy determined that Germany should not recover her overseas colonies. In the face of their inflexible position, he gave in, but not without gaining important concessions. For one thing, although Japan received title to German economic rights in Shantung Province, she promised to return that province to the political control of China. For another, the former German colonies were not awarded outright to new masters, but were made mandates of the League of Nations and given in responsible trusteeship to Great Britain, the Dominions, and Japan. Whether this arrangement represented the "absolutely impartial adjustment of all colonial claims" that Wilson had demanded in Point 5 would in large measure depend upon the development of the mandate system. We can now see that approval of the mandate system marked the end of western colonialism.

A third major problem was the creation, without unduly violating the principle of self-determination, of a Polish state that would have access to the sea and include former German and Austrian territory inhabited mainly by Poles. Wilson and Lloyd George stood firm against Clemenceau and the Polish representatives to win a settlement that vindicated the Fourteen Points. Poland was given a corridor to the Baltic, while Danzig,

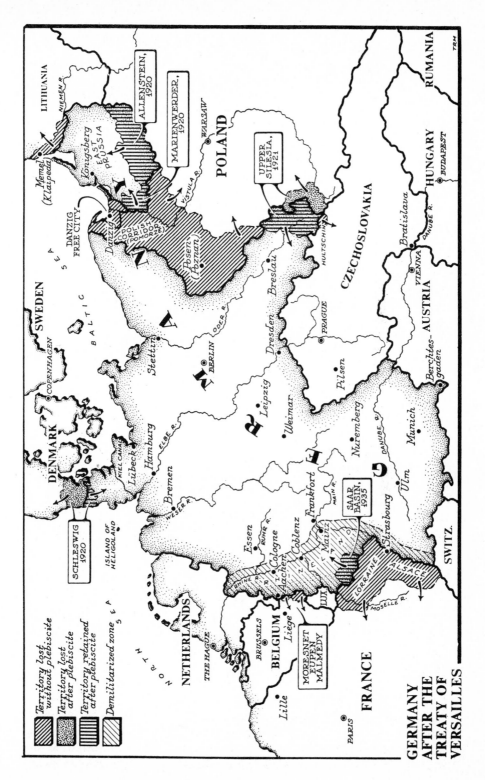

GERMANY
AFTER THE
TREATY OF
VERSAILLES

Territory lost
without plebiscite

Territory lost
after plebiscite

Territory retained
after plebiscite

Demilitarized zone

LITHUANIA

NIEMEN R.

Memel
(Klaipeda)

ALLENSTEIN,
1920

MARIENWERDER,
1920

Konigsberg EAST PRUSSIA

WARSAW

VISTULA R.

POLAND

UPPER
SILESIA,
1921

HULTSCHIN

CZECHOSLOVAKIA

HUNGARY

RUMANIA

BUDAPEST

DANUBE R.

Bratislava

VIENNA

AUSTRIA

Berchtes-
gaden

Danzig

DANZIG
FREE CITY

POLISH
CORRIDOR
(POMORZE)

Posen
(Poznan)

ODER R.

Breslau

Dresden

Prague

Pilsen

Leipzig

Weimar

Nuremberg

DANUBE R.

Munich

Ulm

SWEDEN

B A L T I C   S E A

Stettin

BERLIN

G E R M A N Y

SAAR
BASIN,
1935

Strasbourg

ALSACE

LORRAINE

MOSELLE R.

SWITZ.

COPENHAGEN

DENMARK

KIEL CANAL

Lübeck

Hamburg

Bremen

ELBE R.

WESER R.

ISLAND OF
HELIGOLAND

SCHLESWIG
1920

NORTH   SEA

NETHERLANDS

THE HAGUE

Essen

RUHR R.

Cologne

Aachen

Coblenz

Frankfort

MAIN R.

Mainz

RHINE R.

LUX.

Liège

BRUSSELS

BELGIUM

MORESNET
EUPEN
MALMEDY

Lille

PARIS

FRANCE

her outlet to the sea, was made a free city under the administration of the League of Nations.

The fourth important issue—how much Austrian territory Italy should receive—involved the validity of the secret Treaty of London of 1915. It had brought Italy into the war and promised her the Trentino, the Austrian Tyrol, and a strip of the Dalmatian coast. Wilson was impressed by the plea that control of the Brenner Pass in the Tyrol was absolutely essential to Italian security. He therefore agreed that this area, which contained 200,000 Germans, should go to Italy. The Italians also demanded a long strip of the Dalmatian coast, including the important port of Fiume. Wilson passionately objected, going so far as to appeal to the Italian people over the heads of their government. He argued that Fiume was the only possible outlet to the sea for the new state of Yugoslavia, and he pointed to the Treaty of London, which awarded the port to Yugoslavia. He won his case by main force.

In the struggle over the fifth great issue, reparations, Wilson made his most important concessions. He had agreed during the prearmistice negotiations that Germany should be compelled to pay for all civilian damages incurred by the Allied countries during the war—alone this would be a staggering sum. At the conference he agreed that Germany should also be forced to bear the cost of separation allowances and pensions for Allied veterans. Although he was ill at the time and acted through Colonel House, the president later approved Article CCXXXI of the treaty, in which Germany acknowledged legal responsibility for all losses incurred by the Allied governments and peoples during the war. Wilson agreed, besides, that the Allies might occupy the Rhineland until the potentially astronomical reparations bill was finally paid. Nor was this all. In compensation for wanton destruction of French mines by the retreating German armies, France was given ownership of the mines in the Saar Province of Germany, and the territory was to be governed by a League of Nations commission for fifteen years. The people of the Saar might vote to join the Fatherland at the end of that period. Finally, the treaty compelled the Germans to pay to Britain, France, and Belgium twenty billion gold marks' worth of reparations in kind—merchant shipping, coal, livestock, and the like. In Wilson's defense it should be said that first, he argued consistently in favor of setting a fixed sum for the reparations bill and adjusting it to Germany's capacity to pay; second, he knew that the terms of the reparations were impossible and would have to be revised in the near future—as they were; and third, he gave in to the terms of the reparations only under duress.

In Wilson's mind, the first, last, and overriding issue was the establishment of an international organization to create a concert of world power and preserve the peace. He insisted from the outset of the conference that the covenant, or constitution, of the League of Nations be firmly embedded in the treaty, and that execution of the treaty be entrusted to the

League. Clemenceau was not opposed to the League, but he contended that the organization would be helpless to maintain peace unless it had a powerful army and navy at its command. Convinced that such a proposal was politically impossible, Wilson and the British delegates created a League that would depend upon the wholehearted support of its leading members for its effectiveness. As Clemenceau thought that he had obtained security for his beloved France by other means, he was willing to let Wilson write any kind of covenant he desired.

Wilson must have looked back over his labors at Paris and remembered the tense sessions, the bitter complaints of Orlando, the barbed remarks of Clemenceau, and the compromises that he inevitably had had to make. He was nonetheless certain that he had helped to write a treaty and create a postwar peace structure that would endure. He knew that the treaty was not perfect, but he was sure that time would heal many wounds, and that the United States could obtain modifications within the League of Nations. Moreover, he had high hopes that the new international order that he had helped so significantly to create would be one in which a reformed capitalism, purged of predatory imperialism and led by the United States, would offer an irresistible alternative to the Communist demand for a new order to be achieved through the warfare and dictatorship of the proletariat.

Critics, contemporary and historical, have castigated Wilson in general for failing to win the liberal peace program at Paris, in particular for bargaining all his Fourteen Points away in order to win a League of Nations. Such criticism can come only from one who has never bothered to read the Fourteen Points, for that document was actually honored more in the observance than in the breach. Wilson's chief failures—on the colonial question and reparations—were perhaps inevitable. But the damage done was not irreparable, given forceful American leadership in the League of Nations and the reparations commission. Wilson failed to vindicate the principle of freedom of the seas only because he finally realized during the conference that freedom of the seas was a part of the old system of neutrality, and that neutrality would be impossible in future wars. As he said, there could be no neutrals in the new system of collective security.

Wilson's critics, not content with exaggerating his failures, have also minimized his difficulties. He did not write the treaty alone but in collaboration with three astute and determined negotiators. To be sure, Wilson could have withdrawn from the conference, as on one occasion he seriously threatened to do. But the results of American withdrawal would have been even worse than an unsatisfactory settlement. Furthermore, Wilson's difficulties at Paris were compounded by virulent opposition to his peace program in the United States. Senator Lodge, for example, did not lighten the president's burdens by writing to Clemenceau that Wilson did not speak for the American people, who, Lodge declared, desired a harsh and punitive settlement.

Finally, the historian must ask what kind of a peace treaty would have been written if Wilson had not been at Paris and had not won British support for most of his principles. Wilson and Lloyd George together prevented the dismemberment of Germany in the west and compelled a redrawing of the map of Europe that did not unnecessarily violate the principle of self-determination. As the spokesman of the only disinterested nation represented at the conference, Wilson emerged from the fiery trial with the greatest stature precisely because he was able to accomplish so much in spite of stupendous obstacles.

5. First Phases of the Treaty Fight

There were signs long before the end of the Paris Peace Conference that Wilson would encounter strong opposition in the Senate if he insisted on incorporating the covenant of the League in the treaty. The president returned briefly to Washington in the latter part of February 1919 and conferred with the members of the House and Senate foreign relations committees in an effort to meet the rising criticism. Many senators, he learned, objected because the covenant contained no explicit recognition of the Monroe Doctrine, did not specifically exclude internal affairs from the jurisdiction of the League, and made no provision for the right of a member nation to withdraw. On March 4, 1919, just before Wilson was to return to France, moreover, Senator Lodge presented to the upper house a round robin drawn up by Republican leaders warning that the convenant, "in the form now proposed," was unacceptable. It was signed by thirty-nine senators or senators-elect, considerably more than the one-third plus one necessary to defeat ratification. Back in Paris, Wilson obtained changes in the covenant to meet all the criticisms noted above. The president returned to the United States on July 8 and formally presented the treaty to the Senate two days later. "Our isolation was ended twenty years ago," he declared. "There can be no question of our ceasing to be a world power. The only question is whether we can refuse the moral leadership that is offered, whether we shall accept or reject the confidence of the world."

Wilson spoke confidently of the great new role of "service and achievement" that lay ahead for the American people, whose destiny had been disclosed by the very hand of God. His poetic phrases, however, suggested a unanimity that did not exist. No one could yet say how large a part of the population critics of the treaty represented, but they were already well organized and exceedingly vociferous. Leading the opposition was a small group of extreme isolationists in the Senate, chief among whom were Hiram W. Johnson of California, William E. Borah of Idaho, and James A. Reed of Missouri. These irreconcilables, as they were called, were convinced that membership in the League would violate wise historic policy, and they pledged themselves to keep America free from the entanglements of Europe.

Perhaps even more bitterly opposed to the treaty were the so-called hyphenates, their newspapers, and their chief journalistic allies, the Hearst publications. German-Americans protested that the treaty was a base betrayal of the Pre-Armistice Agreement. Italian-Americans were sulking over Wilson's refusal to award Fiume to Italy. But the most virulent opposition came from Irish-Americans. They were up in arms because Wilson had refused to press the cause of Irish independence at Paris or throw the support of the United States behind the Irish rebellion then in progress.

These opponents were powerful, but the president might yet have triumphed if all Americans who believed in the liberal international program had stood together. Unfortunately for Wilson, such a solid phalanx did not materialize. In the first place, many cautious liberal internationalists—like Elihu Root and Henry L. Stimson, who put their faith in international law and arbitration—feared that Wilson was going too far too fast in breaking with ingrained American traditions. In the second place, many independent progressives and radicals, who had followed Wilson during the war and shared his noble dream of a new world order, drew back in revulsion when the terms of the treaty were published. "The European politicians who with American complicity have hatched this inhuman monster," exclaimed *The New Republic*, the leading liberal internationalist journal, "have acted either cynically, hypocritically, or vindictively." *The Nation* and other liberal journals were equally bitter.

The greatest obstacles to ratification of the treaty, however, were personal and partisan rivalries and prejudices, old traditions of apartness, and the absence in 1919 and 1920 of any popular conviction that membership in the League was essential to American security. Germany had been decisively beaten and disarmed; Russia was in chaos. No war clouds darkened the horizon; no nation menaced the peace and security of the United States. Men might warn of the perils of the future, but who would believe them when it was obvious there could never be another war?

After Wilson presented the treaty to the Senate, the vortex of the struggle over ratification shifted to the upper house, which in the past had upset the plans of many presidents. A fairly distinct alignment was already evident by midsummer of 1919. There were sixteen bitter-end isolationists, mainly Republicans, who would vote against the treaty in any form so long as it contained the covenant. They were a small minority, but they dominated the foreign relations committee and were able to influence its chairman, Lodge, by their frequent threats to bolt the Republican camp. On the other hand, at least forty-three of the forty-seven Democrats would follow Wilson's lead, while the great majority of the forty-nine Republicans favored ratification after making certain reservations to safeguard American interests. Most of these were what were called strong reservationists. Thus considerably more than the necessary two-thirds in the Senate favored ratification of the treaty and membership in the League. The main task of statesmanship in the months ahead would be to find common ground upon which this preponderant majority could stand.

Much, of course, would depend upon the ability of leaders of both parties to suppress partisan ambitions and prejudices and pull together for the common good. The Republican leader in the Senate was Henry Cabot Lodge, a Boston Brahmin, long an intimate of Theodore Roosevelt, and a man of some intellect. Although he had supported a postwar League in 1915 and 1916, Lodge reversed himself after Wilson linked the League plan with the concept of a "peace without victory." Exactly where he stood on the League of Nations in the summer of 1919, it is impossible to say. One historian has recently suggested that Lodge was not an irreconcilable but rather that he was intent upon taking leadership in the treaty struggle out of Wilson's hands and winning credit for ratification for himself and the Republican party.

Lodge's position was, admittedly, extraordinarily difficult. As leader of his party in the Senate he had to preserve some semblance of harmony among the three Republican factions—the irreconcilable isolationists, a small group of so-called mild reservationists, and the large majority who favored strong reservations. Naturally he was buffeted about and appeared all things to all men. But never during the treaty fight or afterward did he act like a sincere friend of the League or a statesman who was able to exalt the national interest above his consuming personal hatred of Wilson and the Democratic party. On the contrary, moving from one calculated step to another, he acted as if his chief purpose was to embarrass the president and prevent ratification of the treaty.

Public sentiment in July 1919 was running so strongly in favor of the treaty that Lodge knew that he could not defeat it outright. Thirty-two state legislatures and thirty-three governors had endorsed the League. Leaders of the League to Enforce Peace were now actively campaigning for unconditional ratification, and a poll of the nation's press indicated that an overwhelming majority of newspapers favored American membership in the League. It was evident to the Massachusetts senator, therefore, that he must work indirectly—first, by packing the foreign relations committee with enemies of the League; second, by appending such strong reservations to the covenant that the president would refuse to accept them.

Meanwhile, Lodge desperately needed time to allow the opponents of the League to agitate. Time he easily obtained, by reading aloud all of the

264 pages of the treaty, which consumed two weeks, and then by holding public hearings on the treaty for another six weeks. In the meantime, the bitter-enders, liberally supplied with funds by the steel manufacturer Henry C. Frick and the banker and aluminum monopolist Andrew W. Mellon, flooded the country with anti-League propaganda.

Opponents of the treaty were gaining momentum by September 1919. At the same time, a series of convulsive strikes had diverted Wilson's attention and prevented him from giving his customary leadership to the League forces. It is true that he had appeared before Lodge's committee on August 19 and conferred individually with some twenty Republican senators, in an effort to detach them from their party. But the more he conferred with senators the more he realized that the situation was passing out of his control. In these circumstances Wilson decided upon bold steps. First, he announced on September 3 that he would not oppose interpretive reservations that did not impair the integrity of the covenant or require new diplomatic negotiations. Second, he decided to carry his fight for the League to the people. He would purify the wells of public sentiment poisoned by the irreconcilables; he would tell the people the truth about their stake in preserving peace through the League of Nations.

No act of his public career so dramatically demonstrated Wilson's sincerity as his decision to undertake this campaign. His health had been poor since he had suffered a severe case of influenza at Paris. He was now weak and exhausted, and his physician warned that a long speaking tour might take his life. He gladly took the risk, however, thinking that he could arouse such a ground swell of support for the League that his senatorial opponents could not resist it. He traveled more than 8,000 miles through the Middle and Far West for three weeks in September and delivered some thirty-seven addresses. The strain on his meager physical resources was great, but the total effect of his outpouring to the people of the West was magnificent. The deeper Wilson moved into the West the larger and more enthusiastic the crowds became. In fact, the irreconcilables were so alarmed by the president's triumphal procession that they sent their two best speakers, Senators Johnson and Borah, to trail him.

The effects of the strain began to tell on Wilson even before the tour was half over. He began to have blinding headaches and to show signs of exhaustion. He delivered one of his longest and most important speeches at Pueblo, Colorado, on September 25. "It always seems to make it difficult for me to say anything, my fellow citizens, when I think of my clients in this case," he exclaimed. "My clients are the children; my clients are the next generation. . . . I intend to redeem my pledges to the children; they shall not be sent . . . [to France]." After this address the president was so near collapse that his physician canceled the remaining speeches and sped the presidential train straight to Washington. Wilson suffered a stroke on October 2, 1919, that paralyzed the left side of his face and body, and for days his life hung in a precarious balance.

6. The Triumph of Partisanship

Meanwhile, the battle in the Senate had begun when the foreign relations committee reported the treaty on September 10, 1919, with forty-five amendments and four reservations. The Democrats defeated all the amendments with the help of some twelve Republican "mild reservationists." Thereupon Lodge, on November 6, presented for his committee a series of fourteen reservations. Most of them merely underlined existing provisions of the covenant and provided that the United States could take no action in important matters without the consent of Congress. The fourth reservation reserved control over all domestic affairs exclusively to the United States; the fifth removed all questions arising under the Monroe Doctrine from the jurisdiction of the League; the sixth declared that the United States withheld assent from the articles of the treaty relating to Shantung. The most important reservation, the second, had been suggested by Elihu Root on June 21, 1919. It asserted that the United States assumed no obligations under Article X of the covenant to preserve the territorial integrity or political independence of any country, interfere in controversies between nations, or use its armed forces to uphold any article of the treaty for any purpose, unless Congress by joint resolution so provided. The Senate approved twelve of Lodge's reservations, including the second, after a bitter partisan battle, and then two others were added.

The next move was up to the ailing president and his Democratic colleagues in the Senate. Colonel House and other friends of the League begged Wilson either to compromise on Lodge's terms or else to accept the Senator's reservations entirely, if that was necessary to get the United States into the League. Gilbert M. Hitchcock of Nebraska, Democratic leader in the Senate, was allowed to visit Wilson in his sickroom on November 7 and 17. He found the president determined never to surrender and disposed to compromise only on his own terms—by accepting reservations that he thought did not impair the obligations of the United States under the covenant. Furthermore, in a public letter to Hitchcock, actually drafted by Hitchcock, Wilson declared on November 18 that the Lodge reservations provided for nullification, not ratification, of the treaty. He virtually ordered Democratic senators to vote against them.

The first showdown came when the Senate voted on the treaty on the following day, November 19, 1919. On a resolution to ratify with the Lodge reservations, the irreconcilables combined with a nearly solid Democratic phalanx to defeat ratification by a vote of fifty-five nays to thirty-nine ayes. A Democratic resolution to ratify without any reservations failed immediately afterward by a vote of fifty-three nays to thirty-eight ayes.

It was apparent from the two test votes that seventy-seven senators, considerably more than the necessary two-thirds, favored ratification with or without reservations. What chance was there for compromise between the two factions? It was clear after the first Senate vote that Lodge would never surrender and that Wilson would have to compromise largely on the senator's terms if he wanted ratification. Colonel House advised the president to wash his hands of responsibility and let the Senate decide; William J. Bryan urged immediate ratification, even with reservations, and most Democratic senators privately agreed. The French and British leaders were, if anything, more frightened by the prospect of the treaty's defeat than were Wilson's friends. The British government sent Sir Edward Grey (now Viscount Grey of Falloden), former foreign secretary, as a special ambassador to Washington to plead for compromise. The president, however, refused to see Grey and was angered when the viscount later issued a public statement declaring that the League would fail without the United States, and that the Allies would accept the Lodge reservations without requiring a reopening of negotiations.

Public sentiment in the United States, moreover, refused to accept the Senate's vote on November 19, 1919, as final. Leaders of the League to Enforce Peace, now called the League of Free Nations Association, appealed for ratification with necessary reservations; newspaper spokesmen were up in arms. Leaders of twenty-six organizations representing some 20 million members demanded on January 13 and February 9, 1920, that Lodge and Wilson compromise their differences. But the weary man in the White House paid scant heed to this ground swell, if, indeed, he knew much about it. He tried to find some constitutional way to challenge his senatorial foes to resign and go before their constituents on the issue of the League. In this plan he would have resigned if his opponents were returned to the Senate. Failing for technical reasons to work this out, Wilson made another proposal in a public letter to Democrats assembled at a Jackson Day dinner in Washington on January 8, 1920. He was certain, Wilson asserted, that the overwhelming majority of Americans desired prompt ratification without crippling reservations. If, however, the Senate refused thus to ratify, then the presidential election of 1920 would be a "great and solemn referendum" in which the voters could decide the issue. It was one of the greatest tactical errors of Wilson's public career. Heretofore he had taken pains to avoid any show of partisanship in the treaty fight. By making ratification a partisan issue, he made it inevitable that most Republicans in the Senate would follow their majority leader. Moreover, public opinion now turned decisively against the president, who had put himself in the position of being the chief obstacle to a solution.

In the face of what seemed to be an overwhelming demand at home and abroad for ratification, the Senate agreed to reconsider and began debate anew in mid-February 1920. While Democratic leaders tried desperately to find common ground with the Republicans, the president, now vastly improved in health and mental vigor, hurled blast after blast at the Lodge reservations and even intimated that he would refuse to proclaim the treaty if the Senate adopted them. The treaty came up for vote on March 19. One reservation, favoring Irish independence, had been added by the Democrats in an effort to embarrass Lodge, while the second reservation regarding Article X had been made even more sweeping than before.

Practically all Democratic senators desperately wanted to accept the reservations. But a majority of them were literally too afraid of Wilson to oppose him; and twenty-three Democrats joined the irreconcilables to defeat approval by a vote of thirty-five nays to forty-nine ayes. A change of only seven Democratic votes would have put the United States in the League of Nations! To end the state of hostilities, Congress adopted a joint resolution on May 15, 1920, repealing the war resolutions against Germany and Austria-Hungary and reserving to the United States all rights under the Treaty of Versailles. Wilson vetoed this resolution on May 27, declaring that he would not be party "to an action which would place an ineffable stain upon the gallantry and honor of the United States."

It was the end, although the tragedy was prolonged during the "great and solemn referendum" that was no referendum at all. Who was responsible for American refusal to enter the League of Nations and for the "ineffable stain" of a separate peace? Certainly Lodge and his Republican friends shared a large measure of guilt for one of the most tragic episodes in American history. Had they been less interested in the election of 1920 and more concerned with their country's good they would have suppressed personal and partisan ambitions and met the champions of the League halfway. In addition, the irreconcilables, who used every device to defeat ratification, shared a large part of the blame, for the unscrupulous propaganda that some of them put forth helped to confuse the public about the implications of American membership in the League.

On the other hand, Wilson, too, was partly responsible. Perhaps because of his hatred for Lodge, perhaps because he believed to the end that the people would force the Senate to his terms, perhaps because his illness had impaired his judgment, he also refused to compromise. He ignored the advice of his best counselors and threw away the only possible chance for ratification. He therefore shared responsibility for breaking the heart of the world. Finally, those Democratic senators who voted against ratification with reservations out of fear of Wilsonian wrath served neither the national interest nor the cause of international peace.

Whatever the causes for the great betrayal of 1919-1920, the consequences remained. The American people were perhaps not yet ready to assume leadership in world affairs, but their leaders denied them an opportunity even to learn the duties of leadership or to grow in wisdom and experience. More important were the catastrophic effects of the American rejection on the infant League and on the future development of European politics. Given American leadership in the postwar era, the League might have developed into the association of free peoples of which its founders had dreamed, and it might have become more efficient in dealing with the maladjustments of European society.

10

Demobilization and the Triumph of Normalcy, 1918–1920

All postwar periods in American history have been times when partisanship runs at fever pitch and passions generated by the war drive people to acts of violence. So it was during the years following the armistice, as war hysteria found new victims in "Reds," foreigners, Jews, blacks, and Catholics. As if further to confuse the domestic scene, labor unrest during 1919 and 1920 was at its highest peak since the 1890s. Politically, the postwar era was marked by extraordinary partisanship. Centering at first on the struggle over ratification of the Versailles treaty, this partisan conflict culminated in 1920, when a reunited Republican party smashed the Wilsonian progressive coalition and swept into control of the federal government. The election results were convincing evidence that the people were determined to put an end to the division of control in the federal government and to return, as the Republican candidate in 1920 said, to "normalcy," to the good days of prosperity and peace.

226

1. Demobilization, 1918-1920

Just as it had adopted the war resolution without any earlier effective preparation for a great war effort, the American government found itself on November 11, 1918, without any plan for demobilization and reconstruction. Indeed, the sudden and unexpected German collapse came at a time when American leaders were planning not for peace, but for an invasion of Germany in 1919.

The president aptly described the manner in which demobilization took place in his Annual Message to Congress in December 1918: "The moment we knew the armistice to have been signed we took the harness off." And that is about what happened. The AEF was brought home and quickly demobilized. Various war agencies began to wind up their affairs. For example, the War Industries Board, refusing to believe there were any problems of demobilization that the business world could not solve, abandoned its control of industry once the fighting stopped. "The magnificent war formation of American industry was dissipated in a day," wrote the board's chief historian.

Everyone, it seemed, expected the country to return quickly to normal without benefit of governmental controls and planning. However, by the time that Wilson returned from Paris in February 1919, prices were rising fast, and large-scale unemployment and industrial conflict seemed inevitable. Unable to obtain legislation from the lame-duck session, Wilson prepared for the impending crisis as best he could. Calling governors and mayors to the White House on March 3, he warned them of the dangers ahead. In addition, he established an Industrial Board to coordinate the efforts of various governmental purchasing agencies to hold the line on prices. The Industrial Board, however, had neither statutory authority nor prestige in the business world. It disbanded in May 1919, after the Railroad Administration refused to permit it to fix prices for steel.

For the most part, therefore, the administration was powerless to meet the larger problems of postwar inflation, business readjustment, and industrial conflict. On the other hand, the period 1919-1920 was not as chaotic or unproductive as this generalization might suggest. For one thing, there were specific problems of demobilization so urgent that Congress could not ignore them. For another, the last two years of the Wilson era witnessed congressional approval of significant measures that brought several phases of the progressive movement to final culmination.

The first requirement was the most urgent—to provide funds to liquidate the war effort at home, care for wounded soldiers and sailors, bring the AEF back from France, and provide relief for Europe. In spite of demands for immediate tax reduction, the lame-duck session courageously adopted a War Revenue bill in February 1919 that increased the tax burden, especially on business and the upper class. (For the provisions of this measure see pp. 192-193.)

The second problem was the disposition of the railroads still being operated by the Railroad Administration at the beginning of 1919. While McAdoo recommended a five-year experiment in public operation and Congress deliberated during the summer of 1919, the so-called Plumb Plan, suggested by Glenn E. Plumb, a lawyer for the brotherhoods, to nationalize the railroads and give the workers a share in their management and profit gained the support of the AF of L and the railroad workers. Wilson took no part in the controversy over the Plumb Plan. He simply announced on December 24, 1919, that he would return the railroads to their owners on March 1, 1920, unless Congress decided otherwise.

Congress responded with the Transportation Act of 1920, drafted largely by two midwestern progressive Republicans, Representative John J. Esch of Wisconsin and Senator Albert B. Cummins of Iowa, and approved February 28, 1920. The Transportation Act was perhaps the most significant measure of the immediate postwar era because it marked the complete fulfillment of the movement for thoroughgoing federal control of railroads. Stopping only short of nationalization, the act gave the ICC complete control over rates, even those set by state commissions; authorized the ICC to supervise the sale of railroad securities and expenditure of the proceeds; permitted railroads to pool traffic in the interest of economy; and empowered the ICC to consolidate existing lines into a limited number of systems.

A third issue was disposition of the huge fleet of merchant vessels that the Shipping Board had purchased, confiscated, or built during and after the war. No one wanted to junk a merchant marine that totaled some 15 million tons by 1920; yet Congress was unwilling to embark upon a long-range program of public operation. A compromise solution was embodied in the Merchant Marine Act of 1920. It directed the Shipping Board to sell as many vessels as possible to corporations of predominantly American ownership and authorized the federally owned Merchant Fleet Corporation to open new shipping lines and operate surplus vessels. As it turned out, the Shipping Board's low prices on easy terms and guarantees against operation losses to private firms lured considerable private capital into the shipping industry and kept a sizable merchant marine afloat in the 1920s. By 1930 the privately owned American merchant marine totaled over 7 million tons.

Four measures—the General Leasing and Water Power acts of 1920 and the woman suffrage and prohibition amendments—rounded out the postwar legislative program and revealed that the reform spirit was by no means dead. The General Leasing Act empowered the secretary of the interior to lease public lands containing mineral and oil deposits to private parties on terms that safeguarded the public interest. The Water Power

Act established a Federal Power Commission, composed of the secretaries of war, the interior, and agriculture. It could license the building and operation of dams and hydroelectric plants on navigable rivers and non-navigable streams in the public domain. We will reserve our discussion of national prohibition for a later chapter. The point here is that Congress acted promptly and, it thought, effectively to implement what many progressives hailed as the greatest triumph for morality since the abolition of slavery. Another important objective of the progressive movement, woman suffrage, also came to fruition at this time. Congress approved the Nineteenth Amendment, which forbade denying the right to vote on account of sex, in June 1919; it was ratified in August 1920. (For details of the struggle for women's rights, see pp. 62–64.)

2. Postwar Inflation and Labor Troubles

Leaders in Washington and the states prepared as best they could during the early months of 1919 to cope with the mass unemployment that they thought would follow demobilization. The anticipated crisis never came. Instead, a boom got under way during the summer of 1919, and industrial production was well above the wartime peak by the following October. In face of what seemed to be insatiable demand, prices began rising in the spring of 1919 and continued to mount until the autumn of 1920. The cost of living rose to 77 percent above the prewar level in 1919 and to 105 percent above that level in 1920.

The postwar inflation's chief significance lay in the fact that it combined with other forces to set off an unprecedented outbreak of labor troubles. All told, during 1919 there were 2,665 strikes involving more than 4 million workers, as organized labor fought to preserve wartime gains and embarked upon ambitious new projects of unionization.

The wave of strikes began four days after the armistice, when the Amalgamated Clothing Workers in New York and Chicago struck for the forty-four-hour week and a 15 percent wage increase. Victory for the union was followed by adoption of the new wage and hours scale in the entire clothing industry. Then in rapid succession followed a general strike in Seattle and strikes by textile workers in New England and New Jersey, telephone operators in New England, telegraph operators throughout the country, the printers' union, the longshoremen of New York, and switchmen in the Chicago railroad yards. Practically all these strikes, and hundreds of others, succeeded, and organized labor was able not only to hold its own against rising prices but also to win an increase in real income.

This outbreak of industrial unrest, however, occurred at a time when the American people were disturbed by a new hysteria—the so-called Red scare. Most of the strikes of 1919 were waged successfully in spite of a growing popular suspicion that they were being provoked by Communist agents and would culminate in a general labor uprising. But organized labor's most important effort in 1919, the AF of L's drive to win collective bargaining in the steel industry, ran afoul of the Red hysteria.

The United States Steel Corporation had stood since 1901 as the chief barrier to unionization of the basic industries. Encouraged by the friendly attitude of federal authorities and what they thought was a sympathetic public opinion, the AF of L convention directed its executive committee in June 1918 to undertake "one mighty drive to organize the steel plants of America"—the first attack in a new general offensive against the mass industries. The union's president, Samuel Gompers, appointed a National Committee for the Organizing of the Iron and Steel Industry on August 1, with William Z. Foster, a left-wing syndicalist, as secretary.

Foster and his committee organized the steelworkers all during late 1918 and early 1919, and the reorganized steelworkers' union claimed a membership of 100,000 by June 1919 and was ready to test its strength in battle. Although the union included a minority of the steelworkers, no impartial observer could doubt that it voiced the protest of the over-whelming majority against old and rankling grievances. Steelworkers lived everywhere under the tyranny of petty bosses, and even mild complaints often brought prompt dismissal. Moreover, about half the iron and steel employees worked from twelve to fourteen hours a day, an additional quarter worked between ten and twelve hours daily, and a minority worked twenty-four hours a day every other Sunday.[1] Wage rates were so low in 1919 that 60 percent of all steelworkers and their families lived below or barely above a minimum subsistence level.

Union officials presented their demands—recognition, the eight-hour day, "an American living wage," and reinstatement of workers discharged for union activities—to Judge Elbert H. Gary, head of United States Steel, in August 1919. Gary refused to negotiate, and some 343,000 workers in the plants of United States Steel went on strike on September 22. Three days later the walkout spread to plants of Bethlehem Steel. The ensuing struggle was marked by widespread violence in which eighteen strikers were killed, by the use of state and federal troops to prevent picketing, and by stern suppression of civil liberties in all strike districts except West Virginia. Perhaps the most significant aspect of the conflict was manage-ment's use of new propaganda techniques learned during the war. By raising and reiterating the false alarm of Bolshevism, management and the vast majority of newspapers diverted public attention from the workers' grievances to the false issue of communism. As a result the workers lost the support of public opinion in this most crucial battle.

---

[1] The average work week in the steel industry in 1919 was 68.7 hours, as compared with 67.6 hours in 1910.

With a large segment of public opinion and most state officials arrayed against them, the strikers could not win, for the steel companies had emerged from the war with full treasuries and resources adequate for a long struggle. The first break came when United States Steel officials imported tens of thousands of strikebreakers and put them to work under military guard. For example, the large works at Gary, Indiana, were operating at 75 percent capacity by November. The struggle dragged on into January 1920, when it was officially ended by the unconditional surrender of the AF of L.

While the steel strike was getting under way a police strike in Boston gave further evidence of deep social unrest and incidentally catapulted an obscure governor of Massachusetts into the vice-presidency of the United States. The police of Boston, like most other public employees during the postwar inflation, were struggling to survive on prewar salaries. When city authorities refused to raise wages and correct other grievances, the policemen's organization, the Boston Social Club, obtained a charter as an AF of L local in August 1919 and threatened to strike. A hastily appointed Mayor's Citizens' Committee was conciliatory and proposed a settlement that would have granted most of the union's demands, except recognition. The police commissioner, however, not only rejected the proposed settlement but also summarily dismissed nineteen leaders of the local.

Thus goaded, the policemen abandoned their posts on September 9, 1919. A volunteer force was unable to control the gangs of looters that menaced the city, and Governor Calvin Coolidge called out the Boston companies of the National Guard and took personal command. The strike was quickly broken; the rebel policemen were dismissed; and a new police force was assembled. And when Gompers appealed to Coolidge to persuade the Boston authorities to reinstate the strikers, the governor replied with a cryptic rebuke that made him at once nationally famous: "There is no right to strike against the public safety by anybody, anywhere, anytime."

The last important strike of the immediate postwar era, the short-lived bituminous coal strike of November 1919, was notable in that it provoked the first test of strength between the federal government and the new president of the United Mine Workers of America (UMW), John L. Lewis. Of all workers in the country bituminous miners probably had the best grounds for discontent. The UMW had concluded a no-strike agreement—the so-called Washington Agreement—with the Fuel Administration in August 1917. Although anthracite miners later received substantial wage increases, bituminous miners received none. Meeting in Indianapolis in September 1919, the UMW adopted a bold program demanding immediate abrogation of the Washington Agreement, a six-hour day and five-day week, and wage increases to 60 percent. And when the operators refused to negotiate until the Washington Agreement had expired, Lewis called a nationwide bituminous strike for November 1. Meanwhile, Attorney General A. Mitchell Palmer had tried vainly to persuade the UMW to cancel the strike order, which, he claimed, was in violation of the Lever Act.

Faced with a complete shutdown of the mines, Palmer obtained one injunction on November 8 from the federal district court in Indianapolis ordering Lewis and other UMW officials to cease all strike activity. Shortly afterward he obtained another injunction commanding union officials to cancel their strike order by November 10. "We cannot fight the government," Lewis declared as he called off the strike. Nonetheless, the miners refused to go back to work until the government, a month later, ordered an immediate 14 percent wage increase and established an arbitration commission to consider the union's demands. The commission, after extended hearings, awarded the miners another 27 percent increase in pay without changing the hours of work.

3. The First Red Scare

The triumph of the Bolshevik revolution in Russia in November 1917, the ensuing spread of communism into Germany, Hungary, and other parts of Europe, and especially the formation in Moscow on March 2, 1919, of the Third International, or Comintern, as it came to be known, dedicated to stimulating immediate world proletarian revolution, set off a wave of new hysteria in the United States. No other development of the postwar era so well reflected the insecurity of the American people as their reactions to fantastic rumors of an equally fantastic Bolshevik uprising in their midst.

An early sign of the excited state of public opinion was the trial of Victor Berger, Socialist congressman from Milwaukee, for conspiracy under the Sedition Act. Reelected to the House in November 1918 after his indictment, Berger was tried in Chicago in the following December, convicted, and sentenced to prison for twenty years. He was released on bail pending appeal (the government finally dropped all charges against Berger in 1922), but denied his seat in the lower house when Congress met in special session in May 1919. Reelected in a special election in December 1919, Berger was again denied his seat in January 1920.[2]

Berger's conviction was the first manifestation of hysteria that developed in response to a series of events during the following months into the first Red scare. Workers in Seattle staged a general strike on February 6, 1919, that brought industry to a standstill and seriously crippled operation

---

[2] He was reelected to the House in 1922, seated promptly when Congress convened, and served until his death in 1929.

of utilities and transportation services. Asserting that the strike was the work of Bolsheviks and the IWW, Mayor Ole Hanson trumpeted that it was the first step in a nationwide workers' uprising. At the same time, committees of the United States Senate and the New York legislature began investigations of Bolshevik activities, while the Justice Department rounded up fifty-three alien Communists on the West Coast on February 11 and shipped them to New York for deportation. A week later a naturalized citizen was quickly acquitted in Indiana for killing an alien who had shouted, "To hell with the United States!"

The climax came with the discovery in April of a plot to assassinate governors, judges, cabinet members, and other public officials. A large bomb was found in Mayor Hanson's mail on April 28; the following day the maid of Senator Thomas W. Hardwick of Georgia had her hands blown off when she opened a package in the senator's Atlanta home. Immediate investigation in the New York Post Office uncovered sixteen bomb packages addressed to such persons as Attorney General Palmer, Postmaster General Burleson, Justice Oliver Wendell Holmes, J. P. Morgan, and John D. Rockefeller. Some twenty other explosive devices were discovered elsewhere in the mails. In addition, later in the spring the residences of Attorney General Palmer, two judges, and others were partially destroyed, with loss of two lives, by bombs in eight cities. The guilty parties, probably a few anarchists, were never apprehended.[3]

Popular retaliation came quickly and indiscriminately. The California legislature outlawed membership in organizations that advocated use of violence. In the wake of the investigations of its Lusk Committee, the New York legislature enacted similar, if less drastic legislation.[4] Some four hundred soldiers and sailors invaded the offices of the New York *Call*, a Socialist daily, and beat up several May Day celebrants. In other parts of New York, and in Boston and Cleveland, there were clashes between May Day paraders and servicemen and police. The most serious outbreak occurred in the lumber town of Centralia, Washington, on Armistice Day. Members of the newly organized American Legion attacked the local headquarters of the IWW, and four of the attackers were killed in the ensuing fracas. In swift reprisal enraged townspeople lynched one of the defenders; police officials raided IWW headquarters throughout the state, arresting more than one thousand leaders of the union; and eleven IWW members involved in the Centralia affair were soon afterward convicted of murder and sentenced to long prison terms.

---

[3] The worst bombing occurred more than a year later, in September 1920, when a wagonload of explosives was set off in front of the offices of J. P. Morgan & Company in New York City. Thirty-eight people were killed, more than 200 were injured, and property damage ran to more than $2 million.

[4] Vetoed by Govenor Alfred E. Smith, the New York anti-Communist bill was reenacted and signed by Smith's Republican successor in 1921.

Scare headlines and sensational newspaper reports magnified the events and stimulated a widespread public alarm,[5] and never was a great nation so afraid of phantom invaders and so agitated by groundless fears. Any threat would have had to come from the newly organized Communist parties, the alleged spearheads of the revolution. One of them, the Communist Labor party, breaking away from the national Socialist convention in Chicago, was formed on August 31, 1919. It had between 10,000 and 30,000 members by the end of the year. Another, the Communist Party of America, was organized on September 1. It had a membership of between 30,000 and 60,000 by the end of 1919.

The danger of social upheaval in 1919 now seems exceedingly remote in view of the extreme weakness of these parties of the Left. The Wilson administration, however, acted as if the menace were dire and launched such a campaign against civil liberties as the country had not witnessed in peacetime since 1799. The organizer and leader of this campaign was the attorney general, A. Mitchell Palmer of Pennsylvania, who thought that he had a good chance to become the next resident of the White House. It is very possible that the sick president knew nothing about Palmer's plans and subsequent actions. Palmer not only set the entire Federal Bureau of Investigation to work ferreting out Communists and boring into their organizations, but he also urged Congress to adopt a measure that went so far as to punish persons guilty even of inciting sedition.

When Congress refused to enact Palmer's sedition bill, the attorney general struck out on his own private campaign. The Labor Department had rounded up some 249 known Russian Communists and shipped them to Finland on December 21, 1919. But Palmer was after bigger game. Without informing the secretary or assistant secretary of labor of his plan, Palmer obtained warrants for the arrest of some three thousand alien members of the Communist and Communist Labor parties from a subordinate official in the Labor Department. Thousands of federal agents and local police executed a gigantic simultaneous raid on Communist headquarters throughout the country on the night of January 2, 1920. Some four thousand persons, many of them non-Communists and American citizens, were hurried off to jails and bull pens in thirty-three major cities in twenty-three states. Persons visiting prisoners in Hartford, Connecticut, were arrested on the ground that they, too, must be Communists.

Eventually one-third of the victims were released for lack of evidence. American citizens suspected of membership in a Communist party were turned over to local authorities for indictment and prosecution under state syndicalism laws. But for the aliens it was a different story. Outraged by

[5]One good index of the state of public opinion was the adoption by state legislatures in 1919 and 1920 of laws outlawing display of the Red flag, prohibiting membership in organizations that advocated the violent overthrow of the government, and forbidding seditious utterances. Thirty-four states and two territories enacted such statutes in 1919; two states adopted such legislation in 1920.

Palmer's procedure, Assistant Secretary of Labor Louis F. Post took charge of the deportation proceedings and saw that justice was done. Only 556 aliens, all of them proved members of the Communist party, were deported.

Palmer continued to warn of gigantic Red plots, but he executed no more raids. The scene now shifted to the states, with investigations by the Lusk Committee of the New York legislature and the subsequent expulsion of five Socialist members of the New York Assembly on April 1, 1920, for no crime except membership in the Socialist party; the arrest and conviction of two anarchists, Nicola Sacco and Bartolomeo Vanzetti, for the alleged murder of a paymaster in a South Braintree, Massachusetts, shoe factory; and the growth everywhere of demands for conformity. As we shall see in a later chapter, the postwar era bequeathed to the 1920s a heritage of hatred and hysteria that permeated and disturbed every aspect of life and thought.

4. Troubled Race Relations

This summer of the first Red scare was also a time of tribulation for American blacks, as postwar intolerances found yet other victims and another form of expression. Tensions burst into the most awful outbreak of interracial warfare in the history of the United States. Let us look first at the causes of this violence on America's most troubled social frontier.

To begin with, a decline in immigration from a little over 1,218,000 in 1914 to 327,000 in 1915 created a scarcity of unskilled labor and stimulated the first large-scale migration of Negroes from the southern countryside to northern and midwestern industrial centers. This stream of black workers swelled in response to increased demands in 1917 and 1918. The nearly half million blacks who went to the North found no warm welcome awaiting them. Forced to crowd into the worst areas, they became the object of the suspicion and hatred of white unskilled workers, most of them immigrants themselves, who resented Negro competition and mores.

At the same time Negro-white relations were considerably worsened by black participation in the war. Some 400,000 Negroes served in the armed forces, about half of them overseas where they were accorded an equality they had never known in their native South. White Southerners were terrified at the thought of so many black men learning the use of firearms and the ways of equality. They were prepared in 1919 to use the rope and the faggot to remind returning Negro veterans that the Great Crusade had been no war for racial democracy in the South.

Thirdly, while the war heightened anti-Negro sentiments in both the North and South, the black people of America and their spokesmen were beginning to demand higher wages, immunity from violence, and a larger voice in politics. Most important, their participation in the war effort had given them a new sense of pride in their own race. The National Association for the Advancement of Colored People, now under control of a militant element, was especially active during the war. One of the NAACP's leaders, William E. B. Du Bois, convoked a Pan-African Congress in Paris during the peace conference to speak for blacks throughout the world.

These tensions burts into full-scale violence in the South as white men resorted to traditional weapons to intimidate black communities. Lynchings increased from thirty-four in 1917 to sixty in 1918, and to more than seventy in 1919. Ten Negro veterans, several of them still in uniform, were lynched in 1919; fourteen blacks were burned publicly. Southern white terrorism also found expression in a form more ominous than these individual acts of violence—in the rapid spread, especially through the Southwest, of the newly revived Ku Klux Klan, about which more will be said later. The Klan grew during 1919 from insignificance into a thriving organization of more than 100,000 members with cells in twenty-seven states. Defying law enforcement officials, hooded Klan night riders flogged, tarred, and hanged their victims in many southern and southwestern communities.

Even worse travail awaited black Americans in the outbreak of the most fearful race riots in American history.[6] They began in July 1919 in Longview, Texas, and spread a week later to the nation's capital, where mobs composed principally of white servicemen pillaged the black section. The worst riot broke out in Chicago on July 27, 1919, after an altercation between whites and blacks on a Lake Michigan beach. Mobs roamed the slum areas of the city for thirteen days burning, pillaging, and killing, with the National Guard unable to subdue them. Fifteen whites and twenty-three blacks were dead when it was over; 178 whites and 342 blacks were injured; and more than 1,000 families were homeless. During the next two months major riots broke out in Knoxville, Omaha, and Elaine, Arkansas, and the final count by the end of 1919 revealed some twenty-five riots, with hundreds dead and injured and property damages running in the millions.

Blacks and liberal whites were dismayed and reacted in varied ways. The NAACP and other militant Negro groups counseled resistance and undertook a public campaign against lynching. It culminated in the passage by the House of Representatives of the first antilynching bill in 1921. This measure was endorsed by twenty-four governors and an overwhelming northern opinion, but it was defeated by a southern filibuster in the Senate. The most significant reaction in the South was the first substantial

[6]That is, in the postwar period. There had been a serious race riot in East St. Louis, Illinois, in July 1917.

awakening of the southern conscience and the organization in Atlanta in 1919 of the Commission on Interracial Cooperation. It would become the spearhead of a growing southern liberal movement in the 1920s and 1930s.

The mass of Negroes, however, were not inspired by antilynching campaigns or encouraged by the beginning of an organized southern effort to combat racial intolerance. They had demonstrated a new militancy during the riots by fighting back courageously and often effectively in self-defense. They were also ready to follow a leader who was proud of his race. Such a black was Marcus Garvey, a Jamaican, who organized his Universal Negro Improvement Association in 1914 and moved to New York City two years later. Garvey urged blacks to be proud of their race and culture and follow him back to Africa to build a "free, redeemed and mighty nation." In the racial upheaval of the postwar years Garvey's schemes stimulated visions of a grand new destiny in the minds of countless Negroes. Claiming 4 million followers in 1920 and 6 million in 1923, Garvey proclaimed himself provisional president of an African Empire in 1921 and raised funds to buy a Black Star steamship line and carry his people home. The empire crumbled in 1923, however, when Garvey was convicted in federal court of using the mails to defraud and sentenced to the Atlanta penitentiary for a five-year term. American blacks, obviously, would not go back to Africa, but the fact that so many of them rallied to Garvey's standard was evidence of important stirrings of black racial self-respect.

5. The Election of 1920

Politicians began their quadrennial preparations for the coming presidential campaign during this season of social conflict and racial unrest. It was obvious by the beginning of 1920 that any passable Republican candidate would win the presidency, and there was much activity in the GOP camp. However, the commanding figures who had led the party since 1900 were absent or in retirement. Into the fight for leadership, therefore, rushed a number of lesser dignitaries. General Leonard Wood, who had inherited most of the following of Theodore Roosevelt, who had died in 1919, made the most formidable campaign for the Republican nomination. Wood was forthrightly independent of party bosses, intensely nationalistic, and a champion of universal military training. Nearly as popular was Governor Frank O. Lowden of Illinois, a former congressman who had the support of the business and farm interests of the Middle West. On the periphery was Senator Hiram W. Johnson of California, vainly trying to rally the old insurgents; Senator Robert M. La Follette of Wisconsin, always a hopeful but never a successful contender; Herbert Hoover, who announced that he was a Republican and would accept the nomination; and a number of favorite sons, including the nondescript Warren G. Harding of Ohio.

The outcome was, therefore, by no means certain when the Republicans met in national convention on June 8, 1920. The Wood and Lowden managers battled fiercely to a standstill during the first four ballots on Friday, June 11. Fearing an impasse, Chairman Henry Cabot Lodge adjourned the convention at seven o'clock, in order, he said, to give the leaders a chance to think. Managers and leaders had little time for reflection during the ensuing hectic hours. The Wood leaders tried unsuccessfully to win the Johnson delegates and refused to make entangling alliances with party bosses and oil lobbyists. At the same time, another group was gathering in the suite of National Chairman Will H. Hays at the Blackstone Hotel. It included Hays and a clique of powerful senators and their allies, among them Lodge, Senator Frank B. Brandegee of Connecticut, George Harvey, caustic New York editor, and other party regulars. They wanted not Wood or Lowden, but a president whom they could control. Their opportunity to name the candidate seemed to be at hand on account of the Wood-Lowden deadlock.

The senatorial clique in the now legendary "smoke-filled" room in the Blackstone continued their search all during the evening on Friday, June 11. They settled upon Senator Warren G. Harding of Ohio, a party hack who met all the qualifications of a perfect dark horse. Harding had many friends, particularly among delegates to the convention, and no enemies in the party; he had voted for the Lodge reservations, and, most important, was thought to be controllable. The decision was made and relayed to other party leaders by eleven o'clock on Friday night. Harvey called Harding to the smoke-filled room at about two o'clock Saturday morning, told him of the decision, and asked if there was any reason why the party should not nominate him. After meditating privately in an adjoining room for ten minutes, Harding returned to reply that there was no reason why he should not be president.

The senatorial clique was proceeding on the assumption that the Wood and Lowden forces would never combine. As it turned out, this was a safe enough gamble. The deadlock continued for four more ballots on Saturday morning, June 12, until Chairman Lodge recessed the convention in the early afternoon. Then, while the Wood and Lowden managers negotiated to no avail, Harvey and the senatorial clique, for reasons that are still obscure, tried to rally the party behind Will Hays. The effort failed, and Harding was nominated on the tenth ballot soon after the convention reassembled Saturday afternoon. The main reason seems to have been that leaders and delegates realized that he was the one candidate who could now be nominated without a grueling, disruptive battle. For vice-president the senatorial clique had settled upon Senator Irvine L. Lenroot of Wisconsin. However, the weary delegates in an unexpected burst of independence nominated Governor Calvin Coolidge, hero of the recent Boston strike.

The Republican platform gave notice of the GOP's intention to destroy Wilsonianism and all its works. It promised tariff increases, tax reductions, immigration restriction, vigorous aid to farmers, and, by implication, an end to further federal social legislation. On the issue of the League the framers made room both for irreconcilables and Republican League men. The platform condemned Wilson's League but approved membership in the World Court and "agreement among nations to preserve the peace of the world."

Meanwhile, the Democrats had been engaged in a preconvention contest even more confused than the struggle that preceded the Republican convention. The chief cause of the Democratic uncertainty was the president himself, for Wilson acted very much like a receptive if silent candidate after his partial recovery during the early months of 1920. He dismissed Secretary of State Lansing and took charge of the government in February. He attended well-publicized cabinet meetings and took long rides in his automobile. And just before the Democratic convention met in June he called photographers to the White House and gave an important interview to Louis Seibold of the New York *World*. All available evidence indicates that the president hoped that he might be chosen to lead a campaign for the League of Nations, and that he intended, if elected, to resign once the treaty had been ratified.

Wilson's potential candidacy cast a long shadow over the aspirations of his son-in-law, William G. McAdoo, the chief contender for the Democratic nomination. As a gesture of filial respect. McAdoo "withdrew" from the race on the same day, June 18, that Wilson's interview appeared in the New York *World*. McAdoo's strongest rival was the attorney-general, A. Mitchell Palmer, who was still beating drums for Americanism. Among the favorite sons, Governor James M. Cox of Ohio had the greatest potential strength, even though President Wilson thought that his candidacy was "a joke." Three times elected governor of a doubtful state, Cox had an excellent progressive record, had survived the Republican victory of 1918, and was more acceptable to the city bosses than McAdoo or Palmer because of his opposition to prohibition.

Because of the division in the Wilsonian ranks, the Democratic convention that opened at San Francisco on June 28 was no less confused than its Republican counterpart. As events turned out, Wilson had no influence over the convention's choice. He had made plans to have his name presented and his nomination effected by acclamation once a deadlock occurred. But this stratagem was never executed because a group of the president's close friends met in San Francisco on July 3-4 and agreed that a third nomination would kill both Wilson and the Democratic party. The Irish bosses who controlled the delegations from Massachusetts, New

York, New Jersey, Indiana, and Illinois held the balance of power and, in the end, named the candidate. The McAdoo and Palmer forces fought to a standstill for thirty-seven weary ballots. Palmer released his delegates on the thirty-eighth ballot; but as most of them went to Cox, a McAdoo drive fizzled, and Cox was named on the forty-fourth roll call on July 5. Cox's choice for running mate was Franklin D. Roosevelt of New York, assistant secretary of the navy, a prominent Wilsonian and League supporter.

Meanwhile the convention had adopted a platform that sidestepped the prohibition question, extended sympathy to Ireland, and promised tax reductions and independence for the Philippines. On the all-important League issue the platform was at the same time straightforward—reflecting Wilson's demands—and evasive—reflecting the arguments of Democrats who wanted to accept the Lodge reservations. We advocate immediate ratification of the treaty without crippling reservations, the platform declared; but we do not "oppose the acceptance of any reservations making clearer or more specific the obligations of the United States to the League associates."

In spite of the convention's straddle, Cox and Roosevelt labored heroically during the ensuing campaign to make the election a "great and solemn referendum" on the League and to warn voters that reactionary business interests would control the government if Harding won. Harding's managers, on the other hand, wisely decided that the less that he said the better his chances would be. Hence Harding made no long tours like Cox, but rather he stayed home in Marion, Ohio, and greeted delegations on his front porch. It was impossible to judge from his sonorous homilies just where Harding stood on any specific issue. Isolationists were certain that he would keep the country out of the detested League. In contrast, a group of thirty-one distinguished pro-League Republicans, including Charles Evans Hughes, Elihu Root, and Herbert Hoover, assured voters that Harding's election was the first necessary step in ratification with reservations.

Harding's ambivalent speeches and the statement of the thirty-one so confused the voters that it is doubtful if the League was even an important issue in the campaign. It was evident long before election day that the Republicans were capitalizing on an accumulation of grievances going back all the way to the progressive legislation of 1916 and the adoption of the war resolution. The disparate elements opposed to Democratic policies—Irish- and German-Americans, blacks, industrialists and businessmen in rebellion against high taxes and policies favorable to labor, champions of civil liberty, independent progressives outraged by the treaty and the Palmer raids, and midwestern and Plains farmers then undergoing a severe depression—moved en masse into the Republican camp.

The result of the combining of the dissident elements with the normal Republican majority was the most smashing electoral triumph since the reelection of James Monroe in 1820. Harding received 16,152,000 popular

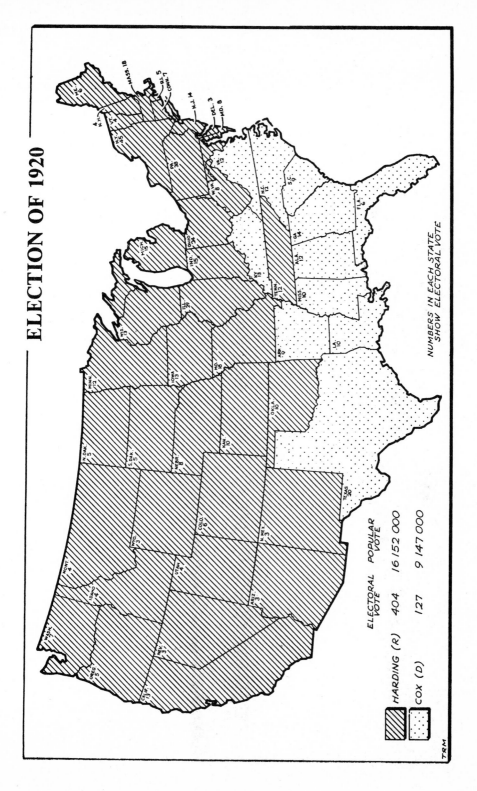

ELECTION OF 1920

ME. 6

MASS. 18
N.H. R.I. 5
VT. CONN. 7
N.J. 14
DEL. 3
MD. 8

PA. 38

MICH. 15

WIS. 13

MINN. 12

N. DAK. 5

S. DAK. 5

MONT. 4

IDAHO 4

WASH. 7

OREG. 5

CALIF. 13

NEV. 3

UTAH 4

ARIZ. 3

WYO. 3

COLO. 6

N. MEX. 3

NEBR. 8

KAN. 10

IOWA 13

ILL. 29

IND. 15

OHIO 24

W. VA. 8

VA. 12

KY. 13

TENN. 12

N.C. 12

S.C. 9

GA. 14

ALA. 12

MISS. 10

ARK. 9

LA. 10

TEXAS 20

OKLA. 10

MO. 18

FLA. 6

NUMBERS IN EACH STATE
SHOW ELECTORAL VOTE

	ELECTORAL VOTE	POPULAR VOTE
HARDING (R)	404	16 152 000
COX (D)	127	9 147 000

TRM

votes, or 61 percent of the total; he won all the states outside the South, for an electoral vote of 404; and he even broke the Solid South by carrying Tennessee. With only 9,147,000 popular and 127 electoral votes, Cox was the worst beaten Democratic candidate since Stephen A. Douglas. The Republican sweep in the senatorial and congressional contests—there would be Republican majorities of 22 in the Senate and 167 in the House in the next Congress—was nearly as impressive as Harding's own majority.

This landslide did not signify a repudiation of the League but rather revealed the confusion and growing popular apathy over that issue. It did not signify a repudiation of progressivism or any great collapse of idealism among the people. It signified, rather, the triumph of the combined forces of dissent and protest. Wilson had created a majority Democratic coalition in 1916 composed principally of Southerners, middle and far western anti-war progressives and farmers, independents, and workingmen throughout the country. Wilson's policies after 1916 consistently alienated independents, antiwar progressives, and, most important, western farmers. By destroying the Wilsonian coalition in 1920, these groups not only registered their protests against Wilson's alleged betrayal of their interests, but they also destroyed the only political alliance capable of carrying on progressive policies in a systematic way. And unwittingly they turned the next administration over to their traditional enemies—the business elements who once again were in control of the Republican party.

11

Aspects

of Economic Development,

1920–1940

The decade 1919–1929 was a period of rapid economic development that brought the standard of living of the American people to a level hitherto unknown in history. Even so, the economic progress of the twenties lacked the overall solidity of economic growth that characterized the period from 1900 to 1914. The prosperity of the twenties was more urban than general; it was confined to some industries more than to others. More dangerous still was the fact that the resources of commercial banks were used to finance a runaway speculative boom in real estate and the stock markets.

Yet these were signs seen only by the wisest economists. By the autumn of 1929 the American people were basking in the golden glow of prosperity but standing on the brink of the greatest depression in their history. Perhaps it was just as well that they did not know the perils and tests that lay ahead in the 1930s.

1. The American People, 1920–1940

These were two decades of revolutionary changes affecting the growth, distribution, and composition of the American people. The decline in the birth rate, which had begun a century before, became really precipitate after 1915. It fell from 30.1 per thousand in 1910 to 27.7 in 1920, and then it dropped to 21.3 in 1930; and the population increase from 106,466,000 in 1920 to 123,188,000 in 1930 was at a rate of 16.1 percent, as compared to 21.2 percent for the period 1900–1910. With the onset of the depression the birth rate fell even further and hovered between 18.5 and 19 per thousand during the last half of the 1930s. Mothers were not having enough children between 1930 and 1940 even to maintain the population, much less to add to future numbers. Studying the statistics at the end of the decade, demographers took a gloomy view of the future of population growth in the United States.

The results of the census of 1940 seemed fully to justify these predictions. From 1930 to 1940 the population of the United States increased from 123,188,000 to 132,122,000. The rate of increase of 7.2 percent was less than half the rate of the preceding decade and about one-third the rate from 1900 to 1910. Offsetting the declining birth rate to some degree, however, was a nearly phenomenal improvement in the health of the American people. The death rate in areas furnishing reliable statistics fell from 17.2 per thousand in 1900 to 13 per thousand in 1920, and to 10.8 per thousand in 1940. Life expectancy for both sexes increased from 47.3 years in 1900 to 62.9 years in 1940.

Americans in 1940 were more than ever white and native-born. The 12,865,518 Negroes and 588,887 Indians, Orientals, and other nonwhites enumerated by the census of 1940 together represented 10.3 percent of the total population, as compared to 12 percent in 1920. The severe restriction and selection of European immigration effected by the legislation of the 1920s (see pp. 315–317) had already begun markedly to alter the composition of the white population. The 11,594,896 foreign-born persons in the United States in 1940 constituted only 8.7 percent of the total population, while 15 percent had been foreign-born in 1910. Total net immigration declined from a prewar peak of 3,015,301 for the period 1911–1915 to 68,789 for the entire decade of the 1930s. As these figures include Canadians and Mexicans unaffected by restrictions, they fail to convey the full impact of the quota system established by legislation in the twenties on immigration from Europe.

The most important internal demographic change of this period was the increasing movement from the countryside to the cities. The American farm population suffered a loss of 10,184,000 by internal migration from 1920 to 1940. It was so tremendous a movement that total farm population

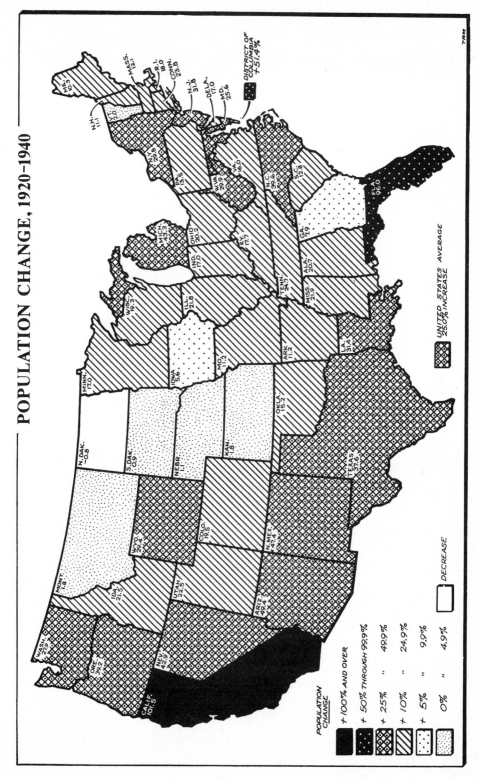

POPULATION CHANGE, 1920–1940

ME.
10.3

N.H.
11.1

VT.
N.Y.
29.6

MASS.
12.1

R.I.
18.0

CONN.
23.8

N.J.
31.8

DELA.
17.0

MD.
25.6

DISTRICT OF
COLUMBIA
+51.4%

PA.
13.5

W.VA.
29.6

N.C.
39.6

S.C.
12.8

MICH.
43.3

OHIO
20.2

IND.
17.0

KY.
17.7

VA.
16.0

FLA.
96.0

WIS.
19.3

ILL.
21.8

TENN.
24.7

MISS.
21.9

ALA.
20.7

GA.
7.9

MINN.
17.0

IOWA
5.6

MO.
11.2

ARK.
11.2

LA.
31.4

N.DAK.
-0.8

S.DAK.
0.9

NEBR.
1.1

KAN.
1.8

OKLA.
5.2

TEXAS
37.6

MONT.
1.8

IDA.
21.5

WYO.
22.1

COLO.
19.5

N.MEX.
47.4

WASH.
25.9

ORE.
30.2

NEV.
43.9

UTAH
22.5

ARIZ.
49.4

CALIF.
101.5

UNITED STATES AVERAGE
25.0% INCREASE

DECREASE

POPULATION
CHANGE

+ 100% AND OVER
+ 50% THROUGH 99.9%
+ 25%   "   49.9%
+ 10%   "   24.9%
+   5%   "   9.9%
    0%   "   4.9%

T.R.M.

245

POPULATION DENSITY, 1940

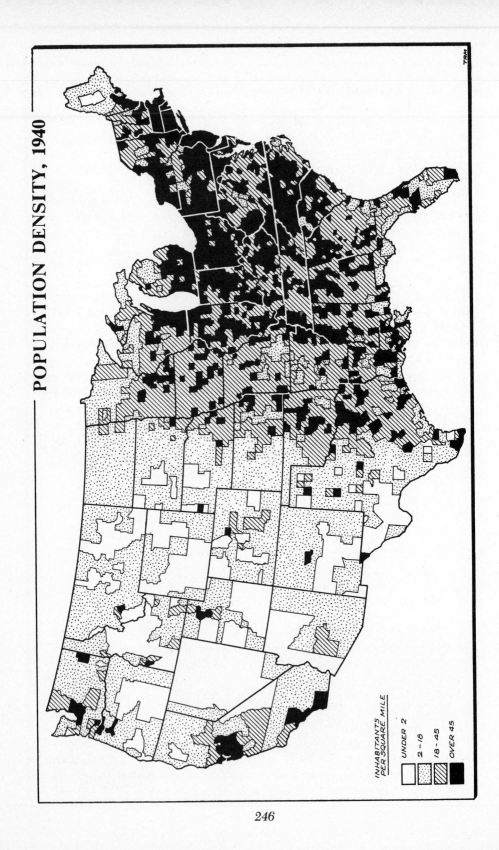

INHABITANTS
PER SQUARE MILE

☐	UNDER 2
▨	2 - 18
▨	18 - 45
■	OVER 45

sustained a net loss of 1,134,000 persons during the two decades, in spite of a high birth rate among farm people. One of the most important changes in the American social fabric during the first four decades of the twentieth century can be read in the following sentences. In 1900 nearly 60 percent of the American people lived in the country and in small towns under 2,500. By 1940, 43.5 percent of the people lived in rural areas, while only 23 percent actually lived on farms.

One direct consequence of this massive movement was the accelerated growth of American cities, particularly in the 1920s. The five cities of 1 million inhabitants or over, for example, alone absorbed more than one-third the total urban increase of 14.6 million during the decade. The so-called satellite cities surrounding the metropolises grew at twice the speed of nonsatellite cities of similar size. This movement was momentarily reversed during the early thirties, but the exodus to the cities began again with the return of prosperity between 1935 and 1937. In 1940 the Census Bureau could count 140 so-called metropolitan districts, in which 48 percent of the people lived. This represented an increase of 9.3 percent for the decade of the 1930s alone.

A final significant internal population change was a steady migration of blacks from the South to the North and Middle West, which had begun on a large scale around 1915. In 1920, 85 percent of all Negroes lived south of the Mason-Dixon line, which was only 7 units lower than the corresponding percentage on the eve of the Civil War. By 1940 nearly 24 percent of blacks lived outside the South, and this was merely the beginning of a movement that would grow enormously after 1940.

2. The American People, 1920–1940:
Income, Wealth, and Industry

The American economy was stimulated from 1917 to 1920 by European purchases, enormous federal war expenditures at home, and a concomitant expansion in bank credits. Then followed a dizzy postwar period of inflation and intense economic activity. Actually, the postwar boom of 1919–1920 was more apparent than real, except in agriculture. National income, adjusted for the cost of living, declined from $64,500,000,000 in 1918 to $57,884,000,000 in 1920, and the index of production in the basic industries fell correspondingly. Yet the decline during 1920 was not precipitate in manufacturing or trade, nor was it marked by any large number of business failures. The greatest shock was the collapse in farm prices that began in the late spring and reached panic proportions during the autumn.

The recession had become a full-fledged depression by the spring of 1921. American foreign trade declined in value from $13.5 billion in 1920 to less than $7 billion in 1921; wholesale prices declined 21 percent; and unemployment reached a peak of 4,754,000. Actually, a general readjustment to a lower world price level was taking place. Recovery set in at the beginning of 1922 and was steady on all fronts until 1927. Then a slight recession was followed by an intensification of economic activity that continued until 1929. This was the period that contemporary economists called the "New Economic Era," when it seemed that production, prices, and wages had reached an equilibrium and a high plateau upon which the economy might run indefinitely. Such hopes were obviously overly confident, but the 1920s were nonetheless a time of marked advancement on most economic fronts.

To begin with, there was a steady increase in the wealth and incomes of the American people during this decade. Adjusted for the cost of living, total national income increased from $65,093,000,000, or $620 per capita, in 1919 to $82,810,000,000, or $681 per capita, a decade later. The spectacular improvement in the material well-being of the American people during the first decades of the twentieth century becomes apparent when we recall that the adjusted per capita income in 1900 was $480.

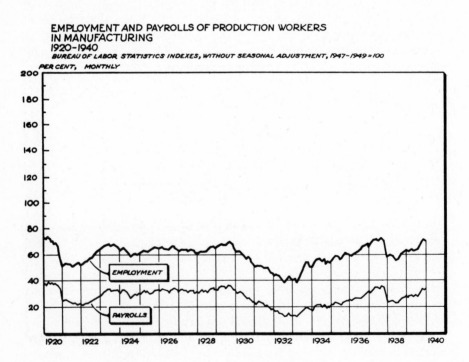

EMPLOYMENT AND PAYROLLS OF PRODUCTION WORKERS
IN MANUFACTURING
1920-1940
BUREAU OF LABOR STATISTICS INDEXES, WITHOUT SEASONAL ADJUSTMENT, 1947-1949=100
PER CENT, MONTHLY

These generalizations illustrate the overall economic progress of the twenties but fail to indicate internal maladjustments that made the prosperity of the period ephemeral for large elements of the population. We can, therefore, obtain a more meaningful picture of the state of the nation during the New Economic Era by seeing the important changes that occurred from 1923 to 1929 in the relative economic status of the major groups.

As we have already seen, farmers suffered a severe deflation in 1920 and 1921. In spite of some recovery in prices from the depression level of 1921, farmers never regained the fine relative balance that they had enjoyed in 1914 and 1919. The share of agriculture in the national private production income had been 22.9 percent in 1919; it was 12.7 percent in 1929.

In contrast, the condition of most workers in industry substantially improved in almost all aspects during the 1920s. Over the decade 1919–1929 there was a rise in annual real earnings of 26 percent; it was perhaps the largest decennial increase up to that time. During the period of greatest expansion, 1923 to 1929, the number of wage earners increased only about .5 percent, but average hourly wages increased 8 percent, average real

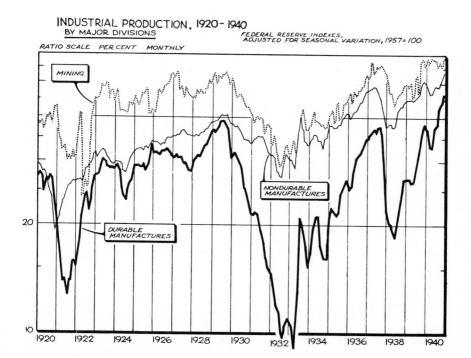

INDUSTRIAL PRODUCTION, 1920–1940
BY MAJOR DIVISIONS

FEDERAL RESERVE INDEXES,
ADJUSTED FOR SEASONAL VARIATION, 1957=100

RATIO SCALE   PER CENT   MONTHLY

MINING

NONDURABLE MANUFACTURES

DURABLE MANUFACTURES

20

10

1920 1922 1924 1926 1928 1930 1932 1934 1936 1938 1940 earnings increased 11 percent, while the average work week decreased from 47.3 to 45.7 hours.

A basic stimulant of prosperity in the 1920s was expansion in the construction industry after 1918. Stable costs and a continued high demand enabled the industry to record one large gain after another from 1922 to 1928, when it began to slacken. The estimated value of construction, based on the value of materials used, rose from a little over $12 billion in 1919 to a peak of nearly $17.5 billion in 1928.

Manufacturing enjoyed an even more significant expansion during the prosperity decade. The number of manufacturing establishments declined through consolidation and elimination of small producers from 274,598 in 1919 to 210,959 in 1929; the number of industrial workers declined during the decade from 9,041,311 to 8,838,743. At the same time, there was an increase of 64 percent in manufacturing output, chiefly because of a 40 percent increase in labor's productivity. The following table illustrates the general character of the shifting pattern of production (see page 251).

These are statistics of dollar volume of production and therefore partially obscure the important growth of certain segments of the economy. Thus the actual production of automobiles increased 255 percent from 1919 to 1929; chemical products increased 94 percent; rubber products, 86 percent; printing and publishing, 85 percent; iron and steel products, 70 percent. At the same time, production of leather, food, tobacco, and textile products increased at a slower pace. On the reverse side, production of coal and railroad equipment sharply declined.

On the surface the American people had never seemed so economically healthy as in 1929. And yet their prosperity was so unevenly divided that it could not long continue without some adjustment. This was true primarily because such an increasing share of the national income was going to industry and finance that workers relatively lost ground, and farmers suffered an absolute retrogression. For example, corporate profits and dividends increased 62 and 65 percent, respectively, from 1923 to 1929, while workers enjoyed an 11 percent increase in real income. By the end of the prosperity decade, such a large portion of the national income was being funneled off at the top by receivers in restricted geographical areas that the men and women on America's assembly lines and farms were finding it difficult to purchase what they produced. For example, there were indications by 1928 of overproduction in residential housing and automobiles.

This fundamental maladjustment is dramatically revealed by the following analysis. There were nearly 27.5 million families in the United States in 1929. Nearly 6 million families, or more than 21 percent of the total, had incomes less than $1,000; nearly 12 million, or more than 42 percent, had incomes under $1,500; nearly 20 million, or some 71 percent, had incomes under $2,500, the sum estimated as being necessary for a decent living standard. On the other hand, the 36,000 wealthiest families received an

The Ten Leading American Industries, Ranked According to Value of Products, 1919 and 1929

	1919			1929	
Rank	Industry	Value of Products (in Thousands of Dollars)	Rank	Industry	Value of Products (in Thousands of Dollars)
1.	Food and allied industries	$12,748,348	1.	Food and allied industries	$12,023,589
2.	Textiles and textile products	9,210,933	2.	Textiles and textile products	9,243,303
3.	Iron and steel and products	5,887,844	3.	Iron and steel and products	7,137,928
4.	Transportation, equipment, including automobiles	5,627,623	4.	Machinery	7,043,380
5.	Machinery	4,768,673	5.	Transportation equipment, including automobiles	6,047,209
6.	Chemicals and allied products	3,803,753	6.	Chemicals and allied products	3,759,405
7.	Forest products	3,113,460	7.	Petroleum and coal products	3,647,748
8.	Leather and its products	2,613,217	8.	Nonferrous metals and products	3,597,058
9.	Nonferrous metals and products	2,519,032	9.	Forest products	3,591,765
10.	Petroleum and coal products	2,289,170	10.	Printing, publishing, and allied products	3,170,140

aggregate income in 1929 nearly equal to the total income received by the more than 11.6 million families receiving less than $1,500 a year.

Since we will relate the course of the Great Depression, the slow progress toward economic recovery, and other changes affecting industry, wage earners, and farmers in the 1930s in some detail in later chapters, a few summary generalizations about economic trends in the 1930s must suffice at this point. The years between the onset of the Great Depression and 1940 were a time of retrogression and despair such as the American people had rarely known in their history, followed by painful and slow recovery. Briefly stated, recovery from the depression was already fairly complete before the great defense spending of 1941 opened a new era in American economic history. The gross national product, measured in constant 1953 dollars, declined from $175.9 billion in 1929 to $123.4 billion in 1933 and then gradually increased to $205.7 billion in 1940. At the same time, per capita disposable income,[1] measured in 1953 dollars, declined from $1,059 in 1929 to $728 in 1933 but recovered steadily to $1,130 by 1940.

[1] That is, income left after taxes and Social Security payments.

3. The Technological Revolution

Underlying the increased industrial output of the 1920s was a revolution in industrial management and technology that made possible the production of larger numbers of units by a smaller number of workers at a lower cost. Of all the causes of America's industrial development in the twentieth century, the technological revolution was most basic and therefore most significant, for the age of mass production could never have come without the techniques it afforded. Like other economic developments of the 1920s and 1930s, the technological revolution had its roots deep in the American past and its greatest impact after 1920.

A young industrial engineer, Frederick W. Taylor, turned to a study of scientific shop management during the 1880s and 1890s and evolved a theory of scientific management. It was that engineers by objective analysis could determine the reasonable capacities of men and machinery. So successful were Taylor and his disciples that scientific management had been accepted to a varying degree by almost every branch of business and industry by the early 1920s.

Meanwhile, another and equally important development had been maturing—mass production by the assembly line technique and production of interchangeable parts by automatic precision machinery.[2] The use of interchangeable parts had begun in the late eighteenth century,[3] but the introduction of the assembly line, or progressive line production, technique was a twentieth-century phenomenon, first developed by Henry Ford in the automobile industry from 1908 to 1914. From 1908 to 1913 Ford used a stationary assembly line. In 1913 and 1914, however, he reorganized the assembly process in a revolutionary way—by introducing the moving assembly line, which reduced labor required for assembly of an automobile chassis from fourteen to less than two man-hours. In the effort to increase production during the First World War, the assembly line technique was applied to shipbuilding, the manufacture of airplane engines, and the production of munitions. The new method was firmly established in many branches of industry by the early 1920s.

Another important component of the technological revolution was industrial research. The war gave the largest stimulus, and by 1920 many corporations had established independent research laboratories. By 1927

---

[2] A whole series of inventions between 1865 and 1900, particularly the micrometer caliper and other measuring devices, the automatic turret lathe, and hard alloys for cutting purposes, contributed to this development.

[3] By 1900, interchangeable parts were being used in the manufacture of firearms, agricultural machinery, sewing machines, typewriters, and bicycles.

at least 1,000 corporations were carrying on either independent or cooperative research for improvement of product or service, reduction of production costs, development of by-products and new products, and the like. Data on total expenditures in 1927 are unavailable, but 208 firms reported expenditures aggregating nearly $12 million. This was a significant beginning, but industrial research was still in its infancy. By 1937, for example, American industrialists were spending $180 million annually for research; four years later the figure stood at $510 million.

THE INCREASE OF PRODUCTIVITY IN THE UNITED STATES, 1891–1950, *BY DECADES*

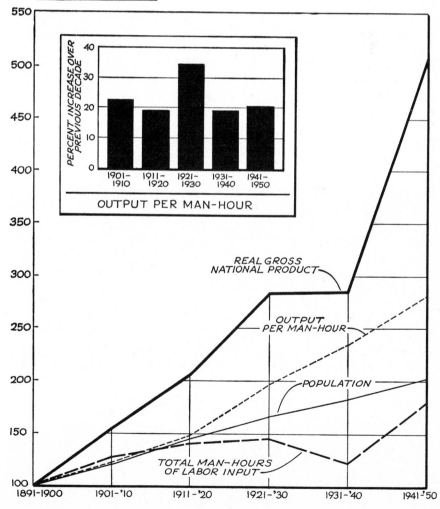

A fourth aspect of the technological revolution paid the largest dividends in human health and happiness. It was the growing acceptance and application of the theory that conditions affecting the health, comfort, and safety of workers had a direct influence on production and productivity. So successful was the safety-in-industry campaign before the First World War that practically every factory erected during the 1920s was constructed according to modern safety standards, while many old factories were modernized in this regard. A study of industrial accidents about 1928 revealed that only 10 percent of them were caused by lack of mechanical safeguards.

By 1929 the technological revolution had gone so far as to cause observers to think that they were living in an age of miracles. That revolution, in its first culmination from 1919 to 1929, caused a gain of productivity of 40 percent in manufacturing and of 26 percent in agriculture—as contrasted with gains in productivity from 1899 to 1909 of 7 percent in manufacturing and 6 percent in agriculture. The technological revolution slowed perceptibly in the 1930s, chiefly because of a severe decline in investment for new capital equipment and the absence of new technological breakthroughs. Indeed, general productivity decreased sharply between 1929 and 1933. For the 1930s as a whole, however, general output per man-hour increased about 20 percent; and productivity in manufacturing and agriculture increased by about the same percentage.

4. The Rise of New Industries

Several industries, in their infancy when the decade began, emerged to positions of key importance during the 1920s. They were not only dynamic economically, in that they stimulated other segments of the economy, but they were also prime movers of a revolution in living habits and social attitudes that was taking shape by 1929 and would come to full flower after the Second World War.

THE RISE OF THE AUTOMOBILE.   Europeans experimented for almost a century with self-propelled carriages, until Carl Benz, a German, built the first automobile powered by a gasoline engine in 1884. Charles and Frank Duryea of Springfield, Massachusetts, and Henry Ford of Detroit built the first successful gasoline-driven carriages in the United States in 1892–1893. There were some 8,000 automobiles in the United States by 1900. Some 181 companies entered the field during the next quarter century; but three major concerns, Ford, General Motors, and Chrysler, accounted for 83 percent of the output by 1930.

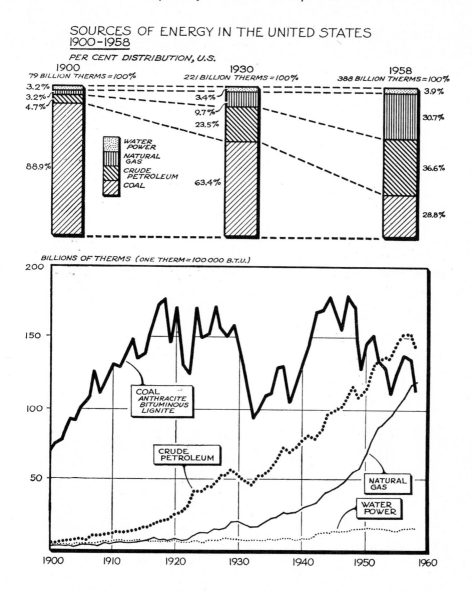

SOURCES OF ENERGY IN THE UNITED STATES 1900-1958

PER CENT DISTRIBUTION, U.S.

Henry Ford was the leader all during this period. After experimenting with low-priced cars, he introduced the Model T in the autumn of 1908. By concentrating on this single unlovely but enduring model, and by introducing the assembly line process and scientific management, Ford realized his dream of producing automobiles for the masses. The price of Ford cars dropped after introduction of the assembly line from $950 to $290. Ford's closest rival in the fierce struggle for supremacy was the General Motors Corporation, organized by William C. Durant in 1908. It fell under the control of the DuPont and Morgan interests in 1921 and produced a wide number of lines, ranging from the luxurious Cadillac to the low-priced Chevrolet. A third but much smaller competitor was the Chrysler Corporation, organized in 1923, which acquired Dodge Brothers in 1928 and Plymouth in 1929.

Meanwhile, the automobile industry had emerged as the largest single manufacturing industry in the United States. Production of automobiles increased from 4,000 in 1900 to 4,794,898 in 1929. Production declined to 1,103,557 in 1932 and then increased steadily to nearly 4,000,000 in 1937. By 1940 there were nearly 32,500,000 automobiles, trucks, and busses in operation in the United States. In 1919 the automotive industry employed 343,115 workers, who earned $491,122,000 in wages and turned out products valued at $2,330,000. In 1939 the industry employed 398,963 workers, paid $646,406,000 in wages, and manufactured products with an aggregate value of $4,047,873,000.

It is no exaggeration to say that manufacture of automobiles was in large measure responsible for the intense economic activity of the 1920s. According to one estimate, it gave employment, directly or indirectly, to 3.7 million persons by 1929. Use of the automobile gave rise to construction and maintenance of hard-surfaced highways, operation of garages and filling stations, maintenance of tourist camps, operation of fleets of motor trucks and busses, and the like. County, state, and federal authorities were spending nearly $2.5 billion annually by the end of the 1930s for construction, maintenance, and financing of highways and bridges alone.

ELECTRIC POWER, MACHINERY, AND APPLIANCES. In a later chapter (pp. 317–318) we will note the rise of the electric power industry, but it might be well to summarize the story briefly at this point. The electric power industry from 1900 to 1929 rose from comparative insignificance to become the second most important economic interest in the United States. Production increased from 6 billion kilowatt-hours to nearly 117 billion; capital invested in the industry grew to nearly $12 billion; and total income to nearly $2 billion. Growth was slower in the 1930s, but in 1940 production was nearly 180 billion kilowatt-hours; capital invested stood at $15.5 billion; and total income was nearly $3 billion. Only 16 percent of American homes were electrified in 1912; nearly 79 percent used electric power by 1940. Almost overnight, also, the manufacture of electric turbines, motors, supplies, and appliances grew into an industry of the first importance. The decade 1919–1929 was the period of greatest growth, as the value of products of this industry increased from $997,968,000 to $2,300,916,000. In 1939 the industry's products were valued at $1,730,000,000.

THE RADIO INDUSTRY. Most inventions basic to the construction of radio transmitters and receivers had been perfected before the First

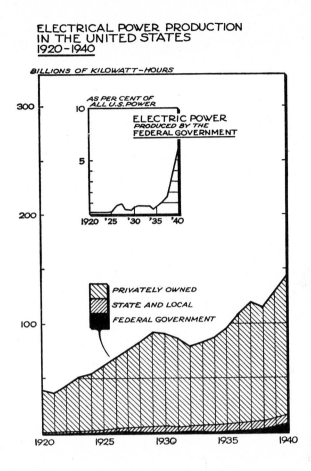

ELECTRICAL POWER PRODUCTION
IN THE UNITED STATES
1920-1940

World War, but it was not until 1919 that the federal government lifted its ban on the private operation of sets. A great new industry came into being during the next decade. The General Electric and Westinghouse companies organized the Radio Corporation of America in 1919 and began to manufacture radio parts on a small scale. Radio soon became a virtual obsession of the American people, and the production of sets increased by leaps and bounds. In 1921 sales of radio parts totaled a mere $10.6 million. By 1939 the industry produced nearly 11 million radios with a total product value of $276 million; and census reporters discovered the following year that 28.5 million American families, or 80 percent of the total number, had radio sets—an increase of 100 percent since 1929.

THE AVIATION INDUSTRY.   Although two Americans, Wilbur and Orville Wright, built and flew the first successful airplane at Kitty Hawk, North Carolina, on December 17, 1903, leadership in aviation soon moved across the Atlantic. With the outbreak of the war, Europeans swiftly developed the flying machine as a fighting weapon. When Congress adopted the war resolution in 1917, however, the American army had no combat planes and only a few inefficient observation craft. The government at once began a gigantic program to train thousands of pilots and established the Aircraft Production Board to build thousands of engines and aircraft.

The United States had twenty-four plants capable of producing 21,000 planes annually when the armistice was signed. But the government hastily canceled its orders, and the entire industry practically collapsed. European governments kept their aviation industries alive through generous mail subsidies, but it was many years before America followed suit. In 1925, Congress authorized the Post Office Department to grant contracts for carrying mail to private companies; in 1926 it enacted the Air Commerce Act, vesting control of commercial aviation in the Commerce Department. As a result of this legislation, scheduled commercial air service first began in 1926. By 1930 the aviation industry was firmly established with 122 airlines in operation over routes covering nearly 50,000 miles. Technological progress was painfully slow until the sluggish and inefficient Ford trimotor aircraft gave way to the all-metal twin-engined Douglas DC-3 in 1936, which at once became the workhorse of the airlines. By 1940 there were 22 airlines in the United States carrying 3,185,000 passengers over routes totaling 94,000 miles.

THE MOTION PICTURE INDUSTRY.   The story of the rise of the motion picture industry from humble beginnings to a position of major importance in American life is one of the great sagas of the twentieth century. Thomas A. Edison and others by 1896 had constructed machines capable of taking motion pictures and projecting them on a screen. For the next few years short feature films were shown in vaudeville houses, and the first movie that told a story, "The Great Train Robbery," was produced in 1903.

The motion picture industry had its first real beginning in 1905—when a Pittsburgh promoter rented a warehouse and displayed one-reel shows for a nickel. Within two years there were some 5,000 "nickelodeons," as these first movie theaters were called, in all parts of the country. From this time on progress in technique and technology was substantial, and promoters began constructing large and ornate theaters on the eve of the First World War. Rapid technological developments, the most important of which were sound movies, brought the industry to full maturity by the end of the 1920s. By 1930 the motion picture industry had a capital investment of some $2 billion and gave employment to 325,000 persons. Motion pictures had become so important a part of American social life that even the depression did not halt the growth or impair the prosperity of the industry.

5. The Age of Big Business

In spite of antitrust crusades, the consolidation movement in industry proceeded inexorably, through Democratic and Republican administrations, through eras of reform and reaction.[4] It slackened from 1904 to 1917, but revived on a large scale at the end of the First World War. A few statistics will illustrate the general trend. The assets of the 200 largest nonfinancial corporations totaled $26,000,000,000 in 1909, $43,718,000,000 in 1919, and $81,074,000,000 in 1929. These 200 corporations by 1929 controlled 49 percent of all corporate wealth and received 43 percent of the corporate income. For various reasons—principally the depression and a political climate unfavorable to big business—the merger movement virtually ceased, and the movement toward concentration in industry was slightly reversed in the 1930s. Five percent of corporations received 85 percent of total corporation income in 1930. The figure declined to 81 percent in 1935 and stood at not quite 84.5 percent four years later.

The favorite instrument of consolidation in the 1920s was the holding company, which enabled an individual or group of men with comparatively small resources to control a utility or railroad empire.[5] Samuel Insull, the Chicago utilities magnate, was most adept at the game. Indeed, so far-flung and complicated was his utilities network by 1930—it had combined assets of $2.5 billion and produced one-eighth of the electric power in the United States—that it is doubtful whether even he understood its structure. Oris P. and Mantis J. Van Sweringen of Cleveland were other masters of the technique. Beginning by controlling the Nickel Plate Railroad before the First World War, they used the holding company technique from 1925 to 1929 to acquire control of the Chesapeake & Ohio, Pere Marquette, Erie, and Missouri Pacific railroads.

[4]Industrial expansion from 1900 to 1929 was in large measure financed by the savings of the rank and file of people, rather than by the investments of a few promoters and industrial leaders. The result was a wide spread in the ownership of America's factories, banks, railroads, and insurance companies and a consequent separation between ownership and management. The 4 million owners of corporate stocks in 1900, for example, grew to a mighty throng of 20 million by 1930.

This separation of ownership from control in industry, which began around 1900, reached major proportions in the 1920s, as the component parts of the dissolved trusts developed into independent concerns and as more and more companies sold stock to the public. Consequently, there developed a significant managerial revolution, in which control passed from single owners or partners, and even from boards of directors, to a salaried bureaucracy, highly trained in production and distribution. In fact American industry was so thoroughly bureaucratized by 1929 that the large majority of routine decisions were made by plant managers and shop foremen even in corporations controlled by owners.

[5]The technique is known as pyramiding and works in the following manner: Using a small investment a promoter might organize a holding company and gain control of it by owning a majority of the voting common stock. By using the proceeds from the sale of the bonds, preferred stock, and nonvoting common stock of this first holding company, the organizer would buy control of operating utility companies. And by following the same method the promoter might pyramid one holding company on top of another almost indefinitely

The American industrial economy had obviously become highly consolidated by the end of the 1930s, but not to the degree that the bare statistics might imply. Actually, few vestiges of industrial monopoly remained by 1940,[6] while many important industries, notably textiles, clothing, furniture, and bituminous coal, remained fiercely competitive. On the other hand, oligopolies, that is, oligarchies of a few large producers, dominated many branches of industry. For example, in 1937-1938 ten large companies controlled approximately 88 percent of the total productive capacity of the steel industry; three corporations controlled 90 percent of the automobile output; four meat packing concerns produced 70 percent of the product of that industry; the four largest rubber companies turned out 80 percent of the automobile tires; four tobacco companies produced 85 percent of the cigarettes.

This trend toward oligopoly, however, did not necessarily signify a diminution of competition. On the contrary, it meant restoration of competition in several important branches of industry. In 1901, for example, United States Steel controlled about 60 percent of the nation's steel ingot capacity. That corporation grew steadily, but its rivals grew even faster; and in 1937 United States Steel controlled only 40 percent of the total steel ingot capacity of the industry. At the time of its dissolution in 1911, the Standard Oil Company of New Jersey enjoyed a virtual monopoly over the refining of petroleum in the United States. The dissolution of the holding company into its constituent corporations was followed by the gradual emergence of these companies as independent concerns. Meanwhile, tremendous new amounts of capital entered the oil refining field, and all the former members of the Standard Oil Trust combined did only about 50 percent of the oil business of the country in 1930. In retailing, also, the rise of mail-order houses and chain stores, which did 25 percent of the retail business in 1935, gave a powerful stimulus to competition in the distribution field.

We could multiply these examples to show that the trend toward oligopoly from 1910 to 1940 actually strengthened competition in many branches of industry in which competition had not existed before 1910. The important phenomenon in this regard, however, was the manner in which competition itself changed during the three decades before 1940. Historic price competition remained in many branches of industry and was always a potential threat in others. But producers in a given branch of industry tended more and more to follow the price leadership of the largest manufacturer and to concentrate on improving and advertising their products.

[6]The Texas Gulf Sulphur Company and the Freeport Sulphur Company controlled virtually the entire sulphur production of the United States; the Aluminum Company of America enjoyed a monopoly in the production of bar aluminum; and the United Shoe Machinery Company was virtually the sole producer in its field. But these were the only important industrial monopolies remaining by 1940, and the aluminum monopoly was soon to be broken.

6. Trends in Banking and Finance, 1919-1940

Industrial growth during the period 1919 to 1929 was accompanied by a rapid accumulation of the financial resources of the American people. Bankers, security promoters and salesmen, and managers of other financial institutions had never before been as numerous or prosperous and had never received such a large share of the national income.[7] Nor had the financial structure of the country ever seemed more solvent. As we shall see, however, there were forces at work changing the character of the banking structure and undermining its foundations.

From 1919 to 1929 the total number of banks in the United States declined from 29,767 to 25,568. The principal reason for this decline was the steady failure of banks in rural areas and in Florida following the collapse of a land boom in that state in 1926. All told, 5,714 banks closed their doors from 1921 through 1929. On the other hand, total bank capital and surpluses increased nearly 100 percent from 1919 to 1929, while total banking resources grew from $47,615,400,000 to over $72,000,000,000.

The statistics afford numerous other evidences of the steady accretion of American financial wealth during the decade. For example, life insurance companies, which had now emerged as the chief depositories of the people's savings, grew in resources much faster than the banks. Life insurance income and policies in force increased nearly 300 percent from 1919 to 1929, and the aggregate resources of life insurance companies grew from $6,759,000,000 to $17,482,000,000. Americans during the same period also increased their savings in banks from $13,040,000,000 to $28,218,000,000 and in building and loan associations from $2,126,620,000 to $8,695,154,-000.

Along with expansion came a relentless movement toward consolidation and the growth of large financial institutions. By 1929, 250 banks, or 1 percent of the total, controlled more than 46 percent of the nation's banking resources, while some 273 chains controlled 18 percent of total banking resources. In addition, there were a number of mergers in Wall Street that greatly concentrated the banking resources of the nation's financial center.

Such consolidations were spectacular, but the most important financial trend of the 1920s was a profound change in the character and functions of great commercial banks. The chief function of commercial banks in the past had been to make short-term loans to care for the needs of industry, commerce, and agriculture. The high prosperity of the period from 1922 to 1929 caused corporations to rely increasingly upon profits and proceeds

---

[7]In 1919 financial institutions earned 2.2 percent of the total private production income. A decade later finance's share had increased to 4.6 percent.

from the sale of securities for expansion or even for current needs. As a consequence, bank loans during the prosperity decade did not keep pace with the rising level of economic activity, and there was no inflation either of bank credit or of the money supply.[8] Coming at a time when banking resources were greatly expanding, this phenomenon caused the managers of great commercial banks to look elsewhere than to business and industry for ways to use idle money. Consequently, they increased bank purchases of stocks and bonds by two-thirds and expanded bank loans against real estate by about 350 percent. Most important, they allowed surplus funds to be used to finance the most reckless speculative campaign in American history. Loans to brokers against stocks and bonds stood at the astounding total of $8.5 billion by the autumn of 1929.

The role of commercial banks in abetting stock speculation did not end at this point, for practically all large commercial banks established investment affiliates, hired thousands of salesmen, organized huge speculative campaigns, and did a flourishing business so long as the upward surge continued. For example, these security affiliates participated in the floating of $19 billion of issues of 1927.

Meanwhile, the great financial leaders—Kuhn, Loeb & Company, the House of Morgan, and their allies—not only survived but also prospered and grew larger during the New Economic Era. They continued to dominate the financial operations of the railroads, in spite of the efforts of the Interstate Commerce Commission to break their control. They took leadership in organizing and underwriting utility holding companies. They continued to play a major role in marketing securities and wielded a certain influence through interlocking directorships in industrial corporations. And yet events and developments of the twenties changed and greatly weakened the Morgan–Kuhn, Loeb & Company imperium. There was too much competition in the money markets as new financial centers emerged and old ones grew in power. Corporations were too independent and prosperous. Finally, there was too vast a growth of the financial machinery to allow continued domination by Wall Street or by one or two firms.

The story of the fortunes of banks and bankers during the following decade is an altogether different one. We need only to sketch the outlines here, as we will come back to this subject (see pp. 351, 373). First came the frightening attrition of the depression and the near collapse of the banking structure in 1933. Heroic federal reorganization and massive assistance had saved the system by 1935 and provided new safeguards for the future. Meanwhile, the American people were slowly rebuilding their ravaged financial resources. By 1940 there were only 15,076 banks in

---

[8]National banks increased their loans and discounts from $11,980,000.000 in 1921 to $14,811,-000,000 in 1929; the total money in circulation actually declined slightly during the period—from $4,911,000,000 in 1921 to $4,746,000,000 in 1929.

operation (as compared with 25,568 in 1929), but they had total resources of nearly $80 billion (as compared with $72 billion in 1929).

7. The Decline of Organized Labor, 1920-1932

As we have seen, the postwar decade was in the main a time of prosperity and economic advancement for American workers. This generalization, however, obscures the important exceptions, for economic sickness in the textile and coal mining industries stimulated labor tensions of fierce intensity that culminated in numerous outbreaks of industrial warfare. Moreover, in spite of steady employment and increases in real wages, the 1920s witnessed a steady decline in the numbers and power of organized labor, a decline that was sharply accelerated by the Great Depression.

For the phenomenon of the decline of organized labor during a prosperous period, both employers and trade union leaders were responsible. State manufacturers' associations and the National Association of Manufacturers began a campaign in 1920 to restore the open shop through the "American Plan."[9] Management's offensive in the twenties had another side—a positive, constructive effort, called welfare capitalism, aimed at eliminating causes of industrial unrest by substituting cooperation for conflict in the field of industrial relations. Accepting the relatively new concept of full production and consumption through high wages, advanced industrialists took labor policy out of the hands of tyrannical foremen, established expert departments of labor relations, and sought to win labor's good will by recreational programs, profit sharing, stock distribution, group health and life insurance programs, and even plans for retirement benefits. Such employers, in addition, usually established an elaborate system, ranging from shop grievance committees to company unions, by which workers might voice complaints and seek rectification of injustices.

All employers in the 1920s did not approve these new concepts and practices, but it was significant for the future that a large majority of the men who determined the policies of great corporations began to think of the needs and aspirations of their workers. For the most part, organized labor heartily reciprocated management's good will. In fact, when management accepted the principle of collective bargaining, labor leaders often went to unusual lengths to prove that cooperation was more profitable than conflict. For example, the Amalgamated Clothing Workers of America willingly assumed responsibility for shop discipline, encouraged

---

[9]This was the name given to the open-shop movement by a conference of the leaders of twenty-two state manufacturers' associations in Chicago in January 1921.

plans to increase efficiency, and even lent money to clothing manufacturers in distress.

With several notable exceptions, tensions between management and organized labor after 1921 lessened perceptibly in the wake of these developments. The average number of strikes per year declined from 3,503 for the period 1916 to 1921 to 1,304 during the years 1922 to 1925, and to 791 from 1926 through 1930. Also, the American Federation of Labor became increasingly conservative, in that its leadership accepted welfare capitalism when accompanied by recognition and the right to bargain collectively. The AF of L, moreover, fought hard and successfully to prevent Communist infiltration. Most important, it generally refused to launch movements to organize the great basic industries.

It was little wonder, therefore, that liberal critics of the AF of L and the railroad brotherhoods charged that organized labor had ceased to speak for the great mass of workers and had become a bulwark of the established order. It was little wonder, also, that organized labor not only did not grow but instead declined precipitately in numbers and influence during the 1920s. Trade union membership declined generally from 5,034,000 in 1920 to 2,857,000 in 1932, while membership in the AF of L fell from 4,079,000 to 2,532,000. Part of this loss resulted from the AF of L's failure to consolidate gains hastily made from 1917 to 1920; part of it was caused by the employers' counteroffensive; and a small part stemmed from losses incurred by unemployment during the depression. But the most important factor was unaggressive and timid leadership.

The violent experiences of workers in coal mining and textiles during the decade 1920–1930 stand in striking contrast to the generalizations of the foregoing discussion. These two industries remained highly competitive, unstable, and plagued by overproduction and dislocations resulting from the movement, especially by textile manufacturers, into the low-wage area of the South. Frontier social conditions still prevailed to a large degree in mining areas and mill towns. Low wages and attempts by employers to preserve an industrial absolutism stimulated efforts at unionization. In turn these organizational campaigns were accompanied by the kind of violent warfare that had often characterized the American industrial scene before the First World War.

The United Mine Workers of America emerged from the bituminous coal strike of 1919 superficially defeated but actually strengthened by the award of the Bituminous Coal Commission and by simultaneous negotiations with the anthracite operators. Along the frontier of the bituminous industry in West Virginia and eastern Kentucky, however, an outbreak occurred that ended in disastrous defeat for the UMW. The union's attempt to organize mines in West Virginia in 1919 and 1920 provoked fierce resistance by operators and pitched battles between striking miners and imported guards. The governor declared martial law in the strike area, and state and federal troops momentarily stopped the fighting. Then violence broke out anew in 1921, after the miners organized an army of 4,000 men and began to invade the strike zone. The uprising quickly collapsed when President Harding dispatched 2,100 troops to the area, and state authorities arrested the strike leaders on charges of treason, murder, and conspiracy.

The West Virginia civil war marked the beginning of a decade of conflict in the troubled coal fields. Negotiations for new contracts with bituminous and anthracite operators failed in early 1922, and President John L. Lewis of the UMW called miners out in the greatest coal strike in American history to that time. There was no violence until the Southern Illinois Coal Company, in Williamson County, Illinois, imported strikebreakers and attempted to resume operations on June 21, 1922. The killing of two strikers by mine guards brought swift retaliation at Herrin. There enraged miners charged a stockade and slaughtered nineteen strikebreakers. Tempers subsided after the Herrin Massacre, and a test of endurance between the UMW and the operators then followed. In the late summer the operators gave in.

Although Lewis forced the operators to renew their contracts in 1924, a series of catastrophes soon befell and nearly wrecked the UMW. For one thing, increased competition from nonunion operators in the South and West forced northern and midwestern operators to cut wages. For another thing progressive and Communist elements in the UMW began a vigorous campaign in 1926 to destroy Lewis's allegedly dictatorial and corrupt control. Although the movement failed, it seriously weakened the UMW and led to the formation of two rival unions, the reorganized United Mine Workers and the Communist-controlled National Miners' Union. Lewis saved the UMW and preserved a semblance of collective bargaining in the coal industry by accepting wage reductions during contract negotiations in 1927. But by 1929 the once proud UMW was so weakened, both from within and from without, that it would be helpless to cope with problems raised by the depression.

Tensions and conflicts also plagued the textile industry during the 1920s. New England manufacturers, pleading southern competition and depressed economic circumstances, cut wages about 20 percent in 1921. They attempted to raise hours and impose another 20 percent wage cut early in the following year. This provoked a series of strikes by the United Textile Workers and left wing unions that forced a restoration of the old wage and hour scales. The conflict shifted to Passaic, New Jersey, three years later, after the large woolen textile mills in that city cut wages 10 percent in September 1925. A United Front Committee under Communist leadership began a strike in January 1926 that soon spread to all the large mills and engendered such disturbances as northern New Jersey had not seen since the IWW's Paterson strike of 1913. After the Communists withdrew from leadership in the strike, the United Textile Workers of the AF of L took control and brought it to a successful conclusion in March 1927.

Northern textile workers staved off wage reductions after 1921 by such violent reprisals. But the rise of southern manufacturers to dominance in the industry and the movement of New England mills to the South in the 1920s posed a serious long-range menace to union wages in the North. Obviously, safety for northern workers lay only in eliminating the sectional wage differential—by unionizing southern mills and imposing a uniform national wage scale.

The United Textile Workers, after a brief and unsuccessful attempt to organize the southern mills in 1919, invaded the South again in 1927 and 1928. They found the mass of workers bitter and resentful over long hours, low wages, the "stretch-out," and above all, high profits. They found, also, a virtual textile barony allied with local police and state officials ready to use any means to prevent unionization. It is not surprising that one of the bloodiest outbreaks of labor violence in recent American history ensued.

The disturbances began in March 1929, when more than 5,000 rayon textile workers in Elizabethton, Tennessee, struck against a low wage scale. Local vigilante groups combined with company guards, state troops, and the courts to drive the organizers of the United Textile Workers from the mills. A month later the Communist-controlled National Textile Workers' Union began a strike against the largest cotton mill in Gastonia, North Carolina, the center of the textile industry. The strike collapsed after the conviction, in October 1929, of seven of the Communist leaders for the second-degree murder of the Gastonia chief of police. At the same time, a United Textile Workers strike in Marion, North Carolina, ended with the slaughter of five and the wounding of nineteen unarmed pickets by a sheriff's posse. The United Textile Workers made their most formidable effort in the autumn of 1930 at the Riverside and Dan River mills in Danville, Virginia. The owners stubbornly refused either to bargain with the union or to submit to arbitration, and the strikers had to surrender to avoid starvation.

Although the decade ended with labor tension running at its highest point since 1919, there were a few signs that official and public opinion was finally beginning to veer strongly in labor's favor. For one thing, the 1920s saw federal endorsement of the principle of genuine collective bargaining between railroads and their employees. The Transportation Act of 1920 had established a Railroad Labor Board that soon proved its uselessness, especially after it failed to prevent a nationwide strike of railway shopmen in 1922. Congress in 1926 therefore adopted the Railway Labor Act. It created effective mediation and arbitration machinery and, more important, virtually compelled railroads to eschew company unionism and deal responsibly with the independent brotherhoods. Then in 1930 the Senate refused to confirm the nomination of Circuit Court Judge John J. Parker to the Supreme Court, in part because Parker had upheld the use of injunctions to prohibit union organizers from attempting to unionize workers who had signed a yellow-dog contract.[10] Finally, Congress in March 1932 adopted the Anti-Injunction Act sponsored by Representative Fiorello La Guardia of New York and Senator George W. Norris of Nebraska. This measure made yellow-dog contracts unenforceable in federal courts; forbade issuance of injunctions against a number of hitherto outlawed union practices; and guaranteed jury trials in cases involving violations of criminal injunctions. Altogether it was not a revolution in federal policy, but it did herald more important changes that would occur after 1932.

[10]This was an agreement between employer and employee by which the latter promised not to join a union in return for the privilege of employment.

12

Social and Cultural Main Currents, 1920–1940, and Tensions of the Twenties

American society between the Spanish-American and First World wars was bound together by common moral and political standards. The two decades between the armistice and the Second World War were also a period of social and intellectual ferment. But it was ferment of a different kind, marked by changes in moral standards, the rise of new faiths among intellectuals, and the flowering of a literary revolt against the polite tradition in letters. To what degree this revolt of the intellectuals affected the masses it is impossible to say. It was, however, surely significant that a large segment of molders of thoughtful opinion repudiated traditional values and thereby destroyed the ideological unity of the prewar period.

As we shall see, however, the 1920s and 1930s were decades of social and artistic accomplishment, as well as a time of revolt and repudiation. The period witnessed the first important beginnings of American literary criticism; achievements that gained new eminence for American literature; and a flowering of American scholarship and research. In addition, Americans poured out money to improve and expand public schools and construct the most extensive system of higher education in the world.

Churches not only survived but grew in social usefulness. Thus, the twenties and thirties, far from being barren of social and cultural accomplishment, were a time of enduring achievement and bright promise for the future. The twenties were also a time of social conflict and tension: fundamentalists fought their last organized crusade to save an antique faith; nativism and intolerance found ugly expressions in organizations like the Ku Klux Klan; and Americans became increasingly divided over the prohibition experiment.

1. The Revolution in Morals and Customs

The most astonishing aspect of the revolution in manners and moral standards that occurred after 1918 was the rapidity with which forces that had long been eroding historic standards suddenly destroyed that code among an influential element. In its ethical aspects the traditional system taught respect for parental authority, idealized the husband-father as the master of the family, and required premarital chastity and marital fidelity. This code provided the basic way of life for most Americans before the First World War. It was often violated, to be sure; but most middle-class Americans accepted it as a standard that was practically and morally sound even if unattainable.

The postwar rebellion was first evidenced by a revolt among young people, especially among "flaming youth" on college and university campuses, against the rules governing sexual relations. Wartime excitement broke down the barriers, but other forces kept them down during the 1920s and 1930s. For one thing, the automobile extended the possibilities of love-making far beyond the sitting room. For another, the increased drinking among middle-class women and young people that accompanied prohibition played a large role in weakening inhibitions. But even more important was the phenomenal spread of the teachings of Sigmund Freud, a Viennese psychoanalyst, whose writings were popularly misinterpreted to mean that the main cause of maladjusted personality was the suppression of the sexual desire, and that a free expression of the libido, or sexual energies, promoted mental health.

Whatever the causes, the breakdown of the traditional moral standard was widespread. F. Scott Fitzgerald's *This Side of Paradise*, a story of undergraduate life at Princeton, and Charles C. Wertenbaker's novels about students at the University of Virginia undoubtedly drew exaggerated pictures. But sexual promiscuity and drinking among college students became to a degree fashionable. High school students, too, indulged in the new freedom on such a scale as to shock their parents.

Indeed, if there was any single striking social phenomenon of the twenties and thirties, it was the popular obsession with sex. While highbrows read James Branch Cabell's erotic novels and applauded Eugene O'Neill's powerful dramas written around Freudian themes, the common people found excitement in a new form of literature, the confession magazines, which featured lurid stories by fallen women or high school girls who had "gone wrong."[1] The motion pictures, also, played upon the sex theme, and it was revealing that the maidenly Mary Pickford was supplanted as "America's sweetheart" by the voluptuous Clara Bow, the "It" girl of the 1920s, and by the equally voluptuous Jean Harlow in the 1930s.

A second manifestation of the revolution in morals and manners was the rise of new forms of ballroom dancing. The waltz and more decorous forms gave way to the fox trot, the Charleston, and, late in the thirties, the jitterbug. To defenders of older forms, the modern dance was simply another evidence of the general breakdown of sexual standards, and church groups launched heroic but vain attacks upon what they called the "syncopated embrace." The modern dance, exclaimed the Reverend John William Porter of Kentucky in his tract, *The Dangers of the Dance* (1922), is based upon and stimulates the sexual instinct. "If this be not true, why is it that women do not dance with women, and men with men? . . . The mix-up is the magnet. A man dancing with a man is about as satisfactory as near-beer to the old drunkard." The elders cried in vain, however, and parents were dancing quite as fast and as artfully as their children before the 1930s had ended.

The most important aspect of the revolution in social life in the long run was the change in the status of women. Political equality was achieved with adoption of the Nineteenth Amendment, and the twenties and thirties saw women not only voting but also holding offices high and low.[2] Although employers still discriminated grossly against women in wages and salaries, women found far greater economic opportunities after 1920 than ever before. There was a sharp decline in the number of women employed in farming, and virtually no increase in the number in domestic service. On the other hand, the rapid expansion of female employment in industry, public schools, service trades and professions, and business enterprise more than compensated for the decline in other fields. By 1940 the

[1] *True Story*, the most successful of these new periodicals, began with a small circulation in 1919 and approached the 2-million mark seven years later.

[2] There were, for example, two women governors and one female United States senator during the 1920s. Mrs. Miriam A. ("Ma") Ferguson served as governor of Texas from 1925 to 1927. Mrs Ferguson represented her husband, former Governor James E. Ferguson, who had been impeached and removed from office in 1917. Her administration did not bear out feminine claims that women in office would purify politics. Mrs. Nellie T. Ross succeeded her husband upon his death in 1924 as governor of Wyoming and served until 1927. Mrs. Rebecca L. Felton of Georgia, appointed to the United States Senate in 1922 after the death of Thomas E. Watson, was the first woman senator. She served for only a short time.

14,160,000 women gainfully employed constituted 25 percent of the entire working force of the nation, as contrasted with 17.7 percent in 1900.

This expansion of economic opportunities for middle-class women was the factor largely responsible for the revolution in feminine attitudes and manners that began in the early 1920s. Masculine supremacy had been based upon man's economic leadership in the family. It rapidly deteriorated as spinster sisters moved into apartments of their own, unmarried daughters went into school teaching or office work, and wives gained independence either by going to work or threatening to do so. As a consequence, women married at a later age, had fewer children, and were more willing to dissolve the marriage bonds. The number of divorces per hundred marriages increased from nine in 1914 to an apparently stable level of around seventeen from 1936 through 1940.

The outward signs of the emancipation were even more frightening to persons who believed in the old way of life. As the barriers fell on all sides women began smoking cigarettes and, what seemed worse to traditionalists, they demanded and asserted the right to drink with men. As women went to work in large numbers they began to discard historic badges of femininity and, ironically, sought to make themselves over in the image of men. The first casualty of feminine independence was the traditional dress that covered the neck and arms and assiduously hid the ankles from masculine view. The average skirt was about six inches from the ground in 1919. From this time on the ascent was spectacular, until the skirt had reached the knees or even above by 1927.

The revolution in morals and customs had run its full course by 1930. Experience soon taught that free expression of the libido produced not mental health but psychological and moral degeneracy. After trying to look and act like men, women finally admitted that there were, after all, certain physical differences between the sexes. They discovered that they did not have to yield their beauty in order to retain the large measure of independence they had won. Most men accepted the new order; in fact, many husbands abandoned authority and responsibility for the rearing of children to their wives. If, as Frederick Lewis Allen has observed, the American people were beginning by 1929 to build a new code on the shambles of the old system and learning to live gracefully again, then that effort would consist mainly of salvaging the enduring values of the traditional system.

While most Americans in the 1930s learned to live with sex without completely losing their heads about it, they also enlarged and made permanent the revolution in mores governing the family that had begun after the First World War. The general acceptance during the thirties of the code exalting happiness as the supreme objective of marriage, permitting divorce for often trivial reasons, and, above all, giving women and children equality with men in family relationships signified that the new code had become the cornerstone of American social life.

2. *Main Currents in American Thought*

Deep and sometimes bitter currents of intellectual unrest converged and swelled into a revolt of considerable proportions in the early 1920s. It is not difficult to understand why this happened. Intellectuals had made a deeply personal commitment to the general reform movement during the progressive period. Most of them, like the group that wrote for *The New Republic,* had answered Wilson's call for an application of progressive ideals to international life during the war. The dream was shattered after Versailles and the subsequent treaty fight. Like the Confederate veteran on the way home from Appomattox, who said he would be damned if he ever loved another country, many intellectuals were damned if they would ever love another ideal.

As it turned out, the reaction against the Versailles settlement was merely the beginning of the disillusionment. Intellectual progressives, who had advocated extension of governmental authority before the war, saw that same authority being used after 1918 to deprive a minority of the privilege of deciding whether they would drink alcoholic beverages. Intellectual progressives had glorified the people and championed adoption of democratic political reforms before 1917. But the people in the 1920s were demanding and enforcing conformity of thought, joining antidemocratic organizations like the Ku Klux Klan, and even attempting to forbid the teaching of evolution in public schools in many states.

Many intellectuals concluded that the old assumptions about the innate virtue of people and the desirability of more democracy were wrong, and they turned in anger and disgust against the democratic ideal. Thus during the 1920s there developed an intellectual leadership at war with the middle classes, separated from the people, tired of crusades and talk about moral idealism and service. Turning from pursuit of social and economic justice, they sought refuge in developing individuality through sexual freedom, esoteric literary and artistic forms, or bitter attacks upon domestic developments. Some of them, but not a large number, repudiated democracy altogether and hailed the Soviet Communist system as the answer to a dying bourgeois democracy. The importance of the defection of intellectuals from the progressive movement can hardly be overestimated. It was as if the spark plugs had been removed from the engine of reform.

In essence, the revolt of the intellectuals was a rebellion against what they thought was the cant, hypocrisy, and low cultural level of American life. "This so-called 'moral idealism,' " cried Harold Stearns in 1921, "is merely what any good psychiatrist would immediately recognise as the morbid perversities which conventionally accompany a deeply dissatisfied human life." The young intellectual of the early twenties simply did not like the society in which he thought he lived. He objected to the "morbid perversities"—the anti-intellectualism of small towns, the "shoddy, cheap" newspapers that gave more space to baseball than to the theater, the demand for conformity, the emphasis upon utilitarian virtues, the "democracy of mountebanks." He felt rejected, unwanted, and overborne by the crowd. He wanted freedom to experiment, to drink, to dream, to write like James Joyce, and to paint in cubes. If he was impecunious he sought fellowship in Greenwich Village in New York City; if he had an independent income he moved to the Left Bank in Paris to find freedom and cultural refreshment with fellow expatriates.

It will perhaps suffice to illustrate the revolt by pointing to H. L. Mencken, the chief intellectual rebel of the decade. A native of Baltimore, Mencken received his literary training as a reporter for the Baltimore *Sun*, wrote an excellent study of the American language, and briefly edited a "little" magazine, *The Smart Set*, with George Jean Nathan. Then, in collaboration with Alfred A. Knopf, Mencken and Nathan began publication in 1922 of *American Mercury*, a monthly addressed to the intellectual rebels.

Mencken's observations on the American scene were barbed and pungent, and *American Mercury* soon became the Bible of the "lost generation." Mencken ridiculed idealism, democracy, organized religion, prudery, cant, prohibition, and ignorance. To him, morality and Christian marriage, for example, were absurdities; patriotism was imbecilic; the American people were mainly a vast collection of peasants, boobs, and hillbillies. It was ironic and revealing that such a purveyor of intellectual snobbishness and antidemocratic views should have become, as Walter Lippmann observed in 1927, the most powerful influence on the contemporary generation of educated people.

To stop at this point, however, would be to give the impression that American intellectuals did nothing but scoff and condemn during the 1920s. Actually, the intellectual rebellion was a phenomenon that passed quickly. Intellectual prodigals returned in huge numbers to their democratic household in response to the challenges of the 1930s. We will discuss this revival of faith in a later chapter (see pp. 425-426). Moreover, the twenties and thirties witnessed the flowering of many fields of intellectual endeavor. It was, for example, a period adorned by important accomplishments in the social sciences. Historians abandoned preoccupation with political institutions and advanced scholarship deep into the frontiers of intellectual, social, and economic history. This advance, aided by the expansion and growing endowments of the country's academic institutions, gave American historiography a breadth that no single European country could match. Sociologists broke loose from the subjective, inductive method, developed new objective criteria, and launched new studies of ecology, urbanization, population, and race relations. The study of anthropology in the United States became an integral part of university curricula rather than an avocation of museum scholars. Social psychology became an independent discipline. A host of economists abandoned preoccupation with economic "laws" and set to work to analyze, describe, and dissect the American economic system. (For further details, see pp. 426–427.)

American accomplishment in the physical sciences during the 1920s and 1930s was on the whole perhaps less impressive than in the social sciences, mainly because the most important theoretical work was still being done by Europeans. The twenties saw the culmination and complete acceptance of new theories of matter, energy, and the structure of the universe fully as revolutionary in meaning as the Copernican and Newtonian theories had been. Robert A. Millikan of the California Institute of Technology and Arthur H. Compton of the University of Chicago won Nobel prizes in 1923 and 1927 for contributions to the new concepts, and Ernest O. Lawrence of the University of California won the prize in 1939 for inventing the first cyclotron, or atom smasher. But leadership in theoretical physics still rested with Europeans like Albert Einstein, Niels Bohr, and Enrico Fermi.

On the other hand, American chemists made extraordinary progress in a seemingly more practical field—production of synthetic chemical fibers, plastics, and products from coal and oil. In biology, Americans like Edmund B. Wilson, T. H. Morgan, and H. J. Muller enlarged man's knowledge of heredity, mutations, and transmission of characteristics from one generation to the next. Following the lead of Europeans, American psychologists abandoned the study for the laboratory, there to attempt to discover the biological bases of human behavior. The 1920s and 1930s witnessed no spectacular discoveries in the field of medicine, but they were marked by steady advancement in knowledge, improvement of medical schools, construction of great medical centers, development of new x-ray and surgical techniques, and growth of the branch of medicine devoted to treatment of mental illness.

3. School and Church in the Twenties and Thirties

Progress in expanding and improving free education had been steady and substantial from the Civil War to 1920. The prosperity of the twenties, however, stimulated such achievement as had not been recorded in any earlier comparable period. Then came heavy blows in consequence of diminished revenues during the depression (for an account of which, see p. 353), followed by slow but steady recovery to new heights in the late 1930s. The following generalizations illustrate the main trends. The number of pupils enrolled in public schools from 1920 to 1940 increased from 21,578,000 to nearly 25,500,000. Total expenditures for education grew during the same two decades from $1,036,000,000 to $2,344,000,000, the number of teachers from 680,000 to 875,000, and expenditure per pupil from $53.52 to $88.09. Illiteracy declined during the same period from 6 percent of the total population to 2.9 percent, and among nonwhites, mainly Negroes, from 23 percent to 11.5 percent.

The goal of free education for all children in elementary schools had been fairly accomplished by 1920, and, except for expansion in kindergartens and schools for black children, progress accomplished in the elementary field from 1920 to 1940 came more from improved instruction, longer terms, and the like, than from any great expansion in sheer numbers. For one thing, state departments of education assumed responsibility for licensing teachers and began to require completion of a four-year college course as a prerequisite for a teaching certificate. For another thing, the progressive methods advocated earlier by John Dewey and others found wider acceptance as schools of education broke away from the formal classical tradition. Traditionalists bemoaned the neglect of genteel subjects, but increased emphasis upon experimentation and participation by children, as well as widespread use of workshops, laboratories, and other material equipment, were certainly well adapted to the capacities of children. They were also indispensable instruments of mass education.

During the two decades under discussion Americans made their greatest relative progress in secondary and higher education. The number of children enrolled in public high schools increased nearly 300 percent, from 2,200,000 to 6,601,000, from 1920 to 1940. And along with growth came important changes in curriculum as high schools ceased to prepare children exclusively for college. Thus, only 16 percent of high school pupils studied Latin in 1934, as contrasted to nearly 50 percent in 1910. On the other hand, music, manual training, home economics, typewriting, agricultural science, and other vocational subjects, most of which had not even been offered in 1910, were beginning to overshadow the so-called classical offerings. Accelerated by the Smith-Lever and Smith-Hughes acts of 1914 and 1917, which provided federal support for agricultural and vocational education, this movement toward more practical training for the large majority of high school students who would not go to college was a frank recognition of the state's enlarged social responsibilities.

The prosperity of the 1920s, and especially the great increase in high school enrollment, in turn stimulated an unprecedented expansion of American colleges and universities. The following statistics illustrate the general trends: from 1920 to 1940 there was an increase in the number of students enrolled from 598,000 to 1,494,000; the number of instructors increased from 48,600 to 147,000; total endowments grew from $556,350,-000 to $1,686,000,000; and total receipts exclusive of new capital funds increased from $199,922,000 to $715,211,000.

This extraordinary growth raised serious new problems concerning the role of higher education in a democracy and inevitably compelled college and university leaders to modify methods and objectives. In short, colleges and universities ceased to prepare students almost exclusively for the professions and became also training schools where young men and women prepared for careers in industry, business, and other walks of life. This fact did not signify any diminution of advanced professional training, research, and writing. On the contrary, graduate schools grew even more rapidly than undergraduate departments,[3] while the growth of medical, law, and other professional schools was substantial if not as spectacular.

How fared the churches, the other great agencies of moral and social enlightenment, during this period? Protestant, Roman Catholic, and Jewish churches continued to grow in membership and wealth during the decades between the religious censuses of 1916 and 1936. Increasing urbanization and use of the automobile caused elimination of many small rural churches and consolidation of others, and church construction proceeded at a much slower pace than the growth in the general population. But church membership in the United States increased more rapidly than the population—from a total of 41,927,000 to 55,807,000, or by 33 percent, while population increased by 27 percent; and churches increased expenditures from $328,810,000 to $518,954,000, or by about 27 percent. But these are only rough figures and do not reveal the significant exceptions. Growth was extraordinarily rapid from 1916 to 1929; church membership increased hardly at all during the depression years from 1929 to 1940. It was a time of such precipitate relative decline as to lead certain observers to conclude that the church in America was a dying institution.

As much as during the early years of the twentieth century, the United States was predominantly a Protestant country in the 1920s and 1930s. Total Protestant membership grew from 25,848,000 in 1916 to 31,251,000 in 1936, and Catholic membership rose from 15,722,000 to 19,914,366. Roman Catholics constituted 37.5 percent of all church members in 1916 and only 36 percent in 1936 because of the more accurate reporting of Jewish congregations. Among the more than 200 Protestant bodies in 1936, the Baptists, with nearly 9,500,000, and various Methodist bodies, with an aggregate of some 7,000,000, continued to command a large superiority in numbers and to account for the greatest increases in membership.

Meanwhile, the 1920s had witnessed the almost complete triumph of liberalism among leaders of American Protestantism. Frankly embracing evolution and the higher criticism, many liberals abandoned theological exegesis for the Social Gospel and hopefully looked toward the early establishment of the Kingdom of God among men. The liberal minority became probably a majority during the 1920s, at least among the Methodist and Congregational churches. One survey in the late twenties revealed

---

[3]For example, there were 16,000 students enrolled in graduate schools and 615 Ph.D. degrees conferred in 1920; in 1940 there were 106,000 graduate students enrolled and 3,290 Ph.D. degrees conferred.

that liberal ideas prevailed among a large minority of ministers and among a large majority of all Protestant seminary students.

Protestant thought was convulsed in the 1930s, and the tide began to turn against liberalism as a consequence of one of the most important intellectual upheavals since the Reformation—the rise of so-called neo-orthodoxy, or reformulated biblical theology. It began in Europe. The Swiss theologians Karl Barth and Emil Brunner, surveying the wreckage of the World War and the failure of the League of Nations in the twenties and early thirties, indicted liberalism for glorifying man instead of God and for forgetting that man's sin produced perpetual crises in history. They were modernists insofar as higher criticism and evolution were concerned, but they were thoroughly orthodox in their emphasis upon the sovereignty and majesty of God, the sinfulness of man, and God's loving grace in justification and election in Jesus Christ. Barth's *Commentary on Romans*, published in 1919, was the fire bell that awakened Europe.

These European theologians of crisis were only faintly heard in the United States during the confident twenties, but they gained many American disciples in the thirties. The leader of neo-orthodoxy in the United States was Reinhold Niebuhr of Union Theological Seminary in New York City. His *Moral Man and Immoral Society* (1932), *Reflections on the End of an Era* (1934), *Beyond Tragedy* (1937), and *The Nature and Destiny of Man* (1941-1943) epitomized the neo-orthodox indictment of shallow liberalism and pointed to the return in the United States to the church's historic knowledge of God and man.

Many American liberals refused to go the whole way but confessed that liberalism had obviously failed in the face of crisis. For example, Harry Emerson Fosdick, pastor of the Riverside Church in New York City, in a notable sermon in 1935 repudiated humanism and called for a return to biblical theology. In addition, the thirties saw a marked revival in interest in the writings of Luther and Calvin; the discovery of the Danish existentialist, Sören Kierkegaard; and stronger emphasis on the Atonement and the concept of the church as the body of Christ.

The Social Gospel was undergoing decline, reconstruction, and revival in a new form while this reformulation of American Protestant theological understanding was taking place. The Social Gospel survived in the twenties, to be sure; but, ironically, it declined during the heyday of the liberalism that had given it birth. The depression, world crisis, and neo-orthodoxy all converged in impact to produce a radical revival and transformation of American Protestant social thought and energies. Older Social Gospel thought survived and was manifested in advanced pronouncements on poverty, the rights of labor and racial minorities, economic justice, and so on. But Protestant social thought was responding more and more to the neo-orthodox doctrines that repudiated utopianism and viewed the church more as the saving remnant in an immoral society

than as the remaker of the social order. This was the conviction popularized by Niebuhr under the name of "Christian realism."

It was not all erosion and decline, for the decades 1920-1940 witnessed
one of the Social Gospel's greatest triumphs of the twentieth century—the
Roman Catholic church's official endorsement and espousal of its cause.
This occurred, most specifically, when the American bishops took command of the inchoate social justice groups within the Church during the
First World War and then, in 1919, endorsed a platform entitled "Social
Reconstruction: A General Review of the Problems and Survey of Remedies." Prepared by Father John A. Ryan, a prophetic sociologist at the
Catholic University of America, it was a ringing document that endorsed
unionization, collective bargaining, and worker participation in industrial
ownership and management. Soon afterward the bishops established the
National Catholic Welfare Council and a special committee of the American hierarchy to coordinate the church's social thought and work. It was
the beginning of what would become a vast enterprise by the end of the
1930s.

Meanwhile, there were numerous signs that forces drawing Protestants
together continued to be far stronger from 1920 to 1940 than old antagonisms keeping them apart. The only disruptive elements in Protestantism
after 1920 were the extreme fundamentalists, who insisted upon verbatim
acceptance of historic creeds, and a lunatic fringe that included a wide
variety of apostles of discord. More than offsetting them was a powerful
ecumenical movement toward either organic union or close fellowship
among the major Protestant bodies. In 1931, for example, the Congregational and Christian churches combined; in 1939 the three main Methodist
bodies healed old wounds and formed the largest single Protestant de-
nomination; and movements for union within Presbyterian and Lutheran
bodies seemed to be gaining ground. Throughout the thirties, moreover,
the Federal Council of Churches of Christ in America continued to speak
for a large majority of American Protestant churches.

4. The Antievolution Crusade

The antievolution crusade was the last organized uprising of fundamentalist America against materialistic concepts that seemed to remove God
from the process of creation, deny His dominion over human affairs, and
attempt to destroy an ethical system based upon divinely revealed moral
law. It was fitting that William Jennings Bryan, spokesman of rural, Protestant America, should have taken leadership in a movement that drew most
of its recruits from rural areas. The spread of scientific materialism and
especially of the belief in the material origins of man presented a personal

challenge to Bryan. Investigation convinced him that evolutionary teaching caused students first to lose faith in the verbal inspiration and inerrancy of the Scriptures and later to repudiate Christianity altogether. What Bryan dreaded most was the possibility of atheistic evolutionists being graduated from the colleges, invading public schools as teachers, and undermining the Christian faith of American schoolchildren.

He sounded the first note in his campaign to purge public schools and colleges with addresses at the University of Wisconsin in April 1921 and before the General Assembly of Kentucky in January 1922. "They have taken the Lord away from the schools," he cried again and again. "Shall teachers paid by taxation be permitted to substitute the unproven hypothesis of scientists for the 'Thus saith the Lord' of the Bible, and so undermine the faith of the children of Christian taxpayers?" The answer, of course, was obvious: legislators should forbid the teaching of evolution in public schools and institutions of higher learning. Bryan soon made his campaign a nationwide crusade. He turned his monthly magazine, *The Commoner*, into a fundamentalist sheet. He spoke before state legislatures through the South and Middle West. He carried his fight to the general assembly of the northern Presbyterian church, there failing to win adoption of an antievolution resolution in 1923. But he had succeeded in beginning one of the liveliest controversies of the decade; legislatures in many states were already being pressed to enact antievolution laws.

Bryan's campaign had significant reverberations in the Middle West, but it met with strong popular support and a measure of success only in the South. Leadership and support for the movement in that region came largely from Baptists and Presbyterians. There was, however, no uniformity of religious opinion in the so-called Bible Belt. Baptists, for example, were badly split by the evolution issue, while the Methodist Episcopal Church, South, and the Episcopal Church taught theistic evolution and refused to be drawn into the controversy.

But Bryan's call to battle in 1921 was answered by a large number of southern fundamentalists. There was, for example, the Reverend J. Frank Norris of Fort Worth, Texas, the *enfant terrible* of the southern Baptist church, who undertook a reign of terror against science teachers at Baylor University in Waco and published a weekly newspaper, *The Searchlight*, devoted to exposing atheists and evolutionists. And there was also the Reverend T. T. Martin, an itinerant Baptist evangelist, who wrote *Hell in the High Schools*, one of the leading antievolution tracts. They and their cohorts carried on vigorous campaigns in most southern and southwestern states from 1921 to 1925. At the same time, liberal leaders in church, school, and journalism met the fundamentalists head on, fought courageously for academic freedom, and, on the whole, won the first round.

In fact, the only state in which the antievolutionists had won a decisive victory by 1925 was Tennessee.[4] Academic circles in the United States were shocked in the spring of 1923 by the dismissal from the University of

Tennessee of a professor of genetic psychology for using James Harvey Robinson's *Mind in the Making*. Five other professors were dismissed at the end of the college year for teaching the evolutionary hypothesis. An antievolution bill was introduced in the Tennessee legislature two years later, and Bryan and a powerful Baptist lobby descended upon Nashville. The legislature and governor surrendered by approving a measure forbidding any teacher in the state's schools and colleges to teach any theory denying the biblical account of creation or asserting that man had descended from a lower order of animals.

The American Civil Liberties Union at once offered to finance defense of any Tennessee teacher who would test the constitutionality of the statute. A young high school biology teacher in Dayton, John Thomas Scopes, volunteered, and a friendly test case was begun in May 1925. When the state's counsel invited Bryan to join the prosecution, the Commoner accepted joyfully, declaring, "This is a matter for the nation." At the same time, the famed trial lawyer, Clarence Darrow, joined the defense counsel, thus setting the stage for one of the great forensic battles of the century.

The little mountain town of Dayton, Tennessee, was crowded with evangelists, traveling performers, and newspaper correspondents from all over the United States and the Western world as the opening day of the trial, July 14, 1925, drew near. Bryan was greeted by huge crowds and ovations; he responded by promising a campaign to amend the Constitution to prohibit the teaching of evolution anywhere in the United States. The presiding judge, John T. Raulston, did his best to preserve a semblance of decorum. But the proceedings soon degenerated into a public circus after the court obligingly adjourned to a vacant lot in order to accommodate the huge crowds. Raulston refused to admit expert testimony concerning the validity of the Darwinian hypothesis, and the trial became a verbal duel between the agnostic Darrow and the fundamentalist Bryan.

It did not take long to prove that Scopes had violated the law, since he admitted as much. The Supreme Court of Tennessee later rescinded the small fine that Raulston had imposed but upheld the conviction and the antievolution law. But the anticlimax came on July 26, 1925, a few days after the Scopes trial, when Bryan died, from exhaustion and overeating, at the scene of his attempt to defend the faith.

The Scopes trial and Bryan's death stimulated a momentary revival of

---

[4] The fundamentalists, however, won qualified victories in Florida, North Carolina, and Texas. Without forbidding the teaching of evolution, the Florida legislature in May 1923 adopted a resolution advising that "Darwinism, Atheism, and Agnosticism" should not be taught as truths in the public schools of the state. The North Carolina State Board of Education on January 22, 1924, forbade the teaching in public schools of any form of evolution affirming that man descended from a lower order of animals. The State Textbook Board of Texas in October 1925 ordered the deletion of all references to evolution in books adopted for public schools in the state.

the antievolution crusade—especially after the formation of the Supreme Kingdom, the Bible Crusaders, the Bryan Bible League, and other fundamentalist organizations. The Supreme Kingdom, modeled after the Ku Klux Klan, was dedicated to winning an antievolution constitutional amendment. It functioned in sixteen states, published a monthly magazine, *Dynamite*, and established a rest home in Florida for "those who grow old in the war against evolution." The Bible Crusaders, under T. T. Martin, was the best organized and most formidable of all the antievolution organizations. It formed mobile squadrons that went from one state capitol to another. It descended upon the Mississippi legislature in 1926, for example, and obtained passage of an antievolution law before the liberal forces of the state could counterattack. It struck next at Louisiana, was turned back, and then moved to North Carolina. The fight that ensued was bitter and prolonged, but liberal spokesmen struck back hard and prevented passage of an antievolution bill in 1927.

Defeat in North Carolina seemed to break the back of the entire fundamentalist crusade. In one state after another—Georgia, Kentucky, Florida, South Carolina, and Oklahoma—antievolutionists met with subsequent defeats. They had one last, curious triumph in Arkansas. After the Arkansas legislature several times had refused to adopt an antievolution bill, fundamentalists obtained adoption of their measure in 1928 by using the initiative to bypass the legislature. For the first time in the history of the world the sovereign people by direct legislation decreed that Darwin was wrong!

Thus ended one of the most significant and also one of the most tragic social movements in American history. Southern Protestants who participated in the antievolution crusade thought that they were fighting to preserve the best features of the American heritage—a belief in the spirituality of the universe and in the God-like character of man. Instead, they tended to identify organized religion with bigotry and ignorance instead of freedom and learning. In several states and many communities fundamentalists instituted witch hunts and inquisitions, the effects of which were felt for many years. On the other hand, the antievolution movement had one beneficial effect. Its great challenge to academic freedom revealed the South's intellectual backwardness and compelled the rising body of southern liberals to take a firm stand against intolerant obscurantism. Their victory in most states was therefore all the more significant for the future.

5. *The Growth of Nativism and Intolerance*

There were, unhappily, numerous other manifestations of a growth of intolerance, bigotry, and chauvinism among all classes and all sections during the decade following the First World War. There was fear of Reds, an intensification of anti-Semitism, organized campaigns against Roman Catholics, and legislation practically to end immigration from southern and eastern Europe. It seemed for a time that champions of arrogant nationalism and religious bigotry spoke for virtually the entire American people.

Fear of communism came out in different ways. Following policy set by the Wilson administration, Republican administrations refused to enter into diplomatic relations with the Soviet Union. The New York legislature, in order to prevent the dissemination of revolutionary propaganda, in 1921 required all nonchurch private schools to obtain approval of their curricula by the Board of Regents. When the Socialist party's Rand School refused to apply for a license, the state began proceedings to close that institution.[5] State officials in California carried on a ruthless campaign from 1919 to 1924 to destroy the Industrial Workers of the World; and 504 persons were arrested, and 264 alleged subversives were tried under the state's criminal syndicalism law for committing sabotage and advocating the violent overthrow of the government.

The case that aroused the most violent controversy involved two obscure Italian-born anarchists, Nicola Sacco and Bartolomeo Vanzetti. Arrested in 1920 for the alleged murder of a paymaster in South Braintree, Massachusetts, Sacco and Vanzetti were tried the following year by a judge, Webster Thayer, who publicly vented his contempt for anarchism and allowed the state's attorney to make the defendants' radicalism a cornerstone of his case. Sacco and Vanzetti were convicted and sentenced to death, but radical and liberal groups throughout the United States and Europe believed that the two men had been sentenced not for murder, but for anarchism.[6] In spite of mass demonstrations abroad and fervent appeals at home, Governor A. T. Fuller permitted Sacco and Vanzetti to die in the electric chair on August 23, 1927.

Anti-Semitism, always a latent menace, was exacerbated by the identification of many Jewish radicals, first with opposition to the war, and then with the Communist party and other radical groups. It was also intensified by the fact that many Jews were recent immigrants, as yet not "Americanized" during a decade when a great majority demanded unquestioning adoption of American manners and customs. It was, moreover, nurtured and used as a rallying cry by leaders of the Ku Klux Klan, who resurrected discredited charges of an international Jewish conspiracy to control the world. These charges were echoed by Henry Ford's newspaper, the *Dearborn Independent*, until Ford, threatened with court action, repudiated the accusation.

---

[5] After the election of Alfred E. Smith as governor in 1922, this legislation was repealed, and proceedings against the Rand School were dropped.

[6] There is now considerable controversy about their innocence.

An uncritical nationalism, stimulated by postwar disillusionment and bitter European criticisms of American life, also seized millions, if not a majority, of Americans during the twenties. Officials in New York and Chicago, agitated by the Hearst newspapers and the *Chicago Daily Tribune*, investigated textbooks to root out works that failed properly to glorify the American past and damn the British. Oregon and Wisconsin forbade use of history texts that defamed American heroism in the Revolution and the War of 1812, while organizations like the American Legion, the Daughters of the American Revolution, and the Ku Klux Klan maintained a steady pressure for "one hundred percent Americanism." And nationalism often shaded into racism, as Madison Grant and Lothrop Stoddard, among others, in their *Passing of the Great Race* and *The Rising Tide of Color*, popularized the contemporary view that the Nordic type was inherently superior to other so-called races.

The most sinister development of the 1920s was the rise in many states of the Knights of the Ku Klux Klan, the American counterpart of Italian Fascists and German Nazis. The Klan was organized by William J. Simmons, a former lay preacher and history teacher, under a blazing cross on Stone Mountain near Atlanta in the autumn of 1915, and was modeled after the hooded organization that had terrorized the South during Reconstruction. Simmons had established a few chapters in Georgia and Alabama by the end of 1919, but loss of membership seemed to threaten his organization with early extinction.

Two expert organizers, Edward Y. Clarke and Mrs. Elizabeth Tyler, rescued the Klan from oblivion early in 1920. Simmons had constructed an imposing empire headed by himself as imperial wizard, but with only a few thousand subjects of dubious loyalty. Recognizing the rich financial opportunity at hand, Clarke and Mrs. Tyler increased the initiation fee to $10.00 and established an imperial promotion department, known as the imperial kleagle, with door-to-door solicitors and heads of state promotion departments.

The Klan gained 100,000 new members in 1920 by a vigorous promotional campaign. The impractical Simmons was ousted as imperial wizard in 1922 and replaced by Hiram W. Evans, a Texas dentist with a bent for making money. The Klan's spectacular growth now ensued. It moved first into the Southwest and stirred violent political storms. From the Southwest the Klan penetrated rapidly into California and Oregon. A Klan-supported governor and legislature were elected in Oregon in 1922 and proceeded to attempt to destroy Catholic parochial schools. Moving at the same time into the Middle West, Klan organizers soon gained a large constituency in this stronghold of democratic idealism. In Indiana, for example, the leading klansman, David C. Stephenson, captured control of the Republican state organization, cowed Indiana's two senators into submission, and helped to elect his henchman, Ed Jackson, to the governorship in 1924.[7]

In summary, the Klan at the peak of its strength in 1925 had a membership throughout the country, but chiefly in the Southwest, Far West, and Middle West, of approximately 5,000,000. At one time or another and to a varying degree, it controlled or had powerful influence in the governments of Texas, Oklahoma, Arkansas, California, Oregon, Indiana, Ohio, and other states. Wherever it went it carried bigotry, violence, and corruption and, as we shall see, posed a dire threat to democracy.

Klan membership was drawn largely from lower middle-class old American stock, chiefly in towns and cities, who were intensely suspicious of anything foreign or different and responded to bombastic expressions of patriotism. As only native-born white Protestants were allegedly "racially" capable of comprehending Americanism, the Klan excluded Catholics, Jews, blacks, and most aliens. The same sort of people who followed demagogues, went to revival meetings, and tried to suppress the teaching of evolution joined the Klan.

The Klan's chief appeal outside the South was anti-Catholicism. Its program in the Middle and Far West was devoted almost exclusively to destroying parochial schools, thwarting the Catholic hierarchy's alleged plot to capture the United States, and preventing the Pope from moving the Holy See to Georgetown. If there was any single issue on which Protestant Americans could be easily aroused, it was this Catholic issue. Thus the Klan gained members and power by appealing to historic fears and perpetuating a strong anti-Catholic tradition that went back to the colonial period of American history.

The Klan was not officially anti-Semitic, but in practice it was almost invariably so, because Jews were not only not Protestants but were also, for the most part, from southern and eastern Europe. However, the Klan stood openly for white supremacy and for keeping the Negro "in his place." Indeed, the most important impetus for the rise of the Klan in the South was fear among whites of returning black veterans and the troubled condition of race relations from 1919 to 1921.

Aside from its anti-Catholic program, the Klan's strongest attraction was its ritual and secrecy and the fact that for a time it was a going concern. Americans have always been a nation of joiners with a strong penchant for high-flown ritual. The Klan also allowed its members to wear weird-looking white robes and hoods; and any ordinary person could pay his ten dollars, become an exalted Knight of the Ku Klux Klan, and parade in exciting anonymity.

---

[7]Stephenson's downfall, however, came swiftly. After a sordid affair in which he kidnaped and assaulted a secretary and caused her to commit suicide, Stephenson was convicted of second-degree murder on November 14, 1925, and sentenced to life imprisonment. His crony, Jackson, was indicted for bribery in September 1927, and the Klan was disgraced and destroyed as a political and social force in Indiana.

Because the imperial headquarters exercised absolutely no control over the klaverns, or local chapters, Klan tactics varied from community to community. The coming of the Klan to the Southwest in 1920-1921, for example, was accompanied by a wave of murders, floggings, kidnapings, and other outrages. And thus it went, though on a lesser scale, wherever the Klan penetrated. Klan leaders piously protested that criminals using the Klan costume were always responsible for the outrages. Klan opponents replied that the Klan was essentially a lawless, terroristic organization, whose chief purpose was the subversion of orderly constitutional government.

Fascism was triumphant in Italy at the end of the 1920s, and the forces of reaction were gathering strength in Germany. In the United States, on the other hand, the Ku Klux Klan stood exposed and discredited, its membership reduced to perhaps 100,000. For this failure of fascism in the United States the American people had to thank their traditions, a free press, and courageous leaders all over the country. Progressive editors, politicians, clergymen, and other public spokesmen everywhere recognized the Klan for what it was. They took the Klan's measure and threw themselves into what seemed in the beginning a losing fight. They triumphed in the end because they fought to preserve traditions that the overwhelming majority of Americans, even most klansmen, cherished.

6. Prohibition: The "Noble Experiment"

The prohibition movement had gained such momentum by the eve of American participation in the First World War that the day could not be far distant when Anti-Saloon leaders would campaign for a constitutional amendment outlawing the manufacture and sale of alcoholic beverages in the United States. (For the origins of the prohibition movement, see pp. 25-26.) By the end of 1914 fourteen states had adopted prohibition; and by the end of 1918 over three-fourths of the people lived either in dry states or counties. Prohibition, obviously, was not the product of sudden impulse or wartime hysteria. On the contrary, it was an important component of the modern reform movement and demonstrated better than any other aspect of that movement the naive progressive faith in the efficacy of legislation in accomplishing fundamental social change.

On the other hand, the Anti-Saloon League might never have won the Eighteenth, or prohibition, Amendment had not the entrance of the United States into the war coincided with the high tide of prohibition agitation. Many champions of local option and state rights had consistently opposed such far-reaching extension of federal authority as national prohibition would compel. But Anti-Saloon spokesmen succeeded in identifying

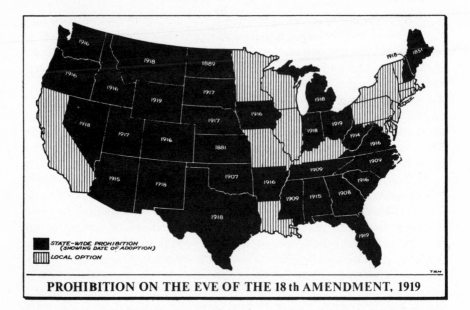

PROHIBITION ON THE EVE OF THE 18th AMENDMENT, 1919

prohibition with patriotism, and these conservative voices were momentarily stilled. Consequently, the dry leaders were able to carry the government and people from one step to another in their relentless campaign.

To begin with, the Anti-Saloon lobbyists forced adoption of an amendment to the Conscription Act of 1917 forbidding the sale of alcoholic beverages at or near army camps and naval bases. Secondly, the Lever Act, to conserve desperately needed grain, prohibited use of grain for distilling and brewing and empowered the president to ban manufacture of other alcoholic beverages. Thirdly, Congress on December 18, 1917, passed and submitted to the states the Eighteenth Amendment. It prohibited, one year after ratification, the manufacture, sale, or transportation of alcoholic beverages in the United States. Fourthly, Congress in October 1919 passed, over Wilson's veto, the Volstead Act extending the wartime ban on distilling and brewing, defining alcoholic beverages as any containing more than one-half of 1 percent alcohol by volume, and prohibiting the manufacture or sale of any such beverages after the Eighteenth Amendment had gone into effect in January 1920.

Meanwhile, in a wave of idealism all the states except Connecticut and Rhode Island approved the Eighteenth Amendment. Nebraska, the home of Bryan, one of the prime leaders of the prohibition crusade, appropriately made the thirty-sixth ratification on January 16, 1919. Nationwide prohibition went into force a year later; but as the country had in effect been dry since the summer of 1917 there were few protest demonstrations. Bryan held a victory celebration in New York in March 1920 and announced that the liquor issue was as dead as slavery. The first prohibition commissioner later promised that no liquor would be manufactured, "nor sold, nor given away, nor hauled in anything on the surface of the earth or under the earth or in the air."

Of course it did not turn out that way. Strict enforcement was impossible unless the government put a million agents in the field and sternly suppressed personal liberty. Partial enforcement was possible only if a large majority of the people were determined to exterminate the liquor traffic. There was probably a considerable decline in drinking and the liquor traffic in rural and strongly Protestant areas, where public opinion generally supported state and federal enforcement authorities. In fact, prohibition was accompanied by a sharp decline throughout the country in the measurable results of drinking—arrests for drunkenness and deaths from alcoholism.

The difficulties of enforcement were, however, enormous from the outset. The politically dry majority in Congress followed the advice of the Anti-Saloon League throughout the twenties in making appropriations and tightening enforcement laws. Even so, such provisions were hopelessly inadequate without the full support of local officials and public opinion. There were only 1,520 agents in the Prohibition Bureau in 1920 and 2,836 ten years later. As a consequence, enforcement was spasmodic, largely ineffective in areas where public opinion was hostile to the Eighteenth Amendment, and often violent and corrupt because of the bad character and strong-arm methods of many agents.

The two chief obstacles to enforcement were the determined resistance of large and important segments of the population and the fanaticism of dry leaders. Probably a majority of people in states with large foreign-born populations—like Massachusetts, New York, New Jersey, Maryland, Illinois, Ohio, and Wisconsin—would have voted against prohibition in a national referendum. Certainly the overwhelming majority in the large cities, native and foreign-born alike, thought that they had an inalienable right to drink. Consequently, neither local nor state officials, nor the masses of people in these states and cities, supported enforcement. Instead, they rallied behind organizations like the Association Against the Prohibition Amendment and political leaders like Governor Albert C. Ritchie of Maryland and Governor Alfred E. Smith of New York, committed to repeal of the Eighteenth Amendment.

In the main, prohibition might have succeeded had dry leaders realized that most opposition to the Eighteenth Amendment stemmed from the ban on the sale of beer and light wine. Immediately after ratification of the amendment, the legislatures of Wisconsin, Massachusetts, New York, Maryland, and New Jersey adopted laws outlawing saloons and sale of hard liquors but permitting sale of light beer. Instead of accepting this slight deviation from perfection, Anti-Saloon lobbyists forced adoption of the Volstead Act and successfully challenged the constitutionality of the beer laws of these states. Inevitably officials and masses of people in the "wet" states not only refused to respect prohibition but began a relentless war against the dry regime.

The consequences of prohibition, that "noble experiment" in federal social control, were as remarkable as the difficulties that the effort raised. For one thing, prohibition brought in its wake a series of social innovations among the wet minority. Speakeasies instead of saloons, hip flasks at football games, bathtub gin, and the increasing popularity of the cocktail party—these were some of the social side products of the Eighteenth Amendment. Another phenomenon was an increase in drinking by women. Saloons before the war had been exclusively male preserves in which no respectable woman would be seen. In contrast, mixed drinking in the home and speakeasy became the rule after 1919—another sign of the emancipation of women.

The most disastrous consequence of prohibition was the tremendous increase in bootlegging that followed adoption of the Eighteenth Amendment. Bootlegging in turn encouraged organization of underworld gangs that went into rackets of various kinds, bought control of city governments, and seriously threatened democratic government in American cities during the 1920s and early 1930s. Prohibition alone was not responsible for this development. Organized vice and gambling had long been the curse of American cities; and gangsterism, racketeering, and organized blackmail developed almost in direct proportion to the speed of the automobile and the ease with which criminals could purchase weapons of wholesale slaughter like the submachine gun. Even so, bootlegging was the chief livelihood and source of income of the gangs.

The truth of this generalization can be demonstrated by a brief recital of the rise of the Capone gang in Chicago, the most important underworld association of the twenties. The story begins in 1920, when young Alphonse, or Al, Capone moved to Chicago after serving a brief apprenticeship in the underworld of New York City. He was soon not only master of his own gang but also the leading bootlegger and gambling and vice operator in the Chicago area, with a gross income by 1927 of $60 million a year. Ironically, most of Capone's income from bootlegging came from the sale of beer. With a private army of from 700 to 1,000 gangsters he ruthlessly crushed rivals who dared to challenge his sovereignty; and Chicago witnessed pitched battles and mass gang killings that made its name a byword in the civilized world. Capone was toppled from his high eminence only when a Treasury agent worked his way into the organization and obtained evidence that led to the gangster's conviction and imprisonment for federal income tax evasion in 1931.

Opposition to the Eighteenth Amendment, sporadic and unorganized at the beginning of the 1920s, mounted after New York repealed its enforcement laws in 1923 and the Democratic party in the eastern states assumed leadership of the antiprohibition movement. Republicans continued from 1920 to 1932 to support the "noble experiment," as Herbert Hoover characterized the prohibition effort, without any important division in their ranks. On the other hand, Democrats were so badly split over prohibition, among other issues, that they practically ceased to be a national party in the twenties.

The end of the "noble experiment" came not long after the people had apparently given it a sweeping endorsement in the presidential election of 1928. Soon after his inauguration President Hoover appointed a commission headed by former Attorney General George W. Wickersham to investigate the problems of enforcement. The commission's report, presented in 1931, revealed what most informed Americans already knew—that the whole process of enforcement had broken down, and that it was virtually impossible to impose aridity upon a determined minority. Moreover, the conviction grew and was shared by many persons who originally had approved the experiment that prohibition simply was not worth the political and social costs—among others, the disruption of the Democratic party, subversion of the right of the states to control social customs, widespread contempt for law that prohibition had bred, and, most important, the stimulus that it gave to organized crime and bootlegging.

By 1932 problems of relief and recovery from the depression overshadowed all other issues. In that year a reunited Democratic party came out frankly for repeal of the Eighteenth Amendment and resumption of state control over the liquor traffic. The deed was quickly done after the smashing Democratic victory in November. The lame-duck session in February 1933 passed and submitted to the people the Twenty-first Amendment. It repealed the Eighteenth Amendment and prohibited the transportation of liquor into any dry state or territory. The same Congress also legalized the sale of light beer in March 1933. Three-fourths of the states had ratified the Twenty-first Amendment by the following December, and the "noble experiment," so auspiciously begun, was over.

7. The Triumph of Naturalism in Literature

The conjunction of circumstances and intellectual currents at the end of the First World War produced one of the most significant literary developments in American history—the flowering of the naturalistic revolt against the genteel tradition in literature among a new group of writers called the Lost Generation. Before the war, Frank Norris, Theodore Dreiser, Jack London, and Edgar Lee Masters had raised the standards of the revolution and pointed the way. For a time after the war it seemed as if literary America had repudiated all ideals and values of the past. The significant fact was the incredible vogue of the new standards among both writers and readers in the 1920s.

In trying to discern the causes for such revolutionary changes in literary standards the historian sees through a glass darkly. Yet writers do not only create, they also reflect the intellectual and spiritual standards and voice the perplexities and doubts of their time. The Lost Generation of the 1920s were creatures of an age characterized on the higher levels of thought by determinism in the physical sciences and relativism in ethics. Naturalism in literature—the study of man as a biological creature entirely enthralled to environment in an amoral universe—was nothing more than the literary reflection of a science that had removed the Creator from the universe, reduced man to a laboratory case study, and solemnly declared that human emotions stemmed from the viscera. The disillusionment of the Lost Generation was, moreover, reflected in a dozen other currents of national thought.

In any event, the converging of naturalistic concepts with the sharp moral deterioration that followed the war set the literary revolution in motion. Inevitably there was a spate of war novels and plays depicting the misery of trench warfare and the complete moral and spiritual bankruptcy of the soldiers. Most notable among the early war novels was John Dos Passos's *Three Soldiers* (1921). Its theme was aptly expressed by one of the leading characters: "This ain't a war, it's a goddam madhouse."

Combining protest against Victorian prudery with a lusty naturalism, Ernest Hemingway wrote a series of stories and novels that set new standards of style in fictional writing. His most notable work during these years, *A Farewell to Arms* (1929), summarized a decade of revulsion against the sham idealism of the war. But in a number of earlier novels and short stories—*The Sun Also Rises* (1926) and *Men Without Women* (1927), for example—he voiced the Lost Generation's revolt against allegedly sham ideals.

Meanwhile, naturalism as a literary form found its apogee in a number of other American writers. Sherwood Anderson, in *Winesburg, Ohio* (1919), *Poor White* (1920), *Many Marriages* (1923), and other novels and stories, attempted to unmask what he considered the perversities of the small-town Middle West. Anderson, however, had too deep a sympathy with his tragic characters to be a true naturalist. More faithful to naturalistic standards were Ring Lardner and Erskine Caldwell. Their stories about small-town and country people of the Middle West and South were marked by a morbid interest in the diseased in mind and body. And it was fitting that in this decade of naturalism Theodore Dreiser, one of the founders of the movement in the United States, should have written his most popular work. His *An American Tragedy* (1925) was even more perfectly mechanistic than *Sister Carrie* (1900), *Jennie Gerhardt* (1911), *The Financier* (1912), and *The Titan* (1914) had been.

Preoccupation with sex, which they often glorified as the primal drive, was characteristic of all the naturalists and quasi-naturalists. There was, however, considerable difference in emphasis. To writers like Dreiser and

Sherwood Anderson, sex was only one of the important drives that determined man's behavior. But there was a group who played upon the sexual theme almost to the point of obsession. One of these was James Branch Cabell, author of *Jurgen* (1919), *Figures of Earth* (1921), and *Something About Eve* (1927), whose vivid symbolism drew the fire of professional defenders of American morality. More indirect was F. Scott Fitzgerald, a superb storyteller and one of the most talented writers among the Lost Generation. In *This Side of Paradise* (1920), *The Beautiful and Damned* (1922), and *The Great Gatsby* (1925), Fitzgerald chronicled the moral and spiritual dissolution of the Lost Generation, to whom, as he said, all gods were dead, all wars fought, all faiths shaken.

As the decade drew to a close a southern rebel, Thomas Wolfe, gave promise of offsetting the Lost Generation's extreme negation. His *Look Homeward, Angel* (1929) was the expression of a young tortured soul in rebellion against the materialism of his mother and, as it seemed to him, the narrow provincialism of his home town of Asheville, North Carolina. But Wolfe was no naturalist. He was too adolescent, too romantic, and too fond of life to be always morbid and introspective, as his later novels, *Of Time and the River* (1935), *The Web and the Rock* (1939), and *You Can't Go Home Again* (1949), revealed.

The most widely read and universally acclaimed American novelist of the 1920s, Sinclair Lewis, stands almost alone as the connecting link between muckraking novelists of the progressive era and social novelists of the New Deal period. He could be harsh and almost captious in depicting the drabness of small-town midwestern life, the provincialism and smugness of the business booster, and the moral sham and materialism of his time. *Main Street* (1920), *Babbitt* (1922), *Arrowsmith* (1925), *Elmer Gantry* (1927), and *Dodsworth* (1929) presented caricatures of types of middle-class Americans and won for their author in 1930 the first Nobel Prize in literature ever awarded an American.

Traditionalists not only survived in spite of the seemingly irresistible vogue of naturalism and negation, but also waged a rear-guard action against the younger generation. It is interesting that most of the novelists among the traditionalists were women. Edith Wharton continued writing her satires of the life and manners of the New York aristocracy. Dorothy Canfield Fisher defended morality and integrity. Ellen Glasgow of Richmond continued her series on life among Virginians high and low. But the greatest of these gentle realists was Willa Cather, who found nobility and spiritual grandeur in human tragedy and divine grace. Her *Death Comes for the Archbishop* (1927) was not only her finest work but also one of the American novels of the 1920s most likely to endure.

In literary criticism the traditionalists were more articulate and aggressive. The leaders in a new humanistic movement, Paul Elmer More, Irving Babbitt, William C. Brownell, and Stuart P. Sherman, met their antagonists, H. L. Mencken, Van Wyck Brooks, and Harold E. Stearns, in a great battle of the books. The neo-humanists not only condemned the naturalists' disdain of graceful style and form; they also boldly championed the Christian ethic and Western cultural tradition. And if they did not convert the writers of the twenties they founded a school and laid the foundations for a later broad humanistic revival in letters. Thus on both sides there was an energy and activity that made the twenties exciting, creative, and fertile.

Nor did the poetic revival, which had begun so auspiciously during the years before the First World War, abate. Among the poets of the people, Vachel Lindsay and Edgar Lee Masters produced little of consequence; but Robert Frost and Carl Sandburg did not lose their voice during the twenties. In *New Hampshire* (1923) and *West-Running Brook* (1928), Frost again expressed his deep love of nature and a sharpened sympathy for man. Edwin Arlington Robinson, after securing his reputation with *The Man Against the Sky* (1916), continued his search for meaning in a trilogy based upon the Arthurian legend, *Merlin, Lancelot,* and *Tristram* (1917–1927). He was, in the eloquent words of one critic, "the solitary poet who absorbed into his thought and art the best of the old in American poetry and became the first of his generation to understand, however darkly, the new."[8]

Meanwhile, leadership among the young intellectual poets who called themselves imagists was shared by two American expatriates, Ezra Pound and T. S. Eliot. Pound had deserted the imagist group in London before the war, spent four years in Paris, and finally settled in Rapallo, Italy. During the 1920s and 1930s he wrote seventy-one *Cantos*, brilliant word pictures often devoid of any readily discernible meaning. Although isolated from British and American friends, he continued to have great influence on young poets.

T. S. Eliot, born in St. Louis and educated at Harvard, moved to London after the outbreak of the war. Convinced that poetry should convey a sense of the complexity of life, Eliot wrote poetry difficult to understand. But the shimmering imagery of his words hid certain profound convictions, especially a belief that life without faith is vain foolishness. *The Waste Land* (1922), Eliot's most important work of the decade, revealed the proportions of his break with the imagists on account of his conviction that the word image was futile unless it conveyed essential meaning about life.

Robinson Jeffers was one poet who more accurately reflected the dominant naturalistic temper among American writers. He wrote romantic poetry before the war and then, in the mid-twenties, turned savagely against humanity. His "Tower Beyond Tragedy" (1924), *Roan Stallion, Tamar, and Other Poems* (1925), and *The Women at Point Sur* (1927) expressed

[8]Stanley T. Williams, "Edwin Arlington Robinson," in Robert E. Spiller *et al., Literary History of the United States* (New York and London, 1963), p. 1170.

the conviction that violence, sexual perversion, and inhumanity character-ize all human behavior, and that the natural world alone has grandeur and dignity.

Convincing proof of the continued vitality of the poetic tradition in the United States was the rise of a generation of young new poets in the 1920s and 1930s. There was, for example, Pound's and Eliot's disciple, Hart Crane. A group of southern regionalists at Vanderbilt University—John Crowe Ransome, Robert Penn Warren, Donald Davidson, and Allen Tate—combined romantic love of the southern past with experiments in new forms. Edna St. Vincent Millay's sonnets expressed the youthful re-volt against Victorian manners. Archibald MacLeish began a distinguished literary career by voicing the dominant mood of discontent. Or, again, there was the experimentalist, E. E. Cummings, whose strange style al-most obscured the simple romantic themes of his poems; and there was also Conrad Aiken, William Carlos Williams, Marianne Moore, and Wal-lace Stevens, among a host of others. The most widely read of the young poets, Stephen Vincent Benét, found his theme in the crisis of the Union. His *John Brown's Body* (1928), an epic poem, depicted the passions and experiences of the American people during the Civil War more convinc-ingly than most social histories have done.

The most significant literary development of the 1920s was the flower-ing of a native American theater. It began around 1915, when young intellectuals established little theaters at Provincetown, Massachusetts, and New York City, and began to experiment for their own pleasure. The New York group reorganized in 1919 under the name of the Theatre Guild, acquired a theater of its own, and began presenting the plays of contemporary European dramatists.

The most distinguished member of the Provincetown group was Eugene O'Neill, whose *Bound East for Cardiff* was first produced by the Province-town Players in 1916. O'Neill emerged during the next six years as the only American dramatist of any consequence at that time. Then, in *Desire Under the Elms* (1924), *Strange Interlude* (1928), and *Mourning Becomes Electra* (1931), he turned to Freudian themes in an attempt to understand human motivation.

O'Neill was beyond cavil the preeminent American dramatist of his generation, but he was joined by such a goodly company after 1922 that almost overnight an American drama of genuine literary significance came into being. Moreover, the American public evinced an encouraging inter-est in the stage and a willingness to accept experimental forms. It was reflected not only on Broadway, but on college campuses and in little theater groups in a hundred American cities. This renaissance first began with the production of Elmer Rice's *The Adding Machine* in 1923. Then during 1924 and 1925 there followed Maxwell Anderson's and Laurence Stallings's *What Price Glory?*, Sidney Howard's *They Knew What They Wanted*, and John Howard Lawson's *Processional*. From this beginning progress was rapid. Although S. N. Behrman and Philip Barry enlivened the theater with sophisticated comedies and Paul Green and Hatcher Hughes tried vainly to stimulate interest in folk drama, the large majority of young playwrights simply mirrored the contemporary determinism, disillusionment, and preoccupation with sex. Not until the depression would the stage become a sounding board for the American social conscience.

8. *Writers in Turmoil, 1929-1941*

American fictional writing during the years between the Great Depression and the Second World War reflected the violent crosscurrents of thought and challenges to democracy that confused the American mind. To begin with, the rebels of the Lost Generation lived on into the thirties. However, their revolt had lost much of its meaning by 1933, and the standards of a new rebellion were being unfurled by other insurgents. There was the tragic spectacle of F. Scott Fitzgerald, caught in the moral and cultural collapse of which he had written so poignantly. His final works, *Tender Is the Night* (1934) and *The Last Tycoon* (1941), were artistically distinguished but revealed a neurotic mind sickened by the corruption that he thought damned American life.

Ernest Hemingway and Sinclair Lewis gave further evidence of the bewilderment that confused and enfeebled the survivors of the Lost Generation. In a series of books—*Death in the Afternoon* (1932), *Winner Take Nothing* (1933), and *The Green Hills of Africa* (1935)—Hemingway violated his own literary standards and nearly renounced human values. Then, alarmed by the challenge of fascism, he replied in 1940 with his most popular novel, *For Whom the Bell Tolls*. In the place of repudiation he now substituted devotion to a cause, the fight of the Spanish Loyalists. But his political ideology was confused, and his characters were out of place. *For Whom the Bell Tolls* marked the end of the Lost Generation, not its rebirth.

The work of Sinclair Lewis after 1930 illustrated in a different way the deterioration of the Lost Generation. Lewis was superbly effective so long as he held a mirror to the absurdities of middle-class thought and manners. But after 1930 he searched for new themes and evidenced less hostility toward society. His *It Can't Happen Here* (1935) depicted the triumph of fascism in America and forecast the salvation of democracy by the middle class. Neither this nor his final novels, written in the forties, displayed the trenchant power that had characterized his work in the twenties.

In contrast, the late twenties and the thirties saw the rise of the brightest star in the whole twentieth-century American literary constellation: William Faulkner of Oxford, Mississippi, who had begun to write in the twenties but who had been culturally too isolated (or intellectually too independent) to be a member of the Lost Generation. From his lonely outpost Faulkner sought to find the meaning of life through reconstruction of the southern past, through the heroes and villains and plain people caught in the vortex of a society in dissolution. From reading his earlier novels—such as *The Sound and the Fury* (1929), *Light in August* (1932), and *Absalom! Absalom!* (1936)—it is difficult for the layman to know whether Faulkner rejected completely the value structure of the past or used a powerful symbolism to reaffirm old values. But in a later volume— *The Unvanquished* (1938)—Faulkner began to exhibit clearer signs of the high purpose that underlay his important novels of the forties and fifties.

Meanwhile, the 1930s witnessed an astounding rebirth of the social and economic novel in America that equaled if it did not exceed the outpouring of the years before the First World War. The mass of human suffering during the depression stimulated despair, while the hope of salvation either through destruction or reform of capitalism stimulated both a cathartic analysis of the American system and a political climate in which such analysis could flourish.

The most loquacious and perhaps the bitterest critic of American capitalism among the fictional writers of the thirties was John Dos Passos. In his trilogy, *U.S.A.—The Forty-Second Parallel* (1930), *Nineteen-Nineteen* (1932), and *The Big Money* (1936)—Dos Passos used a variety of literary techniques to reconstruct the panorama of American life from 1900 to 1929. In a second trilogy—*Adventures of a Young Man* (1939), *Number One* (1943), and *The Grand Design* (1949)—he continued the story through the depression and the New Deal.

Writing in the same vein but on a less panoramic scale and perhaps with less bitterness was James T. Farrell. His *Young Lonigan* (1932), *The Young Manhood of Studs Lonigan* (1934), and *Judgment Day* (1935) recounted the moral and spiritual disintegration of a lower middle-class Irish neighborhood in south Chicago. Another social novelist, John Steinbeck, protested against the injustices of an economic system that allegedly degraded workers and sharecroppers to the level of animal existence. His greatest work, *The Grapes of Wrath* (1939), was a moving odyssey of the flight of a sharecropper family, the unforgettable Joads, from Oklahoma to California. In this and other novels, Steinbeck emerged as a social novelist of the first rank and also as the writer who best understood the tragedy of the lower classes of his time.

The bitterest critics of the depression decade were the so-called proletarian writers—Marxists, Communists, and fellow-travelers (that is, persons who were not members of the Communist party but lent their support to Communist causes)—who used the novel as propaganda to hasten the conversion of the middle classes to revolutionary ideals. The politically devout among them magnified the sins of capitalism, glorified the "little people," and heralded the coming triumph of the disinherited.

The "deviationists" used proletarian themes but would not surrender their artistic integrity to the commissars of Union Square. To a varying degree, Dos Passos, Farrell, and Steinbeck were proletarian writers and the most distinguished members of this group. The black naturalist, Richard Wright, was briefly a party member. His *Native Son* (1940) and *Black Boy* (1945) showed considerable talent if a strong penchant for unrelieved violence. The majority of proletarian writers, however, were important for their economic and social criticism, not for their literary skill.

Not all the writers of the thirties were angry and raucous. There were survivors from the genteel past: Willa Cather, who published one of her most important books, *Shadows on the Rock* (1931), and one of her most poignant tales, *Sapphira and the Slave Girl* (1940); Ellen Glasgow, who continued her satires on life in Virginia; and the southern writers Elizabeth Madox Roberts and Katharine Anne Porter. And there were three new novelists, Pearl S. Buck, John P. Marquand, and Robert Penn Warren, who enriched the literature of the thirties and helped keep alive the traditions of graceful writing and moral purpose.

Judged sheerly by popular standards, the most important literary development after 1930 was the emergence of the historical novel as a mature literary form. Many of the historical novelists of the thirties simply romanticized the past and wrote cheap literature. On the other hand, a large minority, including Margaret Mitchell, Kenneth Roberts, Walter Edmonds, and Conrad Richter, illustrated the timelessness of human experience in graceful prose. Margaret Mitchell's *Gone with the Wind* (1936), for example, was not only an epic of a civilization destroyed and struggling to live again, but it was also something of a literary masterpiece.

It was evident by the Second World War that a great era in American fictional writing had ended. It had begun with the revolt of the naturalists before 1917, flowered in the twenties with the rise of the Lost Generation, and culminated in the thirties in the literature of the people and the search for a symbolic expression of human tragedy in the writings of William Faulkner, Robert Penn Warren, and other authors.

9. *The Flowering of Poetry and the Drama in the Thirties*

There were crosscurrents and new moods in American poetical writing after the brilliant renaissance of the period 1910–1927. Some of the old masters and practitioners of more conventional forms survived in the thirties. For example, the dean of American poets, Edwin Arlington Robinson, confirmed his supremacy during the period between the completion of his Arthurian trilogy in 1927 and his last work, *King Jasper*, published in 1935.

His death in that year deprived America of her greatest poet since Walt Whitman. Robert Frost, whose reputation was already well established by 1930, continued to write with deceptive simplicity about nature and man's struggles. Carl Sandburg, another of the new poets of the earlier renaissance, affirmed his faith in American destiny in *The People, Yes* (1936). Edna St. Vincent Millay, a lyrical poet of some power who had begun her work in the early twenties, came to full artistic maturity in the 1930s, particularly in *Fatal Interview* (1931).

These latter-day traditionalists had some followers in the thirties. There was Stephen Vincent Benét, who continued to voice American democratic idealism in *Litany for Dictatorships* (1936), *Nightmare at Noon* (1940), and, in the year of his untimely death, *Western Star* (1943). Moreover, the challenge of depression at home and the rise of fascism abroad stimulated a brief outburst of democratic and leftist poetry in the 1930s. Muriel Rukeyser's *Theory of Flight* (1935) and *U.S. 1* (1938); Kenneth Fearing's *Poems* (1935); and Archibald MacLeish's *Public Speech* (1936), *America Was Promises* (1939), and other works, were poetic counterparts of the fictional literature of the people.

Despite these survivals of more or less traditional poetry, the most important fact about American poetic thought and writing in the 1930s was the growing influence of the imagist school established by Ezra Pound before the First World War and dominated by T. S. Eliot in the twenties and thirties. Converted to Anglo-Catholicism in the late twenties, Eliot turned to religious themes. His later notable poems, *Ash-Wednesday* (1930) and *Four Quartets* (1943), and his plays, *Murder in the Cathedral* (1935) and *The Cocktail Party* (1950), sought to convey the meaning of life and the universe.

The imagist revolt had long since become a mature movement with elaborate standards by 1940. We can now see that its emphasis upon imagery, symbolism, and intellectual quality produced a new poetry which, in its attempt to recreate the complexity of human experience, often went beyond the ability of the average reader to comprehend and enjoy. But many great poets have done this. The significant contribution of the modern poets was, in the words of one historian of the school, the triumph of "sincerity over sham, of naturalness over affectation, of a striking turn toward precision, analysis, and structure; of a wider range of conception and idea; of a deeper apprehension of meaning."[9]

We have earlier seen how a host of young playwrights, notably Eugene O'Neill, created an American drama in the decade following the armistice. O'Neill's creative energies waned in the early thirties (even though he wrote perhaps his most powerful play, *The Iceman Cometh*, in 1946), and leadership passed to other playwrights. Indeed, so voluminous, varied, and excellent was the outpouring after 1930 that it seemed the drama had

---

[9]Louise Bogan, *Achievement in American Poetry, 1900-1950* (Chicago, 1951), p. 106.

become the chief form of American literary expression. Maxwell Anderson, who had made his literary debut earlier in the twenties, turned to writing historical tragedies in poetic verse. His *Elizabeth the Queen* (1930), *Mary of Scotland* (1933), and *Valley Forge* (1934) established him as perhaps the leading American dramatist of the 1930s. S. N. Behrman and Philip Barry continued to enliven the stage with penetrating social satires that often said more than audiences understood. Marc Connelly depicted black folkways and religious thought in *The Green Pastures* (1930), one of the most beautiful plays of the decade. Thornton Wilder expressed the theme of man's survival in spite of evil, ignorance, and war in *Our Town* (1938) and *The Skin of Our Teeth* (1942).

These and a host of other playwrights celebrated the foibles and follies as well as the enduring values of American life, but they were creative artists rather than social critics. Of greater significance to the political historian of the thirties was the work of a large group who used the stage as a sounding board for all kinds of ideologies and social and political protest. There were, most notably, the leftists—Elmer Rice, John Howard Lawson, and especially Clifford Odets, the most frankly Marxian of them—who joined in the Theater Union and Group Theater to write fierce denunciations of the sins of capitalism. Some of them were also subsidized by the Federal Theatre Project, an enterprise of the New Deal's relief agency, the Works Progress Administration. The most talented social playwright, Lillian Hellman, demonstrated great power in her *The Children's Hour* (1934) and then turned to propaganda in *The Little Foxes* (1939) and *Watch on the Rhine* (1941). Of different political faith was Robert Sherwood, who best reflected the changing temper of the non-Marxist intellectual during the thirties. His *The Petrified Forest* (1935) reflected the pessimistic view of its day that reason was ineffectual as compared with brute force. His *Idiot's Delight* (1936) was one of the most eloquent pieces of antiwar propaganda during the high tide of pacifist sentiment. In response to the challenges of nazism and communism, however, Sherwood replied with two ringing affirmations of faith in man and democracy—*Abe Lincoln in Illinois* (1938) and *There Shall Be No Night* (1940).

13

The Survival of Progressivism: Politics and Problems of the Harding-Coolidge Era

For many years American historians assumed that the return of Republican rule in 1921 signified the end of the progressive movement and ushered in an era in which reactionaries controlled the federal government. Then came progressivism's revival and redemption under Franklin D. Roosevelt. Recent research and reexamination of the Republican era have revealed that the traditional picture is somewhat overdrawn.

To be sure, presidents Harding and Coolidge and their spokesmen in Congress were avowed champions of business and financial enterprise. Believing that American prosperity depended upon the well-being of the upper classes, they sponsored tariff and tax policies to promote special interests, brought federal administrative agencies into close cooperation with the business community, and opposed measures that would have discouraged investment or carried the government into new areas of regulation.

But to stop at this point would be to give a grossly distorted view of American politics in the 1920s. Conservative Republicans gained and held power in the executive branch only because of the peculiar character of the American political system, and only because progressives were divided, not because they were few in number. When the progressive coalition of 1916 was destroyed in 1920, progressives reverted to their traditional voting habits in the national elections of 1920, 1924, and 1928, and they were never able to combine to capture the presidency. On the other hand, they combined in Congress to control the legislative branch during practically all the 1920s, to thwart a conservative executive leadership on several important issues, and to push through a remarkable progressive program, the most advanced parts of which were nullified by presidential vetoes. In addition, progressivism survived on the local and state levels, particularly in movements for administrative efficiency and expansion of state educational and social services. Even the movement for social justice survived. As one authority has written, "The 1920s were not conducive to public action for social reform; but hundreds of social workers were prepared, nevertheless, to maintain their alliance with social reformers. The assumption that the reformers were driven from the field is not valid—they remained on the firing line, beat tactical retreats when necessary, engaged in flank attacks, waited for the breaks, and never for a moment surrendered the initiative. Frustrated and rebuffed, often ridiculed, sometimes despised, they kept alive and vital the crusade for social action, and thus formed a viable link between prewar progressivism and the New Deal."[1]

Thus, as the following sections will reveal, the political developments of the period 1920–1928 refuse to accommodate themselves to sweeping generalizations or pat theories. As we shall see, there were numerous conflicts, crosscurrents, and elements of confusion; but withal progressivism not only survived as an articulate expression of social and economic aspiration, it also widened its horizons.

1. The Harding Debacle

What a contrast the incoming president made with the outgoing chief executive as they rode to the Capitol on March 4, 1921! There was Wilson, aged and infirm, a living mind in a dying body. At his side sat Warren G. Harding, majestic in countenance but awed and still dazed by the trick that fate had played upon him in Chicago in June 1920.

The new president was born at Blooming Grove, Ohio, on November 2, 1865, and owned and edited the *Star*, in the small town of Marion, Ohio, for a number of years. He served two terms in the state senate and one as lieutenant governor, was his party's unsuccessful candidate for governor in

[1]Clarke A. Chambers, "Creative Effort in an Age of Normalcy, 1918–33," in *The Social Welfare Forum, 1961* (New York, 1961), p. 254.

1910, and won election to the United States Senate in 1914. He was his party's keynoter in the national convention of 1916. Realizing his own limitations, he was skeptical about running for the Republican presidential nomination. But ambition overcame his scruples. He permitted his friend Harry M. Daugherty to conduct an undercover campaign; he was popular with the delegates; and he accepted the nomination when it came to him almost by default in June 1920 (see pp. 237–238).

A man of average mental endowment can fulfill the duties of the presidency if his will power and character fortify his determination to rule wisely. It was an unkind act of fate, however, that made Harding president, for he had only average talents, little will power, and a striking inability to discriminate between right and wrong. Easygoing and affable, he possessed an uncanny ability to draw men utterly unworthy of his confidence into his personal circle. He also had at least two adulterous relationships.

The contrast between Wilson and Harding was no more vivid than the dissimilarity between the outgoing administration and many of the men surrounding the new president. Most of the members of the Wilson circle were able and honest public servants. They had carried the nation through a great war effort and spent billions of the public money, and hardly any of them had been guilty of theft or of using their office for private gain. In contrast stands a record of fraud and corruption in high places during the brief Harding regime unparalleled since the Grant era.

The opportunity to honor old friends and enjoy them as drinking and poker companions warmed the president's heart. For example, he appointed Daugherty as attorney general in spite of widespread opposition to the appointment. Another old crony, Senator Albert B. Fall, he named as secretary of the interior. On the whole, however, Harding tried to appoint a cabinet of the best men in the Republican party. Thus he chose Charles Evans Hughes as secretary of state; Andrew W. Mellon, Pittsburgh industrialist and banker, as secretary of the treasury; former Senator John W. Weeks of Massachusetts as secretary of war; Henry C. Wallace, a distinguished Iowa farm editor, as secretary of agriculture; Herbert Hoover as secretary of commerce; and James J. Davis, a Pennsylvania labor leader, as secretary of labor.

During his brief tenure Harding presided over the government of the United States with outward dignity. In contrast to Wilson, Harding was a weak president, never able to command his party forces in Congress. Although he worked slavishly, his undisciplined mind was incapable of mastering the details of important questions, and he stayed in a constant state of confusion. Hence he abdicated leadership of legislative and foreign policies to Congress and his cabinet. He wanted most of all to be loved by everyone, and two acts of his own reveal the very generous side of his nature. The first was the pardoning, in 1921, of Eugene V. Debs, who had spent three years in the Atlanta penitentiary and polled over

900,000 votes as Socialist candidate for president in 1920. The second was his bringing the heads of the steel industry to the White House in 1922 and persuading them to institute the eight-hour day.

Meanwhile, some of the president's subordinates were engaging under his myopic eyes in a mad scramble for bribes and as much loot as they could lay their hands upon. Scandal was inevitable. The first one involved Jesse Smith, an old-time friend of Daugherty's, who had moved to Washington with the attorney general. Smith soon became the liaison between the Department of Justice and violators of the prohibition laws, income tax evaders, and "fixers" of all kinds. Rumors of Smith's behavior reached Harding, and the president told Daugherty that his friend had to go back to Ohio. Smith went home for a while but could not endure the exile. He returned to Daugherty's apartment and killed himself on May 30, 1923.

Smith's suicide was the first event in a chain that culminated in exposure of several enormous scandals. The first to come to light involved the Veterans' Bureau, established by Congress in August 1921, under the direction of Charles R. Forbes. Harding had a profound concern for disabled veterans, especially for those afflicted with mental illness and tuberculosis. Forbes was a bustling, energetic person with a convincing tongue, who gave the impression of an efficient administrator. He supervised the building of hospitals and the expenditure of hundreds of millions of dollars, and Harding was pleased by these visible signs of progress. Unhappily, Forbes could not resist the temptation to make money on the side, and he stole or squandered nearly $250 million before he left office.

Daugherty learned about the corruption in the Veterans' Bureau late in 1922 and passed the bad news on to Harding. The president learned part of the truth from Forbes himself and permitted him to go abroad and resign on February 15, 1923. Rumors soon reached the Senate; it began an investigation on March 2. Twelve days later the legal adviser to the Veterans' Bureau, Charles F. Cramer, committed suicide. This broke the case, and the Senate committee pressed on to expose the full extent of defalcation in the bureau. Forbes was convicted of defrauding the government in 1925 and sentenced to a two-year term in Leavenworth penitentiary.

Meanwhile, Secretary of the Interior Albert B. Fall had been executing one of the most daring criminal forays in American history. He persuaded President Harding in 1921 to transfer control over naval oil reserve lands at Elk Hills in California and Teapot Dome in Wyoming from the Navy Department to his own jurisdiction. On April 7, 1922, Fall secretly leased Teapot Dome to the Mammoth Oil Company, owned by Harry F. Sinclair. The secretary leased Elk Hills to the Pan-American Petroleum Company, owned by Edward L. Doheny, on April 25.

News of the leases leaked out at once. Responding to an early Senate inquiry, Fall declared that he had leased Teapot Dome to Sinclair in the interest of national preparedness and was about to lease Elk Hills to Doheny. The Senate public lands committee, spurred on by Thomas J. Walsh of Montana, began an investigation in October 1923 that was continued the following year by a special commission. These investigations revealed that Sinclair had given Fall $223,000 in government bonds, $85,000 in cash, and some cattle for his ranch at the time that the lease for Teapot Dome was negotiated; and that Doheny had also "lent" $100,000 to Fall at the time that the lease on Elk Hills was being signed.

Eventually—in 1927—the government won its suit to cancel the leases, while Doheny, Sinclair, and Fall were tried for conspiracy to defraud the government and acquitted, although Sinclair spent terms in jail for contempt of Congress and tampering with a jury. Fall was convicted of bribery in October 1929, fined $100,000, and sentenced to a year's imprisonment. After many delays the former secretary went to jail in July 1931, thus becoming the first corrupt cabinet member in American history to receive something like his just reward.

Attorney General Daugherty was suspected of complicity in several frauds. But all during the furor raised by the revelations of the oil scandal in 1923 and 1924 he not only refused to resign but also turned the FBI on senators and other public leaders who were unearthing details of the corruption. Then a scandal involving the return of the American Metal Company to its German owners by the Alien Property Custodian, Thomas W. Miller, broke early in 1924. It came out that a highly placed New York Republican who engineered the deal had paid $50,000 to Miller and $224,000 to Jesse Smith, and that Smith had deposited $50,000 of the loot in an account that he held jointly with Daugherty. President Coolidge dismissed Daugherty when he refused to testify before a Senate committee of investigation in March 1924. Daugherty was brought to trial in New York in 1926 but again refused to testify, saying that his personal relations with President and Mrs. Harding made it impossible for him to do so. After deliberating nearly three days the jury disagreed because Harding's good name seemed to be at stake. The following year Miller was tried, convicted, and sent to jail.

2. The Death of President Harding

Harding made plans early in 1923 for a speaking tour through the West and a vacation in Alaska. Before he left Washington on June 20 the president had learned enough about the corruption of his friends to make him sick at heart and to fill him with a presentiment of impending doom. "My God, this is a hell of a job," he told William Allen White shortly before he left on his western trip. "I have no trouble with my enemies. . . . But my damned friends, my God-damn friends, White, they're the ones that keep me walking the floor nights!"[2]

[2] *The Autobiography of William Allen White* (New York, 1946), p. 619.

Harding, already suffering from a heart condition and hypertension, was physically exhausted and mentally depressed all during the long trip across the continent. The trip to Alaska brought no rest. The president returned to Seattle on July 27 and stood bareheaded under a fierce sun to make a speech. He faltered several times, and members of his party feared that he would collapse. That same evening Harding suffered intense pain. His physician said that he had ptomaine poisoning from eating spoiled crabs. The presidential party went to San Francisco, arriving there on July 29. Harding insisted on walking unaided from the station to his car, but he went to bed at once and developed pneumonia on the following day. Just when it seemed that he was on the road to recovery he suffered a stroke and died on August 2, 1923. As the funeral train bearing the president's body made its way slowly across the country, millions of Americans paid their respects to the man they thought Harding had been.

It was not long, however, before Americans learned the details of the various scandals, read the accusations of Harding's alleged mistress, Nan Britton, and heard absurd rumors that Harding had been poisoned by his wife. In consequence, the deflation of Harding's reputation came at once, not slowly. The people forgot his simplicity and kindliness and remembered only that he had appointed thieves and sheltered scoundrels. And during a later period, when the Republican leadership of the twenties stood discredited in the public mind, "normalcy" became a term of opprobrium, and the scandals of the Harding era, compounded with the ones of the Great Depression, became a heavy liability to the GOP.

3. The Anomaly of American Politics, 1921–1928

Those business leaders and men of wealth who poured nearly $8 million into the Republican campaign coffers in 1920 soon realized part of the expected return on their investment. Through the powerful Senate clique they had a decisive voice in shaping federal policies, both administrative and legislative. The time seemed ripe for complete fulfillment of the business-sponsored program—economy, drastic tax reductions, and sound financing; a return to tariff protection; control of federal regulatory agencies by men friendly to business interests; and an end to quasi-socialistic experiments launched during the war. At the very moment that conservatives were enjoying the election returns on November 2, 1920, however, disruptive economic forces were at work that soon robbed them of many of the legislative fruits of victory. During the autumn and winter of 1920–1921 agricultural prices were falling hard and fast, and a political rebellion, nearly equal in strength to the insurgent revolt of 1910–1912, was brewing.

Congress met in special session in April 1921, business leaders thought, to take the country back to "normalcy." If the president had controlled the enormous Republican majorities in both houses he could have put his program across with ease. As it turned out, the agrarian revolt developed so rapidly that conservatives could not command even a bare majority for measures to which the agrarian insurgents objected.

A month after the special session convened, a group of midwestern farm spokesmen in Congress, led by senators William S. Kenyon of Iowa and Arthur Capper of Kansas, met in the Washington offices of the new and powerful American Farm Bureau Federation to consider the agricultural crisis. Agreeing upon a program of extensive legislation, they at once organized the so-called farm bloc for nonpartisan action. By combining with southern Democrats the Midwesterners were able not only to put a part of their program across but also to block the administration's efforts at substantial tax reductions. (Later sections cover this story in some detail.)

Agricultural prices recovered slightly during the following year, 1922, and business and industry began to recuperate from the sharp depression of 1921. But returning prosperity only stimulated progressive discontent. Republican insurgents made almost a clean sweep in the primary campaigns through the Middle and Far West in the spring and summer of 1922. This was discouraging to administration leaders, but the results of the congressional election in November were even more discouraging. Republican majorities in the Senate and House were reduced to eight and eighteen, respectively, and so many insurgents were elected that the administration lost its small measure of control over Congress.

The congressional election of 1922 not only stimulated hopes of a general progressive revival but also heartened leaders of the farm bloc in Congress. When the lame-duck session convened in December 1922, Midwesterners organized a new and stronger bloc and adopted a platform that appealed as much to independents and workers as it did to farmers. Insurgent leaders insisted that they were merely protesting against conservative Republican policies, not contemplating a campaign to unite the disparate progressive elements in a third party. And yet there were numerous signs even as they spoke that the rebellion among farmers and organized workers was growing to such proportions that a nationwide independent movement might be possible in 1924.

The most important sign was the sudden revival of the Non-Partisan League after 1919. Organized among wheat growers of North Dakota in 1915, the Non-Partisan League advocated a program that was remarkably advanced for its day: state ownership and operation of farm credit agencies, warehouses, and grain elevators; minimum wages; and stringent control of railroads, banks, and private businesses. Capturing the state government of North Dakota in 1916, league organizers moved into Minnesota, Iowa, Montana, Idaho, and other states in 1917 and 1918. The League joined with a number of radical remnants in 1920 to form the

Farmer-Labor party and took second place in Minnesota, South Dakota, and Washington.

As the agricultural and industrial depression of 1920–1922 intensified discontent, leaders of the railroad brotherhoods called a Conference of Progressive Political Action to meet in Chicago in February 1922 for the purpose of considering independent political action. Represented at this gathering were the brotherhoods and many other unions, the Non-Partisan League, the Socialist party, and numerous splinter groups. Instead of launching a third party, the conference decided to endorse congressional and senatorial candidates and to await the outcome of the fall elections.

Encouraged by the success of insurgent Republican and Farmer-Labor candidates in this canvass, Senator Robert M. La Follette of Wisconsin convoked an assemblage of progressive politicians, editors, and labor leaders in Washington in December 1922. The Conference for Progressive Political Action met shortly afterward for a second time in Cleveland. The upshot of these two gatherings was agreement to campaign for La Follette's nomination on the Republican ticket in 1924 and, that failing, to launch a third party.

"The Midwest," said William Allen White, "is on the rampage again"; and, remembering the insurgent revolt of 1910, progressives believed that a second upheaval impended. Much, of course, depended upon the Democrats, for the insurgents alone could never capture the government. If the Democrats could find a strong new leader and unite behind a progressive program, they might win independents, the labor vote, and insurgents, and rebuild their party into the powerful progressive coalition it had been in 1916. This is what they did in 1932.

In 1923 and 1924, however, the Democratic party offered little hope of ever again becoming an effective instrument of the progressive movement. It had become so fragmented since 1920 that it had ceased to be a national party. The majority element, southern Methodists and Baptists, demanded vigorous enforcement of the Eighteenth Amendment. On the other hand, Democratic organizations in the northern cities represented wet constituencies who demanded repeal of that amendment. Southern and midwestern Democrats either supported or feared the Ku Klux Klan, while most northern Democrats were Catholics or foreign-born citizens, opposed to all the Klan stood for. Finally, these two wings of the democracy were hopelessly divided on leading questions of the day. Southerners still supported the League of Nations; the northern Irish bosses wanted to forget the issue. Southerners demanded radical aid to farmers but were unfriendly to labor, uninterested in social reform, and anti-Negro. Northern Democratic organizations opposed radical farm support but sponsored advanced labor legislation and were beginning to develop strength among black voters.

The unbridgeable gulf separating southern and northern Democrats was revealed at the Democratic National Convention that met in New York

City from June 24 to July 10, 1924. During the preconvention contest former Secretary of the Treasury William G. McAdoo had won the support of the South and West and, although he openly repudiated it, the endorsement of the Ku Klux Klan. He might have won the nomination had he not become linked to the Teapot Dome scandal as one of Edward L. Doheny's lawyers. This cost him heavily in support among progressives. His chief and only serious rival was Alfred E. Smith, governor of New York, a Roman Catholic opponent of prohibition and the Klan. He had the support of Irish- and Catholic-dominated eastern and midwestern machines. For an incredible number of weary ballots the McAdoo and Smith forces fought it out and revealed in their struggle the tensions that divided their party. Smith's spokesman, Franklin D. Roosevelt, offered after the ninety-third ballot to withdraw Smith's name if McAdoo would also withdraw. McAdoo refused, and the struggle went on. Then on the one hundred and third ballot the convention turned to John W. Davis, former ambassador to Great Britain and now a lawyer for corporation and banking interests. As a sop to the agrarian element, the convention chose Governor Charles W. Bryan of Nebraska, brother of William Jennings Bryan, as Davis's running mate.

The Democrats found it as difficult to agree upon a platform as upon a candidate. The worst fight centered around a resolution sponsored by the Smith forces condemning the Klan as un-American. It failed by a vote of 543 to 542. Nor could northerners and southerners agree on prohibition: the platform merely scolded the Republicans for failing to enforce the Eighteenth Amendment. Refusing to approve American membership in the League of Nations, the convention called for a public referendum on the issue. Except for denouncing the Republican Fordney-McCumber tariff of 1922 and promising independence to the Philippines, the Democratic platform differed little from its Republican counterpart.

In the meantime, insurgent Republicans had been pressing their campaign to capture the Republican party. The futility of this endeavor had become so apparent by the spring of 1924, however, that La Follette withdrew from presidential primaries in Montana, North Dakota, and Michigan. Control of the party had passed to Harding's successor, Calvin Coolidge, a dour, taciturn man, who was even more intimately associated with big business than Harding had been.

Coolidge and his conservative allies completely dominated the Republican convention that opened in Cleveland on June 10, 1924. Only the Wisconsin and South Dakota delegates objected when the president was nominated almost by acclamation on the first ballot. Rejecting a progressive platform submitted by the Wisconsin delegation, the convention adopted instead a document promising economy, tax reduction, and limited aid to farmers, and approving American membership in the World Court.

Soon afterward, on July 4, the insurgent Republicans and their Conference for Progressive Political Action allies, representing organized labor, disgruntled western farmers, Socialists, and independent progressives, met in Cleveland. Agreeing that both major parties were hopelessly corrupt and reactionary, the delegates formally organized the Progressive party, nominated La Follette for president,[3] and adopted a brief platform demanding nationalization of railroads, public ownership of water power and development of a great public utilities system, abolition of the use of injunctions in labor disputes, the right of Congress to overrule decisions of the Supreme Court, and direct nomination and election of the president.

La Follette made a strenuous campaign, appealing chiefly to midwestern farmers and urban workers. But he was hampered by lack of funds, a gradual withdrawal of AF of L support, refusal of most midwestern Republican leaders to support his party, and most of all by a considerable increase in farm prices a month before the election. President Coolidge took practically no part in the contest, but the other Republican leaders were generously supplied with funds[4] and made a vigorous campaign. Republicans practically ignored Davis and Bryan and concentrated heavy fire against La Follette, who, they said, was un-American and a front for the Communist Third International. Davis tried to campaign on the issues of corruption and Coolidge's intimate association with big business, but his appeals were lost in the anti-Red clamor.

The question whether La Follette would draw enough votes away from Coolidge to throw the election into the House of Representatives was answered emphatically on election day, November 4, 1924. Coolidge received 15,725,000 popular and 382 electoral votes; Davis, 8,387,000 popular and 136 electoral votes; and La Follette, 4,823,000 popular votes and the 13 electoral votes of Wisconsin.

Outwardly the results constituted a thumping endorsement of the Coolidge policies of laissez faire and do-nothingism. Actually, few presidential elections in American history have meant so little. La Follette had frightened numerous voters from Davis to Coolidge in his effort to unite progressives. But it was not La Follette's candidacy that caused the Democratic debacle. The Democratic hopes were wrecked in 1924 by internal dissension, failure to adopt a boldly progressive platform, Davis's inherent weakness as a leader of the forces of discontent, and his failure to appeal to urban, Catholic, and immigrant voters. The fact that only 52 percent of the voters went to the polls was striking proof of Democratic failure to rally the people behind either a candidate or a platform.

The following four years were a prosperous interlude during which Coolidge asserted no leadership in legislation and set about quietly to gain

---

[3] The national committee later named the Montana Democrat, Senator Burton K. Wheeler, as La Follette's running mate.

[4] According to the best estimates the Republicans spent nearly $6,000,000, the Democrats, $1,614,762, and the Progressives, $236,963.

control of the regulatory agencies. The Republicans controlled the Sixty-ninth Congress from 1925 to 1927 by large majorities and the Seventieth Congress during the following two years by a slight margin, but they were constantly at war with one another and with the president. The farm bloc in Congress regrouped after La Follette's death in 1925 and put across two advanced progressive measures in 1927 and 1928—the McNary-Haugen farm relief bill and a measure for governmental operation of the Muscle Shoals dam—both of which were nullified by Coolidge's vetoes. (They are discussed in detail in a later section in this chapter.)

We have thus reviewed in outline the anomalous pattern of American national politics from 1920 to 1928. The pattern was anomalous because conservative administrations, seemingly endorsed overwhelmingly by the American people in 1920 and 1924, were counterbalanced by progressive coalitions in Congress that perpetuated the progressive tradition in legislative policy. How this came about will become more apparent as we discuss the legislative problems and policies of the period in detail.

4. Tariff, Tax, and Bonus Battles of the Twenties

The first item on the Republican agenda after the election of 1920 was upward revision of the tariff, chiefly to meet the demands of midwestern agrarian congressmen then in panic over declining farm prices. In the lame-duck session of the Sixty-sixth Congress in the winter of 1920-1921, eastern Republicans gladly joined midwesterners in adopting an emergency tariff bill that imposed high duties on meat and major farm staples. Wilson vetoed this measure on March 13, 1921, warning that farmers needed new markets for their products, not futile tariff protection. When the Sixty-seventh Congress met in special session on April 11, 1921, however, midwestern leaders obtained the immediate reenactment of the emergency tariff bill, and Harding signed it on May 27.

In the meantime, Chairman Joseph W. Fordney of Michigan and his ways and means committee had set to work to overhaul the Underwood rates. The measure that Fordney reported on June 29, and the House approved three weeks later, incorporated the emergency increases for agricultural products and effected moderate increases in rates on most industrial products. The Senate finance committee, headed by Porter J. McCumber of North Dakota, deliberated during the summer and autumn of 1921 and reported the Fordney bill with over 2,000 amendments in April 1922. After some wrangling it was adopted by the two houses and approved by the president on September 19, 1922.

The Fordney-McCumber Tariff Act revived to a degree the historic Republican policy of economic nationalism. It represented, first of all, a clear-cut victory for the newly formed farm bloc, as duties on farm products—including reindeer meat and acorns—were higher than the Payne-Aldrich rates, while agricultural implements, wagons, and boots and shoes remained on the free list. For the rapidly expanding chemical industry, the act provided the protection that it needed to withstand the destructive competition of the German dye trust. For producers of silk and rayon textiles, toys, chinaware, cutlery, guns, and other items produced more cheaply by the Japanese and Germans, the measure offered almost prohibitive duties. Finally, for the great mass of industrial products the act provided only moderate protection in order to equalize differences in cost of production at home and abroad. The average ad valorem rate for all schedules was 33 percent, as contrasted to the 26 percent of the Underwood-Simmons Tariff Act of 1913.

The great majority of businessmen were clamoring more for drastic tax cuts than for a return to a McKinley-type protection in 1921 and 1922. As the first step toward tax reduction, spokesmen for GOP industrial and banking interests insisted that Harding name Andrew W. Mellon as secretary of the treasury. What Mellon's appointment signified was clear to all who knew him. Head of the aluminum monopoly and of a financial-industrial empire, he was the personification of the American self-made man and seasoned reactionary. His philosophy was honest and simple. Sharing the Hamiltonian trickle-down theory of prosperity, he advocated low taxes on wealth and noninterference by government in business affairs.

Businessmen during 1920 had launched a powerful campaign against the excess profits tax and extremely high surtaxes that still prevailed under the War Revenue Act of 1918–1919 (see pp. 192–193). Mellon reiterated these demands to the special session of 1921, recommending repeal of the excess profits tax, a slight increase in the corporation tax, and reduction of the combined normal taxes and surtaxes on incomes from a maximum of 73 percent to 40 percent for 1921 and 33 percent thereafter. The House of Representatives and the Senate finance committee approved a bill embodying Mellon's program. In the Senate, however, midwestern Republicans joined Democrats to write a tax measure of their own. Commanding a solid majority, these "wild asses of the desert," as insurgents were derisively called at the time, defied the House of Representatives, the president, and the secretary of the treasury and warned that there would be no tax legislation at all unless their bill prevailed. The president signed their measure on November 23, 1921.

The Revenue Act of 1921 was significant, not only because it attested to the power of the combined farm bloc and the Democratic minority, but even more because it gave evidence of the strong survival of advanced progressive tax theories. The measure repealed the excess profits tax entirely—progressives and conservatives alike agreed that it was an unnecessary burden on business during peacetime. But the insurgent senators won all their demands in the critical battle over the income tax. The 1921 act continued the rates under the War Revenue Act for the balance of 1921, set the maximum surtax thereafter at 50 percent, increased the tax on net corporation incomes from 10 to 12½ percent, and left estate taxes unchanged.

Meanwhile, the American Legion, the veterans' organization, had launched a campaign to force Congress to provide additional compensation for men who had served in the armed forces while civilians enjoyed wartime prosperity at home. A measure to provide "adjusted compensation" passed the House in May 1920 but was killed by the Senate finance committee. But the agitation for adjusted compensation redoubled; and Chairman Fordney of the House ways and means committee introduced a revised "bonus" bill in March 1922. It provided payment of twenty-year endowment policies to veterans on a basis of $1.00 a day for service in the United States and $1.25 a day for service overseas. Even after the measure passed both houses by large majorities, Harding vetoed it, successfully, on September 19, 1922.

The tax reduction of 1921 caused a decrease the following year of $1.5 billion in ordinary federal revenues; yet Mellon was able to reduce the national debt by almost $2 billion and to report a surplus of $310 million on hand at the end of the fiscal year. He reopened the tax battle in December 1923, therefore, by urging Congress to cut the maximum surtax on incomes from 50 to 25 percent, decrease proportionately the normal tax on small incomes, and reduce drastically the federal estate tax. However, insurgent Republicans and Democrats in Congress took control once more. Their Revenue Act of 1924 cut the maximum surtax from 50 to 40 percent and halved the normal tax on small and middle incomes. To compensate for these reductions, they increased the maximum estate tax from 25 to 40 percent and imposed a new gift tax. President Coolidge and Secretary Mellon were disgusted, but the president signed the measure on June 2, 1924. In a second display of defiance, Congress in the spring of 1924 reenacted the adjusted compensation bill over Coolidge's indignant veto.

Drastic tax reduction remained the chief objective of the business and propertied classes. The insurgent Democratic coalition finally surrendered control of fiscal policy to the administration when the Sixty-ninth Congress met on December 7, 1925. The country was so prosperous and the needs of the Treasury were relatively so slight that only a tremendous increase in expenditures for public works, housing, and farm relief would have justified maintenance of the prevailing high tax structure. Such a program was far beyond the ken of most progressives at the time.

The Revenue Act that Congress adopted on February 12, 1926, therefore, reduced the normal tax on small incomes, cut the maximum surtax from 40 to 20 percent, abolished the gift tax, and slashed the estate tax in half. One further tax measure—the Revenue Act of 1928, which left income taxes undisturbed but slightly reduced corporation and consumption taxes—rounded out Mellon's fiscal program. He had failed only to obtain complete repeal of the federal estate levy. Organized wealth and its political allies, nevertheless, had succeeded for a time in repudiating the democratic tax policy inaugurated by the antipreparedness radicals of 1916 (see p. 175).

5. *The Farm Problem, 1920–1928*

The most important domestic economic problem of the 1920s was the agricultural depression that began in the summer of 1920 and continued intermittently until 1935. The farmers' happy world came tumbling down when foreign demand decreased sharply in 1920 and the government withdrew price supports from wheat on May 31, 1920. By the autumn of 1921 the price of wheat had dropped to approximately 40 percent of its highest price in 1920, that of corn to 32 percent, and that of hogs to 50 percent. Farm prices recovered slightly between 1921 and 1929, but they were never high enough to make agriculture really profitable. Total net farm income declined from $10,061,000,000 in 1919 to $9,009,000,000 in 1920 and to $4,138,000,000 in 1921. It increased to $5,081,000,000 in 1922 and ran between $6,000,000,000 and $7,000,000,000 from 1923 through 1929. Farmers received 16 percent of the national income in 1919 and only 8.8 percent a decade later.

The first sharp decline in agricultural prices coincided with the return of the Republican party to national power and, as we have seen, stimulated the formation of the farm bloc in Congress. By operating as a non-partisan pressure group, the farm bloc took control of agricultural policy between 1921 and 1924 and pushed through Congress the most advanced agricultural program in American history to that time.

We have already discussed the adoption of high tariff protection for agricultural products. It was the least important item in the farm bloc's program. A more urgent goal in 1921 was legislation to subject meat packers and stockyards to rigorous federal control. The Federal Trade Commission had made a thorough investigation in 1920. It stimulated widespread demand for federal ownership and operation of the stockyards; and Attorney General A. Mitchell Palmer had compelled the packers shortly afterward to accept a consent decree that ended their control over the stockyards. All that remained was to preserve competition in the packing industry and maintain close public scrutiny over the stockyards. These objectives the farm bloc accomplished in August 1921 with adoption of the Packers and Stockyards Act. It empowered the secretary of agriculture to issue cease and desist orders to preserve competition among packers and compel commission merchants and stockyards to charge only reasonable rates.

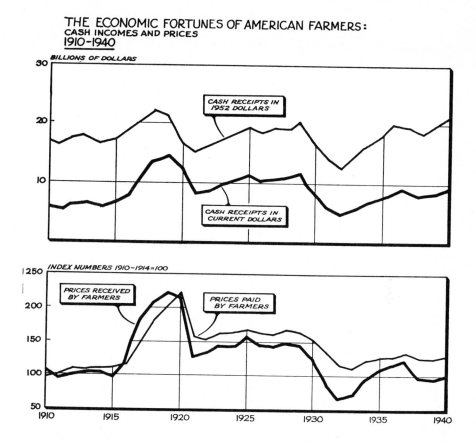

THE ECONOMIC FORTUNES OF AMERICAN FARMERS:
CASH INCOMES AND PRICES
1910-1940

This was not all that the farm bloc won during the hectic special session of 1921. First, Congress extended for three years the life of the War Finance Corporation, established in 1918 to supply capital for war industries, and authorized it to lend up to $1 billion to stimulate the export of agricultural commodities. Second, the lending operations of the Federal Farm Loan System were expanded by increasing the capital of the land banks, established in 1916. Third, the farm bloc obtained passage of the Grain Futures Act, which gave the secretary of agriculture sweeping control over the grain exchanges.

The farm bloc's most important triumph in the early twenties was the enactment in March 1923 of the Agricultural Credits Act—the culmination of a searching inquiry into the farm problem by a joint congressional commission established in 1921. This measure established twelve Intermediate Credit Banks, capitalized by the Treasury and operated in conjunction with the Federal Land Banks, to make loans to organized groups of farmers for periods running from six months to three years.

These were all important measures that greatly strengthened the agricultural program begun by the Wilson administration, and they must be counted as gains for the progressive movement because they further committed federal power to uplift a now depressed minority. But all the agricultural measures of 1921–1923 were based upon the assumption of full recovery in farm prices. When that recovery did not occur farm leaders moved further along the road toward advanced governmental participation.

Since American farmers produced mainly for the world market, the chief problem was to find how to prevent surpluses from depressing domestic prices. Among all the numerous suggestions, the most ambitious and the one that attracted the widest support was the McNary-Haugen plan. It was the invention of George N. Peek and Hugh S. Johnson, two farm machinery manufacturers of Moline, Illinois, whose business had been hard hit by the depression of 1920–1921. The objective—a "fair exchange value" for farm products—would be achieved by segregating the exportable surplus so that the domestic market would not be governed by world prices. How this would be done can be illustrated by a familiar example. The United States during the 1920s annually produced about 800,000,000 bushels of wheat, of which 650,000,000 bushels were consumed at home. If the world price were $1.00 a bushel, then in a free market American farmers would receive $800,000,000 for the wheat crop. Let us assume, however, that the Peek-Johnson plan were in operation. In this event, a federal board would buy the entire wheat crop at a price that would yield a fair exchange value, presumably the world price plus the tariff on wheat, which after 1924 would have totaled $1.42 a bushel. Farmers would thus receive a gross of $1,136,000,000 for 800,000,000 bushels of wheat. The board would sell the surplus of 150,000,000 bushels abroad at the world price of $1.00, and its loss of 42 cents a bushel, or $63,000,000, would be assessed in the form of an "equalization fee" against the farmers. Thus under the plan farmers would receive a net of $1,073,000,000 for the crop, instead of $800,000,000 if the wheat had been sold in a free market at world prices.

The Peek-Johnson proposal seemed such an easy and sensible way of assuring equitable farm prices that it was embodied in the form of the McNary-Haugen bill in 1924. Violently opposed by eastern Republicans and President Coolidge, the measure was defeated by the House on June 3, 1924. This first defeat, however, only spurred farm leaders to redouble their propaganda and seek new allies. Midwesterners won the support of southern farm organizations in 1926 by including cotton, tobacco, and rice in the proposed system; and a southern-western coalition pushed a revised McNary-Haugen bill through Congress in February 1927. Coolidge replied on February 25, with a caustic veto message denouncing the measure as unconstitutional special-interest legislation. Reenacted in May 1928, the McNary-Haugen bill drew a second veto from the president.

Organized farmers, therefore, failed to commit the federal government to the most advanced farm program yet seriously proposed. But they failed only because the eastern business wing of the GOP dominated the presidency. Actually, by 1929 the American Farm Bureau Federation and other organizations in the forefront of the agricultural relief movement had scored one of the most important victories in the history of American progressivism. They had succeeded in promoting a new unity among farm leaders throughout the country. More important, they had compelled the conservative majority in the Republican party to approve a federal farm program that included strict control of grain exchanges, stockyards, and packing houses, support for agricultural cooperatives, and credit facilities on every level. From this advanced program there could be no turning back; in fact, the pathway of progressivism pointed straight ahead to other advanced measures built upon the foundations laid during the 1920s.

6. The Triumph of the Movement for Immigration Restriction

One of the oldest objectives of a certain segment of the progressive movement was exclusion of Oriental immigration to the West Coast and restriction of the numbers of Europeans who came to the United States. Rightly or wrongly, leaders of organized labor believed that large-scale immigration depressed the domestic labor market and impeded the progress of unionization. Additionally, many sociologists and social workers believed that the immigration of eastern and southern Europeans created grave social problems. Finally, most new immigrants were either Catholics or Jews, and their coming aroused fear among Protestant Americans, especially in the rural areas, of a Catholic and Jewish inundation.

Restrictionists sought to accomplish their objective first by imposing a literacy test in 1917, which they thought would exclude large numbers of peasant immigrants from eastern Europe. But the literacy test was only a slight deterrent, as immigrants who went to the trouble to seek a new home were also willing to learn enough to pass a simple test in reading and writing. Some 1,235,000 immigrants poured into the ports between 1920 and 1921, and American consuls warned that millions more were preparing to leave war-ravaged districts.

Labor leaders and social workers found so many new allies in 1920 and 1921 that the movement for restriction became irresistible. For one thing, many leaders of Communist and other radical groups were eastern Europeans; and employers, heretofore the chief opponents of restriction, now joined the movement for new legislation. For another, the Ku Klux Klan

was beginning a powerful campaign aimed at Jews and Catholics. It is only
fair to say, however, that the restrictionists probably would have succeeded without the assistance of the extreme nativistic element, for the
preponderant majority had decided to end the historic policy of free and
almost unlimited immigration.

Congress, therefore, acted with dispatch in 1921. The House approved
a bill sponsored by Representative Albert Johnson of Washington to suspend immigration for one year. It was amended in the Senate to limit the
number of immigrants to 3 percent of the various foreign-born elements in
the United States in 1910 and approved by Congress in the closing days of
the lame-duck session. When Wilson refused to sign the bill, congressional
leaders swiftly pushed it through the special session, and Harding approved the measure on May 19, 1921. The number of immigrants declined
in consequence from 805,228 for the fiscal year ending June 30, 1921, to
309,556 during the following fiscal year.

The reduction effected was obviously drastic, but restrictionists and
especially champions of religious and nationalistic bigotry were still not
satisfied. Congress responded in 1924 with a new and comprehensive immigration statute that satisfied even the exclusionists. Known as the National Origins Act, it prohibited Oriental immigration and limited the total
number of European immigrants to 2 percent of the foreign-born accord-

EFFECTS OF THE QUOTA ACTS ON SOURCES OF IMMIGRATION

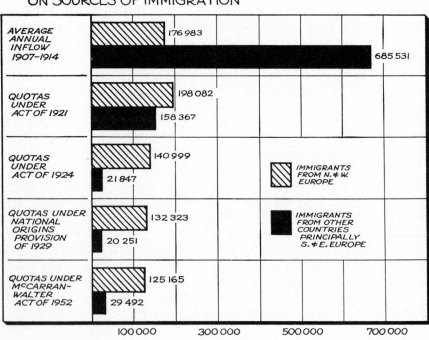

AVERAGE ANNUAL INFLOW 1907–1914	176 983	685 531
QUOTAS UNDER ACT OF 1921	198 082	158 367
QUOTAS UNDER ACT OF 1924	140 999	21 847
QUOTAS UNDER NATIONAL ORIGINS PROVISION OF 1929	132 323	20 251
QUOTAS UNDER McCARRAN-WALTER ACT OF 1952	125 165	29 492

IMMIGRANTS FROM N. & W. EUROPE

IMMIGRANTS FROM OTHER COUNTRIES PRINCIPALLY S. & E. EUROPE

100 000   300 000   500 000   700 000

ing to the census of 1890. The latter stipulation reduced the total number of immigrants to 164,000, discriminated heavily in favor of Great Britain, Ireland, and Germany, and cut the flow of Italians, for example, to less than 4,000 a year. The act provided, additionally, that immigration should be further reduced to a maximum of 150,000 after July 1, 1927, apportioned on a basis of the national origins of the American people in 1920.

The application of the new quota system based upon the national origins of the American people was postponed beyond 1927 because of the difficulty of determining what those origins were; but the quotas finally went into effect on July 1, 1929. Moreover, President Herbert Hoover drastically reduced the quotas in 1931, so that more foreigners left the United States than entered in 1932. The number of immigrants in any one year during the thirties never exceeded 100,000, while the total new immigration for the entire decade was only 68,789.

7. The Power Controversy of the Twenties

The survival of progressivism in the 1920s was nowhere more significantly illustrated than in battles that progressives waged, first, to obtain either municipal ownership and operation of electric power facilities or effective state regulation of the electric industry and, second, to commit the federal government to the operation of important power projects. If progressives in the 1920s did little more than awaken the public and lay the foundations for future action, they gave further evidence that success in great movements comes only after decades of hard struggle.

Compared to the railroads, the electrical industry was still young in the 1920s, but its rise had been spectacular. Production of electric power increased from 6 billion to 117 billion kilowatt-hours between 1902 and 1929. Expansion had been accompanied by consolidation of small operating companies into large systems, and of large systems into great holding-company aggregations. By 1930 eleven well-defined holding-company groups controlled 85 percent of the installed capacity of the industry.

The movement to regulate this vast private interest, the second most important industry in the country, went through the same stages and encountered the same obstacles as did the earlier movement for railroad regulation. The establishment of public utility commissions with rate-making authority in Virginia in 1901 and in Georgia, Wisconsin, and New York in 1907 marked the beginning of the movement at the state level. In spite of public apathy caused by high-pressure utilities propaganda and a downward trend in rates, many state commissions effected a reasonable degree of control over rates and services. On the other hand, probably a majority of the state commissions were timid and incompetent and controlled more often than not by the utilities interest. Therefore, progressives in the 1920s not only sought to strengthen state commissions but also joined a movement for municipal ownership of power plants and distribution facilities.[5]

Like the railroads decades before, power companies during the twenties fought to protect their privileged position, preserve immunity from effective regulation, and prevent public ownership. They executed a gigantic advertising campaign that cost between $28 million and $35 million a year to influence public opinion and indirectly control the editorial policies of hundreds of newspapers. They sometimes bought control of leading dailies. "Information bureaus" working in practically every state on orders from the textbook committee of the National Electric Light Association brought pressure on school boards to force abandonment of civics texts that condemned stock-watering and exorbitant rates and mentioned the benefits of regulation or public ownership. Moreover, the power interests quietly hired a number of college professors for public lectures, subsidized the General Federation of Women's Clubs, influenced bankers through judicious use of deposits, bribed leaders of farm organizations, and worked relentlessly to control local and state politicians and commissions.

The first serious attempt at federal regulation was the adoption of the Water Power Act of 1920, enacted after a long controversy over policy for the licensing of dams on public lands, reservations, or navigable rivers. This measure created a Federal Power Commission, composed of the secretaries of war, interior, and agriculture. It was empowered to license hydroelectric projects on sites within the jurisdiction of the federal government. Such leases ran for fifty years, but the government might purchase the entire property at net cost at the expiration of the lease. In addition, the commission was authorized to regulate the rates, services, and financial operation of companies operating under its license, unless such companies were subjected to state regulation.

The Federal Power Commission licensed 449 projects with 2,489,978 installed horsepower capacity between 1920 and 1930. Because of inadequate staff and the pressure of private interests, however, it did practically nothing to protect the public interest. At President Hoover's request, Congress created a new and independent Federal Power Commission in 1930 but refused to endow it with additional authority because of fear that the president would pack the new agency with men friendly to the power interests. As Hoover soon justified congressional suspicions, effective federal regulation was postponed until the inauguration of an administration less concerned with protecting private enterprise in the production of electricity.

More significant than these largely ineffective efforts at federal regulation was the development of an organized campaign during the 1920s to

[5]By 1930 Los Angeles, Seattle, Tacoma, and some 2,000 other cities and towns owned generating plants or distribution facilities.

commit the federal government to large hydroelectric projects in the Tennessee Valley, the Columbia River watershed, the Southwest, and on the the St. Lawrence River. These regional developments, progressives asserted, would assure an abundance of cheap power for millions of consumers and also provide yardsticks for rates throughout the country. Only one of the proposed projects was begun in the Republican era—Hoover, or Boulder, Dam[6]—but around another proposed development centered one of the most crucial battles of the twenties. This was the struggle for control of a large federally owned dam and nitrogen plants at Muscle Shoals, Alabama, which in time became the focus of the entire controversy over public ownership and operation of power plants.

Congress in 1916 empowered the president and War Department to construct a plant to manufacture nitrates and thus make the United States independent of German and Chilean supplies. Two nitrate plants, with a combined annual capacity of more than 40,000 tons, were built in 1918 at a cost of over $80 million at Muscle Shoals, on the Tennessee River in Alabama. At the same time, the War Department began construction at this site of the gigantic Wilson Dam to provide electric power for the nitrate plants. The war's end found the nitrate plants completed but not yet in production and the dam about three-quarters finished.

Soon after Harding's inauguration the new secretary of war announced that he would urge Congress to appropriate funds to complete the dam if some private company would lease the Muscle Shoals properties and guarantee a fair return on the government's investment. A number of power companies and industrial corporations submitted bids during the next two years, but it was the proposition made by Henry Ford, the automobile manufacturer, that excited the greatest enthusiasm. He offered to lease the Muscle Shoals facilities for one hundred years, to pay an annual rental of $1.5 million, and to produce at least 40,000 tons of nitrates annually for cheap fertilizers.

Ford's proposal was enthusiastically supported by the Harding and Coolidge administrations and farm groups, and the House of Representatives, on March 10, 1924, approved a bill authorizing acceptance of Ford's bid. The Muscle Shoals offers had been referred in the Senate to the agriculture committee, headed by George W. Norris. The Nebraska senator had already concluded that Ford, the power companies, and other industrial-

---

[6]The passage of the Boulder Dam Project Act by Congress in December 1928 represented a compromise between private power interests and the southwestern states and municipalities in a long battle for control of the water and water power resources of the lower Colorado River. The act provided for the construction of a dam 726 feet high and 1,244 feet long in the Black Canyon of the Colorado River on the Arizona-Nevada boundary. The cost of the dam and power plant, $108 million, was to be repaid out of revenues from the sale of electricity. (Actually, the power facilities were to be leased to private companies.) In addition, the act authorized the building of the so-called All-American Canal to divert water from the Colorado River to the Imperial and Coachella valleys in California. The cost of this 75-mile canal, $38.5 million, was to be paid by the users of the water.

ists were deceiving the people in an attempt to steal one of the nation's greatest natural assets—the potentially enormous hydroelectric resources of the Tennessee Valley. As early as 1922 a bold alternative had begun to take shape in Norris's mind: creation of a public corporation to control the waters of the Tennessee Valley—and afterward of other such watersheds—for flood control and production of vast quantities of cheap electric power.

Norris's first move was to push a bill through Congress in 1922 for completion of Wilson Dam; his second move involved persuading the Senate agriculture committee, in May 1924, to approve a bill for governmental operation of the Muscle Shoals properties. When the Nebraskan presented his measure to the Senate on December 3, 1924, Senator Oscar W. Underwood of Alabama countered with a substitute bill providing for private operation. The Senate approved the Underwood bill on January 14, 1925; two weeks later a conference committee met to iron out differences between the Senate and House measures. Just when it seemed that the Senate would approve the conference report, Norris, on February 19, made what was probably the most important parliamentary point of order in American history. He objected that the conference committee had improperly added new provisions to the Muscle Shoals bill. The point of order was sustained, and Norris was able to prevent a vote by threat of filibuster when the conference committee reported a proper bill on February 26, 1925. Norris did not relax his vigilance during the next two years. Indeed, he won new allies among the southern senators and the Senate's approval, on March 13, 1928, of his bill for governmental operation of the Muscle Shoals power plant. Insurgent Republicans and Democrats in the House soon afterward adopted a measure that was in many respects superior to the Norris bill. It provided for creation of a federal corporation to operate Wilson Dam and the nitrogen plants, as well as for construction of an additional dam at Cove Creek, Tennessee, to insure flood control and a steady flow of water through the Muscle Shoals turbines. It was this House measure that Congress approved in the latter part of May 1928.

Spokesmen of a large part of the business community appealed to Coolidge to prevent such a far-reaching experiment in socialism. Coolidge did not disappoint his friends; he gave the Muscle Shoals bill a pocket veto. In spite of President Hoover's open opposition, Norris and the progressive coalition adopted a second Muscle Shoals bill in February 1931. Hoover replied on March 3 in a veto message that was a ringing defense of private enterprise. Thus the fight to launch one of the most significant progressive experiments in American history was again momentarily defeated by a conservative president. Even so, Norris and progressives in Congress had saved Muscle Shoals and the water power resources of the Tennessee Valley for the American people. The time was not far distant when this aspect of the progressive movement would come to fruition.

8. The Supreme Court and Social
and Economic Policy, 1918–1929

The conflict between conservative and progressive theories in the postwar decade was as evident in the Supreme Court as in the political arena. The court had validated a whole series of advanced social and economic legislation from 1908 to 1917 (see pp. 61–62, 108). Then, beginning with the child labor case in 1918, discussed below, reaction against advanced progressivism set in and was enormously strengthened by the appointment of a new conservative majority between 1921 and 1930. So retrogressive, in fact, was the new court that on occasion it tended to be blindly reactionary in cases involving economic and social policies.

The decade from 1919 to 1929 was no time of triumph for defenders of the American tradition of civil rights. On the contrary, the prevailing demand for conformity and suppression of radical ideas was in part reflected in a series of Supreme Court decisions that destroyed old judicial barriers against assaults on the right of free expression. In *Schenck* v. *United States*, a unanimous court had agreed that the government had the right to suppress sedition during wartime, on the ground that sedition constituted, to quote Justice Holmes's famous words, a "clear and present danger" to national security (see pp. 201–202). In *Abrams* v. *United States*, 1919, and other cases, Holmes and Louis D. Brandeis tried to persuade their colleagues to accept a narrow interpretation of the "clear and present danger" doctrine. But the bars were down, and the two dissenters pleaded in vain for a return to the old freedom. Morever, in *Gitlow* v. *New York*, 1925, and *Whitney* v. *California*, 1927, the court—with Holmes and Brandeis again eloquently dissenting—upheld criminal anarchy and syndicalism laws of New York and California. The effect of these decisions, in brief, was to give federal and state officials practically unlimited discretion in determining what constituted a "clear and present danger."

In contrast, the court exhibited more boldness in protecting racial and religious minorities. In 1923 it overturned state wartime statutes forbidding the use of foreign languages in schools.[7] In a momentous decision two years later—*Pierce* v. *Society of Sisters*—the court unanimously outlawed a Klan-sponsored Oregon statute to destroy parochial schools by requiring all children between eight and sixteen to attend public schools. Finally, when the Texas legislature excluded Negroes from the Democratic primary and soon afterward authorized the Democratic state committee to exclude black voters, the court, in 1927 and again in 1932, nullified the

---

[7]These decisions were rendered in *Meyer* v. *Nebraska*, 1923, and *Barteis* v. *Iowa*, 1923; both cases involved the use of German in parochial schools.

statutes on the ground that they obviously violated the Fourteenth and Fifteenth amendments.[8]

As for social and economic policies, it would be an exaggeration to say that the Supreme Court set out willfully to overturn the whole body of progressive state and federal statutes. But on two important frontiers of the social justice movement the court not only called a halt to reform but also completely nullified gains already made. The first controversy involved the constitutionality of the Child Labor Act of 1916. By a five-to-four decision in *Hammer* v. *Dagenhart*, 1918, the court declared that the act involved an unconstitutional invasion of the police power of the states. In other words, Congress could not use its power over interstate commerce to regulate the conditions of labor. Congress in 1919 levied a prohibitive tax on products manufactured in whole or in part by children, and the court, in *Bailey* v. *Drexel Furniture Company*, 1922, again applied its veto. Congress, the majority declared, could not use the taxing power to accomplish an unconstitutional regulation.

The court's inflexible opposition to any form of federal regulation of hours, wages, and conditions of labor—for such opposition was clearly implied in the child labor decisions—was discouraging enough to social justice reformers with ambitious plans for extensive federal regulation through the commerce power. Even more disheartening was the court's destruction of all state efforts to regulate the wages of women workers. The case of *Adkins* v. *Children's Hospital*, involving the constitutionality of a District of Columbia minimum wage statute for women, came before the new conservative Supreme Court in 1923. Felix Frankfurter defended the statute by marshaling economic and social data to prove a direct connection between the wages that women received and their health and morals. Justice George Sutherland, speaking for the majority, dismissed this argument as irrelevant. He also resurrected the decision in *Lochner* v. *New York* to affirm that state efforts to regulate the wages of grown women violated their freedom to make a labor contract. Progressives were enraged by this reversion to obsolete interpretations and launched propaganda that seriously weakened the court's prestige.

Another long and bitter controversy erupted when the court denied that the labor provisions of the Clayton Act of 1914 had conferred any substantial new benefits and privileges on labor unions. The question, in essence, was: Did the Clayton Act give unions immunity from prosecution and injunctions against methods of industrial warfare—the secondary boycott, the blacklist, and mass picketing, among others—which the federal courts had earlier outlawed under the Sherman Antitrust Act? The Supreme Court in a number of decisions in the 1920s ruled that the Clayton

---

[8]In 1935, however, the same conservative court, in *Grovey* v. *Townsend*, allowed the Democratic state convention of Texas to exclude Negroes from party membership and to deny them the privilege of voting in the party primary election.

Act had neither conferred upon labor unions immunity from prosecution for violating the antitrust laws nor legalized labor practices that were illegal before the Clayton Act was adopted. Although the majority correctly interpreted the intentions of the framers of the Clayton Act (see pp. 50–51), Justices Holmes, Brandeis, and John H. Clarke dissented and lent authority to the AF of L's contention that organized labor had been unjustly deprived of the benefits of its "Magna Charta."

Continuing a policy begun in the 1880s, the Supreme Court during the 1920s insisted on wielding the power to review state action regulating economic enterprises. Generally speaking, however, Supreme Court policy concerning state regulation was neither capricious nor reactionary. The court readily acknowledged the right of states to regulate businesses clothed with a public interest. At the same time, it insisted that such regulation be nondiscriminatory and according to due process of law. Railroad regulation, both state and federal, had become in practice thoroughly institutionalized by the 1920s. But state regulation of public utilities was not as well developed by precedent and experience, and there was considerable confusion over the proper constitutional basis for rate-making. State commissions usually determined rates on a basis of original cost; during the prosperous twenties, on the other hand, public utility companies contended that the cost of reproducing the properties was the proper basis. Although the court usually accepted the latter contention before 1933, it did not evolve any definite formula for determining the basis for a fair return.

As for federal regulation, there occurred a marked expansion of the federal power during the 1920s, in spite of the conservative temper of the men who determined Republican policies and controlled the Supreme Court. In *Massachusetts* v. *Mellon*, 1923, the court upheld the system of federal grants-in-aid to the states and repudiated Massachusetts's argument that such grants unduly infringed the police power of the states because of conditions attached to acceptance of the grants. The result of the decision was a significant erosion of state sovereignty. Moreover, in all cases in which the United States could demonstrate that the regulated activity was interstate in character the Supreme Court sanctioned an expansion of federal authority. In *Stafford* v. *Wallace*, 1922, for example, the court upheld the Packers and Stockyards Act, which subjected the meat packing industry to strict federal control. While nullifying the Grain Futures Act in 1923, because Congress had used the taxing power to regulate grain exchanges, the court declared that Congress might use its commerce power to accomplish the same result. When Congress established the Federal Radio Commission and gave it complete control over the airways, the court agreed in 1933 that such regulation was proper and constitutional.

14

Foreign Relations

in the 1920s

The development of American foreign policy during the years between the armistice and the Great Depression presents an anomaly between the popular desire for extrication from entangling obligations on the one hand and the necessary adoption of measures of cooperation on the other. In brief, the United States in the 1920s largely abandoned isolation and sought to strengthen and protect the peace structure of the world. At the same time it sought the advantages of peace without being willing to assume obligations to preserve peace. And in some measure because of this fact, new aggressors were able to make a hollow mockery of these vain efforts in the following decade.

Events of the thirties lay in the distant future, however, as the Harding administration set about in the spring of 1921 to extricate the United States from obligations that Wilson had assumed. First, the new president made it clear that the United States would not join the League of Nations—"We do not mean to be entangled," he declared in his inaugural address. Second, the administration moved to end the state of war between the United States and the Central Powers. Soon after Congress, on July 2, 1921, approved a joint resolution declaring the war with Germany at an end, the new secretary of state, Charles Evans Hughes, negotiated separate peace treaties with Germany, Austria, and Hungary. They gave the United States the benefits without the responsibilities of the Versailles treaty.

By concluding a separate peace with Germany, the Harding administration made it clear that the United States would assume no responsibility for enforcing the peace it had helped impose. Meanwhile, however, a crisis of dangerous magnitude involving the United States, Great Britain, and Japan was nearing culmination just as Harding took office. Let us now examine the causes of this menace to peace and see how the new administration met the first challenge to its leadership and courage.

1. War Clouds over the Pacific

The reader will recall that Japanese-American relations on the eve of America's entrance into the First World War were troubled, and that the effort of Viscount Ishii and Secretary of State Lansing to come to comprehensive understanding on all aspects of the Far Eastern question in October and November 1917 had brought no real relief from the tension (see pp. 151–152). Events following negotiation of the Lansing-Ishii Agreement only further embittered relations. For one thing, in order to prevent Japanese economic domination of northern China and Manchuria, Wilson revived the international banking consortium that he had roundly condemned in 1913. For another thing, as a result of the Russian Revolution and ensuing civil war, Japanese and American troops had been brought face to face in Siberia (see p. 212). By early January 1919, the Japanese army controlled all the strategic centers of eastern Siberia. Perceiving that the Japanese meant to seize the Russian Maritime Province, Lansing at once brought heavy pressure on Tokyo for withdrawal of most of its troops.

Japanese-American relations were further embittered at the Paris Peace Conference. Wilson was maneuvered into opposing a Japanese demand for inclusion of a provision in the covenant of the League of Nations affirming the principle of racial equality. Failure of the demand greatly embittered public opinion in Japan. Even more exacerbating were the controversies between Wilson and the Japanese delegates over disposal of the former German-owned Marshall, Mariana, and Caroline islands and Shantung Province of China, all of which Japan had occupied in 1914. Unable to win British and French support, Wilson had to agree that the disputed islands should be mandated to Japan but never fortified. Wilson made a much harder fight to force the Japanese out of Shantung Province. Supported by a rising anti-Japanese sentiment in the United States, the president pressed his fight to the verge of disrupting the conference; he gave in only at the last moment because he had no alternative. Nonetheless, American opinion was bitter, and the Japanese left the conference convinced that Wilson had tried to thwart their legitimate expansion and challenge their predominant position in the Far East.

The event that made the tension immediately dangerous was the development of a naval race among the United States, Britain, and Japan at the end of the war. The United States was, ironically, immediately most responsible. The United States had but sixteen battleships at the end of the war, as compared with Britain's forty-two. However, the Navy Department soon after the armistice prepared to resume construction of the ships authorized in 1916, completion of which would give the United States a dreadnought and battle cruiser fleet nearly equal to Britain's. In addition, the department presented plans to Congress in December 1918 for a second three-year building program to give the American navy definite superiority over the British fleet.

Actually, the president permitted introduction of the second three-year building program in order to increase his bargaining power with the British at the peace conference. He cheerfully abandoned it in return for British support for the League of Nations. However, the Navy Department's general board in December 1919 presented a new one-year program for construction of two battleships, one battle cruiser, and lesser craft, completion of which would give the United States command both of the Atlantic and western Pacific. Rebuffed by Congress, the general board returned the following year to urge a new three-year program. The navy's plans for a fleet as large and powerful as the British had considerable support in the American press.

The fear of an uncontrollable upsurge of navalism in the United States alarmed British leaders as no other event had done since Germany in the 1890s set out to challenge the mistress of the seas. "Great Britain would spend her last guinea to keep a navy superior to that of the United States or any other Power," Prime Minister Lloyd George had declared; and the British government in March 1921 revealed plans to resume construction on a large scale. Japanese leaders were equally alarmed. The Diet, or Japanese parliament, by 1920 had authorized a construction program to give the empire a force of twenty-five capital ships by 1927. More immediately disturbing to the Japanese than the threat of new American naval construction was the stationing by the end of 1919 of an American fleet in the Pacific nearly as powerful as the entire Japanese navy, together with development of plans by the Navy Department to enlarge naval bases in Hawaii and the Philippines and to fortify Guam.

2. *The Washington Conference*

Moderate opinion in the United States, Britain, and Japan rose against a senseless arms rivalry. In no country was this popular uprising more powerful than in the United States. The old antipreparedness bloc in Congress revived after the armistice and coalesced in the winter of 1920–1921 into a strong movement for an international conference for naval disarmament. The Senate on May 25 and the House on June 29, 1921, overwhelmingly approved a resolution introduced by Senator William E. Borah of Idaho requesting the administration to begin negotiations with Britain and Japan looking toward disarmament.

Meanwhile, achievement of a naval agreement with the United States had become one of the principal objectives of the British foreign office. The British were as anxious as ever to maintain naval superiority, but the prospect of an arms race with the United States caused His Majesty's government to count the costs. Convinced that the expenditures would be exorbitant, the British foreign office informed the State Department that it would make the first move for disarmament if the Washington government did not. On the same day, July 8, 1921, that this message reached Washington, Harding and Secretary Hughes agreed that action could no longer be postponed. After preliminary overtures met with friendly responses, Hughes issued formal invitations on August 11 to Britain, Japan, China, France, Italy, Belgium, the Netherlands, and Portugal, all with interests in the Far East, to join the United States at a conference in Washington in November 1921.

Hughes next set to work to find a disarmament formula that would neither impair American security nor threaten the security of Japan and Great Britain. Hughes concluded that the only hope lay in persuading the powers to agree to abandon present building plans and set definite limits for capital ships. Hughes made these points vigorously when the conference assembled for its first session on November 12, 1921. The only way to end the naval race, he asserted, was to end it now, not sometime in the future. He then outlined a bold plan for a ten-year holiday in construction of capital ships, to be accompanied by agreement to set the maximum capital tonnage of the United States and Britain at 500,000 tons and of Japan at 300,000 tons. This could be accomplished, Hughes said, if the United States scrapped 845,740 tons, the British 583,375 tons, and the Japanese 448,928 tons of capital ships already built or under construction.

The British, American, and Japanese delegates announced agreement on all essential points on December 15, and the French and Italian governments, after some acrimony, agreed to a capital tonnage of 175,000 tons each. Thus the Five Power Naval Treaty, signed in Continental Hall on February 1, 1922, not only ended the naval armaments race in capital ships but also preserved a balance of power in the Far East that left the relative security of the great powers unimpaired. Under the treaty the naval powers agreed to abandon capital ship construction for ten years, to follow with a few exceptions Hughes's proposal for destruction of existing tonnage, and to limit auxiliary craft to 10,000 tons and aircraft carriers to

27,000 tons.[1] In addition, Japan, the United States, and Great Britain promised not to fortify further their outlying island possessions in the western Pacific.

The Five Power Naval Treaty was the first agreement in modern history by which major powers undertook disarmament of any kind. It represented a remarkable triumph of reason over selfish nationalism, but it was not enough. The naval arms race had in large measure reflected America's quest for security in the Pacific and Japan's fear of future American encroachments. Any agreement for naval disarmament would soon prove worthless unless the causes for mutual distrust were removed and the three major powers were willing to forgo aggression in the future.

Such an understanding was achieved at the Washington Conference because Britain and the United States desired only to preserve a status quo that safeguarded their interests in the Far East, but above all because the existing government of Japan sought the friendship of the democracies of the West. To Americans the chief obstacle to a comprehensive understanding was the Anglo-Japanese Alliance, which obligated Britain to assume a benevolent neutrality toward Japan in the event of a Japanese-American war. Months before the Washington Conference met, when renewal of the alliance was under consideration, Hughes had brought strong pressure upon the British Foreign Office for abrogation or modification of the treaty. The Dominion governments were even more insistent upon abrogation than was the United States.

Japan and Britain were willing to abrogate the alliance, which had now seemingly outlived its original purpose of restraining Russian expansion in the Far East, provided they could obtain a new triple alliance that included the United States. Hughes rejected this proposal and insisted upon bringing France into the new understanding. The outcome was the Four Power Treaty, presented to a plenary session of the conference on December 10, 1921, by Senator Henry Cabot Lodge of the American delegation. It pledged Britain, America, Japan, and France to respect each other's possessions in the Pacific area and to confer jointly if disputes among them or aggression by nonsignatories threatened the peace. The pact provided also that the Anglo-Japanese Alliance would be abrogated upon ratification of the Four Power Treaty.

The question of China's status and of Japan's intentions toward that so-called republic still remained unanswered. Under steady Anglo-American pressure the Japanese yielded their imperialistic ambitions and approved an agreement, the Nine Power Treaty, that reaffirmed the historic American policy of the Open Door and noninterference. Signed on February 6, 1922, by representatives of the United States, Britain, Japan, France, Italy,

---

[1] Each signatory, however, was permitted to convert two capital ships to aircraft carriers as large as 33,000 tons. This provision was inserted to permit the American navy to convert the battle cruisers *Lexington* and *Saratoga* into carriers.

China, the Netherlands, Belgium, and Portugal, it pledged the signatories to respect the sovereignty, independence, and integrity of China; to give China full opportunity to establish a stable government; to uphold the Open Door in China; and to refrain from seeking special rights and privileges in China that would impair the rights of friendly states.

Nor was this all, though it did represent the most sweeping affirmation of self-denial that Japan had yet made. Hughes meanwhile had been hard at work on the Japanese and Chinese delegates to effect a direct settlement of the Shantung question. Actually, the Japanese were more reasonable than the Chinese; and the treaty concluded on February 4, 1922, conceded everything that Hughes had asked—restoration of full Chinese sovereignty over Shantung and the sale by Japan to China of the Shantung Railroad. Finally, as if to demonstrate their determination to liquidate all sources of potential trouble, the Japanese promised to evacuate Siberia, conceded the American demand for special cable rights on the island of Yap, and joined the United States in abrogating the Lansing-Ishii Agreement.

It became fashionable in the United States years later to condemn the Harding administration for surrendering naval supremacy and failing to obtain ironclad guarantees against future disturbers of the peace. Such criticism, however, ignores some large historical facts. First, the Five Power Naval Treaty required the United States to yield only potential naval supremacy. Actual naval supremacy could have been achieved only if the American people had been willing to maintain a long and costly arms effort. But the evidence is overwhelming that the people and Congress were not willing, for Congress refused until 1938 even to maintain the fleet at the authorized treaty strength. Second, although the absence in the Washington treaties of any enforcement machinery undoubtedly weakened them, enforcement would have involved the giving of guarantees that the Senate would never have approved. In spite of the omission of any such guarantees, the Senate, in consenting to ratification of the Four Power Treaty in March 1922, insisted upon declaring that the United States had made "no commitment to armed force, no alliance, no obligation to join in any defense."

The expressed determination of the American people to avoid a naval rivalry and even the suggestion of binding obligations to preserve the peace was a compelling historical reality to which Hughes had to yield. But by yielding he obtained for his country parity in capital ships with Great Britain and considerable supremacy over Japan under an agreement that ended the most dangerous phase of the naval race for a decade. He cleared the air of suspicion and distrust and won the abrogation of the Anglo-Japanese Alliance. Best of all, he helped to erect a new peace structure for the Far East that seemed to make it possible for Britain, the United States, and Japan to live and work together in mutual trust and respect.

3. *The Japanese-American Crisis of 1924*

Relations between Japan and the United States were unusually cordial for a short time after the Washington Conference. Then a catastrophic event in 1924 renewed anti-Japanese agitation in the United States and poisoned the wells of sentiment against the United States in Japan. It was the adoption by Congress of legislation specifically prohibiting Japanese immigration.

Japanese immigration to the United States had been regulated since 1907 by the Gentlemen's Agreement. (For the negotiation and provisions of this agreement, see pp. 144–145.) When the House immigration committee in 1923 began work on a permanent immigration bill to supplant the emergency measure of 1921, the AF of L, American Legion, and other organizations joined Californians in what seemed to be an overwhelming demand for statutory exclusion. News of the impending legislation prompted the Japanese embassy to remind the secretary of state of the dangers it would raise. In turn, Hughes urged House leaders to put Japanese immigration on the quota basis, permitting only 246 Japanese to enter a year. On the high ground of national interest he pleaded against insulting the Japanese people by an open and invidious exclusion. The House committee disregarded this solemn advice and reported a bill forbidding the immigration of persons "ineligible to citizenship"—words hateful to the Japanese.

This was the situation in March 1924, when the secretary of state called in the Japanese ambassador, Masanao Hanihara, and asked him to write a letter summarizing his government's attitude toward the Gentlemen's Agreement. This Hanihara did on April 10; but he warned in closing that "grave consequences" would follow enactment of the House immigration bill. Hughes read the letter before it was published and unwisely let the words "grave consequences" pass without comment. Published in the press with Hughes's approval, Hanihara's letter provoked a storm of comment. The aged Senator Lodge exclaimed that it was a "veiled threat" to the United States; he persuaded the Senate to reject an amendment tacitly extending the Gentlemen's Agreement. The senators approved the House bill seventy-one to four on April 16, 1924, and Coolidge reluctantly signed it after vainly attempting to persuade the conference committee to delete the controverted provision.

It is no exaggeration to say that Congress by this action virtually nullified all the progress that Hughes and Japanese leaders had made since 1921 in restoring cordial relations between their two countries. "Our friends in the Senate have in a few minutes spoiled the work of years and done a lasting injury to our common country," Hughes wrote in disgust on April 24, 1924. Unfortunately, reaction in Japan fully justified the secretary's gloomy observation. The day upon which the immigration law went into effect was a day of national mourning and humiliation, and millions of Japanese lived thereafter in shame and anger.

4. *The United States and the World Economy, 1919–1929*

While international political developments in the early 1920s refused to permit a reversion to isolation, the American people were projected into the arena of world affairs by still another force—the dissipation of European economic power during the war and sudden emergence of the United States as the chief source of capital for so-called backward areas and the debt-ridden countries of Europe. American citizens by 1914 had invested some $3.5 billion abroad but still owed to Europe a net debt of almost $3.7 billion. As a consequence of the sale of British- and French-owned American securities between 1914 and 1919, the aggregate investment of foreigners in the United States was reduced from a little over $7 billion to nearly $4 billion. During the same period private American investments abroad increased to nearly $7 billion. By 1920, therefore, foreigners owed Americans a net private debt of nearly $3 billion. In addition, European governments owed the United States more than $10.3 billion borrowed during the war and postarmistice periods.

This fundamental shift in the world's economic balance of power demanded bold American leadership in establishing a workable system of international exchange. Unfortunately, the American leaders and people were too inexperienced to be farsighted in meeting this, the most important economic challenge of the postwar era. Instead of insisting upon mutual cancellation of all intergovernmental debts and reparations—the most disturbing factors in the postwar international economy—the United States insisted on full payment of war debts. Instead of lowering tariffs to enable Europeans to pay their debts in goods, Congress increased tariff rates.

The result was by no means international economic chaos. Private bankers constructed a new system of international exchange that worked remarkably well. But given the balance of payments situation, the new system was bound to be entirely dependent upon the maintenance of a high level of American export of capital for successful operation. During the 1920s the United States bought raw materials and other goods on the world market in large quantities—imports in the peak year totaled almost $4.5 billion. On the other hand, Americans consistently sold more abroad than they bought, the excess ranging from a low of $375.5 million in 1923 to a high of slightly over $1 billion in 1928.

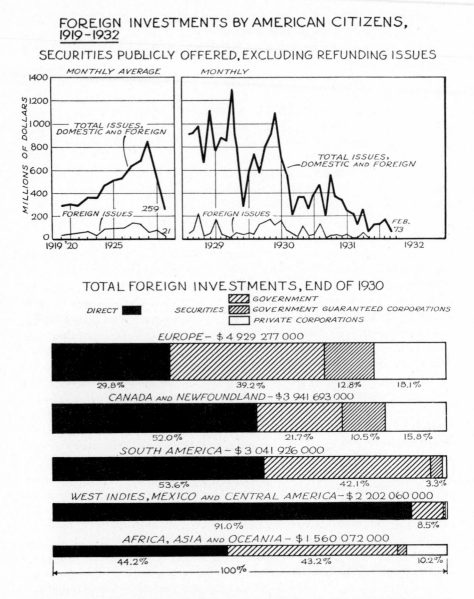

FOREIGN INVESTMENTS BY AMERICAN CITIZENS, 1919-1932

SECURITIES PUBLICLY OFFERED, EXCLUDING REFUNDING ISSUES

TOTAL FOREIGN INVESTMENTS, END OF 1930

DIRECT ■   SECURITIES ▨ GOVERNMENT
                        ▨ GOVERNMENT GUARANTEED CORPORATIONS
                        ☐ PRIVATE CORPORATIONS

EUROPE – $4 929 277 000
29.8%   39.2%   12.8%   18.1%

CANADA AND NEWFOUNDLAND – $3 941 693 000
52.0%   21.7%   10.5%   15.8%

SOUTH AMERICA – $3 041 926 000
53.6%   42.1%   3.3%

WEST INDIES, MEXICO AND CENTRAL AMERICA – $2 202 060 000
91.0%   8.5%

AFRICA, ASIA AND OCEANIA – $1 560 072 000
44.2%   43.2%   10.2%
100%

The manner in which foreigners found dollars to meet trade deficits and pay their war debts to the United States in 1929 was typical for the decade. The United States in that year had a favorable trade balance of $842 million and received additionally about $800 million from payments on war debts. Europeans met this aggregate deficit of more than $1.6 billion in a variety of ways—by the expenditure of $500 million by American tourists abroad, the remittance of $200 million to Europe by immigrants in the United States, and by dollar earnings from the carrying trade, foreign investments in the United States, and the like. The remaining deficit was supplied by American investments abroad of more than $1 billion. Thus foreign bankers and merchants actually accumulated a surplus of $508 million in 1929. And so it went throughout the 1920s. By the annual export of about $1 billion between 1919 and 1930 American bankers and businessmen supported the huge volume of American foreign trade and the world economy as well. The fatal weakness of the system was that its maintenance depended upon a continuing flow of American dollars in the form of purchases and investments abroad. As long as the system lasted, however, it seemed to work well.

5. American International Economic Policy, 1919–1930

The Harding, Coolidge, and Hoover administrations followed the policy begun by the Wilson administration of withdrawing the federal government from the realm of international economic activity. At the same time, the State and Commerce departments worked vigorously and often successfully to protect economic interests abroad and to expand the frontiers of American foreign trade and investments. One notable victory was the Nine Power Treaty, which for a time preserved an area of freedom for American merchants and capitalists in China. More important was Secretary Hughes's fight to break the monopoly over middle eastern oil reserves that the British, French, and Dutch governments had established at the end of the First World War. Seven American oil companies were given a quarter share in the future exploitation of oil in Iraq in 1925 as a result of Hughes's intervention. In all these and other economic aspects of diplomacy, the State Department continued the well-established policy of opposing special concessions and exclusive rights for Americans and insisting only upon equal commercial opportunity abroad.

The most perplexing international economic issues of the 1920s were war debts and reparations, and the stubborn refusal of American leaders to work out an enlightened solution. These factors disturbed the economies of Europe and engendered antagonisms that persisted until the Second World War. The United States lent the Allied governments a little over $7 billion during the war and an additional $3.25 billion in cash and supplies during the months immediately after the armistice. But this was only one aspect of the complicated structure of intergovernmental debts. The British, for example, had lent more than $4 billion to seventeen nations; the French had lent to ten nations.

Congress established a World War Foreign Debt Commission in February 1922 to negotiate long-term funding agreements with the European

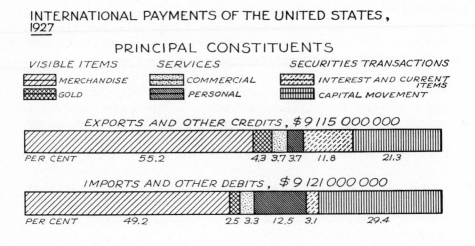

INTERNATIONAL PAYMENTS OF THE UNITED STATES, 1927

PRINCIPAL CONSTITUENTS

VISIBLE ITEMS
MERCHANDISE
GOLD

SERVICES
COMMERCIAL
PERSONAL

SECURITIES TRANSACTIONS
INTEREST AND CURRENT ITEMS
CAPITAL MOVEMENT

EXPORTS AND OTHER CREDITS, $9 115 000 000

PER CENT   55.2   4.3 3.7 3.7   11.8   21.3

IMPORTS AND OTHER DEBITS, $9 121 000 000

PER CENT   49.2   2.5 3.3 12.5 3.1   29.4

debtors. The British, with their reputation for financial integrity at stake, agreed in June 1923 to pay $4.6 billion in principal and accrued interest over a 62-year period at 3 percent for the first decade and 3½ percent thereafter. The French and Italians, however, at first refused to acknowledge either the moral or financial validity of their indebtedness to the United States. The State Department retaliated by imposing a ban on all private loans to citizens and governments in default; and the French and Italians finally surrendered under this pressure in 1925 and 1926. In the same manner the smaller nations of Europe were brought to terms.

Thus did the United States bludgeon Europeans into obligating themselves for a debt that they could never possibly pay from their own resources through normal channels of exchange. In the end a solution was found, but not before the American government had intervened decisively though unofficially, to help settle the most perplexing issue of all—Germany's reparations payments, upon which the entire structure of intergovernmental payments was based. Let us review briefly the background of this story.

The Reparations Commission on May 1, 1921, presented to the German Republic a reparations bill of $33 billion, in addition to the total Belgian war debt and the costs of the armies of occupation. The German government was forced at the point of a gun to accept responsibility for this sum; it tried to make payments but had to default in 1922. The French retaliated by occupying the Ruhr, the center of German industry and coal mining. Thereupon the Germans inaugurated a program of passive resistance that soon resulted in a spectacular inflation of the German currency. The German government was bankrupt by the end of 1923, and the Reich tottered on the brink of total economic ruin. Alarmed by the prospect of chaos in central Europe, Secretary Hughes intervened to find a way out of the impasse. With British support he negotiated patiently with the French government and persuaded the Reparations Commission to attempt to work out a plan of reparations payments based upon Germany's capacity to pay.

The upshot was the appointment by the Reparations Commission in November 1923 of a committee upon which two Americans, Charles G. Dawes and Owen D. Young, served unofficially. This so-called Dawes Committee submitted a plan in April 1924 that saved Europe from financial collapse. It provided elaborate financial machinery to collect and distribute reparations payments, established a schedule of payments that Germany could bear, and arranged for a gold loan of $200 million by American bankers to the German government to stabilize the German mark on a gold standard. A new committee of experts, headed by Owen D. Young, reexamined the reparations question in 1929, set the total bill at a little more than $2 billion exclusive of interest, and provided for an end of payments by 1988.

The significant point of this somewhat complicated story is the manner in which the American government and private bankers participated to help establish a system of intergovernmental debt and reparations payments that worked so long as the dynamic factor in the system continued to operate. That dynamic factor was private American loans to the central government, states, municipalities, and corporations of Germany totaling some $2.5 billion from 1924 to 1930. During the same period Germany made reparations payments under the Dawes Plan totaling nearly $2 billion, while the former Allies in turn paid to the United States more than $2.6 billion on their war debt accounts, or about the same amount that American bankers had lent to Germany. Thus, in spite of the refusal of the State Department ever to admit the fact, payment of war debts under this complicated structure became contingent upon the payment of reparations by Germany. They in turn depended upon the flow of dollars from the United States.

6. The Further Search for Peace, 1924–1930

Peace was the prevailing passion of the American people in foreign affairs in the 1920s. A small but influential minority of public leaders continued to agitate for entrance into the League of Nations, but probably a majority preferred to advance the cause through less entangling means—disarmament, membership in the World Court, cooperation with the League, treaties outlawing war, and the like. But the American peace sentiment was conceived in naiveté concerning European affairs and born of a romantic delusion as to the manner in which the United States could best serve mankind. Americans wanted peace, to be sure, but they were unwilling to assume obligations to enforce an international system. Moreover, as the Immigration Act of 1924 revealed, Americans were not yet ready to forgo nationalistic prejudices that impaired international friendship. It is against this background climate of opinion that we must consider the further search for peace without obligations.

One significant manifestation of this search was the campaign for American membership in the World Court. It was a project upon which both advanced and cautious internationalists could agree, for the Permanent Court of International Justice was an agency apart from the League, and membership did not involve any obligation to help enforce the court's decisions. Hughes won Harding's approval for membership in February 1923 and began a campaign to stimulate public discussion. Sentiment was so aroused by the summer of 1924 that both major parties endorsed membership, and the House of Representatives adopted a resolution approving a membership protocol in March 1925. Bitter-end isolationists like Senator Borah failed to prevent passage of the resolution by the Senate on January 27, 1926, but they forced adoption of a reservation restricting the right of the court to render advisory opinions. When the member nations refused to accept the reservation, presidents Hoover and Roosevelt, in 1930 and 1935, again vainly urged membership in the court. Meanwhile, a number of Americans, including Charles Evans Hughes, John Bassett Moore, and Frank B. Kellogg, had served as judges on the tribunal.

A second manifestation of the American search for peace in the 1920s was the gradual change in official policy toward the League of Nations. The State Department during the early months of the Harding administration had not only refused to cooperate with the League's nonpolitical agencies but had also failed, either accidentally or deliberately, even to acknowledge communications from the League's secretariat. Evidence indicates that Hughes was trying to avoid giving offense to Senate isolationists while devising a means by which the United States might cooperate with the League's humanitarian endeavors.

In any event, the secretary of state launched a new policy of cooperation in the spring and summer of 1922 by sending "unofficial observers" to speak for the United States in various League agencies and commissions. This policy developed rapidly, and the American government cooperated in conferences to control the traffic in arms, women, and opium, in the work of the Reparations Commission, in the League Health Organization, and in the International Labor Organization. The United States by 1930 had participated in some forty League conferences and had five permanent representatives stationed at Geneva, Switzerland, headquarters of the League.

Even so, there were few indications by the late twenties that the American people were willing to undertake responsibilities for preserving the peace in times of crisis. This fact was vividly revealed by the peculiar American peace movement that culminated in the signing of the Kellogg-

Briand Pact in 1928. American peace organizations voiced the passion for peace during the early twenties but could not agree on the most crucial issue, American membership in the League of Nations. It fell to Salmon O. Levinson, a Chicagoan interested in the peace cause, to devise a program upon which all the disparate and sometimes warring peace elements could unite—a program to outlaw war as an instrument of national policy. Levinson's crusade, begun in 1921, became somewhat formidable when he won the support of Nicholas Murray Butler and James T. Shotwell, two officials of the Carnegie Endowment for International Peace.

Shotwell visited the French foreign minister, Aristide Briand, in Paris in March 1927 and suggested that the French government could best allay American fears of French militarism by taking leadership in the movement to outlaw war. Perceiving an opportunity to draw the United States and France together in a sympathetic alliance, Briand on April 6, 1927, addressed an open letter to the American people, proposing that the two countries join hands in a pact forever outlawing war between them. Briand's message went virtually unnoticed in the American press until Butler called attention to it in a letter published in the *New York Times* on April 25. At once the various peace organizations and Senator Borah took up the hue and cry for a peace pact.

Secretary of State Frank B. Kellogg, who had succeeded Hughes in March 1925, planned at first to ignore Briand's appeal. Then on May 21, 1927, the young American flier Charles A. Lindbergh landed his *Spirit of St. Louis* outside Paris after making the first nonstop solo flight from New York. Lindbergh's feat provoked such a demonstration of Franco-American friendship and so stimulated the peace forces in America that the administration had to capitulate. Unwilling to sign a bilateral pact with France, which they regarded as a negative military alliance,[2] Coolidge and Kellogg suggested on December 28, 1927, that France and the United States invite other powers to join them in a treaty renouncing war as an instrument of national policy.

Kellogg's counterthrust came as an alarming move to Briand, who well knew that France's security rested upon her willingness to go to war to preserve her dominant position in Europe. Negotiations went smoothly, however, once the State Department made it clear that the proposed pact should outlaw only aggressive war and not legitimate defensive efforts. Representatives of all the great powers except the Soviet Union, which later ratified, signed the Pact of Paris in the French capital on August 27, 1928. "The High Contracting Parties," it read, "solemnly declare in the names of their respective people that they condemn recourse to war for the solution of international controversies, and renounce it as an instrument of national policy in their relations with one another."

---

[2]In other words, an alliance requiring the United States to remain neutral in the event that France had to go to war under her far-flung military alliance system.

Although idealists romanticized the significance of the Pact of Paris and cynics sneered at what they called an "international kiss," its negotiation constituted another milestone along the road away from isolation for the American people. To be sure, the treaty established no enforcement machinery and would be only as effective as the signatories made it. But it was not meaningless. For one thing, by outlawing aggressive war it changed international law in an important way. For another, it brought the United States, however tenuously, into the peace system established by the Treaty of Versailles.

7. *Continued Efforts at Naval Disarmament*

The Five Power Naval Treaty of 1922 ended the rivalry in the construction of battleships and aircraft carriers; and for a short time after the Washington Conference it seemed that the signatory powers would also refrain from expanding their fleets of cruisers, destroyers, and submarines. However, Great Britain launched a new construction program in 1924 by laying keels for five heavy cruisers of 10,000 tons each. The following year she adopted a program for building nine 10,000-ton and seven 8,000-ton cruisers. The Japanese countered by beginning work on four heavy cruisers, while the American Congress in December 1924 authorized the president to undertake, prior to July 1, 1927, construction of eight 10,000-ton cruisers. Obviously, the major naval powers stood by 1927 on the verge of another costly naval race that threatened to upset the fine balance established so auspiciously at the Washington Conference.

In response to urgings by the House of Representatives and peace organizations in the United States, President Coolidge issued a hasty call on February 10, 1927, for a five-power naval disarmament conference to meet at Geneva that same year. Alleging that they preferred to work for general disarmament through the League, the French refused to attend; and French refusal gave the Italians good excuse for staying away. Thus only the three major naval powers sent delegates to the conference that met in Geneva from June 20 to August 4, 1927. Negotiations went badly from the outset because the State Department had made no diplomatic preparations for the meeting. The British were willing to accept parity in heavy cruiser tonnage with the United States. But the two delegations were never able to agree upon the limitation of light cruisers, and the conference broke up in complete disagreement.

Public opinion in the United States and Britain refused to accept the Geneva failure as final, despite the passage by Congress in February 1929 of a second and larger cruiser bill. The coming to power of the Hoover administration in the United States and the Labour government under Ramsay MacDonald in Great Britain in 1929 raised new hopes for Anglo-

American accord, and MacDonald and the new American ambassador, Charles G. Dawes, set to work to prepare the way for understanding. By July 26, 1929, the two governments had agreed on equality in combat strength, to be determined in all categories of fighting ships.

Only minor details remained for discussion, therefore, when Hoover invited MacDonald to visit the United States for final talks preparatory to calling a new five-power naval conference. The two men agreed to end "all competitive building"; and the prime minister, speaking before the Senate on October 7, ended all doubts about British willingness to go all the way. On that same day the British government invited the other four naval powers to send delegates to a conference in London the following year.

The conference opened on January 21, 1930. The American, British, and Japanese representatives readily agreed to extend the construction "holiday" on capital ships for five years and to scrap a total of nine battleships. However, Japanese insistence upon greater cruiser strength than the 10:10:6 ratio would allow threatened for a time to disrupt negotiations. In the end the Japanese accepted a compromise by which they obtained a 10:10:6 ratio for heavy cruisers, a 10:10:7 ratio for light cruisers and destroyers, and equality in submarines. In addition, the delegates fixed a definite tonnage quota based upon these ratios for cruisers, destroyers, and submarines.[3]

Coming at the end of a decade of popular agitation, the London Treaty was a striking victory for the peace movement and further evidence of the determination of the British, American, and Japanese peoples to live in close friendship. As President Hoover declared in 1930, the alternative to naval agreement was mutual "suspicion, hate, ill-will and ultimate disaster." The British, American, and Japanese governments chose mutual trust instead, at least for a moment, in this, the last successful effort to preserve the peace system of the postwar era.

8. *Toward a New Latin American Policy*

Relations between the United States and Latin America were at probably their bitterest point in hemispheric history when Harding took office in 1921. American troops stationed in Nicaragua were sustaining a minority government in that country. American naval commanders were running the governments of the Dominican Republic and Haiti. And the State Department and the government of Mexico, headed by Álvaro Obregón,

[3]Under this quota the United States was awarded 325,000 tons of cruisers, 150,000 tons of destroyers, and 52,700 tons of submarines; Great Britain received 339,000 tons of cruisers, 150,000 tons of destroyers, and 52,700 tons of submarines; and Japan got 208,850 tons of cruisers, 105,500 tons of destroyers, and 52,700 tons of submarines.

were not even on speaking terms, even though President Wilson in 1919 had sternly and successfully resisted a strong movement in Congress for military intervention in Mexico.

It is ironic that Republican administrations of the 1920s, allegedly the special protectors of American investors, should have set in motion liquidation of a good part of the American imperium in the Caribbean area. For this phenomenon a number of factors were responsible. First and most important was the elimination of every threat to American security in the approaches to the Panama Canal. This meant that the American government could afford to be more relaxed about revolutions and debt repudiations after 1920. A second factor was the accidental injection of Latin American policy as an issue in the campaign of 1920, when Franklin D. Roosevelt, Democratic vice-presidential candidate, indiscreetly boasted that the United States would control twelve Latin American votes in the League assembly and inaccurately bragged that he had written the Haitian constitution. This provoked Harding to give a sweeping pledge of nonintervention toward Caribbean republics.

A third and certainly not unimportant factor was the attitude of the new secretary of state in 1921, Charles Evans Hughes. He was determined to withdraw American power as fast as circumstances would permit. The new secretary was also fortunate in finding an able young career diplomat, Sumner Welles, at the Latin American desk in 1921. Welles left the department in the following year but returned on several occasions to help implement the policy of withdrawal.

The first testing ground of the new policy was the Dominican Republic. Convinced that Dominicans were ready to resume self-government, Hughes superintended the holding of elections and the formation of a native government from 1922 to 1924. After the inauguration of President Horatio Vásquez on July 12, 1924, the American occupation forces were gradually withdrawn; and, except for the American customs receivership, Dominicans were once again masters in their own house. Planning to restore self-government also to the Haitians, the secretary sent a special commissioner to the black republic in 1922 to work with local leaders. When the commissioner warned that renewed anarchy would follow American withdrawal, and after a special Senate committee confirmed his findings, Hughes had to postpone the day of liberation.

Nicaragua, however, seemed at last ready to stand on its own; and Hughes withdrew the United States marine guard at Managua in August 1925, after the Liberal, Carlos Solórzano, won the presidency in 1924. Immediately afterward, the Conservative leader, Emiliano Chamorro, forced Solórzano out of office and installed himself in the presidential palace. When the United States withheld recognition, the Nicaraguan Congress, in October 1926, elected Adolfo Díaz, another Conservative and long-time friend of the United States, to the presidency. Secretary of State Kellogg unwisely accorded immediate recognition.

At this point the exiled Liberal vice-president, Juan B. Sacasa, returned to Nicaragua and raised a general revolt against the Díaz government. In response to frenzied appeals from Díaz, President Coolidge dispatched some 5,000 marines to suppress the uprising early in 1927. The president's action evoked a storm of protest in the United States; and Coolidge sent Henry L. Stimson to Nicaragua to mediate. Stimson by tact and patience persuaded the Liberals to give up the fight. In return, Stimson guaranteed a fair presidential election—under American military supervision—and compelled Díaz to admit Liberals to his Cabinet.

The result of Stimson's mediation became apparent when the Liberals, General Moncado and Sacasa, were elected to the presidency in 1928 and 1932. The United States had used military force from 1909 to 1927 to keep unpopular but pro-American Conservative governments in power, in defiance of the wishes of a large majority of Nicaraguans. When Stimson offered impartiality in return for the cooperation of the Liberals, he was in effect reversing the historic policy of the State Department. American troops remained in Nicaragua to help the government suppress the bandit leader, Augusto Sandino, and were gradually withdrawn from 1931 to 1933.

Setting the withdrawal from the Dominican Republic, Haiti, and Nicaragua in motion was easy as compared with the task of reestablishing Mexican-American relations on a friendly basis. The high tension between the two countries, which had been provoked by Wilson's interventions, was increased during the war by American charges that Mexico was a hotbed of German espionage, and especially by Carranza's decree of February 19, 1918, applying Article XXVII of the Mexican Constitution of 1917. This highly controverted provision vested ownership in the Mexican people of all subsoil rights to oil and mineral properties acquired by foreigners before 1917 and, moreover, required foreign owners of such properties to obtain new concessions from the revolutionary government. Vigorous protests from the United States and Great Britain forced Carranza to postpone operation of the decree.

A revolution led by General Obregón deposed Carranza and put Obregón and a less anti-American group in power in Mexico City in April 1920. The Wilson administration refused recognition because Obregón would not promise to respect American holdings in Mexico, and diplomatic relations were thus in a ruptured state when Hughes assumed office. By firm but cordial dealing, Hughes won all his demands[4] and recognized the Obregón regime in 1923. The accession to the presidency in 1924 of Plutarcho Elias Calles, however, brought a more radical wing of the revolutionary party to power, and relations between Mexico and the United States suddenly worsened. Calles threatened to overturn the Mexican-American agreement of 1923 by requiring American owners of oil lands to

---

[4]They were compensation for or return of American-owned land seized by the revolutionary government before May 1, 1917; validation of the title to mineral and oil properties owned by Americans in Mexico before 1917; and the establishment of a joint commission to consider claims of American losses suffered during the revolution.

exchange their titles for fifty-year leases. He also launched a bloody campaign against the Catholic church that greatly inflamed Catholic opinion in the United States.

Relations were brought to a crisis point early in 1927 when Secretary of State Kellogg foolishly charged that the Calles government was working with Russian agents to establish a "Mexican-fostered Bolshevik hegemony intervening between the United States and the Panama Canal." Although Kellogg's sensational charge stimulated a serious war scare, the State Department was actually then preparing a new campaign to win Mexican friendship. President Coolidge inaugurated this campaign in September 1927 by sending Dwight Morrow, a partner of Morgan & Company and a man of extraordinary tact and ability, as ambassador to Mexico City. By offering genuine friendship, Morrow won the affection of the Mexican people. By his shrewd handling of Calles, he also won a compromise settlement of the oil lands dispute, a surcease of the anticlerical campaign, and a new Mexican-American accord.

Republican leaders not only retreated from empire in the Caribbean area but also set in motion repudiation of the Roosevelt Corollary to the Monroe Doctrine, which Theodore Roosevelt had devised in 1904 to justify a policy of intervention (see pp. 141–142). Hughes began the reversal in 1923 by attempting to explain to the American people that the Monroe Doctrine was exclusively a policy of self-defense. It neither infringed the independence of any American state, he said, nor warranted interference by the United States in the affairs of neighboring countries.[5] That such interpretation did not imply complete American abandonment of the alleged right to intervene, however, was dramatically revealed at the Pan American Conference at Havana in January 1928. There Hughes, as head of the American delegation, stubbornly refused to yield to overwhelming Latin American demands that his country give an unequivocal pledge of nonintervention.

Even so, there were numerous signs from 1928 to 1933 that the United States could not long maintain its traditional position in face of a growing Latin American demand. President-elect Hoover made a good-will tour of Latin America in early 1929; a short time later he promised never to intervene to protect American property rights abroad. He courageously honored this promise, even when the depression set off a wave of revolutions and debt repudiations throughout Latin America. It was little wonder, therefore, that relations between the United States and Latin America were on a more cordial basis when Hoover left office than they had been at any time since 1901.

[5] This position was later affirmed by the State Department in a *Memorandum on the Monroe Doctrine*, prepared by J. Reuben Clark in 1928 and published in 1930. The *Memorandum* did not renounce the alleged right of the United States to intervene but pointed out that such intervention could not be justified by the Monroe Doctrine.

15

Hoover and
the Great Depression,
1929–1933

The Great Depression brought an end to a long era of economic expansion and social progress that had begun in the 1890s. There had been momentary recessions in 1907, 1913, and 1921, to be sure; but these reversals had never been severe enough or long enough to shake the deeply rooted popular confidence in the American economic system or generate any comprehensive national discontent.

It would be inaccurate to say that the depression that began in 1929 destroyed the faith of the American people in the essential worth of the capitalistic system or the enduring value of democratic institutions. However, the Great Depression caused widespread suffering and profound discontent among all classes in all sections, and this in turn revived the American progressive movement in full strength. Thus the chief consequence of the Great Depression was not the havoc that it wrought for a decade. It was, rather, the impetus that it gave for completion of the metamorphosis in popular attitudes regarding the role of government in the economy that had been in progress for nearly half a century.

The depression not only caused deflation at home but also stimulated the withdrawal of American capital from abroad, and this culminated in the collapse of the international economy in 1931. In this chapter we will explore why and how this happened, and why political leadership seemed incapable of overcoming this most serious international crisis since the First World War.

1. The Election of 1928

As we have seen, conflicts over the Klan, race and religion, and prohibition so rent the Democrats that they ceased to be an effective opposition from 1924 to 1928. That these same tensions would weaken the Democratic party during the campaign of 1928 became apparent long before the national convention met in Houston, Texas, on June 26, 1928. Governor Alfred E. Smith of New York had emerged as the only Democrat of presidential stature and had won most of the nonsouthern states during the preconvention campaign of 1928. But he had failed utterly to win any popular support in the South on account of his Roman Catholicism, Tammany connections, and avowed opposition to prohibition. Indeed, all signs pointed to a southern rebellion of large proportions if the northern and western majority insisted upon nominating the New York governor and standing for repeal of the Eighteenth Amendment.

After praying, drinking, and struggling in the Houston convention, southerners concurred in Smith's nomination only after the northern leaders had agreed to give up their demand for a platform plank favoring repeal of the controverted amendment. Without this concession, the southern politicians warned, they could not hold their constituents in the party. Ignoring these warnings, Smith notified the convention that although he would enforce the prohibition laws if elected, he also reserved the right to advocate and work for repeal of the Volstead Act and perhaps also of the Eighteenth Amendment.

Meanwhile, the Republicans had met at Kansas City on June 12 and nominated Secretary of Commerce Herbert Hoover, the ablest representative of the business leadership of the Harding-Coolidge administrations and a preeminent champion of individualism and regulated and orderly private enterprise. During the ensuing campaign Hoover reiterated his frank opposition to all advanced progressive proposals like support of agricultural prices, public power projects, and special-interest legislation in organized labor's behalf. Time and again, also, he reiterated his conviction that only a continuation of the Harding-Coolidge policies could make prosperity permanent. "We in America today are nearer to the final triumph over poverty than ever before in the history of any land," he exclaimed in his acceptance speech. "The poorhouse is vanishing from among us. We have not yet reached the goal, but, given a chance to go forward with the policies of the last eight years, we shall soon, with the help of God, be in sight of the day when poverty will be banished from this nation."

Smith had a moderately progressive platform upon which to campaign[1] and a distinguished record as a champion of civil rights and social legislation. But progressives who expected him to revive and rally their scattered forces must have been badly disappointed. He advocated federal operation of Muscle Shoals and development of power projects in the West and accepted the principle of the McNary-Haugen plan. But otherwise Smith's campaign was thoroughly conservative in tone. He discussed almost exclusively the evils of prohibition and religious bigotry, while his peripheral remarks were aimed at convincing voters that a Democratic victory would not endanger prosperity.

Smith campaigned gallantly, but his obstacles were nearly insuperable. His attacks on prohibition cost more votes in the South and Middle West than they gained in the East. The fact that he was a devout Roman Catholic stirred bigots and Protestant leaders who feared the aggrandizement of Catholic power. Republicans and Hoover Democrats in the South blamed the New Yorker for all the misdeeds of Tammany Hall. Social snobs whispered that Smith and his wife would not grace the White House because they had risen from New York City's Lower East Side. The campaign to defeat the Democratic nominee assumed the proportions of a religious crusade in the South. Throughout that region Protestant clergy and laity, under the leadership of Bishop James Cannon, Jr., of the Methodist Episcopal Church, South, were up in arms, chiefly because of Smith's opposition to the Eighteenth Amendment.

Cannon's organization broke the Solid South and carried Virginia, North Carolina, Tennessee, Florida, Kentucky, Oklahoma, and Texas for Hoover. The prohibition issue undoubtedly played some role in the outcome. However, Smith's Catholicism was the dominant factor. Outside the South, Smith carried only Massachusetts and Rhode Island. His combined popular vote was 15,016,443, as compared with Hoover's 21,392,190. Yet there were perhaps signs of things to come in the election returns of 1928. First, Smith carried the twelve largest cities—in contrast to Cox's and Davis's failure in the metropolitan areas in 1920 and 1924—and ran impressively in all counties in which Catholics and recent immigrants were significant elements. Second, Smith ran far better in the midwestern farm states, particularly in the wheat belt, than any Democrat had done since the election of 1916. Whether these new currents would produce a tide, only the future could reveal.

The prevailing prosperity was also a factor in the election. There was still acute unrest in the farm areas, especially in the western Middle West.

---

[1] The Democratic platform promised farm relief without specifying details, approved collective bargaining and an anti-injunction act, demanded strict control of hydroelectric power, and promised immediate independence to the Philippines. It did not mention the League of Nations or demand drastic tariff reductions. The Republican platform approved prohibition and the protective tariff and promised some farm relief without artificial price supports.

In Minnesota, Nebraska, North Dakota, Wisconsin, and Washington insurgent Republicans, who violently opposed the conservative leadership of their party, were elected by large majorities. These were signs for the future, to be sure; but a large majority of Americans in the autumn of 1928 apparently desired only continuation of the leadership and policies that had seemingly accomplished economic stability and offered the promise of even better times ahead.

2. *Underlying Causes of the Depression*

The American people in November 1928 reveled in the prospects of the economic millennium that lay just around the corner. All seemed well with the Republic: the government was in safe hands, and a great engineer, pledged to abolish poverty and carry on policies that had made America prosperous, would soon occupy the White House. Except for a speculative boom in Wall Street, there were few obvious signs of impending disaster. And yet, more discerning eyes could see subtle signs of weakness in the economy, apart from the dangerous stock market boom. In themselves these weaknesses did not set off the depression. But once the stock market collapse destroyed business confidence and caused huge withdrawals of capital, the subsidiary economic strains combined to prolong and intensify the severity of the depression.

The first and perhaps the most important maladjustment of the 1920s was the unstable nature of the international economy, stemming from a complex of difficulties reviewed in an earlier chapter (see p. 335). The fundamental weakness of the new international exchange system—Europe's financial dependence upon the United States—proved fatal when the wellsprings of American credit dried up. Secondly, the long depression in agriculture that began in 1920 impoverished American farmers and caused them to operate at a net capital loss during most of the decade (see p. 312). The effects of this agricultural depression were apparent in the decline in farm incomes, values, and purchasing power, and in the failure of thousands of country banks. Farmers dragged the rest of the nation with them in their decline when nothing really effective was done after 1929 to halt the downward plunge of farm prices. A third maladjustment was the lack of any proper balance between private and public control of financial institutions and practices. The fundamental weakness here was a rigid gold standard that tied the government's hands in expanding the money supply when it would have been advantageous to do so. Finally, there were no state or federal agencies with power to prevent the stock market excesses and malpractices that abetted speculation.

In other ways, too, the American political economy was badly out of joint by 1929. Large segments of American industry were concentrated and bureaucratized and able to maintain prices at artificially high levels for a time after the depression began. Abnormally high industrial profits and a federal tax policy that favored the rich also aggravated an unequal distribution of incomes that gave 26 percent of the national income to the top 5 percent of income receivers in 1929. These internal maladjustments were beginning to impair the health of the economic system at least two years before the stock market crash occurred. Even so, the development that threw the financial machinery out of gear and set off the cumulative forces of dissolution was the stock market boom that ended in the crash of October 1929.

3. The Wild Bull Market: Boom and Bust

The speculative craze that seized a large minority of the American people in 1927 was by any reckoning one of the most remarkable developments in the nation's history. It seemed as if the mania for quick profits had infected everyone from bank presidents to street-corner grocers and school teachers.

One of the most startling aspects of the wild bull market was the suddenness with which it developed. In response to increased business activity and rising profits, trading on the New York Stock Exchange increased from 236 million shares in 1923 to 451 million in 1926, while the average price of 25 representative industrial stocks rose from $108 to $166 a share, that is, an increase of about 54 percent. This forward movement represented only the normal response of the market to higher earnings in industry. Then a tremendous upward surge of the market began in 1927. Brokers' loans—that is, loans with stock for collateral—increased from a little over $3 billion in January 1927 to nearly $4.5 billion by the end of December. The volume of shares traded on the New York Stock Exchange rose from 451 million in 1926 to 577 million in 1927.

Obviously, a boom was developing; and conservative bankers, sensing a disastrous inflation of stock prices, urged caution. During the early weeks of 1928 it seemed briefly that the market might break. Instead, it held firm when Treasury officials and President Coolidge declared that the volume of brokers' loans was not too great, and that the country had never been more soundly prosperous. Thus reassured, a group of the largest operators on the New York Stock Exchange, on March 3, 1928, opened a gigantic buying campaign in the stock of General Motors and the Radio Corporation of America. As the price of these and other stocks rose, the fever spread, and the wild bull market had begun.

The first phase of the speculation lasted until nearly the middle of June 1928, when prices declined slightly. Rallies alternated with declines during the next sixteen months, but prices always recovered and surged to new heights. The boom was totally out of control by the beginning of 1929. Industrial issues were then selling at more than sixteen times their earnings, although the traditional safe ratio was ten to one.

A few summary statistics will illustrate the dimensions of the stock market inflation that occurred from 1925 to September 1929. The market value of all stocks listed on the New York Stock Exchange increased from $27 billion in 1925 to a peak of $87 billion on October 1, 1929. The average price of common stocks increased nearly 300 percent, and the volume of trading on the exchange rose from 454 million shares in 1925 to 1.1 billion shares in 1929. Brokers' loans, which were used to finance the speculation, rose from $3.5 billion in January 1926 to $8.5 billion on September 30, 1929.

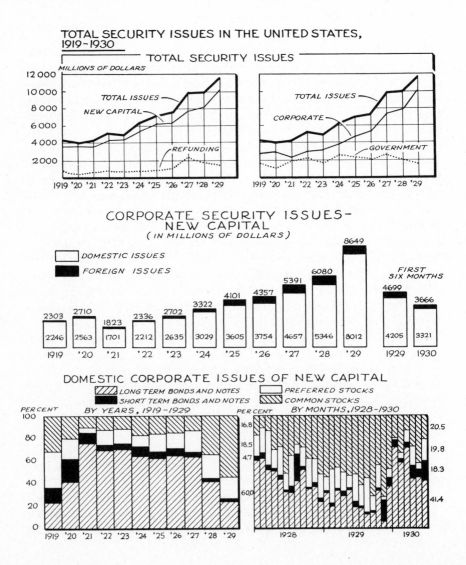

The boom had reached such irrational proportions by the summer of 1929 that some kind of readjustment, if not a collapse, was inevitable. Prices could not rise forever, and the financial structure was so precarious that even a slight recession would set off a panic. The first storm signals came from London, when the Bank of England, on September 26, 1929, raised the rediscount rate, or the interest rate for banks, to 6½ percent in order to halt the outward flow of gold and protect the pound in international exchange. The withdrawal of at least several hundred million dollars from New York to London caused prices to decline on September 30; but the market rallied during the next two weeks. Then dissolution and withdrawal began on October 15, gradually at first, as large operators unloaded discreetly. However, total panic seized the stock market on October 24, 1929, "Black Thursday." Nearly 13 million shares changed hands, and prices fell so rapidly that tickers could not keep pace with their descent.

The panic subsided momentarily in the afternoon of "Black Thursday" when J. P. Morgan & Company and other large banks formed a $240 million pool and bought heavily to buoy the market and protect their loans and investments. Thousands of brokers and hundreds of thousands of petty speculators had been ruined by the end of the day, to be sure. But Treasury officials, leading economists and bankers, and the metropolitan press all hastened to assure the public that the decline in stock prices would have a salutary effect by freeing more money for genuine investment purposes. "The fundamental business of the country, that is, production and distribution of commodities," said President Hoover on October 25, "is on a sound and prosperous basis."

Hoover's reassurance was echoed a hundred times in the inner circles of Wall Street. Nonetheless, the bankers let prices slide when the bottom dropped out of the market again on October 29. Nearly 16.5 million shares changed hands in the wildest trading in the New York Stock Exchange's history to that time, and the average price of fifty leading stocks declined almost forty points under the pressure. Rallies alternated with declines during the remaining weeks of 1929 and afterward, but the declines were always greater than the subsequent advances, until it seemed as if there could be no end except a final smashup of the entire financial system.

4. The Progress of the Depression, 1929-1932

The tremendous decline in stock values—a loss of some $40 billion during the last four months of 1929 alone—set off intricate forces that interacted to carry the United States into the depths of industrial and financial stagnation. The essential fact was that American prosperity was in large measure dependent upon the smooth functioning of the basic cogs of the economic machinery—world trade, investment in capital plant and equipment, the construction industry, and production of automobiles. The oil that lubricated this economic machinery was confidence that goods could be sold and investments would yield a profitable return.

The stock market crash did not at once utterly destroy but it did severely shake the confidence of the business community, weaken financial institutions, slow down industrial expansion, and cause a diminution in American purchases and investments abroad. The practical withdrawal of the American dollar props from beneath the foundations of the international economy in turn precipitated a severe financial crisis in Europe in 1931. Europeans met this crisis only by adopting policies that virtually destroyed the system of international exchange. The European collapse in turn caused further strain on American banks and deepened the industrial

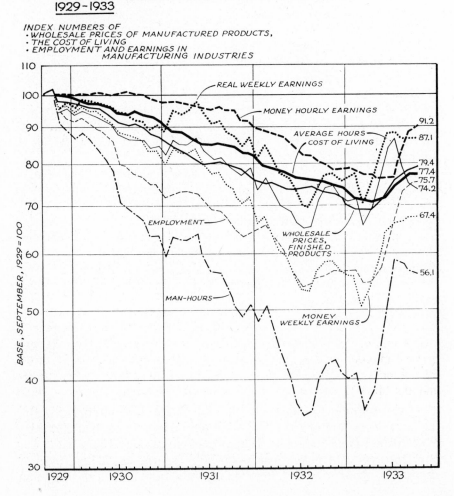

THE PROGRESS OF THE GREAT DEPRESSION, 1929-1933

INDEX NUMBERS OF
· WHOLESALE PRICES OF MANUFACTURED PRODUCTS,
· THE COST OF LIVING
· EMPLOYMENT AND EARNINGS IN
MANUFACTURING INDUSTRIES

and business depression. Meanwhile, from 1930 to 1932, the Federal Reserve Board, in order to protect the dollar and gold standard, disastrously raised the discount rate and reduced the money supply. By so doing, it made even moderate recovery virtually impossible.

The progress of the depression and its effect on the basic generative components of the economy are revealed by the following statistics. New capital issues, representing the investment of the American people in industrial, railroad, public utility, and other stocks and bonds, declined from $10 billion in 1929 to $7 billion a year later, to $3 billion in 1931, and to a little over $1 billion in 1932. Foreign capital issues, governmental and corporate, declined from a high of nearly $1.5 billion in 1928 to a paltry $88 million in 1932. American imports of goods and raw materials dropped from almost $4.5 billion in 1929 to about $1.3 billion in 1932; exports declined from $5.3 billion to $1.7 billion. At home the two basic industries of construction and automobiles declined even more alarmingly.

The progressive slowing down of these important cogs in the economic machinery of course had an immediate and catastrophic effect on all other segments of the economy. Twenty-five representative industrial stocks fell from an average closing price of $366.29 a share in 1929 to $96.63 a share in 1932. There were 659 bank failures, involving deposits of nearly $250 million, in 1929; in the following year 1,352 banks, with deposits of $853 million, failed. In 1931, when the European financial crisis intensified the severity of the depression, a total of 2,294 banks, with aggregate deposits of nearly $1.7 billion, closed their doors. In 1932, 1,456 banks, with deposits of nearly $750 million, failed. Equally dismal was the record of 109,371 commercial failures, with aggregate liabilities of nearly $3 billion, from 1929 through 1932, and a decline in the net profits of all private corporations from $8.4 billion in 1929 to $3.4 billion in 1932. This plummeting provoked an even more serious crisis among the railroads. Already beginning to feel the effect of competition from the trucking industry in 1929, they staggered under heavy blows, and great systems, with an aggregate of some 45,000 miles, passed into receivership from 1929 to 1933.

The cumulative momentum of the depression can perhaps best be illustrated by the statistics on industrial production and unemployment. By the last quarter of 1930 industrial production in the United States was 26 percent below the peak level of 1929. By midsummer of 1932 the production curve had declined 51 percent below the level of the peak year. In response, unemployment grew by the month and year: 3 million in April 1930; 4 million in October 1930; almost 7 million in October 1931; nearly 11 million a year later; and from 12 million to 14 million during the first months of 1933. Moreover, workers fortunate enough to find or retain employment suffered severely from wage reductions, especially after 1931. Total labor income from 1929 to 1933 fell from $53 billion to $31.5 billion; manufacturing wages, from nearly $12 billion to approximately $7 billion. American farmers, already in economic straits by 1929, lost more in cash income and general economic standing during the depression years

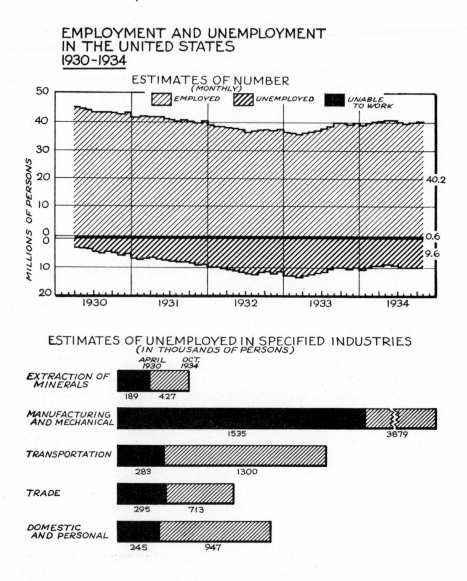

EMPLOYMENT AND UNEMPLOYMENT IN THE UNITED STATES 1930-1934

ESTIMATES OF NUMBER
(MONTHLY)

EMPLOYED   UNEMPLOYED   UNABLE TO WORK

MILLIONS OF PERSONS

40.2

0.6

9.6

1930   1931   1932   1933   1934

ESTIMATES OF UNEMPLOYED IN SPECIFIED INDUSTRIES
(IN THOUSANDS OF PERSONS)

APRIL 1930   OCT. 1934

EXTRACTION OF MINERALS — 189   427

MANUFACTURING AND MECHANICAL — 1535   3879

TRANSPORTATION — 283   1300

TRADE — 295   713

DOMESTIC AND PERSONAL — 245   947

than any other important group. Gross farm income shrank from more than $11.9 billion to $5.3 billion between 1929 and 1932.

The dimensions of the economic misfortune that befell the American people can perhaps be comprehended by the following summary view. National income declined from $87.8 billion in 1929 to $40.2 billion in 1933; adjusted for the cost of living, per capita income declined from $681 to $495. Salaries decreased 40 percent, dividends nearly 57 percent, and manufacturing wages 60 percent. The total picture of these years of the locusts, therefore, is one of extreme deflation everywhere except in the debt structure. As the American people struggled to save their financial system, interest payments on long-term debts declined only 3.3 percent from 1929 to 1933.

5. *The Social Impact of the Depression*

The social impact of the depression could be seen in all aspects of life. The first place affected was the home, to which women who had formerly been employed returned by the hundreds of thousands, even though the incidence of unemployment was less among women than among male workers. Most middle-class families had to dispense with domestic servants; and women responded to "live at home" appeals by gardening, canning, making soap, and the like.

Americans sometimes acted curiously under the impact of shattered hopes. They practically stopped buying new automobiles, to be sure, but they stubbornly refused to give up their old ones; and gasoline consumption increased slightly from 1929 through 1933. Jewelry sales declined precipitately; but women would not give up silk and rayon hosiery or even radios, for soap operas were just coming into vogue. And never would people give up smoking. Cigarette consumption, in fact, rose steadily during the depression years, as if the nervous strains engendered by distress demanded a sedative.

One of the most unfortunate social effects of the depression was its impact on family relationships and marriage and birth rates. Tens of thousands of families were forced to double up in homes and apartments, and tensions between fathers and sons increased as the latter found it impossible to find work. Young people out of work married later and had fewer children. Thus the number of marriages declined from 1,233,000 in 1929 to 982,000 in 1932, while the birth rate declined from 21.3 per thousand in 1930 to 18.4 in 1933.

Schools and colleges were of course profoundly affected, but Americans struggled successfully to maintain school plant, equipment, and salaries until 1932. The tide began to turn in that year, and the retreat had turned into a rout on all educational fronts by the end of the school year 1933–1934. Expenditures for school purposes declined from more than $1.8 billion to $1.5 billion, or about 18 percent, from 1930 to 1934. But in many states the decrease exceeded 30 percent, and in Michigan and Mississippi it was 41 and 52 percent, respectively. Colleges and universities experienced even greater adversity. Total enrollment in institutions of higher learning declined 8.5 percent throughout the country between 1931 and 1934. Generally speaking, state colleges and universities were hardest hit, suffering a 31 percent decline in income from state appropriations, as compared with a 19 percent decline in income from endowments owned by private institutions.

Perhaps the most important, because it was the most lasting, social effect of the depression was the way it caused a shift in responsibility for alleviating social distress from private to public agencies and resources. City and state governments formed emergency relief administrations almost at once and took over the burden of relief and public health services from old charitable agencies. In spite of early optimism, excellent administration, and the cooperation of federal authorities, the cities and states could not meet the relief emergency after 1931. Staggering under financial burdens they could not bear, forced to default on obligations and pay public employees in scrip, the cities and states simply could not borrow the money necessary to meet the elementary needs of the unemployed. Appeals for private support yielded only paltry sums; "give-a-job" campaigns, "block aid" programs, and so on, were largely futile.

The impossibility of using only private, city, and state resources to meet the crisis had been amply demonstrated by social workers and statisticians by the winter of 1932. The destitute congregated in cardboard shacks in so-called Hoovervilles on the edges of cities across the nation; hundreds of thousands of the unemployed roamed the country on foot and in boxcars in futile search of jobs. There was perhaps little outright starvation, but there was much hunger; and the malnutrition rate among patients admitted to certain community health centers in New York City and Philadelphia increased 60 percent. Nor were hunger and malnutrition confined to the great cities, for five-cent cotton meant a lean diet of salt pork and hominy for southern poor whites and blacks, and unemployment in the mining areas brought destitution unequaled on a large scale anywhere in the cities.

6. Rumblings of Social Discontent

Americans were baffled by the anomaly of a country with abundant resources, the largest force of skilled labor, and the most productive plant in the world being unable to find the right formula for getting the wheels of industry turning once again. Moreover, it was difficult to understand why millions of people should go hungry in a country groaning under the burden of huge food surpluses. The people, as they are wont to do during periods of economic distress, searched for scapegoats and soon concluded that speculators and bankers in Wall Street had been responsible.

This discrediting of an economic leadership that had hitherto been warmly admired did not, of course, occur all at once. Until the summer of 1931 probably a majority of the people believed the assurances of Republican spokesmen and financial leaders, who since the stock market crash had predicted that the economic system would soon right itself again. However, the European collapse in 1931 (to be described below) caused more banks to fail and bread lines to lengthen, and the Senate banking committee in the winter of 1931–1932 exposed corruption and malfeasance in the banking community. Consequently, public confidence in the economic leadership and the Hoover administration sagged and then nearly collapsed during the summer of 1932.

The rumblings of discontent grew from a scarcely audible whisper into a mighty chorus after the spring of 1931. In the late summer of 1931, for example, a commission of the Federal Council of the Churches of Christ in America prepared a statement to be read from pulpits on Labor Sunday. It was one of the most sweeping indictments of American capitalism ever drawn up by a middle-class group.

Many businessmen, alarmed by the menace of revolutionary upheaval and moved by the misery of the lower classes, abandoned faith in automatic mechanisms and began to doubt the worth of an economy in which there could be so much abundance and misery at the same time. One of the most startling proposals for amelioration, in fact, came from Wall Street. It was a suggestion by Gerard Swope, president of the General Electric Company, that industrial leaders cooperate to increase production and protect workers against unemployment and poverty. Swope's warning that government would surely assume this responsibility if industry did not was echoed by the banker-industrialist, Owen D. Young, and by the president of the United States Chamber of Commerce.

Nor were labor spokesmen any less disturbed. Leaders of the AF of L for a time waited patiently for the return of prosperity. But unrest among AF of L members was so great by the autumn of 1931 that spokesmen of organized labor could no longer remain silent. The executive committee of the AF of L prepared a statement in October 1931 declaring that the prime cause of the depression had been the unequal distribution of wealth and incomes and calling upon President Hoover to convoke a great national economic conference to consider ways and means of combating the foe from within.

These protests and proposals were, of course, more a reflection of the important ideological upheaval that was transforming popular attitudes toward government and the economy than manifestations of any disposition toward social violence. Signs of dangerous social eruption, actually, were few. There were hunger marches and a serious riot of unemployed persons in Dearborn, Michigan, in the spring of 1932. Embattled farmers organized to prevent mortgage owners from profiting by foreclosure (see p. 386). But the only outbreak that threatened to get out of hand was the descent of the so-called Bonus Expeditionary Force of some 12,000 to 14,000 unemployed and homeless veterans on Washington in May and June 1932. They demanded passage of a bill providing immediate full payment of the bonus by the issuance of $2.4 billion in paper money, built a shanty town on Anacostia Flats outside the capital, and threatened to sit it out all summer. The Senate, under strong presidential pressure, refused to approve the bonus bill, and about half the marchers went home when

Congress appropriated funds to provide transportation. But some 5,000 to 6,000 veterans, many with wives and children, remained: gaunt representatives of the millions of destitute in every state and section.

Then a riot occurred on July 28, 1932, when police attempted to clear a throng of bonus marchers out of a construction area. Two veterans were killed, and several policemen were injured. The District commissioners warned that they could not preserve order without extensive use of force, and President Hoover at once called upon the army to control the situation.[2] The army chief of staff, General Douglas MacArthur, assembled a formidable small army with machine guns and tanks, dispersed the bonus marchers from Anacostia Flats and, accidentally or deliberately, burned the shanty town. The very "institutions of our Government" would have been severely threatened, MacArthur declared, if the president had not acted decisively.

No doubt the general exaggerated the dimensions of the threat. To be sure, there was much talk of revolution if Hoover should be elected again, but it never got beyond street corners. Actually, the wonder is that there were so few organized uprisings like the bonus march, that people suffered so much without losing their sense of humor or falling prey to Communist and fascist agitators. The American democracy survived one of its severest testings only because the people never lost hope of finding a democratic solution through new political leadership.

7. Hoover and the Crisis of American Capitalism

No man ever came to the presidency with broader experience in world and domestic affairs than Herbert Clark Hoover. He was a self-made man, whose success story should become as much a part of the American legend as Horatio Alger's tales of boys who made good. Born of Quaker parents at West Branch, Iowa, in 1874, Hoover migrated in his youth to Oregon, attended the newly established Stanford University, and was graduated with a degree in mining engineering in 1895. He proved to be resourceful, in fact, a sheer genius at running large enterprises. Rising from one high position to another, Hoover had won an international reputation and amassed a large personal fortune by 1914. During the early years of the First World War, Hoover did an extraordinary job as head of the Belgian Relief Commission. He was called to Washington to direct the Food Administration when his country entered the war. His reputation was so great by 1920 that he was seriously mentioned for the Democratic presidential nomination. The movement foundered when he decided that he was a Republican.

[2] In a public statement issued on July 28, 1932, President Hoover declared that Communists and persons with criminal records were stirring the bonus army to violence.

He was appointed secretary of commerce by Harding in 1921 and served in this post until his nomination for the presidency in 1928. Hoover was the chief spokesman of free regulated enterprise, mass consumption, and welfare capitalism during a decade when the businessman was the hero of the urban middle classes. He was never intimate with professional politicians, but the popular demand for his nomination in 1928 was so overwhelming that the professionals had to submit.

Hoover must have idealized the presidency as the culmination of his long career of service to the people of the world. As one historian has put it, "Hoover the engineer would be the symbol of the coming age of material fulfillment, as Jefferson had been of democracy and Lincoln of emancipation." With supreme confidence that his administration would witness the maturing of humanitarian capitalism, he entered the White House with such popular approval as few presidents have ever enjoyed. He left office, on the other hand, rejected and despised as few presidents have ever been, his name an article of common sneering and associated with horse-drawn carts and assemblages of human misery.

What was wrong? How can we account for this almost total deflation of a great reputation? Why was it that a great engineer and expert in alleviating human suffering should have failed to provide the leadership and techniques so desperately needed in this interval of domestic crisis?

In the first place, Hoover was as inept at politics as he was superb at administration. Before 1928, he had never run for or been elected to political office. He had grown accustomed to obedience during a long career of holding appointive positions of command. In his rigorously honest and orderly mind he had contempt for mere politicians. Thus, when it came to dealing with Congress he was poorly equipped for effective leadership. Indeed, he could not establish leadership even of the members of his own party, much less of the Democrats. He could command men's respect in times of prosperity but not their love and devotion to a great vision during times of adversity.

Hoover's chief handicap, however, was a rigid, unyielding mental quality that made it difficult for him to adapt to new circumstances and undertake unusual experiments. Out of long experience and careful thought he had come to certain convictions concerning government and the economy. He was no laissez-faire economist of the classical school. He approved regulation of business enterprise clothed with the public interest, and he championed order and efficiency in business rather than destructive competition. On the other hand, he believed fervently that American progress and prosperity depended upon private initiative and striving. Thus he opposed all measures, like federal operation of Muscle Shoals, that would diminish private energies or impede private investment and enterprise. Out of a sincere belief in local government and the inherent goodness of the American people, Hoover just as strongly opposed any measures that would transfer responsibility for social alleviation from localities and states to the federal government. Finally, his almost mystical faith in the gold standard prevented him from adopting bold fiscal measures to spur the economy, although it must be added that the Federal Reserve Board might well have thwarted any fiscal innovations if Hoover had proposed them.

With Hoover these principles constituted not only a political philosophy but a religious faith as well. During his own lifetime the American system of comparatively free enterprise, powered by private initiative and what he called "rugged individualism," had worked the greatest material miracle of the modern age. Free capitalism, unhampered by binding controls, had brought a good material life within the reach of the average man. Hoover saw no reason why it should not continue to carry the masses ever upward toward a higher standard of living. When the stock market crash set off a business depression, he refused to believe that the downswing was anything more than a passing phase in the business cycle, like the Panic of 1907 or the depression of 1921-1922.

Once the recession of 1929-1930 turned into a full-fledged depression in 1931, Hoover was forced to recognize that complete economic ruin would ensue without positive and unprecedented action by the federal government. Abandoning momentarily the main tenets of his philosophy, he approved ambitious measures to save the economy. At the same time, he never lost confidence in the gold standard, the inherent soundness of American economic institutions, and the altruism of businessmen and bankers. Recovery was bound to come, he was certain, if only the federal government did not destroy business confidence by tampering with the gold standard or launching wild fiscal experiments.

8. *The Hoover Policies:*
Agricultural Stabilization

Disturbed by the rising insurgency in the Middle West and the Far West, Hoover and other GOP spokesmen during the campaign of 1928 promised sane farm relief and upward revision of the tariff rates on agricultural products. Soon after his inauguration Hoover called the Seventy-first Congress into special session to redeem these campaign pledges. Farm leaders still contended that only the McNary-Haugen or some other price-fixing plan would give agriculture parity with industry, and they had long since ceased to believe that higher tariff rates would mean higher agricultural prices at home. But the president had his way, and Congress approved his two measures for farm relief—the Agricultural Marketing Act of June 15, 1929, and the Hawley-Smoot Tariff Act of June 17, 1930.

The draft of the Agricultural Marketing bill that Hoover presented to Congress provided a remedy that would not, the president explained, undermine the initiative of the individual farmer or involve the government in any schemes of price control. It created a nonpartisan Federal Farm Board and gave it the use of a revolving fund of $500 million. This money would be lent to agricultural marketing cooperatives, to enable them to market products efficiently, build warehouses, and hold farm products in the event of a price decline. In order to win the support of the Senate, however, the president made one concession that changed the character of the proposed stabilization program. It was an amendment authorizing the Federal Farm Board to establish corporations to stabilize farm prices through direct intervention in the market.

The Agricultural Marketing Act, therefore, launched the federal government upon the most ambitious program of agricultural stabilization and support in American peacetime history to that date. The Federal Farm Board from 1929 to 1931 organized producers of major staples into national cooperatives and established corporations to stabilize farm prices through large-scale market operations. By lending to cooperatives and buying wheat and cotton in large quantities, the board maintained domestic farm prices a little above the world price level until the summer of 1931. However, the financial crisis in Europe that same year caused a sudden shrinking of foreign markets for American agricultural exports, and dumping by Russia, Argentina, and Australia drove prices to fantastically low levels. From this point on, the board was powerless to prevent the collapse of the price structure at home.

The Federal Farm Board recognized its inability to cope with the situation as early as 1931. Having lost some $354 million in market operations by the summer of 1932, the board openly admitted its helplessness. Finally, on December 7, 1932, it urged Congress to establish an effective system for regulating acreage and production as the only alternative to continued agricultural bankruptcy. Hoover's ambitious experiment obviously failed; but out of failure came experience and a profound conviction that cooperation and voluntary action would not suffice. The transition from the Hoover stabilization program to the bolder and more advanced New Deal measures was as natural as it was inevitable.

Hoover's program of tariff relief for agriculture was an even greater fiasco than his ill-fated effort at price stabilization. His intentions undoubtedly were excellent, but all the old lobbies and pressures set diligently to work once deliberations on a tariff bill began. The result was the Hawley-Smoot tariff bill of 1930, which provided about 75 increases for farm products and 925 for manufactured commodities.[3] As a device for supporting domestic agricultural prices, the Hawley-Smoot tariff was completely futile, except, perhaps, with regard to meat and dairy products. Its

---

[3]This measure increased the average level of agricultural duties from 20 to 34 percent and the general average of all duties from 33 to 40 percent. As a result of the Hawley-Smoot Act, moreover, the average ad valorem duties on imports subject to the tariff increased from 26 percent for the period 1921–1925 to 50 percent for the period 1931–1935.

sheerly economic effect on foreign trade was probably unimportant. Its psychological impact abroad, however, was unfortunate, as it seemed to signal an intensification of economic nationalism in the United States just at the moment when the world desperately needed enlightened leadership. One thousand members of the American Economic Association pointed out this elementary fact in an urgent appeal to the president to veto the Hawley-Smoot bill. Their warning was justified if unheeded. The British, for example, adopted protection and a system of imperial preference in 1932. Germany in the following year embarked upon a program of autarky that severely damaged world trade. The passage of the Hawley-Smoot bill was not responsible for the international economic demoralization that occurred in 1931 and afterward, but its enactment set a bad example for the rest of the world.

9. *The Hoover Policies:*
Combating the Depression

Hoover moved with a new kind of presidential boldness during the first and relatively mild phase of the depression that lasted from October 1929 to the spring of 1931. He met with railroad presidents on November 19, 1929, and obtained their promise to proceed with normal construction. Calling leaders of finance, industry, and trade to the White House two days later, Hoover frankly warned them that a serious recession would follow in the wake of the storm in Wall Street. The leaders of American business responded to his urgent pleading by agreeing to maintain production and refrain from severe wage reductions, provided labor leaders would cooperate by withdrawing demands for wage increases. On the same afternoon the president obtained a promise of full cooperation from labor leaders. The following day, November 22, Hoover met with leaders in the construction industry and won their promise to maintain current wages and hours standards. Then on November 23 he called upon governors and mayors throughout the country to join the federal government in increasing expenditures for public works.

It seemed by the spring of 1930 that Hoover's program of cooperation had carried the country through the worst phase of the storm. Bankers had reduced brokers' loans from $8.5 billion to $3 billion; the index of industrial employment, which had stood at 99 in December 1929, dropped only two and a half points during the next four months. A nationwide census of unemployment taken in the following April revealed that only some 3,000,000 workers were unable to find jobs. Congressional action in the spring of 1930, authorizing expenditure of $145 million for river and harbor improvements, $530 million for public buildings, and $75 million for highways, also had a steadying effect.[4] Moreover, employers were honoring their pledges not to cut wages and workers their promise not to strike.[5]

Then, beginning in May and June 1930, employers began slowly to reduce production. From April to November 1930 the index of industrial employment fell from 96.3 to 84.6, and the index of payrolls dropped from 97.7 to 76.8. When unemployment reached about 4 million in October, Hoover appointed a Committee for Unemployment Relief and called upon city and private agencies to redouble their relief efforts. Moreover, he ended immigration and declared that he would ask Congress for larger appropriations for public works.

Meanwhile, Democratic leaders had begun the congressional campaign of 1930 with such confidence as they had not felt since Wilson's first administration. Aided by a mounting public fear and by a smear campaign against Hoover personally, the Democrats made a much better showing in the November elections than they had done two years before.[6] The election was no landslide or mass repudiation of Hoover's leadership. Yet by giving control of the legislative branch to the president's political foes on the eve of a presidential election, it divided responsibility in the federal government and led inevitably to bitter wrangling.

In fact, there were some manifestations of tension between Hoover and the progressive bloc in Congress even during the lame-duck session of the Seventy-first Congress that sat from December 1930 to March 1931. Progressives, Republican and Democratic, demanded that the president abandon voluntarism and meet the crisis boldly—by a federal relief program, part payment of the veterans' bonus, and development of the Muscle Shoals facilities. Hoover replied that private and local relief resources were still ample and set himself sternly against any projects for direct federal relief. He successfully vetoed the Norris bill for federal operation of Muscle Shoals, but Congress overrode his veto of a bill allowing veterans to obtain half the value of their certificates in cash.

At the same time, it seemed again that the president's policies had turned back the depression tide and set the nation on the road to recovery. Indices of employment, payrolls, and production steadied in February 1931 and then rallied slightly until about the first of June. Bank failures abated; unemployment slackened. To many observers these encouraging developments signified that the recession was nearly over.

---

[4] Actually, federal expenditures for public works totaled $493 million in 1930, as compared with $384 million in 1929. State and municipal expenditures totaled more than $2.8 billion in 1929 and over $3 billion in 1930.

[5] Only 7 percent of firms reporting to the Bureau of Labor Statistics reduced wages during 1930.

[6] The Democrats elected seventeen governors, the Republicans twelve. The GOP lost some forty seats but retained control of the House of Representatives by a plurality of one. When the Seventy-second Congress met in December 1931, however, enough Republican incumbents had died to give control to the Democrats. The new Senate consisted of forty-eight Republicans, forty-seven Democrats, and one Farmer-Laborite; but so many Republican senators were midwestern insurgents that an insurgent-Democratic coalition easily controlled the upper house.

Unhappily, the second and catastrophic phase of the depression was now about to begin in the United States as the result of a financial panic in Europe that paralyzed the international economy. Central European and South American countries had been borrowing heavily in short-term loans since 1927 to compensate for a drying up of the sources of long-term credit.[7] French bankers, who held large sums of German and Austrian short-term notes, demanded immediate payment, partly for political reasons, in March 1931. To avert bankruptcy, Germany and Austria appealed to London and New York for aid. British bankers did what they could, but it was not enough, and the Kreditanstalt of Vienna, the largest bank in Austria, was "reorganized" on May 11, 1931. Its virtual failure stimulated such heavy withdrawals of gold from Germany that the republic was unable by June to meet reparations payments, much less its short-term obligations. Desperately, almost pathetically, the aged president of Germany, Paul von Hindenburg, appealed personally to Hoover on June 18 for immediate assistance.

Hoover and his advisers, meanwhile, had been contemplating proposing a one-year moratorium on all intergovernmental debt and reparations payments. As these obligations would total about $1 billion, any attempt to force payment would bankrupt Germany and cause the entire international economy to collapse. Hoover proposed the moratorium on June 21, 1931, after delaying too long for fear of political repercussions. Britain and Germany accepted at once; but the French government balked for two weeks, and further withdrawals from Germany compelled the German government to adopt severe measures to stave off repudiation.

No sooner had the German crisis passed than French bankers began withdrawing large sums of gold which they had earlier deposited in British banks. The Bank of England negotiated a short-term gold loan in France and the United States on August 1 and another in the United States at the end of the month. But the withdrawals were so heavy that the Bank of England defaulted on gold payments on September 21, 1931, and the British cabinet took the government off the gold standard. Within six months, only the United States, France, Italy, Belgium, Holland, and Switzerland remained committed to payment in gold.

The financial crises of the spring and summer of 1931 virtually destroyed the existing system of international exchange and trade and set off a sharp depression in western Europe. More significant for our story was the effect of the European crisis in deepening the depression in the United States. For one thing, before the European crisis erupted, British, French, and other European nationals and banks had deposited some $1.5 billion

---

[7]By March 1931 Germany alone had more than $4 billion in short-term debts outstanding. Normally, short-term loans are made to finance business and trade operations. The Germans, however, had invested the money in a variety of nonliquid assets. Any crisis leading to demand for payment of these obligations would, therefore, immediately imperil the entire German financial structure.

in gold in American banks, and American banks in turn had lent out most of this money. Europeans demanded payment of most of this gold when their own crisis came in the spring of 1931, and American depositories had to call in domestic loans. In the second place, American banks held more than $1 billion of German short-term trade paper and bank acceptances. Fear that these obligations could not be paid gave additional cause for American bankers to call loans to amass liquid reserves. Third, the panic in Europe prompted foreigners to unload large quantities of securities on the New York Stock Exchange. Finally, devaluation and demoralization of exchange caused a virtual stoppage of foreign trade, the consequences of which were catastrophic for the commodity markets.

These and other factors combined during the summer of 1931 to destroy all the encouraging progress toward recovery that the American economy had made since January and to plunge the country deeper into depression. Contraction of loans set off panic, hoarding of cash, and runs by depositors; bankers in turn had to contract further. Dumping of securities drove the price of stocks and bonds to new depths. The loss of foreign markets caused agricultural prices to fall to very low levels. Above all, fear seized the American business and financial communities. Men began hoarding instead of spending; employers cut production and wages; investors tried to recover money instead of investing it. The downward spiral is well illustrated by the following table.

1931	Index of Employment (Monthly Average 1923-1925 = 100)	Index of Payrolls (Monthly Average 1923-1925 = 100)	Number of Bank Failures
May	80.1	73.4	91
June	78.4	69.7	167
July	77.0	66.2	93
August	77.1	65.9	158
September	77.4	63.4	305
October	74.4	61.3	522
November	71.8	58.1	175
December	71.0	57.6	358

It was obvious by the late summer of 1931 that unrestrained liquidation could lead only to total collapse of the American financial structure. Now President Hoover moved more boldly than before. Still hoping to defeat the depression by the voluntary cooperation of the business community, he called some thirty leading New York bankers and insurance executives to a secret conference on October 4, 1931. He wanted the banks to form an emergency credit pool of $500 million and the insurance companies to agree not to foreclose mortgages when creditors were in honest straits. Moreover, he warned that he would call Congress into special session if the financial leaders did not cooperate. The warning sufficed to bring early compliance. The bankers formed the credit pool soon afterward and organized the National Credit Corporation to administer it. Moreover, the president met with congressional leaders of both parties on October 6 and won their promise of support in the impending Seventy-second Congress.

Hoover outlined the recovery program upon which he had been working since September when Congress convened in early December. He proposed drastic reductions in administrative expenditures and an expansion of federal public works; expansion of the lending powers of Federal Farm banks; creation of a system of home-loan banks to prevent foreclosures; and a gigantic emergency reconstruction corporation to strengthen the entire economy. Fear of national collapse had obviously forced the president to abandon old assumptions about the sufficiency of voluntary measures and to support a program that implied more extensive federal intervention than had ever been attempted in peacetime. But he had come to this position reluctantly. He had accepted the proposal for an emergency reconstruction agency only after the National Credit Corporation had collapsed, and only under heavy pressure from New York bankers and particularly Eugene Meyer, a member of the Federal Reserve Board and author of the idea.

At first, during the early months of 1932, Democratic leaders in Congress cooperated with Hoover to complete his recovery program speedily. The main cog of the recovery machinery was the Reconstruction Finance Corporation (RFC), chartered by Congress on January 16, 1932, with a capital of $500 million and authority to borrow up to $1.5 billion more in tax-free obligations. The RFC opened offices in thirty cities and set to work immediately to save banks, railroads, building and loan associations, and other financial institutions. In all, the RFC lent $1.5 billion during 1932 to more than 5,000 concerns, restored a large measure of public confidence, and successfully halted the undermining of the financial structure.

Through other measures the president and Congress cooperated to strengthen the financial machinery. Thus, the Glass-Steagall Act of February 27, 1932, made government bonds and new classes of commercial paper acceptable as collateral for Federal Reserve notes. This measure not only permitted the Federal Reserve banks to expand the currency but, more important, released $1 billion in gold to meet foreign withdrawals. The Federal Home Loan Bank Act of July 22, 1932, established home loan banks with a total capital of $125 million to enable building and loan associations, savings banks, and insurance companies to obtain cash without foreclosing on home owners. In addition, an act of January 23, 1932, provided more capital for Federal Land banks.

On the whole these were nonpartisan measures, adopted after a minimum of bickering. Conflicting tax and relief proposals, however, engendered bitter controversies between the administration and Democratic and progressive Republican leaders in Congress. Many of the progressives were frank inflationists, who proposed to extend direct aid to the unemployed by printing paper money. Hoover blocked their efforts at almost every turn. A case in point was the controversy provoked by the agitation for full and immediate payment of the so-called bonus. The House of Representatives on June 15, 1932, approved a measure sponsored by Wright Patman of Texas for full payment of the bonus with $2.4 billion in newly printed money. The Senate rejected the Patman bill on June 19 under threat of a presidential veto.

Progressives also demanded adoption of a large-scale public works and direct relief program, to be financed through borrowing; and Congress, in early July 1932, adopted the Garner-Wagner relief bill providing direct aid to individuals and a vast expansion of public works. Hoover vetoed the Garner-Wagner bill on July 11, calling it "impractical," "dangerous," and "damaging to our whole conception of governmental relations." Congress then followed his advice and adopted a new relief bill on July 16. It authorized the RFC to lend $300 million to states whose resources were exhausted and an additional $1.5 billion to states and municipalities for self-liquidating public works.

To repeat the old allegation that Hoover fiddled while the country burned would merely add undue dignity to an important part of the American political mythology. Hoover was surely no old-fashioned conservative, willing to let the depression run its full course in the confidence that the automatic machinery of the economy would eventually start the wheels to roll again. On the contrary, he was a cautious progressive, whose campaign for recovery was grounded ideologically on the assumption that only strong federal leadership and action could carry the country through the storm. His philosophy and policies, especially during 1931 and 1932, represented a turning point, a transition toward a future characterized by increasing federal participation in economic affairs.

It was Hoover's personal misfortune that he lost the confidence of a large majority of the American people at the very time that he was going to greater lengths to combat depression than any president before his time. This was true in part because he had the bad luck to be president during a time of widespread social and economic misery. It was true even more because he saved the financial structure but stubbornly refused to countenance measures for direct federal relief. In the minds of most Americans, Hoover's program seemed inadequate and too heavily weighted in favor of the upper classes. Moreover, the majority of people were beginning to demand not a holding action, but a thoroughgoing overhauling of the economic machinery. Hoover still talked as if it would suffice merely to revive the business machinery of the 1920s. In contrast, millions of Americans were turning their eyes toward a new and, they hoped, brighter future in which they, not businessmen and bankers, would make important economic decisions.

16

The First New Deal:

Experiment in Compromise

The Hoover administration had seemingly halted the most destructive attrition of the depression by the summer of 1932, but most Americans were now somewhat weary of the president's talk about prosperity being just around the corner. Farmers in debt, workers without jobs, and bankrupt businessmen demanded bolder federal action than Hoover was willing to approve. Rejecting the president and the now discredited business leadership, the disparate forces of discontent came together in a new coalition in November 1932 and voted to entrust the government of the United States to a new leader and a party long out of power.

The consequence was a new era in American political history—the age of Franklin D. Roosevelt. A word of warning should perhaps be said at the outset. The key to understanding this period lies in the realization that there was no single set of Roosevelt policies carried out according to a prearranged plan. There were, roughly speaking, two New Deals, two reform programs. Given historical circumstances at the time, the second was an inevitable extension of the first. The first New Deal, from 1933 to 1935, marked a transition from a cautious progressivism, such as Wilson and Hoover had espoused, to new programs with expanded social and economic horizons. In the second New Deal, from 1935 to 1939, the American progressive movement found fulfillment. We will pause briefly at the beginning of this chapter to try to see what all this implied for American political traditions.

1. The Election of 1932

While Republican fortunes declined in direct ratio to the intensity of economic distress after 1930, Democratic leaders looked forward with growing confidence to victory in the presidential election of 1932. Alfred E. Smith of New York was still titular head of the Democratic party, but a number of other contenders entered the preconvention contest. Franklin D. Roosevelt was easily Smith's most dangerous rival. Elected governor of New York in 1928, Roosevelt was reelected in 1930 by 725,000 votes. The magic of this majority at once made him a leading contender for the Democratic nomination in 1932. But the situation in New York was discouraging, for Tammany Hall, the New York City Democratic organization, was still loyal to Smith. Therefore, Roosevelt's managers—Louis M. Howe, his secretary, and James A. Farley, a former Smith lieutenant who had come into the Roosevelt camp in 1929—began to build support for the New York governor in the South and West. They succeeded so well that they had amassed a majority of the delegates, but not the then necessary two-thirds, by the time that the Democratic National Convention opened in Chicago on June 27, 1932.

Smith's only hope of stopping Roosevelt was to form a coalition with other favorite sons, particularly Speaker John Nance Garner of Texas, who had the support of the California and Texas delegates. The anti-Roosevelt managers maneuvered desperately, but Farley played a shrewd game. Instead of showing his full strength on the first ballot, he held off part of his delegates and added them to the Roosevelt column on the second and third ballots in order to create the impression of a landslide. But the expected landslide did not occur on the third ballot, and Farley turned in desperation to the Texas and California delegates. Garner could not have taken his chances for the presidency very seriously; he was certainly eager to avoid a futile deadlock. When consulted on Friday evening, July 1, he swung Texas and California into the Roosevelt column and precipitated the landslide on the fourth ballot. Only Smith's Tammany followers refused to make the nomination unanimous. Garner was named as Roosevelt's running mate, perhaps as a reward—there is some evidence of a bargain—more certainly because he was from the Southwest and a powerful figure in the party.

Flying to Chicago to accept the nomination in person, Roosevelt went down the planks in the platform, endorsing them one by one. "I pledge you, I pledge myself, to a new deal for the American people," he concluded on a high note of dedication. "This is more than a political campaign; it is a call to arms." Roosevelt's promises of work, security, and a fairer distribution of incomes encouraged the country, but what it foretold no man could say. Moreover, a reading of the Democratic platform would neither have yielded knowledge nor provided inspiration. Indeed, in view of later New Deal policies, it was a poor prophecy.[1]

The Republicans had meanwhile assembled at Chicago on June 14 and renominated President Hoover on the first ballot. The Republican convention was a gloomy conclave, and it seemed that the delegates knew they were going through necessary motions. Most of the speeches and a good part of the platform[2] were devoted to proving that the depression was the product of outside forces, and that Hoover had met the enemy on home ground and conquered him through bold measures of relief and reconstruction.

Hoover campaigned vigorously, but he spoke gravely, recounting the things that he had done to combat the depression, "the battles on a thousand fronts . . . the good fight to protect our people in a thousand cities from hunger and cold." To the unemployed he declared that he would mobilize the nation's resources rather than permit a single person to starve. To farmers he promised enlarged tariff protection and additional federal credit. To investors he promised maintenance of the gold standard. To the country at large he promised abundance if the Republicans won. And he warned that grass would grow "in the streets of a hundred cities, a thousand towns" if Roosevelt was elected.

In sharp contrast to Hoover's unencouraging defense was Roosevelt's brilliant campaign. He said many things about economy and a balanced budget that he must have regretted afterward. But with the help of his advisers, called the "brain trust," Roosevelt also forecast at least the shadow of future New Deal policies. Thus at Topeka, Kansas, he sketched the outline of a crop control measure. At Portland, Oregon, he promised federal hydroelectric projects. Before the Commonwealth Club of San Francisco he demanded that businessmen work together to assure full production and employment. To millions of investors who had been fleeced by Wall Street operators he promised to bring the stock exchanges under strict control. To the unemployed he declared that he was "utterly

[1]The Democratic platform was brief but neither radical nor bold. Among other things, it demanded repeal of the Eighteenth Amendment; promised to balance the budget and reduce federal expenditures by 25 percent; demanded the removal of government from all fields of private enterprise, "except where necessary to develop public works and natural resources." It also promised to maintain "at all hazards" a sound currency and reform the banking system; advocated lending money to the states to care for the unemployed; endorsed unemployment and old-age insurance "under state laws"; and promised lower tariffs and "effective control of crop surpluses" without specifying the nature of such controls.

[2]The Republican platform, among other things, advocated economy, emergency relief loans to states unable to cope with the unemployment crisis, maintenance of the gold standard, and banking reform. It endorsed cooperative efforts by farmers to control agricultural production and maintenance of tariff protection. And it approved a constitutional amendment to allow the states to resume control of the liquor traffic.

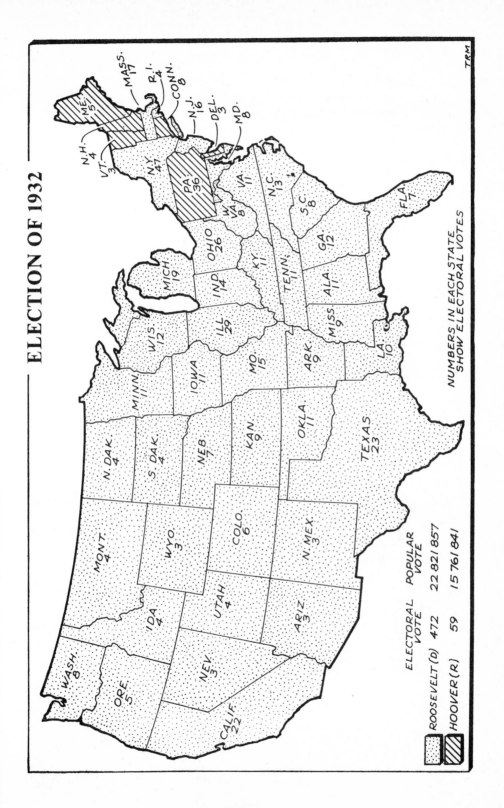

ELECTION OF 1932

NUMBERS IN EACH STATE
SHOW ELECTORAL VOTES

	ELECTORAL VOTE	POPULAR VOTE
ROOSEVELT (D)	472	22,821,857
HOOVER (R)	59	15,761,841

MASS. 17
R.I. 4
CONN. 8
N.J. 16
DEL. 3
MD. 8
N.H. 4
ME. 5
VT. 3
N.Y. 47
PA. 36
W. VA. 8
VA. 11
N.C. 13
S.C. 8
GA. 12
FLA. 7
OHIO 26
IND. 14
KY. 11
TENN. 2
ALA. 11
MICH. 19
ILL. 29
MO. 15
ARK. 9
MISS. 9
LA. 10
WIS. 12
IOWA 11
MINN. 11
N. DAK. 4
S. DAK. 4
NEB. 7
KAN. 9
OKLA. 11
TEXAS 23
MONT. 4
WYO. 3
COLO. 6
N. MEX. 3
IDA. 4
UTAH 4
ARIZ. 3
WASH. 8
ORE. 5
NEV. 3
CALIF. 22

T.R.M.

unwilling that economy should be practiced at the expense of starving people." Strange to say, organized labor was the only group to which Roosevelt did not promise some specific benefit.

Any Democrat could probably have won in that autumn of depression. But there can be no doubt that Roosevelt's contagious smile, reassuring voice, and ability to inspire confidence helped to make the election of 1932 one of the most impressive mandates in American history. Retaining business and a large middle-class support, Hoover received 15,761,841 votes and carried Pennsylvania, Connecticut, Delaware, Maine, New Hampshire, and Vermont. In contrast, Roosevelt received 22,821,857 popular votes, carried the electoral votes of the rest of the states, and helped give the Democrats staggering majorities in both houses of Congress. Certainly the revolution of 1932 was as sweeping as any Democrat could have wished for.[3]

2. *Franklin D. Roosevelt and the Progressive Movement*

No man, except perhaps Washington, Lincoln, and Truman, ever assumed the duties of president with more baffling problems than Franklin D. Roosevelt. But if the tasks were overwhelming, the opportunity for bold leadership was also great. That opportunity arose from more than just the weakness of the Republican opposition and the strength of Roosevelt's forces in Congress after 1932. It arose even more importantly because of the strong survival in the 1930s of the progressive movement, especially in its economic and social manifestations. Divided and thwarted in the 1920s, the various components of progressivism came tentatively together in 1932. Roosevelt's most urgent political task, therefore, was to weld disparate groups that had not been able to cooperate effectively for long into a solid majority coalition.

This task proved deceptively easy in the dire emergency of 1933, for practically all classes and interests demanded action. Once the worst phase of the depression had passed, however, large conservative and business elements deserted the New Deal coalition, and Roosevelt had to fashion a new alliance and a new program. Abandoning many of his early policies, he resurrected the Jacksonian alliance of farmers and workingmen in 1935, added to it the social justice forces and the mass of the unemployed, and then set in motion the most far-reaching program of federal, social, and economic legislation in American history to that time. It was ironic that Roosevelt in 1932 neither foresaw nor planned this

[3]In spite of a vigorous campaign and a comprehensive program for combating the depression, the Socialist candidate, Norman Thomas, polled only 884,781 votes. The Communist candidate, William Z. Foster, enjoyed considerable support in intellectual and literary circles, but he also failed utterly to profit by the prevailing discontent and polled a mere 102,991 votes.

culmination of the American progressive movement. And yet when necessity compelled a new departure he took firm control of the progressive forces and won congressional approval for a program that satisfied their historic demands. This, in brief, was his chief contribution to the progressive movement in the United States.

What manner of man was he who guided the destinies of the American people from the Great Depression to victory in global war and became almost the personal embodiment of the democratic movement?

Roosevelt came up the easy way, at least before 1921. Born at Hyde Park, New York, on January 30, 1882, the son of James and Sara Delano Roosevelt, Franklin received a proper education at Groton and Harvard without demonstrating ambition or much intellectual promise. After graduating from Harvard in 1904, he moved to New York, studied in a desultory way at the Columbia University Law School, married his distant cousin Anna Eleanor Roosevelt in 1905, and settled down in 1907 for a comfortable career with a prominent New York law firm.

Following the example of his uncle-in-law and fifth cousin, Theodore Roosevelt, Franklin went into politics in 1910. He accepted the Democratic nomination for the New York State Senate in a Hudson Valley district that had gone Republican in every election but one since the Civil War. By virtue of hard campaigning and a split in the Republican party he won his first election. He led a small group of antimachine Democrats at Albany in 1911 in a fight to prevent the election of a Tammany leader to the United States Senate. Seeming success in this first skirmish brought Roosevelt a measure of national publicity; soon afterward he organized the anti-Tammany Democrats in support of Wilson's candidacy for the presidential nomination in 1912.

Roosevelt was appointed assistant secretary of the navy in 1913 by Wilson at the suggestion of Josephus Daniels (who remembered that Theodore Roosevelt had used the same office as a stepping stone to the presidency). The young New Yorker was an able administrator and popular in the second rank of the Wilson circle from 1913 to 1920, even if he agreed more with Theodore Roosevelt than with Wilson and Secretary Daniels on issues like preparedness and intervention in the European war. Coming to friendly terms with the new young leaders of Tammany Hall, Roosevelt supported Alfred E. Smith in Smith's first bid for the governorship in 1918. Indeed, Roosevelt won the Democratic vice-presidential nomination in 1920 because he was the leading New York Wilsonian acceptable to Tammany.

Roosevelt lost the election, to be sure, but he gained invaluable experience, a host of friends, and a position of considerable prominence in Democratic councils. In brief, he was rapidly changing from a patrician reformer into a practical politician with a bright future. Then disaster struck in August 1921, when an attack of polio laid Roosevelt low. Courageously he fought to regain his strength and use of his withered legs; slowly, painfully he won a partial victory. Meanwhile, his wife and his devoted secretary and adviser, Louis M. Howe, stayed by his side and helped him to extend his influence among Democratic politicians through voluminous correspondence.

Roosevelt had recovered sufficiently by 1924 to nominate Smith for the presidency at the Democratic convention in New York's Madison Square Garden. He had discarded his crutches in public and had achieved maximum recovery when he placed Smith's name before the national convention at Houston in 1928. Nominated for the governorship of New York soon afterward, Roosevelt surprised friends and opponents by his vigor during the campaign of 1928; except for Smith he was the best vote-getter that the Democrats had. But the greatest surprise came on election day. Smith lost New York by a narrow margin, but enough Republicans voted for Roosevelt to put him in the governor's chair by a plurality of 25,000.

We have seen how Roosevelt won the presidency in 1932 and established himself as the spokesman of a large part of the American people. During the fateful years of his tenure he abandoned old policies and adopted new ones, and he emerged with greater stature in the contemporary public eye during war than in peace. But throughout the conflict and turmoil he remained remarkably the same man.

Roosevelt's personality was extraordinarily complex; he had many sides, and the whole is not equal to the sum of its parts. Personally, he was urbane and witty; yet for all his patrician upbringing he had a deep affection for people as individuals, not en masse. This was true in part because his long illness and fight for recovery purged him of any social snobbishness that he might once have had. It stirred a deep compassion in his heart for the physically afflicted and troubled in spirit. Moreover, he so much wanted people to like him that he often gave the impression of duplicity because he found it difficult to disagree with a good friend. Finally, in spite of his great courage in times of national peril, he rarely had the heart to dismiss a loyal but incompetent friend. On this account he was often a poor administrator,[4] although it must be added that Roosevelt's canny refusal to permit any subordinate to exercise too much power was the chief cause of the administrative snarls that vexed his regime.

Roosevelt's religious beliefs underlay all his attitudes toward men and society. He believed in a personal God, an absolute ethic, and the essential goodness of his fellow men. Hence his views toward government and what government should do for people stemmed from his belief in decency, justice, and fair play. To his friends he was playful, radiant, and warm, and few could resist his charm, which he used in the confidence that he could "get through" to any person. Toward his enemies, on the other hand, he could appear vain, deceptive, petty, and vindictive.

Intellectually, Roosevelt was at once naive and sophisticated. He was not widely read in literature, preferred to obtain information from conver-

---

[4]But see the extended analysis in Arthur M. Schlesinger, Jr., *The Coming of the New Deal* (Boston, 1959), pp. 533–552.

sation rather than from study, and gave the impression of relying upon intuition more than hard thinking in solving difficult problems. The latter he himself characterized as "playing it by ear." He was not a particularly original thinker, but he demonstrated great capacity for learning and for thinking in broad terms, and he had a flexibility that freed him for experimentation. In economic matters Roosevelt displayed considerable virtuosity in assimilating, mastering, and reducing complex data. But he was not as competent in economic theory and was often at the mercy of advisers in formulating economic policies.

In spite of all his shortcomings, Roosevelt won such affection and loyalty from the American people as few presidents have earned. He was the champion campaigner of American history, the president for life after 1932. In brief, Roosevelt succeeded, first, because he was able to communicate—either in person, over the radio, or in newsreels—directly with individuals and to radiate his warmth and confidence into the hearts and minds of all manner of people. He succeeded, secondly, because he was able to articulate great ideals in simple language; in other words, he had the ability to express the hopes and aspirations of the average person in homely yet moving words. He succeeded, above all, because he possessed an uncanny ability to know and understand what the majority of people wanted and the courage to defy powerful forces of privilege and fight for measures of social and economic justice. By his character and the techniques of his leadership he restored the presidency to the high eminence that it had enjoyed under Woodrow Wilson.

3. Interregnum: The Banking Panic and the Change of Government

The event that gave the new administration its tremendous emergency power was the practical collapse of the banking structure of the United States in the last months of Hoover's tenure. American banking strength began to give way after the European collapse in the summer of 1931. Banking resources declined from $70,209,000,000 to $57,245,100,000 between June 30, 1931, and June 30, 1932, while bank deposits shrank nearly $9,000,000,000. Thus by the summer of 1932 the forces of dissolution were beginning to imperil the very foundations of American capitalism. Whatever the cause, fear spread and grew into panic in January 1933. The strain of runs and heavy withdrawals was too great for the banks to bear. The first sign of crisis came on October 31, 1932, when the governor of Nevada declared a twelve-day banking holiday in his state to avert the failure of an important chain of banks. Banks were either closed or doing business under severe restrictions in forty-seven states when Roosevelt was inaugurated.

Meanwhile, President Hoover had been trying to win Roosevelt's approval for policies that would stabilize the financial situation and restore public confidence. Hoover in private conference and by letter exhorted the president-elect to announce that he would balance the budget, maintain the dollar at its current value in gold, and cooperate with European powers in stabilizing currencies and exchange rates. Roosevelt refused, not only because he had already decided to inflate the currency, but also because he suspected that Hoover was trying to transfer some of his own unpopularity to the incoming administration. Thus, irreconcilable differences over policy prevented effective teamwork between the two men.

Throughout all the turmoil Roosevelt was hard at work constructing an administration. For secretary of state he chose Senator Cordell Hull of Tennessee, probably the most influential Democrat in the upper house. As secretary of the treasury, Roosevelt wanted Senator Carter Glass of Virginia, author of the Federal Reserve bill and former head of the Treasury under Wilson, whose financial orthodoxy would reassure the banking interests. Glass, however, refused because Roosevelt would not promise to eschew inflation. The post went instead to William H. Woodin of New York, president of the American Car & Foundry Company and a heavy contributor to the Democratic party. Woodin was succeeded by Henry Morgenthau, Jr., in 1934. The secretaryships of agriculture and of the interior went to two midwestern progressive Republicans, Henry A. Wallace of Iowa and Harold L. Ickes of Chicago. By selecting Frances Perkins, a social worker with long experience in New York, as secretary of labor, the president-elect honored women and accorded signal recognition to the men and women who had been pressing the cause of social and labor reform. The important job of dispenser of the patronage, otherwise known as the postmaster general, went to the astute Jim Farley, while the remaining cabinet appointees were an assortment of party hacks and wheelhorses.

The men who stood close to Roosevelt and made important decisions with his approval were not the cabinet, although a few cabinet members were in the charmed inner circle. They were Roosevelt's unofficial advisers—the earlier brain trust—now considerably enlarged in number: Raymond Moley, A. A. Berle, Jr., Rexford G. Tugwell, Hugh S. Johnson, George N. Peek, Louis M. Howe, Samuel I. Rosenman, and others. All of them were given posts in various agencies and the White House.

It was a gloomy day, March 4, 1933, when Franklin Delano Roosevelt took the oath as president of the United States. The economic machinery of the country was almost at a standstill, and people looked toward Washington for some word of hope. The new president struck at the frights and anxieties of the last three years and called out defiantly: "This great Nation will endure as it has endured, will revive and will prosper. So, first of all, let me assert my firm belief that the only thing we have to fear is fear itself." He was ready, he declared, to assume supreme command, and he called upon the people to follow him as if he were their commander in chief in battle. There were many urgent tasks ahead, Roosevelt continued.

People had to be put to work; the banking, credit, and currency systems had to be overhauled and strengthened; the nation had to learn to use its resources wisely. If Congress failed to provide adequate remedies, he warned, he would ask Congress for "broad Executive power to wage a war against the emergency, as great as the power that would be given to me if we were in fact invaded by a foreign foe."

The meaning of this pronouncement was not lost upon the people of the United States as they sat huddled around their radios. They knew little about the finely spun rationalizations of the orthodox economists and understood even less the abstruse mathematical logic of the new school who talked of managed currency. They did not have to know or understand these things in order to sense that this day, March 4, 1933, was a fateful moment in the nation's history. One order was dead beyond recall. Another, ill-defined and uncertain though it was, had been born.

4. Financial Reinforcement and Reform Under the New Deal

So desperate was the crisis on March 4, 1933, and so frightened were congressmen and the people, that Roosevelt possessed a power unprecedented in American peacetime history. Had he harbored imperial ambitions, he probably could have obtained dictatorial powers from Congress. Had he been a Socialist, he might have nationalized the banks and set the country upon the road toward extreme collectivism. However, Roosevelt was neither a Fascist, Socialist, or Communist. He was simply an old-fashioned American—as he once put it, simply "a Christian and a democrat"—with traditional views on the benefits of the system of private enterprise and ownership of property. He believed that the capitalistic system was worth saving. And the manner in which he and his helpers achieved this goal revealed the true character of the first New Deal.

The hope for national salvation, Roosevelt thought, lay in quick action to overcome the menace of economic collapse. He closed all banks on March 6, 1933, for a four-day period and forbade all gold payments and exports. Congress met in a special session on March 9 and within four hours enacted the Emergency Banking Act. It revealed that the administration had decided to retain private ownership and management in the financial field. It authorized Federal Reserve banks to issue currency against bank assets, empowered the RFC to provide liquid funds to banks by buying their preferred stock, directed Treasury officials to supervise the reopening of banks,[5] and forbade hoarding and export of gold.

[5]Treasury officials divided banks, on a basis of relative soundness, into four classes. Over half the banks, with 90 percent of all deposits, were given a clean bill and allowed to reopen by March 15, 1933.

Coupled with the Economy Act, approved March 20, which drastically reduced federal expenditures in an effort to balance the budget, swift Treasury action under the Emergency Banking Act at once restored the confidence of the business classes. Roosevelt explained what the government was doing and appealed for public confidence in the banking system in his first "fireside chat," or direct radio talk, with the American people on March 12. The response was immediate. By the first week in April more than $1 billion in currency had flowed back to the banks; hoarders had returned gold to the Federal Reserve banks; and Treasury officials had had to issue only a small amount of new Federal Reserve currency.

The worst crisis was over, and now the Treasury began the immense task of strengthening weak banks and eliminating unsound ones. First, the RFC between March 1933 and July 1935 extended more than $1 billion in aid to 6,468 banks that were deemed essentially sound. Second, Treasury and state officials liquidated 2,352 banks, with aggregate deposits of $2,756,946,000, during the same two-year period. Hence the administration strengthened and restored to private hands the most vital and sensitive part of the capitalistic economy, although, as we will see, that segment would be subjected to thoroughgoing public control.

In fulfilling his promise to reform the financial system, the president merely encouraged a bipartisan congressional determination that the speculative debacle of 1929 should never happen again. Thus the Glass-Steagall Act, or Banking Act of 1933, sought to prevent banks from using the resources of the Federal Reserve system for speculation—chiefly by compelling the absolute divorcement of commercial banks from their investment affiliates.[6] The Truth-in-Securities Act of 1933 and the Securities Exchange Act of 1934 left operation of stock exchanges in private hands but compelled all underwriters and brokers to furnish complete information regarding the true value of securities being offered for sale and the arrangements under which the sale was being made. To the Securities and Exchange Commission (SEC), a nonpartisan agency established by the act of 1934, was entrusted the task of preventing and helping to punish misrepresentation and fraud.

Administration leaders set to work after the banking crisis had been liquidated to prepare a comprehensive measure to supplant the temporary Banking Act of 1933. The result, the Banking Act of 1935, was the first fundamental overhauling of the Federal Reserve Act since its adoption in 1913. In contrast to the Wilsonian legislation, which had diffused power within the Federal Reserve system, the Banking Act of 1935 concentrated enormous power in the central board, now called the Board of Governors. The board now had direct authority over discount, or interest, rates, re-

---

[6]For a discussion of the growth of these investment affiliates and their contribution to the speculation of the late 1920s, see p. 262. At the insistence of southern and western Democrats, the Banking Act of 1933 also established the Federal Deposit Insurance Corporation, which insured deposits, first up to $2,500, then up to $5,000 in 1935, and finally up to $40,000 after the Second World War.

serve requirements, and open market operations of Federal Reserve banks. In addition, a number of highly technical provisions established new classes of securities and commercial paper against which Federal Reserve currency might be issued.

Roosevelt's own contribution to this edifice of financial reform—the Public Utility Holding Company Act of 1935—gave the SEC complete supervisory control over the financial operations of holding companies, compelled destruction of the giant utilities empires within five years, but allowed small holding companies controlling single, integrated operating systems to survive.

The task of reforming the country's financial institutions was now fairly complete. To progressives the changes that had been accomplished during the past two years were good because they transformed financial operations from a private into a quasi-public business. At long last the progressive demand for complete federal control of banks, stock markets, and the money supply had been satisfied.

Two other aspects of the first New Deal's program to save the capitalistic structure remain to be noted here. The first was the establishment on June 13, 1933, of the Home Owners Loan Corporation (HOLC). Authorized to borrow up to $2 billion, later increased to $4.75 billion, the HOLC refinanced mortgages of home owners in dire peril of foreclosure. The agency lent more than $3 billion to more than 1 million home owners and assumed about one-sixth of the entire urban mortgage load during its three years of life. Secondly, to stimulate the nearly defunct housing construction industry,[7] Congress on June 28, 1934, established the Federal Housing Administration (FHA), which insured mortgages for new construction and home repairs. The FHA played a large role in the resumption of private home construction by providing a system of long-term repayment at low interest rates. Between 1934 and 1940 it insured 2.3 million loans totaling $945 million for home repairs and 554,000 loans totaling $2.3 billion for new construction.

5. *The Problem of Recovery and an Unsuccessful Experiment*

The philosophy underlying the administration's recovery program was compounded of a curious mixture of pessimism about the future of the economy and naive faith in the ability of government to work miracles by easy solutions. Roosevelt and his advisers accepted the then popular view that the American economy had reached a stage of full maturity—that the closing of the agricultural frontier, restriction of immigration, and sharp decline in the birth rate had removed the self-generating forces from the

---

[7]Urban home construction numbered only 60,000 units in 1933, as compared with 900,000 units in 1925.

economy. The age of expansion and confidence, when businessmen invested in the future and expanded economic frontiers, was allegedly over. Indeed, Roosevelt several times observed, the American industrial plant was overbuilt because it could produce more than people could consume.

The chief task ahead, therefore, was to conserve human and natural resources, restore prices to a level that would yield profits to farmers, manufacturers, and businessmen, and assure fair distribution of goods and incomes. This could be accomplished not by stimulating foreign trade and encouraging new investment, but by close cooperation among workers, farmers, businessmen, and government to raise prices, increase purchasing power through shorter hours and higher wages, and limit production to actual needs.

This is not to say that Roosevelt took the helm with any grand plan for recovery, for his most elaborate undertaking, the National Recovery Administration and the Public Works Administration, which we will soon discuss, were afterthoughts and improvisations. The administration's original program was aimed chiefly at stimulating recovery by raising the prices of agricultural products through restriction of output and by increasing the general price level through controlled inflation.

Roosevelt took the first step toward controlled inflation on March 6, 1933, by prohibiting redemption of currency in gold coin and export of gold without the Treasury's approval. Subsequent presidential decrees and acts of Congress nationalized gold and forbade fulfillment of private and public contracts calling for payment of debts in yellow coin. This action took the country off the traditional gold standard at home but retained a gold bullion backing for the currency and allowed limited gold payments in international exchange.

The dollar had fallen in value by mid-May 1933 to 85 cents in gold on international exchanges. Wholesale prices in the United States were rising as a result, and the entire economy seemed on the verge of invigoration. Having apparently set recovery in motion, would the president now agree to stabilize the gold content of the dollar, or would he embark upon a course of frank inflation?

This was perhaps the most important question confronting the administration in the late spring of 1933. On the one hand, an overwhelming majority of Congress favored outright inflation through the issue of paper currency.[8] On the other hand, an international conference would meet in London in June 1933 to lower tariffs, stabilize currencies, and find other means to stimulate a revival of international economic activity. Thus the president was caught in an embarrassing dilemma by the end of May. He

---

[8] It required all the president's influence to restrain these congressional demands, but he won control over monetary policy with the passage of the Thomas Amendment to the Agricultural Adjustment Act of May 12, 1933. The Thomas Amendment authorized but did not require the president to increase the money supply by six different methods, including the printing of $3 billion in paper currency, free coinage of silver at 16 to 1, lowering of Federal Reserve requirements, and devaluation of the gold content of the dollar up to 50 percent.

had pledged support to the London Economic Conference, yet he was not willing to stabilize the gold content of the dollar and forgo the advantages of further inflation.

By the time that the London Economic Conference met,[9] Roosevelt had been converted to the so-called commodity dollar theory and had decided upon further inflation. Advocates of the commodity dollar argued that the best hope for sound recovery lay in devaluing the dollar to its purchasing power of 1926. This could be done, they said, by decreasing its gold value by 43 percent. Such inflation, these economists further contended, would not only stimulate production through substantial price increases but would also enable the American people better to carry their debt burdens.

Before acting, however, the president first waited to see how far the dollar would fall naturally in the exchanges and whether the recovery that had set in would last. The dollar had depreciated about 30 percent by October, and commodity prices had risen 19 percent. Meanwhile, the country had gyrated from depression to near recovery and back to depression again, as the following table reveals.

1933	Manufacturing Production[°]	Employment[°]	Payrolls[°]	Wholesale Prices[‡]
March	56	58.8	37.1	60.2
April	65	59.9	38.8	60.4
May	77	62.6	42.7	62.7
June	93	66.9	47.2	65.0
July	101	71.5	50.8	68.9
August	91	76.4	56.8	69.5
September	83	80.0	59.1	70.8
October	65	79.6	59.4	71.2

[°]Monthly average 1923–1925 = 100.
[‡]1926 average = 100.

Resolved to try any expedient rather than permit the nation to suffer through another winter of subdepression, Roosevelt decided that the time had come to put the commodity dollar theory to work. He announced his decision in a fireside chat on October 22, 1933. Three days later he instructed the RFC to purchase gold, then selling at $29.80 an ounce, at $31.36 an ounce.[10] The president gradually increased the price of gold during ensuing months until he had finally achieved the commodity dollar, which was theoretically equal in purchasing power to the dollar of 1926. Now willing to stabilize, he persuaded Congress to establish a new gold reserve standard.[11] Then on January 31, 1934, he set the price of gold at

[9]For Roosevelt's "torpedoing" of the London Economic Conference, see pp. 439–440.

[10]The pre-1933 price had been $20.67 an ounce.

[11]This was accomplished in the Gold Reserve Act, adopted on January 30, 1934. This measure impounded in the Treasury all gold in Federal Reserve banks, authorized the president to set the gold content of the dollar at between 50 and 60 percent of its pre-1933 value, made gold bullion an unredeemable reserve against Federal Reserve notes, and established from the "profits" of devaluation a fund of $2 billion to be used to stabilize the dollar in international exchanges.

$35.00 an ounce and the gold content of the dollar at 59.06 percent of its pre-1933 value. Not long afterward he approved a Trade Agreements Act and permitted Secretary Hull to undertake a vigorous campaign to expand foreign trade (for details, see pp. 446–447).

It is impossible to measure precisely the effect of this monetary manipulation. By 1935 the nation was definitely, if slowly, on the road to recovery (see pp. 407–408). However, the increase in the total currency from $9 billion in 1933 to $15.1 billion in 1935 by a cooperative Federal Reserve system and the government itself was probably more decisive in spurring recovery than devaluation had been.

6. The NRA: Unsuccessful Experiment in a Planned Economy

Perhaps the most interesting and revealing fact about the Roosevelt administration when it came into power was its utter lack of any plan for industrial recovery other than devaluation. The first stimulus came from organized labor and its spokesmen in Congress. In December 1932 Senator Hugo L. Black of Alabama introduced a bill sponsored by the AF of L to limit hours of labor in industry to thirty a week. Roosevelt's advisers regarded the Black bill as a dangerous threat to recovery, but they were so engrossed in the banking crisis that they paid scant attention to the congressional situation. Then the Senate passed the measure on April 6, and the president commissioned Secretary Perkins to prepare an administration alternative. Miss Perkins went before the House labor committee a few days later, half-heartedly approved the thirty-hour principle, and suggested addition of provisions for minimum wages and federal control of production. By this time leaders of the business community were up in arms, and Roosevelt asked Raymond Moley to find out what they wanted.

Business spokesmen were ready with an answer, for the Chamber of Commerce of the United States had been at work on a recovery plan since 1931. It proposed creation of a national council of industrialists and businessmen who would work through trade associations to control production, raise prices, and stabilize wages. It was the business community's old dream of self-regulation brought to full maturity.

While Congress debated the Black bill, Moley and two other brain trusters, Hugh S. Johnson and Rexford G. Tugwell, set to work to reconcile the chamber of commerce plan with the principle of federal control. Moley and Johnson presented a draft of their recovery bill to the business leaders when the Chamber of Commerce met in Washington on May 3, 1933. Although it included substantial concessions to labor, the Chamber of Commerce approved it as the only practical alternative to the Black bill. Thus fortified, the administration presented its measure, the National Industrial Recovery Act (NIRA), to Congress on May 15.

It was one of the most pretentious pieces of legislation ever presented to Congress to that time. Its objectives were to end cutthroat competition, raise prices to a profitable level by limiting production to actual needs, and guarantee a reasonable work week and a living wage to labor. These aims would be accomplished through the adoption of codes for all branches of industry and business by committees representing management, labor, and the public. In the event of irreconcilable disagreement, the president might intervene and impose a code of his own making. Section 7a of the bill—added, incidentally, at the demand of Secretary Perkins and William Green, president of the AF of L—affirmed labor's right to organize and bargain collectively. All these provisions were included in Title I of the measure. Title II, which appropriated $3.3 billion for a public works program, was incorporated in the measure at the last minute.

The two houses held slipshod hearings and debates on the bill for several weeks. A few senators were skeptical; but business, labor, and the administration united in a solid front, and Congress willingly concurred. Roosevelt signed, as he called it, "the most important and far-reaching legislation ever enacted by the American Congress" on June 16, 1933. On the same day he established the National Recovery Administration (NRA) and named Hugh S. Johnson as administrator.

Johnson plunged into work with great energy and bustle. To provide for the interim period before specific codes could be drawn up, he proposed adoption of a blanket code. Almost 2.5 million employers with 16 million workers had signed the blanket code within a few weeks. The NRA was on its way. Now began the laborious task of preparing individual codes to fit the needs of every industry and trade in the United States. Theoretically the code-making process involved mutualization of the interests of management, labor, and the consuming public. In actual practice it was the trade associations, dominated usually by their large members, that wrote the codes in the first instance. After hasty reviews by the Code Analysis Division and various advisory boards, these codes were adopted as bodies of law governing the industries or trades involved.

From October 1933 to early 1935, when the code-making process was completed, the NRA approved 557 basic codes and 208 supplementary codes. All of them contained provisions confirming labor's right to organize and establishing minimum wage and maximum hours scales. But business leaders, in making these concessions, obtained far-reaching benefits from the government: price stabilization,[12] production controls,[13] and out-

[12] Although the NRA tried to discourage outright price-fixing, the bituminous coal, petroleum, and lumber codes contained schedules of minimum prices; most of the codes forbade sales below cost; and over half the codes required establishment of the open-price system, that is, a system of prices openly published and adhered to.

[13] Production control was achieved in various ways in the codes. The petroleum, copper, and lumber codes, for example, set definite production limits and assigned quotas to individual producers. The cotton textile code limited mills to two eight-hour shifts daily. Other codes forbade the expansion of plant without approval of the code authority.

lawry of allegedly unfair competition. More important, business leaders won the right to govern themselves, for each code was administered by a code authority, almost invariably composed of trade association officials representing the large corporations. Finally, businessmen won another long-sought objective—exemption from antitrust prosecution for restrictive practices heretofore deemed illegal by the courts.

In the beginning this "self-regulation" of industry went smoothly on the surface, so long as the NRA gave free rein to businessmen. By the spring of 1934, however, Johnson had assembled his own staff of experts to run the NRA. They soon discovered the obvious fact that the codes discriminated against small producers, especially in pricing and sales policies. But the codes were already written and in force. All that the NRA staff could do was to try to compel code authorities to implement the broad objectives of the NIRA. This effort brought the NRA into increasingly frequent and bitter conflict with business leaders. As if to compound the NRA's perplexities, the inchoate opposition of small businessmen and manufacturers to codes written and administered by big business swelled into a mighty storm of protest in the early months of 1934. Actually, there is little evidence that small businessmen were much injured by the codes; they objected mainly to the provisions for minimum wages and prevention of sharp practices. To palliate this discontent, Roosevelt on February 19 appointed a National Recovery Review Board, headed by the famed criminal lawyer, Clarence Darrow, to investigate and recommend. Darrow, instead of trying to evaluate impartially, dealt with the NRA as if he were the prosecutor in a murder trial.

The fortunes of the NRA fell hard and fast after Darrow's pillorying. In the face of mounting criticism the president asked Johnson to resign, abolished the office of National Recovery Administrator, and, on September 27, 1934, created a National Recovery Board composed of representatives of management, labor, and the public. Any overhauling of the codes themselves, however, had to await congressional action, as the NIRA's life of two years would soon expire. The Supreme Court ended the discussion before Congress could respond to the president's request for extension of the NIRA by declaring the measure unconstitutional on May 25, 1935.

Economists and historians agree that although the NRA brought substantial benefits to workers (discussed in the following section), it failed to achieve many of the objectives of the act that gave it birth. In the final analysis the NRA failed because it was based upon false assumptions about human nature and the American economy. The framers of the NIRA assumed, for example, that businessmen would use self-regulation to promote the general interest. As any serious student of human nature could have predicted, businessmen used the NRA for other purposes, and they fought the NRA when they could not control it. Secondly, the NIRA was based upon the assumption that full production and employment could be achieved by outlawing price competition and either limiting or discouraging full production. Here was the basic contradiction and the most egregious error. What the United States needed in 1933 was new investment and a massive increase in production. Because the NRA discouraged both prerequisites of prosperity it dampened the recovery already under way. Finally, the NIRA failed because it attempted to achieve something like a planned economy without conferring any powers necessary to attain this objective. It gave no power to the NRA, for example, either to determine desirable production goals for the entire economy or to compel manufacturers to meet them. Looking back, old brain trusters like Tugwell have said that the NIRA might have been the first step toward development of rational economic planning. Perhaps hindsight has brought the wisdom that administration leaders seemed to lack at an earlier time.

7. Relief, Labor, and the First New Deal, 1933–1934

In no area of federal action was the basically emergency character of the first New Deal more fully revealed than in the matter of relief policies. So long as Roosevelt's original advisers had the president's ear, the administration rejected long-range comprehensive plans and followed Hoover's policies of public works and indirect relief through the cities and states.

From the outset, however, Roosevelt was more responsive to the needs of the millions in distress than Hoover had been. For example, Roosevelt personally devised a new plan to save both human and natural resources— the Civilian Conservation Corps (CCC), authorized by Congress in late March and put into operation on April 5, 1933. The CCC, with an initial grant of $300 million, enrolled 250,000 young men from relief families[14] in some 1,500 camps. They worked under the direction of the War Department at reforestation, flood control, and soil conservation. The CCC had reached a maximum strength of 500,000 by 1935. More than 2.75 million youths had served in the corps when the project was ended in 1942.

The administration's primary concern in the spring of 1933 was the plight of the millions of unemployed and the survival of the nearly 6 million persons on city and state relief rolls. In response to the president's appeal, Congress approved the Federal Emergency Relief Act, signed on May 12, 1933. It appropriated $500 million, one-half of it to be given outright to impoverished states and the balance to other states on a basis of one federal dollar for every three dollars spent by states and municipalities. Creating the Federal Emergency Relief Administration (FERA), Roosevelt appointed Harry L. Hopkins, chairman of the New York Temporary Emergency Relief Administration, as administrator.

Actually, Roosevelt regarded these measures as stopgaps to keep people

---

[14]Men between the ages of eighteen and twenty-five, who were in need and who were capable of performing hard labor, were eligible. They received subsistence and $30 a month, $25 of which was sent to their families.

from starving until recovery had set in. The administration's ace in the hole was a gigantic public works program to be launched with the NRA to stimulate depressed industries, mainly construction, not immediately affected by the main recovery program. Title II of the NIRA, which established the Public Works Administration (PWA) and appropriated $3.3 billion for the program, gave specific authorization.

The effect might have been invigorating had this huge sum been poured immediately into the economy. As it turned out, the president unwittingly prevented any such result. Fearing that Johnson was too unstable to spend the money wisely, the president separated the PWA from the NRA and gave control of the PWA to Secretary of the Interior Ickes. He was a cautious, honest man, determined that not one cent of the $3.3 billion should be stolen or wasted. Thus he insisted upon scrutinizing the details of all projects. His loving care bore fruit eventually in the form of new highways, hospitals, university buildings, municipal water works, and the like. But it prevented the PWA from being a great spur to recovery in 1933. Thus the president faced a critical situation in September of that year. The false boom of the spring and summer had ended; the PWA was mired in red tape; and millions of families faced the coming winter with no hope of employment.

It was during this crisis that Harry Hopkins first had decisive influence in the administration. He saw the president on about November 1 and urged him to launch a vast new program of work relief—a kind of primitive public works on a direct basis—for 4 million of the unemployed. Readily concurring, Roosevelt created the Civil Works Administration (CWA) on November 8, appointed Hopkins as administrator, and took $400 million from PWA funds to get the program under way. Within thirty days the CWA was a thriving concern and a means of living for 4 million men and their families.

It seemed for a time that Roosevelt's approval of the CWA signified capitulation to what were then considered to be radical doctrines—that it was the federal government's duty to provide work if private industry did not. Then, in response to the advice of conservative Democrats and bitter Republican criticism of waste, Roosevelt told Hopkins in mid-January 1934 that he would have to end the CWA. Hopkins obtained an additional $450 million from Congress in February to carry the agency through the winter, but he liquidated his CWA projects in March and April. The burden of relief for the balance of 1934, therefore, fell again on the FERA, for which Hopkins had obtained an additional $500 million from Congress on February 15.

An experimental approach and indecision over general objectives also characterized the first New Deal's labor program. Administration leaders sincerely wanted to help labor, and they succeeded to some degree. To begin with, incorporation of labor provisions in all NRA codes won immediate gains that organized labor in its then weakened position could not have won on its own. The forty-hour week was established by codes covering 13 million workers, while the average work week for all industries fell from 43.3 hours in June 1933 to 37.8 hours in the following October. All codes, moreover, contained provisions outlawing child labor and establishing minimum wages, ranging generally from 30 to 40 cents an hour. Finally, adoption of the codes helped to stimulate a decrease in unemployment from 24.9 percent of the total labor force in 1933 to 20.1 percent in 1935 and an increase in average weekly earnings in manufacturing from $16.73 in 1933 to $20.13 in 1935.

More important to labor in the long run was Section 7a of the Recovery Act. It asserted that workers should have the right to organize and bargain collectively "through representatives of their own choosing." The act also outlawed the yellow-dog contract and declared that workers should not be required to join a company union as a condition of employment. Experience soon demonstrated that Section 7a was more an affirmation than a grant of essential protection. Nonetheless, it marked an epochal turning point: for the first time the federal government endorsed organized labor's historic objectives in general legislation.

Under the aegis of Section 7a, the AF of L roused with new hope and vigor. AF of L membership increased from 2,127,000 to 3,045,000 between 1933 and 1935, while membership in all unions grew from 2,857,-000 to 3,728,000. It was substantial growth. A minority of employers, particularly in the building trades and the coal and garment industries, tried faithfully to honor Section 7a. For the most part, however, management was as determined as ever to prevent unionization, and employers by the thousands defied the NRA in labor disputes and harassed it by frequent appeals to the courts. More important, employers somewhat frantically organized company unions as a foil to independent unionism. Some 2,500,000 workers were organized in company unions by 1935.

Labor's striving and management's continued determination to preserve the open shop inevitably collided; and a wave of bloody strikes followed adoption of the NRA codes. To help bring peace to the industrial world, the president, on August 5, 1933, established a mediation commission to cooperate with the NRA—the National Labor Board, composed of distinguished labor leaders and industrialists, with Senator Robert F. Wagner of New York as chairman.

The National Labor Board settled many disputes during the ensuing year by common sense, persuasion, and an ability to find a compromise. More important was the fact that a group of public leaders studied, for the first time since 1915, the whole problem of industrial relations and discovered the full extent of management's opposition to the very principle of collective bargaining. They also learned that many employers would use almost any method, including the use of labor spies and force, to prevent unionization.

The experience convinced Senator Wagner that the movement for unionization could never succeed until the federal government came strongly to labor's support. When an employer refused to recognize a union or to bargain in good faith, for example, there was nothing that the National Labor Board could do but appeal to the NRA and the courts for uncertain redress. Following a wave of strikes in the spring of 1934, the president abolished the National Labor Board and established the National Labor Relations Board, a three-man commission empowered to hold elections to determine the right of unions to conduct collective bargaining. Wagner vainly tried to persuade the president and Congress to give the new board authority to prevent so-called unfair practices by management. Lacking such authority, the National Labor Relations Board was even less successful in settling disputes than its predecessor had been.

The first New Deal's labor policies in part represented the fulfillment of the most advanced objectives of the social justice program—abolition of child labor, minimum wages, and maximum hours. Long overdue though they were, these reforms were not enough. In the final analysis, industrial democracy could be achieved only by the workers themselves, not by a beneficent government. In refusing to give the protection and positive support that organized labor needed for the full success of its movement, the president acted in the spirit of compromise that permeated the first New Deal.

8. Toward Agricultural Stability, 1933-1935

Farmers everywhere were on the verge either of despair or rebellion by the spring of 1933, but in no section was agrarian discontent so intense and dangerous as in the corn belt of the Middle West. The farmers' most immediate concern was the threat of foreclosure. Farm owners everywhere in the Middle West banded together to save their farms, either by direct action or through their state governments. The legislature of Minnesota enacted a two-year moratorium on foreclosures; the governor of North Dakota forbade forced sales of farm properties. Vigilante committees threatened to shoot bank or insurance agents and went en masse to foreclosure sales and bought back properties for nominal sums. The most famous outbreak occurred at Le Mars, Iowa, when some 600 enraged farmers dragged a foreclosing judge from his bench and beat him into unconsciousness on April 27, 1933.

The Roosevelt administration acted quickly in this crisis to save the farmers and avert the likelihood of even more violent revolt. The president consolidated all federal agricultural credit agencies into the Farm Credit Administration on March 27, 1933; Congress provided abundant new credit shortly afterward.[15] Moreover, Congress in response to radical

[15]The Emergency Farm Mortgage Act of May 12, 1933, for example, authorized emergency loans to save farmers in immediate peril. Within less than two years the Farm Credit Administration had refinanced one-fifth of all farm mortgages in the United States.

farm demands adopted the Frazier-Lemke Farm Bankruptcy Act on June 28, 1934; it enabled farmers to recover lost property on easy terms.

These, however, were all stopgaps. The major need was a long-range program for agricultural recovery. Here the difficulty lay not in originating measures but in persuading agricultural spokesmen to unite upon a common plan. Secretary of Agriculture Henry A. Wallace began a series of conferences with farm leaders on March 6, 1933. The outcome was the Agricultural Adjustment Act, approved by Congress on May 10, 1933, and signed by the president two days later. It was easily the most ambitious agricultural legislation in the history of the country, but all its major features had long been discussed and advocated by important farm groups. The framers of the act announced their objectives in clear language: to establish and maintain such a balance between production and consumption of agricultural commodities that farm income would have the same relative purchasing power that it had enjoyed during the stable parity period from 1909 to 1914. To achieve so-called parity prices, the act authorized the imposition of various production controls[16] on major staples. The money to finance the program would come from taxes on the processing of agricultural commodities and customs duties on certain enumerated commodities.

While farm leaders and administration spokesmen were agreeing upon what was called the domestic allotment plan, the Agriculture Department received frightening reports of bountiful crops for the coming summer and autumn of 1933. In response, Wallace and George N. Peek, the new head of the Agricultural Adjustment Administration (AAA), sent agents through the South and Southwest to persuade farmers to plow under 10 million acres, or one-fourth, of the cotton crop in return for benefit payments. The AAA in addition bought 220,000 sows and over 6 million pigs for immediate slaughter. A similar destruction of part of the wheat crop was averted only by weather reports indicating that there would be drastic natural reductions in that staple.

Cotton farmers plowed under with a vengeance, but they fertilized the remaining crop so heavily that total output in 1933 was 13,047,000 bales, as compared with 13,002,000 bales in 1932. In the following year, therefore, Congress adopted the Bankhead Cotton Control Act, approved April 21, 1934. It permitted the AAA to assign marketing quotas and imposed a prohibitive tax on cotton sold in excess of the quotas.[17] Cotton production fell in consequence to 9,636,000 bales in 1934, and to 10,638,000 bales in 1935.

The AAA meanwhile used its vast powers in other ways to restrict production and restore prices. After the "plow under" and the slaughter

---

[16] Among these controls were benefit payments for voluntary crop reduction, commodity loans to farmers who cooperated, marketing agreements and quotas, export subsidies, and purchase of surpluses by the Department of Agriculture.

[17] The Kerr-Smith Tobacco Control Act, also approved in 1934, gave the AAA similar powers of control over tobacco growers.

of the pigs, the AAA set production goals for 1934 in the major staples and sent out 100,000 agents to persuade farmers to sign contracts. In addition, the AAA established the Commodity Credit Corporation on October 18 to enable cotton and corn producers to borrow against their crops and hold them until prices rose to higher levels.

The AAA worked almost an economic miracle through these and other measures until the Supreme Court called a halt in January 1936. In the case of cotton and tobacco, the effects of the AAA program were direct and calculable. Cotton production, for example, was cut one-third during the period 1933-1935; had controls and price supports not been in effect the price of cotton would not have risen much above the depression level. The effects of the AAA program on corn, wheat, and livestock are more difficult to calculate, but it seems likely that the droughts of 1933 and 1934 caused vastly greater reductions than could ever have been accomplished by crop controls. It was as if nature cooperated with the AAA to end for a time the problem of uncontrollable surpluses in the basic food commodities.

Whatever the cause, farmers were well on the way toward stability and parity by the end of 1935. Net farm income rose from $1,928,000,000 in 1932 to $4,605,000,000 in 1935, with startling results. For one thing, the ratio of farm prices to prices that the farmer paid for manufactured goods rose from 58 in 1932 to 88 in 1935.[18] For another, moderate prosperity and increased governmental credit enabled farmers not only to hold their own in the battle against bankruptcy but even to turn the tide for the first time since 1920—by reducing the farm mortgage load from $9,630,768,000 in 1930 to $7,584,459,000 in 1935. On the other hand, the benefits of the farm program went mainly to commercial farmers, not to the great majority of subsistence farmers, and only rarely did it go to tenant farmers and sharecroppers and tenants. In the South, for example, the effect of large reductions in cotton acreage was to throw about 300,000 black and white sharecroppers out of work.

In the long run, however, the economic results of the first AAA program were not as significant as its political implications. Representatives of the urban majority in Congress, acting on the assumption that a bankrupt agriculture could mean only an impoverished economy, converted agriculture into a subsidized industry by taxing consumers and diverting a portion of the national income to the farming minority. To be sure, the organized farmers who benefited most from the AAA program were a powerful pressure group who were almost able to impose demands on the two parties. Even so, the first AAA stemmed as much from genuine progressive convictions concerning government's duty toward submerged groups as from considerations of political advantage.

[18]One hundred equals the ratio prevailing during the parity period 1909-1914.

17

The Second New Deal: The Culmination of American Progressivism

The first New Deal coalition of businessmen, workers, and farmers came apart at the seams in the spring and summer of 1934. A large part of the business and industrial leadership came out against the administration's program, while the masses of voters—workers, farmers, and those who were unemployed—rallied more overwhelmingly to Roosevelt's support in the congressional election of 1934 than they had done two years before. Roosevelt had neither foreseen nor desired the realignment in American politics that occurred as the nation divided roughly into a Right and a Left during the last months of 1934 and early 1935. Yet the realignment occurred, and spokesmen of labor, the unemployed and destitute, and the aged were beginning campaigns to commit the federal government to new and often absurd schemes. Indeed, it was evident by January 1935 that the administration would have to undertake measures to allay the forces of discontent or else run serious risk of being overwhelmed by those forces.

Roosevelt moved with remarkable agility to construct a new coalition and program in order to bring the political situation under his control. Gradually discarding conservative advisers, he gathered a new retinue of rasher friends and espoused a program designed to ameliorate the misfortunes of the masses through deficit spending, redistribution of wealth, and the most far-reaching program of social and economic legislation in American history. This was the second New Deal, the full flowering of social justice progressivism.

This shift was certainly leftward in one sense. The first New Deal was grounded in large measure upon technocratic assumptions about the possibilities of national planning through the NRA, among other agencies. The effort collapsed both in constitutional theory and in practice. The second New Deal, for all its concern for legislation to help disadvantaged groups, was based at least in practice upon the assumption that competition was still the life of trade, and that it was government's main duty to regulate in order to prevent the imposition of shackles upon private economic energies.

Actually, it is extremely risky to try to fit either the first or second New Deal in any Procrustean bed of ideology. The NIRA in one sense marked a radical departure from the main traditions in American political economy. Yet it represented the triumph of a movement for self-regulation in the business community itself that was at least as old as the second administration of Theodore Roosevelt. Whatever radical departures it might have implied were more than offset by the first New Deal's conservative reinforcement of the financial sector, even though this effort also brought final satisfaction of the old progressive demand for popular control over banks and the money supply.

It seems safest to conclude in retrospect that both the first New Deal and the second New Deal moved inexorably toward fulfillment of the main historic objectives of the American progressive movement. There were deviations like the NIRA, to be sure, but they did not survive for long. Much of the first New Deal did survive: financial reform and restructuring, expanded federal relief activity, the Tennessee Valley Authority's experiment in regional planning (to be discussed in the next chapter), the federal agricultural program launched in 1933 and later overhauled, and an inchoate policy of support of labor, among other things. To this foundation the second New Deal added a vast new structure of advanced legislation and policies, as we will soon see. It is somewhat far-fetched to say that this culmination marked any important deviation from main traditions. Every single important policy of both the first and second New Deals had deep roots in the progressive tradition.

1. Launching the Second New Deal

The normally conservative middle and upper classes began to judge the first New Deal by conventional standards and to turn receptive ears toward its critics once the worst phase of the depression was over in 1934.

The developments that turned the business classes decisively against the administration stemmed mainly from the NRA. On the one hand, small businessmen rebelled against codes that favored big business. On the other hand, when the NRA tried to bring the code authorities under some measure of public control, the great industrial leaders turned sharply against the administration. Moreover, practically all manufacturers, large and small, resisted when the National Labor Board endeavored to implement Section 7a of the NIRA.

The conservative revolt took shape with the formation in August 1934 of the American Liberty League. Its voices were those of conservative lawyers and Democratic politicians led by Alfred E. Smith and John W. Davis, but its financial support came from certain big business interests, notably the Du Pont family. It opposed New Deal bureaucracy and capricious presidential tyranny and championed state rights, "free enterprise," and the "American" system of the open shop. In their zeal to turn back the tide of progressivism, Liberty Leaguers entered the congressional campaign of 1934 to help elect conservatives of both parties.

Roosevelt viewed this revolt of the business community at first as the opposition of a small minority. Much more disturbing to him and his political advisers was the rising tide of opposition to the first New Deal program from disgruntled reformers and demagogues. The frightening thing was the fact that the New Deal had obviously failed to bring hope to sharecroppers, tenant and subsistence farmers, the millions still unemployed, and especially indigent old people. These lower-class elements seemed ready in their desperation to follow any crackpot with a plan.

One of these was the generous Dr. Francis E. Townsend of Long Beach, California, and his creation, the so-called Townsend Plan. Townsend proposed that the federal government pay $200 monthly to all unemployed persons over sixty. The proposal spread like wildfire among the destitute aged; there were thousands of Old Age Revolving Pension, or Townsend, clubs by 1935, and the good doctor claimed 5 million followers.

More disquieting to the administration were movements being promoted from 1933 to 1935 by the Reverend Charles E. Coughlin and Senator Huey Pierce Long. Coughlin was a Roman Catholic priest in a Detroit suburb who fell to discussing politics and economic issues in radio sermons around 1930. His animadversions against bankers and Republican leaders were soon more popular than his religious messages. Advocating a program of far-reaching socialization of industry and credit, Coughlin at first supported the New Deal. However, he soon fell out with Roosevelt over monetary policies and turned his National Union for Social Justice against the New Deal in 1935. Coughlin claimed 9 million followers—an absurdly exaggerated estimate—at the height of his influence.

Huey P. Long was a much more dangerous menace. He was not a mere demagogue of the anti-Negro, anti-Catholic type. Rising out of the piney woods section of northern Louisiana, he won a reputation in the early 1920s because he addressed himself realistically to the needs of the lower classes. Elected governor of Louisiana in 1928, Long redeemed his promises to the common people. Elected to the United States Senate in 1930, he continued to dominate the government of his state as completely as if he had remained at Baton Rouge. So powerful was his hold over the lower classes that he established a virtual dictatorship in 1934–1935 and could declare, "I am the law." He was the idol of the common people of Louisiana when an assassin's bullet cut short his career on September 8, 1935.

Long's significance on the national scene lay chiefly in the fact that he was the chief agitator of lower-class protest against the first New Deal compromise. Long, like Coughlin, was an ardent Roosevelt supporter in 1932. But the Louisianan turned savagely against the administration and set out to win control of the Democratic party when Roosevelt refused to nationalize banks, expropriate wealth, and knuckle under to Long's patronage demands in 1933. Organizing the Share Our Wealth Society in that same year, Long promised to make every man a king. His methods were simple enough. He would give every family a homestead worth $5,000 and an annual income of $2,500, and he would confiscate large fortunes to provide this bounty to the poor.[1]

President Roosevelt in late 1934 and early 1935 launched a program frankly designed to provide larger security and incomes for the masses. This sudden leftward shift, if such it may be called, was one of the really significant turning points in twentieth-century American politics. It occurred not because the president "planned it that way," but in response to the developments just discussed. In these circumstances Roosevelt converted challenge into opportunity. First, he accepted leadership of the new progressive coalition of farmers, workers, the lower middle classes, and the unemployed that came into existence during the congressional campaign of 1934. Second, he reconstituted his program to satisfy the basic aspirations of these various groups.

The catalyst was the election of a Congress eager to implement a comprehensive reform program in November 1934. As the election results were in part interpreted as an emphatic mandate for a work relief program, the prestige of Harry L. Hopkins, the chief advocate of the program, increased enormously. "Boys—this is our hour," Hopkins told his friends in the FERA soon after the election. "We've got to get everything we want—a works program, social security, wages and hours, everything—now or never." Hopkins joined Roosevelt soon after Thanksgiving at Warm Springs, Georgia, and apparently won his approval for "everything." Then the president launched the second New Deal in his Annual Message to Congress on January 4, 1935. Dismissing the achievements of

---

[1] A survey published by *Fortune* magazine in July 1935 revealed the extent to which Long's attack on the wealthy reflected widespread popular opinion. When asked whether they believed that the government should permit a man who had investments worth more than $1 million to keep them, "subject only to present taxes," 45.8 percent of the persons polled replied in the negative. In the Middle West 54.6 percent and on the Pacific Coast 54 percent replied in the negative.

the past two years, he declared that the mandate of the people in the recent election was clear: the time had come to fulfill a bold new social mission and to subordinate profits and wealth to the general good. This he proposed to accomplish, first, by ending the dole; second, by putting the 3.5 million able-bodied persons on relief rolls to work in new programs of slum clearance, rural housing, rural electrification, and expanded public works; and, third, by inaugurating a comprehensive social security program to reduce the hazards of unemployment and old age.

2. The WPA: The Second New Deal as the American Social Conscience

Advanced progressives hailed the president's full-fledged conversion to the cause of social justice, while Congress for the most part responded eagerly to the administration's suggestions from 1935 to 1937. The outcome of this converging of reform impulses was the enactment of legislation that marked the full flowering of the humanitarian-progressive movement and the construction of at least the framework of the welfare state.

The first item—the work relief program—was authorized by Congress and the president on April 8, 1935, with the adoption and signing of the Emergency Relief Appropriation Act, providing nearly $5 billion for the fiscal year 1935–1936. It was launched by the president on May 6, 1935, with the establishment of the Works Progress Administration (WPA) and allied agencies. Hopkins was appointed WPA administrator and directed to transfer unemployables and indigent persons to local relief rolls. More important, he was authorized to begin small work projects designed to put as many as 5 million jobless men and women to work.

Actually the number of workers on WPA rolls never reached this large figure. The average monthly number from 1935 to 1941 was 2,112,000, and the peak of WPA employment was 3,238,000 in November 1938. The agency, along with cooperating sponsors, spent $11,365,000,000 on some 250,000 projects. Seventy-eight percent of WPA money went for public construction and conservation. The balance was expended for a variety of community projects which, on the theory that professional people also had to eat, enrolled musicians, actors, writers, artists, and even historians.

In addition, Hopkins and his colleagues used their broad authority in ambitious experiments that well exemplified the humanitarian impulses of the second New Deal. The first of these new agencies of social reform, funded by money taken from the Emergency Relief appropriation, was the Resettlement Administration (RA), which the president established as an independent agency under Tugwell in the Department of Agriculture on

May 1, 1935.[2] Secondly, the president established the Rural Electrification Administration (REA) on May 11, 1935, to provide loans and WPA labor for extension of power lines into rural areas not served by private companies. The REA made such a successful beginning that its authority and resources were greatly expanded in 1937. Thirdly, the administration embarked upon a long-range program to benefit young people with the establishment of the National Youth Administration (NYA) in the WPA on June 26, 1935, and with a doubling of appropriations for the Civilian Conservation Corps. Under the NYA some 750,000 high school, college, and graduate students were earning from $5 to $30 a month by 1939–1940 as typists, laboratory and library assistants, tutors, and the like.

All these developments were signs of the rise of Harry Hopkins's star, of the triumph of the social worker over the businessman, in the Roosevelt inner circle. Believing that it was government's duty to provide jobs if private industry could not,[3] Hopkins regarded the WPA not as a stopgap but as a means of fulfilling society's obligations to its citizens. Roosevelt's approval of the work relief concept also committed the administration to a program of pump-priming by deficit spending on a huge scale. Although

THE NATIONAL DEBT
1910–1960

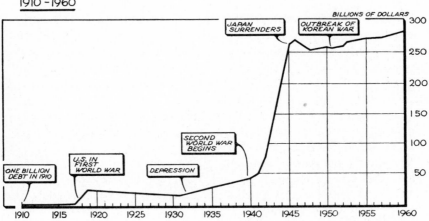

[2]The RA during its two years of independent existence purchased 5 million acres of submarginal land and resettled 4,441 families on farms and in thirty-one homestead communities. In addition, it built three so-called Greenbelt towns, experiments in planned suburban communities for low-income city workers, near Washington, Cincinnati, and Milwaukee.

[3]Contemporary surveys of public opinion indicated that an overwhelming majority of Americans at the time shared Hopkins's conviction. In a *Fortune* poll in July 1935, for example, 76.8 percent of all persons queried agreed that "government should see to it that every man who wants to work has a job." Even 46.6 percent of the prosperous and 69 percent of the upper middle-class persons replied in the affirmative.

Congress increased income and estate taxes in 1935, the administration did not attempt to redistribute the national income through drastic tax increases but financed the WPA program mainly through borrowing.[4]

The WPA's accomplishments were substantial, and to progressives they far outweighed the costs. From the social point of view, the WPA greatly relieved the discontent of the millions of persons formerly on the dole. Considered in sheerly economic terms, WPA expenditures contributed importantly to substantial progress toward recovery between 1935 and 1940. Politically, the WPA helped fasten the control of the Democratic party on the country, although not usually in the manner that Republicans alleged. To be sure, local politicians used WPA staffs and funds, and their activities became so flagrant during the congressional and senatorial campaign of 1938 that Congress intervened the following year to put an end to them.[5] The chief political significance of the WPA, however, was the fact that workers on WPA rolls and their families rarely voted against an administration that had befriended them.

3. Expanding the Second New Deal, 1935–1936

For all its immediate and long-run significance, the work relief program was the most ephemeral phase of the second New Deal. Other measures adopted at the high tide of progressivism more permanently altered American social and economic institutions.

The first was the Social Security bill, prepared in 1934 by a nonpartisan Committee on Economic Security and presented to Congress in January 1935. Congress approved the measure with only minor amendments, and the president signed it on August 14, 1935. "If the Senate and the House of Representatives in this long and arduous session had done nothing more than pass this Bill," he told a happy assemblage at the White House as he signed it, "the session would be regarded as historic for all time."

For old people the Social Security Act provided two kinds of assistance. First, the federal government offered to share equally with the states the burden of caring for persons over sixty-five who would have no opportuni-

[4]The Hoover administration operated at a total deficit of $3,844,010,531 during 1931 and 1932; the Roosevelt administration accumulated a total deficit of $25,279,670,735 from 1933 through 1940. The gross national debt increased from $16,931,000,000 in 1929 to $19,487,000,000 in 1932, and to $42,967,000,000 in 1940.

[5]This was accomplished with the passage of the Hatch Act, forbidding federal office-holders below the policy-making level from participating actively in political campaigns or soliciting or accepting contributions from WPA workers.

ty to participate in the new old-age insurance program.[6] Second, the act established a nationwide system of old-age insurance, participation in which was compulsory except for public servants, domestic servants, farm and casual workers, merchant seamen, and employees of educational, religious, and philanthropic institutions.[7] Benefit payments ranging from $10 to $85 a month would begin in 1942.

The Social Security Act nominally left the establishment of unemployment insurance systems to the states but actually gave state governments no alternative but to cooperate. It imposed on employers an unemployment tax beginning at 1 percent of all payrolls in 1936 and rising to a permanent level of 3 percent after 1937. However, employers might pay 90 percent of the tax to approved state unemployment compensation commissions; and most of the balance paid directly into the federal Treasury would be returned to the states to finance the administration of their systems. On the other hand, states that failed to establish unemployment compensation systems would lose all the taxes paid by employers within their jurisdiction. Needless to say, all states had complied within two years and provided a schedule of benefits that met minimum federal standards and afforded protection for some 28 million workers.[8]

Finally, the measure offered federal aid to the states on a matching basis for the care of the crippled, the blind, and dependent mothers and children, and for public health services. It also established a nonpartisan Social Security Board to administer the entire system.

Roosevelt and the authors of the Social Security Act knew that the measure was experimental and inadequate; they were also confident that the system would be strengthened and enlarged with the passage of time.[9] Of all the New Deal measures, the Social Security Act was indubitably one of the most important. Between 1935 and 1939, when the system was

[6]The federal contribution was limited to $15 monthly per person but was increased to $20 in 1939. Some 2 million persons were receiving assistance under this provision by 1940, and combined federal and state payments averaged $20 a month per person.

[7]Employees and employers were required to pay at the rate of 1 percent each on all wages under $3,000 a year from 1937 through 1939; 1½ percent each from 1940 through 1942; 2 percent each from 1943 through 1945; 2½ percent each from 1946 through 1948; and 3 percent each after 1948. The measure contemplated the accumulation of a reserve fund invested in government bonds, which would total some $47 billion by 1980 and make the system self-sustaining.

[8]Unemployment benefits varied in different states and sections. Maximum weekly payments ran $15-$18 a week, while duration of payments ranged from twelve to twenty-six weeks in any single year.

[9]This, of course, did occur. In response to widespread criticisms, congressional leaders and the Social Security Board undertook a study in 1937 looking toward revision of the Social Security Act. The upshot was legislation in 1939 completely overhauling the old-age retirement program by (1) extending the act's coverage to include 1.6 million additional workers, (2) advancing the date of the beginning of retirement benefits from 1942 to 1940, (3) increasing monthly payments to persons who had been insured for a short time, (4) providing benefits for wives and dependent children of retired workers, as well as survivors' benefits for widows and dependent children when insured workers died before reaching sixty-five, and (5) continuing the old-age payroll tax of 1 percent each on workers and employers until 1943. For further changes, see *passim* in vol. II.

launched and strengthened, the administration and Congress effected a lasting revolution in American public policy. Discarding ingrained traditions of self-help and individual responsibility, they set the United States upon the high road leading to the welfare state.

The question of new labor legislation also arose during the early months of 1935, but there was no such unanimity of administration and congressional opinion regarding wise labor policy as had prevailed during the drafting of the Social Security bill. Senator Robert F. Wagner was working almost single-handedly in Congress for passage of his labor disputes bill to give unions federal protection. But the president opposed the measure, saying that he preferred to obtain protection for labor through renewal of the NIRA.

The Senate under administration pressure voted to renew the NIRA. Then it approved the Wagner bill on May 16, 1935. There seemed to be a strong possibility of a presidential veto if the House approved the measure. Less than two weeks later the Supreme Court declared the code system of the NIRA unconstitutional. In response, the president reversed himself on the Wagner bill (actually, he had indicated on May 24 that he favored it), persuaded House leaders to bring it to the floor, and signed the measure on July 5 after speedy approval by the House of Representatives.

The Wagner, or National Labor Relations, Act reaffirmed the principles set forth in the now defunct Section 7a. But the Wagner Act was specific and strong where Section 7a had been vague and weak. By making the organization of company unions virtually impossible and outlawing so-called unfair practices,[10] it deprived employers of their most formidable antiunion weapons. By establishing a nonpartisan National Labor Relations Board (NLRB) empowered to issue cease and desist orders and compel obedience from employers, the act provided machinery for its own enforcement. Finally, by setting forth the explicit conditions under which unions should be entitled to recognition,[11] it threw the power of the federal government behind a union seeking to compel an employer to bargain in good faith. Coming at a time when the advance guard of the AF of L was making plans to organize the basic industries, the Wagner Act and the NLRB straightaway became the charter of liberty and shield of the American labor movement.

Work relief, Social Security, and legislation to reinforce the labor movement were only the beginning of a new program designed to increase and strengthen public control over business and industry and benefit the masses of people. The fact that the Supreme Court invalidated the NIRA

[10]For example, the act outlawed interference with employees in the exercise of guaranteed rights, discharge or blacklisting of employees for union activities, and discrimination against employees who brought charges against the company.

[11]A union was entitled to recognition by the employer as the sole bargaining agent when it won—usually in a secret election conducted by the NLRB—majority support among workers in an industry, company, shop, or craft.

just at the moment when the president and his advisers were formulating these new measures meant that they could decide what features of the NRA experiment were worth salvaging. Earlier, after the Supreme Court had invalidated Section 9c of the NIRA, which established special controls for the oil industry, the president in February 1935 had approved the Connally Act prohibiting shipment in interstate commerce of oil produced in violation of interstate compacts. With adoption of the Guffey-Snyder Coal Conservation Act in August 1935, the administration salvaged the bituminous coal code and reestablished the NRA coal code authority in a different form.[12] Refusing to approve a general wages and hours bill on the ground that such a measure was probably unconstitutional, Roosevelt instead supported and signed the Walsh-Healey Act on August 30, 1936. It attempted indirectly to establish fair labor standards for manufacturing and the construction industry.[13] Other measures preserved the sections of the NRA codes prohibiting destructive price competition and reenacted the NRA liquor code.

To these measures for regulation were added other more important substantive reforms during 1935 and 1936. We have seen how the Banking Act of 1935 established comprehensive federal control over the Federal Reserve system and how the president obtained destruction of the public utility giants and strict federal control of the smaller holding companies. The Federal Power Act of 1935 enlarged the jurisdiction and rate-making authority of the Federal Power Commission. The Motor Carrier Act of 1935 and the Transportation Act of 1940 brought trucking concerns and domestic water carriers under the regulation of the ICC. The Merchant Marine Act of 1936 created a new Maritime Commission and authorized it to help create an American merchant marine. And the Civil Aeronautics Act of 1938 established a Civil Aeronautics Authority, later called the Civil Aeronautics Board, to regulate the operation and services of airlines.

These were all nonpartisan measures of reform and regulation, and, except for the Holding Company Act, they excited little opposition. More indicative of the second New Deal's social and economic purposes was Roosevelt's campaign in 1935 to democratize the federal tax structure. Roosevelt replied to his critics on the Left on June 19, 1935, by calling

[12]This measure established a National Bituminous Coal Commission composed of representatives of management, labor, and the public; it was empowered to control production and prices of the raw material. The act, moreover, guaranteed collective bargaining in the coal industry and stipulated that when wages and hours agreements were signed by the miners' union and producers of two-thirds of the national tonnage, such agreements should go into effect in the entire industry. The Supreme Court declared the Guffey-Snyder Act unconstitutional in 1936, on the grounds that the labor provisions conferred legislative authority on the Coal Commission, and that a tax levied by the act on noncooperating producers resulted in an unconstitutional regulation of an industry that was not interstate in character. Omitting the provisions to which the court had objected, Congress reenacted the Guffey-Snyder Act in April 1937.

[13]The Walsh-Healey Act required the inclusion, in all federal contracts involving the expenditure of $10,000 or more, of provisions limiting hours to eight a day and forty a week, prohibiting child labor, and empowering the secretary of labor to set minimum wages.

upon Congress to increase the tax burden on the upper classes and large corporations in order to check the growing concentration of economic power, reduce "social unrest and a deepening sense of unfairness," and encourage the wider distribution of wealth. Congress, with astonishing alacrity, wrote most of the president's suggestions into the wealth tax bill, or the Revenue Act of 1935, and Roosevelt signed it on August 30. It left the normal income tax unchanged but increased the surtax to the highest rates in American history,[14] increased the federal estate tax to a maximum of 70 percent, and imposed a graduated income tax on net corporation income.

4. The Election of 1936

The Republican leaders must have surveyed the political scene during the early months of 1936 with considerable dismay. Not since Andrew Jackson's day had the Democratic party been so firmly entrenched and so popular with the masses. Probably never before had there been such a dearth of able leadership in the GOP. The only really serious candidate was Governor Alfred M. Landon of Kansas, who had survived the Democratic landslide of 1934 and had the support of William Randolph Hearst and his chain of newspapers. Republican delegates assembled in Cleveland on June 9, 1936, named Landon on the first ballot on June 11, and afterward nominated Frank Knox, publisher of the *Chicago Daily News*, as his running mate. Orators denounced the New Deal in the generalities of campaign rhetoric. But the Republican platform did not threaten to destroy the New Deal reform structure, except to revise the corporation tax structure and the Trade Agreements Act of 1934, which empowered the president to make tariff agreements (see p. 446). On the contrary, Republicans in 1936 reaffirmed their own progressive tradition by promising to provide better relief, farm subsidy, and labor programs.

The Democrats met in Philadelphia on June 23, 1936, in a convention that was riotous and triumphant. So prevalent was the good feeling that Roosevelt and Garner were nominated by a mighty shout on the first ballot. Southern Democrats, in a moment of exhilaration or perhaps intoxication, even agreed to abrogate the historic party rule that required a two-thirds majority for a presidential nomination.

The Democratic platform was a frank reiteration of the social ideals of the second New Deal and a recital, with emphatic endorsement, of the

[14]The Revenue Act of 1935 increased the surtaxes only on net incomes over $50,000, rising in a graduated scale from a surtax of 31 percent on net incomes over $50,000 to 75 percent on incomes over $5 million.

good works of the Roosevelt administration. Declaring that "government in a modern civilization has certain inescapable obligations to its citizens," the platform promised more rural electrification and a stronger farm program, public housing, additional legislation to protect workers, and vigorous enforcement of the antitrust laws. The foreign policy planks, like those of the Republican platform, reflected the then dominant isolationist temper and the popular determination to avoid, as the Democrats said, "being drawn, by political commitments, international banking, or private trading, into any war which may develop anywhere."

Both candidates conducted dignified and strenuous campaigns. Landon spoke forcefully and made it clear that he approved the basic features of the New Deal program, but he did not fire the public imagination or inspire much confidence. On the other hand, Roosevelt was at his magnificent best as a campaigner and phrase-maker in this battle. His acceptance speech was a declaration of war against "economic royalists" who had supposedly regimented and enslaved the people in an "industrial dictatorship." It was also a new call for dedication to the cause of democracy. "This generation of Americans," Roosevelt concluded, "has a rendezvous with destiny. . . . We are fighting to save a great and precious form of government for ourselves and the world." Taking nothing for granted, the president stumped the country as if his election were in doubt; the themes of social and economic democracy ran strongly through all his speeches.

Two developments of the campaign were significant because they indicated long-range realignments. One was the development of a vigorous political consciousness among organized labor and the participation of the major unions in an all-out effort to return the Democrats to power. The leaders in labor's first important political crusade since 1924 were George L. Berry of the AF of L and John L. Lewis and Sidney Hillman, two spokesmen of the newly formed CIO. They organized Labor's Non-Partisan League in April 1936, raised some $1 million, half of which came from Lewis's United Mine Workers, and turned their unions into momentary political machines. The second significant development in 1936 was the shift of a majority of black leaders and newspapers in northern and midwestern states from the GOP to the Democratic party. For the first time in American history, a majority of black voters supported a Democratic candidate in 1936.

It was obvious by mid-October that Landon simply did not have a chance, in spite of the fact that more than two-thirds of the metropolitan newspapers supported him. Even so, most observers were startled by the magnitude of the Democratic victory on November 3. Landon won 16,679,583 popular votes and carried only Vermont and Maine for a total of eight electoral votes. Representative William Lemke, radical farm leader from North Dakota, running on a Union party ticket supported by Dr. Townsend, Father Coughlin, and Huey Long's successor, the Reverend Gerald L. K. Smith, polled nearly 900,000 votes. The Socialist Norman Thomas and the Communist Earl Browder trailed far behind. In contrast, Roosevelt won 27,751,597 popular and 523 electoral votes and carried huge Democratic majorities with him in the greatest sweep since 1920. The verdict of the people was unmistakable: it was an emphatic mandate for continuation of the second New Deal.

5. The Supreme Court Controversy

High Democratic spokesmen uttered veiled threats against the Supreme Court during the presidential campaign of 1936 for overturning New Deal measures, but the president gave no indication then that he intended to bring the court before the bar of public opinion. Nor was there any strong hint of an impending attack in Roosevelt's Annual Message of January 6, 1937, or in his second inaugural address, delivered on January 20. Yet he presented a plan for judicial reorganization to Congress on February 5, the purpose of which was nothing less than to bring the Supreme Court under his control. We cannot understand Roosevelt's purpose unless we understand the gravity of the constitutional crisis that he thought compelled him to take this momentous step.

As one authority has put it, "five willful Supreme Court Justices . . . had in fact contrived well-nigh complete absence of the power to govern" by the early months of 1937. In short, the court's majority had nearly paralyzed the executive and legislative branches. Responsibility for this situation lay primarily with the court, not with the president or Congress. Four of the justices—James C. McReynolds, George Sutherland, Willis Van Devanter, and Pierce Butler—were reactionaries who lived in a nineteenth-century world of extreme individualism and liberty of contract. They were so consistently hostile to advanced progressive legislation that they were popularly called the "Four Horsemen." In a small minority were the three progressive justices, Louis D. Brandeis, Benjamin N. Cardozo, and Harlan F. Stone. Somewhere between the reactionaries and the progressives stood the chief justice, Charles Evans Hughes, and Owen J. Roberts.

A majority of the court seemed capable before 1935 of recognizing an emergency when they saw one, but what soon became prodigious judicial nullification began in January 1935. In the so-called hot oil cases,[15] the court invalidated Section 9c of the NIRA on January 7, on the ground that it conferred improper legislative authority upon the president to regulate the petroleum industry. More alarming to the administration was the court's decision,[16] rendered on May 6 in a five-to-four verdict, which nul-

[15] *Panama Refining Company* v. *Ryan* and *Amazon Petroleum Corporation* v. *Ryan.*
[16] *Railroad Retirement Board* v. *Alton Railroad.*

lified the Railroad Retirement Act of 1934. The majority alleged, first, that the government had deprived railroad companies of property without due process of law by compelling them to contribute to pensions for their employees and, second, that Congress's control over interstate commerce did not warrant such interference in labor relations. The Social Security bill then pending was also surely unconstitutional if this was true.

These two decisions constituted a kind of prelude to "Black Monday," May 27, 1935, when the court set a new record in judicial review. In *Louisville Joint Stock Land Bank* v. *Radford*, it nullified the Frazier-Lemke Farm Mortgage Act on the grounds that it deprived creditors of property without due process of law. In *Humphrey's Executor* v. *United States*, the majority reprimanded the president for removing William E. Humphrey, a reactionary Republican, from the Federal Trade Commission and laid down a new constitutional rule of considerable importance.[17] The most fateful decision on this fateful "Black Monday" was rendered in *A. L. A. Schechter Corporation* v. *United States*. In this decision all the justices agreed that the NIRA was unconstitutional, either on the grounds that the statute conferred essential legislative authority on the president, or on the grounds that the corporation involved in the case was engaged in intrastate commerce.

Stunned by the *Schechter* decision, the president went to the root of the issue in a press conference on May 31. He pointed out that the court's objection to a plenary grant of legislative power to the executive could be easily overcome. The danger, he said, lay in the court's narrow view of interstate commerce as consisting only of goods in transit.[18] How could the federal government seek to remedy *any* national economic problem if this "horse and buggy" definition of interstate commerce prevailed?

The court answered the president's query after a period of anxious waiting in a series of epochal decisions that emphatically confirmed the Schechter doctrine. Justice Roberts, speaking for himself, Hughes, and the "Four Horsemen" in *United States* v. *Butler* on January 6, 1936, held that the Agricultural Adjustment Act of 1933 was unconstitutional. It was a strained decision, but its meaning was clear: production of agricultural commodities was local activity, not interstate commerce; therefore Congress could not use the taxing power to regulate agriculture. Then an even clearer reaffirmation of the Schechter doctrine came on May 18, 1936. Justice Sutherland, in *Carter* v. *Carter Coal Company*, rendered an opinion invalidating the Guffey-Snyder Coal Conservation Act. The mining of coal, Sutherland asserted, was obviously not interstate commerce, and Congress could not use the taxing power to regulate an industry over which it had

---

[17]Namely, that independent regulatory commissions were arms of Congress, not of the executive, and that the president could not remove their members except for reasons stipulated by Congress.

[18]For this obsolete definition of interstate commerce, Chief Justice Hughes had gone back to the notorious *Knight* decision of 1895, for which see p. 104.

no constitutional control. Having thus denied the federal government jurisdiction over manufacturing, mining, agriculture, and labor conditions, the conservative majority went all the way on June 1, 1936, and denied to the states the right to regulate hours and wages. This decision, rendered by Justice Butler in *Morehead* v. *New York* ex rel. *Tipaldo*, nullified a New York State minimum wage law for women and children by resurrecting the doctrine enunciated in *Adkins* v. *Children's Hospital* in 1923.[19]

Only a blind man could fail to see that the country was in an intolerable constitutional situation by the summer of 1936. The Supreme Court had wrecked several key New Deal enterprises. It seemed certain that the justices would soon invalidate the Social Security and Wagner acts; and the president and Congress knew that they proceeded with further reform legislation only at the risk of additional judicial reversals. Nor was this all. Inferior federal courts were also hard at work in a campaign of judicial nullification and obstruction. They issued no less than 1,600 injunctions against federal administrative officials before 1937; for intermittent periods they paralyzed such important agencies as the NLRB and the SEC.

The president must have concluded that the reckoning could no longer be postponed after the people gave him their emphatic mandate in the election of 1936. He submitted a Judiciary Reorganization bill on February 5, 1937. It empowered him to appoint a new federal judge whenever an incumbent failed to retire within six months after reaching the age of seventy. The number of additional judges would be limited to fifty, and not more than six of them would be named to the Supreme Court. Roosevelt explained in an accompanying message why he desired to enlarge the federal courts. He pointed to the crowded dockets and delay in judicial business caused by insufficient and infirm personnel; described the confusion created by hundreds of injunctions issued by inferior courts; and frankly asserted that the courts needed new blood and a modern outlook.

The whole plan was of course grounded upon Roosevelt's assumption that he could control the huge Democratic majorities in both houses of Congress. He was consequently surprised, even stunned, when violent opposition developed in his own party, from progressives and conservatives alike.

Actually, the original Judiciary Reorganization bill was never brought to a vote in Congress, and Roosevelt might have won most of his measure if an extraordinary change in the opinions of the Supreme Court had not occurred at the height of the controversy in Congress. But such a change did occur—and with dramatic suddenness. For the rupture in his party, Roosevelt was himself in large measure responsible. In his cocksureness he had not taken Democratic leaders into his confidence before submitting the Judiciary Reorganization bill. He allowed Postmaster General Farley

---

[19]In this decision the Court had ruled that minimum wage laws violated the freedom of contract guaranteed by the Fourteenth Amendment.

to use the patronage stick too bluntly after the controversy had begun. Worst of all, he refused to listen to compromise proposals that might have succeeded. "All his sagacity seemed to desert him," one contemporary has written of the president; "he was arrogant to those who counseled caution, disbelieving when they warned him of defeat, and neglectful until too late of their alternative suggestions."[20] Consequently, he probably lost control of Congress for the first time since 1933.

The court rendered judgment on a minimum wage statute of the state of Washington in the case of *West Coast Hotel* v. *Parrish* on March 29, 1937. Roberts had joined the "Four Horsemen" only a year before to invalidate a similar New York law. Now he joined Hughes and the progressives to approve the Washington statute in sweeping language that left room for almost any reasonable form of state wages and hours legislation. The crowning irony came when the new progressive majority upheld the Wagner Act in *National Labor Relations Board* v. *Jones and Laughlin Steel Corporation* on April 12, 1937. Here the issue was essentially the same as in the *Schechter, Butler,* and *Carter Coal Company* cases: did the power of Congress to control interstate commerce include the power to control the actual production of commodities? In the *Jones and Laughlin* decision the chief justice in effect reversed the earlier decisions without openly admitting that any change in interpretation had occurred. Congress's control over interstate commerce was absolute, Hughes declared, and included power to encourage and protect such commerce. The peaceful movement of goods was essential to the life of the nation, he concluded. Hence Congress might even prescribe the labor relations prevailing at factories in which goods were manufactured. In addition, the court approved the Social Security Act on May 24, 1937, in three decisions[21] by justices Stone and Cardozo that upheld the compulsory features of the unemployment and old-age retirement systems.

Thus the president had in large measure already won the war by the end of May 1937. Moreover, Justice Van Devanter retired on June 1, thus allowing Roosevelt to buttress the new progressive majority on the supreme bench. Now that the constitutional crisis was resolved in favor of broad interpretation, the advocates of compromise, Vice-President Garner and Majority Leader Alben W. Barkley of Kentucky, came forward with a new judiciary bill that denied the president power to enlarge the courts but conceded badly needed procedural reforms. The Judicial Procedure Reform Act, which Roosevelt accepted and signed on August 26, 1937, empowered the attorney general to participate in cases involving the constitutionality of federal statutes when they were first tried before district courts. It also made provision for moving such cases, when they went

---

[20] Rexford G. Tugwell, *The Democratic Roosevelt, A Biography of Franklin D. Roosevelt* (Garden City, N.Y., 1957), p. 403.

[21] *Carmichael* v. *Southern Coal Company, Charles C. Steward Machine Company* v. *Davis,* and *Helvering* v. *Davis.*

against the government, from district courts directly to the Supreme Court and severely circumscribed the right of federal judges to stay the execution of federal laws.

6. Additions to the New Deal: 1937

The president reaffirmed his determination to broaden and complete the reform structure of the second New Deal on several notable occasions following the election of 1936. His Annual Message of January 6, 1937, and his second inaugural address of January 20 were clarion calls to Congress for aid to the millions of people in city and country on low incomes, the "one-third of a nation ill-housed, ill-clad, ill-nourished," over whom disaster hung like a pall. "The test of our progress," he declared in his inaugural, "is not whether we add more to the abundance of those who have much; it is whether we provide enough for those who have too little."

Roosevelt presented his new program cautiously during the early months of 1937 in step with changing circumstances. Thus in his Annual Message of January 6 he merely asked Congress to consider measures for public housing, aid to tenant farmers, and broader social security coverage. On January 12 he submitted a plan for reorganization of the Executive Department. On February 5 he added his plan for reorganization of the judiciary. This was as far as he could go until the constitutional crisis had been resolved. But he moved quickly to round out his program once the Supreme Court had executed its reversal in March and April. On May 24 he urged Congress to "extend the frontiers of social progress" by enacting legislation establishing minimum wages and maximum hours in American industry. Finally, on July 12 he asked Congress to reestablish the AAA.[22]

[22]Congress had adopted the Soil Conservation and Domestic Allotment Act a month after the Supreme Court's invalidation of the Agricultural Adjustment Act on January 6, 1936. The former was a hastily drawn and unsatisfactory substitute. It simply appropriated $500 million to be paid to farmers who diverted part of their land from staple to soil-building crops.

It was the time of the great dust bowl in the Southwest and Plains states, and the nation had been profoundly alarmed by the spectacle of millions of tons of topsoil being blown away in the parched area. The epic documentary film, *The Plow That Broke the Plains,* had further dramatized the urgent need to save American soil resources. Thus the conservation program under the legislation of 1936 evoked widespread popular approval and support by farmers, two-thirds of whom signed contracts with the Department of Agriculture to plant soil-building crops. However, the Soil Conservation Act was woefully inadequate as a means of crop control because the Agriculture Department had no power under its provisions to compel cooperation by the recalcitrant minority. Severe drought in the corn and wheat belts continued in 1936, and there were consequently no grain surpluses. But, as we shall see, return of good weather and prosperity in 1937 stimulated the planting and harvesting of huge cotton, wheat, corn, and tobacco crops and demonstrated the need for new and more effective controls.

This, then, was the administration's program to complete the second New Deal. Unfortunately for the president, the Judiciary Reorganization bill consumed much of Congress's energies during the spring and early summer of 1937, disrupted the party's ranks, and gave conservative Democrats in both houses an excuse for defying the president's leadership on other questions. They combined with the Republican minority to defeat the Executive Reorganization bill by charging that it was a twin of the Judiciary Reorganization bill and another step toward presidential dictatorship.[23] The Senate approved the administration's wages and hours, or Fair Labor Standards, bill on July 31, 1937, but conservative Democrats and Republicans on the House rules committee prevented the House from voting on the measure. The president's proposal for a new agricultural act received scarcely any attention from the lawmakers.

Even so, the first session of the Seventy-fifth Congress that sat from January to September 1937 left a memorable record of achievement: the Judicial Procedure Reform Act; the Guffey-Vinson Bituminous Coal Act, which reenacted most of the provisions of the Guffey-Snyder Act; and, most important, the Bankhead-Jones Farm Tenancy Act and the Wagner-Steagall National Housing Act. The last two measures were landmarks in the history of federal policy.

The Bankhead-Jones Farm Tenancy Act was the outgrowth of the investigations of the president's Committee on Farm Tenancy. Its report, issued in February 1937, revealed that more than half the farmers in the South, nearly a third in the North, and one-fourth in the West were sharecroppers or tenants. Highlighting the poverty and misery of this important segment of the farm population, the report also took serious notice of a new group of the rural destitute—the hundreds of thousands of migratory farm workers and displaced cotton sharecroppers from the Southwest, the "Okies," who were moving en masse to California in search of jobs. To turn back the tide of tenancy, the committee suggested a remedy in keeping with the spirit of the second New Deal. It proposed that the Resettlement Administration (RA) be reorganized as the Farm Security Administration (FSA). The FSA should help enterprising tenants to become landowners, refinance and rehabilitate small farmers who were in danger of losing their lands, promote withdrawal of submarginal land, and help migratory workers. With the support of southern Democrats keenly responsive to the needs of small farmers and white tenants, the Bankhead-Jones Act, embodying the committee's recommendations, became law on July 22, 1937.

---

[23]The Senate passed a revised reorganization bill in 1938, but conservatives in the House, led by the reactionary chairman of the rules committee, John J. O'Connor of New York, defeated it. Finally, both houses approved a new administration Reorganization Act in 1939. It deprived the president of power to reorganize the independent regulatory agencies but permitted him to appoint six administrative assistants and to reorganize and consolidate a number of lesser agencies.

The FSA was the social conscience of the second New Deal in action on the rural front from 1937 until the end of the Second World War.[24] It established some thirty camps that accommodated from 12,000 to 15,000 migratory families, helped farmers scale their debts, organized rural medical and dental care groups, sponsored cooperative leasing of land and purchase of machinery by tenants and small farmers, and carried on homestead projects already begun by the RA. Moreover, the FSA had lent over $800 million in short-term rehabilitation loans by June 1944 to 870,000 farm families. Finally, it lent nearly $260 million to 41,000 families—on a forty-year basis at 3 percent interest—between 1937 and 1946 for purchase of farms.

The Wagner-Steagall National Housing Act, approved September 1, 1937, was the culmination of several years of planning and investigation by various agencies of the government. Large-scale public housing was one objective of the PWA from 1933 to 1937; and the PWA Housing Division by 1937 had constructed fifty-one projects in thirty-six cities with new homes for 21,700 families. The housing program launched by the Wagner-Steagall Act of 1937, on the other hand, reflected the administration's determination to meet the housing problem comprehensively and not as part of a public works and recovery program. This measure established the United States Housing Authority (USHA) in the Interior Department, with a capital of $1 million and authority to borrow up to $500 million, increased to a total of $1.6 billion in 1940.

The USHA worked through public housing agencies in all important cities—by lending up to 100 percent of the costs of housing projects on a long-term basis, making annual subsidies to local agencies, and establishing standards of cost, construction, and eligibility to tenants.[25] All told, before 1941, when the USHA turned to providing housing for defense workers, the agency lent over $750 million to local housing authorities for 511 projects with a total of 161,162 units. It was, obviously, only the beginning of what would perforce be a long campaign to destroy slums and provide adequate housing for America's urban poor.

7. Recovery, Recession, and the Last Surge of Reform, 1937–1938

Health began to return to the ailing American economy between 1933 and 1936. National income rose from nearly $42.5 billion in 1933 to $49 billion

[24]Congress created a new Farmers' Home Administration in August 1946 and transferred to it the functions of the FSA.

[25]Residents of public housing projects, for example, had to be from among the lowest third of income receivers. The average income of all families living in USHA projects on December 31, 1941, was $837 a year; the average rental of all USHA units was $12.64 a month.

in 1934, and to $57.1 billion in 1935. The indices of production, employment, and payrolls in manufacturing[26] rose from 56, 62.3, and 38.3, respectively, in March 1933 to 104, 94.2, and 80.5, respectively, in December 1935. All indices of economic activity began to rise sharply in the spring of 1936. Removal of NRA restrictions on production perhaps gave one stimulus. Certainly increased farm income and enormous federal expenditures for work relief beginning in the spring of 1935 and payment of the bonus in 1936 all had an important impact. From May 1936 to September 1937 the index of employment rose from 96.4 to 112.2—higher than the peak figure in 1929—while the payroll index increased from 84 to 109, and the index of industrial production rose from 101 to 117 during the same period. Disposable per capita income, measured in 1952 dollars, increased from $906 in 1935 to $1,048 in 1937. It had been $1,045 in 1929.

There was a speculative upsurge on the stock markets, but the upswing from 1935 to 1937 was essentially sound because it was based on increased investment and production and larger purchasing power through higher wages and public spending. Instead of welcoming the return of prosperity and making certain that the volume of credit was equal to business needs, however, the administration acted as if it feared prosperity. The board of governors of the Federal Reserve system, assuming that another runaway boom was in the making, increased reserve requirements of member banks drastically in 1936 and again in 1937, while Federal Reserve banks took sharp action on their own to prevent monetary and bank credit inflation. In addition, the president made plans drastically to cut the work relief program, reduce other federal expenditures, and balance the budget in 1939. Consequently, WPA rolls were reduced from 3 million to 1.5 million workers between January and August of 1937.

Credit restrictions, reduced federal expenditures, and other factors combined in September and October 1937 to cause a severe slump that set the indices tumbling and threatened to wipe out all gains toward recovery that the country had made since 1935. There was grave danger that price rigidity accompanied by widespread wage cutting would accentuate the downward spiral, and that farm prices would fall to subdepression levels because of extraordinarily large production in 1937. Roosevelt therefore called Congress into special session on October 12, 1937. Then in a fireside chat with the nation and in a message to Congress on November 15 he presented a program to halt the recession and complete the second New Deal. That program included a new and comprehensive agricultural act, legislation to abolish child labor and establish minimum wages and maximum hours, and revision of the antitrust laws to root out monopolistic control over prices.

Profoundly frightened by the prospect of returning depression during an election year, Democrats in Congress closed ranks and set to work with

[26] Monthly average, 1923-1925 = 100.

resolution and dispatch. The most urgent necessity was legislation to prevent the complete collapse of agricultural prices. Drought and soil conservation contracts had kept farm production in 1936 at the lowest point since the First World War, except for the drought year of 1934. High prices stimulated tremendously increased plantings in 1937, however, and the return of good weather made possible the harvesting of the largest aggregate yield in American history.

It was simply to avert agrarian catastrophe that Congress enacted and the president signed a new Agricultural Adjustment Act in mid-February 1938. It provided up to $500 million for soil conservation payments annually to farmers who cooperated in restricting production. In addition, marketing quotas might be applied to cotton, wheat, corn, tobacco, and rice if production exceeded normal requirements and two-thirds of the producers of each crop voted to institute such controls. To achieve parity for agricultural prices, the act of 1938 provided a number of devices.

The Second World War soon ended the farm problem for a time, but there can be little doubt that the second AAA brought stability to American agriculture during the interim years 1938 to 1941. Huge surpluses threatened to depress prices to the level of 1932 when the measure went into effect. The Agriculture Department averted a rural depression in the critical years of 1938 and 1939 by vigorous action on many fronts and helped farmers to return to the near-prosperity level of 1937 in 1940. Cash farm income, including governmental payments, was $9,176,000,000 in 1937, $8,130,000,000 in 1938, $8,658,000,000 in 1939, and back to $9,120,000,000 in 1940.

Meanwhile, the widespread wage cutting that occurred during the first months of the recession of 1937 prompted the administration to muster all its strength to force passage of the Fair Labor Standards, or wages and hours, bill. Signed by the president on June 25, 1938, it was the last of the great New Deal measures and joined the Social Security and National Labor Relations acts to round out a comprehensive structure of advanced labor legislation. The Fair Labor Standards Act represented the culmination of perhaps the most important aspects of the social justice movement. First, it established a minimum wage of 25 cents an hour, to go into effect at once and to be gradually increased to 40 cents. Second, it limited hours of labor to forty-four a week, to be reduced within three years to forty a week, and provided for payment at the rate of time and a half for overtime work. Third, it forbade shipment in interstate commerce of any goods manufactured in whole or in part by children under sixteen. Finally, it created a Wage and Hour Division in the Department of Labor to supervise application of the new law. Thus the act abolished the worst sweatshops and ended the exploitation of children even though it left many workers unprotected. Nearly 13 million persons were protected by the Wage and Hour Division by April 1939; an additional 700,000 workers, chiefly in the South, received immediate pay increases when the minimum wage was increased from 25 to 30 cents in October 1939.

Meanwhile the president waited to see whether the economy would recover without new efforts at pump priming. The economic situation was steadily worsening instead of improving during the winter of 1937-1938, as the following table reveals.

	Index of Employment in Manufacturing	Index of Payrolls in Manufacturing	Index of Production
1937			
October	110.3	104.9	102
November	104.2	93.3	88
December	97.7	84.6	84
1938			
January	91.0	75.4	80
February	91.6	77.7	79
March	91.2	77.8	79

Therefore, the president sent a special message to Congress on April 14, 1938, announcing a loosening of credit restrictions, demanding a drastic revival of deficit spending, and calling upon business and labor to unite in a common war against the recession.

A frightened Congress hastily responded by making some $3 billion immediately available to expand the WPA, launching a huge public works program in conjunction with the states, and increasing the activities of other agencies. Expanded bank credits and renewed pump priming reversed the tide almost at once. Indices of manufacturing production, payrolls, and employment started upward beginning in July and August 1938; recovery to the near-prosperity level of 1937 was almost complete by the end of 1939.

The last surge of New Deal reform was the inauguration by the administration and Congress in the spring and summer of 1938 of the most intense antitrust campaign since the presidency of William Howard Taft. Thurman Arnold of the Yale Law School, an ardent foe of monopoly, was appointed head of the Antitrust Division of the Department of Justice and given large new appropriations and increases in staff. To sharpen federal antitrust policy, he set in motion within a short time 215 major investigations and 92 test cases. In addition, the president sent a special message to Congress on April 29, 1938, calling for a thorough study of the concentration of economic power and its effect on the American system of free enterprise.

Congress responded on June 16, 1938, by creating the Temporary National Economic Committee (TNEC), composed of members of Congress and representatives of various executive agencies. For seventeen months, from December 1, 1938, to April 26, 1940, the TNEC heard witnesses, while its economists wrote forty-three monographs covering almost every phase of economic life. The result was such a stocktaking of the American economy as had never before been attempted. It seemed at first that the administration contemplated some drastic new form of public control over business, industry, and finance. Such plans, however, did not long survive, if they ever existed. The TNEC, after taking mountains of testimony, submitted a final report on March 31, 1941, that was neither original nor bold. It recommended only traditional remedies like strengthening the antitrust laws and reform of the patent system. By the date of the publication of the final report, of course, the administration was more concerned with preparation for war than with sweeping reform of the economic system.

8. The Passing of the New Deal

The administration's reform impulses and plans came to an abrupt halt in the early months of 1939 as the result of portentous developments in Europe and Asia and political reversals at home. Hitler's triumph at Munich in September 1938 and his subsequent partition of Czechoslovakia in March 1939 convinced Roosevelt that the Nazi menace to European and American democracy demanded a stronger foreign policy and preparation for possible conflict. Moreover, Japan's invasion of China in 1937 and threat of future expansion seemed to raise threats to American security in the Far East. In brief, the president believed that a worldwide cataclysm impended in the near future, and that his chief duty was now the protection of American security.

A firm defense of American interests, however, would almost inevitably require a radical alteration of the policy of strict nonintervention embodied in the neutrality legislation from 1935 to 1937 (see pp. 450–451). Such a reversal could not be accomplished unless Roosevelt had a strong majority in Congress, but the Democratic party was split wide open on foreign policy. Midwestern and western Democrats were ardent supporters of second New Deal domestic policies. But they, like Republicans from their own regions, were determined to avoid any action that might conceivably lead to American participation in a Second World War. Eastern Democrats generally supported progressive measures and, except for representatives of Irish-American districts, were willing to support a stronger foreign policy. Southern Democrats were the most vociferous champions of defense and cooperation with Britain and France. But they were growing acutely fearful that the administration's advanced reform measures would impinge upon race relations in their region. Roosevelt might have to call a halt to further reform legislation in order to win their support for a stronger foreign policy. He might even have to jettison midwesterners and westerners and try to build a new coalition of southerners and internationally minded easterners. The implications of such a new departure for continuation of the second New Deal were clear enough.

Political developments in 1938 emphasized this dilemma and revealed that the second New Deal coalition of midwesterners and easterners was beginning to crumble. The first sign came in December 1937 and January 1938 during struggles in Congress over the proposed Ludlow Amendment and the Wagner-Van Nuys antilynching bill.[27] The president addressed a strong plea to Congress for defeat of the Ludlow resolution on January 6, and the House defeated it by a vote of 209 to 188 four days later. But Roosevelt must have perceived the significance of the alignment on the measure: three-fourths of the Republicans and a majority of midwestern and western Democrats combined in support of the proposed amendment, while an overwhelming majority of southern and eastern Democrats voted against it. The conflict over the antilynching bill came to a head in the Senate at the same time. Although Roosevelt undoubtedly approved the measure, he said no word in condemnation when southern senators by filibuster prevented a vote.

The development that decisively compelled Roosevelt to make peace with the conservatives in order to build strength for his foreign policy was the failure of his campaign to purge conservative southern Democrats in the primary campaigns during the summer of 1938. The president announced his determination to participate in the Democratic primary campaigns on June 24 and threw himself into the fight during the next two months. What Roosevelt said to southerners was honest enough. He declared that conditions that made the South "the Nation's No. 1 economic problem" could be remedied only by united progressive action in which southerners played a leading part. As was perhaps inevitable, the president's intervention boomeranged. Two staunch southern progressives, Representative Lister Hill of Alabama and Senator Claude W. Pepper of Florida, had won notable victories in earlier primary campaigns in which Roosevelt took no part. In contrast, not a single southern conservative was dislodged by Roosevelt's attempted purge.

The outcome of the congressional elections in November, moreover, left Roosevelt no alternative but to draw his party together in a solid front. The Republicans made enormous gains in the Middle and Far West and, by gaining seven seats in the Senate and eight in the House, became a formidable power for the first time since 1932. Roosevelt would desper-

---

[27] Introduced by Representative Louis Ludlow, Democrat of Indiana, the proposed amendment required majority approval of a war resolution in a national referendum, except in the event of an invasion of the United States or its territories. It had the support of numerous church and pacifist groups and apparently a large majority of the American people.

The Wagner-Van Nuys antilynching bill made lynching a federal crime and allowed families of lynch victims to sue counties in which the lynching occurred for damages running to $10,000. It was supported by the National Association for the Advancement of Colored People and by liberal labor, church, and political groups in all sections except the South, where sentiment was divided.

ately need the support of southerners on foreign policy in the next Congress. He would not be able to run the risk of driving them into alliance with the Republicans by further antagonism on domestic issues.

Therefore the president in effect announced the end of the great reform movement of the second New Deal in his Annual Message to the Seventy-sixth Congress on January 4, 1939. Pleading only for continuation of deficit spending until recovery had returned, he asked for no new reform legislation and declared: "We have now passed the period of internal conflict in the launching of our program of social reform. Our full energies may now be released to invigorate the processes of recovery in order to preserve our reforms." The major theme of this address, in fact, was the enormity of the totalitarian threat to religion, democracy, and international peace.

Thus it came about that the forward motion of progressivism came to a halt in the early uncertain months of 1939. And yet it would be erroneous to conclude that the failure of the "purge," the Republican revival, or even the increasing peril of the international situation alone accounted for the president's decision to abandon the fight for further reform legislation. More important was the fact that with one exception—development of new regional hydroelectric projects like the Tennessee Valley Authority— the president and his party had by 1939 brought to full completion the progressive program first formulated by agrarian, social justice, and labor progressives from the 1890s to 1917 and then enlarged in the 1920s and 1930s. In other words, progressives had nearly reached the limits of achievement within the framework of their ideology. It embodied a faith in the middle way, in regulation and activity on behalf of disadvantaged classes, rather than in socialistic ownership of the means of production. Progressives in the years after the Second World War would find that their own ideological limitations made it difficult for them to do more than round out and strengthen the structure of the second New Deal.

"As a Nation we have rejected any radical revolutionary program," Roosevelt observed in 1938. "For a permanent correction of grave weakness in our economic system we have relied on new applications of old democratic processes." And what student of American history could disagree with this judgment on the whole New Deal effort? The chief significance of the reform legislation of the 1930s was its essentially conservative character and the fact that it stemmed from half a century or more of discussion and practical experience and from ideas proposed by Republicans as well as by Democrats.

18

The New Deal and

the American People

Many old progressives must have been as much astonished as gratified in 1941 by all the changes they had seen. Most important was the profound metamorphosis in popular attitudes toward the federal government that had occurred in the four decades after 1900. By 1941 most Americans agreed that the federal government should be the most powerful organized force in their democracy: a guarantor of solvency to farmers, a beneficent protector to workers, a friend in adversity to tenant farmers and the unemployed, and a powerful safeguard as well as a regulator of businessmen and bankers.

Historians might argue that popular acceptance of progressive assumptions represented more a pragmatic response to obvious need than a reasoned acceptance of an elaborate ideology. Nonetheless, analysts were quick to perceive the significance of the institutional changes wrought by the New Deal legislation and the new spirit that permeated the American democracy by 1941. We have noted many of these changes in agriculture, industry, finance, and politics in the preceding two chapters. Now let us look at other, and in the long run perhaps more important, effects of the New Deal. We will observe how the intellectual and political upheaval of the 1930s affected the labor movement; promoted the growth of bold concepts concerning the development of regional resources, constitutional interpretations, and the treatment of minority groups; and stimulated the expansion and maturing of the progressive ideology.

1. Labor's Civil War

The labor movement experienced its most spectacular growth from 1933 to 1941 and finally won its old and hitherto elusive goal of unionization of the mass industries. However, this triumph was accomplished at the cost of a bitter civil war that split the ranks of organized labor and left deep scars for years to come. Leadership in the AF of L had fallen to cautious men after the death of Samuel Gompers in 1924. Convinced that craft or trade unionism offered the only solid basis for the American labor movement, they abhorred the concept of industrial unionism, that is, organization of all workers in a given industry into one big union. In opposition stood an aggressive minority among the leaders of the AF of L. One was John L. Lewis, who had built his United Mine Workers (UMW) into the most powerful union in the United States by 1935. Another was Sidney Hillman, one of the founders and president of the Amalgamated Clothing Workers. A third was David Dubinsky, head of the International Ladies' Garment Workers. These and others argued that labor's hope lay in meeting strength with strength—by organizing mass industries on a mass, or industrial, basis and by attempting to bring the great body of black workers into the ranks of organized labor.

The AF of L convention voted in 1934 under strong pressure from Lewis, Hillman, and Dubinsky to charter so-called federal, or industrial, unions in the automobile, cement, aluminum, and other mass industries. But the conservatives had no intention of allowing the infant unions to grow into lusty giants and seize control of the AF of L. In fact, no sooner were the new unions launched than the old craft unions began to raid them.

The struggle came to a head at the AF of L convention in October 1935. Then Lewis bluntly proposed that craft unions should have no jurisdiction over workers in mass industries and made a ringing plea for a great campaign to organize unskilled workers. The majority of the convention rejected this resolution on October 16. Lewis and other leaders of eight AF of L unions met in Atlantic City on November 10 and formed the Committee for Industrial Organization, allegedly to help the AF of L unionize the basic industries. President William Green and the AF of L executive council struck back in January 1936, ordering the CIO to disband. The rebels defiantly welcomed new allies and laid plans for unionization campaigns. Then the AF of L executive council suspended ten unions in August 1936 and expelled them in March 1937.

Ensuing months saw a bitter struggle for control of the masses of unorganized workers and CIO triumphs on almost every front. Beginning with 1.8 million members in March 1937, the new union could claim a membership of nearly 3.75 million six months later. Peace negotiations with the AF of L in October 1937 failed to yield an agreement satisfactory to Lewis. At the conclusion of these negotiations the rebel leaders finally declared their independence of the parent organization and reorganized the CIO soon afterward as the Congress of Industrial Organizations.

2. The Progress of the CIO

Meanwhile, the CIO had begun its offensive against the mass industries in June 1936 with the formation of the Steel Workers' Organizing Committee (SWOC) under Philip Murray, a lieutenant of Lewis in the UMW. The SWOC campaigned in the steel industry for over seven months, and discontented workers everywhere broke away from company unions and joined the CIO. In the past, company managers could always rely upon the military assistance of the states and the moral support of the federal government. In that year of New Deal grace, 1936, however, the Washington administration was openly friendly to the workers, while the Democratic governor of Pennsylvania promised relief assistance if a strike should occur.

It soon became evident that the executives of United States Steel, if not other captains of the industry, preferred surrender to a long and costly strike. Myron C. Taylor, chairman of the board of United States Steel, held a series of private conferences with John L. Lewis beginning in December 1936. The talks led to friendly understanding and agreement by officials of the corporation to recognize the SWOC. Consequently, Benjamin Fairless, president of the Carnegie-Illinois Steel Company, a United States Steel subsidiary, signed on March 2, 1937, what was perhaps the most important contract in American labor history—important because it signified surrender of the corporation which since 1901 had taken leadership in the movement to block unionization of the basic industries. All the rest of United States Steel's subsidiaries had signed similar contracts within a short time. They granted recognition, a 10 percent wage increase, the forty-hour week, and time and a half for overtime work.

It was an epochal victory, and Murray and the SWOC expected the remainder of the steel companies, known collectively as Little Steel, to come to terms quickly. Several of them, notably Inland Steel, made no effort to break the strike; but the leaders of the Bethlehem Steel, Republic

Steel, and Youngstown Sheet and Tube companies fought back with all the force they could command. Republic Steel officials in Massillon, Ohio, organized a small army of deputies that killed two strikers in a wanton attack on July 11, 1937. Police in South Chicago killed ten and wounded scores of strikers at the Republic Steel plant on Memorial Day, 1937.

So violent was Little Steel's counterattack that the SWOC's momentum was almost entirely halted. Inland Steel agreed to recognize the union in July 1937, but the other companies held out. In pre-New Deal days this would probably have been the end of the story, at least until the workers organized for another bloody battle. Now, however, the workers' new ally, the federal government, went into action. First, a Senate subcommittee, headed by Robert M. La Follette, Jr., of Wisconsin, conducted a thorough investigation into all aspects of the strike during the spring and summer of 1938. It reported numerous violations of the Wagner Act and the civil liberties of the strikers by the steel companies, local police, and the National Guard. It also discovered that the companies maintained corps of spies and *agents provocateurs*, and it revealed that the same companies had collected arsenals of guns, tear gas, and ammunition for use against strikers. Second, the NLRB moved into the case upon appeal of the SWOC and compelled the Little Steel companies to recognize and bargain in good faith with the SWOC in 1941. By the end of that year, therefore, the steelworkers' union, now 600,000 strong, stood triumphant throughout the entire industry.

The key automobile industry became the CIO's next target, although the union's leaders did not plan it that way. The AF of L had chartered some 100 local unions in the automobile industry in 1933 and 1934 and launched the United Automobile Workers in August 1935. Homer Martin, an industrial unionist and former Baptist preacher, gained control of the UAW in May 1936 and took it into the CIO. The following summer and autumn saw an intensive and successful unionization campaign among workers in General Motors and Chrysler plants. The workers were so determined to win full recognition that the national CIO leaders could not refuse to support them, even though their chief concern now was the impending strike in the steel industry.

Martin invited officials of the General Motors Corporation to a bargaining conference in December 1936. When company spokesmen declined, workers in the Fisher Body Plant in Cleveland sat down by their machines on December 28. Within a few days the sit-down strike had spread through key General Motors plants. There had been minor sit-down strikes before, but none so well organized and on such a spectacular scale as this one. Company officials for the most part did not dare molest the occupying forces, for fear that violence would lead to destruction of machinery. But there was one pitched battle on January 11, 1937, when police tried to prevent the delivery of food to strikers inside Fisher Body

Plant No. 1 at Flint, Michigan. Strikers in this melee turned back the police, reopened food lines, and retained possession of the plant.

General Motors officials called upon the recently inaugurated governor of Michigan, Frank Murphy, to use the National Guard to dislodge the trespassers. But Murphy was a Democrat, elected with the support of labor, who sympathized with the objectives if not the methods of the strikers. Instead of using force, he tried to conciliate. Mediation conferences in Lansing and Washington failed to bring peace. Then the corporation appealed to Circuit Court Judge Paul V. Gadola on January 29, 1937, for an injunction ordering the strikers from the plants. Gadola signed an injunction on the following day ordering all strikers from the property of General Motors under pain of a $15 million fine and imprisonment if they refused. When the strikers defied the injunction, Judge Gadola ordered the sheriff to arrest them; the sheriff refused and appealed to Governor Murphy. Murphy in turn refused to use the National Guard and redoubled his efforts at mediation. After days of tense negotiations, General Motors finally surrendered on February 11, 1937. The UAW won all its demands except the closed shop—that is, they gained dismissal of the injunction proceedings, recognition of the union as the sole bargaining agent for the workers, and collective bargaining looking toward agreement on hours and wages.

Flushed with their victory over General Motors, UAW leaders moved next against the smaller Chrysler Corporation and applied sit-down and mass picketing techniques at eight Chrysler plants on March 8, 1937. Judge Allen Campbell of Detroit ordered the arrest of CIO leaders and 6,000 sitting strikers (they had defied his earlier injunction), and the workers prepared to resist. But public opinion throughout the country by this date was growing alarmed by a wave of sit-down strikes in many branches of industry and was turning sharply against the new technique.[1] Governor Murphy announced that he would enforce the injunction; at the same time he succeeded in bringing Walter P. Chrysler and John L. Lewis together in high-level peace talks. The upshot was an agreement altogether favorable to the UAW. Lewis called the strikers out of Chrysler plants on March 24, and the corporation surrendered on April 6 on the terms to which General Motors had recently agreed.

Henry Ford had the lowest wage scale of any of the major automobile producers in 1937; he also had the most efficient "service department," a collection of labor spies and company police dedicated to destroying any incipient union. The UAW began an organization campaign in the Ford Company soon after Chrysler capitulated, but it was badly managed and failed to win the workers in Ford's huge River Rouge plant. However, the UAW was consistently successful among smaller producers like Packard

[1] Some 500,000 workers were engaged directly in sit-down strikes from September 1936 through May 1937 and forced the shutting down of other plants employing 600,000 workers. The peak came in March 1937, when nearly 200,000 workers participated in sit-down strikes.

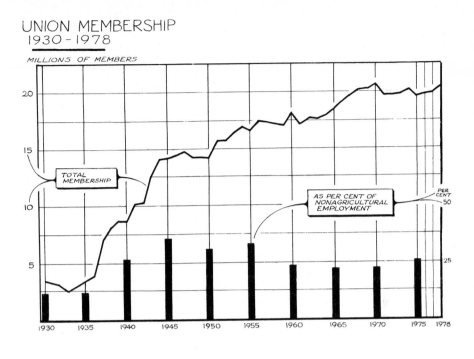

UNION MEMBERSHIP
1930-1978

MILLIONS OF MEMBERS

TOTAL MEMBERSHIP

AS PER CENT OF NONAGRICULTURAL EMPLOYMENT

PER CENT
50

25

1930 1935 1940 1945 1950 1955 1960 1965 1970 1975 1978

THE TEN LARGEST UNIONS
1977

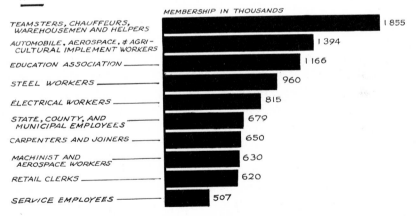

MEMBERSHIP IN THOUSANDS

TEAMSTERS, CHAUFFEURS, WAREHOUSEMEN AND HELPERS — 1855

AUTOMOBILE, AEROSPACE, & AGRI-CULTURAL IMPLEMENT WORKERS — 1394

EDUCATION ASSOCIATION — 1166

STEEL WORKERS — 960

ELECTRICAL WORKERS — 815

STATE, COUNTY, AND MUNICIPAL EMPLOYEES — 679

CARPENTERS AND JOINERS — 650

MACHINIST AND AEROSPACE WORKERS — 630

RETAIL CLERKS — 620

SERVICE EMPLOYEES — 507

and Hudson; by September 1937 the union had over 300,000 members and boasted bargaining agreements with every automobile producer except Ford. Even the crusty old individualist surrendered to the UAW in the spring of 1940.

Meanwhile, CIO unions had won the right to bargain for workers in most of the other basic industries. An uprising of rubber workers in Akron, Ohio, in February 1936 led to the formation of the United Rubber Workers Union and the CIO's rapid conquest of the rubber industry. The United Textile Workers Union organized the textile mills of the North and made a heroic but generally unsuccessful effort to penetrate the southern area in 1937 and 1938. Harry Bridges organized longshoremen on the Pacific Coast into a powerful CIO union. And so it went in dozens of other industries, until by the time that the United States entered the Second World War the CIO had some 5 million members, the AF of L had grown to a membership of about 4.6 million, and independent unions could count an additional 1 million. By this date, 28.2 percent of all workers in non-agricultural employment were unionized, as compared to 11.5 percent in 1933. In short, labor was well on its way toward achieving the organization of all important American industries and its long-sought goal of equality with management in the determination of labor policies. Offsetting and to a degree counterbalancing the power of big business now stood big labor, a new institution brought into being not merely by labor's own efforts but also because the federal government had thrown its moral and legal support to labor's side during the critical period of the CIO's life.

3. The TVA and the Concept of the Region

No New Deal enterprise so fired the imagination of progressives as the creation and development of the Tennessee Valley Authority (TVA). The greatest hydroelectric project in history, it harnessed the water resources of an area 40,000 square miles in size and made possible utilization of vast quantities of electric power in a once impoverished region. It dramatically demonstrated man's ability to control the primeval forces of nature and repair the damage done to the good earth during two centuries of wasteful exploitation. Even more significant was its conception as a regional under-taking and operation by a nonpartisan agency as much responsible to the people of the region as to its owner, the federal government. The TVA was the first really significant experiment in public planning on a regional scale. Its concepts and techniques might well prove to be the New Deal's most important contribution to the theory and practice of government in the United States.

The reader will recall the struggle for control of Wilson Dam at Muscle Shoals, Alabama, in the 1920s, and how Senator George W. Norris of Nebraska helped save the power resources of the Tennessee Valley for the American people (see pp. 318–320). Progressives bided their time and enlarged their objectives even while their plans for federal development were being thwarted by presidents Coolidge and Hoover. Their opportunity came with Roosevelt's election in 1932, for the new Democratic leader came out for public power projects that would serve as yardsticks

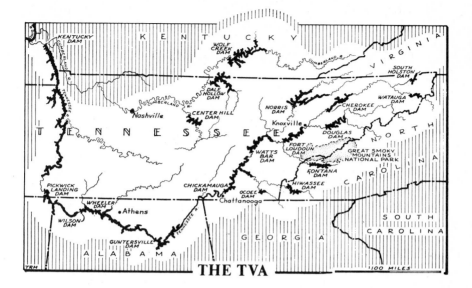

THE TVA

for electric rates and make possible the wider consumption of power. The president-elect visited the Tennessee Valley in January 1933 in company with Norris. Roosevelt's fertile imagination must have been excited by the opportunities that unfolded as he stood on Wilson Dam.

Roosevelt converted opportunities into objectives on April 10, 1933, when he asked Congress to establish a Tennessee Valley Authority, "a corporation clothed with the power of Government but possessed of the flexibility and initiative of a private enterprise," to plan for the full development of the natural resources of the valley. Congress responded quickly by creating the TVA, a corporation controlled by a three-man board and endowed with sweeping authority subject to the general supervision of the president and Congress.

The TVA directors conceived their first task to be control of the Tennessee River and its tributaries to stop erosion, prevent floods, and improve navigation. The authority designed and constructed twenty new dams and improved five existing ones between 1933 and 1952, using enough material to build thirty-five Hoover or ten Grand Coulee Dams. By 1978 the authority's investment stood at $6.65 billion.

The result was the completion of a nearly perfect system of water control in one of the areas of heaviest rainfall in the United States. There were no more floods in the Tennessee Valley once the TVA dams were completed; and TVA engineers could also greatly reduce the flood menace in the Ohio and Mississippi valleys by holding back the Tennessee and its tributaries. In addition, the TVA created an inland waterway 652 miles long with a minimum depth of nine feet, connecting the interior of the

South with the Great Lakes, Ohio River, and Missouri-Mississippi river systems. By 1977, more than 27 million tons of barge freight moved on the river annually.

Flood control and development of navigation required technical planning on a regional scale, to be sure, but the TVA directors viewed their task in the broader terms of helping the people of the region to stop erosion and recover the valley's lost fertility. To accomplish this goal, the TVA used facilities at Muscle Shoals to produce phosphatic fertilizers and distributed them through the AAA. It also conducted a demonstration program to teach farmers how to prevent erosion and rebuild soil and worked with the CCC in the reforestation of hundreds of thousands of acres of gullied lands.

From a strictly legal point of view, the TVA was not established to manufacture and distribute electric power. If the authority should manufacture electric power as a by-product of its main activities, the act of incorporation declared, it might then dispose of such electricity. This of course was said for the benefit of the Supreme Court, for there was grave doubt in 1933 whether the federal government could constitutionally engage in such an activity. No sooner had the TVA begun its work than a group of stockholders in the Alabama Power Company sued to prevent that company from selling certain properties to the TVA. In deciding the case in February 1935, the federal district judge in Birmingham ruled that the TVA had no right intentionally to manufacture and sell electric power; moreover, he forbade seventeen municipalities from buying TVA power produced at Wilson Dam.

This judgment was reversed by the Supreme Court in *Ashwander* v. *T.V.A.* in February 1936. But in this decision the Supreme Court ruled only on the constitutionality of the sale of electricity produced at Wilson Dam. Seeing the loophole, nineteen utility companies brought suit against the TVA in May 1936, praying for an injunction forbidding the authority to produce or distribute electric power except at Wilson Dam. The companies won a temporary injunction in December 1936, but the Supreme Court summarily disposed of the case in *Tennessee Electric Power Company* v. *T.V.A.* in January 1939, by ruling that private companies had no right to complain of competition by the government. The leader of the utility interests, Wendell L. Willkie, president of the Commonwealth & Southern Corporation, gave up the fight after this rebuff. He sold the entire facilities of the Tennessee Electric Power Company to the TVA in August 1939 at his own price of nearly $79 million.

Commonwealth & Southern's withdrawal marked the end of private enterprise in the utilities field in the Tennessee Valley, for numerous smaller operating companies had either already sold out to the TVA or soon followed Commonwealth & Southern's example. The TVA soon emerged as the largest producer of electric power in the United States.

Over the period 1933–1978 total generating capacity in the valley increased from 800,000 kilowatts to 28 million kilowatts, while actual production of electricity increased from 1.5 billion to 118 billion kilowatt-hours.

President Roosevelt, on June 3, 1937, urged Congress to plan for six additional regional authorities.[2] He was thinking, however, more in terms of future than of immediate development. Meanwhile, the administration pushed forward in a more limited way with other regional projects. One was Hoover Dam and the All-American Canal, completed in 1936 with the aid of PWA funds at a total cost of about $165,000,000, which was producing 6 billion kilowatt-hours annually by the late 1970s. Another was Grand Coulee Dam on the Columbia River in Washington, the largest masonry structure in the world, completed in 1942 at a cost of $435,734,-000, with a total power capacity of nearly 2 million kilowatt-hours. A third was the great earthen Fort Peck Dam on the Missouri River in Montana, completed in 1939 and used principally for flood control. Whether these projects should constitute the basis for new regional developments like the TVA would be one of the major issues confronting the American people in the years after 1945.

4. The New Deal in the Supreme Court

Although it was the last branch of the federal government to fall under New Deal influence, the Supreme Court effected a profound and rapid revolution in constitutional interpretation after 1937. Sweeping away all doubt about the constitutionality of advanced social and economic legislation, it became the chief practitioner of sociological jurisprudence, gave a larger degree of freedom to state and federal regulatory agencies than they had enjoyed before, and added strong new safeguards for the protection of civil liberties, labor, and minorities. This revolution in American law occurred in the first instance because Roosevelt was privileged by virtue of his long tenure and the advanced age of incumbent judges to appoint virtually a new federal judiciary, from district courts to the supreme tribunal. By the end of 1941, for example, the president had appointed the chief justice and seven of the eight associate justices of the Supreme Court.

Convinced that the Constitution must serve the needs of an urbanized and industrialized democracy, the members of the "Roosevelt Court"

[2] They were to be in the following areas: the Atlantic Seaboard; the Great Lakes and the Ohio Valley; the Missouri River and the Red River of the North; the drainage basins of the Arkansas, Red, and Rio Grande rivers; the basin of the Colorado River; and the Columbia River Valley.

completed and clarified the constitutional revolution begun by the unreformed court in 1937. In a series of cases from 1938 to 1942 testing the constitutionality of the TVA's power operations, the Fair Labor Standards Act, the Public Utility Holding Company Act of 1935, the second Railroad Retirement Act, the second Agricultural Adjustment Act, and other measures, the court gave Congress virtually unlimited authority under the interstate commerce clause. While accepting the principle of stringent federal regulation, the new court also gave to federal and state administrative agencies broad new freedom to act in the public interest—a reversal of the old court's insistence on imposing judicial criteria on the regulatory agencies.

The New Deal court made its most important contribution in the development of broad federal protection of religious, civil, and political liberty and defense against arbitrary police authority. Chief Justice Hughes had already firmly laid the basis for new safeguards in the 1930s, in decisions establishing the doctrine that because of the adoption of the Fourteenth Amendment no state could deprive a person of any of the basic rights guaranteed by the first ten amendments.[3] The significant fact was the way in which the New Deal court, with Hughes still its spokesman until his retirement in 1941, expanded the concept of basic liberties guaranteed by the Fourteenth Amendment.

To begin with, the court reaffirmed Hughes's earlier condemnation of so-called third-degree methods of obtaining confessions by beating and torture and applied this ban against all subtler forms of torture as well. Again, the court majority went to the defense of Jehovah's Witnesses, a fanatical sect that disavowed loyalty to any earthly state, by ruling in 1943 that local or state authorities could not require children of Jehovah's Witnesses to salute the flag in school, since such action violated the Witnesses' religious scruples and liberty. The court also nullified local ordinances requiring religious groups to obtain licenses to conduct open-air services or distribute literature.

Blacks, who had most often been denied civil rights on account of race, benefited most from the court's increased vigilance. As a result of decisions cited above, they enjoyed a larger degree of personal safety and the right to a fair trial in which members of their race would participate. It was perhaps more important that the new court began to open the gates to educational opportunities for Negroes. On this front the court took the first step toward abandoning the legalism which, under the "separate but

[3]In *Stromberg* v. *California* and *Near* v. *Minnesota*, both rendered in 1931, Hughes invalidated a California statute forbidding the display of the red flag and a Minnesota censorship law, on the ground that the measures contravened fundamental civil rights guaranteed by the Fourteenth Amendment. In another decision in the second Scottsboro case in 1935—*Norris* v. *Alabama*—involving the conviction of seven Negroes for rape, Hughes reversed the conviction on the grounds that blacks had been excluded from the jury that convicted the Scottsboro boys. Exclusion on grounds of race, Hughes asserted, was a denial of the citizen's right to a trial by a jury of his peers.

equal" concept, had permitted southern states to maintain segregated educational facilities for blacks for three-quarters of a century. Chief Justice Hughes set in motion the reversal that would end in repudiation of the theory that separate public schools, colleges, and universities for Negroes could in fact be equal in the case of *Missouri* ex rel. *Gaines* in 1938. In this decision the court simply required the University of Missouri Law School to admit a black student because the state had not provided separate but equal facilities for Negroes. In the forties, as we shall see in the next volume, the New Deal court handed down a series of decisions that removed many of the legal roadblocks on the Negro's avenue to full citizenship, preparing the way for the spectacular advances—social, political, economic, educational—made by the nation's black inhabitants from the 1950s to the present.

Nearly as important were decisions that freed organized labor from the bonds imposed by the courts under the Sherman Antitrust Act. The fundamental issue was whether labor unions, in the conduct of industrial warfare, might employ methods that restrained interstate commerce. The Roosevelt Court formulated a new doctrine in *Apex Hosiery Company* v. *Leader*, 1940, and *United States* v. *Hutcheson*, 1941, that labor unions might restrain commerce when such restraint was incidental to achievement of legitimate objectives. The *Apex* and *Hutcheson* rulings reversed earlier decisions and gave organized labor its long-sought immunity from prosecution under the antitrust laws, except when unions sought directly to restrain commerce through monopolistic and restrictive practices or attempted to defy the government when it was an employer.[4]

5. The Return of the Prodigals: Intellectuals and the New Deal

The hope of reform and redemption under Roosevelt's leadership stirred intellectuals as they had not been roused since 1917. Political thinkers, professors in various disciplines, editors, and socially minded lawyers, clergymen, and writers threw off the torpor and cynicism that had ruined their influence and separated them from the middle classes in the 1920s. They reclaimed their high position as leaveners of progressivism and chief interpreters of the American democratic tradition. In a sense this was the

[4]For example, in *United States* v. *United Mine Workers of America*, 1947, the Supreme Court upheld a district court judge's injunction ordering John L. Lewis and the UMW to terminate a strike against the coal industry, then technically operated by the United States. In this important decision the court ruled that the Norris Anti-Injunction Act did not apply when the United States was the employer. Again, in *United States* v. *Petrillo*, 1947, the Supreme Court upheld an act of Congress of 1946 that made it unlawful for the musicians' union to attempt to compel radio stations to employ more musicians than they actually needed.

natural response of a sensitive group to challenges to democracy raised at home by the depression and abroad by the rise of totalitarianism. The significant fact, however, was that Roosevelt personally drew large numbers of intellectuals, particularly professors, into governmental service and used them to construct his program of reform and rehabilitation.

This was true in the first two years of the New Deal, when the brain trust wrote much of the emergency legislation, and when the president called into the public service men like William O. Douglas of the Yale Law School and Dean James M. Landis of the Harvard Law School to serve as chairmen of the SEC. It was true on a much broader scale when Roosevelt utilized the services of trained scholars and experts to formulate and carry out the important measures of the second New Deal. A mere listing of the host of men and women who left university and foundation posts to launch and direct the Social Security, Farm Security, and kindred agencies would require more space than we could give.

Intellectuals working with the administration did more than staff New Deal agencies. They were organized in various president's committees on social security, farm security, executive reorganization, natural resources, the problem of southern poverty, and the like, and they issued reports that stirred thoughtful Americans to the necessity for action in these fields. Sociologists and economists working with the National Resources Planning Board surveyed the problem of population redistribution and other such subjects. A large group of economists working in conjunction with the TNEC revealed the concentration of control in American industry, exposed the quasi-monopolistic practices of big business, and pointed the way ahead to reform.

The result of these manifold labors was such a thoroughgoing examination of every phase of American economic and social life as the country had not experienced since the early years of the progressive period. In other words, professors and other intellectuals were the muckrakers of the 1930s and catalysts of the latter reform movement. They had greater resources than the earlier muckrakers had, and their audience was different, but their task and accomplishment were much the same. It is not surprising that a generation of intellectuals should have regarded the New Deal era as a time bright with the hope of good things.

The 1930s were a time also when social scientists, under the impact of the depression crisis, discarded old concepts and matured new ones to justify a broad expansion of public authority. Following the trail blazed years before by the iconoclastic Thorstein Veblen, economists analyzed American economic institutions critically and apart from a priori assumptions about the nature of economic activity. These institutional economists taught the necessity of governmental participation in economic affairs. The disciples of John Maynard Keynes, a British economist, for example, evolved a theory of governmental compensatory spending to prevent or end depressions and adduced intricate mathematical formulas to buttress an otherwise common-sense theory. The institutional economists of the 1930s were collectivists to the degree that they recognized the interdependent character of the economy and the necessity for a larger measure of public participation in economic affairs. But, like their earlier counterparts in the United States, they believed not in utopian socialism but in democratic capitalism controlled in the interest of all the people.

A group of political scientists working in an allied field abandoned the ivory tower of abstract principles to discover how and why the American political system actually functioned. It was the sociologists, however, who won the largest audience and had the most significant impact on the thoughtful American public. They were learned, sophisticated, and "scientific," to be sure. But, like the muckrakers, they performed the task, indispensable to the preservation of democracy, of laying bare the unpleasant facts of American social life. The most important new developments in this field accurately reflected the major concerns of the second New Deal—the South and the concept of the region, the Negro, and rural poverty. Led by Howard W. Odum and Rupert B. Vance of the University of North Carolina, southern sociologists courageously examined their region's institutions and social structure. Moreover, southerners joined other sociologists in an almost frantic drive to understand and destroy the bases of racial prejudice. The culmination of this campaign was a cooperative study financed by the Carnegie Corporation of New York and synthesized by the Swedish sociologist, Gunnar Myrdal, in a huge volume entitled *An American Dilemma: The Negro Problem and Modern Democracy* (1944).

Progressive intellectuals in the New Deal era made their most lasting contribution by expanding the horizons of democratic ideology to encompass fundamentals that earlier progressives had often ignored. New Deal progressives assumed that the political institutional structure was essentially sound and made few suggestions for political change.

Their one important contribution was to broaden the meaning of democracy by vastly increasing the participation of farmers, workers, and others in making fundamental decisions concerning their own welfare. The vehicle was the secret ballot, now used, for example, by farmers to determine whether to limit production, or by workers to choose their agent for collective bargaining. New Deal progressives gave major attention to economic justice and security, advanced concepts of civil liberty, and experiments in compensatory spending and planning. The pioneers in the progressive movement had been principally concerned with constructing new forms for democracy and with bringing uncontrolled property under public control. It fell, therefore, to the latter-day progressives to broaden the horizons and objectives of the movement to include programs for the benefit of hitherto neglected disadvantaged groups: blacks, the unemployed, tenants and sharecroppers, industrial workers, and the like. The dimensions of their accomplishment can be seen in the social and economic legislation of the second New Deal. The significance of this accomplishment lay in the fact that the great majority of Americans, Republicans and Democrats alike, accepted and approved the new ideals of social welfare democracy.

6. *The Survival of the Democratic Faith*

The 1930s were a time of severe testing for democracy throughout the world, as fascism, nazism, and militarism grew audacious, and the democracies trembled in fear of aggression and war. At the same time, the totalitarian powers used all weapons of modern psychological warfare in a great campaign to capture the minds of men. The American democracy was throughout the decade a vast free marketplace where contenders peddled their ideological wares, often by deceit and cunning but always with such freedom as befits a democracy.

On one side were a crowd of Fascist and Nazi-financed demagogues and their organizations, whose themes ranged from social justice to violent anti-Semitism. The Reverend Charles E. Coughlin, Catholic priest of Royal Oak, Michigan, quickly emerged as the preeminent leader of the Fascist forces after 1935. Coughlin discarded his social justice disguise in 1938, came out frankly as a pro-Nazi and anti-Semite, and formed the Christian Front in 1939 to unite the widely scattered antidemocratic organizations. The Christian Front had mobilized strong-arm gangs in cities throughout the country by the autumn of 1939, and Coughlin counted his followers by the hundreds of thousands and his audience by the millions.

Working for the same objectives and using the same anti-Semitic, anti-Communist propaganda were a group of lesser Fascist demagogues. There was, for example, William Dudley Pelley, who organized the Silvershirt Legion, a counterpart of Hitler's Brown Shirts, in 1933. Lawrence Dennis, author of *The Coming American Fascism* and other works, was the intellectual leader and principal adviser of the Fascist groups. Huey P. Long's chief organizer and successor, the Reverend Gerald L. K. Smith of Shreveport, Louisiana, moved to Detroit, converted the Share Our Wealth organization into the Committee of One Million, and began a campaign against Jews, Negroes, and Communists. In the Northeast, Fritz J. Kuhn, a naturalized German American and veteran of Hitler's Munich beer-hall *putsch* in 1923, formed the *Amerikadeutscher Volksbund* in 1936. As *Bundesführer* he hailed the day when the swastika would replace the Stars and Stripes.

These and lesser evangels of fascism and religious hatred flooded America with Nazi propaganda, nurtured anti-Semitic passions, and formed an important component of the large isolationist faction after 1939. They had the support of a small but vocal element in Congress, and they reached a combined audience running into the millions. They were potentially dangerous, but they failed to subvert democracy or to become anything more than a lunatic fringe. Most of them were sheer moneymakers rather than conspirators working under the control of the Nazi government. Factionalism and personal rivalries prevented the little führers from uniting. Most important, practically the entire civil and religious leadership of the United States recognized the rabble-rousers for what they were and effectively neutralized their propaganda.

The Communist movement in the United States, on the other hand, was better organized, used a more insidious propaganda, and was part of an international conspiracy directed and controlled by the Soviet government. Its menace to American democracy varied, however, according to changing circumstances and party lines. The Communist party in the United States was torn during the 1920s by the struggle for power between Joseph Stalin and Leon Trotsky then going on within the Soviet Union. Stalin, after winning absolute power in Russia in 1927–1928, called the leaders of the American section to Moscow, removed the Trotskyites, and established a party hack, Earl Browder, as secretary general of the party.

This purging of the Trotsky element weakened American communism just when the depression offered some opportunity to the party. Communists tried to bore into the AF of L unions and were turned back. They then organized rival but successful unions in the clothing, coal, textile, and other industries. They also tried to organize the unemployed. The net effect of all these efforts was only to confirm the dominant popular conviction that communism was at war with American institutions. Party membership, which stood at 8,000 at the beginning of the depression, was only 12,000 in 1932 and, after two years of vigorous recruiting, only 24,000 in 1934. William Z. Foster, the party's presidential candidate in 1932, polled a mere 102,991 votes.

One of the chief causes for Communist failure during the depression years was the inability of American comrades to develop an ideology and a program of their own. They were forced to follow tactics and a party line dictated by the Comintern, or Communist International. International communism from 1928 to 1935 was in its so-called third period, in which Stalin adhered to exaggerated notions of world revolution in order to diminish Trotsky's influence. Convinced that the depression would culminate in the downfall of capitalism in the West, the Russian dictator declared war on labor unions and democratic leaders who seemed to offer the best hope of recovery and reform. In the United States this assault was directed chiefly at the New Deal, which the Communist party declared in 1934 was "the aggressive effort of the bankers and trusts to find a way out of the crisis at the expense of the millions of toilers . . . [and] a program of fascization and the most intense preparations for imperialist war."

Stalin obviously made a bad guess as to the outcome of the world depression. The consequences of his policy were particularly tragic in Germany, where Communist refusal to cooperate with the Social Democrats
was the decisive factor in Hitler's rise to power in 1932-1933. The German Fascists did not collapse as Stalin expected, but soon won complete
control of the Fatherland and began to prepare for an all-out struggle with
Russia. Stalin too late perceived the enormity of his blunder and effected
a swift and complete reversal of policy. He announced the new line at the
seventh Comintern meeting in Moscow in the summer of 1935. Hereafter
Communists should take leadership in a movement to contain fascism by
cooperating in so-called Popular Front organizations with democratic and
"anti-Fascist" forces in political parties, labor unions, and even church
groups. Quietly putting revolutionary doctrines and heroes in temporary
storage, American Communists now proclaimed the slogan "Communism
Is Twentieth Century Americanism," disclaimed any intention forcibly to
subvert the Constitution, and made a bold bid for the friendship of old-
line groups. Their chief aim after 1935 was not rapid expansion of party
membership but infiltration and control of labor unions, writers' groups,
Popular Front organizations with mass memberships, and, finally, the federal government itself.

Communists scored their most important successes on the labor front.
To be sure, they were in no way responsible for events that led to the split
of the AF of L and the formation of the CIO in 1935. But Lewis, Hillman,
and other CIO leaders needed thousands of trained organizers and accepted such support as the Communists could give, without asking questions about Communist motives. As a consequence, Communists by 1938
controlled several major unions, including the electrical workers, the West
Coast longshoremen, and the seamen, and were in strategic positions in
the powerful UAW. Moreover, two fellow travelers if not party members,
Lee Pressman and Len De Caux, were highly placed in the leadership of
the CIO as, respectively, general counsel and editor of the *C.I.O. News.*
Even more important, the general counsel and a member of the NLRB,
Nathan Witt and Edwin S. Davis, were strong Communist sympathizers if
not card-bearing party members during the period of the critical struggle
between the CIO and AF of L from 1935 to 1940.

To a large group of writers, Communist doctrine and propaganda either
appealed with the force of a new religion or else held out the hope of
genuine cooperation to halt the spread of fascism and anti-Semitism at
home and abroad. Many intellectuals were sickened by the plight of the
lower classes in the United States and inspired by the seeming material
progress and social stability of the Soviet Union during the depression
period. Hence a number of distinguished American novelists, including
Sherwood Anderson, Erskine Caldwell, and Granville Hicks, publicly supported Foster for president in 1932. Moreover, left wing writers and artists banded together in John Reed clubs to nurse the cult of proletarian

literature from 1932 to 1935. The John Reed clubs metamorphosed into the League of American Writers in 1935. It held annual conferences until 1939 and included a hard core of Communists and a host of momentary cooperators like Ernest Hemingway, Richard Wright, Archibald Mac-Leish, Upton Sinclair, and James T. Farrell. Left wing actors also banded together in the Group Theater, Theater Union, and Theater Collective to enjoy the bohemian life and salve their social consciences by producing plays of Clifford Odets, John Howard Lawson, Elmer Rice, and other "proletarian" playwrights.

Communist leaders executed their most ambitious schemes in trying to gain control of large segments of public opinion through the formation of more general "front" organizations. In these, distinguished non-Communist progressives lent their names and energies to bodies actually controlled by a Communist minority. Three such front organizations were the American League for Peace and Democracy, which claimed an affiliated membership of over 7 million, the American Student Union, and the American Youth Congress, which won the sponsorship of Eleanor Roosevelt, the president's wife, and pretended to speak for nearly 5 million young people.

On the political front, Communists pursued a two-pronged campaign from 1935 to 1939: first, to bore into and gain control of independent non-Communist political groups and, second, to build a powerful machine within the federal government to influence federal policies and carry on political espionage. In both its aspects this campaign met with some success. The Communists put a ticket, headed by Browder, into the field during the campaign of 1936; under cover, they worked very hard for Roosevelt. Only in New York City, however, did they gain any power in an important political party.[5]

More successful was the Communist effort to establish a conspiratorial underground in Washington. The leader of the principal group was Harold Ware, who had managed a large collective farm in Russia in the early 1920s. Ware organized a Communist cell soon after Roosevelt's inauguration that included a number of party members strategically placed in various departments and agencies. Several of the conspirators and cooperators, notably Alger Hiss, Harry Dexter White, Julian Wadleigh, and Nathan Witt, rose to positions of high responsibility and carried from their offices thousands of documents to be photographed and passed on to the head of the Soviet underground, Colonel Boris Bykov. Witt and later John

[5]This was the American Labor party, formed by labor leaders and Socialists to support the Democratic cause in 1936. Communists entered the ALP at the outset but kept well under cover for a number of years. However, Sidney Hillman, the CIO's chief political spokesman, joined forces with the Communists in 1944 to capture the ALP and drive the anti-Communist right wing from control of the party. The right wing group, headed by George S. Counts and David Dubinsky, thereupon seceded and formed the American Liberal party. The complete measure of Communist control of the American Labor party became evident after Hillman's death in 1946, when the devout admirer of Stalin, Representative Vito Marcantonio, became state chairman of the party.

Abt became leaders of the cell after Ware's death in an automobile accident in 1935.

The American Communist movement began to lose strength in 1937, suffered mortal blows in 1938 and 1939, and had shrunk to its hard conspiratorial core in 1941. For this swift decline in prestige American comrades could only blame the actions of their Soviet masters and the fundamental democratic convictions of the great body of American intellectuals. Several thousand Americans, many of them non-Communists but inbued with the Popular Front psychology, fought on the Loyalist side in the Spanish Civil War from 1936 to 1939. Many young idealists saw Communists at work, conspiring to control the Loyalist government and betraying and killing comrades-in-arms to achieve this goal. John Dos Passos, one of the most distinguished of the Popular Front novelists, was thus disillusioned by what he saw in Spain.

Also shattering to illusions were the purges, trials, and executions from 1936 to 1938 by which Stalin eliminated his closest friends and rivals and established a ruthless monolithic dictatorship. The crowning disillusionment came when the Soviet government signed a Non-Aggression Pact with Hitlerite Germany in August 1939. Communists changed at once from ardent "anti-Fascists" into apologists for nazism and vehement opponents of any form of support for Britain and France in their war against Germany. Thus events on the international scene ripped off the democratic disguise of American communism and revealed the true character of the movement for all to see and know the truth.

What shall we say about American communism's significance in the 1930s—its strength, its hold over American intellectuals, and the danger that it posed to the American democracy? In brief, how red was the so-called Red Decade? It was not as red as the above discussion might indicate. To begin with, few Popular Front Americans actually embraced the Communist ideology, for historical materialism and a philosophy of class warfare were doctrines abhorrent to people imbued with the democratic tradition. It must be remembered, also, that the Communists succeeded only to the degree that they were able to identify communism with democracy and resistance to brutal aggression and anti-Semitism.

However, the significant fact was not the momentary alignment of these Americans but the proof, furnished by events of the 1930s, that communism could not prosper when the channels of exposure and criticism were kept open. Because of free debate and objective reporting of events, practically all Americans affected by the concept of Popular Front recognized the character of international communism and then rallied courageously to the defense of the democratic ideal. The American democracy survived in the face of the Communist assault, moreover, because the reforms of the second New Deal healed the wounds of the body politic and gave proof that democracy could effect fundamental institutional changes without recourse to revolution, purges, and executions.

19

---※✕※---

The United States
and the Collapse of
the International Structure,

1931–1938

We come now to that time of trouble when aggressors in Europe and the Far East made a mockery of the peace structure so hopefully constructed during the Versailles conference and the 1920s. Depression, fear, mutual suspicion, and a guilt complex arising from the alleged injustices of the Versailles settlement destroyed the democratic coalition, prevented the western democracies from finding a new modus vivendi for collective defense, and so paralyzed the peoples of Britain, France, and the United States that they were impotent in the face of the rising tide of aggression.

It was an ironic circumstance that an overwhelming majority of the people of the world, with unrivaled resources and technology and a great superiority in military and naval power, should have been unable to curb aggression because they were unwilling to run the risk of war. Why this was so will become evident as we review events of the 1930s and relate the part that the American people played in the unfolding tragedy.

1. Stimson, Hoover, and the Manchurian Crisis

The first important assault upon the post–World War peace structure occurred when Japan occupied Manchuria and made war on China in 1931–1932, and the western powers with interests in the Far East failed to cooperate in any effective measures to halt Japanese aggression. The background can be briefly told. The Japanese government enjoyed such large privileges in southern Manchuria after the Russo-Japanese War that the province soon became an economic colony of the island empire, although it remained technically under Chinese political jurisdiction. The Japanese imperial government by and large attempted to protect its interests in Manchuria by a policy of friendship with China and the great powers. Such a peaceful policy, however, could prevail only so long as China and the western powers acknowledged Japanese supremacy in Manchuria. All Japanese, liberals and militarists alike, regarded the province as the economic lifeline of the empire and the bulwark against Russian expansion.

Two developments in the 1920s excited Japanese fears for the safety of Manchuria and strengthened the clique who had long been clamoring for a "positive" policy of direct action. One was the resurgence of Soviet Russia as a Far Eastern power after Russian withdrawal from northern Manchuria and the Maritime Province following the Bolshevik revolution. Sun Yat-sen, leader of the Chinese Nationalist party, the Kuomintang, joined forces with the Chinese Communists and the Soviet government in 1924 in a drive to conquer and unite his country. Sun's successor, Chiang Kai-shek, succeeded in this campaign. Then he broke with the Chinese Communists in 1927 and next endeavored to oust the Russians from northern Manchuria. The result was an undeclared war between China and Russia in 1929. Soviet armies invaded northern Manchuria and compelled the Chinese to respect the Sino-Soviet treaty of 1924 providing for joint Chinese and Russian control of the Chinese Eastern Railway that ran from Siberia to Harbin and Vladivostok. At the same time, the Soviet government was busily engaged in constructing huge air and naval bases at Vladivostok that pointed at the heart of Japan.

The return of Russian power to the Far East made the Japanese all the more determined to reinforce southern Manchuria as a barrier against Soviet expansion. But the development that incited Japan to so-called positive action was the spread of Chinese nationalism into Manchuria and Chiang Kai-shek's attempt to control that province. A number of minor incidents had increased the tension to the breaking point by 1931. The Japanese army, taking control of policy out of the hands of the foreign minister, attacked and occupied Mukden, Changchun, and other Manchurian cities on September 18–19, 1931.

The blow was well timed, for Britain and the United States were then struggling to stave off international economic collapse. China appealed to the League of Nations for protection on September 21, and the whole world turned to Britain and the United States. The British were in general opposed to strong measures against Japan and waited to see what policy the Washington government would follow.

Secretary of State Henry L. Stimson moved cautiously during the first weeks following the outbreak of the crisis because he assumed that strong American action might embarrass the Japanese cabinet in bringing the army under control. The Tokyo Foreign Office talked of direct negotiations with China and withdrawal, but the imperial army drove steadily forward and consolidated its hold over all southern Manchuria. The moderate cabinet gave way in December to a cabinet that supported the army, and Japanese forces occupied Chinchow, the last Chinese stronghold in Manchuria, on January 2, 1932.

Stimson was now convinced that Japanese militarists and imperialists had ruthlessly violated treaties and destroyed the entire security system erected at the Washington Conference. He was eager to rally Britain and America in defense of China, even if that meant economic sanctions and possible war. However, no statesman ever faced more discouraging obstacles than Stimson did in late 1931 and early 1932. He had to content himself with expressing his government's abhorrence of Japanese aggression while he knew that he could do nothing to bring the Japanese to book.

To begin with, evidence was overwhelming that the American people strongly condemned Japanese ruthlessness but even more strongly opposed any measures that might conceivably lead to war. The same public spokesmen who were loudest in condemning Japan advised complete withdrawal of American forces from China. If this overwhelming popular resistance to warlike moves had not been enough, then President Hoover's inflexible determination to avoid the risk of war would have proved an insurmountable barrier to forceful action. Stimson suggested as early as October 1931 that the United States might have to cooperate with the League of Nations in imposing sanctions against Japan. Hoover was startled and concluded that his "able Secretary was at times more of a warrior than a diplomat." The president learned through personal inquiry in London that the British government would not support the United States in a strong policy. He was convinced that the American people did not want war, and that the imposition of sanctions would goad Japan into a war which the United States might have to fight alone. He therefore sternly vetoed Stimson's plan for economic measures in early 1932.

There were, the president thought, moral weapons in the arsenal of diplomacy. He suggested that Stimson should revive the doctrine of nonrecognition of territorial and political changes effected by military force, which Secretary Bryan had first enunciated in 1915 at the time of the crisis over Japan's twenty-one demands upon China (see p. 151). Hence Stimson issued an identical warning to Japan and China on January 7, 1932: the American government would recognize no changes in the Far East

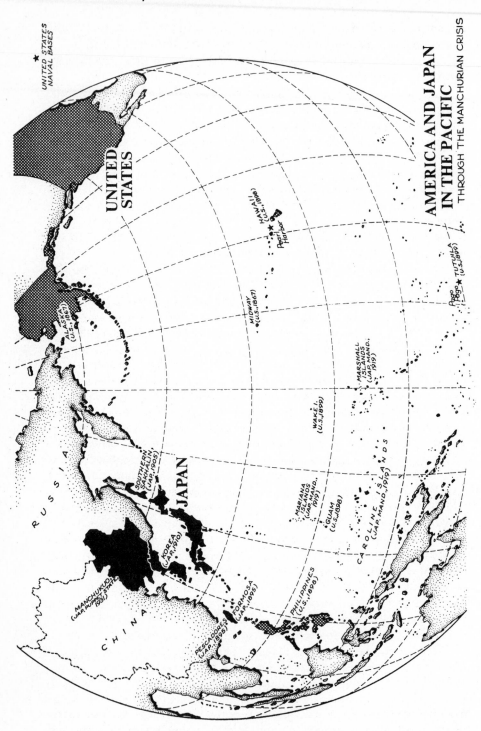

UNITED STATES NAVAL BASES

AMERICA AND JAPAN IN THE PACIFIC

THROUGH THE MANCHURIAN CRISIS

UNITED STATES

RUSSIA

JAPAN

CHINA

HAWAII (U.S., 1898)

Pearl Harbor

MIDWAY (U.S., 1867)

ALASKA (U.S., 1867)

Pago Pago (U.S., 1899) TUTUILA (U.S., 1899)

MARSHALL ISLANDS (JAP. MAND., 1919)

WAKE I. (U.S., 1899)

SOUTHERN SAKHALIN (JAP., 1905)

KOREA (JAP., 1910)

MANCHUKUO (JAP. PUPPET STATE, 1931)

MARIANA ISLANDS (JAP. MAND., 1919)

GUAM (U.S., 1898)

CAROLINE ISLANDS (JAP. MAND., 1919)

PHILIPPINES (U.S., 1898)

PESCADORES (JAP., 1895)

FORMOSA (JAP., 1895)

brought about by force which impaired the treaty rights of the United States and the independence and administrative integrity of China.

The British Foreign Office refused to concur, while the Japanese Foreign Office replied sarcastically to the State Department on January 16, 1932. Then, less than two weeks later, on January 28, the Japanese fleet and marines invaded Shanghai in retaliation against a Chinese boycott, wantonly bombarded the city, and killed thousands of civilians. The Shanghai attack strengthened Stimson's hand but pointed up the fatal weakness of his method. On the one side the British foreign secretary now joined Stimson in vigorous diplomatic condemnations of this new Japanese aggression. On the other side, when Stimson suggested imposing economic sanctions, Hoover refused even more emphatically than before. Thus Stimson once again was forced back to the use of moral weapons. In a long public letter to Senator Borah on February 23, 1932, he reiterated the American position in order to keep the record clear.

It was a triumph for Stimson when the assembly of the League of Nations, with the Japanese representative abstaining, unanimously adopted a resolution on March 11, 1932, incorporating almost verbatim the Bryan-Stimson doctrine of nonrecognition. Events in the Far Eastern crisis now moved swiftly to conclusion. A League commission of inquiry presented a report naming Japan as the aggressor, and the League assembly on February 24, 1933, called upon Japan to observe the covenant and return Manchuria to China. The Japanese replied by withdrawing from the League.

These are the bare facts of this episode. Their meaning is still not altogether clear. This much, at least, can be said by way of conclusion: the policy of the United States and the League of Nations was for from being realistic however one views the merits of the case. If the Japanese attack on Manchuria was a gross violation of the covenant and the Nine Power Treaty, then only willingness to go to war, not moral exhortation, would have sufficed to bring the Japanese to book. If the Japanese were justified in securing their hold on Manchuria, then wisdom would have demanded a policy of acquiescence. Hoover and Stimson in effect simply perpetuated a policy that had long been irrelevant to the facts of international life in the Far East. More than this, they gave a simple moral gloss to an enormously complicated situation. Without knowing it, they staked out a policy that would eventually culminate in war between their country and imperial Japan.

2. The United States and the Collapse of European Stability, 1931–1933

We have seen how President Hoover issued his plan for a one-year moratorium on all intergovernmental debt and reparations payments in the late spring of 1931, and how this move eased the strain on the international economy (see p. 362). The late summer or autumn of 1931 was clearly the time for the president to urge a mutual cancellation of all intergovernmental debt and reparations obligations. Hoover was personally willing to extend the moratorium until the worst of the depression had passed, but he regarded Europe's debts to the United States as sacred obligations and would never consent to cancel them or connect them officially with Germany's reparations obligations. In this matter he, not Stimson, who wanted mutual cancellation, spoke for the vast majority of Americans and Congress. The latter voiced its emphatic opposition to any reduction or cancellation of the war debts by joint resolution on December 23, 1931.

The truth was, however, that Germany could not pay reparations in 1932, and most of the European debtors were thus unable to meet their debt payments to America without running the risk of bankruptcy. Europeans consequently did what they had to do. Representatives of the western and central European powers, meeting in Lausanne, Switzerland, in June 1932, reduced Germany's reparations obligations to $714 million and tacitly agreed that this sum would never have to be paid. However, this final settlement would go into effect only when the nations in debt to the United States and one another had reached a "satisfactory settlement" of the war debts question. Stimson urged a graceful acceptance of the inevitable, but Hoover condemned the Lausanne agreement and continued to apply diplomatic pressure on Europe.

The denouement of this story can be briefly told. Germany ceased reparations payments altogether after the Lausanne Conference. Then, when the time for renewal of semiannual payments to the United States came in December 1932, Britain, Czechoslovakia, Italy, Finland, Latvia, and Lithuania met their obligations, while France, Greece, Poland, Belgium, Estonia, and Hungary defaulted. Britain, Italy, Czechoslovakia, Rumania, Lithuania, and Latvia made token payments in June 1933, while the remaining debtors, except Finland, again defaulted. Congress replied on April 13, 1934, with the Johnson Act. It forbade any American citizen or corporation to lend money to any nation in default on its debt payments to the United States. When the attorney general ruled that token payments did not meet the requirements of the Johnson Act, all of America's debtors except Finland defaulted in 1934 and afterward.

However, there seemed to be some hope in early 1933 that American and western European leaders would unite in the forthcoming World Economic Conference to attack two other impediments to international economic recovery—high tariffs and unstable currencies. President Hoover had taken leadership in calling the conference, and the new president, Roosevelt, promised cooperation. Prime Minister Ramsay MacDonald of Great Britain, former Premier Edouard Herriot of France, and other spokesmen from Europe descended upon Washington in late April and early May for preliminary conversations with Roosevelt and his economic advisers. The upshot of these discussions was a firm American refusal to discuss suspension of war debt payments, agreement that the conference

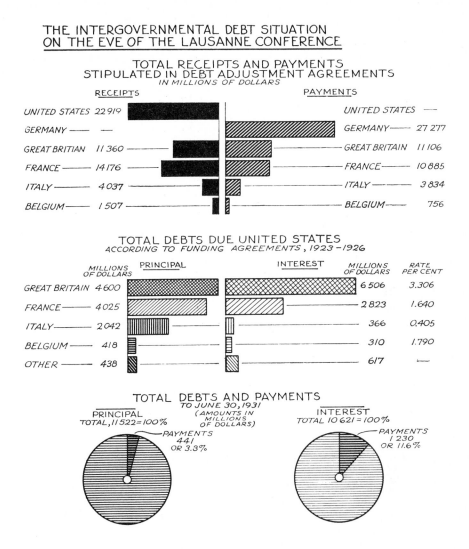

THE INTERGOVERNMENTAL DEBT SITUATION
ON THE EVE OF THE LAUSANNE CONFERENCE

TOTAL RECEIPTS AND PAYMENTS
STIPULATED IN DEBT ADJUSTMENT AGREEMENTS
IN MILLIONS OF DOLLARS

RECEIPTS		PAYMENTS
UNITED STATES 22 919		UNITED STATES —
GERMANY — —		GERMANY — 27 277
GREAT BRITIAN 11 360		GREAT BRITAIN 11 106
FRANCE 14 176		FRANCE 10 885
ITALY 4 037		ITALY 3 834
BELGIUM 1 507		BELGIUM 756

TOTAL DEBTS DUE UNITED STATES
ACCORDING TO FUNDING AGREEMENTS, 1923-1926

	MILLIONS OF DOLLARS	PRINCIPAL	INTEREST	MILLIONS OF DOLLARS	RATE PER CENT
GREAT BRITAIN	4 600			6 506	3.306
FRANCE	4 025			2 823	1.640
ITALY	2 042			366	0.405
BELGIUM	418			310	1.790
OTHER	438			617	—

TOTAL DEBTS AND PAYMENTS
TO JUNE 30, 1931

PRINCIPAL
TOTAL, 11 522 = 100%
(AMOUNTS IN MILLIONS OF DOLLARS)
— PAYMENTS 441 OR 3.3%

INTEREST
TOTAL 10 621 = 100%
— PAYMENTS 1 230 OR 11.6%

should meet in London in June 1933, and vague assurances by Roosevelt that the United States would cooperate in lowering tariff barriers and stabilizing currencies.

Once again the United States had an opportunity to take bold leadership in formulating a program to repair the ravages of the depression. Once again the American government refused the opportunity, because Roosevelt had no intention of agreeing to the first necessary step, currency stabilization, unless the dollar had fallen sufficiently in value to stimulate a considerable price increase at home and an increase of American exports abroad. A large American delegation, headed by the new secretary of state, Cordell Hull, sailed for London on May 31, 1933; but they sailed in deepest ignorance of the president's intentions and in confusion among themselves. Hull believed that his government should agree to lower its tariffs and peg the dollar at its then present value in gold; moreover, he thought that Roosevelt agreed with him. On the other hand, a majority of the delegates opposed tariff reductions and were confused on stabilization.

The conference opened on June 12 and got off to a bad start when Prime Minister MacDonald raised the war debts question. After a week of indecisive debate, Roosevelt sent his economic adviser, Raymond Moley, to London with a tentative proposal to stabilize the dollar, then worth $4.00 to the British pound, at between $4.05 and $4.25 to the pound. But while Moley was on the high seas the dollar began to fall rapidly in value, until it reached $4.38 to the British pound on June 28. Roosevelt was delighted by this development. He was convinced that further depreciation of the dollar was essential to recovery at home, and so he decided to end the agonizing debate at London. Therefore, he sent his "Bombshell Message" on July 3 to the conference announcing that the United States could not agree to immediate currency stabilization. Hull kept the conference alive for another three weeks by heroic efforts, but all the delegates knew that further talk was futile.

American leadership in the movement for disarmament was considerably more vigorous than in international economic policies. Various commissions of the League worked on the problem of disarmament from 1921 to 1926; and the United States joined the European powers from 1926 to 1931 in a League Preparatory Commission to a draft a treaty. The World Disarmament Conference finally met at Geneva on February 2, 1932, amid alarming developments in Asia and Europe. The Japanese had attacked Shanghai only a few days before, while the Nazi party, frankly committed to rearmament and repudiation of the Versailles treaty, was growing daily in Germany.

From February 2 to June 21, 1932, the conference intermittently discussed a French proposal for an international army and compulsory arbitration, and American proposals for abolition of offensive armaments like tanks and bombing planes. President Hoover tried to end what seemed to be the hopeless deadlock by using the same techniques of shock and surprise that Secretary Hughes had employed successfully at the Washington Naval Conference. The head of the American delegation presented Hoover's plan on June 22, 1932. It proposed immediate abolition of all bombers, tanks, large mobile artillery, and instruments of chemical warfare, and the reduction of all land and naval forces by approximately one-third. Hoover's proposal revived the conference; and American, British, and French leaders soon afterward promised revision of the Versailles treaty and equality in land armaments to Germany. But these concessions came too late to save the future peace of Europe. Hitler became chancellor of Germany on January 30, 1933. Roosevelt renewed Hoover's plea for action on May 16 and promised American participation in a new collective security system on May 24, but Hitler withdrew his delegations from the World Disarmament Conference and the League on October 14, 1933.

One development in 1933—American recognition of the Soviet Union—at first seemed a positive step in the direction of common action to prevent aggression. The Washington government since 1917 had consistently withheld diplomatic recognition from the Moscow regime, chiefly because it refused to honor the debt of the czarist government to the United States, confiscated American-owned property, denied religious freedom to Americans in the USSR, and waged covert warfare against American institutions through the Comintern and its branch in the United States. However, international circumstances made an abrupt change in Russian policy imperative by 1933. In that year Russia feared a Japanese attack against the Maritime Province, and Soviet authorities now wanted American friendship and the right to purchase supplies on credit in the United States in the event of war with Japan.

President Roosevelt informed the Soviet government on October 10, 1933, that he would receive a commissioner to explore "all questions outstanding between our countries." The Russian foreign minister, Maxim Litvinov, arrived in Washingon on November 7 to open negotiations. The upshot was an agreement embodied in a formal exchange of notes on November 16, 1933. In return for American recognition, the Soviet government promised to abstain from propaganda activity in the United States, guarantee religious freedom and fair trials to Americans in the Soviet Union, and negotiate a settlement of the czarist debt to the United States.

The Washington administration, eager to promote full economic intercourse with the Soviet Union, established an Export-Import Bank on February 12, 1934, to facilitate exchange. Secretary Hull's bright hopes of friendship and mutual accommodation were soon blasted, however, by Russian failure to honor its pledges of November 16, 1933. Negotiations over a debt settlement failed, and the State Department blocked the extension of any credits to the Soviet Union. More damaging to Russian-American relations was the Kremlin's refusal to call off the dogs operating in the guise of the American Communist party. Relations between the two governments were formally correct but far from cordial before 1941.

3. *The Good Neighbor Policy, 1933–1936*

Franklin D. Roosevelt and Cordell Hull came into control of American foreign policy at a time when the forces of international anarchy seemed about to engulf the New World as much as the Old. With courage and unflagging consistency they repudiated Wilsonian missionary interventionism, completed the Hoover-Stimson reversal of the Roosevelt Corollary (see pp. 339–342), and then went on to construct an edifice of inter-

American friendship and peace. Let us see how this so-called Good Neighbor policy[1] developed and what its larger consequences were.

Much remained to be done in 1933 to put the relations of the United States with its Latin American neighbors on a really cordial footing. For one thing, although the Hoover administration had tacitly repudiated the Roosevelt Corollary, it had steadfastly refused to surrender the alleged right to intervene in the internal affairs of the Caribbean republics. No Latin American could take its professions of friendship seriously so long as the United States maintained this position. Moreover, tragic circumstances were conspiring in Latin America in 1932 and early 1933 to present the new administration with perplexing difficulties. In the first place, American trade with Latin America had declined from $2,079,817,000 in 1929 to $573,814,000 in 1932. The effect was to blast the foundations of Latin American prosperity and cause wholesale economic disorganization, bankruptcy, and repudiation. Secondly, the peace of the New World was threatened by dissension from within as Roosevelt came into office. The so-called Chaco War between Paraguay and Bolivia was raging intermittently in the jungles, a border conflict between Colombia and Peru threatened to explode into full-scale war, and unrest was rising in Cuba against the brutal dictatorship of Gerardo Machado.

Roosevelt's and Hull's determination to establish a genuine Pan-American accord was put immediately to test as a result of these and other developments. When the League of Nations offered to mediate the Peruvian-Colombian border dispute, the State Department approved and, in May 1933, appointed a member of the commission that settled the controversy a year later. Soon afterward, on August 7, 1933, the State Department concluded an agreement with Haiti for withdrawal of American marines from the black republic by October 1, 1934. The real test of the new administration's sincerity came when a revolution against the Machado government broke out in Cuba in the spring of 1933. There were numerous demands for American intervention, but Roosevelt and Hull stubbornly resisted them. The State Department stood by patiently.

These developments were a prelude to the Seventh Inter-American Conference that met in Montevideo, Uruguay, in December 1933. Hull arrived in Montevideo to be greeted by an angry reception from the local press and deep hostility among many of the Latin American delegates. First he called upon all the foreign ministers in their hotel suites. Next he told the Argentinian foreign minister, Doctor Saavedra Lamas, who had given evidences of wanting to turn the conference into an anti–United States rally, that the American government stood ready to renounce any right it once claimed to intervene in the affairs of sister states.

---

[1] Roosevelt in his first inaugural dedicated the United States to the policy of the good neighbor in foreign affairs generally. He reiterated the phrase a few weeks later, in an address on Pan-American Day, and applied it specifically to the Latin American policy of the United States. The slogan at once caught the popular fancy and was thereafter associated only with the administration's Latin American policy.

Hull's actions assured the entire success of the Montevideo Conference, and the result of the newly found spirit of friendship was the signing of a number of important inter-American treaties. The most important was the Convention on Rights and Duties of States. It represented a sweeping triumph for Latin American jurisprudence on such important issues as recognition of de facto governments, equality of states, nonintervention, the sovereignty of states in dealing with foreign nationals, inviolability of territory, and territorial changes effected by forceful means.

The months following the Montevideo Conference were a critical period. Any refusal by the United States to observe the letter and spirit of the Convention on Rights and Duties of States would have destroyed all the progress made thus far. For the second time Cuba became the testing ground of the Good Neighbor's sincerity, for the Cubans demanded abrogation of the Cuban-American Treaty of 1903 that embodied the Platt Amendment and gave the United States a legal right to intervene in Cuba's internal and external affairs. Hull hastened to honor his promises after recognizing the government of Carlos Mendieta, who came to power with the support of General Fulgencio Batista on January 18, 1934. The secretary of state signed a treaty on May 29, 1934, formally abrogating the Platt Amendment and ending all special American rights in Cuba, except the right to maintain a naval base at Guantánamo.[2] In addition, Hull moved soon afterward to restore the basis of Cuban prosperity, the sugar trade, which had been hard hit by the Hawley-Smoot Tariff[3] and the depression. The tariff on Cuban sugar was reduced by 25 percent in May and by an additional 40 percent in August. As a result, American trade with Cuba increased nearly 100 percent during the next year.

There still remained three Caribbean countries—Haiti, the Dominican Republic, and Panama—in which the United States might intervene by treaty right to protect property and maintain order. By special agreement with the Haitian government, American marines were withdrawn from Port-au-Prince on August 15, 1934, instead of on October 1 as the treaty of 1933 had stipulated. Moreover, Washington allowed the Haitian-American Treaty of 1916, which had made Haiti a semiprotectorate of the United States, to expire in 1936 and relinquished its control over Haiti's financial affairs. Panama and the United States concluded a treaty in 1936 that ended the American right to intervene in Panamanian affairs granted in the Panamanian-American Treaty of 1903.[4] The Dominican-American Treaty of 1924, which had continued American receivership of the Do-

---

[2] Ratifications were exchanged on June 9, 1934, and the Cubans held a three-day festival to celebrate.

[3] American imports from Cuba declined in value from $207,421,000 in 1929 to $90,059,000 in 1931.

[4] A special article provided, however, that the two nations would consult with each other and take action to protect the Panama Canal should war or aggression endanger its security. The United States Senate approved the treaty in 1939, but only after the Panamanian government had agreed that in emergencies the United States might act first and consult afterward.

minican customs after the withdrawal of American troops and which did not expire until 1945, was abrogated by a new treaty between the two countries in 1940, and the receivership was ended in 1941.

Thus did the United States surrender rights and privileges that few nations in the history of the world have voluntarily given up once they obtained them. No act of the Roosevelt administration better illustrated its good faith than the execution of this retreat from empire in the Caribbean. It is only fair to add that the administration was not motivated by sentimental altruism but rather by a desire to protect the security of the people of the United States. Roosevelt and Hull believed that only a policy of nonintervention would win the friendship of Latin America. They further believed that Latin American friendship was essential to the security of the United States. Hence they adhered firmly to nonintervention, even when that policy involved possible capital losses by American citizens. Their action came none too soon, for events in Europe and Asia demanded concerted cooperation for peace by the American republics.

The Eighth Inter-American Conference was scheduled to meet in Lima, Peru, in 1938, but the international situation was so foreboding by 1936 that the State Department did not dare to wait to sound a warning against potential Nazi aggression in the New World. At Roosevelt's suggestion, therefore, a special inter-American conference assembled at Buenos Aires in December 1936. The president went in person to Buenos Aires and opened the conference on December 1 to emphasize the seriousness of the international crisis heightened by the recent outbreak of civil war in Spain.

The delegates made easy progress on matters about which there was no disagreement. A new treaty—an Additional Protocol Relative to Non-Intervention—pledging the American republics not to intervene "directly or indirectly" in the affairs of neighboring states, for example, was signed by representatives of all twenty-one republics. On the overshadowing issue of mutual defense against aggression, however, Hull and the American delegation ran head on into the opposition of the Argentine foreign minister, Saavedra Lamas.

Rather than disrupt the conference, the American and Argentine delegations accepted a compromise offered by the Brazilians. It was embodied in a Convention for Collective Security and a Convention to Co-ordinate, Extend and Assure the Fulfillment of Existing Treaties. These treaties omitted Hull's suggestion for a permanent consultative committee, but they pledged the signatories to consult with one another in the event that war threatened the peace of the hemisphere; to refrain from hostile action against one another for six months while consultation was in progress; and to adopt a common neutrality in the event that war should break out. The Convention for Collective Security was weakened by the inclusion, at Argentina's insistence, of a reservation giving each signatory freedom to refuse to join in mutual consultation in the event that war outside the hemisphere threatened the peace of the Americas. Hull, nonetheless, was convinced that a beginning toward mutualization of the Monroe Doctrine had been made. Finally, the delegates at Buenos Aires proclaimed their unity and peaceful purposes in a Declaration of Principles of Inter-American Solidarity and Co-operation. It pledged the American republics to peaceful settlement of all disputes and outlawed territorial conquest, collection of debts by force, and intervention by one state in the affairs of another.

Thus the Roosevelt administration had laid the groundwork for friendship and mutual defense in the Western Hemisphere by the time that Hitler's threats had imperiled hopes for peace in Europe. We shall see in the following section, moreover, how Washington reinforced political unity with measures of economic support and refused to use even the threat of force to protect American property interests in Latin America. Let us now examine another phase of the American retreat from empire during the 1930s—the ironic way in which domestic self-interest combined with old anti-imperialistic impulses to impose independence upon the Filipinos.

Following the award of near-autonomy to the Philippines by the Jones Act of 1916, President Wilson recommended full independence in 1920. President Harding, committed to a more cautious policy, sent a commission in 1921 headed by General Leonard Wood and former Governor General W. Cameron Forbes to Manila to investigate. Wood stayed on as governor general and thoroughly antagonized local leaders by his insistence upon prerogative. The new governor general after Wood's death in 1927, Henry L. Stimson, quickly won the confidence of Filipino politicians.

All Filipino leaders continued in the 1920s publicly to demand immediate independence and privately to wonder whether independence was worth losing the free American market for Philippine sugar and other agricultural products. The Philippine-American trade had reached $183 million in value by 1930, and almost two-thirds of the people of the islands were dependent upon it for the highest standard of living in the Orient. Moreover, fear of an expansive Japan after 1931 caused Filipino leaders to count the blessings of American protection and conclude that dominion status in an American Commonwealth was safer than a perilous independence.

It was the depression that gave the greatest impetus to the movement for the independence that most Filipino leaders privately opposed by 1932. Western sugar beet growers, American investors in the Cuban sugar industry, southern cotton growers, and dairymen throughout the country were determined to end the competition from Philippine sugar and cocoanut oil. Their spokesmen in Congress on January 17, 1933, adopted over Hoover's veto an act for Philippine independence after a ten-year transition period, provided that the Filipinos established a republican form of government. The Philippine legislature rejected the act and sought dominion status instead. But Congress was adamant, and the Filipino leaders had to accept the Tydings-McDuffie Act of March 24, 1934. It was almost an exact replica of the Independence Act of 1933. Filipino voters and President Roosevelt subsequently approved a Philippine Constitution drafted by a constitutional convention in 1934 and 1935; Manuel Quezon became first president of the Commonwealth of the Philippines in 1935; and July 4, 1946, was set as the date for launching the Philippine Republic.

4. The Good Neighbor in Foreign Economic Policy

Roosevelt tried to ride two horses at the same time during the first year of his presidency. On the one hand, he pursued a thoroughly enlightened policy of political cooperation and friendship with foreign countries. On the other hand, he experimented with nationalistic economic measures. The president would obviously have to make up his mind and coordinate his political and economic foreign policies. He would either have to pursue a course of political and economic autarky, such as Germany embarked upon in 1933, or else he would have to stabilize the dollar, lower tariffs, and make serious efforts to reopen the channels of international trade.

From the beginning, Roosevelt's secretary of state, Cordell Hull, was obsessed with the conviction that the United States could never find prosperity and friendship abroad unless it was willing to act like a good neighbor in economic affairs. He saw his suggestions for currency stabilization and a reciprocal trade program go unheeded for almost a year while proponents of economic nationalism had the president's ear. But he waited patiently, and Roosevelt was ready to stabilize the dollar and conclude his little experiment in autarky by the end of 1933.[5] With the White House's blessing, therefore, Hull and his assistants set to work on a reciprocal trade bill in January 1934. It empowered the president to negotiate trade agreements, which would go into effect without congressional approval, and to raise or lower existing Hawley-Smoot rates by as much as 50 percent in order to obtain concessions from other countries. All tariff reductions made by the United States would apply to all nations that accorded the benefits of their lowest tariff rates to the United States. The Trade Agreements bill passed Congress easily, and the president signed the measure on June 12, 1934.

The State Department concluded its first trade agreement with Cuba on August 24, 1934, and began negotiations with other nations soon afterward. It had concluded trade agreements by the end of 1936 with Belgium, Sweden, Holland, Canada, France, Switzerland, Finland, and six Latin American nations as well. American exports to these countries in-

---

[5] As we have seen, he stabilized the price of the dollar on January 31, 1934. Moreover, in October 1936 the American, British, and French governments agreed to stabilize their currencies, use large stabilization funds to maintain the value of these currencies in the international exchanges, and adopt a common gold standard for purposes of international trade.

creased 14 percent during 1936, as compared with an increase in exports to other nations of only 4 percent.

Congress renewed the Trade Agreements Act for a second three-year period in 1937, and Hull's chief objective now became a trade agreement with Great Britain and a breakdown of the imperial preference barriers that Britain and the Dominions had erected in 1932. He achieved some success in the British-American and Canadian-American trade agreements signed at the White House on November 17, 1938. The Trade Agreements Act was renewed again in the spring of 1940. By this time Hull had negotiated agreements with twenty-one nations, including all the leaders of the democratic bloc. They covered nearly two-thirds of the total foreign commerce of the United States.

Hand in hand with the reciprocal trade program went policies to reconcile the broad political objectives of the Good Neighbor policy with the protection of American investments in Latin America. To begin with, the Roosevelt administration merely continued Hoover's policy of refusing to use force or the threat of force to protect such investments. Actually, outright confiscations of American property in the 1930s were rare and were largely confined to Bolivia and Ecuador, both of which had irresponsible dictators during the period. Next, the Washington government established a second Export-Import Bank in March 1934 to stimulate foreign trade with Latin American and other countries. The bank lent some $66 million from 1934 through 1938, most of which went to help stabilize Latin American currencies and exchange rates. Because of Hull's fierce opposition to barter deals, however, the bank never became an important direct factor in expanding the commerce of the Western Hemisphere.

This, in brief, was the Good Neighbor policy at work in the economic field; it was usually unspectacular and generally ignored by the public. However, one case, the Mexican expropriations of American-owned land and oil properties, exploded rather violently in the 1930s, involved the fate of property worth many millions of dollars, and put the principles of the Good Neighbor to severe test.

Beginning in 1934 the Mexican government of Lázaro Cárdenas began to expropriate land holdings of American citizens in Mexico. Secretary Hull followed the advice of the extraordinarily popular ambassador in Mexico City, Josephus Daniels, in refusing to deny Mexico's right to expropriate. But through Daniels the secretary of state did apply pressure on Mexico City to obtain fair compensation to former owners. The controversy over land expropriations, heated though it threatened to become, was of minor importance as compared to the storm set off when the Mexicans moved against the British and American oil companies within their territory.

As we have seen, the Mexicans agreed in 1928 that foreign oil companies might retain possession of properties acquired before 1917 (see p. 342). Cárdenas did not openly repudiate this agreement but rather began a flanking movement against the British and American companies soon after his accession in 1934. This campaign culminated in demands by the government-sponsored union of oil workers in 1936 that would have crippled, if not bankrupted, the companies. They refused to surrender, and the Mexican government thereupon declared that an "economic conflict" existed and ordered them to comply. The Mexican Supreme Court upheld the government's decree, and the companies made a counterproposal that won Cárdenas's approval. Then the companies made the fatal mistake of demanding that Cárdenas put his approval in writing. Outraged by what he considered to be a slur on the national honor, the Mexican president told his people on March 15, 1938, that the government had decided to nationalize the oil industry and expropriate the property of the large foreign companies.

Loud was the protest in the United States and Great Britain from the oil companies. Their spokesmen claimed that the expropriated properties had a potential value of $450 million. The British Foreign Office protested in such a way as to cause the Mexican government to hand the British minister his passports. Reaction in Washington was only slightly less violent, and for a time it seemed that Secretary Hull might hurl his own stern demands. But under pressure from Daniels—and perhaps because of President Roosevelt's direct intervention—the secretary of state began negotiations that culminated on November 19, 1941, in a general settlement of the land and oil claims,[6] conclusion of a Mexican-American trade agreement, and a promise by the United States to help stabilize the peso and obtain loans for Mexico through the Export-Import Bank.

Thus Roosevelt, with Daniels's vital help, turned the expropriation affair to the advantage of the people of the United States. By refusing to interfere in a controversy that was essentially Mexican in character, he won the lasting friendship of the Mexican people and a valuable ally during the Second World War. More important, he convinced most Latin Americans that there were no strings attached to the Good Neighbor policy.

5. *The Triumph of Isolationism*

Roosevelt well understood the consequences to the United States of the breakdown of the international system in Europe and Asia. But he was so acutely sensitive to political and popular pressures from 1932 to 1938 that he was more often a captive of public opinion than an audacious leader.

---

[6]The Mexican government promised to pay a total of $40,000,000 during the next fourteen years to satisfy all American general and agrarian claims. By the agreement on the oil issue, the United States and Mexico appointed a joint commission of experts to determine the value of the expropriated American oil properties. Both governments agreed, however, that oil in the ground was the property of the Mexican people. The joint commission reported on April 17, 1942, that the value of the expropriated American property was $23,995,991, plus interest of some $5,000,000. The American companies grudgingly accepted the award, which, incidentally, was apparently a fair one, after the State Department told them they must accept it or receive no compensation at all.

There were signs during these years that the administration might have pursued a different course had the public been willing to approve collective action for peace. The important facts, however, were the determination of the American people to avoid international commitments and participation in all future wars, and the administration's refusal to run perhaps fatal risks by flouting the popular will.

As we have observed earlier, isolationism—the feeling of apartness coupled with a belief in the degeneracy of Europe and the unique virtue of American institutions and motives—had been one of the oldest traditions and perhaps the dominant ideological force in American history. The American people caught the internationalist vision for a brief moment during the First World War. But events at Versailles and afterward turned American idealism into disgust and confirmed traditional beliefs about Europe's congenital perversity.

Moreover, intellectuals in the 1920s nursed a nagging guilt feeling about American participation in the war and peace conference. American historians set to work as European archives were opened to discover the causes of the war; many concluded that Germany had been among the powers least responsible for the tragedy. This "new" history soon mushroomed into the cult of so-called revisionism. If Germany had not been primarily responsible for the war, the revisionists argued, then the Versailles treaty was a monstrous fraud and injustice, and the American people had been tricked into fighting for an unworthy cause.

This belief, popular among American intellectuals during the late 1920s, was fired by sensational exposures after 1932 and spread rapidly among the masses of people. The House foreign affairs committee conducted an investigation of the arms traffic and its allegedly sinister influence in world politics in 1933. In April 1934 the Senate approved a resolution for a special investigation of the munitions industry offered by Senator Gerald P. Nye, an extreme isolationist Republican from North Dakota. Nye himself was appointed chairman of the investigating committee. What ensued was not a restrained inquiry but rather a ruthless investigation to prove the old progressive thesis that wars are always primarily economic in origin. The committee's report grossly exaggerated the influence of bankers and businessmen and distorted the causes for America's entry into the First World War, but it set off a virtual wave of hysteria among thousands of thoughtful Americans. They resolved that such tragic mistakes should not happen again.

Thus the dominant temper of the American people in the mid-1930s was even more doggedly isolationist than before. A whole raft of books by scholars, journalists, and professional pacifists played upon the antiwar theme and reiterated the assertion that Americans could make their best contribution by staying out of Europe's troubles and strengthening democracy at home. High school and college students organized Veterans of Future Wars, joined pacifist movements like the Fellowship of Reconciliation, and vowed that they would not fight if the nation went to war again.

A wave of pacifism swept over the clergy. It was little wonder that nearly two-thirds of the people questioned in a Gallup poll in April 1937 said that American participation in the First World War had been a mistake.

So strong was the popular feeling by 1935 that neutrality legislation of some kind was inevitable; the only question was whether Congress would take control of foreign policy out of the president's hands. Senator Key Pittman of Nevada, chairman of the foreign relations committee, introduced a resolution on August 20, 1935, prohibiting, "upon the outbreak or during the progress of war between, or among, two or more foreign States," the export of arms and munitions from the United States. It also made it unlawful for American ships to carry arms for or to any belligerent and empowered the president to warn American citizens against traveling on belligerent ships. The president had no discretion and no authority under this resolution to discriminate in favor of the victims of aggression. The Senate approved the bill on August 21. The best that Hull could do was to persuade the House to amend the measure by limiting the life of the mandatory arms embargo provision to six months. Thus amended, the Pittman Resolution was quickly adopted by Congress and approved by the president with some misgiving on August 31, 1935.

6. *The United States and the Ethiopian Crisis, 1935–1936*

Even while Congress sought to outlaw American participation in future wars, events in Europe and Asia began to spell the end of international stability and make a hollow mockery of American hopes. The year 1935 opened on an international situation dangerous for the peace of the world. In the Far East the Japanese were pushing forward in northern China. In Europe Hitler was feverishly rearming Germany in defiance of the Versailles treaty, while Benito Mussolini, Italian dictator, was laying plans to conquer Ethiopia.

Hitler made the opening move on March 16, 1935, by denouncing all provisions of the Versailles treaty for German disarmament and inaugurating conscription. The British, French, and Italian governments had the power to compel German compliance with the treaty, but they contented themselves with verbal protests. Meanwhile, a skirmish between Italian and Ethiopian troops on December 5, 1934, had given Mussolini the pretext for picking a quarrel with Haile Selassie, emperor of Ethiopia. Rejecting mediation by the League of Nations, Mussolini launched an invasion from Eritrea and Italian Somaliland on October 3, 1935. President Roosevelt applied an arms embargo two days later, and the State Department waited to see what the League would do. The League council under strong British pressure condemned Italy as the aggressor on October 7; the League assembly voted four days later to impose economic sanctions.

Then the British moved their main fleet to the Mediterranean, and it seemed that the stage was at last set for a real test of the collective security system.

Britain and France, however, preferred compromise rather than show-down. The League's sanctions against Italy went into effect on November 18; but the embargo did not include oil and coal, without which the Italian fleet and war machine could not function. Actually, the president and secretary of state would have been prepared to cooperate in stern measures of economic coercion had the League given the lead.[7] But Pierre Laval, French foreign minister, feared that such action would drive Italy into the arms of Germany. He therefore blocked all suggestions for an oil embargo. And while the League debated, Mussolini completed his conquest of Ethiopia on May 9, 1936.

Meanwhile, consultation with Democratic leaders had convinced Hull that Congress was determined to enact permanent neutrality legislation to supplant the Pittman Resolution, which would expire on February 29, 1936. They also led the secretary to believe that the Senate would not give the president discretionary authority to apply the embargo only against aggressors. Hull tried to persuade Senator Pittman and Representative Sam D. McReynolds, chairman of the House foreign affairs committee, to introduce a bill extending the nondiscretionary arms embargo but adding provisions for a virtual embargo on the export of essential raw materials and extension of credits to belligerents. Isolationists led by Senators Hiram Johnson, William E. Borah, and Gerald P. Nye counterattacked furiously, charging that Hull's measure was aimed at Italy and designed to strengthen the League system of sanctions. The attack was so effective that the Senate foreign relations committee refused even to report Hull's measure. Instead, Congress extended the provisions of the Pittman Resolution to May 1, 1937, and added amendments that gave the president discretionary power in finding that a state of war existed, prohibited extension of war loans and credits to belligerents, required the president to apply the neutrality legislation in the event other nations went to war after hostilities had begun, and exempted any American republic at war with a power outside the Western Hemisphere.

7. The United States and New Aggressions in Europe and Asia, 1936-1937

Mussolini's successful defiance of the League revealed England's and France's fatal timidity and indecision—caused in large part by the conviction that they would get no help from America in the event of war—and

---

[7]On November 15, 1935, for example, Hull announced the institution of a "moral," or voluntary, embargo against the shipment to Italy of coal, oil, cotton, and other raw materials in excess of normal Italian purchases in the United States.

cleared the road for new assaults on the peace structure by Germany, Italy, and Japan. Indeed, Hitler denounced European security treaties and sent his troops into the demilitarized Rhineland on March 7, 1936, at the height of the Ethiopian crisis. Hitler and Mussolini joined hands eight months later, on October 25, in the so-called Rome-Berlin Axis, which afterward metamorphosed into a political and military alliance between the two dictators. Then the Germans and Japanese joined forces in an Anti-Comintern Pact on November 16, 1936, and the stage was at last set for a new alliance of the militaristic-imperialistic nations to destroy the old balance of power.

The leaders of the Soviet Union recognized the new coalition as a dire threat to the security of their own regime and appealed to the western democracies for stern collective action to contain fascism. The British and French, however, feared the Communist threat from within as much as the Fascist danger from without; were obsessed by fear of a general war, which they would have to fight without even a modicum of support from the United States; and hopefully assumed that satisfaction of legitimate German and Italian complaints would preserve the peace of Europe. Had the American government been able to provide the necessary leadership and rally the Atlantic powers in this time of crisis, the world might have been spared the worst tragedy in the history of mankind. Lacking American support, the dominant western powers stood by helplessly from 1936 to 1939 while Germany and Japan marched from one triumphant conquest to another.

No sooner had the Ethiopian crisis ended than Europe's peace was again threatened by the outbreak of civil war in Spain on July 18, 1936. The conflict was in the beginning simply a Spanish affair—a revolt of the army under General Francisco Franco, supported by great landowners, the Roman Catholic church, and the business classes, against a Popular Front government. However, Spain soon became an arena in which Spanish, Italian, and German Fascists joined battle against an incompatible coalition of democrats and Communists.

Before the civil war developed into this international contest, the British, French, German, Italian, Russian, and other European governments applied a policy of seemingly strict nonintervention to prevent the Spanish cauldron from boiling into a general war. Representatives of the European powers on September 9, 1936, established a Non-Intervention Committee in London to prevent men and supplies from going to either side; and the committee established a naval blockade of Spain in March 1937. But the committee's efforts were totally futile, as the Italians, Germans, and Russians made a laughingstock of the blockade, and the Italian government openly boasted of its aid to Franco.

The American government in the meantime had joined the British and French in applying a policy of nonintervention. The Neutrality Act of 1936 did not apply to civil wars, but the State Department imposed a moral embargo against the export of arms and war materials as a means of strengthening the Non-Intervention Committee. Then, when a dealer in secondhand airplanes sought to export some 400 airplane engines to the Loyalist government in December 1936, the administration hastily requested Congress to apply the arms embargo to Spain. A joint resolution granting the president's request passed with only one dissenting vote in both houses on January 6, 1937. It became law two days later with the president's approval. Even after the true character of the civil war became evident and a large body of opinion favorable to the Loyalists, or the forces of the legitimate government, developed in the United States, the administration, fearful of alienating Catholic opinion, blocked all efforts at repeal of the joint resolution. Thus Franco destroyed the Spanish democracy with the open support of Germany and Italy and secured his dictatorship in 1939 while the western democracies stood by.

The overriding American determination to avoid entanglement in European troubles was again demonstrated in the late winter and spring of 1937, when Congress adopted a new and permanent neutrality law to supplant the temporary measure of 1936. Hull knew that he could not prevent legislation, and so he worked quietly and to a degree successfully to win larger discretion for the executive branch of the government in the enforcement of the new statute. Approved by Congress on April 29 and signed by Roosevelt on May 1, 1937, it authorized the president to determine when a state of war existed or a civil war threatened the peace of the world. If the president should find that such international or civil wars existed, an embargo against the export of arms, ammunition, and credits would go immediately into effect. In addition, a "cash-and-carry" provision, to run for two years, empowered the president to require belligerents who purchased nonmilitary commodities in the United States to pay cash for such goods and to transport them in their own vessels.

It was a fateful time for a great nation thus to bind its hands. For one thing, the Japanese army, after absorbing Manchuria and Outer Mongolia in 1932 and 1933, began a campaign to wrench the five northern provinces of China from the control of the Nationalist government at Nanking. At the same time, the Nationalist leader, Chiang Kai-shek, consolidated his administrative power and strengthened his armed forces in preparation for the inevitable showdown. A minor clash between Chinese and Japanese troops at the Marco Polo Bridge near Peking on July 7, 1937, gave the Japanese army an excuse for launching full-scale war. Instead of submitting, however, the Chinese fought back; thus what the Japanese military leaders thought would be a mere incident quickly settled into a long and bloody war.

Hull circulated a note on July 16 in which he implicitly condemned the Japanese and called upon the powers to reaffirm allegiance to the principles of international morality. Next, the president dispatched 1,200 marines to Shanghai on August 17 to reinforce the 2,200 American soldiers already stationed in China. In order to stir public support for a stronger policy, Hull persuaded the president to include a plea for international cooperation in an address he was scheduled to deliver in Chicago on October 5. But Roosevelt, going far beyond the draft prepared by the State Department, appealed to the American people to see the facts of international life and implied that peace-loving nations might have to co-operate to quarantine aggressors to prevent the spread of international anarchy. Roosevelt hoped that the slogan "Quarantine the Aggressors" would catch the public fancy, as the phrases "New Deal" and "Good Neighbor policy" had done. Instead, the quarantine speech stirred such violent reactions that it probably injured the movement for a larger degree of collective action.

On the day following the president's address the League assembly adopted reports condemning Japanese aggression and suggesting that a conference of the signatories of the Nine Power Treaty meet to consider proper measures of redress. The British strongly endorsed the suggestion as they feared a Japanese threat to their far-flung interests in the Orient. Secretary Hull also approved and recommended Brussels as the meeting place. What might have become the first great experiment in forceful cooperation against aggression, however, was wrecked before it could be launched—by the overwhelming American determination to avoid the risk of war, and by the president's refusal to defy this popular will. Press polls revealed a two-to-one congressional majority against cooperation with the League in applying sanctions against Japan. Roosevelt beat a quick retreat from the advanced position of his quarantine address. For example, he assured the country in a fireside chat on October 12 that the purpose of the Brussels Conference was settlement of the Sino-Japanese War by agreement and cooperation, obviously not to propose use of strong measures of economic warfare.

The British and French leaders probably had no more heart for risky policies than Roosevelt and Hull. To Anthony Eden, British foreign secretary, it was obvious that the Brussels Conference would take no effective action, anyway. Hence he maneuvered to throw the onus for its failure on the United States. Eden had a long talk at Brussels with the American delegate on November 2, 1937. His Majesty's government, Eden declared, was prepared to stand shoulder to shoulder with the United States and would cooperate in any measures against Japan. But Britain would go only so far as the United States and would "base her policy upon American policy during the present crisis." Other delegates demanded that the Americans take leadership in formulating a program of action when the conference opened on the following day. The Washington government could not lead because it believed that it was impotent in the face of public opinion at home. Since no one dared to act, the conference adjourned on November 24 after adopting a pious reaffirmation of the principles enunciated in the Nine Power Treaty.

The Japanese gave their answer on December 12 by bombing and sinking the United States gunboat *Panay* and three Standard Oil tankers in the Yangtze River near Nanking. The chief reaction in the United States was a loud demand for withdrawal of all American forces in China,[8] and Japan was allowed to apologize and pay an indemnity on December 23, 1937.

8. *The President's Plan and Its Aftermath*

At the time that he made his quarantine address Roosevelt was contemplating some bold stroke—perhaps a meeting of the leaders of the great powers at sea—to prepare the way for the Brussels Conference. Undersecretary of State Sumner Welles sent the president a memorandum on October 6, 1937, suggesting that he call for a world conference in which the powers would seek to reconstruct international law and find a basis for political and economic cooperation. Roosevelt approved and contemplated summoning the diplomatic representatives on Armistice Day. He postponed action when Hull strenuously opposed the plan on the ground that Japan and the European dictators would of course pay lip service to peace and brotherhood, and that their seeming concurrence would lull the democracies into a false sense of security.

Significant events in Europe soon afterward caused the president to take up his plan again. The British government embarked upon a policy in November 1937 aimed at appeasing Germany's legitimate grievances and establishing a new European accord. Lord Halifax, speaking for the Cabinet, described the new British policy in conversations with Hitler in Berlin; Hitler in turn promised sincere cooperation. Roosevelt learned of this development and decided to launch his campaign for a new international modus vivendi in order to support Britain's attempt to come to an understanding with Germany.

First, however, the president sent a secret message describing his plan to Prime Minister Neville Chamberlain on January 11, 1938. In delivering the message to the British ambassador, Welles warned that "all the progress which had been made in Anglo-American cooperation during the previous two years would be destroyed" if the British cabinet did not cooperate.[9] Chamberlain replied on January 13 without consulting the absent Eden that the president's proposal would interfere with his, Chamberlain's, plan to appease Germany and recognize Italy's conquest of Ethiopia in return for certain guarantees. This news that Britain intended to condone Mussolini's conquest of Ethiopia dumbfounded Washington, and Roosevelt and Hull both replied in words that scarcely concealed their disgust.

Eden meanwhile had returned to London and virtually forced Chamberlain to inform the president on January 21, 1938, that the British gov-

---

[8] In a Gallup poll taken in January 1938, 70 percent of the persons queried said that they favored total American withdrawal from the Far East. Four months before, only 54 percent had favored such withdrawal.

[9] The quotation is from Winston S. Churchill, *The Gathering Storm* (Boston, 1948), pp. 251-252.

ernment would cordially cooperate in his plan but could not take responsibility for its failure. We do not know whether Roosevelt would have acted had circumstances not changed drastically soon afterward. In any event, Eden resigned on February 20, primarily in protest over Chamberlain's Italian policy, while Hitler occupied and annexed Austria to Germany on March 12 and 13. In consequence, the president's plan sank out of sight.

The prospect for peace was now obviously uncertain, and Washington began seriously to consider the naval and military impotence of the nation. The president and Congress had slightly augmented the army's feeble strength since 1933 but had not provided enough new naval construction to maintain the fleet even at the strength authorized by the London Treaty of 1930. Japan had denounced the Five Power Naval Treaty in December 1934. A renewal of Japanese construction and especially the outbreak of the Sino-Japanese War in 1937 convinced the president that the time had come for the United States to look to its own defenses. He sent a special message to Congress on January 28, 1938, urging an immediate increase of 20 percent in expenditures for naval construction. Congress in May 1938 approved the Vinson Naval Expansion Act authorizing the expenditure over the next decade of some $1 billion to create a navy presumably strong enough to meet the combined fleets of Japan, Germany, and Italy.

The adoption of the naval expansion bill was one sign, among others, of profound changes that were taking place in American opinion by the spring of 1938. The American people were still determined to avoid participation in Asia's and Europe's wars. Even so, most thoughtful Americans were beginning to perceive the enormity of the rising dangers, and were willing at least to admit the necessity for strong defenses against potential threats to the security of the Western Hemisphere.

20

The Second Road

to War,

1938–1941

Hitler brought Europe to the brink of war soon after his seizure of Austria in March 1938 by threatening to seize the German-speaking Sudeten provinces of Czechoslovakia. The British and French rejected Russian cooperation and submitted to Hitler's demands during this so-called Munich crisis. They thus postponed war but lost a powerful ally. Then Hitler's betrayal of his Munich pledges and attack against Poland in September 1939 caused the two western democracies to stand up and fight to prevent Nazi power from overwhelming all of Europe.

The policies demanded by the American people and followed by their government between September 1939 and June 1940 were certainly neither bold nor helpful to the western democracies. But it is easy to criticize in retrospect and to forget how divided and distraught the American people were in this time of crisis, and how the administration could not lead where Congress and the people would not follow. The important fact was that Americans, or a majority of them, rallied behind the president in bold if belated efforts once they understood the dimensions of the Nazi threat.

While the Washington government sought to help stem the Nazi tide in the West by measures short of war, it used stern diplomacy to turn back the rising tide of Japanese imperialism that threatened to engulf the Far East. At any time during the period from 1939 to December 1941 the American leaders could have come to terms with Japan—by accepting Japanese control of China and Japanese demands for leadership in the Orient. The supreme tragedy was that by 1941 the situation had passed beyond the point of reasonable solution. As compromise on any terms that did not violate everything the American people had stood for in the Far East seemed impossible by 1941, the two nations reached the point where diplomacy could not harmonize fundamentally divergent objectives.

In this chapter we will describe how the American government and people, haltingly at first, but boldly afterward, emerged from the chrysalis of isolation and assumed a position of decisive power in the affairs of mankind.

1. From the Munich Crisis to the Outbreak of War

After the annexation of Austria, Hitler began a campaign for incorporation of the German-speaking Sudeten provinces of Czechoslovakia into Greater Germany and made plans for a campaign in the East.

Prime Minister Chamberlain flew to Germany for a personal meeting with Hitler on September 15, 1938, where he learned that Germany would accept nothing less than outright cession of the Sudetenland. Chamberlain and the French premier, Edouard Daladier, knuckled under and agreed that Czechoslovakia must surrender to the führer's demands. The Czech leaders had no alternative but to submit. Then Hitler rejected Chamberlain's arrangement for the transfer of the disputed provinces, and it seemed that war was inevitable. Chamberlain in a last-ditch plea on September 27 suggested that Hitler, Daladier, Mussolini, and he meet personally to find a solution. The world was surprised when Hitler accepted and relieved when the four leaders met at Munich on September 29 and quickly agreed to a scheme for the dismemberment of the Czech republic.

Chamberlain and Daladier by a stroke of the pen confirmed Hitler's supremacy over his generals, who had opposed his recent reckless moves; made Germany absolutely dominant on the Continent; weakened the attractiveness of a western alignment for the Soviet leaders; and demonstrated their own incompetence as diplomats. All that they received in return was Hitler's unctuous promise that he would make no more territorial demands in Europe, respect Czech sovereignty, and settle all future disputes by peaceful negotiation.

Roosevelt had acted as an unhappy partner in appeasement by making several appeals to the European leaders for a peaceful settlement, but he was never guilty of believing that the Munich Pact offered any hope for real peace in Europe. On the contrary, he began to reorient his domestic and foreign policies soon afterward in preparation for the conflict that he was certain would ensue. He abandoned his "purge" of conservative Democrats, called a halt to the reform energies of the New Deal, and began a campaign for speedy rearmament in the autumn of 1938. Hitler announced an expansion of German military strength on October 9. Roosevelt countered two days later by announcing a $300 million increase in American spending for defense purposes and calling upon his military advisers to plan for huge increases in aircraft production. In his Annual Message to Congress and his Budget Message on January 4 and 5, 1939, he asked for $1.3 billion for the regular defense establishment and an additional $525 million, most of it for airplanes. These appeals fell upon receptive ears, for the Munich tragedy had opened the eyes of millions of Americans to the Nazi danger to world peace, while violent anti-Jewish pogroms in Germany in November 1938 had revealed anew the brutal character of the Nazi regime.[1] Thus Congress responded by increasing the military and naval budgets by nearly two-thirds and by authorizing the president to begin accumulating stockpiles of strategic raw materials for use if war occurred.

In addition, the administration intensified its campaign to strengthen the collective security system in the Western Hemisphere. This was now a more urgent and difficult task than during the early years of the Good Neighbor policy, for the German government had begun a tremendous economic and propaganda campaign aimed at establishing German hegemony in Latin America. Nazi agents had organized National Socialist parties among German immigrants in Brazil and Argentina, threatened economic reprisals against any Latin American nation that dared to cooperate with the United States, and engaged in wholesale military espionage under the cover of German steamship and air lines.

Roosevelt and Hull therefore determined to form a solid hemispheric anti-Nazi front at the Pan-American Conference that opened at Lima, Peru, on December 9, 1938. Hull, as chairman of the American delegation and chief advocate of hemispheric solidarity, had the cordial support of most Latin American governments. As during the conference in Buenos Aires two years before, however, the Argentine delegation seemed determined either to dominate or wreck the proceedings. Hull marshaled a nearly solid Latin American opinion and conducted patient negotiations with the president and foreign minister of Argentina. The result was unanimous approval of the Declaration of Lima on Christmas Eve. It reaffirmed

---

[1] It would be difficult to exaggerate the importance of the American reaction to this outbreak of terrorism against the Jews of Germany. Leaders of both parties joined in expressing the revulsion of the American people, while Roosevelt recalled Ambassador Hugh Wilson from Berlin in protest.

the twenty-one American republics' determination to resist jointly any Fascist or Nazi threat to the peace and security of the hemisphere.

Roosevelt's chief objective during the uneasy months following Munich was repeal or drastic amendment of the Neutrality Act of 1937. Hull was in constant communication with Key Pittman, chairman of the Senate foreign relations committee, urging him to take leadership in repealing the arms embargo, that "incitement to Hitler to go to war." But Pittman warned that a repeal measure could not pass, and Roosevelt and Hull momentarily gave up the fight and concentrated on measures for stronger defense.

The international situation suddenly deteriorated when Hitler sent his armies into Prague on March 15, 1939, and took control of what remained of unhappy Czechoslovakia. The dictator's cynical violation of an agreement upon which the ink was hardly dry caused such a profound revulsion of sentiment in Great Britain that Chamberlain was forced to abandon appeasement. The prime minister almost at once began negotiating treaties guaranteeing the independence and territorial integrity of countries believed to be next in Germany's line of march—Poland, Rumania, Greece, and Turkey.

Reaction in Washington to Hitler's latest move was nearly as violent as in London. Speaking for the president on March 17, Acting Secretary of State Sumner Welles condemned Germany's "wanton lawlessness" and use of "arbitrary force." On the same day the president decided not to recognize the destruction of Czechoslovakia and to continue to deal with the Czech minister in Washington. Accompanying this strong talk now went even stronger administration action to obtain revision of the neutrality statute. In order to win Senator Pittman's support, Roosevelt and Hull accepted a compromise measure—introduced by Pittman on March 20— that extended the cash-and-carry provision but amended it to include arms, ammunition, and other war materials.

The president ventured all his prestige in the fight to obtain either passage of the Pittman bill or outright repeal of the arms embargo, but the campaign was to no avail. Roosevelt called House leaders to the White House on May 19 and declared that repeal of the arms embargo might prevent war and would certainly make an Axis victory less likely if war occurred. But Congress would not budge; both houses decisively refused to approve measures of revision. Then the president invited Senate leaders to the White House on July 18 for a frank discussion of the European situation. All senators present but one thought that revision of the Neutrality Act was impossible, and Vice-President Garner turned to Roosevelt and said: "Well, Captain, we may as well face the facts. You haven't got the votes, and that's all there is to it." The president replied that he had done his best, and that the Senate would have to shoulder responsibility for refusing to take action to protect the nation's security.

2. *The Impact of the War upon the American People*

Leaders of Europe engaged in last-minute negotiations during the summer of 1939 in preparation for Armageddon. Chamberlain and Daladier by signing the Munich Pact had not only isolated Russia but had also intensified Russian suspicions that they were trying to turn Hitler eastward. The British and French premiers, once they had abandoned appeasement, appealed to the Kremlin to sign an alliance to contain nazism. The Russians demanded as their price a guarantee of the security of all eastern Europe and the Baltic states and acknowledgment of Russia's right in certain circumstances to occupy this broad zone stretching from Finland to Bulgaria.

While Chamberlain and Daladier were negotiating, Stalin and his new foreign minister, Vyacheslav Molotov, were simultaneously sounding out the possibilities of agreement with Germany. Hitler was glad to make temporary concessions to prevent Russia from joining his adversaries in the West. The upshot of these negotiations was the signing of a Nazi-Soviet treaty of nonaggression in Moscow on August 23, 1939. The published terms provided simply that Russia and Germany would refrain from attacking each other. The secret provisions provided that in the event of a territorial rearrangement in eastern Europe, Russia should have Finland, Estonia, Latvia, eastern Poland, and the Rumanian province of Bessarabia, while Germany might annex Lithuania[2] and western Poland.

Hitler was now protected against the danger of a two-front war and increased his demands on Poland. Chamberlain warned that Britain would go at once to Poland's aid if Germany attacked but offered to discuss the Polish question, and Roosevelt added a new appeal for peace. Hitler responded by sending his armies into Poland on September 1; two days later Britain and France declared war on the Reich. Thus the chips were finally down for a last play after four years of intolerable tension.

Most Americans had seen that war was inevitable and took the outbreak of hostilities in stride. The president issued an official proclamation of neutrality on September 5, 1939, and put the Neutrality Act into force,[3] as he was bound to do; but he did not ask the people to be impartial in thought as well as in deed, as Wilson had done in different circumstances in 1914.

The administration moved swiftly to strengthen the defenses of the Western Hemisphere by arranging for a conference of the foreign ministers of the American republics. They met at Panama City on September 23

[2] By subsequent negotiation Germany exchanged Lithuania for Polish territory.

[3] Thus the arms embargo went into effect, causing an immediate cancellation of Anglo-French war orders worth $79 million. Belligerents, however, were free to buy raw materials and food, although the Johnson Act prevented extension of credits to the British and French governments.

and agreed with surprising unanimity upon common neutrality regulations and mutual consultation in the event that a transfer of territory from one European power to another threatened the security of the New World. The most striking work of the conference was the adoption of the Declaration of Panama, marking out a broad zone 300 miles wide around the Americas, excluding Canada and European colonies, into which the belligerents were forbidden to carry the war. It was, actually, only a verbal prohibition and had no practical effect.

The president's primary objective, however, was still repeal of the arms embargo provision of the Neutrality Act. He called Congress into special session to plead earnestly for repeal on September 21. His main theme was maintenance of American neutrality, for he shared the prevalent view that Britain and France could defeat Germany if only they could obtain weapons of war. As if to prove that he believed that neutrality was desirable, he urged Congress to prohibit American ships from entering European war zones and to apply the cash-and-carry principle to all European purchases in the United States.

The request was modest and thoroughly neutral, but it stirred isolationists to frenzied activity. Senator Borah in a radio broadcast warned that lifting the arms embargo would be tantamount to taking sides in a war in which American interests were not involved. Pacifists, who argued that the only way to prevent war was to have nothing to do with the instruments of destruction, were joined by Communists, who charged that Britain and France were fighting to preserve imperialistic capitalism. On the other side, in support of the president, was ranged a powerful new combination of southern and eastern Democrats in Congress. They were joined in the country at large by such preparationist Republicans as Stimson and Frank Knox, a vast majority of the business interests and the metropolitan press, and a large segment of the intellectual leadership of the country. It was evident by the middle of October that the tide had turned in the president's favor. Meanwhile, Senator Pittman had drafted a new neutrality bill that lifed the arms embargo, applied the cash-and-carry principle, and forbade American ships to trade with belligerent countries and Americans to travel on belligerent ships. Pittman persuaded the foreign relations committee to report this measure favorably on September 28. Congress approved the Pittman bill after a month of debate, and the president signed it on November 4, 1939.

Meanwhile, Hitler's armies had overrun Poland before the French could mount an offensive on the western front, and the Russians had shocked the world by joining the Germans in devouring Poland. The Germans built their offensive power for a drive in the West during the following months, while the British and French acted as if the war could be won merely by waiting for the Nazi regime to collapse. This so-called phony war lulled Americans even more than the British and French into believing that the Germans could never win.

American attention was diverted from the western front by a Russian invasion of Finland in November and December 1939, which was mounted in order to protect Russia's northern flank against a potential German attack. A hot wave of anger swept over the American public, but the administration acted cautiously. Roosevelt indignantly denounced the "dreadful rape of Finland" and castigated the Soviet Union as "a dictatorship as absolute as any other dictatorship in the world." The State and Treasury departments instituted an effective moral embargo on the export of war supplies to the Soviets. But beyond this action the administration could not go. Roosevelt and Hull perceived that the marriage between Germany and Russia was incompatible, and they may well have understood the strategic reasons for the Russian attack against Finland.

3. *The Menace of a Nazi Victory*

The so-called phony war ended on April 9, 1940, when Hitler hurled his armies into Denmark and Norway, and German airplanes and *Panzer* (armored) divisions struck hard at Belgium, Holland, and northern France on May 10. Terror swept over the American people as this blitzkrieg (lightning war) developed. All Americans except a few diehard isolationists recognized that a Germany completely dominant in Europe would pose a dire threat to their peace and security. And now it was about to happen, the catastrophe that only a week before had seemed impossible. There was France, her dispirited armies reeling and scattering under the impact of Nazi power; there was the British expeditionary force, driven to the sea at Dunkirk and forced to execute a nearly impossible evacuation.

The immediate threat to American security was the possibility that Hitler might claim Iceland and Greenland, both of which commanded the American sea lanes to Britain, by virtue of his conquest of their mother country, Denmark. Roosevelt refused to order the occupation of Iceland but was obviously pleased when the British occupied it on May 10. Greenland, however, was too close to the United States and Canada to be ignored. Roosevelt declared on April 18 that the island enjoyed the protection of the Monroe Doctrine. Washington refused a request by Greenlanders that it assume a temporary protectorate. Instead, it furnished military supplies and established a Greenland Patrol by the Coast Guard.

Chamberlain resigned on May 10, 1940, the same day the Germans hurtled into the Low Countries, and Winston Spencer Churchill, long the chief British opponent of appeasement, took the helm as prime minister. He had nothing to offer the people of the empire but "blood, toil, tears, and sweat" and the hope of ultimate victory. Churchill sent a cable to Roosevelt when the blitzkrieg was in its fifth day in which he frankly acknowledged the likelihood of German conquest of Europe and asked the president to proclaim a state of nonbelligerency, lend Britain forty or fifty old destroyers, and supply several hundred aircraft and quantities of ammunition. Roosevelt had to reply that the moment for such action was not opportune since Congress would have to approve a transfer of the destroyers.

Roosevelt had determined even before he received Churchill's urgent plea to ask Congress to hasten the nation's armament campaign.[4] This he did in a special message on May 16, 1940, warning Americans that their own security would be gravely imperiled if an enemy should seize any outlying territory, and calling for production of 50,000 planes a year and large new expenditures for the armed forces. Moreover, after the Allied collapse on the western front, he asked Congress on May 31 for an additional $1 billion for defense and for authority to call the National Guard and reserve personnel into active service.

Meanwhile, Roosevelt had also been trying to bolster French morale and to dissuade Mussolini from joining Hitler. Mussolini was deaf to such appeals and rushed to join the Nazis in devouring the carcass of France on June 10. This act of aggression gave the president an opportunity to say in clear and ringing words what the United States would do. In an address at the University of Virginia on the same day that Italy entered the war, Roosevelt announced the end of American isolation and the beginning of a new phase of nonbelligerency. Hereafter the United States would "extend to the opponents of force the material resources of this nation."

This was the week in which France was tottering on the brink of ruin. German armies entered Paris on June 14. The government of Paul Reynaud, who had succeeded Daladier as premier on March 21, gave way on June 16 to a government headed by the aged Marshal Henri-Philippe Pétain. He surrendered to the Germans on June 22. The supreme moment of decision had now come for the president and his advisers. Hitler stood astride the Continent. Italian entry into the war seemed to presage early Axis control of the Mediterranean and North Africa. The British army was stripped of virtually all its heavy equipment after the Dunkirk evacuation. Churchill had warned in repeated messages that the British Isles might be overrun without immediate American assistance, and that a successor government might have to surrender the fleet in order to save the realm. Should the Roosevelt administration assume that the British were lost, abandon aid to them, and prepare to defend the Western Hemisphere? Or should it strip American defenses in the hope that the British could survive?

Not only isolationists but many "realistic" Americans demanded adherence to the former course. They were joined by the Joint Planners of the

---

[4]The War Department had made plans for increasing the army's strength to 500,000 men by July 1941, to 1 million by January 1942, and to nearly 2 million by July 1942; for production of 50,000 aircraft a year; and for manufacture of vast numbers of tanks and guns.

War and Navy departments, who warned on June 27, 1940, that Britain might not survive and urged the president to concentrate on American defenses. It was the kind of advice that military leaders, who think in terms of the worst contingencies, have to give. But Roosevelt decided to gamble on Britain. In this decision he had the support of his new secretaries of war and of the navy, Henry L. Stimson and Frank Knox, whom he had appointed on June 20 to gain Republican support for the defense effort. Roosevelt rejected Churchill's ambitious proposals for turning the United States into a gigantic arsenal for Britain, but he ordered the War and Navy departments to "scrape the bottom of the barrel" and turn over all available guns and ammunition to private firms for resale to Britain.[5] In addition, officials of the War, Navy, and Treasury departments conferred with a British Purchasing Mission and promised to deliver 14,375 aircraft by April 1942. Roosevelt's decision to gamble on British survival was the most momentous in his career to this time, for he acted in the certain knowledge that war with Germany was probable if Britain should go down.

4. The Great Debate

The fall of France and the seeming imminence of British defeat shocked the American people and stimulated much wild talk of an immediate German invasion of the Western Hemisphere. More significant was the way the threat of Nazi victory intensified the great debate over American foreign policy that had been in progress since the Munich crisis. Upon the outcome of this controversy would depend the fate of the world.

Hitler's destruction of Czechoslovakia had convinced a small but influential minority of Americans that the United States would live in deadly peril if nazism ever enveloped Europe. Soon after the outbreak of the war they formed the Non-Partisan Committee for Peace through Revision of the Neutrality Law, with William Allen White of Kansas as chairman. The Non-Partisan Committee had branches in thirty states by the end of October 1939. Its propaganda was a decisive factor in swinging public opinion behind repeal of the arms embargo provision. The committee quietly disbanded during the so-called phony war but reorganized on May 17, 1940, as the Committee to Defend America by Aiding the Allies. The committee had over 600 local branches within a few months and had taken leadership in a nationwide campaign to combat isolationism and stimulate public support for the government's policy of all aid short of war.

[5] Some 970,000 rifles, 200,500 revolvers, 87,500 machine guns, 895 75-mm guns, 316 mortars, and a huge quantity of ammunition were shipped to Britain from June to October 1940.

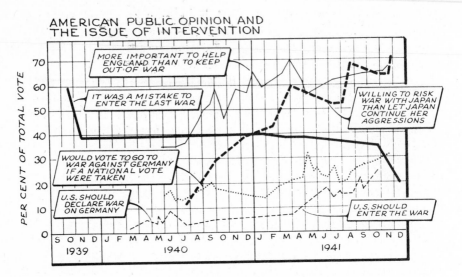

AMERICAN PUBLIC OPINION AND
THE ISSUE OF INTERVENTION

Reproduced by permission of Professor Hadley Cantril and the Public Opinion Research Project of Princeton
University.

The committee's success was reflected in the transformation in public
opinion that occurred during the summer of 1940. When polls revealed in
July that probably a large majority favored aid to Britain, the committee
next worked to generate public support for a transfer of destroyers to the
British.[6] A Gallup poll in mid-August indicated that a majority of the
people would approve if the president followed the committee's lead. In
addition, White and other Republican leaders headed off an isolationist
bloc in the Republican national convention and obtained a platform plank
approving aid to "all peoples fighting for liberty."

It was inevitable that this movement to draw America closer to the
war's orbit would not go unchallenged by isolationist leaders. Their ranks
were considerably thinned by the fall of France, but they were still a
powerful if incongruous group by the autumn of 1940. They included pro-
Nazi spokesmen like Father Coughlin, Gerald L. K. Smith, and William
Dudley Pelley. A large body of midwestern businessmen joined their ranks
mainly out of hatred of the New Deal. Old progressives like senators
Burton K. Wheeler and Gerald P. Nye still identified cooperation with
England with the machinations of Wall Street. Many Protestant ministers
and idealists had embraced a philosophy of nonresistance. The Hearst
papers, the *Chicago Tribune*, the *New York Daily News*, the *Washington
Times-Herald*, and other newspapers lent editorial support. Cooperating

---

[6]The president told White about the contemplated destroyer transfer at a conference on June 29,
1940, and won White's and the committee's support for the project.

also were the Socialists, led by Norman Thomas, who still thought of war in economic terms, and the Communists, who had become suddenly pro-Nazi after the signing of the Nazi-Soviet Non-Aggression Pact.

The leading isolationist organization was the America First Committee, incorporated in September 1940 with Robert E. Wood, chairman of the board of Sears, Roebuck and Company, as national chairman. The America First movement soon included thousands of patriotic Americans who sincerely believed that defense of the Western Hemisphere and nonintervention in Europe's war were the only course of safety for the United States. But the America First Committee also had the support of all pro-Nazi groups in the country.

The debate between proponents of strong support for Britain and the noninterventionists did not end until Japanese bombs fell on Pearl Harbor, but it was evident that the former had won the battle for control of the American public mind long before this date. The polls showed the metamorphosis that occurred. In September 1939 some 82 percent of persons queried thought that the Allies would win; by July 1940 only 43 percent were sure that Britain would win. More important, the proportion of Americans who believed that a German victory would menace their security increased from 43 percent in March 1940 to 69 percent in July 1940. All through the period 1939-1941 an overwhelming majority of Americans indicated a desire to avoid active participation in the war. The important fact was that this same majority approved strong assistance to Britain; and by the spring of 1941 a majority favored extending such aid even if it led to hostilities with Germany.

The president, administration leaders, and the Committee to Defend America played a significant role in this erosion of isolationist sentiments, but events in Europe and the Far East from 1939 to 1941 played an even more significant part. The American people, not wanting to defend obsolete neutral rights or to engage in a second crusade for democracy, supported the administration in a strong policy and accepted the risk of war. They were concerned only with defending their own security and freedom. The tragedy was that it required the momentary triumph of Hitler and the near defeat of the British Empire to awaken Americans to the simple facts of international life.

5. *The Presidential Election of 1940 and the World Crisis*

Meanwhile, the crisis of the spring and summer had no less an impact upon the national conventions and presidential campaign of 1940 than upon popular attitudes regarding the American stake in an Allied victory.

It seemed certain at the beginning of the year that either Senator Robert A. Taft of Ohio, Senator Arthur H. Vandenberg of Michigan, or young Thomas E. Dewey of New York—all of them ardent noninterventionists at the time—would win the Republican presidential nomination. Almost at the last moment Wendell L. Willkie of Indiana, president of the Commonwealth & Southern Corporation and an old antagonist of the TVA, had entered the preconvention campaign. For all his big business connections, Willkie was a former Democrat who approved most of the New Deal reform measures. More important, he had long supported the president's program of aid to Britain. In more normal times Willkie would not have had a chance, but the Republican convention opened in Philadelphia on June 24 amid the panic created by the French surrender two days before. Willkie's managers were able to execute a miraculous whirlwind campaign in the fear and excitement of the time. They achieved his nomination on June 28 by marshaling the young progressive and internationalist element in the GOP. They won a second notable victory over the diehard isolationist bloc with adoption of a platform approving "prompt" and "realistic" defense and aid to victims of aggression.

The nomination of the rugged, popular Willkie—the first colorful Republican candidate since 1904—compelled President Roosevelt to come to some decision concerning the Democratic nomination. Roosevelt probably intended all along to run for a third term, for he made his nomination inevitable by refusing to support another candidate and by failing to discourage efforts in his own behalf. In any event, he sent a message on July 16 to the Democratic National Convention, which had opened in Chicago the day before, saying that he had no desire to remain in office and wanted the convention to be free to make a choice, but implying that he would accept the nomination if the convention insisted. Few of the party bosses wanted Roosevelt, but there was nothing that they could do except nominate him on the first ballot. The delegates rebelled, however, when the president insisted upon Secretary of Agriculture Henry A. Wallace as his running mate. Roosevelt's spokesman, Harry Hopkins, was able to force the Iowan upon an unwilling party only by using the most ruthless methods.

The president delivered his acceptance speech by radio to the convention early in the morning of July 19 and then did not make another campaign address until September 11. In the meantime he gave all his energies to more urgent problems: military, air, and naval expansion, which he obtained easily from Congress, and approval of the Burke-Wadsworth bill for selective service, which he won in September with Willkie's support.

There was danger at this time that the Nazis might seize the French islands in the Caribbean, Guadeloupe and Martinique. Washington first warned Berlin against trying any such stratagem; then it arranged for a conference of the Pan-American foreign ministers to meet at Havana on July 21, 1940, to consider countermeasures. Hull won unanimous approval on July 27 of a declaration that an attack on any American republic was an attack against all of them, as well as adoption of a convention providing that an Inter-American Commission for Territorial Administration should take temporary control of any European possessions in the New World about to be transferred to another sovereignty.

The most urgent necessity confronting the administration during this summer of campaign and crisis, however, was devising some means of transferring forty or fifty destroyers[7] to Britain for antisubmarine operations and assistance in defense of the British Isles against the invasion that Hitler planned for mid-September. The chief obstacle was an amendment to the naval appropriations bill that Congress had adopted on June 28. It forbade the president to transfer defense equipment to a foreign power unless the army chief of staff and the chief of naval operations first certified that the equipment was not essential to the national defense.

Roosevelt found a way out of this dilemma after the Nazis had begun a great air assault against Britain preparatory to the invasion. The upshot was an agreement signed in Washington on September 2, 1940. The United States gave fifty destroyers to the British government in return for a formal pledge that Britain would never surrender its fleet and ninety-nine-year leases on air and naval bases on British territory in Newfoundland, Bermuda, and the Caribbean. Because the agreement vastly enhanced the security of the Western Hemisphere, General George C. Marshall, army chief of staff, and Admiral Harold R. Stark, chief of naval operations, could in good conscience approve it, as the amendment of June 28 required. Churchill, however, rebelled at the idea of a deal and insisted upon giving outright the leases for American bases in Newfoundland and Bermuda. The destroyer-bases agreement meant the end of formal neutrality and marked the beginning of a period of limited American participation in the war. Henceforth the extent of that participation would bear a direct relation to German strength and British needs.

While Roosevelt was thus engaged, Wendell Willkie had undertaken a one-man campaign against a silent opponent. He was ebullient and confident during the early weeks in his strictures against Democratic inefficiency and a third term. He was fatally handicapped, however, by his own basic agreement with most of Roosevelt's domestic and foreign policies. Willkie apparently realized around the first of October that he might be defeated. In desperation, because he badly wanted to win, he jettisoned his progressive, internationalist advisers and accepted the counsel of the Old Guard professionals. They "begged Willkie to abandon this nonsense about a bipartisan foreign policy—to attack Roosevelt as a warmonger—to scare the American people with warnings that votes for Roosevelt meant wooden crosses for their sons and brothers and sweethearts."[8]

The more Willkie played upon the war issue the more his campaign

---

[7]They were to be supplied from a reserve of 172 destroyers built during the First World War, which the Navy Department had reconditioned and returned to service.

[8]Robert E. Sherwood, *Roosevelt and Hopkins, An Intimate History* (New York, 1948), p. 187.

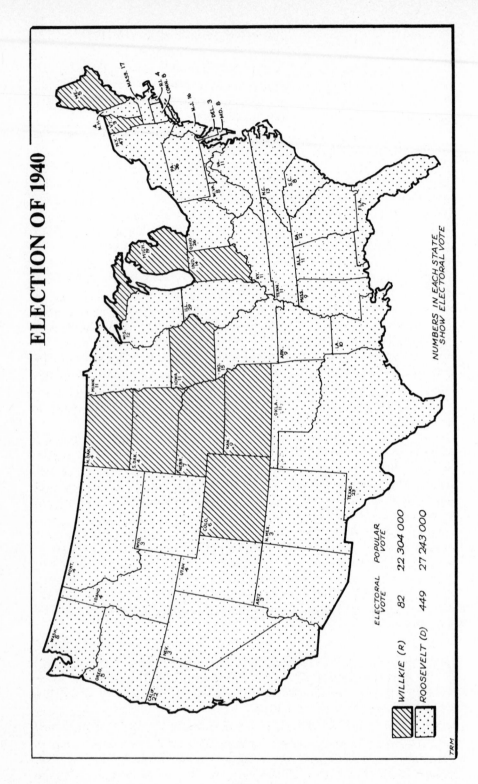

ELECTION OF 1940

NUMBERS IN EACH STATE
SHOW ELECTORAL VOTE

	ELECTORAL VOTE	POPULAR VOTE
WILLKIE (R)	82	22 304 000
ROOSEVELT (D)	449	27 243 000

caught fire, and Democratic managers throughout the country were appalled lest the rising antiwar tide sweep the Republican candidate into the White House. Worried Democrats begged Roosevelt to tell the country that he stood for peace. In response, the president reversed his field. He assured voters in a speech at Philadelphia on October 23 that he had made no secret agreement to involve the United States in the war, "or for any other purpose." He made a grand tour of New York City on October 28, climaxed by an evening address in Madison Square Garden. Reviewing his long efforts to strengthen the nation's defenses, he warned that Americans could keep war from their shores only by stopping aggression in Europe. He called this the "realistic" way to preserve the peace that all Americans desired.

The Madison Square Garden address was in the main a forthright enunciation, but it neither reversed the rising Willkie tide nor quieted the fears of Democratic politicians. On October 30 the president began a tour of New England, to be climaxed by a speech in Boston during the evening. He was inundated all during the day by telegrams warning that defeat impended unless he gave more explicit pledges to maintain peace. For once the great campaigner seemed unsure of himself. At the last minute he included the following promise in his Boston address: "I have said this before, but I shall say it again and again and again: Your boys are not going to be sent into any foreign wars. . . . The purpose of our defense is defense."

It was evident by the late evening of election day, November 5, that the president had won again, although the margin of his victory was considerably smaller than it had been in 1936. He received 27,243,000 popular and 449 electoral votes, as compared with 22,304,400 popular and 82 electoral votes for Willkie. In addition, the Democrats retained large majorities in both houses of Congress. The Socialist and Communist candidates, Norman Thomas and Earl Browder, received 100,264 and 48,579 popular votes, respectively.

6. Lend-Lease: Implementing Nonbelligerency

The chief concern of British and American leaders by the autumn of 1940 was the danger that the entire flow of American goods would be cut off as a result of the exhaustion of British dollar reserves. Out of their total dollar resources of $6.5 billion at the beginning of the war, the British had spent $4.5 billion in the United States by November 1940. By that date they were ready to place new orders for American airplanes, armored equipment for ten divisions, and cargo ships. But the Neutrality Act of 1939 required cash payment for all supplies, and the British were nearing the end of their ability to pay. Roosevelt and Treasury officials well knew that the entire system of American aid would soon collapse unless some solution was quickly found.

The president embarked upon a cruise of the Caribbean aboard the cruiser *Tuscaloosa* on December 2, 1940, when the crisis seemed darkest. A navy seaplane landed alongside the ship on the morning of December 9 and delivered a long letter from Churchill. The prime minister reviewed the naval and military situations and emphasized the grave danger of the growing submarine threat. That threat could be overcome, and Britain could mount air and land offensives, he wrote, only if American shipping and naval forces helped to keep the North Atlantic sea lanes open, and only if the British had enough American aircraft, especially heavy bombers, "to shatter the foundations of German military power." Moreover, Churchill went on, the time was approaching when Britain could no longer pay for shipping and other supplies. He was confident, he concluded, that the president could find the means to implement a common effort for victory.

Roosevelt pondered Churchill's message for two days and then acted swiftly. On December 17, the day after his return to Washington, he intimated to reporters the plan that had taken shape in his mind. Brushing aside suggestions that the United States either lend money to the British or else give them military supplies, he told a homely parable about a man who lent his neighbor a garden hose—without first demanding payment for it—in order to help put out the fire in his neighbor's house. Then, in a fireside chat on December 29, the president told the people frankly what he had in mind. Britain and the British fleet, he declared, stood between the New World and Nazi aggression. Britain asked for war materials, not for men. "We must be the great arsenal of democracy," he concluded. "I call upon our people with absolute confidence that our common cause will greatly succeed."

Public reaction was immediate and overwhelmingly favorable. Roosevelt reiterated the danger from Nazi aggression in his Annual Message on January 6, 1941, and asked Congress "for authority and for funds sufficient to manufacture additional munitions and war supplies of many kinds, to be turned over to those nations which are now in actual war with aggressor nations." These, he went on, would be paid for, not in dollars, but in goods and services at the end of the war. The president's measure, called the Lend-Lease bill, was drafted by Treasury officials during the first week in January 1941 and approved by administration and congressional leaders on January 9. It was introduced in Congress on the following day. The House approved the Lend-Lease bill on February 8, the Senate, on March 8. The president signed it on March 11, 1941, and promptly asked Congress for $7 billion for lend-lease production and export; Congress complied two weeks later.

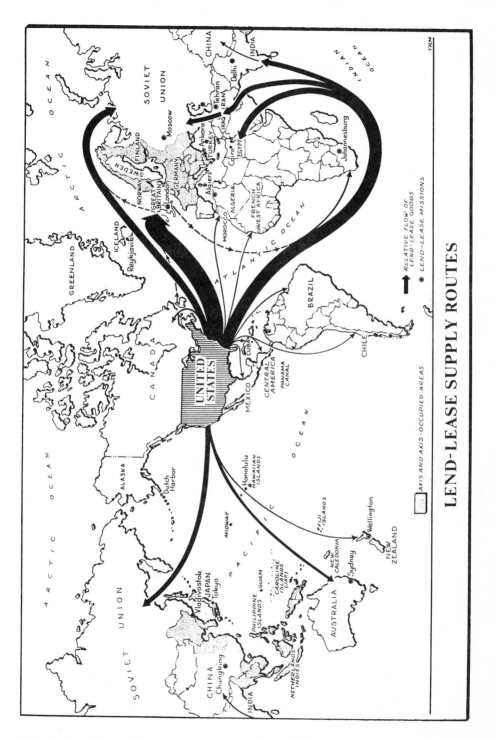

LEND-LEASE SUPPLY ROUTES

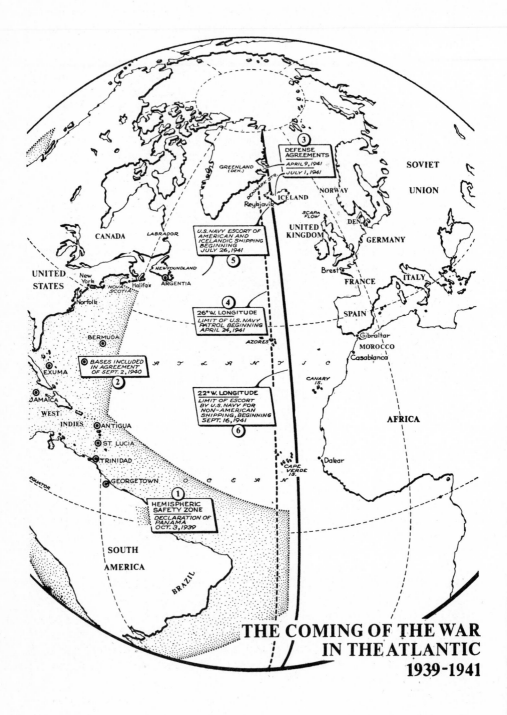

THE COMING OF THE WAR
IN THE ATLANTIC
1939-1941

No man could doubt what the enactment of the Lend-Lease Act signified. "Through this legislation," the president said on March 12, "our country has determined to do its full part in creating an adequate arsenal of democracy." Actually, Roosevelt's characterization was an understatement. Adoption of the Lend-Lease Act converted the United States from a friendly neutral, which sometimes helped more than the rules of traditional neutrality permitted, into a full-fledged nonbelligerent, committed to pour out all its resources if need be to enable Britain to bring Germany to her knees. If there had ever been any doubts before that the American people would falter or refrain from taking the risk of war, those doubts were now resolved.

Having committed itself to underwriting a British victory, the Washington government was not willing to watch Nazi submarines prevent the delivery of goods vital to German defeat. German depredations on British and neutral shipping from the beginning of the blitzkrieg to the end of 1940 had been staggering enough,[9] but the spring of 1941 witnessed an even more powerful German attack. The Nazis extended their war zone on March 25 to include Iceland and Denmark Strait between Greenland and Iceland and sent dozens of new submarines into the North Atlantic to hunt their prey in "wolf packs." They also used surface vessels in daring raids and threw a large part of their air force into the battle to choke off the stream of supplies flowing from American to British ports. The Germans destroyed 537,493 tons of merchant shipping in March 1941; 653,960 tons in April; and 500,063 tons in May. As Churchill repeatedly warned, the outcome of the Battle of the Atlantic might well determine the entire course of the war.

To the president, therefore, the choice did not seem to lie between action and inaction but rather among various means of participating in the Battle of the Atlantic. Consequently, on March 25 and April 2, 1941, he authorized American naval yards to repair British vessels; on March 28 he transferred ten Coast Guard cutters to the British fleet to assist in antisubmarine operations; on March 31 he had the Coast Guard seize thirty Axis and thirty-five Danish merchant ships in American ports. It was bold action, but it was not enough to clear the sea lanes. Secretary Stimson urged Roosevelt to order the navy to convoy British and Allied merchant ships all the way from American to British ports.

The president rejected Stimson's advice but decided on April 10 to extend the American Neutrality Patrol far out into the Atlantic—to longitude 25° west, a line between Brazil and the west coast of Africa in the south and slightly west of Iceland in the north. American naval vessels would search out, but not attack, Nazi submarines, and they would warn British vessels of the presence of U-boats within the area between the

[9]British, Allied, and neutral shipping losses totaled 3,139,190 tons from May through December 1940.

American coast and longitude 25° west.[10] In addition, the president issued a proclamation on April 10 removing the area of the Red Sea from the list of war zones forbidden to American ships.

Isolationists in Congress were meanwhile pressing the charge that Roosevelt had begun an undeclared naval war by ordering American vessels in the patrol area to convoy British ships and attack Nazi U-boats. A German submarine torpedoed an American freighter, *Robin Moor*, in the South Atlantic on May 21. The president had a fireside chat with the people six days later and told them what their navy was doing in the North Atlantic. He said that German control of the Atlantic would imperil American security, and he revealed that the Nazis were sinking ships twice as fast as British and American shipyards could replace them. The hope of victory, he continued, lay in increasing shipbuilding and in helping to reduce losses at sea. To accomplish the latter objective, he explained, "Our patrols are helping now to insure delivery of the needed supplies to Britain." He ended by warning that "all additional measures necessary to deliver the goods" would be taken, by calling upon industry and labor to redouble their efforts, and by declaring an unlimited state of national emergency.

7. The Invasion of Russia

An overwhelming majority of Americans had thought no better of the Russians than of the Nazis ever since the Soviet Union sealed its pact of friendship with Hitlerite Germany and then seized eastern Poland, absorbed the Baltic states, launched war against Finland, and afterward tore the province of Bessarabia from Rumania. This anti-Russian tension was increased during the period from August 1939 to June 1941 by efforts of American Communists to cripple defense production through strikes in airplane factories and otherwise to impair American solidarity. Congressional vexation at such subversion took form in the Smith Act in the spring of 1940. It made it unlawful for any group to advocate or teach the violent overthrow of government in the United States, or for any person to belong to such a group.

We now know that the Soviet leaders would have been prepared to come to agreement with Hitler for a division of Europe and the Middle East. Conversations between Hitler and Molotov in Berlin in November 1940 failed to bring agreement, but only because Hitler thought the Rus-

[10]This was the substance of orders issued by Roosevelt to Admiral Ernest J. King on April 19–21, 1941. The Navy began intensified patrol activities on April 24. Meanwhile, the State Department on April 9 concluded an agreement with the Danish minister in Washington, authorizing the United States to build naval and air bases on Greenland.

sians wanted too much. He was enraged by Russian demands and ordered preparations on December 18, 1940, for an invasion of Russia in the coming spring. Hitler launched his attack against the Soviet Union in the early morning hours of June 22, 1941. Washington reacted circumspectly, for the American public probably welcomed a showdown battle between the dictatorships, while Roosevelt's military advisers warned that Russia would collapse within three months and any aid given to the Soviet armies would only fall into Hitler's hands.

Meanwhile, Roosevelt used the breathing space afforded by the German attack to strengthen home defenses and the American position in the North Atlantic. The most urgent defense necessity in the early summer of 1941 was extension of the terms of service of the 900,000 men drafted in the preceding autumn. The defense effort would have practically collapsed if the men had been allowed to go home at the end of their one-year term. The president, therefore, permitted General Marshall to ask Congress on July 3 to extend the term of service and also to remove the provisions in the Selective Service Act of 1940 that prohibited sending draftees outside the Western Hemisphere. The Senate extended the term of service by six months on August 7, 1941. On the other hand, the struggle in the House of Representatives was bitter and long in doubt until that body approved extension by a vote of 203 to 202 on August 12.

While this controversy was in its first stage the president moved decisively to strengthen American control of the North Atlantic sea lanes. Negotiations among Roosevelt, Churchill, and the prime minister of Iceland culminated in the occupation of Iceland by American marines on July 7, 1941, and the inauguration of United States naval escorts for convoys of American and Icelandic ships between the Atlantic Coast and Iceland on July 26. Thus by one stroke the character of American operations in the North Atlantic was changed drastically. Henceforward the navy would not merely patrol the area between Iceland and the United States but would destroy "hostile forces" that threatened American and Icelandic shipping in that broad expanse of water.

8. The Atlantic Conference and the Brink of War

Harry Hopkins, lend-lease administrator and now Roosevelt's closet confidant, left Washington on July 13, 1941, for London to pave the way for a personal meeting between Roosevelt and Churchill. Roosevelt not only wanted to renew acquaintance with the "Former Naval Person"; he also wanted the military and naval leaders of both countries to coordinate plans for future operations. Churchill was delighted and agreed to come to a secret meeting "in some lonely bay or other" on August 9. Hopkins flew next to Moscow for conversations with Stalin and other Soviet leaders. From Stalin the American envoy heard the news that the Russian armies would withstand the first Nazi onslaught and take the offensive during the coming winter. Hopkins also learned that the Kremlin would welcome lend-lease aid and facilitate its delivery, and that the Russian government desired American entry into the war above all other things.

Hopkins was back in London in time to join Churchill and his party aboard the new battleship, *Prince of Wales*, for the journey to the rendezvous with Roosevelt off Argentia, Newfoundland. The president arrived aboard the cruiser *Augusta*, and the two leaders met on the American vessel on the morning of August 9.[11] The British tried to obtain some commitment of American support if Japan attacked British possessions in the Far East. In this, as in all other matters discussed, Roosevelt and his advisers refused to make any promises of a military or naval character.

The most important work of the Argentia meeting was the approval, after some stiff argument about Britain's imperial policy, by Roosevelt and Churchill on August 12 of the joint declaration known as the Atlantic Charter. It was the product of careful thought and patient negotiation and recorded Anglo-American agreement on "certain common principles" on which the two governments based "their hopes for a better future for the world." These principles were no territorial aggrandizement, no territorial changes that did not accord with the wishes of the people involved, the right of all peoples to choose the form of government under which they lived, economic collaboration in the postwar world, and the right of all peoples to live in peace and in freedom from fear, want, and aggression.

News of the Argentia conference and the text of the Atlantic Charter were published in the press on August 15 and provoked isolationist editors and politicians to new outbursts. But the overwhelming majority of Americans believed Roosevelt's assurances that he had made no commitment to intervene actively and approved the Wilsonian aspirations embodied in the Atlantic Charter. Obviously, the preponderant majority continued to approve giving aid to Hitler's enemies and to hope that the United States would not have to enter the "shooting war." Roosevelt shared these sentiments. Like the great majority of his fellow countrymen, he continued to hope for peace while announcing objectives that could be attained only by full-fledged American participation in the war.

The president set about to provide greater assistance to Russia soon after his return from Argentia. This undertaking was made immensely difficult by the opposition of isolationists, the Catholic press, and many anti-Communist Americans. Even though he was uncertain of public and congressional reaction, Roosevelt began discussions that led to an Anglo-American-Soviet conference in Moscow in late September 1941 and an

[11]It was, incidentally, their second meeting. They had met casually in London on July 29, 1918.

Anglo-American promise to furnish $1 billion worth of aid to Russia before June 30, 1942. When Congress, while voting a new $6 billion appropriation for lend-lease production and export in October, rejected an amendment forbidding extension of aid to Russia, Roosevelt declared the Soviet Union eligible for lend-lease assistance on November 7.

More significant for the immediate future, however, was Roosevelt's decision further to relieve the British position in the North Atlantic. The president decided at Argentia to allow British and Allied vessels to join American convoys between the United States and Iceland. This was done unofficially before the end of August, although orders to this effect were not issued until September 13.

Roosevelt pondered the best way to break the news of this new policy to the people. Then a German submarine attacked the destroyer *Greer* south of Iceland on September 4, after the *Greer* had joined a British airplane in trailing the U-boat. The incident gave the president the "provocation" he needed to justify a change of policy. In a radio address on September 11, he declared in seeming seriousness that the attack on the *Greer* was part of a Nazi plan to control the Atlantic, in preparation for an assault upon the Western Hemisphere. The time for active defense had come, he added; hereafter American ships and planes would protect all ships within the area between the United States and Iceland. Moreover, he continued, he had ordered the army and navy to shoot on sight at all German and Italian war vessels in the American patrol area.

The president's speech was in effect a declaration of an undeclared naval war against Germany—the perhaps inevitable outcome of the adoption of the Lend-Lease Act and the American decision to get supplies through the troubled waters to Great Britain. Not only did a large majority of Congress and the public approve this forward step; the majority also approved when Roosevelt finally asked Congress on October 9, 1941, to revise the Neutrality Act of 1939. He requested permission to arm American merchantmen and indirectly suggested that Congress should permit American ships to enter war zones and belligerent ports. While debate on these proposals proceeded, a German submarine torpedoed the destroyer *Kearny* on the night of October 16-17, with the loss of eleven lives. The Senate on November 7 and the House on November 13 voted to allow merchantmen to arm and to pass through the war zone to British ports.

Meanwhile the undeclared naval war in the North Atlantic proceeded. A submarine sank the destroyer *Reuben James* with the loss of 115 lives on October 31, but there was no such general agitation for war as had followed German attacks on American ships in early 1917. The American people now clearly understood their immediate task—to deliver supplies to Britain and Russia regardless of the peril. They assumed that task not gladly, for they knew that it involved the risk of war, but with grim determination and still fervent hope that somehow they could avoid full-scale participation.

9. Futile Negotiations with Japan, 1938-1941

Relations between the United States and Japan were in a state of suspended hostility between the adjournment of the Brussels Conference of 1938 and the outbreak of the German-Polish crisis in the spring of 1939. During this period the military clique in the Tokyo government were pressing for an alliance with Germany to offset Soviet and American power. The Japanese army was also undertaking extensive military operations against Russian forces along the Manchurian border. The army's hopes for an alliance with the Nazis were momentarily blasted by the Nazi-Soviet Pact in August 1939; meanwhile, however, Japan undertook a diplomatic campaign to force the British to recognize Japanese conquests in China. The Chamberlain government surrendered to these demands on July 24, 1939, by recognizing that the Japanese army was supreme in the areas it occupied.

The announcement of this agreement galvanized Washington's determination to play a stronger role in the Far East. Therefore, the president sent to Tokyo on July 26 the necessary six months' notice of the possible abrogation of the Japanese-American Commercial Treaty of 1911. It was no idle warning but a stern threat that after January 26, 1940, the United States might deny Japan access to the source from which it obtained more than half the raw materials, especially iron, steel, and oil, for its war machine.

The threat of full-scale war with Russia and economic retaliation by the United States restrained the extreme militarists in Japan and prevented the imperial government from embarking upon new conquests following the outbreak of war in Europe. Instead, the Japanese ended the border conflict with Soviet forces in September and next launched a strenuous effort to liquidate the China Incident. Moreover, the Japanese opened negotiations with the State Department in December 1939 to prevent imposition of the threatened American embargo. These talks ended in a stalemate because neither government would recede on the basic issue of China. Washington simply reaffirmed its traditional position and declared that for the time being it would not end the export of American war supplies.

Japanese-American official relations were relatively quiescent during the early months of 1940, especially after a new moderate government under Admiral Mitsumasa Yonai came to power in Tokyo on January 14, 1940. In the United States, however, public opinion was moving strongly toward the application of an embargo. In fact, sentiment in Congress was so vociferous that administration leaders suppressed it only with difficulty.

THE COMING OF THE WAR
IN THE **PACIFIC, 1939-1941**

481

The State Department's policy of threatening economic retaliation might well have succeeded had not Germany's triumph in western Europe convinced the Japanese military leaders that the power of Britain, France, and the Netherlands was gone, and that henceforth they would have to deal only with the United States. Army leaders and expansionists were excited by the opportunity to seize or fall heir to French Indochina and the Netherlands East Indies and by the hope of an alliance with Germany. They caused the fall of the Yonai cabinet on July 16, 1940, and created a new government headed by Prince Fumimaro Konoye, with the boastful Yosuke Matsuoka as foreign minister and the ardent expansionist, General Hideki Tojo, as minister of war.

The new cabinet, as a first step toward achieving a "new order in Greater East Asia," demanded and after some negotiation obtained from the Vichy government the right to build airfields and station troops in northern Indochina. As a second and more important step, Konoye, Tojo, Matsuoka, and other leaders approved a program for future action on July 27 and September 4, 1940. It envisaged conquest of British, French, and Dutch Far Eastern possessions *if circumstances permitted* and a military alliance with Germany if Hitler approved these plans of conquest. The bargain was struck following the arrival of a new German ambassador in Tokyo on September 7. It was formally sealed in Berlin on September 27, 1940.[12]

Washington moved cautiously to apply such counterpressure as would not provoke an immediate Japanese thrust into the South Pacific. First, it applied an embargo on the export of aviation gasoline, lubricants, and prime scrap metal to Japan on July 26, 1940. Then, after the Japanese occupied northern Indochina, the American government announced extension of a new $25 million loan to China on September 25.[13] On the following day it decreed an embargo on the export of all types of scrap iron and steel. Following this action came a virtual embargo in December on the export of iron ore and pig iron, certain chemicals, certain machine tools, and other products. Churchill was encouraged to reopen the Burma Road, the chief supply route between Nationalist China and the outside world, on October 8, 1940.[14] The Japanese protested, but Washington's firm stand and rumors of Anglo-American naval cooperation in the Pa-

[12]This was the Tripartite Agreement, or Triple Alliance, in which Japan recognized German and Italian leadership in Europe, Germany and Italy recognized Japan's leadership in the establishment of a "new order" in Greater East Asia, and the three signatories agreed to cooperate militarily, politically, and economically "if one of the three Contracting Powers is attacked by a Power at present not involved in the European War or in the Chinese-Japanese conflict."

[13]Moreover, Roosevelt announced on November 30, 1940, after the Japanese had recognized a puppet Chinese government in Nanking, that the United States would extend a $100 million loan to Nationalist China. This assistance, incidentally, came in the nick of time to save Chiang Kai-shek's government at Chungking from collapse.

[14]The British had closed the Burma Road in response to Japanese threats on July 12, 1940.

cific[15] caused the Konoye government to beat a momentary diplomatic retreat.

The United States by a policy of implicit threatening had, therefore, prevented the Japanese from striking while Britain and America were in direst peril following the fall of France. Moreover, Japan was not yet prepared to engage the western democracies. There was still the danger that the Soviet Union would strike in the north if Japan turned southward; and there was still the faint hope that somehow the United States might be frightened into acquiescing in Japanese plans. In order to safeguard Japan's long exposed northern flank, Matsuoka made a pilgrimage to Berlin, Rome, and Moscow in March and April 1941. Hitler urged that Japan strike immediately at Singapore. Foreign Minister Joachim von Ribbentrop, intimating that a German-Russian conflict was no longer inconceivable, promised that Germany would attack Russia if the Soviets attacked Japan after she was involved in war with Britain and America. Matsuoka was pleased but not entirely satisfied by these assurances. His supreme objective—a pledge of Soviet neutrality—he obtained in Moscow on April 13, in a Neutrality Pact in which Japan and Russia promised to remain neutral if either power were attacked by one or more countries.

Meanwhile, Tokyo had begun secret discussions with Washington on the other side of the world in a desperate effort to see if any ground for accommodation existed. The background of these negotiations was somewhat odd. An American Catholic bishop and priest discussed the problem of Japanese-American relations with certain Japanese leaders in Tokyo in December 1940. In consequence Premier Konoye asked them to convey a startling message to President Roosevelt—that Japan would for all practical purposes nullify the Tripartite Pact, withdraw its troops from China, and discuss closer economic relations with the United States. The two Catholic emissaries delivered the message to the president in the latter part of January 1941. They were followed soon afterward by two unofficial Japanese representatives, who urged that Roosevelt and Konoye could come to a comprehensive agreement[16] in a personal meeting. After this,

[15]The Washington government, alarmed by the conclusion of the Tripartite Pact, also began in the late autumn of 1940 to consider joint British, American, and Dutch planning for defense of the western Pacific. Discussions between Washington and London culminated in elaborate Anglo-American staff meetings from January 27 to March 27, 1941, and in British-American-Dutch-Commonwealth staff discussions in Singapore in late April. During both conferences, known respectively as ABC-I and ADB, the American representatives refused to make political or military commitments. Instead, they simply joined potential allies in making tentative plans for common action in the event that a Japanese attack forced the United States into the war.

It should be added that the American conferees at the ADB Conference named certain circumstances—notably a Japanese attack on British and Dutch possessions—in which the United States would enter the war. General Marshall and Admiral Stark, however, refused to approve the ADB report because it contained this commitment.

[16]As elaborated in a proposal brought to the State Department on April 9 by a messenger from the imperial army, the Japanese proposed withdrawal of Japanese troops from China by agreement between China and Japan, reaffirmation of the Open Door policy, merger of the Chinese Nationalist regime with the Japanese puppet government in Nanking, resumption of normal economic relations between Japan and the United States, and an American loan to Japan.

they said, the emperor would dismiss Matsuoka. Hull doubted that Konoye could carry through, but he began discussions in March 1941 with the new Japanese ambassador, Admiral Kichisaburo Nomura, who had meanwhile been brought into the secret discussions. Hull did not reject the Japanese proposal, which had been put into writing in language much less promising between April 2 and April 5 as a "Draft Understanding." The secretary of state simply countered on April 16 with a four-point program that embodied traditional American demands concerning China and disavowal of expansion by forceful means.

The Japanese leaders were encouraged by Nomura's report that Hull was eager to negotiate and failed utterly to see the significance of the secretary's four-point program because of the ambassador's incompetence. Instead, they gained the impression that the "Draft Understanding" was the American government's own proposal. A liaison conference in Tokyo on April 21, 1941, decided to continue the discussions and to defer making definite reply until the return of Matsuoka from Moscow. The foreign minister was infuriated by the negotiations that had proceeded during his absence. Japan's destiny, he argued, lay with Germany and in expansion; he was certain that strength, not weakness, would prevent the United States from interfering. He countered on May 7 with the suggestion that Japan and the United States sign a neutrality pact. Hull at once rejected the proposal as a carte blanche for Japanese seizure of British, French, and Dutch Far Eastern possessions. Matsuoka next submitted to the State Department on May 12 a revised and remarkable proposal for a comprehensive understanding. It provided that the United States would cut off aid to Britain, urge Chiang Kai-shek to come to terms with Japan, resume normal trade relations with Japan, and end its ban on Japanese immigration.

Matsuoka's proposal was obviously unacceptable, but Roosevelt and Hull agreed to continue the negotiations, chiefly to buy time in the hope that moderates in the Tokyo government would depose the unruly foreign minister. Hull, therefore, restated the American position on May 31 and then again repeated it more fully on June 6 and 21. He proposed that the Japanese agree that American aid to Britain was defensive in character and that the Tripartite Pact would not apply if such aid led to a German-American clash. At this moment, when it seemed that the opponents of war with the United States might gain the upper hand in Tokyo, the German attack on Russia removed the threat of Soviet interference and encouraged the Japanese leaders to decide to occupy all of Indochina, perhaps preparatory to an attack on Singapore.

The German assault on Russia also momentarily disrupted the desultory Japanese-American talks then in progress. Matsuoka apparently wanted to end the negotiations altogether and loudly demanded that Japan strike at once at the Soviet Union. But he carried his arrogance too far and was deposed on July 16 and replaced by the more moderate Admiral Teijiro Toyoda. As Washington knew from intercepted Japanese messages to Berlin,[17] the cabinet shake-up did not mean any immediate change in Japanese policy. In fact, the imperial government presented a demand to Vichy on July 14 for the immediate occupation of land, air, and naval bases in southern Indochina by Japanese forces. It was the first step in a general program adopted at an imperial conference on July 2. Under its provisions Japan would attempt to conclude the China Incident, avoid war with the USSR for the time being, and advance southward (this provision was intentionally vague) even at the risk of war with the United States and Great Britain.

The Washington government reacted swiftly and violently. The United States, Hull told Nomura on July 23, 1941, could only conclude that the occupation of southern Indochina was the prelude to further Japanese conquests and could see no point in further discussions. On the following day, after Vichy had surrendered to the Japanese demands, the president received the Japanese ambassador, hinted that he was contemplating an embargo on the export of oil to Japan, and warned that a Japanese attack on the Dutch East Indies would result in serious consequences. On the other hand, Roosevelt continued, if Japan would withdraw from Indochina he would take leadership in a movement to neutralize that French colony and help Japan to find access to raw materials.

The president, however, was done with mere parleying. He impounded all Japanese funds in the United States, closed the Panama Canal to Japanese shipping, and called the Philippine militia into active service on July 26. On August 1 he forbade the export to Japan of a number of vital materials, including oil that could be refined into aviation gasoline, while the British and Dutch governments applied similar sanctions.

This decisive retaliation put Tokyo in the dilemma of having to choose between a modified retreat or a desperate war with the United States. Although some extremists welcomed the prospect of war, the naval leaders were reluctant to risk hostilities and warned that the empire would probably be defeated in a protracted conflict. The Cabinet, therefore, maneuvered to find a solution that would include both Japanese occupation of southern Indochina and peace with the United States. Premier Konoye proposed on August 7 that the president meet him in personal conference to discuss means to relieve the tension. Roosevelt gave his reply on August 17, after his return from the Atlantic Conference. If Japan made any further aggressive moves the United States would take all necessary steps to safeguard American security. However, if Japan sincerely desired to come to agreement along lines already laid down by the United States, then Washington would be willing to resume the exploratory discussions disrupted by the Japanese occupation of Indochina.

Faced squarely with the choice of war or agreement with the United States, Konoye now moved desperately to persuade the president to join

[17]Experts in the American government had earlier deciphered the Japanese diplomatic code.

him in a personal conference. Foreign Minister Toyoda reiterated Konoye's proposal to Ambassador Joseph C. Grew on August 18, while Konoye ordered a ship to stand in readiness to take him to the meeting. Then
on August 28 Nomura presented the imperial government's reply to Roosevelt's note of August 17. Japan would withdraw its troops from Indochina as soon as the China Incident was settled; it would not undertake
expansion southward or make war on the Soviet Union unless attacked;
and it agreed that the principles set forth in the American note were "the
prime requisites of a true peace." In a subsequent note of clarification
dated September 4 the Japanese government made perhaps its most important offer, namely, that Japan would not feel bound by the Tripartite
Pact to go to war if the United States became involved in a defensive war
with Germany.

Roosevelt was so pleased by the Japanese response that he was ready to
give immediate consent to the proposal for a meeting with Konoye. But
Hull urged caution and insisted that the two governments agree upon the
fundamental issue of China before the chiefs of state met. Despite warnings from Tokyo that only some bold stroke could restrain the war party,
the president accepted the State Department's view that Japan would not
attack and that a policy of continued firmness would force the imperial
government to surrender. Thus Roosevelt replied on September 3 that he
would be glad to confer with Konoye, but that basic differences, particularly on China, would have to be cleared up first.

The president's reply in the circumstances spelled the doom not only of
the projected conference, but of peace as well. Whether the momentous
decision was wise or foolish will be long debated by historians. Defenders
of the administration have argued that agreement on important issues was
impossible, and that in any event Konoye could not have forced the army
to make the concessions necessary to preserve the peace. On the other
hand, Roosevelt's antagonists have maintained that the administration rejected Konoye's invitation in order to goad Japan into attacking the United
States. At least on the point of the administration's intentions the records
are full and revealing. They indicate that the president and the State
Department, far from desiring war, were convinced that the Japanese
could not undertake hostilities and would retreat in the face of a firm
American policy.

In view of the primacy of the Nazi danger and the likelihood that the
United States would soon be drawn into the European war, American
policy in the Far East might well have been directed at one objective
only—maintenance of peace with Japan on any terms short of countenanc-
ing further Japanese aggressions in the southwestern Pacific. Such a policy
might have necessitated unfreezing Japanese assets, lifting the embargo on
export of oil and metals, and easing the pressure on Japan to withdraw
immediately from China. There is considerable evidence that such concessions by the United States at this time—that is, early September 1941—

would have enormously strengthened the Japanese moderates and might have sufficed to preserve the status quo and gain precious time.

Roosevelt and Hull were influenced by a group of Sinophiles in the State Department into believing that Japan would not fight, and that it would not matter much if she did. Instead of making any concessions they continued to press demands for Japanese withdrawal from China, demands that were impossible in the circumstances. The time might have come when the United States and Britain could have forced a showdown on China without having to go to war.[18] But that time would be after the defeat of Germany, when the two democracies were invincible, not in the late summer of 1941, when they were weak, and when wisdom demanded a policy of delay.

10. Pearl Harbor

Events following the delivery of Roosevelt's reply of September 3 support the thesis that the effect of American policy was to strengthen the extremists and perhaps tip the balance in Tokyo in favor of the war party. An imperial conference met for a showdown on policy on September 6, soon after receipt of the president's reply. The army chief of staff urged immediate preparations, if not a decision, for war. The navy chief of general staff agreed that Japan might have to resort to hostilities to avoid economic destruction as a consequence of the American embargo. Emperor Hirohito, however, demanded that negotiations be continued in the hope of peaceful understanding. The imperial conference ended in agreement to continue military preparations, to be completed by the end of October, and to seek for the last time American acquiescence in the minimum Japanese program.[19]

Premier Konoye met secretly with Ambassador Grew during the evening of September 6, immediately after the imperial conference, and reit-

[18]From a sheerly strategic point of view, the continuation of the Sino-Japanese War served Anglo-American interests by keeping large Japanese forces occupied, draining Japanese resources, and deterring the Japanese from expanding into the southwestern Pacific. Perceiving the rather obvious fact that involvement in China in part prevented the Japanese from expanding northward, the Soviet leaders played a skillful game of preserving peace with Japan while at the same time sending a modicum of supplies to Nationalist China to make certain that the Japanese would have to continue their now useless war in China.

[19]This imperial conference defined as (1) Anglo-American agreement to close the Burma Road, cease all aid to Nationalist China, and not obstruct a settlement of the China Incident by Japan; (2) Anglo-American agreement to make no offensive preparations in the Far East; and (3) Anglo-American agreement to resume normal trade relations with Japan and assist Japan in her negotiations with Siam and the Netherlands Indies. In return Japan would (1) agree not to use Indochina as a base for offensive operations except against China; (2) withdraw troops from Indochina after establishment of peace in the Far East; (3) guarantee the neutrality of the Philippines; (4) refrain from war against Russia unless attacked; and (5) agree to clarify Japanese obligations under the Tripartite Pact.

erated his desire for a personal meeting with Roosevelt. Konoye renewed his invitation on September 22, and Grew added a plea for acceptance. Hull replied on October 2, again declaring that the two governments must agree on fundmental issues, principally China, before a general conference could succeed. To Konoye, Washington's final refusal spelled the doom of his efforts to prevent war. He and the naval leaders tried to persuade the army chieftains that Japan could not defeat America and that they had to evacuate China as a prerequisite to peace. The army adamantly refused and insisted that there was no recourse but war. Then Konoye sent a special emissary to Washington to plead the absolute necessity for some kind of speedy agreement. Japan was even willing to evacuate China, the messenger told Welles on October 13.

But the situation in Tokyo was passing out of Konoye's control. The premier had a long conference with high military and naval officials on October 12 and argued in behalf of agreement to withdraw from China. But the war minister, General Tojo, instantly vetoed the proposal. Further discussions revealed that the premier and the army group had reached an impasse, and Konoye resigned on October 16. As his successor the emperor named Tojo himself, after the general had promised that he would continue negotiations.

The fall of the Konoye government only intensified the conflict in Tokyo between the army and the antiwar group. The emperor, supported by the navy, demanded reconsideration of the provisions for early military operations adopted by the imperial conference on September 6. Debate proceeded from mid-October through November 5. The new foreign minister, Shigenori Togo, tried to find a solution for the evacuation of China, but the army would not yield and insisted that war was preferable to the gradual economic ruin of the empire. Togo did persuade the army to agree to one last effort at compromise with the United States. The military chieftains agreed on November 5 but won the emperor's consent to preparations for immediate attack if the negotiations had yielded no agreement by about November 25. On November 5 the army and navy also issued war orders, to go into effect in early December if diplomacy had failed.

As a consequence negotiations proceeded anew in Washington between November 7 and December 7. The repetitious details need not be given here. It suffices to say that neither government retreated from its irrevocable position on the key issue of China, and that the American leaders continued the discussions mainly in the hope of deferring the conflict that they now thought was practically inevitable.

The utter hopelessness of the deadlock was further revealed after a special Japanese envoy, Saburu Kurusu, arrived at the White House on November 17. After talking with Roosevelt and Hull, Kurusu and Nomura were unable to persuade their government to agree to a stopgap proposal providing for immediate evacuation of southern Indochina, which the United States was willing to accept. Then Nomura on November 20 presented what was in fact Japan's final offer, actually, in Japanese eyes, an ultimatum. It was not entirely impossible as a basis for bargaining;[20] indeed, Foreign Minister Togo was confident that it would provide the basis for agreement.

Actually, Roosevelt had already drafted in his own hand a proposal for a temporary modus vivendi not entirely dissimilar from the Japanese proposal, except that the president's draft also provided for Japanese neutrality in the event of American hostilities in Europe. Thus the State Department, after receiving the Japanese note of November 20, drafted a counterproposal of its own, which was to run for three months. Its crucial provisions embodied mutual pledges against military action in the South Pacific, a Japanese promise to evacuate southern Indochina "forthwith," an American promise to restore normal trade relations with Japan, and a statement to the effect that the United States would "not look with disfavor upon the inauguration of conversations between the Government of China and the Government of Japan directed toward a peaceful settlement of their differences."

We will never know whether the American proposal could have saved the peace of the Pacific. Roosevelt and Hull decided not to submit the modus vivendi as a consequence of two events on November 25—receipt in Washington of news of the movement of Japanese troopships off Formosa, and the violent reaction of the British and Chinese governments to the proposed modus vivendi. The Chinese frankly warned that adoption of the modus vivendi would cause a collapse of their resistance. Receipt of a cable from Churchill on that same day evidently clinched Hull's decision to abandon the project. Hull called in Nomura and Kurusu on the following day, November 26, and formally rejected the Japanese proposal of November 20. He then proceeded to read the text of a draft "Mutual Declaration of Policy" and "Steps to be taken by the Government of the United States and by the Government of Japan." The mutual declaration was a reaffirmation of the principles that Hull had somewhat tediously enunciated many times. The proposed steps to be taken provided for Japanese evacuation not only of Indochina *but of China as well*, and for support of the Nationalist government by the Japanese.

In the circumstances, Hull's note came close to being an ultimatum. In any event, it spelled the doom of the negotiations. Its receipt in Tokyo on November 27 stunned the Japanese leaders, who concluded that it signified American insistence upon war. The Japanese deferred final decision until Nomura and Kurusu had conferred with President Roosevelt on No-

[20]It included (1) Japanese-American agreement not to invade any area in Southeast Asia and the South Seas, except for Indochina; (2) Japanese-American cooperation in guaranteeing mutual access to raw materials in the Netherlands Indies; (3) resumption of normal Japanese-American trade relationships; (4) American promise to put no obstacle in the way of Japan's attempts to make peace with China; (5) Japanese promise to withdraw from all of Indochina upon conclusion of a Sino-Japanese peace; and (6) Japanese promise to withdraw from southern to northern Indochina upon the conclusion of this agreement.

vember 27. When news of the president's refusal to consider any modus vivendi reached Tokyo, an imperial conference on December 1 decided on hostilities. To responsible Japanese leaders an uncertain war, which they really did not expect to win, seemed the only way to avoid slow economic strangulation or humiliating surrender that would spell Japan's end as a great power.

Meanwhile, Japanese preparations for probable conflict had been proceeding on the assumption that one must be prepared to fight if diplomacy fails. A carrier task force left the Kuriles on November 25 to attack the great American naval base at Pearl Harbor in Hawaii, while large army forces were poised in southern Indochina to strike at Malaya. The Washington leaders knew from intercepted messages only that the Japanese would attack somewhere soon. They recognized that an assault on the Philippines and Guam was possible, but they concluded that Tokyo would avoid such direct provocation to the United States. Thus the American government on the eve of war was more concerned with what to do in the event of a Japanese attack on Malaya and the Dutch East Indies than with immediate defense of American territory. When news of the movement of large Japanese forces against Malaya reached Washington on December 6, Roosevelt dispatched an urgent personal appeal to Hirohito, warning that the present tension could not last much longer and urging him to take some action to dispel the threat of war.

The Japanese reply to Hull's note of November 26 began to come to Washington over the wires in the afternoon of Saturday, December 6. The first sections, which were decoded by early evening, revealed Japan's rejection of the note; the final section, which announced termination of the negotiations, was in the president's hands by the morning of December 7. The attack on Pearl Harbor had already occurred, and first reports from the stricken base had reached Washington by the time that Nomura and Kurusu were able to deliver the message to Hull.

Meanwhile, American military and naval commanders in the Pacific had been duly but not strenuously warned on November 24 and 27 that surprise Japanese attacks were likely. Like their superiors in Washington, however, they expected the Japanese to strike at Malaya, not at them. The commanders in Hawaii, Admiral Husband E. Kimmel and General Walter C. Short, were unconcerned as what Roosevelt would call the "day of infamy" approached. Kimmel had concentrated virtually his entire fleet in Pearl Harbor; fearing sabotage, Short had disposed his airplanes and anti-aircraft guns in such a manner as to make successful defense impossible. Neither commander had established an effective air patrol. Thus the carrier task force under Admiral Chuchi Nagumo approached Hawaii from the northwest undetected.

The first wave of Japanese airplanes attacked airfields at 7:55 A.M. on December 7, 1941, and then struck the fleet anchored in the harbor. A second wave followed at 8:50. The navy and marine corps were unable to get a single plane off the ground. An army fighter squadron at Haleiwa, which the Japanese overlooked, got a few planes into the air and destroyed several of the attackers. A few antiaircraft batteries were operating by the time of the second major assault. And several naval craft were able to get into action and attack Japanese submarines. Otherwise, the Japanese were unopposed and raked and bombed at will. When the last planes turned toward their carriers at about 9:45 the great American bastion in the Pacific was a smoking shambles. Practically every airplane on the island of Oahu was either destroyed or disabled. All eight battleships in Pearl Harbor were disabled—two of them, *Oklahoma* and *Arizona*, were destroyed or sunk. Three cruisers and three destroyers were heavily damaged or destroyed. And 2,323 men of both services were dead. The cost to the Japanese was twenty-nine airplanes, five midget submarines, and one fleet submarine.

First reports of the attack came to Washington at about two in the afternoon, while later news told of other Japanese attacks on the Philippines, Hong Kong, Wake Island, Midway Island, Siam, and Malaya, and of a Japanese declaration of war against the United States and Great Britain. After cabinet meetings in the afternoon and evening, the president called congressional leaders to the White House and reviewed dispatches he had received. He appeared before the two houses on the following day, December 8, excoriated the "unprovoked and dastardly attack by Japan," and asked Congress to recognize the obvious state of war that existed. It was done within an hour and with only one dissenting vote in the House of Representatives. Roosevelt had deliberately avoided mention of Germany and Italy in his war message, in order to leave the decision for full-fledged war for the time being to Hitler. The führer was delighted by the Pearl Harbor attack and responded to the Japanese request for a German declaration of war against the United States on December 11. Mussolini followed suit at once. The president and Congress reciprocated during the afternoon of the same day.

Shock and indignation surged through the American people as they heard the news of the Japanese attack over their radios on the afternoon of Pearl Harbor day. They did not know that their armed forces had suffered the most humiliating defeat in American history by a foreign foe, or the desperate circumstances that impelled the Japanese to undertake a suicidal war. The American people only thought that they had been treacherously attacked. And in their anger they forgot all the partisan quarrels and debates over foreign policy that had so long divided them and resolved with firm determination to win the war that the Japanese had begun. The agony of doubt was over; the issue was now fully joined. The American people had embarked not gladly upon a second crusade, but grimly upon a war for survival.

21

The Second World War:

The American

Home Front

Not since the dark days of the Revolution had the American people confronted so dire a military menace or so staggering a task as during the Second World War. Within a few months after Japanese bombs fell on Pearl Harbor, the ensign of the Rising Sun floated triumphantly over all the outposts and bastions of the far Pacific region, while Hitler and his armies stood poised to strike at the Middle East and join forces with the Japanese in India.

It was perhaps fortunate that the American people in December 1941 little knew how long the war would last and what the costs would be. However, they had certain advantages that made victory possible: courageous allies, unity unprecedented in American history, enormous resources and industrial capacity, superb political and military leadership, and, most important, determination to win. These factors combined from 1941 to 1945 to achieve miracles of production that made earlier American war efforts look small by comparison.

The astonishing thing, however, was the fact that Americans could engage in total war without submitting to the discipline of total war at home. To be sure, the war intensified certain social tensions and created new problems of adjustment; but the mass of Americans took the war in stride, without emotional excitement or hysteria.

1. Manpower for War

The adoption of the war resolutions found the United States in the midst of a sizable rearmament campaign, the momentum of which was daily increasing. Congress at once ordered the registration of all men between the ages of twenty (lowered to eighteen in 1942) and forty-four for war service and of men between forty-five and sixty-five for potential labor service. All told, draft boards registered some 31,000,000 men, of whom 9,867,707 were inducted into service. Including volunteers, a total of 15,145,115 men and women served in the armed services before the end of the war—10,420,000 in the army, 3,883,520 in the navy, 599,693 in the marines, and 241,902 in the Coast Guard.

Because the first offensive blows could be delivered from the air, the army air forces were authorized at the outset to increase their strength to 2.3 million men and were given highest priority on manpower and materials. When the Japanese attacked Pearl Harbor the AAF had 292,000 men and 9,000 planes (1,100 of which were fit for combat). When the Japanese

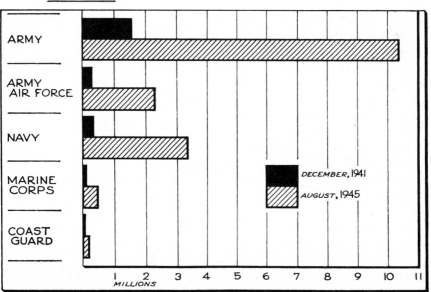

EXPANSION OF U.S. ARMED FORCES
1941-1945

surrendered in August 1945, the AAF enlisted 2.3 million men and women and had 72,000 planes in service.

Thanks to the wealth, technology, and industrial and agricultural capacity of his country, the American soldier was the best-paid, best-clothed, and by 1943 the best-equipped fighting man in the world. In that year, for example, Americans achieved not only a quantitative but also a decided qualitative superiority in fighter planes and bombers. Even in areas of research in which the Germans had a head start, such as atomic fission, American scientists and engineers had won decisive advantages by 1945. On the battlefield the best American weapons were the light semiautomatic Garand rifle and the multiple-driven truck. They combined to give a superiority in firepower and mobility that the Germans were never able to overcome in spite of general equality in machine guns, mortars, rocket-launched missiles, and artillery.[1]

In the meantime, the navy, marines, and Coast Guard had grown from relative weakness after Pearl Harbor to dimensions of gigantic strength at the time of the Japanese surrender. On December 7, 1941, the navy had a complement of 337,349 men, in addition to 66,048 in the Marine Corps and 25,336 in the Coast Guard. By the summer of 1945, the navy's manpower had increased to 3,408,347 officers and men, the Marine Corps' to 484,631, and the Coast Guard's to 170,480. Before Japanese bombs disabled or sank part of the Pacific Fleet at Pearl Harbor, the navy had in operation some 4,500 ships, including 17 battleships, 7 fleet carriers, 18 heavy and 19 light cruisers, 200 destroyers and torpedo boats, and 114 submarines. By the end of 1945 the navy had grown to more than 91,000 ships of all sizes, including 24 battleships, 2 large cruisers, 29 fleet carriers, 73 escort carriers, 23 heavy and 45 light cruisers, 489 destroyers and torpedo boats, 500 escort vessels, and 274 submarines.

Finally, there was mobilization of women for war service. The Women's Auxiliary Corps, which grew in size to 100,000, sent 17,000 WACs overseas; the navy's counterpart, the WAVEs, numbered about 86,000 at the end of the war. There was also the Coast Guard's SPARs and the Marine Corps' Women's Reserve. Working as stenographers, clerks, technicians, cryptographers, and the like, female contingents not only performed indispensable functions but released over 200,000 men for service on the battle fronts.

Measured in human costs, the price of victory in the Second World War came high to the American people—253,573 dead, 651,042 wounded, 114,204 prisoners, and 65,834 men missing. For the men who died, how-

---

[1] In certain categories, however, the Germans retained a marked advantage. The German 88-mm rifle, for example, was superior to the American 90-mm rifle. Use of a smokeless, flashless powder gave the German infantryman a great advantage over his American foe, who had to use powder that exposed his position every time he fired. Moreover, the American medium Sherman tank was no match from 1943 to 1945 for the heavy German Tiger and Panther tanks. Not until production of the heavy Pershing tank in the winter of 1944–1945 were American armored divisions able to meet German *Panzer* forces on equal terms.

ever, Americans and their allies exacted a fearful retribution. Germany and Italy suffered 373,600 dead and lost 8,108,983 prisoners to the Allies on the western front alone. The Japanese gave up 1,093,000 battle dead in areas outside China.

For their comparatively low death lists, Americans in large measure could thank the medical corps of the several services. Although American soldiers lived and fought in deserts and jungles as well as in the temperate zones, the death rate from nonbattle causes was no higher than the rate for similar groups at home. And for the sick and wounded there was extraordinary care, while use of sulfa drugs, penicillin, and whole blood brought such healing and relief from wounds and shock as would not have been possible a decade before. The result was to cut the rate of deaths from disease and battle wounds in half from the rate of the First World War.

2. Scientists Against Time

In the last analysis the war was won as much in the laboratory and on the testing ground as on the battlefield. American scientists at the outset of the war lagged far behind the Germans in research in atomic fission, jet propulsion, and rockets, and they were behind the British in work on jet propulsion, radar, and other electronic devices. Alarmed by the prospect of his country entering the war scientifically unprepared, Dr. Vannevar Bush, president of the Carnegie Institution of Washington, persuaded the president in June 1940 to establish the National Defense Research Committee (NDRC), with representatives from the defense departments, universities, and private industry. Then Roosevelt reorganized the government's research program in June 1941 by creating the Office of Scientific Research and Development (OSRD). Bush was director of the OSRD, with power to approve or veto all projects and to initiate research.

Bush and his colleagues had accomplished a full mobilization of scientific personnel and facilities by the autumn of 1941. Let us look briefly at some of the most significant results of this great effort—the development of radar and electronic devices, rockets for combat use, the proximity fuse, and, finally, the atomic bomb.

It was the British who first perfected radar and put it to large-scale use during the great German air assault of 1940-1941. Radar sets in patrol planes enabled the British and American navies to bring the German submarines under control.[2] Radar in fighters enabled the air forces to launch powerful night interceptors; in bombers, it provided a generally accurate bombsight. As the basis of a new method of fire-control, it gave eyes to guns as well as to airplanes and ships. The American armed services alone

---

[2] Perhaps even more effective in antisubmarine operations was so-called sonar, or underwater sound detection apparatus, developed by the NDRC in conjunction with the Harvard Underwater Sound Laboratory.

had received $3 billion worth of radar equipment and $71 million worth of Loran, a long-range navigational aid, by July 1945.

The outbreak of the war found research in the field of rocket warfare well advanced in Britain and Germany and practically nonexistent in the United States. But NDRC scientists had a sizable research program under way by the end of 1941. One of the first results was the "bazooka," a tube rocket-launcher perfected in 1942, which could be operated by two infantrymen and discharged a rocket powerful enough to destroy a tank. Subsequently, scientists developed an incredible variety of rocket-launchers and rockets for use in land combat and antiaircraft operations, by airplanes, and in ship-to-shore bombardments. What this meant in terms of increased firepower can perhaps best be illustrated by the fact that a single fighter plane carrying rockets could discharge a salvo as heavy as a destroyer's.

One of the most brilliant scientific achievements of the war was the development, exclusively by the OSRD, of the proximity fuse. It was a miniature radio set in the head of the shell that detonated it by proximity to the target. Proximity fuses were first used by the navy against Japanese aircraft in 1943. Fearing that the Germans would recover an unexploded shell and put the fuse into production, the Joint Chiefs of Staff did not allow the ground forces in Europe to use the new weapon until December 1944. Put into use against the Germans in their Ardennes counteroffensive (see pp. 550–551), the proximity fuse compounded the effectiveness of American artillery and proved devastating against German ground troops.

The mobilization of American scientists paid numerous other dividends—among them the development of more powerful explosives and fire bombs, of DDT and other weapons in the warfare against insects and vermin, of advanced techniques in the use of blood plasma and whole blood, of penicillin, and of new and deadly gases, which were never used. But the greatest triumph of American scientific and productive genius was the development of the atomic bomb. The perfection of this weapon marked a decisive turning point in history.

The Danish physicist Niels Bohr startled a group of American physicists assembled in Washington on January 26, 1939, by announcing that two Germans at the Kaiser Wilhelm Institute in Berlin had recently accomplished atomic fission in uranium. Nuclear physicists had long understood the structure of the atom and known that atomic fission was theoretically possible. But the deed had now been done, and the road was open for the development of a bomb more powerful and deadly than the world had ever dreamed of. The grave danger was that the Nazis would produce atomic bombs and literally conquer the world. Therefore, Enrico Fermi of Columbia University, Albert Einstein of the Institute for Advanced Study, and others persuaded the president to begin a small research program. It was not until 1940, however, that work began in earnest. By the summer of 1941 research at Columbia, California, and other universities had confirmed the possibilities of atomic fission through a chain reaction. The chief problem now was to find a fissionable element in sufficient quantity.

Earlier experiments had proved that the uranium isotope, U-235, was fissionable; but since U-235 was an infinitesimal part of uranium, the chances were remote of ever accumulating enough of the element to manufacture atomic bombs. This problem was solved by Dr. Ernest Lawrence of the University of California at Berkeley, who used a huge cyclotron, or "atom smasher," to convert the plentiful uranium element, U-238, into a new element, plutonium, which was as fissionable as U-235 and much easier to obtain in quantity.

The next objective became a chain reaction in uranium, that is, the almost simultaneous fission of the uranium atoms through a chain bombardment by neutrons. A group of physicists under the direction of Dr. Arthur H. Compton built the first atomic pile, or apparatus, under the stadium at Stagg Field of the University of Chicago. They produced the first controlled chain reaction on December 2, 1942. Production of an atomic bomb was now possible, provided a means of production could be devised. OSRD turned the problem over to the Manhattan District of the Army Engineer Corps, headed by General Leslie R. Groves, on May 1, 1943. Drawing upon the combined resources of the OSRD, universities, and private industries, Groves pushed the project with incredible speed. Work on the bomb itself was begun in the spring of 1943 at a laboratory built on a lonely mesa at Los Alamos, outside Santa Fe, New Mexico. Here a group of American, British, and European scientists under direction of Dr. J. Robert Oppenheimer worked night and day to perfect the bomb. They began the final assembly of the first atomic bomb on July 12, 1945, and tension mounted as the fateful day of testing drew near. Nearly $2 billion had been expended in an effort which yet might fail. The bomb was moved to the air base at Alamagordo and successfully detonated at 5:30 A.M. on July 16. A searing blast of light, many times brighter than the noonday sun, was followed by a deafening roar and a huge mushroom cloud; and relief mixed with a feeling of doom filled the minds of the men who watched the beginning of a new era in human history.

3. American Industry Goes to War

The story of how changing agencies mobilized the American economy for staggering tasks is a tale full of confusion and chaos, incompetence and momentary failure, political intrigue and personal vendetta, but withal one of superb achievement on many home fronts. Government and industry accomplished one of the economic miracles of modern times before it was too late—the production of a stream of goods that provided a high standard of living at home and also supplied the American armed forces with all and the British, French, and Russians with a large part of the resources and matériel for victory.

The task during the first period of industrial mobilization, from August

1939 until about the end of 1941, was the comparatively easy one of utilizing idle plants and men to supply the inchoate American armed forces and the British. The president in August 1939 established the War Resources Board, headed by Edward R. Stettinius, Jr., of the United States Steel Corporation, to advise the administration on industrial mobilization. It soon fell victim to labor and New Deal critics, who charged that it was dominated by Morgan and Du Pont interests.

This was, of course, the time of the so-called phony war, when Allied victory seemed assured and the necessity for total economic mobilization seemed remote. Nevertheless, the War Resources Board, before its dissolution in October 1939, prepared an industrial mobilization plan that envisaged dictatorial economic authority for a single administrator in the event that the United States entered the war. Roosevelt rejected this plan and asked the former chairman of Wilson's War Industries Board, Bernard M. Baruch, to prepare another. Baruch presented a plan that met all Roosevelt's objections to the earlier proposal and provided for gradual transition to a total war economy.

Roosevelt, for reasons still unknown, suppressed the Baruch plan and permitted the partial mobilization effort of 1939–1940 to drift aimlessly. The fall of France, however, galvanized the president into action, inadequate though it was. Calling for vast new defense appropriations and the production of 50,000 planes a year, he reestablished the Advisory Commission to the old and nearly defunct Council of National Defense on May 28, 1940. It was charged with responsibility for getting defense production into high gear. In addition, Congress on June 25 authorized the RFC to finance the building of defense plants and, in the Revenue Act of October 8, 1940, permitted businessmen to write off construction costs over a five-year period.

The Advisory Commission abdicated control over priorities to the Army-Navy Munitions Board and had lost all control of industrial mobilization by December 1940. Roosevelt still stubbornly refused to institute the kind of mobilization plan that Baruch had earlier suggested. Instead, on January 7, 1941, he established the Office of Production Management (OPM), headed by William S. Knudsen of the Advisory Commission and Sidney Hillman of the CIO. It was directed to cooperate with the president and defense secretaries in stimulating and controlling war production. In addition, an Office of Price Administration and Civilian Supply, established on April 11, would work to protect consumers' interests.

The OPM went to work to improve the priorities system, to coordinate British and American orders, and especially to help automobile manufacturers prepare for conversion to production of tanks and planes. The result was a gradual shift during the spring and summer of 1941 to a wartime economy. Shortages of electric power, aluminum, steel, railroad stock, and other materials became acute. The priorities system nearly broke down, and internal bickering and public criticism mounted. Roosevelt attempted another superficial reorganization. He suspended the OPM on August 28,

1941, but left an OPM Council. Then he created a Supplies Priorities and Allocation Board, headed by the Sears-Roebuck executive, Donald M. Nelson, and added other agencies, many of which overlapped in a confusing way. The central force in the new apparatus, however, was the Supplies Priorities and Allocations Board, for it had the power to determine and allocate requirements and supplies for the armed forces, the civilian economy, and the British and the Russians.

The president at last attempted to establish a comprehensive economic mobilization on January 16, 1942, by creating the War Production Board (WPB), under Donald Nelson, to take supreme command of the economic home front. Nelson was an excellent technician, but he failed to meet the test of leadership. He continued to allow the military departments to control priorities; consequently, he never established firm control over production. He permitted the great corporations to obtain a practical monopoly on war production, and this caused a near scandal when the facts were disclosed by a special Senate committee headed by Harry S Truman of Missouri. Finally, he allowed industrial expansion to get out of hand and occur in the wrong areas.

American industry was booming by the autumn of 1942, but chaos threatened. Alarmed by the prospect, Roosevelt brought Justice James F. Byrnes to the White House as head of the new Office of Economic Stabilization on October 3 and gave him supreme command of the economic effort. One of Byrnes's first moves was to force adoption of a plan that established such complete control over allocation of steel, aluminum, and copper that the priorities difficulty vanished almost at once. Then Roosevelt in May 1943 created the Office of War Mobilization, a sort of high command with control over all aspects of the economy, with Byrnes as director or "assistant president." Representative Fred M. Vinson of Kentucky succeeded Byrnes as head of the Office of Economic Stabilization. The home front was at last well organized and under control.

4. The Miracle of Production

In spite of all its shortcomings, the American industrial mobilization did succeed far beyond any reasonable expectations. We can gain some understanding of the total achievement by considering the general performance of the American economy from 1939 through 1945. Measured by depression standards, 1939 was a relatively prosperous year. Gross national product stood at $91.3 billion—higher in real dollars than during the boom year of 1929. On the other hand, the gross national product had risen, in 1939 dollars, to $166.6 billion by 1945. Moreover, from 1939 to 1945 the index of manufacturing production increased 96 percent; agricultural production was up 22 percent; and transportation services increased 109 percent. Contrasted with the performance of the economy during the First

World War, when the total national output increased hardly at all, this was a remarkable achievement.

American war production in 1941 was a mere trickle, only $8.4 billion in value. It totaled $30.2 billion in value in 1942 and equaled that of Germany, Italy, and Japan combined. American factories by 1944 were producing twice the volume of the Axis partners. A few illustrations will give point to the generalizations. The American airplane industry employed 46,638 persons and produced 5,865 planes in 1939. At the peak of production in 1944, the industry employed more than 2.1 million persons and turned out 96,369 aircraft. All told, American factories from Pearl Harbor to the end of the war produced 274,941 military aircraft.

Production of merchant ships in the United States was an essential ingredient of Allied victory in the battle of supply. The construction of merchant shipping, which had totaled only 1 million tons in 1941, rose to a peak of over 19 million tons in 1943, and, as the need diminished, declined to nearly 16.5 million tons in 1944 and nearly 8 million tons from January through July of 1945. All told, from July 1, 1940, to August 1, 1945, American shipyards produced a total of more than 55.2 million tons of merchant shipping—a tonnage equal to two-thirds of the merchant marines of all Allied nations combined.

Perhaps the most remarkable miracle of production was the creation, almost overnight, of a new synthetic rubber industry. Japanese conquest of Malaya and the Netherlands East Indies deprived the United States of 90 percent of its natural rubber supply at a time when the total stockpile of rubber in the United States amounted to only 540,000 tons and normal consumption exceeded 600,000 tons annually. Total imports could not exceed 175,000 tons during 1942, and the rubber shortage threatened to hobble the entire war effort. On August 6, 1942, Roosevelt appointed a special committee headed by Bernard M. Baruch to investigate and recommend. The Baruch committee reported on September 10, warning that the war effort and civilian economy might collapse if a severe rubber shortage occurred and urging immediate construction of a vast industry to produce rubber synthetically from petroleum. Roosevelt acted at once, appointing William M. Jeffers, president of the Union Pacific Railroad, as rubber director in the WPB on September 15, 1942. Jeffers ruthlessly cut his way through the existing priorities system. By the end of 1943 he had brought into existence a synthetic rubber industry that produced 762,000 tons in 1944 and 820,000 tons in 1945.

5. *The Greatest Tax Bill in History*

Federal expenditures aggregated in excess of $321.2 billion from 1941 to 1945. Some 41 percent of the money for the war effort came from tax receipts, which totaled nearly $131 billion during the fiscal years

1941–1945. The balance was raised by borrowing, which in turn increased the gross national debt from $49 billion in 1941 to $259 billion in mid-1945.

Meanwhile, the administration and Congress had joined hands to revolutionize the tax structure. On the one hand, the president, Congress, and a vast majority of Americans, rich and poor alike, agreed that the few should not profit from the sacrifices of the many, and that there should be no new millionaires as a result of the defense and war efforts. On the other hand, it became increasingly evident that it would be hopelessly inadequate to use the income tax as a tax principally on wealth, and that the costs of the war would have to be borne in part also by the lower and middle classes.

The administration's tax program evolved gradually in response to the Treasury's need for funds and the necessity for curbing inflation. For example, Congress approved two revenue acts in 1940 that increased income and corporation taxes and imposed an excess profits tax graduated to a maximum of 50 percent. Congress again increased old taxes in 1941 and devised new means of finding revenue. Even so, the income tax still touched only the small minority with upper middle- and upper-class incomes. The turning point came when the president presented his Budget Message to Congress on January 5, 1942, proposing a $7 billion increase in the tax burden. After months of agonizing delay, Congress responded with the Revenue Act of 1942, approved October 21.

EXPENDITURES OF THE UNITED STATES GOVERNMENT,
1914–1952

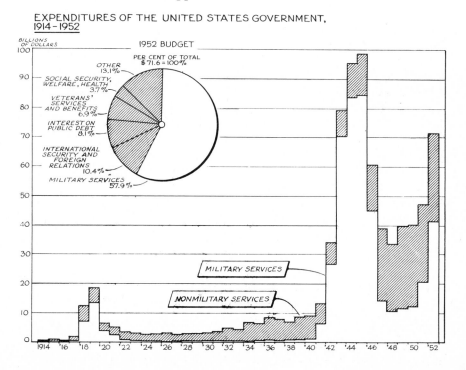

FEDERAL EXPENDITURES AND RECEIPTS, 1939-1953

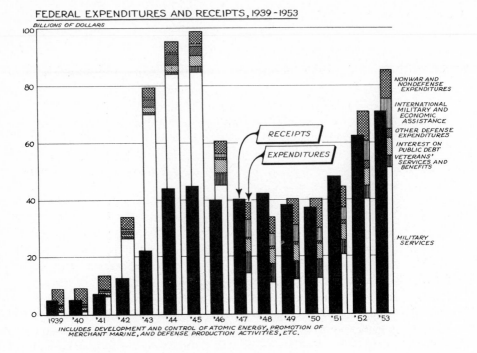

INCLUDES DEVELOPMENT AND CONTROL OF ATOMIC ENERGY, PROMOTION OF
MERCHANT MARINE, AND DEFENSE PRODUCTION ACTIVITIES, ETC.

It was, as the president said, "the greatest tax bill in American history," designed to raise more than $7 billion additional revenue annually, a sum exceeding total federal revenues in any peacetime year before 1941. The measure increased the combined corporate income tax to a maximum of 40 percent and raised the excess profits tax to a flat 90 percent. Moreover, it increased excise taxes and levied a host of new ones, and stiffly increased estate and gift taxes. The revolutionary feature of the Revenue Act of 1942, however, was its broadening of the income tax to tap low incomes as well as practically to confiscate large ones. Only 13 million persons had paid federal income taxes in 1941; in contrast, some 50 million persons were caught in the net cast in 1942.[3] The difficulty of collecting income taxes from 50 million persons by the conventional method of individual returns led to the adoption, in 1943, of a measure requiring employers to collect the tax by payroll deductions.

Meanwhile, personal incomes, governmental expenditures, and inflationary pressures continued to mount. The president therefore came back

[3]Specifically, the Revenue Act of 1942 lowered exemptions to $500 for single persons and $1,200 for married persons and increased the normal income tax from 4 to 6 percent. On top of this normal tax came a surtax ranging from 13 to 82 percent and a Victory tax of 5 percent, collected at the source on all incomes above $624 a year. The act of 1942 promised that part of the Victory tax would be refunded after the war, but Congress revoked this pledge in 1944. A married person with two dependents and a net income of $500,000 paid $344,476 in federal income taxes in 1941; he paid $439,931 under the act of 1942. A married person with two dependents and a net income of $3,000 paid $58 in the first instance and $267 in the second.

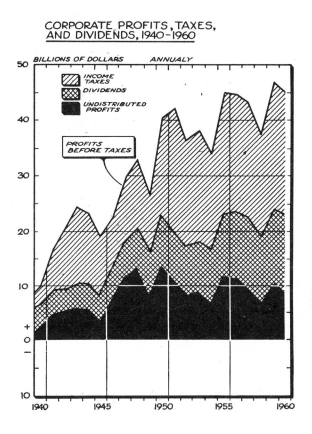

CORPORATE PROFITS, TAXES,
AND DIVIDENDS, 1940-1960

BILLIONS OF DOLLARS   ANNUALY

INCOME TAXES
DIVIDENDS
UNDISTRIBUTED PROFITS

PROFITS BEFORE TAXES

in his Budget Message of 1943 to demand an increase of $16 billion in the
federal tax load. Treasury officials later lowered the request to $10.5 bil-
lion. Even so, congressional leaders rebelled and adopted a Revenue Act
in early February 1944 that yielded additional revenue of only $2.2 billion,
chiefly by increasing the excess profits tax to 95 percent and by heavy
increases in excise taxes. The president replied on February 22 with a veto
so stinging that his spokesman in the Senate, Alben W. Barkley of Kentucky, resigned his post as majority leader. The Senate Democratic caucus
promptly and unanimously reelected Barkley, and an angry House and
Senate overrode the veto by enormous majorities on February 24 and 25,
1944. From this time forward administration and congressional leaders
were concerned not with increasing the tax burden, but with simplifying
the withholding system and planning for the reconversion that would soon
come with the end of the war.

In retrospect, perhaps the most significant aspect of the tax program
from 1941 to 1945 was the way it reflected the nation's conviction that a
war for survival should not become a war for the enrichment of the few.
There could be no "swollen fortunes" when the federal income tax
reached a maximum of 94 percent of total net income, to say nothing of

state income and local property taxes. Indeed, the nation's top 5 percent of income receivers suffered their severest relative economic losses in the history of the country during this period. Their share of disposable income fell from 25.7 percent in 1940 to 15.9 percent in 1944. The relative status of the top 1 percent of income receivers declined even more. Their share of disposable income decreased from 11.5 percent in 1940 to 6.7 percent in 1944. And with an excess profits tax of 95 percent and corporation income taxes reaching a maximum of 50 percent there were few cases of swollen profits. Net corporation income was $9.4 billion in 1941 and 1942, increased slightly in 1943 and 1944, and fell back to $8.5 billion in 1945.

6. *Combating Inflation on the Home Front*

Aside from the mobilization of fighting men and the maintenance of a steady flow of materials to the battle fronts, perhaps the most important problem at home was prevention of a runaway inflation that would compound the costs of the war and increase the burdens of many classes. To state the problem in its simplest terms, inflationary pressures existed after 1941 because the volume of disposable personal income greatly exceeded the supply of goods and services available for civilian consumption at the prevailing price level. Disposable personal incomes rose from $92 billion in 1941 to $151 billion in 1945, but the supply of civilian goods and services, measured in constant dollars, rose from $77.6 billion to only $95.4 billion during the same period. The danger of inflation stalked the home front because of this inflationary gap.

The most obvious weapon against inflation and the first to be tried was control of prices and rents. It will be recalled that Roosevelt, while reorganizing the defense mobilization machinery, had established an Office of Price Administration and Civilian Supply (OPA), headed by Leon Henderson, to work in conjunction with the Office of Production Management. Without any real power, Henderson was helpless to control prices during 1941. Consequently, retail prices were rising at the rate of 2 percent a month by February 1942. The president pleaded for new authority, and Congress responded with the Emergency Price Control Act of 1942. It empowered the price administrator to fix maximum prices and rents in special areas and to pay subsidies to producers, if that was necessary to prevent price increases. On the other hand, the powerful farm bloc denied the price administrator authority to control agricultural prices until they reached 110 percent of parity.

The OPA during the next three months launched a two-pronged campaign—to stabilize prices piecemeal, and to establish a system of rationing for tires, automobiles, gasoline, and sugar and, somewhat later, for shoes, fuel oil, and coffee. Moreover, the OPA followed the president's lead on April 28 by issuing its first General Maximum Price Regulation. It froze

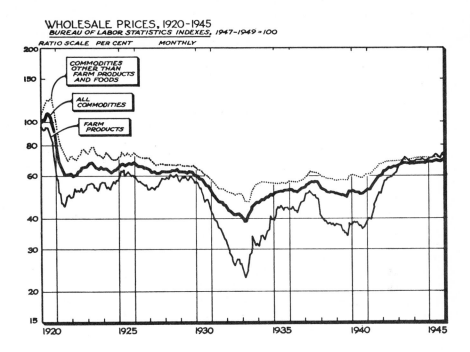

WHOLESALE PRICES, 1920-1945
BUREAU OF LABOR STATISTICS INDEXES, 1947-1949 = 100
RATIO SCALE PER CENT   MONTHLY

COMMODITIES OTHER THAN FARM PRODUCTS AND FOODS

ALL COMMODITIES

FARM PRODUCTS

most prices and rents at their level of March 1942. Events soon revealed
large loopholes in the stabilization program. The most obvious was the ban
on a ceiling for food prices until they reached an extraordinary level. As
food prices continued their inexorable rise—they increased a total of 11
percent during 1942—organized labor redoubled its demands for pay increases that in turn would mean higher prices for manufactured products.
Somehow, somewhere, the inflationary spiral had to be stopped, the president exclaimed in a special message on September 7, 1942. "I ask Congress to take . . . action by the first of October. . . . In the event that the
Congress should fail to act, and act adequately, I shall accept the responsibility, and I will act."

Congress responded swiftly if grudgingly with the Anti-Inflation Act of
October 2, 1942, empowering the president to stabilize wages, prices, and
salaries at their levels on September 15. The president established the
Office of Economic Stabilization on the following day, October 3, and
forbade any further increase in wages and salaries without the approval of
the stabilization director, James F. Byrnes. In addition, he froze agricultural prices at their level on September 15 and extended rent control to all
areas of the country.

It was a heroic beginning, but even rougher storms lay ahead. The OPA
administrator, Leon Henderson, had never been popular with Congress
and the public. Roosevelt permitted him to resign in December 1942 and
appointed Prentiss S. Brown, former senator frcm Michigan, in his stead.

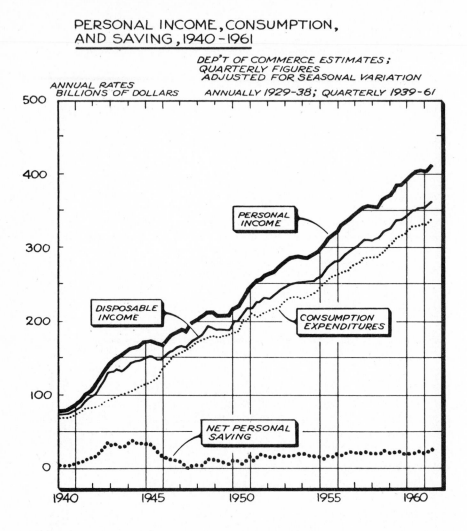

PERSONAL INCOME, CONSUMPTION,
AND SAVING, 1940-1961

Unfortunately, business, farm, and labor groups took his appointment as a signal for an all-out campaign against stabilization. Congress tried to open a large hole in the dike in March 1943 by approving a bill to exclude subsidy and parity payments in determination of parity levels for agriculture. Roosevelt vetoed the measure on April 2, pointing out that it would increase the cost of living by more than 5 percent. At the same time, labor spokesmen were growing restive under a formula by which workers had been allowed a 15 percent wage increase in 1942, and were threatening to break the no-strike pledge they had given after Pearl Harbor.

It was a dangerous situation, but the president acted decisively on April 8 by ordering the stabilization agencies to "hold the line" against any further unwarranted price and wage increases. Nor was this all. When John L. Lewis called a general coal strike on May 1 in defiance of the hold

CONSUMER PRICES
1940 – 1960

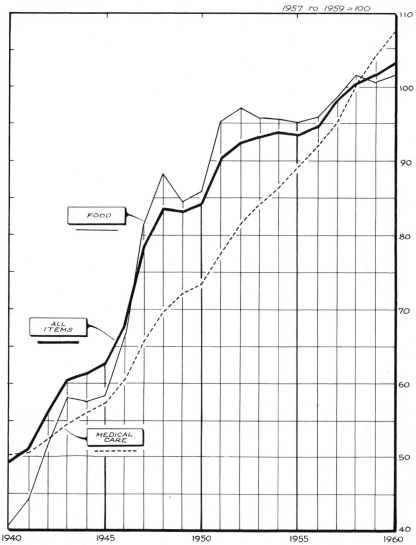

the line order, the president seized the coal mines and virtually ordered miners back into the pits. Moreover, the OPA began an aggressive campaign to roll back food prices. It culminated in a 10 percent reduction in the retail prices of meat, coffee, and butter on May 7. The tide had turned, and the cost of living increased less than 1.5 percent between the spring of 1943 and the summer of 1945. The Consumer Price Index had increased by 28.3 percent during the entire period 1940-1945. This was a remarkable record in view of the power of organized pressure groups and inevitable public vexation at the inconveniences of direct controls.

7. *Workers, Farmers, and the War Effort*

The nearly insatiable demands of the American and Allied war machines solved the unemployment problem almost overnight, as the number of civilian workers increased from about 46.5 million to over 53 million from 1940 to the middle of 1945. The chief factor in this expansion was the addition of about 7 million workers from the reservoir of the unemployed. To all these workers the war boom brought such prosperity as they had

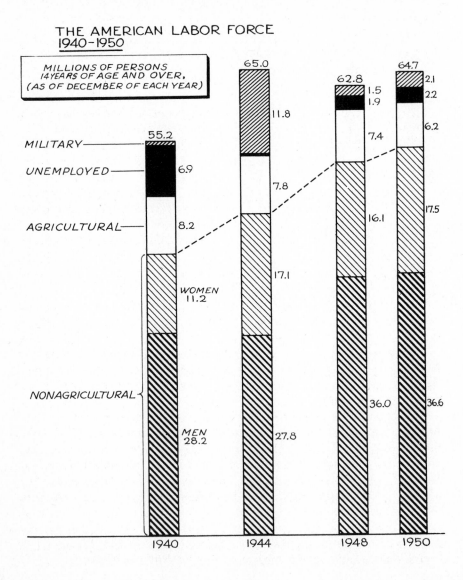

THE AMERICAN LABOR FORCE
1940-1950

MILLIONS OF PERSONS
14 YEARS OF AGE AND OVER,
(AS OF DECEMBER OF EACH YEAR)

never known before. The Consumer Price Index advanced 23.3 percent between 1941 and 1945, but weekly earnings of persons employed in manufacturing increased 70 percent.

It was no easy task to mobilize this huge labor force, restrain labor's natural desire for higher wages, and bridle irresponsible labor leaders. Indeed, the administration never did achieve comprehensive control over manpower resources. The president created the War Manpower Commission (WMC) in April 1942 and appointed former Governor Paul V. McNutt of Indiana to direct the flow of workers into war industries. The WMC gradually evolved coercive measures that prohibited workers in defense industries from leaving their jobs without approval of the United States Employment Service. This system worked reasonably well, but it did not solve the more important problem of recruiting new workers and shifting workers from nondefense to war industries. One solution, of course, was national service legislation to draft men for war work. The CIO and AF of L bitterly opposed such legislation, but the manpower shortage seemed so critical by the end of 1943 that the president finally came out in support of a national service act in his Annual Message in January 1944. The House approved a labor draft bill in December 1944, but Germany collapsed before the Senate could act on the measure.

Much more important and difficult was the task of preventing strikes and reconciling labor's natural desires for economic advancement and union security with the general objective of winning the war without runaway inflation. This gigantic and at times nearly impossible task was entrusted to the War Labor Board (WLB), created by the president on January 12, 1942. The WLB was established simply to settle labor disputes, but it soon discovered that mediation was impossible without a complete edifice of labor policy. Inevitably, therefore, the WLB emerged as a powerful policy-making body in the war economy.

To the leaders of organized labor the fundamental issue was protection of the right of collective bargaining. The WLB stood firm in defense of labor's rights under the Wagner Act, even the right to the closed shop when a majority of workers voted in favor of it. Moreover, it applied a compromise—the so-called maintenance of membership plan—that protected unions in rapidly expanding war plants.[4] Union membership expanded under its aegis to nearly 15 million by the end of the war.

The thorniest problems of wartime labor administration were inexorable demands for higher wages and strikes to enforce such demands. Here the issue lay not between labor and management, for management was usually eager to increase wages in order to hold and attract labor, but rather between the public interest and combined private interests. The WLB defended labor's right to enjoy a standard of living "compatible with

---

[4]Under this arrangement unions retained their membership and the right to bargain for all workers during the life of a bargaining contract. On the other hand, new workers coming into an industry or plant were not required to join the union as a condition of employment.

health and decency." It also endorsed union demands for equal pay for blacks and women and elimination of sectional differentials. On the other hand, it also asserted that workers should be content to maintain and not improve their standard of living during wartime. In theory most labor leaders concurred; the trouble was that they could never agree with the WLB on what that standard of living was. The rise in the cost of living during the early months of 1942 precipitated the first crisis. The WLB responded on July 16, 1942, with the so-called Little Steel formula. It granted most workers a 15 percent wage increase to offset a similar increase in the cost of living since January 1, 1941. But employers began to award pay increases that exceeded the Little Steel formula, and the president, under authority of the Stabilization Act of October 2, 1942, empowered the WLB to forbid increases that imperiled the stabilization program.

Meanwhile, the WLB's determination to hold the line on wages had driven a minority of labor to irresponsible action. The AF of L and CIO had given a no-strike pledge soon after Pearl Harbor and promised to "produce without interruption." Responsible labor leaders kept this promise for the most part, but a few reckless leaders and a minority of the rank and file accumulated a sorry record during the Second World War. All told, there were 14,731 work stoppages involving 6,744,000 workers and resulting in the loss of 36,301,000 man-days from December 8, 1941, through August 14, 1945. To cite only the bald record, however, would be to do injustice to the great majority of workers who remained faithful to the no-strike pledge. Most work stoppages were short-lived and occurred in defiance of union leadership. Moreover, they caused a loss of only one-ninth of 1 percent of total working time.

Even so, it was difficult for the mass of Americans to think in terms of averages when they saw workers in airplane factories and shipyards striking for higher pay or over union jurisdiction. Two major incidents—a coal strike and the near occurrence of a nationwide railroad strike in 1943—particularly alarmed the American people. John L. Lewis refused to appear before the WLB and called a general coal strike on May 1, 1943. The president seized the mines, but the miners struck again on June 11 because the WLB would not break the Little Steel formula and grant high wage increases. Miners returned to work when Roosevelt threatened to ask Congress to draft them, but Lewis forced the administration to surrender by threat of a third strike.[5]

Lewis's cynical defiance of federal authority was more than Congress would tolerate. In hot resentment it approved and reenacted over the president's veto on June 26, 1943, the Smith-Connally, or War Labor Disputes, Act. It empowered the president to seize any struck war plant. It also required unions to wait thirty days before striking, and to hold a secret vote of the workers before a strike was executed. More indicative of

[5] Under the agreement concluded between Lewis and Secretary of the Interior Ickes the miners received normal wage increases under the Little Steel formula. In addition, they received pay increases to compensate for reduced lunch periods and for time spent going to and from the pits.

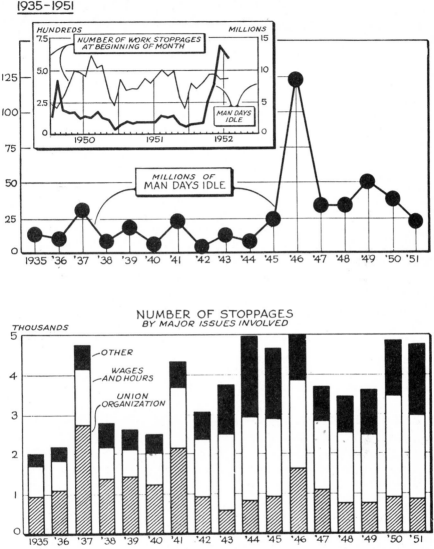

WORK STOPPAGES IN THE UNITED STATES, 1935-1951

NUMBER OF STOPPAGES BY MAJOR ISSUES INVOLVED

the rising antilabor sentiment was the enactment by many state legislatures of laws to prevent certain union practices and to subject unions to a measure of public regulation.[6]

For agriculture, the war boom brought new problems but also a stability and prosperity unknown since 1919. Net cash income from farming increased from $2,300,000,000 to $9,458,000,000 from 1940 to 1945, or by

---

[6]For example, these laws forbade the closed shop, mass picketing, secondary boycotts, and the like, and required unions to file financial reports and obtain licenses for labor organizers.

more than 300 percent. Two factors—increased production and higher prices, both of them stemming from vastly increased demands at home and abroad—made possible this return of agriculture to its long-sought position of parity in the American economy. Agricultural prices more than doubled between 1940 and 1945. During the same period, the index of all farm production rose from 108 to 123, while increases in food crops were even more spectacular. Incredible though it sounds, this expansion was accomplished in spite of a declining farm population and without any significant increase in acreage planted and harvested.[7]

8. Public Opinion, Civil Rights, and War

Never before had Americans gone to war with such determination and unity. Significant opposition to the war effort simply did not exist after the Pearl Harbor attack, mainly because Communists rallied to the defense and war efforts after the Germans attacked Russia. And because disloyalty was rare, there were no volunteer leagues of patriots, no committees of public safety, no high-powered propaganda campaigns and war madness. This is not to say that the government abandoned control over news and expressions of opinion,[8] or that it was not ready to act ruthlessly to suppress dangerous dissent. For example, the Justice Department at the president's command convened a special grand jury in Washington in July 1941 and laid before it and two succeeding grand juries voluminous evidence on the far-flung network of Nazi and Fascist organizations in the United States. The upshot was the indictment under the Smith Act of thirty leading seditionists for conspiring to establish a Nazi government in the United States and incite disloyalty among the armed forces. The trial proceeded for more than seven months in 1944 until the judge died, apparently a victim of the badgering of defense attorneys. The seditionists were in-

[7]The total number of agricultural workers declined from 11,671,000 in 1940 to 10,873,000 in 1945. On the other hand, the index of productivity in agriculture increased from 112 in 1940 to 136 in 1945 because of increased use of tractors, trucks, and other machinery. Two factors making possible larger yields without significant increases in acreage were a large expansion in the use of fertilizers and the spread of hybrid corn.

[8]Some kind of censorship was inevitable. The president entrusted censorship of war news to the War and Navy departments and the FBI on the day after the Pearl Harbor attack. Then, following passage by Congress of the first War Powers Act on December 18, 1941, the President established an Office of Censorship, with Byron Price, executive news director of the Associated Press, as director. Roosevelt next established the Office of War Information (OWI) on June 13, 1942, with Elmer Davis, veteran correspondent and commentator, in charge. The OWI happily never became a second Creel committee—the government's propaganda agency during the First World War. It produced motion pictures and published pamphlets and posters reminding Americans of their duty and depicting the dangers of an Axis victory. On the other hand, it did not spread manufactured atrocity stories—the truth was horrible enough—or attempt to engender hatred of the enemy. Indeed, such hatred, especially for the Japanese, already existed in full measure and was fanned by the radio, press, and motion pictures. The overseas branch of the OWI also broadcast daily programs to the Axis peoples.

dicted a second time in 1945, and government attorneys rushed to Germany to obtain new evidence. However, the Circuit Court of Appeals of the District of Columbia ended the fiasco in November 1946 by dismissing the indictment on the ground that the government's proceedings were a travesty of justice.

The government was scarcely more successful when it tried to imprison individual champions of nazism and opponents of the war. The critical test arose when the Justice Department invoked the Espionage Act of 1917 against a man named Hartzel, who published a diatribe against American participation in the war in 1942 and mailed copies to army officers. The Supreme Court, in *Hartzel* v. *United States*, 1944, made enforcement of the Espionage Act virtually impossible by declaring that the government had to prove specific intent to obstruct the war effort before it could obtain convictions under the law. Again, when the government obtained the conviction of twenty-four leaders of the German-American Bund for violating the Espionage Act, the court reversed the conviction on the ground of insufficient evidence of criminal intent.

Actually, the government knew that the assorted crackpots who made up the Bund and other pro-Nazi organizations were no menace, for the FBI had penetrated these groups and placed their leaders under surveillance. Espionage and sabotage, however, were different matters, and the Justice Department moved swiftly and sternly in dealing with them. The FBI broke a small Nazi espionage ring in 1938, destroyed the major Nazi network in 1941, and was prepared to move against potential spies and saboteurs on the eve of American entrance into the war. The FBI had taken more than 1,700 enemy aliens into custody within less than three days after the Pearl Harbor attack.[9] By such effective countermeasures the Justice Department completely destroyed the elaborate German intelligence and sabotage systems, with the results that not a single known act of sabotage was committed in the United States after December 7, 1941.

Deprived of its underground in America, the German high command resorted to audacious plans. It trained two teams of saboteurs—they were Germans who had lived in America and Americans citizens of German descent—and sent them by submarines in May 1942 to destroy the American aluminum industry and blow up bridges and railroad facilities. One team landed on Long Island, the other on the Florida coast. The eight invaders were captured almost immediately by the FBI, tried by a special military commission, sentenced to death, and executed on August 8.[10] The father of one of the saboteurs, Hans Haupt of Chicago, was also convicted of treason for hiding his son and given life imprisonment. Another German

[9] All told, the Justice Department arrested some 16,000 enemy aliens during the war, one-fourth of whom were imprisoned.

[10] The president commuted the sentences of two saboteurs who gave evidence to life imprisonment in one case and thirty years' imprisonment in the other.

American, Anthony Cramer, was convicted of treason for assisting one of the saboteurs.[11]

The one great blot on the administration's otherwise excellent civil liberties record during the war was the detention and forced removal of Japanese Americans from the West Coast to internment camps in the interior. It was the greatest single violation of civil rights in American history. The issue was not the arrest of Japanese subjects who were potential saboteurs, for they were rounded up immediately after the Pearl Harbor attack. It was the loyalty of some 41,000 Japanese ineligible to citizenship and 71,000 Nisei, or American citizens of Japanese ancestry. The general staff declared the West Coast a theater of war in the panic following December 7, 1941, and newspapers and political leaders in California began a widespread campaign for removal of all Japanese Americans, whether citizens or not. The demand was taken up in Washington by the congressional delegations from the Pacific Coast states, and was seconded by the commanding general on the West Coast, John L. De Witt. The president on February 19, 1942, authorized the army to take control. General De Witt soon afterward ordered removal of *all* Japanese Americans from an area comprising the western third of Washington and Oregon, the western half of California, and the southern quarter of Arizona. Some 110,000 Japanese and Nisei were ruthlessly ejected from their homes, herded into temporary stockades surrounded by barbed wire, and then transported to ten relocation centers established by the War Relocation Authority in western deserts and the swamplands of Arkansas. Eventually some 18,000 persons suspected of disloyalty were confined in a camp at Tule Lake, California, while the remainder were allowed to find new homes or go to colleges in the Midwest and East. Some 36,000 chose resettlement during the war.

The most disappointing aspect of the whole affair was the Supreme Court's refusal to vindicate the principle of civilian supremacy or defend elementary civil rights. A divided court, in *Korematsu* v. *United States*, December 1944, apologetically approved the evacuation on the ground that military leaders were justified in taking extreme measures against persons on account of race to protect national security, even though the situation was not serious enough to justify imposition of martial law. The

[11] The Supreme Court reversed Cramer's conviction in 1945 on the ground that the government had not proved that he gave aid and comfort to the enemy within the meaning of the treason clause. However, the Court upheld Haupt's conviction in 1947. Only one other person was tried for treason during the war. He was a Detroit Bundsman, Max Stephan, who was sentenced to death in 1942 for helping a German prisoner of war to escape. The president commuted his sentence to life imprisonment one day before the execution was to take place. However, the Justice Department obtained indictment of a number of turncoat Americans—among them Ezra Pound, the poet; Robert H. Best, a former foreign correspondent; Mildred Gillars, known to servicemen as "Axis Sally"; and Mrs. Iva d'Aquino, better known as "Tokyo Rose"—who broadcast for the Axis during the war. Most of them were apprehended at the end of hostilities, convicted of treason, and sentenced to long prison terms. Pound, however, was declared insane and incarcerated in St. Elizabeth's Hospital in Washington.

meaning of the decision was clear and foreboding: in future emergencies no American citizen would have any rights that the president and army were bound to respect when, *in their judgment*, the emergency justified drastic denial of civil rights.

9. Blacks and the Home Front

The Second World War was a time of unrest and new striving on America's troubled frontier of black-white relations. There were race riots, and national discriminations like continued segregation of nearly a million blacks in the armed services and separation of black and white blood in Red Cross blood banks. Racial tensions rose to the danger point in the South as blacks acquired a measure of financial independence and social self-respect. Yet, withal, Negroes emerged from the war with a larger measure of self-esteem and economic and political security than they had ever enjoyed.

The most dangerous racial tensions developed in industrial areas outside the South, as a result of the sudden immigration of nearly 1 million southern blacks in search of jobs and new social opportunities. There were numerous minor clashes in many cities, and New York escaped a major race riot in early 1944 only because of the quick action of its mayor and police force. Tensions flared into large-scale rioting in Detroit, home of Gerald L. K. Smith and other Negro-baiters. A fight between a black and a white man on June 20, 1943, led to other clashes. Soon mobs of whites were roaming the Negro section, killing and burning as they went. By the time that federal troops had restored order, twenty-five blacks and nine whites had been killed.

This was the dark side of an otherwise bright picture, for the Second World War was a time also of great advancement for American blacks. Blacks in the South enjoyed greater acceptance and security and larger political and economic opportunities than ever before. Lynching, long the extreme form of southern race control, became almost a historic phenomenon, as the number of Negroes thus put to death declined from five in 1942 to one in 1945. A distinguished body of southern leaders, black and white, met in Atlanta in 1944 and organized the Southern Regional Council to combat prejudice and misunderstanding by concerted action in communities and states. Equally significant was the growth during the war of an advanced equalitarian movement outside the South. Assuming the proportions almost of a crusade, this campaign against Jim Crow won many triumphs, the most important of which was a growing concern for civil rights by the major parties.

Negroes made greatest progress during the war, in both the North and the South, on the economic front. Of all groups they had suffered most during the depression and profited least from New Deal measures; nor did the defense boom of 1940–1941 bring relief, as employers stubbornly refused to hire black workers. The administration moved slowly, until A. Philip Randolph, president of the Brotherhood of Sleeping Car Porters, called upon 50,000 blacks to march on Washington to protest. Randolph called off the threatened march; but he did so only after Roosevelt had issued his notable Executive Order 8802 on June 25, 1941. It directed that blacks be admitted to job training programs, forbade discrimination in work on defense contracts, and established a Fair Employment Practices Committee to investigate charges of discrimination on account of race.

The FEPC made progress slowly and performed its most effective service during 1942 and 1943 by conducting hearings on discrimination in most of the large cities of the country. It set to work more vigorously when the president, in May 1943, reorganized the agency, expanded its budget, and directed that antidiscrimination clauses in contracts be enforced. Establishing fifteen regional offices, it heard some 8,000 complaints and conducted thirty public hearings from 1943 to 1946. The results were unexpectedly gratifying. Nearly 2 million Negroes were at work in aircraft factories, shipyards, steel mills, and other war plants in the South and elsewhere by the end of 1944.[12]

The millennium had not come for American blacks when the war ended. To men of good will, however, the steady enlargement of economic, social, and political opportunities for blacks during the war years was perhaps the most encouraging development on the American home front. Blacks in 1945 could look forward to a postwar era full not only of struggle but also of hope for a new era in which they might stand erect as free men and women and citizens of the great democracy.

---

[12]In addition, New York, New Jersey, and Indiana established Fair Employment Practices commissions, while many cities set up antidiscrimination boards.

22

The Second World War: Diplomatic and Military Aspects

The American people were destined to play a leading and decisive role in the military operations that brought victory for the United Nations in 1945. In this chapter we will follow the Allies on the long and tortuous road from near defeat to victory. Since the war was won not only in the factory and on the battlefield but around the conference table as well, we will also note how Roosevelt and Churchill forged the bonds of Anglo-American unity, drew the Russian leaders into close association, and gave such an effective demonstration of allied cooperation in wartime as the world had rarely seen before.

1. The Formation of the Grand Alliance

American and British leaders gathered in Washington soon after the Pearl Harbor attack to lay plans for combined conduct of the war. Liaison with the Russians would come later, as soon as circumstances permitted. Prime

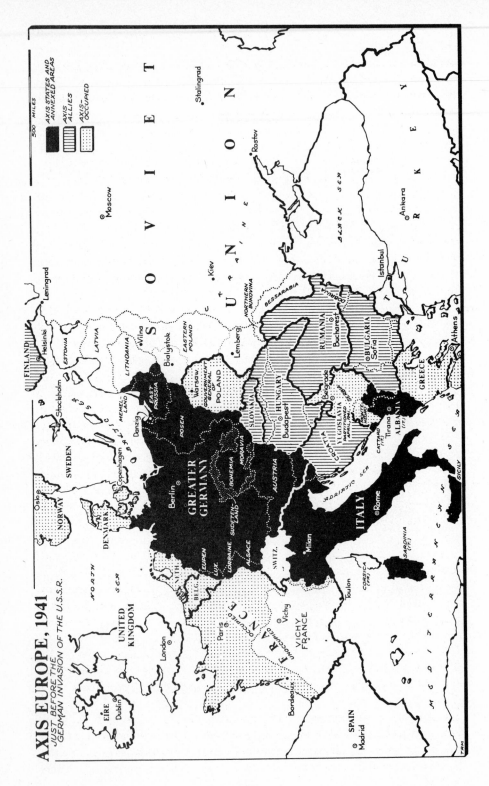

AXIS EUROPE, 1941

JUST BEFORE THE GERMAN INVASION OF THE U.S.S.R.

AXIS STATES AND ANNEXED AREAS

AXIS ALLIES

AXIS OCCUPIED

500 MILES

Minister Winston Churchill arrived in Washington on December 22, 1941, for a week of conferences known by the code name of ARCADIA. These discussions continued on the military level until January 14, 1942. This was a time when Allied military fortunes were at their lowest ebb since the fall of France, but negotiations proceeded smoothly and yielded complete agreement on all important points: American production goals for 1942 and 1943, pooling of Anglo-American munitions and their disposal by a joint Munitions Assignment Board, and immediate establishment of a Combined Chiefs of Staff in Washington and a combined British, American, and Dutch command in the Pacific. ARCADIA's most important work was reaffirmation of the earlier staff decision to defeat Germany first since that nation was the stronger enemy and controlled industry and manpower superior to the Japanese. Therefore the Allies would launch their first major offensives against the Continent and conduct holding operations in the Pacific until Nazi power had been subdued.

On the diplomatic level, moreover, Roosevelt and Churchill worked in complete harmony for the formation of a grand coalition of the Allies. The fruit of their labor was the Declaration of the United Nations, signed at the White House on New Year's Day, 1942, by Roosevelt, Churchill, Maxim Litvinov for the USSR, and representatives of twenty-three other nations at war with the Axis. The signatory powers reaffirmed the principles set forth in the Atlantic Charter, pledged their full resources to the defeat of the Axis nations, and promised one another not to make a separate peace.

The most uncertain link in the new Allied chain was Russia. By hearty cooperation, the USSR could hasten victory and help lay the groundwork for postwar cooperation; by making a separate peace, on the other hand, Russia could postpone the hope of Allied victory perhaps indefinitely. The president's and the prime minister's most pressing diplomatic problem during early 1942 was Russian territorial ambitions in Europe and a Russian demand that Britain and the United States guarantee those ambitions in advance. The Kremlin presented the first installment of its demands during a visit of Foreign Secretary Anthony Eden to Moscow in December 1941. Stalin then requested Britain's immediate approval of Russia's absorption of the Baltic states and parts of Finland, Poland, and Rumania. He warned, moreover, that conclusion of a British-Soviet alliance would depend upon British endorsement of these territorial claims.

The issue came to a head when the Soviet foreign minister, Vyacheslav Molotov, arrived in London on May 20, 1942, to press Russian territorial and military demands. Churchill and Eden had been strengthened by a warning from Washington that the United States might publicly denounce any Anglo-Russian agreement conceding Stalin's ambitions. They stood firm and persuaded Molotov to sign, on May 26, a general twenty-year Treaty of Alliance that included no reference to boundaries.

2. *The Ebb Tide of Allied Military Fortunes*

Axis victories were so swift and far-reaching during the first six months of 1942 that it seemed that the United Nations might lose the war before they could begin fighting. The Japanese, following air attacks on British and American possessions on December 7, launched seaborne invasions of Hong Kong, Malaya, the Philippines, and lesser islands. They were free to roam and strike almost at will, for the once mighty Anglo-American Pacific naval power was nearly gone by the end of 1941. Guam fell on December 11, 1941; Wake Island, on December 23; Hong Kong, on Christmas Day. Meanwhile, Japanese forces pressed forward in conquest of Malaya, Burma, and the Philippines. Singapore, the great British naval base in the Far East, surrendered on February 15, 1942, to a Japanese force that came down from the north through Malaya. Most of Burma fell in March and April 1942, while Ceylon and India were threatened by a large Japanese naval force that momentarily controlled the Indian Ocean and the Bay of Bengal in April.

In the Philippines General Douglas MacArthur, with a force of 19,000 American regulars, 12,000 Philippine Scouts, and 100,000 soldiers of the new Philippine army, fought a desperate delaying action. When Japanese troops threatened Manila, MacArthur declared the capital an open city, moved to Corregidor, and withdrew his troops into Bataan Peninsula for a hopeless but gallant last stand. MacArthur was transferred to Australia on March 17, 1942. His successor, General Jonathan Wainwright, continued the fight from Corregidor and other forts off the tip of the peninsula and held out there until disease, starvation, and superior enemy forces made further resistance impossible. He surrendered May 6.

Meanwhile, large new Japanese forces were poised in Malaya and the Philippines by the end of December 1941 to strike at Borneo, the Celebes, New Guinea, and the Dutch East Indies. Only the small American Asiatic Fleet and a few Dutch and British cruisers stood athwart the path of Japanese conquest of the Indies. In the Battle of Macassar Strait, January 24, 1942, American destroyers executed a daring night attack against a Japanese convoy and forced it to turn back. But in the subsequent engagements, known as the Java Sea campaign, the Allies lost their entire naval force, except for four American destroyers. By the end of March 1942 the Japanese were in possession of the East Indies, had pushed into New Britain and the Solomon Islands, and were in position to strike at Port Moresby, the Allied base in southern New Guinea, and at Australia itself. In little more than three months they had gained control of a vast area extending from the Gilbert Islands in the Central Pacific west and south through the Solomons and New Guinea to Burma. India and Australia lay virtually undefended.

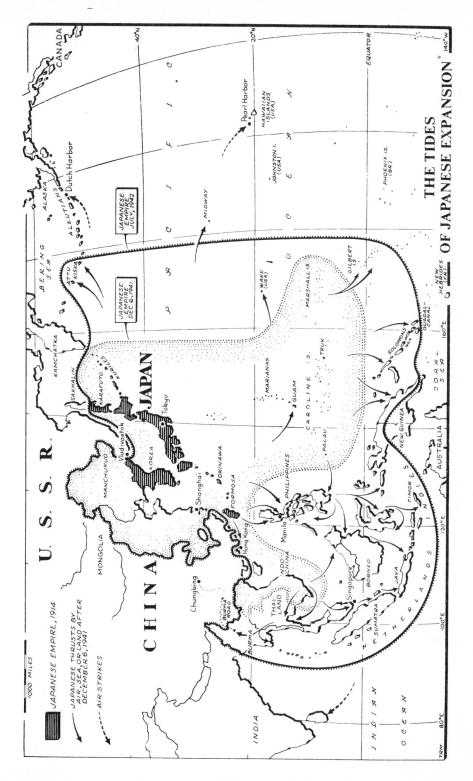

THE TIDES OF JAPANESE EXPANSION

Japanese Empire, 1914

Japanese Thrusts by Air, Sea, or Land After December 6, 1941

Air Strikes

JAPANESE EMPIRE JULY, 1942

JAPANESE EMPIRE DEC. 6, 1941

1000 MILES

CANADA

ALASKA

Dutch Harbor

ALEUTIANS

ATTU

KISKA

BERING SEA

KAMCHATKA

SAKHALIN

KARAFUTO

KURILES

U. S. S. R.

MONGOLIA

MANCHUKUO

Vladivostok

KOREA

JAPAN

Tokyo

OKINAWA

Shanghai

FORMOSA

Hong Kong

CHINA

Chungking

BURMA ROAD

BURMA

THAILAND

INDO-CHINA

Manila

PHILIPPINES

Singapore

SUMATRA

BORNEO

JAVA

NETHERLANDS INDIES

INDIA

INDIAN OCEAN

TIMOR

NEW GUINEA

AUSTRALIA

CORAL SEA

SOLOMONS

GUADAL-CANAL

NEW HEBRIDES (FR)

PALAU

CAROLINE IS.

TRUK

GUAM

MARIANAS

MARSHALL IS.

GILBERT IS.

WAKE (USA)

MIDWAY

P A C I F I C   O C E A N

JOHNSTON I. (USA)

PHOENIX IS. (BR)

HAWAIIAN ISLANDS (USA)

Pearl Harbor

EQUATOR

20°N

40°N

80°E

100°E

120°E

160°E

140°W

TRM

521

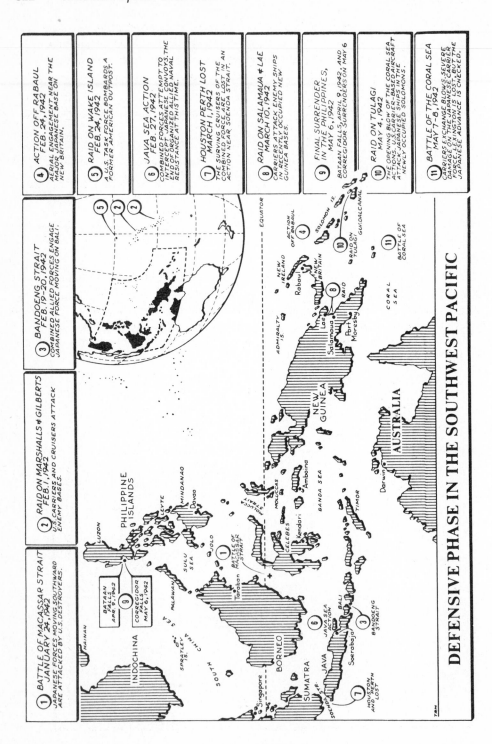

DEFENSIVE PHASE IN THE SOUTHWEST PACIFIC

① BATTLE OF MACASSAR STRAIT
JANUARY 24, 1942
JAPANESE FORCES MOVING SOUTHWARD
ARE ATTACKED BY U.S. DESTROYERS.

② RAID ON MARSHALLS & GILBERTS
FEB. 1, 1942
U.S. CARRIERS AND CRUISERS ATTACK
ENEMY BASES.

③ BANDOENG STRAIT
FEB. 19-20, 1942
COMBINED ALLIED FORCES ENGAGE
JAPANESE FORCE MOVING ON BALI.

④ ACTION OFF RABAUL
FEB. 24, 1942
AERIAL ENGAGEMENT NEAR THE
MAJOR JAPANESE BASE ON
NEW BRITAIN.

⑤ RAID ON WAKE ISLAND
FEB. 24, 1942
A U.S. TASK FORCE BOMBARDS A
FORMER AMERICAN OUTPOST.

⑥ JAVA SEA ACTION
FEB. 27, 1942
COMBINED FORCES ATTEMPT TO
INTERCEPT JAPANESE CONVOYS. THE
END OF ORGANIZED ALLIED NAVAL
RESISTANCE AT THIS TIME.

⑦ HOUSTON PERTH LOST
MARCH 1, 1942
THE SURVIVING CRUISERS OF THE
COMBINED FORCE ARE LOST IN AN
ACTION NEAR SOENDA STRAIT.

⑧ RAID ON SALAMAUA & LAE
MARCH 10, 1942
CARRIERS ATTACK ENEMY SHIPS
IN RECENTLY OCCUPIED NEW
GUINEA BASES.

⑨ FINAL SURRENDER
IN THE PHILIPPINES,
MAY 6, 1942
BATAAN FALLS, APRIL 9, 1942, AND
CORREGIDOR SURRENDERS ON MAY 6

⑩ RAID ON TULAGI
MAY 4, 1942
THE OPENING BLOW OF THE CORAL SEA
ACTION. CARRIER-BASED AIRCRAFT
ATTACK JAPANESE SHIPS IN THE
NEWLY OCCUPIED SOLOMONS.

⑪ BATTLE OF THE CORAL SEA
MAY 7-8, 1942
CARRIERS EXCHANGE BLOWS. SEVERE
DAMAGE DONE TO JAPANESE CARRIER
FORCE. U.S.S. LEXINGTON IS LOST, BUT THE
JAPANESE ADVANCE IS CHECKED.

Events almost as catastrophic for the Allies were transpiring in the Atlantic, on the eastern front in Russia, and in North Africa. German submarines came perilously close to winning the Battle of the Atlantic during 1942, when Allied and neutral shipping losses aggregated nearly 8 million tons. "The disaster of an indefinite prolongation of the war," to quote Churchill's phrase, threatened to upset Allied plans for military operations.

Meanwhile, the Germans had mounted a large offensive to drive through North Africa, cut the Suez Canal, and penetrate Arabia and the Middle East. General Erwin Rommel, the "Desert Fox," opened the campaign in Libya on May 26. The British, after several sharp defeats, retreated to El Alamein in Egypt, only seventy-five miles from Alexandria, to regroup and reinforce their shattered Eighth Army. The German lines were overextended by July 1, and Rommel's Afrika Korps was too exhausted to press the offensive.

These reversals during the spring and summer of 1942 had a nearly fatal impact on the Grand Alliance when the hard-pressed Russians demanded assistance in the form of a second front in the West. The issue first arose prominently when Molotov arrived in Washington on May 29, 1942, for

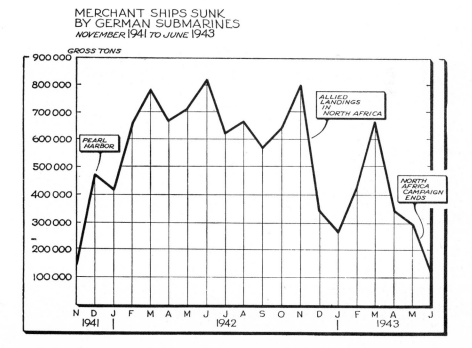

MERCHANT SHIPS SUNK
BY GERMAN SUBMARINES
NOVEMBER 1941 *TO JUNE* 1943

conferences mainly of a military nature with the president and his advisers. Stalin wanted, Molotov declared, an Anglo-American invasion of western Europe strong enough to draw forty German divisions from the eastern front. Without a second front in 1942, he continued, Germany might deal the USSR a mighty, crushing blow. "If you postpone your decision," he concluded in ominous words, "you will have eventually to bear the brunt of the war." Roosevelt turned to General Marshall for an answer. Marshall replied that there were enough men and supplies for the undertaking; the chief problem was to obtain adequate shipping for an expeditionary force without cutting off supplies to the Soviet Union.

Molotov returned to Moscow with a virtual promise that the United States would launch a cross-Channel invasion in 1942. The Germans drove deeper into southeastern Russia and penetrated the Caucasus, and the pressure from Moscow for relief in the West increased. At this point the president and his advisers began to consider the feasibility of an Anglo-American thrust at the northern coast of France, known by the code name SLEDGEHAMMER, as a means of averting total disaster in eastern Europe. This was the issue that dominated the conferences among Roosevelt, Churchill, and their chiefs of staff that began in Washington on June 21. Churchill stubbornly opposed any limited diversionary attempt. He admitted that the British would have six or eight divisions available for an invasion by September; they would participate if the Americans could guarantee the success of the undertaking. But were there not other ways, perhaps an invasion of North Africa, in which combined Anglo-American forces could attack more successfully? In the midst of these heated deliberations came news of Rommel's threatened drive into Egypt. It diverted the conferees' attention from the coast of France to the imperiled area, enabled Churchill to drive home his arguments for a North African invasion, and caused him to hurry home to face his critics in the House of Commons.

The president and his military staffs moved swiftly to bolster British defenses in Egypt during the last week of June 1942. But this crisis soon passed, and Roosevelt decided to have the issue of the second front determined once and for all. He sent Harry Hopkins, General Marshall, and Admiral Ernest J. King, American naval commander, to London on July 16. They joined General Dwight D. Eisenhower, now commander of the European theater of operations, and other Americans in London on July 18 for preliminary conferences. Marshall and Eisenhower were enthusiastic for an invasion of France, which they contemplated beginning on a limited scale until a large offensive could be mounted. But British staff officers refused to budge from their adamant opposition; and American naval officers agreed that a cross-Channel operation in September or October would be dangerous. Informed of the stalemate, Roosevelt replied that his spokesmen should now insist upon offensive operations somewhere, preferably in North Africa. When it seemed that the conferees would also postpone decision on GYMNAST, as the North African operation was then called, the president replied that plans must be made at once, and that landings in North Africa should occur no later than October 30, 1942. Churchill agreed, and there now remained only the task of preparing for TORCH—the new code name of the North African operation—and the unpleasant job of telling Stalin why his western Allies could not open a second front in France in 1942. All apprehensions about a premature second front were confirmed in August. A commando raid by a force of 5,000 men, mainly Canadians, against Dieppe, on the French coast, was a disaster with nearly 3,000 casualties inflicted by the strongly entrenched Germans.

3. *The Tide Begins to Turn*

Events of the autumn of 1942 began for the first time to bring some hope to the embattled United Nations. The American navy and marines finally stemmed the onrushing tide of Japanese conquest and began their slow and painful progress on the road to Tokyo. The Anglo-American Allies began a campaign in North Africa that ended the Nazi threat to the Middle East and culminated in an invasion of Sicily and Italy in 1943. The Russians finally held firm on the banks of the Volga and then began a counteroffensive that would not cease until Soviet armies had captured Berlin.

The American Pacific Fleet, commanded by Admiral Chester W. Nimitz, had regrouped and given warning even during the high tide of Japanese expansion. A spectacular blow came on April 18, 1942, when United States Army medium bombers under Colonel James Doolittle took off from the carrier *Hornet* to raid Tokyo. But the most decisive engagement during this defensive phase was the Battle of the Coral Sea, May 7 and 8, when planes from *Lexington* and *Yorktown* turned back a large Japanese force moving around the southeastern coast of New Guinea to attack Port Moresby.

The Japanese, shocked by the raid on Tokyo and unaware that the planes had come from a carrier, concluded that the Americans had launched the attack from one of the outlying islands in the Central Pacific. To avoid repetition of this air attack, they decided to extend their perimeter and sent a large armada and invasion force against Midway Island, an outpost guarding the Hawaiian Islands, in a bold bid to cut American communication lines in the Pacific and perhaps establish bases in the islands themselves. Warned of this attack by intercepted Japanese code

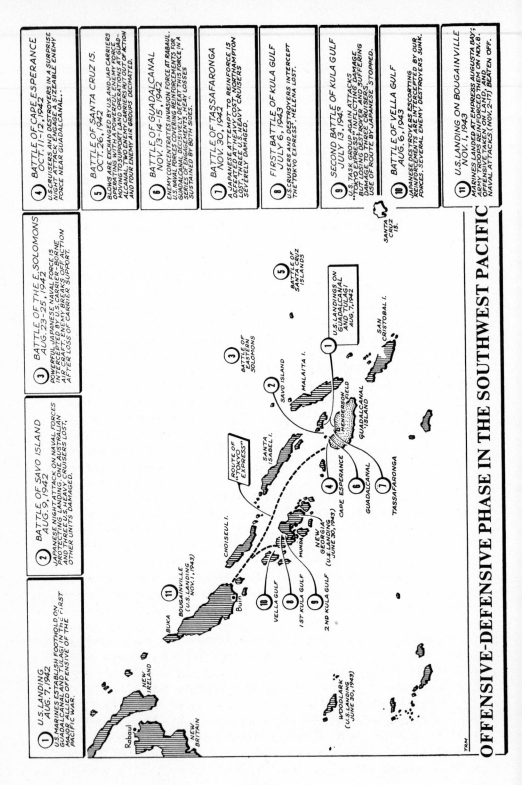

OFFENSIVE-DEFENSIVE PHASE IN THE SOUTHWEST PACIFIC

messages, Nimitz had moved his carriers and cruisers into the Central Pacific, and one of the most decisive battles of the Pacific war raged with incredible fury from June 3 to June 6. Dive bombers and B-17s from Midway joined with dive bombers and torpedo planes from *Enterprise, Hornet,* and *Yorktown* to sink four Japanese carriers, a heavy cruiser, and three destroyers, and to damage one heavy cruiser and two destroyers. In contrast, the Americans lost only *Yorktown* and a destroyer. The Battle of Midway not only removed the threat to the Hawaiian Islands but also restored the balance of naval power in the Pacific. It was, moreover, convincing proof of the importance of air power, for warships in this battle, as in the Battle of Coral Sea, did not exchange a single salvo during the engagement.

Now it was the Americans' turn to go on the offensive. The Japanese had recently moved into the southern Solomon Islands and were building an airfield on Guadalcanal, which imperiled the Allied position in the entire South Pacific and the line of communication to Australia. Assembling a large force of warships, transports, and marines in New Zealand, Admiral Robert L. Ghormley attacked Tulagi and Guadalcanal in the Solomons on August 7 and soon won control of Tulagi and the airfield on Guadalcanal. A Japanese cruiser and destroyer force surprised the Allies and sank four cruisers and damaged other ships in the Battle of Savo Island on August 8 in one of the most humiliating defeats ever suffered by the United States Navy. The Japanese did not know what damage they had done, and they withdrew without attacking the Allied transports. But they soon returned with troops, and the battle raged on Guadalcanal and for control of the air and seas in the area of the Solomons during the next six months. The issue was long in doubt, as the Japanese enjoyed an advantage in land-based aircraft from their base in Rabaul in New Britain Island. However, the American navy won control of the seas in a number of violent battles. Then American army forces, relieving the battle-weary First Marine Division, gradually overcame the enemy on Guadalcanal. The Japanese withdrew on the night of February 7–8, 1943.

In the meantime, Allied planners and diplomats had been at work preparing TORCH, the offensive in North Africa under General Eisenhower. The British Eighth Army opened an offensive against Rommel's forces at El Alamein on October 24, 1942, and three great Anglo-American convoys converged west of Gibraltar soon afterward. They struck simultaneously on November 8 at Oran and Algiers in Algeria and Casablanca on the Atlantic coast of French Morocco. They encountered heavy French resistance only around Casablanca. Marshal Henri-Philippe Pétain, head of the Vichy French government, severed diplomatic relations with the United States on November 9 and called upon his forces in North Africa to resist. But Pétain's deputy in North Africa, Admiral Jean Darlan, took control when the Germans invaded unoccupied France on November 11. He concluded an armistice agreement with the Allied supreme commander, General Eisenhower, that recognized Darlan's control and promised the cooperation of some 50,000 French colonial troops in North Africa.[1]

American and British policy toward France had diverged since 1940. Britain had given moral and material support to General Charles de Gaulle as the leader of the French forces carrying on outside France, and as representative to some extent of the growing underground resistance in France itself. The Americans, on the other hand, had regarded the de Gaullist movement as a minor military auxiliary. Roosevelt, in fact, was to continue to resist the political claims of de Gaulle's movement until after the liberation of France, when the support of the French people for the gallant general was unmistakable.

During the two weeks following the conclusion of the Darlan agreement, American and British units from Algiers engaged in a race with the Germans for control of Tunisia, then occupied by small French forces. The Germans reached the province in large numbers first and poured additional men, tanks, and planes into North Africa, and the ensuing campaign became a crucial test of strength. Fighting began in earnest on February 11, 1943. It mounted in intensity as General Sir Bernard Montgomery's British Eighth Army in the east and Eisenhower's combined armies in the west gradually closed the jaws of a gigantic vise on the Germans. The result was a complete Allied victory, signaled by German surrender on May 12, which cost the Axis fifteen divisions, and 349,206 men killed and captured, 250 tanks, over 2,300 airplanes, and 232 ships. In contrast, the Allies suffered 70,000 casualties in a campaign that seasoned their troops and opened the Mediterranean once again to Allied shipping.

In the meantime, Roosevelt, Churchill, their political advisers, and the American and British chiefs of staff had met at Casablanca for a full-dress conference in January 1943. When the conference opened on January 12, the chiefs of staff talked about operations to be launched after the Tunisian campaign had ended. These discussions continued after Roosevelt arrived on January 14. The upshot was a decision, agreed to reluctantly by the Americans (who preferred to concentrate upon an early second front in France) first, to invade Sicily in order to secure complete control of the Mediterranean and advanced air bases and, second, to defer the invasion of France at least until 1944. General Marshall argued strenuously for a cross-Channel invasion in 1943, but without success.

Roosevelt and Churchill also plunged into French politics at Casablanca. Darlan had been assassinated on December 24, 1942, and the de Gaull-

---

[1] Eisenhower's agreement with Darlan nearly cost him his post as supreme commander. The Americans had brought with them General Henri H. Giraud, who had escaped from German captivity, in the hope that he could command the loyalty of all French forces in North Africa. When Giraud failed to win that support, Eisenhower recognized Darlan because he was the de facto French chief of state. Nonetheless, liberal groups in the United States and Britain were outraged by what they charged was American collaboration with the worst reactionary elements in the Vichy regime.

ist Free French group in London and the supporters of General Giraud, Darlan's successor, were contending for the right to speak for the French nation. All that the president wanted was cooperation in the common cause of liberation, and agreement that the French people should decide the question of sovereignty after the war was over. Roosevelt and Churchill persuaded the austere and sensitive de Gaulle to come to Casablanca on January 22, meet with Giraud, and work out plans for future cooperation.

The work of the conference completed, Roosevelt and Churchill held a joint press conference at Casablanca on January 24 in which they reviewed their work and looked forward to victories ahead. But more important was Roosevelt's declaration, made after previous consultation with Churchill that the Allies would insist upon the unconditional surrender of the Axis enemies. "It does not mean the destruction of the population of Germany, Italy, and Japan," he explained, "but it does mean the destruction of the philosophies in those countries which are based on conquest and the subjugation of other people." It was, as one critic afterward said, one of the "great mistakes of the war." It hardened the German popular will to resist and shut the door to negotiations by an anti-Hitler faction. Worse still, it virtually precluded a negotiated settlement of the Pacific war, the one conflict that might well have been terminated by negotiation.

4. 1943: The United Nations on the Offensive

The decisive turning point of the European war in 1942–1943 occurred when the Russians held Stalingrad from September to November 1942 against furious German attacks. Then the Russians launched a counteroffensive that destroyed or captured a large German army in the blazing city on February 2, 1943. From this point on, the Soviet armies pressed forward along the entire length of the eastern front. By October 1943 the Red armies had driven deep into the Ukraine and stood on the east bank of the Dnieper River, poised for a winter offensive that would drive through the Ukraine into Rumania.[2]

The year 1943 also witnessed the turning of the tide in the Battle of the Atlantic. The Germans had more than 100 U-boats constantly at sea by the spring of 1943. But the Anglo-American Allies had finally found the means of victory—aggressive offense through new methods of detection, air patrols both from land bases and escort carriers, and fast destroyers and destroyer escorts to protect the convoys. The turning point came from

[2]One factor in the Soviet victories was the increasing stream of lend-lease supplies from the United States. Supplies worth $4.25 billion went from the United States to Russia from October 1941 to January 1944. They included 7,800 planes, 4,700 tanks and tank destroyers, 70,000 trucks, and huge quantities of ammunition, food, and clothing.

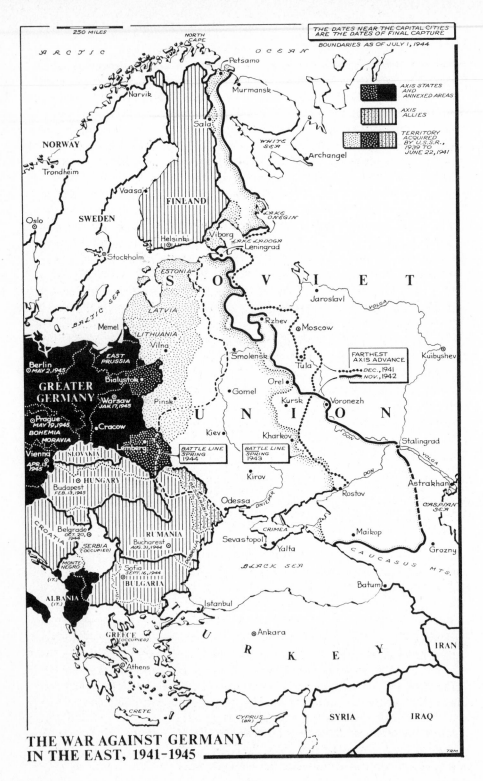

THE WAR AGAINST GERMANY
IN THE EAST, 1941-1945

March through May 1943, when U-boat sinkings in the Atlantic declined from 514,744 tons in March to 199,409 tons in May, and the number of submarines destroyed rose from 12 to 40. Allied shipping losses had declined to 29,297 tons by May 1944, and not a single Allied ship was torpedoed in the summer of 1944. And for decreasing results the Germans paid such a high price—237 submarines sunk in 1943, 241 in 1944, and 153 during the first four months of 1945—as to make their underseas campaign a useless drain on resources and manpower.

Allied power increased so swiftly in the Pacific from March 1943 to March 1944 that the two major commanders in the area, Admiral Nimitz and General MacArthur, were able not only to overwhelm or neutralize the Japanese bastions in the Central and South Pacific, but also to launch new offensives that pierced the outer perimeter of Japanese defenses.

The objective of the first great offensive was Rabaul in New Britain Island, the most important Japanese air and naval base in the Southwest Pacific area. The Allied attack was two-pronged. First came a tortuous drive up the New Guinea coast from Port Moresby to Hollandia by American and Australian ground forces, paratroops, and the American Fifth Air Force and Seventh Fleet—all under MacArthur's general command. The enemy had been cleared from the eastern part of New Guinea by February 1944. Meanwhile, American and New Zealand ground forces and strong air and naval forces under Admiral William F. Halsey began a drive through the central and northern Solomon Islands that carried to New Georgia on June 30, 1943, Bougainville on November 1, and Green Island on February 15, 1944. Finally, with the occupation of the Admiralty Islands north of New Guinea on February 29, Rabaul was cut off from communication with the Japanese base of Truk, and its encirclement was complete. Thereafter, Allied commanders were content to reduce Rabaul to impotence through aerial bombardment, without attempting to capture it.

While Allied forces under MacArthur were thus securing their hold on the South Pacific, the forces under Admiral Nimitz launched two major offensives in the Central Pacific that cracked the outer rim of Japanese defenses in that area. A new Central Pacific Force, including marine and army units, under the command of Admiral Raymond A. Spruance, attacked Tarawa and Makin islands in the Gilberts on November 20, 1943. Makin was lightly garrisoned and fell quickly to army troops; but the Second Marine Division that invaded Tarawa after an inadequate bombardment met fierce resistance from Japanese marines and had to fight for every inch of ground until the last defenders were wiped out on November 24. Striking next at the Marshall Islands, army and marine divisions rooted out Japanese defenders on Kwajalein, Roi, Namur, and Eniwetok between February 1 and 19, 1944. Next the American navy steamed into the enemy's interior defenses in daring raids against Truk on February 16

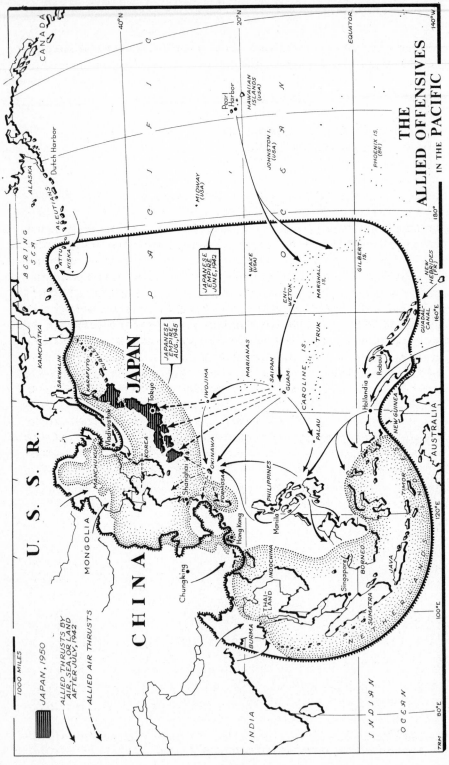

THE
ALLIED OFFENSIVES
IN THE PACIFIC

JAPAN, 1950

ALLIED THRUSTS BY
AIR, SEA, OR LAND
AFTER JULY, 1942

ALLIED AIR THRUSTS

1000 MILES

JAPANESE EMPIRE, JUNE, 1942

JAPANESE EMPIRE, AUG., 1945

U. S. S. R.

MONGOLIA

CHINA

JAPAN

KOREA

INDIA

BURMA

THAILAND

INDOCHINA

Chungking

Hong Kong

Shanghai

Tokyo

Vladivostok

MANCHURIA

KAMCHATKA

SAKHALIN

KARAFUTO

KURILES

Hollandia

NEW GUINEA

AUSTRALIA

PHILIPPINES

Manila

FORMOSA

OKINAWA

IWOJIMA

SAIPAN

GUAM

PALAU

TRUK

CAROLINE IS.

MARIANAS

ENI-WETOK

MARSHALL IS.

GILBERT IS.

WAKE (USA)

MIDWAY (USA)

JOHNSTON I. (USA)

PHOENIX IS. (BR)

HAWAIIAN ISLANDS (USA)

Pearl Harbor

NEW HEBRIDES (FR)

GUADAL- CANAL

Rabaul

BORNEO

JAVA

SUMATRA

Singapore

TIMOR

N E T H E R L A N D S   I N D I E S

ATTU

KISKA

ALEUTIANS

Dutch Harbor

ALASKA

CANADA

BERING SEA

P A C I F I C   O C E A N

INDIAN OCEAN

40°N

20°N

EQUATOR

140°W

180°

160°E

120°E

100°E

80°E

TRM

532

and against Saipan in the Marianas, only 1,350 miles from Tokyo, on February 21, 1944.

5. Planning for Victory and the Surrender of Italy

No sooner had the Anglo-American Allies taken the offensive than they began to look forward to victory and an uncertain postwar future. Roosevelt, Hull, and Hopkins began exploratory discussions in Washington with the British foreign secretary, Anthony Eden, in March 1943. The president was reluctant to approve Russia's absorption of the Baltic states and parts of Finland and Poland, but he agreed that there was probably nothing the United States and Britain could do to dislodge the Russians from territory that they had occupied. Roosevelt and Eden emphatically agreed that Germany should be completely disarmed and broken into a number of states. In addition, they talked in a general way about the organization of a postwar security agency, the United Nations.

Roosevelt and Hull were determined to avoid Wilson's mistake of ignoring congressional leaders and assiduously drew them into discussions of plans for a United Nations. There had been considerable debate in Congress and the press since Pearl Harbor looking toward American leadership in a postwar organization, and the public demand for strong American leadership in planning for the future was obviously overwhelming by the spring of 1943. The House on September 21 and the Senate on November 5 approved by large majorities the Fulbright and Connally resolutions pledging the United States to membership in an international organization, "with power adequate to establish and to maintain a just and lasting peace."

Meanwhile, Churchill and his advisers arrived in the United States on May 11, 1943, for another grand conference on war strategy known as TRIDENT. In brief, the conferees agreed that the British should seize the Azores Islands to provide new air and naval facilities;[3] approved plans for a tremendous increase in the aerial bombardment of Germany; instructed Eisenhower to plan for an invasion of Italy after the conquest of Sicily; set May 1, 1944, as the date for OVERLORD (the new code name for the invasion of France); and mapped plans for new offensive operations in the Pacific.

The war in the Mediterranean erupted again according to the Allied schedule soon after the TRIDENT conference. A huge Anglo-American ar-

[3]The British cabinet, however, won permission from the Portuguese government to establish these bases, and thus the projected invasion never came off.

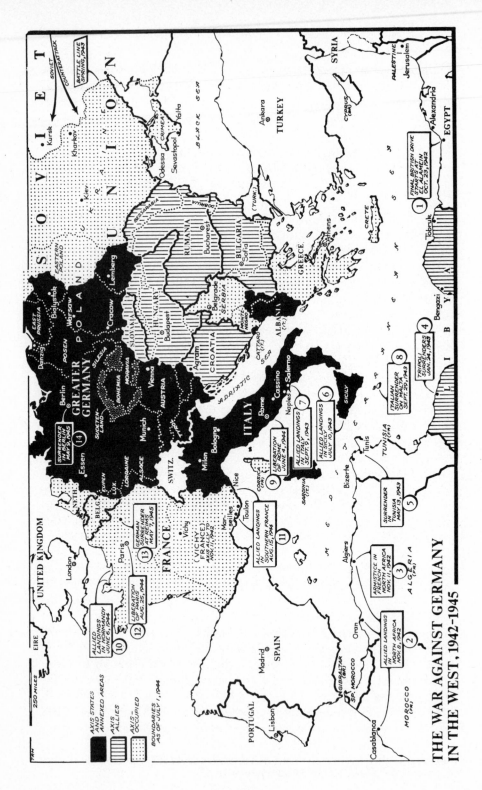

THE WAR AGAINST GERMANY
IN THE WEST, 1942–1945

AXIS STATES
AND
ANNEXED AREAS

AXIS
ALLIES

AXIS-
OCCUPIED

BOUNDARIES
AS OF JULY 1, 1944

250 MILES

mada disgorged 160,000 troops, 600 tanks, and 1,800 guns on the beaches of Sicily on July 10, 1943. The British Eighth Army under General Montgomery and the American Seventh Army, under General George S. Patton, had routed the Italian and German defenders and overrun the island by August 17. It was an important turning point, for a group of Italian conspirators persuaded King Victor Emmanuel to connive at the deposition and arrest of Mussolini on July 25[4] and formed a new government under Marshal Badoglio. He proceeded to open negotiations looking toward the surrender of Italy.

This sudden turn of events raised new perplexities for Roosevelt and Churchill—whether to negotiate with the Badoglio government, as Eisenhower and other Allied leaders requested, or to demand unconditional surrender in accordance with the Casablanca declaration. The situation was so uncertain that the president, the prime minister, and their respective entourages met in Quebec on August 17, 1943, for a conference known by the code name of QUADRANT.

The new Italian government made secret contact with the Allies. The Italians were eager to surrender but insisted that the Allies protect Rome, the king, and the government from the Germans, who had meanwhile taken control of most of Italy. Roosevelt and Churchill agreed to send an airborne division to capture the airfields around Rome, and the armistice was signed on September 3. By the time that preparations for an airborne assault on Rome were completed, however, the Germans had surrounded the city in force and seized the airfields.

Meanwhile, the British Eighth Army crossed the Straits of Messina on September 3 and began the invasion of the Italian mainland, known as operation AVALANCHE. A week later a British airborne division seized the large Italian naval base at Taranto, while the United States Fifth Army, under the command of General Mark Clark, landed in the Gulf of Salerno south of Naples. The Fifth Army occupied Naples on October 7 in spite of furious German counterattacks and pushed northward to the Volturno River. Meanwhile, British forces had cleared the central and eastern sections of the Italian boot. Allied forces had pushed to a winter line south of Cassino by January 1, 1944.

A long and bloody campaign for Italy still impended, but the Italian surrender and successful invasion of Italy yielded large dividends to the Anglo-American Allies. It brought the surrender of the Italian fleet and guaranteed complete Allied control of the Mediterranean. It gave the Allies advanced air bases from which to bomb the Balkans and Central Europe. It consumed some of Hitler's best divisions. Most important, it gave the British and Americans the incalculable advantage of being on the offensive.

---

[4]A German parachute force rescued Mussolini on September 12, 1943. He then established a new Fascist government at Lake Como under German protection.

6. Slow Progress Toward Accord with Russia

The QUADRANT conferees at Quebec turned to other urgent problems after approving final arrangements for the Italian surrender. They reaffirmed May 1, 1944, as the date for OVERLORD. Hull and Eden discussed postwar plans for Germany and approved the draft of a Four Power Declaration—to be submitted to the coming conference of foreign ministers in Moscow—pledging America, Britain, Russia, and China to work for establishment of an effective postwar security organization. The conference was over on August 24, and Churchill accompanied Roosevelt back to Washington and stayed with him intermittently during the next three weeks. During this time the Badoglio government surrendered, and the Allies began their invasion of the Italian mainland.

Soon afterward, Secretary Hull made the arduous air journey to Moscow for the conference of foreign ministers that opened in the Russian capital on October 18. Before this time no one in Washington or London knew what Russian postwar ambitions were, except for the territorial demands that Stalin had outlined to Eden in December 1941. Hull, Molotov, and Eden discussed immediate and postwar problems in Moscow from October 18 to 30, 1943, with so little disagreement that future accord seemed assured. They agreed, for example, upon a plan for the postwar treatment of Germany that the State Department had prepared and the president had tentatively approved. Indeed, Molotov declared that it expressed Stalin's views and had his complete endorsement.[5] They agreed, moreover, that Austria should be reconstituted an independent nation and regarded as a liberated and not an enemy state, while Hull persuaded Stalin and Molotov to sign the Four Power Declaration. In addition, at a state dinner on October 30 Stalin told Hull the welcome news that Russia would join the war against Japan after the defeat of Germany.

There were differences over Poland,[6] but the Moscow Conference was

---

[5] As this plan eventually became the cornerstone of Allied postwar policy toward Germany, it would be well to examine it in some detail. It called for the unconditional surrender of Germany by whatever government exercised power at the end of the war. An Inter-Allied Control Commission would supervise the surrender and occupation of Germany by Soviet, American, and British troops. During the occupation the Control Commission would undertake to destroy all vestiges of nazism and take necessary steps to encourage establishment of a democratic government and restore freedom of religion, speech, the press, and political activity. Moreover, Germany should be denied a standing army and general staff and prohibited from manufacturing any war materials or aircraft of any kind. The Hull plan was vague on future German boundaries, except to say that East Prussia should be separated from the Reich. Finally, Germany should be required to pay reparations in goods, equipment, and manpower, but not in money.

[6] The Kremlin had severed diplomatic relations with the Polish government-in-exile in London, because the Poles had demanded that the International Red Cross investigate a German charge that the Russians had murdered 8,000 to 10,000 Polish officers in 1939 and buried their bodies near Smolensk. Moreover, the Russians were beginning to deal with a group of Polish Communists in the Soviet Union. In Moscow, Hull urged the Russians to restore relations with the Polish government in London, but Molotov made it clear the Kremlin would deal only with a Polish government it could control.

nonetheless a resounding success. To be sure, no one in the West knew absolutely whether Russia would cooperate in the postwar era, but such cooperation now seemed at least possible. As one milestone along the road to Allied unity, the conference prepared the way for the next—a personal meeting of the Big Three.

Roosevelt had long wanted to meet with the Russian leader, and he had invited Stalin before the Moscow Conference to join him and Churchill at Ankara, Bagdad, or Basra in Iraq. Stalin replied that he would go only to Teheran, since he could maintain personal control over his high command from the Iranian capital. The president agreed and left Hampton Roads on the new battleship *Iowa* on November 13, 1943, for the long journey to Cairo. There he conferred with Churchill, Chiang Kai-shek, Lord Louis Mountbatten, Allied commander in Southeast Asia, and General Joseph W. Stilwell, American commander in the China area and adviser to Chiang, from November 23 to 27 on the situation in Burma and China. Most of these discussions revolved around an Allied drive in Burma to open supply lines to China, and a Chinese offensive in northern China.[7]

The president and his party next flew from Cairo to Teheran on November 27. For security reasons Roosevelt moved into a villa in the Russian compound on the next day. The Big Three thrashed over practically all outstanding military and political problems during the next four days. These included military operations in Italy and American plans for offensive operations in the Pacific, during discussions of which Stalin again promised that Russia would join the war against Japan after Germany's surrender.

The Russians were most concerned about OVERLORD and seemed desperately anxious to pin Roosevelt and Churchill to a definite time and place for the great invasion. Stalin pressed Roosevelt to name a supreme commander for OVERLORD and implied that he would believe that the operation would come off only after the president had named the commander. Roosevelt had long wanted General Marshall, for whom he had warm affection and respect, to have the honor of leading the liberation of Europe; but he wisely refused to follow the impulse to give Stalin an immediate answer. As it turned out, Roosevelt and his advisers concluded that Marshall could not be spared from his vital post in Washington. The president decided on his return from Teheran to name Eisenhower as supreme commander of OVERLORD.

The Big Three also discussed the future of Germany and plans for postwar collaboration. They now seemed to favor partition. Stalin empha-

---

[7]The Allies opened this campaign in December 1943, when General Stilwell's Chinese divisions moved from Ledo against Japanese forces in northern Burma, and British forces moved down the southwestern coast of Burma in January 1944. Japanese counterattacks against Chittagong and Imphal, both in India, were eventually repulsed but delayed British liberation of Rangoon and southern Burma until the spring of 1945. To the north, however, Stilwell's American and Chinese forces were more successful and assured completion of the new supply line to China, the Ledo Road. It was opened in January 1945.

sized the danger of future German resurgence and added that he did not think that the State Department plan submitted at the Moscow Conference was severe enough. Roosevelt outlined his plan for a future United Nations organization, which would assume responsibility for preventing wars and aggression. During all these conversations the utmost frankness and usually a spirit of cordiality prevailed. In fact, the president was convinced that he had broken through the wall of suspicion and distrust surrounding Stalin, won Russian trust and friendship, and laid the basis for fruitful collaboration in the future. His feeling was well expressed in the concluding sentences of the Declaration of Teheran, issued on December 1: "We came here with hope and determination. We leave here, friends in fact, in spirit, and in purpose."

The president said good-by to Stalin after a final dinner on December 2 and then went to Cairo for conferences with Churchill and Turkish leaders about Turkey's entrance into the war. In addition, Roosevelt and Churchill and the Combined Chiefs of Staff held conferences of tremendous military importance from December 4 to 6. Thus the end of the year 1943 found the Allies on the offensive on all fronts, Allied unity existing in fact as well as name, and Anglo-American leaders completing plans for final assaults against Germany and Japan.

7. *The Allied Air Offensives in Europe, 1940-1945*

Superiority in the air passed to the British after the failure of the German air blitz against England in 1940-1941. The RAF Bomber Command conducted a limited number of night raids against selected industrial and transportation targets in Germany from 1940 to early 1942. Results were so unsatisfactory that the new chief of the Bomber Command, Sir Arthur Harris, executed a complete change in British bombing tactics—from the target system to mass bombing of industrial areas in order to disrupt the German economy and lessen the will of the German people to fight. The first 1,000-plane RAF raid, against Cologne on May 30, signaled the beginning of the new campaign. It was followed in 1942 by others against centers in the Ruhr, Bremen, Hamburg, and other German cities. This was only a small beginning, for less than 50,000 tons of bombs fell on Axis Europe in 1942, and German war production and civilian morale were not visibly impaired.

Meanwhile, the United States Eighth Air Force had established bases in England in early 1942 and joined in the air war on August 17, 1942. The offensive power of the Eighth Air Force grew and was reinforced by the Ninth Air Force and the Fifteenth Air Force, and the Americans became a powerful factor in the air campaign during the summer of 1943. While the British continued their devastating night attacks, the Americans used their heavier armored Flying Fortresses and Liberators in daring daylight raids—until extremely heavy losses in a raid on Schweinfurt on October 14, 1943, convinced American commanders that further large daylight operations must await production of long-range fighters to protect the bombers. All told, American and British bombers dropped 206,188 tons of bombs on European targets in 1943.

A new phase in the air campaign began in February 1944. The arrival in England of substantial numbers of long-range American fighters made resumption of daylight raids possible. The introduction of radar bombsights had already greatly increased the accuracy of night bombing. And there was a use of increasingly heavy bombs and a rapid build-up of the Eighth and Fifteenth Air Forces. The Americans first began a systematic campaign to destroy the German aircraft industry. Then the attack shifted in March to French and Belgian marshaling yards, railroads, and bridges. And after the invasion of France, the American and the British air forces began a coordinated and relentless round-the-clock assault upon German synthetic oil and chemical plants. Some 8,000 to 9,000 Allied planes turned to the task of paralyzing the German transportation system in February 1945. Finally, the air forces joined the advancing Allied armies in April in reducing the German nation to utter impotence and ruin.

The overall dimensions of the Anglo-American air effort in Europe stagger the imagination: 1,442,280 bomber and 2,686,799 fighter sorties, which dropped 2,697,473 tons of bombs on Germany and Nazi-occupied Europe, cost the Allies some 40,000 planes and 158,000 personnel. All told, Allied bombs dropped on Germany killed 305,000 persons and wounded 780,000 others, destroyed or damaged 5.5 million homes, and deprived 20 million persons of essential utilities. By the beginning of 1944, according to a poll taken by the Strategic Bombing Survey immediately after the war, some 77 percent of the German people were convinced that the war was lost; and by May 1945 most Germans had lost all will to continue the uneven struggle.

8. Victory in Europe: To the Westwall

General Dwight D. Eisenhower, supreme commander of the Allied Expeditionary Forces, arrived in London on January 15, 1944, with orders from Roosevelt and Churchill to "enter the continent of Europe and, in conjunction with the other Allied Nations, undertake operations aimed at the heart of Germany and the destruction of her armed forces." The Combined Chiefs of Staff and various technical staffs in Britain and America had been hard at work on OVERLORD since 1942. Planning for the actual invasion and subsequent operations proceeded apace in Eisenhower's London headquarters after mid-January 1944.

The appointed time, June 5, 1944,[8] for which the world had long waited now approached rapidly. The great invasion armada was delayed by a sudden storm and put out to sea early in the morning of June 6. The Germans expected the invasion to come in the Pas de Calais area, where the English Channel is narrowest. Instead, the Allies struck at five beaches along a sixty-mile stretch of the Cotentin Peninsula in Normandy. First there were furious air and naval bombardments of the invasion area and beaches. Next came the landing of three airborne divisions behind the German lines a few minutes after midnight on June 6. Finally, the sea-borne troops hit the beaches at 7:30 in the morning. German resistance was generally light; but American invaders met a fierce defense on Omaha Beach and suffered heavy casualties.

The German commanders, field marshals Rommel and Karl von Rundstedt, mistook the Normandy invasion as a screen for a larger invasion in the Pas de Calais. They were not able to bring up their reserve divisions in time to prevent the Allies from securing and capturing a bridgehead in Normandy. Within two weeks after D day the Allies had landed more than 1 million troops with enormous quantities of supplies in a broad sector along the Normandy coast. They had also captured Cherbourg, Caen, and St. Lô, "eaten the guts out of the German defense," and were poised for a grand sweep through northern France.

The battle of the breakthrough began on July 25, with a lightninglike thrust by General Patton's Third Army into Brittany and a breakthrough to Avranches and Falaise by the American First Army and the British Second Army. Soon the battle for Normandy turned into the battle for France. The German Seventh Army in the area between Falaise and Argentan was under orders to stand firm. It was surrounded and partially destroyed or captured during a furious battle from August 19-23. The Allies completed the liberation of France in blitzkrieg fashion while the surviving German armies moved back to their Siegfried line. The American Seventh Army invaded southern France on August 15 and joined the race for the German frontier. Paris fell to French and American troops ten days later. By mid-September American and British armies had captured Brussels and Antwerp, occupied Luxembourg, and crossed the German border at Aachen.

The Allies were on the move on other fronts as well. They had tried vainly to break the German lines in southern Italy. Then they tried to turn the German flank on January 22, 1944, by landings at Anzio and Nettuno on the Italian western coast, only thirty-six miles from Rome. This effort failed. But the British Eighth Army and the American Fifth Army pushed

[8]The date for the launching of OVERLORD was postponed from May 1 to the more unfavorable first week in June 1944 because of a shortage of landing craft.

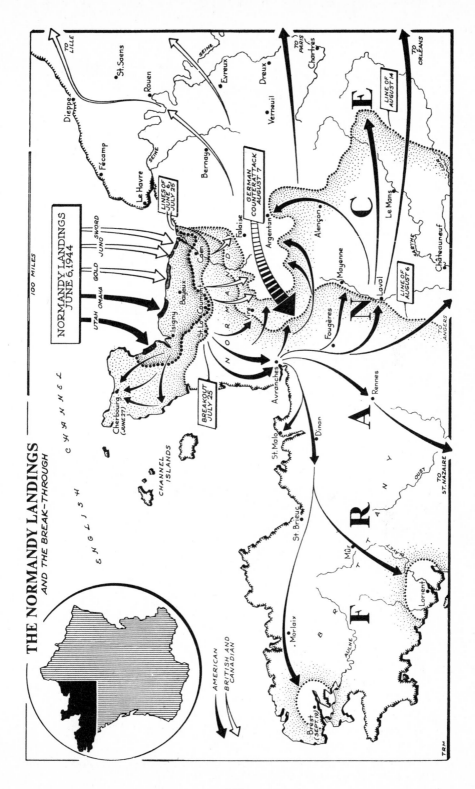

THE NORMANDY LANDINGS
AND THE BREAK-THROUGH

NORMANDY LANDINGS
JUNE 6, 1944

UTAH OMAHA GOLD JUNO SWORD

LINES OF JUNE 6, JULY 25

GERMAN COUNTERATTACK AUGUST 7

LINE OF AUGUST 14

LINE OF AUGUST 6

BREAKOUT JULY 25

CHANNEL ISLANDS

ENGLISH CHANNEL

100 MILES

AMERICAN
BRITISH AND CANADIAN

TO LILLE

St. Saens

Dieppe

Fécamp

Le Havre

Rouen

SEINE

Evreux

Dreux

Verneuil

Bernaye

TO PARIS

Chartres

TO ORLEANS

Falaise

Caen

Bayeux

Isigny

St. Lô

Caumont

Vire

NORMANDIE

Argentan

Alençon

Mayenne

Fougères

Le Mans

SARTHE

Châteauneuf

TO ANGERS

Avranches

Laval

Cherbourg (JUNE 27)

St. Malo

Dinan

Rennes

FRANCE

St. Brieuc

Morlaix

Mûr

BRITTANY

BLAVET

AULNE

OUST

TO ST. NAZAIRE

Lorient

Brest (SEPT. 19)

FRANCE

TRM

northward in the spring, joined the beleaguered divisions on the Anzio beachhead, and captured Rome on June 4, 1944. Under heavy Allied pressure and harassment, the Germans pulled back to their Gothic line, which ran across Italy some 150 miles north of Rome. There they managed to stabilize the fighting around September 1, 1944.

Meanwhile, the Russians, during the spring of 1944, began offensives along the entire eastern front fully as important in the Allied strategy as the Anglo-American sweep across France. One Russian drive on the northern sector forced Finland to sue for peace on August 25. The greatest Russian offensive, however, opened on June 23 to coincide with the Anglo-American drive in the West. Soviet armies captured the German stronghold of Vitebsk and then broke through to the Baltic on August 1. Five Russian armies in the central sector rolled into Poland, reached the Vistula River in late July, captured Warsaw on January 17, 1945, and reached the Oder River, only forty-five miles from Berlin, the following month. Farther to the south, two Red armies overran Rumania in August 1944. Then they marched into Bulgaria, captured Belgrade on October 20, and entered Budapest in February 1945.

It was obvious to almost everyone by the autumn of 1944 that the German military situation was hopeless. Germany was now a beleaguered fortress awaiting final destruction because her fanatical master preferred complete destruction to unconditional surrender. Some high German officers, foreseeing inevitable ruin under Hitler's leadership, in cooperation with certain anti-Nazi groups perfected plans to take control of the German government and assassinate Hitler. Their agent left a time bomb in Hitler's headquarters on July 20, 1944. Thinking Hitler dead, the conspirators proceeded to take first steps to seize control of the army and government. Unfortunately, Hitler was only injured by the bomb's blast. With the support of loyal troops he rounded up the opposition, executed about 5,000 persons after drumhead trials, and sent another 10,000 enemies to concentration camps. In consequence, the war would proceed to its bitter end.

9. The Campaign and Election of 1944

Meanwhile, partisan politics had persisted in the United States. The Republicans made a hard fight to win control of Congress in 1942. They failed, but they made such sweeping gains in the elections on November 3 that a GOP victory in 1944 seemed at least possible.[9] Actually, what oc-

[9]The Democrats elected 222 and the Republicans 209 members to the House—a Republican gain of 47 seats. The Republicans, moreover, gained 9 seats in the Senate.

curred in the federal and state elections in November 1942 was not merely a Republican revival but also a strong conservative upsurge. The significance of the upheaval became apparent after the organization of the Seventy-eighth Congress in January 1943, when many southern Democrats joined Republicans to form a majority coalition and seize control of legislative policy. This coalition gave the president aggressive support in all matters relating to the war and postwar policies. In domestic matters, however, they proceeded as fast as they could to destroy certain parts of the New Deal.

Politicians in both camps began preparations for the coming national conventions and presidential campaign while the conservative coalition and the president engaged in frequent verbal duels during the winter and spring of 1944. Wendell L. Willkie was still titular head of his party, but he had no support among party leaders and had become so closely identified with the Roosevelt administration as to lose his status as leader of the opposition. He withdrew from the preconvention campaign after suffering an impressive defeat in the Wisconsin presidential primary in April. Meanwhile, Willkie's chief rival, Governor Thomas E. Dewey of New York, was fast emerging as the new Republican leader. The presidential nomination went to him on the first ballot when the Republican national convention met in Chicago on June 26, with the vice-presidential nomination going to Governor John W. Bricker of Ohio. The convention adopted a platform that was aggressively internationalistic and essentially progressive in tone.[10]

In view of Roosevelt's precarious health and poor chances of serving out a fourth term, the crucial struggle revolved around the nomination of a vice-presidential candidate. This battle was bitter and created divisions in the party that persisted for years afterward. Vice-President Henry A. Wallace enjoyed the support of the advanced progressive wing and large elements in the CIO. But he was almost unanimously opposed by party bosses, southerners, and many moderates who suspected that he was temperamentally unfit for the presidency and hopelessly inept in political leadership. Roosevelt endorsed Wallace publicly but refused to insist upon his nomination. In fact, the president had apparently promised the succession to Byrnes and actually tried to obtain the nomination for the South Carolinian.

The president's plans, however, were upset on the eve of the convention by a newcomer in high Democratic councils, Sidney Hillman, a vice-president of the CIO and former co-director of the defense effort. Alarmed by the rising tide of antilabor sentiment and the failure of workers to go to the polls in 1942, Hillman organized the Political Action

---

[10]The Republican platform roundly condemned the Roosevelt administration's alleged inefficiency, waste, excessive centralization, and destruction of private enterprise. However, it made it clear that Republicans had no fundamental quarrel with Democrats on domestic issues by promising to strengthen the New Deal's labor, social security, and agricultural programs. All in all, it was the most significant endorsement of the Roosevelt policies yet written.

Committee (PAC) of the CIO in 1943. His purpose was not only to rally workers and progressives but also to win new bargaining power for labor within the Democratic party.

Hillman used his power in a spectacular way at the Democratic national convention. He virtually vetoed Byrnes's nomination by warning the president that the South Carolinian was unacceptable to labor and northern blacks. The president concluded that his assistant must give way to a compromise candidate. He therefore declared that either Senator Harry S. Truman or Justice William O. Douglas would be an agreeable running mate; and he agreed with Hillman that the PAC should shift its support from Wallace to Truman when it became obvious that Wallace could not be nominated. In any event, Roosevelt declared in his final instructions to National Chairman Robert E. Hannegan, that the party managers must "clear it with Sidney," that is, must win Hillman's approval for any vice-presidential candidate.

The issue was actually settled during the three days before the Democratic convention opened in Chicago on July 19, 1944. Hillman declared that he would fight Byrnes's nomination to the bitter end, and the president on July 17 asked the South Carolinian to withdraw. Byrnes's withdrawal narrowed the field to Wallace, who still enjoyed the PAC's seeming support, and Truman, upon whom administration and party leaders had finally agreed. During the balloting for the vice-presidential nomination on July 19 and 20, Wallace led on the first ballot and Truman won on the third, as the leaders had planned. The convention had nominated the president on the first ballot a short time before. The Democratic platform promised continuation of progressive policies at home and vigorous American leadership abroad in the postwar era.

Dewey campaigned hard under tremendous handicaps during the ensuing summer and autumn. He was beaten before he started by smashing Allied victories in Europe and the Pacific, a general reluctance to change governments in the midst of the world crisis, and above all by his own general agreement with basic administration policies. This latter handicap forced him to make criticisms that could only sound captious. Dewey's chief advantage was Roosevelt's failing health and growing suspicion that perhaps the president was incapable of managing affairs of state. This suspicion increased after his address at Bremerton, Washington, during which he was halting and ineffective because he was suffering at this very time from an attack of angina pectoris. However, Roosevelt, his health substantially recovered, came back in a speech before the Teamsters' Union in Washington on September 23 that convinced millions of voters that he was still the champion campaigner. He followed this masterpiece with strenuous tours and speeches in Chicago, New York City, Wilmington, Delaware, and New England.

This aggressive campaign gave Roosevelt the initiative that he had seemingly lost. He also recovered lost ground by committing himself

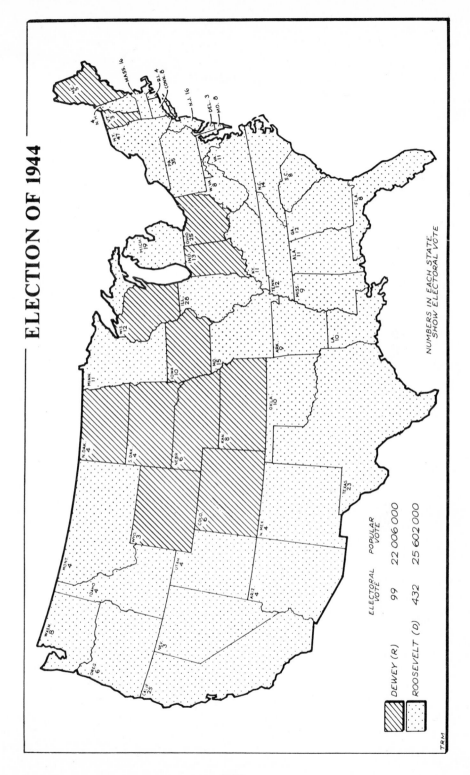

ELECTION OF 1944

NUMBERS IN EACH STATE
SHOW ELECTORAL VOTE

	ELECTORAL VOTE	POPULAR VOTE
DEWEY (R)	99	22 006 000
ROOSEVELT (D)	432	25 602 000

545

squarely to a full resumption of progressive policies in the postwar era. Almost as decisive was the PAC's success in getting workers to the polls. In the election on November 7, Roosevelt received 25,602,505 popular and 432 electoral votes; Dewey, 22,006,278 popular and 99 electoral votes. The Democrats lost one seat in the Senate, but they gained twenty seats in the House, all but four of them in the large cities, and captured governorships in Ohio, Massachusetts, Missouri, Idaho, and Washington. The most important outcome of the election was not the continuation of Democratic control but rather the fact that Americans of both parties were now irrevocably committed to assume the leadership in world affairs that they had so often rejected before 1941. For better or for worse, there could be no turning back on the high road to international responsibility.

10. Yalta: The High Tide of Allied Unity

The rapid progress of Allied and Russian armies raised the possibility that war in Europe might end before the three great powers had come to definitive agreement on plans for future collaboration. Indeed, there was little evidence that the American leaders yet knew even their own minds on the most important aspect of postwar planning, a policy for the control of Germany.[11] More disturbing, however, were signs of growing Allied dissension that threatened to split the Grand Alliance and prevent organization of a postwar United Nations. British, American, and Russian delegates met at Dumbarton Oaks in Washington in September 1944. They agreed on a basic structure for a United Nations but could not agree upon certain fundamental aspects of voting procedure. Following this the State Department and the British Foreign Office engaged in heated controversies over organization of a new Italian government and the methods and objectives of British intervention in Greece. The most dangerous potential source of trouble was Russian policy in eastern Europe, especially in Poland.

Roosevelt's thoughts inevitably turned toward another meeting of the Big Three to discuss matters that could be settled only on the high level. Churchill and Stalin were agreeable, although Stalin insisted that he could

---

[11] American confusion on this aspect of postwar policy was revealed during a heated controversy in the administration in the late summer of 1944 around the so-called Morgenthau Plan. Prepared by Harry Dexter White in the Treasury Department and presented by Secretary of the Treasury Henry Morgenthau, Jr., it proposed to give parts of Germany to Poland, Russia, Denmark, and France and to divide the remaining rump, strip it of all industrial capacity, and convert it into a large "goat pasture." Roosevelt approved it over the violent opposition of Hull and Secretary of War Stimson. Moreover, at a conference with Churchill in Quebec in September 1944, the president was so insistent that Churchill reluctantly agreed to consider the Morgenthau Plan as a basis for postwar German policy. Yet the president had dropped the plan altogether within six weeks.

not leave Russia because he was personally directing the Russian armies. The three leaders soon agreed upon Yalta in the Crimea as the place and early February 1945 as the time of the conference.

The Yalta meeting would obviously be the last Big Three conference before the surrender of Germany, and the president and the new secretary of state, Edward R. Stettinius, Jr.,[12] went to unusual effort, first, to formulate an American program and, second, to come to firm agreement with the British before the Big Three met. Stettinius took his staff to Marrakech in French Morocco for a briefing session from January 26 to 29, 1945. Then they went to Malta for conferences with Churchill and Eden on January 31 and February 1. Roosevelt arrived with his party aboard the cruiser *Quincy* on February 2, and it was soon evident that recent Anglo-American difficulties had not done fatal damage to his relationship with Churchill.

The Anglo-American-Russian conferees assembled at Yalta on February 3 and 4, 1945, for the opening of the conference called ARGONAUT on the latter day. The Big Three discussed almost every conceivable problem related to the future of Europe, Asia, and the United Nations from February 4 through 11. In addition, the foreign ministers and military and naval leaders of the three powers worked behind the scenes to smooth out minor differences and lay the groundwork for major understandings. Without following the conferees in their long deliberations, let us now summarize their major agreements and decisions.

GERMANY.   The discussions relating to Germany revolved around the questions of dismemberment, reparations, future Allied control, and French participation in the Inter-Allied Control Commission. The conferees approved dismemberment in principle and agreed to consider details in future negotiations. However, they agreed that northern East Prussia, including Königsberg, should go to Russia; that Poland should annex the southern half of East Prussia; that Russia should annex certain former eastern Polish provinces; and that Poland should receive territory in eastern Germany as compensation.[13] As for reparations, the Russians proposed exacting a total bill of $20 billion, half of which should be paid to the USSR. Roosevelt and Churchill would not approve any fixed sum. But they agreed to accept the Russian proposal as the basis for future negotiations and to establish a reparations commission with headquarters in Moscow. The Russians withdrew their objection to French participation in the

---

[12]Cordell Hull had resigned because of ill health on November 21, 1944, after thirteen and a half years as secretary of state.

[13]Roosevelt and Churchill refused to agree to a definite cession of this territory to Poland. However, the American and British leaders agreed at the Potsdam Conference in July 1945 that the Poles should occupy the region between the Oder-Neisse rivers and the old eastern German boundary, pending settlement of the boundary by a future peace conference. The Poles at once proceeded to incorporate the territory, expel the German population, and settle the region with Poles.

occupation of Germany, and Stalin agreed also that France should have a seat on the Control Commission. As the several occupation zones had already been drawn by the European Advisory Commission in London, there was no discussion of this matter at Yalta.

THE GOVERNMENTS OF POLAND AND EASTERN EUROPE.   The crucial question was Poland's political future. Stalin and Molotov said quite frankly that they would not tolerate a Polish regime unfriendly to the USSR. As they pointed out, the Germans had twice within twenty-five years used Poland as the corridor for attacks against Russia. They insisted that Britain and the United States recognize a provisional Polish government in Lublin that Russia had sponsored and recognized. Roosevelt and Churchill adamantly refused. Then Stalin suggested that the Lublin government be enlarged to include some of the leaders of the Polish government-in-exile that the western powers supported and which was now in London. Roosevelt and Churchill again refused. Stalin finally agreed that the Lublin government should be reorganized to include Polish democratic leaders at home and abroad, and that free elections should be held at an early date to determine the future government of the country. Roosevelt made it clear that the British and American ambassadors in Warsaw would judge whether this pledge had been honestly kept.

The three powers pledged themselves to assist the peoples of other so-called liberated countries of eastern Europe to establish, through free elections, democratic governments responsive to popular will.[14]

THE ORGANIZATION OF THE UNITED NATIONS.   The Russians conceded practically everything for which Americans had contended at the Dumbarton Oaks Conference in discussions at Yalta over organization of the United Nations. First, they accepted the American formula for voting in the Security Council.[15] Second, the Soviets withdrew their demand for sixteen votes in the General Assembly and received in return additional representatives and votes for the Ukraine and White Russia.[16] Third, Stalin

[14]It should be added that Churchill and Eden had had conferences with Stalin in Moscow over the future of the Balkans in October 1944. They agreed that during the coming months Russia should have predominance in Rumania and Bulgaria, that Britain should have predominance in Greece, and that the two countries would share responsibility in Yugoslavia and Hungary. Churchill tried to make it clear, however, that the arrangement provided merely a temporary modus vivendi to prevent a conflict of British and Russian forces during the period of German withdrawal and should not be construed to authorize interference in the domestic affairs of the Balkan states. In any event, the Yalta agreements superseded the Churchill-Stalin agreement.

[15]The main issue here was whether the permanent members of the Security Council, that is, the great powers, should have the right to veto consideration of disputes to which they were a party. The Americans fought against use of the veto in such circumstances and overcame Russian objections at Yalta. The right of the great powers to use the veto in all important matters was not involved, for Americans and Russians alike insisted upon having veto over any proposed action by the Security Council.

[16]In return, Stalin and Churchill agreed that the United States might have three votes in the General Assembly if it so desired.

agreed to Roosevelt's proposal that all nations at war with Germany by March 1, 1945, might become members of the United Nations.

THE FAR EAST.   By secret agreement between the Americans and Russians, which Churchill approved but did not help make, and which was not published until February 11, 1946, Stalin agreed to bring Russia into the war against Japan within two or three months after the surrender of Germany. In return, the president approved the transfer of the Kurile Islands from Japan to Russia, recognized Russian control of Outer Mongolia, and agreed that Russia should recover all rights and territory lost at the end of the Russo-Japanese War.[17] Finally, Stalin agreed to recognize Chinese sovereignty over Manchuria and to conclude a treaty of friendship and alliance with the Nationalist government of China.

Millions of words have since been spoken and written about the Yalta agreements. Critics have called them base appeasement of Russia, betrayal of Poland and eastern Europe to Soviet imperialism, and useless surrender to communism in the Far East—all by a mentally incompetent president who was hoodwinked by the wily Stalin. Defenders have replied that the agreements were necessary and realistic.

The charge that Roosevelt was mentally incompetent is most easily disposed of. Roosevelt was obviously tired at Yalta and exhausted afterward by the strain of the grueling sessions and of his long journeys. But there is no evidence that he was not in full possession of his mental faculties during the conference itself.[18] The consensus of historical judgment rather emphatically supports the conclusion that Roosevelt and Churchill achieved nearly everything that circumstances permitted. They undoubtedly knew the risks they were running in the agreements on Poland and eastern Europe. They knew also that they had no alternative but to accept a compromise and hope that the Russians would honor it. The Russians were already in eastern Europe. The United States and Britain might conceivably have driven them out, but neither the Anglo-American peoples nor soldiers would have tolerated even the suggestion of a long and bloody war to save Poland or Rumania from Communist domination. These were the two prime historical realities with which Roosevelt and Churchill had to reckon, and from which Stalin could benefit, at Yalta. The Anglo-American leaders obtained important concessions from Stalin in spite of their weak bargaining positions. Future conflicts with the Soviet

[17]This commitment involved (a) transfer of the southern half of Sakhalin from Japan to Russia; (b) internationalization of the port of Dairen and safeguarding of "the pre-eminent interests of the Soviet Union in this port"; (c) restoration of the Russian lease on Port Arthur as a naval base; and (d) joint Soviet-Chinese operation of the Chinese Eastern Railway and the South Manchurian Railway.

[18]It might be well in passing to mention the charge that Alger Hiss, who was a member of the State Department staff at Yalta, and who had been an agent for the Soviet spy ring in the 1930s, was the principal author of the Yalta agreements. It has never been demonstrated that Hiss had any influence in determining any important decisions at the conference.

Union developed not because the Russians honored the Yalta agreements, but precisely because they violated them.

We now know that Roosevelt concluded the secret Far Eastern agreement with Stalin because he and his military advisers believed that the Japanese would not surrender unconditionally without invasion and occupation. Moreover, no one yet knew whether the atomic bomb would explode or what damage it would do. Acting on the advice of his military advisers, Roosevelt made the agreement with Stalin, he thought, in order to prevent the death of perhaps 1 million American men in bloody campaigns in Japan and on the Asiatic mainland. To avert this catastrophe, the president virtually let Stalin name his own price for Soviet participation. Actually, Soviet Far Eastern policy was neither determined nor defined at Yalta. It is a fair assumption that the Russians would have entered the war against Japan and reestablished themselves as a major Far Eastern power whether the Americans liked it or not.[19]

Critics of the Yalta agreements tend to forget that the Russians, also, made substantial concessions. They agreed to participate in a United Nations that would certainly be controlled by the Anglo-American bloc; to give France a share in the control of Germany; and to respect the integrity of the peoples of eastern Europe. They seemed determined to act reasonably and to meet Churchill and Roosevelt halfway on all important issues. Roosevelt and Churchill, therefore, acted in the only manner that was historically possible. As Churchill put it, "Our hopeful assumptions were soon to be falsified. Still, they were the only ones possible at the time."

11. Victory in Europe

The British and American armies approached the Siegfried line in September 1944. Eisenhower made an effort to turn the northern flank of the German defenses by landing three airborne divisions to capture bridges across the Meuse, Waal, and Rhine rivers. This effort failed when the British First Airborne Division was unable to hold a bridge across the Rhine at Arnhem, and the Allies were denied the opportunity to make a rapid drive across the north German plain. Instead, they brought up reinforcements for a winter campaign through the heavy German defenses manned by armies now regrouped and strengthened.

While American and British armies were probing along the length of the Siegfried line, Hitler laid plans for one final gamble—a counteroffensive

---

[19]It might be added, also, that Chiang Kai-shek, who was not informed until much later of the details of the Far Eastern agreement, was delighted by the Russian promise of a treaty of alliance because he thought that it meant Soviet neutrality in the Nationalist government's war with the Chinese Communists.

through the weak center of the Allied lines in the Ardennes Forest. This he hoped would split the enemy's forces and carry to Liège and perhaps Antwerp. Bad weather in late November and early December enabled Von Rundstedt, the German commander, to bring up his forces in secret. They struck furiously in the Ardennes on December 16 and scored heavily until Allied counterattacks forced them to withdraw. The Battle of the Bulge, as the German offensive is commonly known, was over by January 1945. Hitler's gamble had cost him his last reserves of aircraft and some of his best divisions.

In fact, the German army in the west was so weakened by ruinous losses in the Ardennes counteroffensive that it could no longer prevent the Allied armies from advancing to the Rhine. Forces under Field Marshal Montgomery captured Cleves, in the north, on February 12. Cologne fell to the American First Army on March 6. Troops of the French First and the American Third and Seventh armies had cleared the Saar and Palatinate areas in the south by March 25. Meanwhile, American troops by an unbelievable stroke of good luck captured the Ludendorff Bridge across the Rhine at Remagen on March 7 before it could be demolished. They quickly established a bridgehead on the other side of the river.

Anglo-American armies were now poised along the Rhine for a final drive into the heart of Germany, and Russian armies were massed on the Oder River for an assault upon Berlin. But new tensions between the western democracies and Russia gave warning of troubled times ahead. For one thing, the Russians in February 1945 had imposed a Communist government on Rumania. For another thing, Anglo-American negotiations with a German general for surrender of German forces in Italy had caused Stalin to address a letter to Roosevelt virtually accusing him and Churchill of treacherously negotiating for surrender of all German forces in the west so that British and American armies could occupy Berlin before the Russians.

Even more ominous were Russian actions in Poland. The Russians had not only refused to honor the Yalta agreement to reorganize the puppet Lublin government, but they had also refused to allow American and British observers to enter Poland and had proceeded to liquidate the leaders of the democratic parties in that unhappy country. It was plain that Stalin would tolerate no Polish government that he could not completely control; indeed, he admitted as much in correspondence with Churchill. The Polish dispute was nearing the point of open rupture by mid-March, but Roosevelt was now so weak that he had lost his grasp and could not take leadership in opposing Soviet violations of the Yalta agreements. Actually, Poland was irretrievably lost to Soviet domination, as Stalin's blunt replies to Churchill's vigorous protests revealed.

Poland was lost, but not yet Prague and Berlin, if the Allies resolved to act quickly and send their armies hurtling across Germany. Churchill perceived clearly enough that "Soviet Russia had become a mortal danger to

ALLIED OFFENSIVES TO THE RHINE
1944-1945

GREAT BRITAIN

Norwich

NORTH SEA

NETH.

Amsterdam

BATTLE LINE
DECEMBER 15
1944

Ipswich

The Hague
Rotterdam

Arnhem

Münster

G E R M A N Y

London

Dover

BELG.

WAAL
MAAS

Essen
Dortmund
Düsseldorf
Cologne

Kassel

Dunkirk

Ghent
Brussels

Antwerp

Bonn

Brighton

Portsmouth

Calais

Lille

Aachen

REMAGEN
BRIDGE
MAR. 7, 1945

Boulogne

BATTLE OF
THE BULGE
DEC. 1944

Coblenz

Frankfurt

ENGLISH CHANNEL

Abbeville

Cambrai

Dinant

Bastogne

Mainz

Cherbourg

BREAKOUT
AT ST. LO
JULY 25, 1944

Amiens

Sedan

LUX.

SAAR

Mannheim

Le Havre

Rouen

Compiegne

Reims

Verdun

Metz

Karlsruhe

St. Lo
Caen
Falaise

SEINE

Paris

Nancy

Strasbourg

Avranches

Evreux

MEUSE

Rennes

Chartres

SEINE

Sens

Epinal

Colmar

Freiburg

Laval

Le Mans

Orléans

Belfort

Loriant

Basel

St. Nazaire

Angers

LOIRE

Sombernon

Dijon

Besançon

Bern

SWITZ.

Nantes

Tours

Bourges

Nevers

SAONE

F R A N C E

La Rochelle
Rochefort

Vichy

Bourg

Geneva

Limoges

Clermont
Farrand

Lyon

Grenoble

Turin

ITALY

GARONNE

Bordeaux

RHONE

Montélimar

Savona

Sisteron

Nice

Avignon

Bayonne

Toulouse

Montpellier

St. Raphaël

Narbonne

Marseille

St.
Tropez

Toulon

LANDINGS
IN SOUTHERN FRANCE
AUGUST 15, 1944

Perpignan

SPAIN

Lérida

Barcelona

Pamplona

AMERICAN
BRITISH AND
CANADIAN
FRENCH

100 MILES

TRM

the free world." He pleaded all through April and early May with his American colleagues to push as rapidly as possible toward the two central European capitals. Even more important, he proposed that the Allies stay in force on this forward eastern line until the Russians had honored earlier promises.[20]

The reasons for failure to attempt to seize strong outposts in Central Europe can best be seen in an account of military and political events. The combined Anglo-American armies began their crossing of the Rhine on March 24. Montgomery's forces in the north and Bradley's in the center had converged by April 1 to encircle the Ruhr and trap more than 250,000 German troops. General Montgomery was all for driving straight to Berlin. But Eisenhower, for what seemed to be sound military reasons, decided to "push his main force from the Kassel-Frankfurt area to the Elbe, split the German forces, cut off Berlin from the so-called 'National Redoubt' area [the Bavarian mountains, where Hitler was reputed to be preparing for a last stand], and then turn his forces directly to the north and to the southwest of the Elbe. These maneuvers would enable him to seize ports on the North Sea and the Baltic and also clean up the area to the south before the enemy could assemble a force there."[21]

Eisenhower relayed this decision to Stalin directly on March 28. Stalin approved, but Churchill was so distressed that he appealed personally to Roosevelt to join him in ordering the supreme commander to move against Berlin. "I deem it highly important," the prime minister wrote to Eisenhower on April 2, "that we should shake hands with the Russians as far to the east as possible." Eisenhower, however, argued that his plan was sound on military grounds; and he had the firm support of other American field generals. "I could see no political advantage accruing from the capture of Berlin that would offset the need for quick destruction of the German army on our front," Bradley writes. "As soldiers we looked naïvely on the British inclination to complicate the war with political foresight and nonmilitary objectives."[22]

The vanguard of the American army reached the Elbe, only fifty-three miles from Berlin. The Russians were still on the banks of the Oder, thirty to forty miles from the German capital. Churchill now redoubled his pleading, but his voice was no longer heard in Washington. Roosevelt was tired and unable to stand any longer at the helm. He wanted rest and recovery, not a new quarrel with the Russians. He went to Warm Springs

[20]The Big Three at Yalta had approved the occupation zones drawn earlier by the European Advisory Commission, but Roosevelt and Churchill had made no agreement anywhere to stop their armies at any certain point. Churchill argued that Russian violations had already invalidated the Yalta agreements. He proposed to occupy as much of the Soviet zone of Germany and of Czechoslovakia as possible, and to stay there until the Russians lived up to the agreement on Poland and consented to a real integration of the occupation administration in Germany.

[21]Forrest C. Pogue, "The Decision to Halt at the Elbe," in K. R. Greenfield (ed.), *Command Decisions* (New York, 1959), p. 378.

[22]Omar N. Bradley, *A Soldier's Story* (New York, 1951), pp. 535–536.

early in April to renew his strength before opening the San Francisco Conference of the United Nations on April 25. On April 12 he complained of a terrific headache, lost consciousness, and died at 4:35 P.M. of a massive cerebral hemorrhage.

Roosevelt's growing weakness and death came at a fateful time in the history of the world. The new president, Harry S. Truman, had been utterly unprepared by his predecessor. Eisenhower had submitted a plan for further action to the Combined Chiefs of Staff on April 7. He proposed pushing through to the Elbe near Leipzig and then turning northward to the Baltic coast in order to prevent the Russians from occupying any part of the Danish peninsula. He added that he saw no point in making Berlin a military objective, but that he would cheerfully accept the decision of the Combined Chiefs of Staff on this matter. The military leaders did not discuss the question of Berlin. President Truman supported Eisenhower's proposal. Even Churchill agreed on April 19 that the Anglo-American forces were "not immediately in a position to force their way into Berlin." Eisenhower informed Stalin of his plan on April 21, adding that he intended to send forces not only northward but also southward into the Danube Valley. He sent General Patton into Bavaria on the following day.

Even at this date Eisenhower could have captured Prague with ease, and Churchill pleaded for action that "might make the whole difference to the postwar situation in Czechoslovakia." Eisenhower in response decided to send Patton into Prague and so informed the Soviet high command. But he called Patton back after receiving a vehement protest from Stalin. Thus while the Americans waited the Russians occupied Prague on May 9.

Meanwhile, Hitler remained in Berlin, confident that a miracle would yet save the Third Reich. He was heartened by Roosevelt's death and certain that the western Allies and Russia would soon turn against each other. But *Götterdämmerung* was near. Marshal Georgi K. Zhukov began a massive offensive across the Oder on April 15 that reached the suburbs of Berlin a week later. American and Russian troops met on the Elbe near Torgau on April 27. Italian partisans captured and shot Mussolini on the following day. Hitler married his mistress, Eva Braun, in his bunker in Berlin and appointed Admiral Karl Doenitz his successor on April 29. He committed suicide on the next day, and his body was burned in the garden of the Reichschancellery.

Nothing remained but to end the war as quickly as possible. Nearly 1 million German troops in northern Italy and Austria surrendered on May 2. Two days later German troops in northwest Germany, Holland, Schleswig-Holstein, and Denmark laid down their arms. Then Colonel General Alfred Jodl surrendered unconditionally the remnants of the German army, air force, and navy at Eisenhower's headquarters at Rheims at 2:41 A.M. on May 7. All hostilities ceased at midnight May 8, 1945.

12. Victory in the Pacific

American ground, naval, and air power in the Pacific was overwhelmingly preponderant by the early summer of 1944. The American navy was now five times stronger than the imperial fleet. The time had come to close in on the stronghold of the enemy's inner ring. Admiral Raymond A. Spruance with a huge force of ships, aircraft, and troops moved against the strongly held Marianas, about 1,350 miles south of Tokyo. After a bitter struggle, in which the Japanese fought fanatically, the three principal islands in the group, Saipan, Tinian, and Guam, fell before the overpowering assault. While Americans were invading Saipan a large Japanese force of 9 aircraft carriers, 5 battleships, and other ships sailed from the Philippines to intercept the invaders. Over 500 Japanese airplanes attacked and slightly damaged a battleship and 2 carriers on June 19, 1944. But the Japanese lost 402 airplanes and pilots, the core of their naval aviation. Pursuing American submarines and aircraft caught up with the Japanese fleet on June 20. On that date they sank 3 Japanese carriers and 2 destroyers and severely damaged 1 battleship, 4 carriers, and other craft in the first Battle of the Philippine Sea. American naval and ground forces then attacked the western Caroline Islands in September, overpowering fierce resistance on Peleliu, Angaur, and Ngesebus islands, and neutralizing the main Japanese garrisons on the islands of Babelthuap and Yap.

While Admiral Nimitz's forces were clearing the Central Pacific route to the Philippines, General MacArthur farther in the Southwest Pacific was making final preparations for an invasion of the islands. First came an Allied drive in April and May 1944 that cleared the northern coast of New Guinea; next, amphibious offensives against Wakde, Biak, Noemfoor, and other islands off the northwestern coast of New Guinea that cleared the lower approaches to the Philippines; finally, capture of Morotai Island in September, which put the Southwest Pacific forces within striking distance. As prelude to the great invasion, land-based bombers and planes from carriers of the Third Fleet scourged Japanese airfields and installations in Mindanao, Luzon, and Formosa during September and October. These operations practically destroyed Japanese air power in the area and disrupted Japanese sea communications. Then Americans returned on October 20 to redeem their pledge to liberate the Philippines—with an invasion of Leyte Island by the Sixth Army, the Seventh Fleet under Admiral Thomas C. Kinkaid, and the Third Fleet under Admiral Halsey.

The Japanese admirals well knew that American conquest of the Philippines would spell the doom of the empire, because it would cut communication between Japan and Indochina, Malaya, and the East Indies. They made one last desperate effort to destroy the American invaders in Leyte

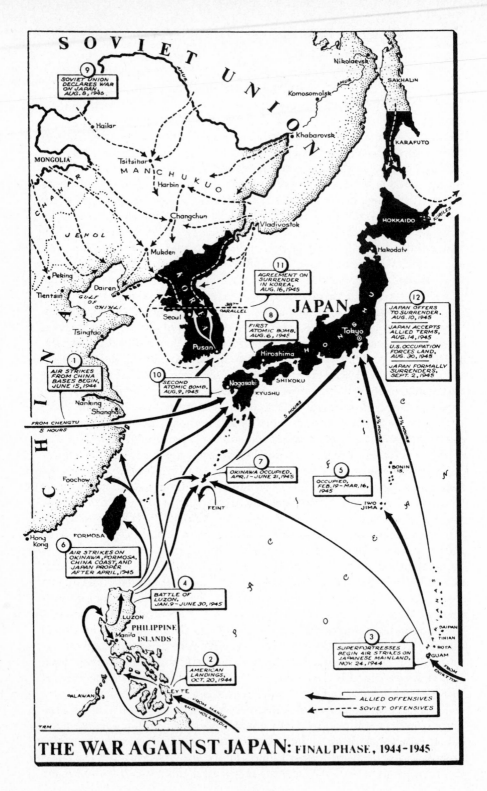

9 SOVIET UNION DECLARES WAR ON JAPAN, AUG. 8, 1945

11 AGREEMENT ON SURRENDER IN KOREA, AUG. 16, 1945

12 JAPAN OFFERS TO SURRENDER, AUG. 10, 1945

JAPAN ACCEPTS ALLIED TERMS, AUG. 14, 1945

U.S. OCCUPATION FORCES LAND, AUG. 30, 1945

JAPAN FORMALLY SURRENDERS, SEPT. 2, 1945

8 FIRST ATOMIC BOMB, AUG. 6, 1945

1 AIR STRIKES FROM CHINA BASES BEGIN, JUNE 15, 1944

10 SECOND ATOMIC BOMB, AUG. 9, 1945

FROM CHENGTU 5 HOURS

7 OKINAWA OCCUPIED, APR. 1 – JUNE 21, 1945

5 OCCUPIED, FEB. 19 – MAR. 16, 1945

6 AIR STRIKES ON OKINAWA, FORMOSA, CHINA COAST, AND JAPAN PROPER AFTER APRIL, 1945

4 BATTLE OF LUZON, JAN. 9 – JUNE 30, 1945

3 SUPERFORTRESSES BEGIN AIR STRIKES ON JAPANESE MAINLAND, NOV. 24, 1944

2 AMERICAN LANDINGS, OCT. 20, 1944

FROM MANUS AND HOLLANDIA

FEINT

→ ALLIED OFFENSIVES
--→ SOVIET OFFENSIVES

THE WAR AGAINST JAPAN: FINAL PHASE, 1944-1945

Gulf. The three naval engagements that ensued between October 24 and 25—the battle of Surigao Strait, the battle off Samar, and the battle off Cape Engaño, collectively known as the Battle for Leyte Gulf—ended disastrously for the Japanese. In this greatest naval battle in history the Japanese lost practically their entire fleet—three battleships, four carriers, nine cruisers, and eight destroyers.

The threat of Japanese naval intervention was forever ended, and MacArthur could now press forward with his overwhelming campaign in the Philippines. While the invasion of Leyte was at its height, he launched an attack against Mindoro in December and then attacked Luzon from Lingayen Gulf in early January 1945. Not until July 5, however, were the Japanese rooted out of the mountains of northern Luzon and out of Mindanao and dozens of smaller islands. All told, Japan lost over 400,000 men and 9,000 planes in the entire Philippines campaign.

The American conquest of the Marianas, western Carolines, and Philippines blasted the inner rim of Japanese defenses, cut communications between the home islands and Indochina, Malaya, and the East Indies, and reduced the Japanese navy to the size of a single task force. Equally important, it afforded advanced bases from which to bomb the homeland of the empire. Indeed, the air war against Japan had already begun in June 1944, when a force of large new B-29 Superfortresses of the Twentieth Air Force, operating from bases in China, attacked steel works in Kyushu. The Twentieth Air Force made subsequent raids on Japan and Manchuria, but its operations were limited because all its supplies and bombs had to be flown over the Himalayan Hump from India. A massive B-29 attack became possible only with the capture of Saipan in the Marianas. The capture of Iwo Jima later yielded bases for American fighter planes and fighter-bombers that joined in the increasing aerial assault. All told, American planes dropped about 160,000 tons of bombs on the Japanese home islands from November 1944, when the bombardment from the Marianas began, to September 1945, when the war ended.

Although the tonnage of bombs dropped on Japan was about one-ninth of that dropped on Germany, the physical destruction in Japan almost equaled that in Germany. American bombs killed 330,000 Japanese civilians and injured nearly 500,000; moreover, they destroyed 2,510,000 buildings and 40 percent of the built-up areas of sixty-six cities. The effects on the Japanese war economy were equally devastating. Air attacks by July 1945 had reduced the productive capacity of Japanese oil refineries by 83 percent, aircraft engine plants by 75 percent, electronics and communication equipment plants by 70 percent, and munitions factories by some 30 percent. For a nation with an industrial capacity only 10 percent that of its chief enemy, these losses were fatal.

Let us now turn back to the last phase of the relentless American drive by land and sea toward Japan. While MacArthur was bringing the Philippines campaign to its climax, marine divisions invaded Iwo Jima, 750 miles south of Japan, on February 19, 1945. The Japanese defenders had made the island virtually one vast pillbox. They fought so courageously that the Iwo Jima operation was the bloodiest in the history of the United States Marine Corps. However, the entire island, with its two airfields, was in American hands by March 16. Next came a larger attack, beginning April 1, by marine and army forces against Okinawa, a large island in the Ryu-kyus only 350 miles southwest of Japan. The Japanese and American lead-ers both knew that the fall of Okinawa would spell the early doom of the empire. The defenders, therefore, fought fanatically during the battle that raged from April 1 to June 21 and lost nearly 111,000 dead and 9,000 prisoners. The most spectacular aspect of the defense was the unrelenting and often effective Kamikaze, or suicide, attacks by Japanese aircraft against American warships and transports. All told, the Japanese lost some 4,000 aircraft, 3,500 of them in Kamikaze attacks, during the Battle of Okinawa.

By this time the main question was whether Japan would collapse inter-nally before the Americans had launched their final invasion of the island empire. We have noted the terrible devastation wrought by the Superfor-tresses from Saipan. They were joined in February 1945 by thousands of planes of the Third Fleet and in April by fighter-bombers from Iwo Jima and Okinawa. American battleships and heavy cruisers joined in the attack in mid-July by shelling steel works, synthetic oil plants, and other indus-trial targets on the mainland and by heavy attacks upon Japanese shipping. But Japan was suffering most from a combined sea, air, and mine blockade that had reduced her once large merchant fleet to ineffectiveness and deprived her people of food and her industries of vital raw materials.[23]

Indeed, it had been evident to certain Japanese leaders since the au-tumn of 1943 that they were fighting a losing battle, and that the imperial government should seek peace, even at the cost of giving up China, Korea, and Formosa. On July 18, 1944, soon after the American invasion of the Marianas, a moderate group led principally by the naval chieftains forced Tojo to resign and establish a new cabinet under General Kuniaki Koiso. An important element in the new government, led by Navy Minister Mi-tsumasa Yonai and allied with officials in the imperial court, were deter-mined to end the war as quickly as possible. The emperor threw his full support to the peace party in February 1945. After the invasion of Oki-nawa on April 8, he appointed Baron Kantaro Suzuki as premier and ordered him to end the war. Suzuki, however, did not control the army. It was determined to fight to the bitter end and threatened to revolt if the cabinet moved for peace. Thus the cabinet began secret discussions in

---

[23] Japan entered the war with 6 million tons of merchant shipping and constructed an additional 4.1 million tons between 1941 and 1945. Of this total of 10.1 million tons, the Japanese lost 8.9 million—54.7 percent to submarines, 16.3 percent to carrier-based planes, 14.5 percent to land-based planes, 9.3 percent to mines laid by B-29s, 4 percent to marine accidents, and less than 1 percent to surface gunfire.

May with the Russian ambassador, Jacob Malik, looking toward Russian mediation. In addition, the emperor appealed directly to the Soviet government in June and July to help arrange peace talks with the United States.

This was the situation when Truman, Churchill, Clement Attlee, soon to be Churchill's successor, and Stalin met at Potsdam on July 17, 1945, for the last conference of the Big Three. Truman almost certainly knew about the Japanese peace overtures even before the Potsdam Conference met; in any event, Stalin soon gave full information about them. The president was not inclined to take the overtures seriously. He did not trust the Japanese, and his military advisers believed that Japan would not surrender until Allied forces had invaded and occupied the islands. He therefore approved a discouraging Soviet reply to Tokyo.

Meanwhile, word had come to the American leaders at Postdam on July 16 that an atomic bomb had been exploded in New Mexico. Knowing that the bomb was a reality (there were materials on hand to assemble two additional bombs at once), and that its use might avert the necessity of a long and bloody campaign, Truman now concentrated on a public warning to Japan. It was the Potsdam Declaration issued on July 26 under Truman's, Churchill's, and Chiang Kai-shek's signatures. It promised stern justice to Japanese war criminals and enforcement of the Cairo Declaration stripping Japan of all conquests. But it also held out the hope of generous treatment of a Japan purged and reformed. "The alternative for Japan," it concluded, "is prompt and utter destruction."

The leaders of the Suzuki government in Tokyo agreed to accept the Potsdam Declaration but could not persuade the army leaders to surrender. When Suzuki declared on July 28, only for home consumption, that the Potsdam Declaration was "unworthy of public notice," President Truman and his advisers took this as a refusal and decided to use the atomic bomb.[24] The decision was made largely on military grounds. The Japanese were doomed, to be sure, but they still had large supplies of weapons and an army of 2 million in the home islands. An invasion would surely have succeeded only at great human costs on both sides.

Thus a lone B-29 flew over Hiroshima on August 6 and dropped the first atomic bomb used in warfare. It leveled 4.4 square miles of the city and killed between 70,000 and 80,000 persons. On the same day President Truman announced the news to the world and warned the Japanese that if they did not surrender they could expect "a rain of ruin from the air, the likes of which has never been seen on this earth." Still the Japanese army

---

[24]This decision to use the bomb if the Japanese refused to surrender was actually made at Potsdam on July 22, after intensive discussions among Truman, American military leaders, and Churchill, and after earlier discussions in the War Department and among the scientists involved in the Manhattan Project. Most of the scientists either opposed using the atomic bomb or else proposed dropping one on an uninhabited area as a demonstration and warning to the Japanese leaders.

refused to surrender. Then, on August 9, news came to Tokyo that Russia had entered the war,[25] and that the Americans had dropped a second atomic bomb on Nagasaki. When hurried conferences failed to yield agreement to accept the Potsdam ultimatum, the emperor made the decision for peace. The cabinet informed Washington on the following day that it accepted the Potsdam terms, provided that the status of the emperor would not be changed. The military and naval chieftains balked when Washington replied on August 11 that the emperor must be subject to the supreme commander of the Allied powers. But the emperor insisted, and the Suzuki government formally accepted the Allied demands on August 14. The emperor at once prepared records of an imperial rescript ordering his armed forces to surrender; and the cabinet, after suppressing an insurrection of army fanatics, sent emissaries to General MacArthur to arrange the details of surrender. A great Allied fleet entered Tokyo Bay on September 2. Soon afterward Foreign Minister Mamoru Shigemitsu and a representative of the imperial general staff signed articles of surrender on board the battleship *Missouri*. General MacArthur and representatives of the Allied powers accepted on behalf of their respective governments.

[25]The conferees at Potsdam had given careful attention to Russian plans for participation. American leaders still welcomed Russian intervention even though they were by no means as eager for it as they had been earlier.

Suggested Additional Reading

---

1. AMERICAN POLITICS FROM THEODORE ROOSEVELT THROUGH
   FRANKLIN D. ROOSEVELT

A. *Aspects of the Progressive Revolt*

For the origins and immediate background, see Charles A. Barker, *Henry George* (1955); Chester McA. Destler, *Henry Demarest Lloyd and the Empire of Reform* (1963); Sidney Fine, *Laissez Faire and the General Welfare State* (1956); and Harold U. Faulkner, *Politics, Reform, and Expansion, 1890-1900* (1959). The best single account of the origins of progressivism is David P. Thelen, *The New Citizenship: Origins of Progressivism in Wisconsin, 1885-1900* (1972). Among other general works are John D. Buenker, *Urban Liberalism and Progressive Reform* (1973); Robert H. Wiebe, *The Search for Order, 1877-1920* (1967); Richard Hofstadter, *The Age of Reform* (1955); Samuel P. Hays, *The Response to Industrialism, 1885-1914* (1957); Eric F. Goldman, *Rendezvous with Destiny* (1953); Harold U. Faulkner, *The Quest for Social Justice, 1898-1914* (1931); Benjamin P. De Witt, *The Progressive Movement* (1915); Russell B. Nye, *Midwestern Progressive Politics* (1951); C. Vann Woodward, *Origins of the New South, 1877-1913* (1951); Jack T. Kirby, *Darkness at the Dawning: Race and Reform in the Progressive South* (1972); and Hugh C. Bailey, *Liberalism in the New South* (1969). Significant phases are illuminated by James H. Timberlake, *Prohibition and the Progressive Movement, 1900–1920* (1963); Samuel P. Hays, *Conservation and the Gospel of Efficiency: The Progressive Conservation Movement, 1890–1920* (1959); L. E. Fredman, *The Australian Ballot: The Story of an American Reform* (1968); Robert H. Wiebe, *Businessmen and Reform: A Study of the Progressive Movement* (1962); Samuel Haber, *Efficiency and Uplift: Scientific Management in the Progressive Era* (1964); and Mark H. Haller, *Eugenics: Hereditarian Attitudes in American Thought* (1963).

Still the classic accounts of the progressive revolts in the cities and states are Lincoln Steffens, *The Shame of the Cities* (1904) and *The Struggle for Self-Government* (1906), which should be read with *The Autobiography of Lincoln Steffens* (1931). The secondary literature on urban and state progressivism and problems is growing by leaps and bounds. For general introductions to the former, see Charles N. Glaab, *The American City* (1963); Blake McKelvey, *The Urbanization of America, 1860–1915* (1963) and *The Emergence of Metropolitan America, 1915–1966* (1968); Frank M. Stewart, *A Half-Century of Municipal Reform: The History of the National Municipal League* (1950); Mel Scott, *American City Planning Since 1890* (1969); and John W. Reps, *The Making of Urban America: A History of City Planning in the United States* (1965).

Among the particular studies that highlight urban reform are James B. Crooks, *Politics and Progress: The Rise of Urban Progressivism in Baltimore, 1895 to 1911* (1968); Zane L. Miller, *Boss Cox's Cincinnati: Urban Politics in the Progressive Era* (1968); Melvin G. Holli, *Reform in Detroit: Hazen S. Pingree and Urban Politics* (1969); William D. Miller, *Memphis During the Progressive Era, 1900–1917* (1957); George S. Reynolds, *Machine Politics in New Orleans, 1897–1926* (1936); and Bradley R. Rice, *Progressive Cities: The Commission Government Movement in America, 1901–1920* (1977). Joel A. Tarr, *A Study in Boss Politics: William Lorimer of Chicago* (1971), makes a strong case for the social usefulness of the city boss.

Excellent state studies include Ransom E. Noble, Jr., *New Jersey Progressivism Before Wilson* (1946); George E. Mowry, *The California Progressives* (1951), which should be supplemented by Olin C. Spencer, Jr., *California's Prodigal Sons: Hiram Johnson and the Progressives, 1911–1917* (1968), and Michael P. Rogin and J. L. Shover, *Political Change in California: Critical Elections and Social Movements, 1896–1966* (1970); Robert S. Maxwell, *La Follette and the Rise of the Progressives in Wisconsin* (1956); Herbert F. Margulies, *The Decline of the Progressive Movement in Wisconsin, 1890–1920* (1968); Stanley P. Caine, *The Myth of a Progressive Reform: Railroad Regulation in Wisconsin, 1903–1910* (1970); Carl H. Chrislock, *The Progressive Era in Minnesota, 1899–1918* (1971); Irwin Yellowitz, *Labor and the Progressive Movement in New York State, 1897–1916* (1965); Richard M. Abrams, *Conservatism in a Progressive Era: Massachusetts Politics, 1900–1912* (1964); Sheldon Hackney, *Populism to Progressivism in Alabama* (1969); Albert D. Kirwan, *The Revolt of the Rednecks: Mississippi Politics, 1876–1925* (1951); Raymond H. Pulley, *Old Virginia Restored: An Interpretation of the Progressive Impulse* (1968); Allen W. Moger, *Virginia: Bourbonism to Byrd, 1870–1925* (1968); and Charles Granville Hamilton, *Progressive Mississippi* (1978). Prohibition was often an important aspect of progressivism on the state level. There are studies on Tennessee by Paul E. Isaac, on Virginia by C. C. Pearson and

J. Edwin Hendricks, on Alabama by James Benson Sellers, on North Carolina by Daniel J. Whitener, and on California by Gilman M. Ostrander.

Among the biographies of city and state leaders, some of the following range far beyond the scope of this section: Alpheus T. Mason, *Brandeis: A Free Man's Life* (1946); Melvin I. Urofsky, *A Mind of One Piece: Brandeis and American Reform* (1971); Belle C. and Fola La Follette, *Robert M. La Follette* (2 vols., 1953); Aubrey L. Brooks and H. T. Lefler (eds.), *The Papers of Walter Clark* (2 vols., 1948-1950); Joseph L. Morrison, *Josephus Daniels: The Small-D Democrat* (1966); Dewey W. Grantham, *Hoke Smith and the Politics of the New South* (1958); Oliver H. Orr, Jr., *Charles Brantley Aycock* (1961); William Larsen, *Montague of Virginia: The Making of a Southern Progressive* (1965); Richard Lowitt, *George W. Norris, The Making of a Progressive* (1963); G. Wallace Chessman, *Governor Theodore Roosevelt: The Albany Apprenticeship, 1898-1900* (1965); Robert F. Wesser, *Charles Evans Hughes: Politics and Reform in New York, 1905-1910* (1967); Nancy Joan Weiss, *Charles Francis Murphy, 1858-1924: Respectability and Responsibility in Tammany Politics* (1968); Robert M. Crunden, *A Hero in Spite of Himself: Brand Whitlock in Art, Politics, and War* (1969); Jack Tager, *The Intellectual as Urban Reformer: Brand Whitlock and the Progressive Movement* (1968); William B. Hixson, Jr., *Moorefield Storey and the Abolitionist Tradition* (1972); Rupert N. Richardson, *Colonel Edward M. House: The Texas Years, 1858-1912* (1964); William D. Miller, *Mr. Crump of Memphis* (1964); Edwin R. Lewinson, *John Purroy Mitchel, the Boy Mayor of New York* (1965); J. Joseph Huthmacher, *Senator Robert F. Wagner and the Rise of Urban Liberalism* (1968); and William F. Holmes, *The White Chief: James Kimble Vardaman* (1970). Daniel Levine, *Varieties of Reform Thought* (1964), dealing with Jane Addams, Samuel Gompers, Robert M. La Follette, and others, is an important contribution.

We are now well on the way toward a comprehensive history of the social justice movement. Don D. Lescohier, "Working Conditions," and Elizabeth Brandeis, "Labor Legislation," in John R. Commons et al., *History of Labour in the United States* (4 vols., 1918-1935), Vol. III, contain much of the basic information. Robert H. Bremner, *From the Depths: The Discovery of Poverty in the United States* (1956), is a rich and eloquent general account, which should be supplemented by his brief *American Philanthropy* (1960). Roy Lubove, *The Professional Altruist: The Emergence of Social Work as a Career, 1880-1930* (1965) and *The Struggle for Social Security, 1900-1935* (1968), are important studies, as is Allen F. Davis, *Spearheads for Reform: The Social Settlements and the Progressive Movement, 1890-1914* (1967). On child labor reform, see Walter I. Trattner, *Crusade for Children* (1970); Jeremy P. Felt, *Hostages of Fortune: Child Labor Reform in New York State* (1965); and Elizabeth H. Davidson, *Child Labor Legislation in the Southern Textile States* (1939). Excellent biographies of social justice leaders are Daniel Levine, *Jane Addams and the Liberal Tradition* (1971); John C. Farrell, *Beloved Lady: A History of Jane Addams' Ideas on Reform and Peace* (1967); Josephine C. Goldmark, *Impatient Crusader: Florence Kelley's Life Story* (1953); Dorothy R. Blumberg, *Florence Kelley: The Making of a Social Pioneer* (1966); Louise C. Wade, *Graham Taylor: Pioneer for Social Justice, 1851-1938* (1964); Walter I. Trattner, *Homer Folks: Pioneer in Social Welfare* (1968); and Hugh C. Bailey, *Edgar Gardner Murphy: Gentle Progressive* (1968). (The Social Gospel movement is covered in Section 4D of this bibliography.)

On the muckrakers, there is a rich literature: Cornelius C. Regier, *The Era of the Muckrakers* (1932); Louis Filler, *Crusaders for American Liberalism* (1939); Harold S. Wilson, *McClure's Magazine and the Muckrakers* (1971); Daniel Aaron, *Men of Good Hope* (1951); Lloyd R. Morris, *Postscript to Yesterday* (1947); David Mark Chalmers, *The Social and Political Ideas of the Muckrakers* (1964); John E. Semonche, *Ray Stannard Baker: A Quest for Democracy in Modern America, 1870-1918* (1969); Robert C. Bannister, Jr., *Ray Stannard Baker: The Mind and Thought of a Progressive* (1966); Peter Lyon, *Success Story: The Life and Times of S. S. McClure* (1963); and Mary E. Tomkins, *Ida M. Tarbell* (1974). The writings of the muckrakers and the literature of revolt are discussed in Chapter 3 of this volume.

We still have no general history of intellectual progressivism, but see Henry S. Commager, *The American Mind* (1950); Charles Forcey, *The Crossroads of Liberalism: Croly, Weyl, Lippmann and the Progressive Era, 1900-1925* (1961); Benjamin G. Rader, *The Academic Mind and Reform: The Influence of Richard T. Ely in American Life* (1966); Jean B. Quandt, *From the Small Town to the Great Community: The Social Thought of Progressive Intellectuals* (1970); John Adam Moreau, *Randolph Bourne: Legend and Reality* (1966); Richard Hofstadter, *The Progressive Historians: Turner, Beard, Parrington* (1968); and Daniel M. Fox, *The Discovery of Abundance: Simon N. Patten and the Transformation of Social Theory* (1967). Eric F. Goldman, *Rendezvous with Destiny* (1953), and Alpheus T. Mason, *Brandeis: A Free Man's Life* (1946), also provide valuable insight. For the most important contributions by the intellectual progressives, see Chapter 3 of this volume.

The struggle for women's rights and woman suffrage, long neglected by professional historians, can now claim an imposing literature: Eleanor Flexner, *Century of Struggle, the Woman's Rights Movement in the United States* (1975); Aileen S. Kraditor, *The Ideas of the Woman Suffrage Movement, 1890-1920* (1965); Mildred Adams, *The Right to Be People* (1967); Andrew Sinclair, *The Emancipation of the American Woman* (1966); William L. O'Neill, *Everyone Was Brave: The Rise and Fall of Feminism in America* (1969), *The Woman Movement: Feminism in the United States and England* (1969), and *Divorce in the Progressive Era* (1967); Alan P. Grimes, *The Puritan Ethic and Woman Suffrage* (1967); David M. Kennedy, *Birth Control in America: The Career of Margaret Sanger* (1970); Anne Firor Scott, *The Southern Lady* (1971); and William H. Chafe, *Women and Equality: Changing Patterns in American Culture* (1977).

The literature on socialism and left wing unionism is large and excellent: David A. Shannon, *The Socialist Party of America: A History* (1955); John P. Diggins, *The American Left in the Twentieth Century* (1973); Donald D. Egbert and S. Persons (eds.), *Socialism and American Life* (2 vols., 1952); Howard H. Quint, *The Forging of American Socialism* (1953); Ira Kipnis, *The American Socialist Movement, 1897-1912* (1952); James Weinstein, *The Decline of Socialism in America, 1912-1925* (1967); John H. M. Laslett, *Labor and the Left: A Study of Socialist and Radical Influences in the American Labor Movement, 1881-1924* (1970); Laslett and Seymour Martin Lipset (eds.), *Failure of a Dream? Essays in the History of American Socialism* (1974); Henry F. Bedford, *Socialism and the Workers in Massachusetts, 1886-1912* (1966); Garin Burbank, *When Farmers Voted Red: The Gospel of Socialism in the Oklahoma Countryside, 1910-1924* (1976); Robert Laurence Moore, *European Socialists and the American Promised Land* (1970); Melvyn Dubofsky, *We Shall Be All: A History of the Industrial Workers of the World* (1969); Robert L. Tyler, *Rebels of the Woods: The I. W. W. in the Pacific Northwest* (1967); Ray Ginger, *The Bending Cross: A Biography of Eugene Victor Debs* (1949); Kent and Gretchen Kreuter, *An American Dissenter: The Life of Algie Martin Simons* (1969); and W. A. Swanberg, *Norman Thomas: The Last Idealist* (1976).

B. *The Republican Era, 1901–1913*

Arthur M. Schlesinger, Jr. (ed.), *History of U. S. Political Parties* (4 vols., 1973), and Schlesinger, Fred L. Israel, and William P. Hassen (eds.), *History of American Presidential Elections* (4 vols., 1971), are basic for the entire political history covered by this entire volume. George E. Mowry, *The Era of Theodore Roosevelt, 1900–1912* (1958), has filled the need for a good, concise political history of the Republican era. The first four volumes of Mark Sullivan, *Our Times: The United States, 1900–1925* (6 vols., 1926–1935), are racy and informative. Gabriel Kolko, *The Triumph of Conservatism: A Reinterpretation of American History, 1900–1916* (1963), and James Weinstein, *The Corporate Ideal in the Liberal State: 1900–1928* (1968), are provocative Marxist interpretations of the period. For other general studies, see Horace S. and Marion G. Merrill, *The Republican Command, 1897–1913* (1971); James Holt, *Congressional Insurgents and the Party System, 1909–1916* (1967); and Norman M. Wilensky, *Conservatives in the Progressive Era: The Taft Republicans of 1912* (1965).

For legislative issues, battles, and policies, see Frank W. Taussig, *Tariff History of the United States* (1931); Albro Martin, *Enterprise Denied: Origins of the Decline of American Railroads, 1897–1917* (1971), a highly revisionist study; Sidney Ratner, *American Taxation* (1942); M. Nelson McGeary, *Gifford Pinchot, Forester-Politician* (1960); Elmo P. Richardson, *The Politics of Conservation: Crusaders and Controversies, 1897–1913* (1962); Alpheus T. Mason, *Bureaucracy Convicts Itself: The Ballinger-Pinchot Controversy of 1910* (1941); James R. Penick, *Progressive Politics and Conservation: The Ballinger-Pinchot Affair* (1968); Hans Thorelli, *The Federal Antitrust Policy* (1954); William Z. Ripley, *Railroads: Rates and Regulation* (1912); Gabriel Kolko, *Railroads and Regulation, 1877–1916* (1965); Paul P. Van Riper, *History of the United States Civil Service* (1958); and Oscar E. Anderson, Jr., *The Health of a Nation: Harvey W. Wiley and the Fight for Pure Food* (1958).

The general biographical literature of this period grows increasingly richer. Henry F. Pringle, *Theodore Roosevelt, a Biography* (1931), long the standard, has been supplanted by William H. Harbaugh, *Power and Responsibility: The Life and Times of Theodore Roosevelt* (1961). Significant additions to Rooseveltian biography are Edmund Morris, *The Rise of Theodore Roosevelt* (1979), a brilliant portrayal of his subject to 1901; G. Wallace Chessman, *Theodore Roosevelt and the Politics of Power* (1968); and Willard B. Gatewood, Jr., *Theodore Roosevelt and the Art of Controversy: Episodes of the White House Years* (1970). However, no student should overlook Elting E. Morison and John M. Blum (eds.), *The Letters of Theodore Roosevelt* (8 vols., 1951–1954), and John M. Blum, *The Republican Roosevelt* (1954), for new information and insights. Henry F. Pringle, *The Life and Times of William Howard Taft* (2 vols., 1939), covers the entire period and beyond.

For other political leaders in this period, see Philip C. Jessup, *Elihu Root* (2 vols., 1938); Richard W. Leopold, *Elihu Root and the Conservative Tradition* (1954); Merlo J. Pusey, *Charles Evans Hughes* (2 vols., 1951); Carolyn W. Johnson, *Winthrop Murray Crane: A Study in Republican Leadership, 1829-1920* (1967); John A. Garraty, *Henry Cabot Lodge* (1953); Francis B. Simkins, *Pitchfork Ben Tillman* (1944); Richard Lowitt, *George W. Norris, The Making of a Progressive* (1963); John Braeman, *Albert J. Beveridge: American Nationalist* (1971); A. Bower Sageser, *Joseph L. Bristow: Kansas Progressive* (1968); Hermann Hagedorn, *Leonard Wood* (2 vols., 1931); Elting E. Morison, *Turmoil and Tradition: A Study of the Life and Times of Henry L. Stimson* (1960); Paul W. Glad, *The Trumpet Soundeth: William Jennings Bryan and His Democracy, 1896-1912* (1960); Paolo E. Coletta, *William Jennings Bryan: Political Evangelist, 1860-1908* (1964); and Louis W. Koenig, *Bryan: A Political Biography* (1971). George E. Mowry, *Theodore Roosevelt and the Progressive Movement* (1946), and Kenneth W. Hechler, *Insurgency: Personalities and Politics of the Taft Era* (1940), are excellent for the rise of the insurgents and the rupture of the GOP. J. Rogers Hollingsworth, *The Whirligig of Politics: The Democracy of Cleveland and Bryan* (1963), relates the fortunes of the Democratic party during this period of Republican ascendancy.

C. *The Wilson Era*

The only general works on the period 1912-1921 are Frederick L. Paxson, *The American Democracy and the World War* (3 vols., 1936-1948); and Arthur S. Link, *Woodrow Wilson and the Progressive Era* (1954). Louis Filler, *Appointment at Armageddon: Muckraking and Progressivism in the American Tradition* (1976), is excellent on the election of 1912. For aspects of domestic history, see Henry Parker Willis, *The Federal Reserve System* (1923), and J. Laurence Laughlin, *The Federal Reserve Act* (1933), for the background and writing of the Federal Reserve bill; John D. Clark, *The Federal Trust Policy* (1931), for the writing of the Clayton and Federal Trade Commission bills; and Stephen B. Wood, *Constitutional Politics in the Progressive Era: Child Labor and the Law* (1968), for the two child labor acts of the Wilson administration. George B. Tindall, *The Emergence of the New South, 1913-1945* (1967), discusses the relation of the South to Wilsonian policies. A. L. Todd, *Justice on Trial: The Case of Louis D. Brandeis* (1964), is a good account of the fight over the confirmation of Brandeis's appointment to the Supreme Court. Graham Adams, *Age of Industrial Violence, 1910-1915: The Activities and Findings of the United States Commission on Industrial Relations* (1966), is excellent on this subject.

The American home front during the war is treated by Seward W. Livermore, *Politics Is Adjourned: Woodrow Wilson and the War Congress, 1916-1918* (1966); Frederick Palmer, *Newton D. Baker: America at War* (2 vols., 1931); and Daniel R. Beaver, *Newton D. Baker and the American War Effort, 1917-1919* (1966). Arthur S. Link (ed.), *The Impact of World War I* (1969), reprints some of the significant articles on this subject. Bernard M. Baruch, *American Industry in War* (1941), discusses the problems of industrial mobilization. For special studies, see Alexander D. Noyes, *The War Period of American Finance, 1908-1925* (1926); Charles Gilbert, *American Financing of World War I* (1970); Walker D. Hines, *War History of American Railroads* (1928); Edward N. Hurley, *The Bridge to France* (1927); Frank M. Surface and R. L. Bland, *American Food in the World*

War and Reconstruction Period (1931); George Creel, *How We Advertised America* (1920); James R. Mock and C. Larson, *Words That Won the War: The Story of the Committee on Public Information, 1917-1919* (1939); Stephen Vaughn, *Holding Fast the Inner Lines: Democracy, Nationalism, and the Committee on Public Information* (1979), a highly revisionistic study; George T. Blakey, *Historians on the Home-Front: American Propagandists and the Great War* (1971); Carol S. Gruber, *Mars and Minerva: World War I and the Uses of Higher Learning in America* (1975); Frank L. Grubbs, Jr., *The Struggle for Labor Loyalty: Gompers, the A. F. of L., and the Pacifists, 1917-1920* (1968); Melvin I. Urofsky, *Big Steel and the Wilson Administration* (1969); Joan M. Jensen, *The Price of Vigilance* (1968); and H. C. Peterson and Gilbert C. Fite, *Opponents of War, 1917-1918* (1957).

There is a growing literature on demobilization and the politics and problems of the immediate postwar era. Mark Sullivan, *Our Times: The United States, 1900-1925* (6 vols., 1926-1935), Vols. V and VI; Frederick L. Paxson, *The American Democracy and the World War* (3 vols., 1936-1948), Vol. III; Frederick Lewis Allen, *Only Yesterday, an Informal History of the Nineteen-Twenties* (1931); William E. Leuchtenburg, *The Perils of Prosperity, 1914-1932* (1958); and Preston W. Slosson, *The Great Crusade and After, 1914-1928* (1930), are all good introductions. James R. Mock and E. Thurber, *Report on Demobilization* (1944), is more detailed. For good studies of the race riots from 1917 to 1920, see Elliott M. Rudwick, *Race Riot at East St. Louis* (1964); Charles F. Kellogg, *NAACP: A History, Volume I: 1909-1920* (1967); William M. Tuttle, Jr., *Race Riot: Chicago in the Red Summer of 1919* (1970); and Arthur I. Waskow, *From Race Riot to Sit-In* (1966). David Brody, *Labor in Crisis: The Steel Strike of 1919* (1965), is superb. For the Red scare, see Zechariah Chaffee, Jr.'s, indispensable *Free Speech in the United States* (1941); Robert K. Murray, *Red Scare: A Study in National Hysteria, 1919-1920* (1955); Stanley Coben, *A. Mitchell Palmer: Politician* (1963); Theodore Draper, *The Roots of American Communism* (1957); William Preston, Jr., *Aliens and Dissenters: Federal Suppression of Radicals, 1903-1933* (1963); Robert L. Friedheim, *The Seattle General Strike* (1964); and Woodrow C. Whitten, *Criminal Syndicalism and the Law in California, 1919-1927* (1969).

William T. Hutchinson, *Lowden of Illinois* (2 vols., 1957); Frank Freidel, *Franklin D. Roosevelt: The Apprenticeship* (1952); James M. Cox, *Journey Through My Years* (1946); Robert K. Murray, *The Harding Era: Warren G. Harding and His Administration* (1969); and Randolph C. Downes, *The Rise of Warren Gamaliel Harding, 1865-1920* (1970), are all informative about the presidential campaign of 1920. But see especially the fine general study by Wesley M. Bagby, *The Road to Normalcy: The Presidential Campaign and Election of 1920* (1962).

The most voluminous and sometimes the best literature on the Wilson era are the biographies and memoirs of the leaders of that period. Arthur Walworth, *Woodrow Wilson* (2 vols., 1958), is a good personal biography. Arthur S. Link, *Wilson: The Road to the White House* (1947), *Wilson: The New Freedom* (1956), *Wilson: The Struggle for Neutrality, 1914-1915* (1960), *Wilson: Confusions and Crises, 1915-1916* (1964), and *Wilson: Campaigns for Progressivism and Peace, 1916-1917* (1965), cover Wilson's public career from 1902 to 1917 in some detail. Arthur S. Link, *Woodrow Wilson, a Brief Biography* (1963); John M. Blum, *Woodrow Wilson and the Politics of Morality* (1956); and John A. Garraty, *Woodrow Wilson* (1956), are brief studies. Arthur S. Link et al. (eds.), *The Papers of Wood-*

row Wilson (1966——), has now reached Wilson's first administration. Meanwhile, for Wilson's speeches and public papers, the student may consult Ray S. Baker and William E. Dodd (eds.), *The Public Papers of Woodrow Wilson* (6 vols., 1925–1927), and John Wells Davidson (ed.), *A Crossroads of Freedom: The 1912 Campaign Speeches of Woodrow Wilson* (1956). An indispensable but sometimes unreliable source is Charles Seymour (ed.), *The Intimate Papers of Colonel House* (4 vols., 1926–1928). For biographies of persons active in the Wilson era, see John M. Blum, *Joe Tumulty and the Wilson Era* (1951); Frank Freidel, *Franklin D. Roosevelt: The Apprenticeship* (1952); Monroe L. Billington, *Thomas P. Gore: The Blind Senator from Oklahoma* (1967); C. H. Cramer, *Newton D. Baker, a Biography* (1961); Margaret L. Coit, *Mr. Baruch* (1957); Stanley Coben, *A. Mitchell Palmer: Politician* (1963); Lawrence W. Levine, *Defender of the Faith, William Jennings Bryan: The Last Decade, 1915–1925* (1965); Paolo E. Coletta, *William Jennings Bryan: Progressive Politician and Moral Statesman, 1909–1915* (1969) and *William Jennings Bryan: Political Puritan, 1915–1925* (1969); and Richard Lowitt, *George W. Norris: The Persistence of a Progressive* (1971).

D. *The Supreme Court and Social and Economic Policy, 1900–1920*

Charles Warren, *The Supreme Court in United States History* (2 vols., 1937); William F. Swindler, *Court and Constitution in the Twentieth Century* (2 vols., 1969–1970); Alfred H. Kelly and W. A. Harbison, *The American Constitution* (1963); and Paul L. Murphy, *The Constitution in Crisis Times, 1918–1969* (1972), are excellent surveys. Louis B. Boudin, *Government by Judiciary* (2 vols., 1932), focuses on the Supreme Court and social and economic legislation. Biographies of leaders in the court for this period include Merlo J. Pusey, *Charles Evans Hughes* (2 vols., 1951); Alpheus T. Mason, *Brandeis: A Free Man's Life* (1946); Max Lerner (ed.), *The Mind and Faith of Justice Holmes* (1943); and Kathryn Griffith, *Judge Learned Hand and the Role of the Federal Judiciary* (1973). David Wigdor, *Roscoe Pound: Philosopher of Law* (1974), is an excellent biography of the founder of sociological jurisprudence. John E. Semonche, *Charting the Future: The Supreme Court Responds to a Changing Society, 1891–1920* (1978), is a significant reappraisal.

E. *The Politics and Problems of the Twenties*

For general histories, see Robert K. Murray, *The Harding Era: Warren G. Harding and His Administration* (1969); Eugene P. Trani and David L. Wilson, *The Presidency of Warren G. Harding* (1977); Donald R. McCoy, *Calvin Coolidge: The Quiet President* (1967); George E. Mowry, *The Urban Nation, 1920–1960* (1965); John D. Hicks, *Republican Ascendancy, 1921–1933* (1960); William E. Leuchtenberg, *The Perils of Prosperity, 1914–1932* (1958); Frederick L. Paxson, *The American Democracy and the World War* (3 vols., 1936–1948), Vol. III; Paul A. Carter, *The Twenties in America* (1975); Burt Noggle, *Into the Twenties: The United States from Armistice to Normalcy* (1974); Mark Sullivan, *Our Times, the United States, 1900–1925* (6 vols., 1926–1935), Vols. V and VI; and Paul A. Carter, *Another Part of the Twenties* (1977). John Braeman et al. (eds.), *Change and Continuity in Twentieth-Century America: The 1920's* (1968), includes some good essays on various developments during the decade.

Valuable for Republican politics and policies of the period are Samuel H. Adams, *Incredible Era: The Life and Times of Warren Gamaliel Harding* (1939), a scathing account; Andrew Sinclair, *The Available Man: The Life Behind the Masks of Warren Gamaliel Harding* (1965); Francis Russell, *The Shadow of Blooming Grove: Warren G. Harding and His Times* (1968); William A. White, *A Puritan in Babylon* (1938), a biography of Coolidge; Herbert Hoover, *Memoirs* (3 vols., 1951-1952), Vol. II; Robert H. Zeiger, *Republicans and Labor, 1919-1929* (1969); and Donald L. Winters, *Henry Cantwell Wallace as Secretary of Agriculture, 1921-1924* (1970).

William H. Harbaugh, *Lawyer's Lawyer: The Life of John W. Davis* (1973), is a biography that tells much about the politics of the 1920s. For the Democratic and liberal politics of the period, see also David Burner, *The Politics of Provincialism: The Democratic Party in Transition, 1918-1932* (1968); Frank Freidel, *Franklin D. Roosevelt: The Ordeal* (1954); Oscar Handlin, *Al Smith and His America* (1958); Matthew and Hannah Josephson, *Al Smith: Hero of the Cities* (1969); Richard O'Connor, *The First Hurrah: A Biography of Alfred E. Smith* (1970); Edmund A. Moore, *A Catholic Runs for President: The Campaign of 1928* (1956); Allan J. Lichtman, *Prejudice and the Old Politics: The Presidential Election of 1928* (1979); D. Joy Humes, *Oswald Garrison Villard: Liberal of the 1920's* (1960); Arthur Mann, *La Guardia Comes to Power, 1933* (1965); Howard Finn, *La Guardia in Congress* (1959); and Le Roy Ashby, *The Spearless Leader: Senator Borah and the Progressive Movement in the 1920s* (1972). J. Joseph Huthmacher, *Massachusetts People and Politics, 1919-1933* (1959), and Franklin D. Mitchell, *Embattled Democracy: Missouri Democratic Politics, 1919-1932* (1968), are pioneering state studies. James W. Prothro, *The Dollar Decade: Business Ideas in the 1920's* (1954), tells us much about the conservative politics of the period.

There is an abundant and fast-growing literature on specific problems of the postarmistice decade. Theodore Draper, *The Roots of American Communism* (1957) and *American Communism and Soviet Russia During the Formative Period* (1960), are superb contributions. Major aspects of postwar intolerance and bigotry are related by Arnold S. Rice, *The Ku Klux Klan in American Politics* (1962); David M. Chalmers, *Hooded Americanism: The First Century of the Ku Klux Klan, 1865-1965* (1965); Charles C. Alexander, *The Ku Klux Klan in the Southwest* (1965); Kenneth T. Jackson, *The Ku Klux Klan in the City, 1915-1930* (1967); Walter Lippmann, *American Inquisitors* (1928); and Howard K. Beale, *Are American Teachers Free?* (1936). The facts and significance of the greatest legal cause cèlébre of the 1920s are related in Felix Frankfurter, *The Case of Sacco and Vanzetti* (1927); G. Louis Joughin and E. M. Morgan, *The Legacy of Sacco and Vanzetti* (1948); and David Felix, *Protest: Sacco-Vanzetti and the Intellectuals* (1965). Norman F. Furniss's judicious *The Fundamentalist Controversy, 1918-1931* (1954), is the best work on that subject, but see also Willard B. Gatewood, Jr., *Preachers, Pedagogues, and Politicians: The Evolution Controversy in North Carolina* (1966); Richard Hofstadter, *Anti-Intellectualism in American Life* (1963); and Ray Ginger, *Six Days or Forever? Tennessee v. John Thomas Scopes* (1958). For the origins of the twentieth-century prohibition movement, see James H. Timberlake, *Prohibition and the Progressive Movement, 1900-1920* (1963), and Peter H. Odegard, *Pressure Politics, the Story of the Anti-Saloon League* (1928). The failure of the "noble experiment" is recounted by Herbert Asbury, *The Great Illusion, an Informal History of Prohibition* (1950), and Norman H. Clark, *The Dry*

Years: Prohibition and Social Change in Washington (1965). John Kobler, *Capone: The Life and World of Al Capone* (1971), is a racy biography of one of prohibition's chief beneficiaries. Burl Noggle, *Teapot Dome: Oil and Politics in the 1920's* (1965), is excellent on the major scandal of the 1920s.

For three major legislative issues of the 1920s—tariff, taxes, and federal policy toward the electric power industry—see Frank W. Taussig, *Tariff History of the United States* (1931); Sidney Ratner, *American Taxation* (1942); and George W. Norris, *Fighting Liberal* (1945). Judson King, *The Conservation Fight: From Theodore Roosevelt to the Tennessee Valley Authority* (1959), is highly condemnatory of the private utilities. Preston J. Hubbard, *Origins of the TVA, the Muscle Shoals Controversy, 1920-1932* (1961), is a superb scholarly account of the greatest single power fight of the 1920s, but see also Richard Lowitt, *George W. Norris: The Persistence of a Progressive* (1971). The farm problem, revival of insurgency, and the Progressive party of 1924 are amply treated in Russel B. Nye, *Midwestern Progressive Politics* (1951); Theodore Saloutos and John D. Hicks, *Agrarian Discontent in the Middle West, 1900-1939* (1951); Theodore Saloutos, *Farmer Movements in the South, 1865-1933* (1960); and Gilbert C. Fite, *George N. Peek and the Fight for Farm Parity* (1954). See also James H. Shideler, *Farm Crisis, 1919-1923* (1957); Robert L. Morlan, *Political Prairie Fire: The Nonpartisan League, 1915-1922* (1955); and Kenneth C. MacKay, *The Progressive Movement of 1924* (1947). Clarke A. Chambers, *Seedtime of Reform: American Social Service and Social Action, 1918-1933* (1963), provides a provocative answer to the question: What happened to the progressive movement in the 1920s?

For the Supreme Court between 1920 and the great court controversy of 1937, see the following excellent general surveys: Charles Warren, *The Supreme Court in United States History* (2 vols., 1937); William F. Swindler, *Court and Constitution in the Twentieth Century* (2 vols., 1969-1970); Alfred H. Kelly and W. A. Harbison, *The American Constitution* (1963); and Paul L. Murphy, *The Constitution in Crisis Times, 1918-1969* (1972). Louis B. Boudin, *Government by Judiciary* (2 vols., 1932), focuses on the Supreme Court and social and economic legislation. Alpheus T. Mason, *The Supreme Court from Taft to Warren* (1958) and *William Howard Taft, Chief Justice* (1965), cover the 1920s.

F. *Herbert Hoover and the Great Depression*

For brief and objective surveys of the Hoover period, see John D. Hicks, *Republican Ascendancy, 1921-1933* (1960); William E. Leuchtenberg, *The Perils of Prosperity, 1914-1932* (1958); and George E. Mowry, *The Urban Nation, 1920-1960* (1965). Arthur M. Schlesinger, Jr., *The Age of Roosevelt: The Crisis of the Old Order, 1919-1933* (1957)—the first volume in a monumental series noted more fully below—marks the beginning of a reevaluation of the Hoover administration, as does David Burner, *Herbert Hoover, the Public Life* (1979); Joan Hoff Wilson, *Herbert Hoover: Forgotten Progressive* (1975); Harris G. Warren, *Herbert Hoover and the Great Depression* (1959); Albert U. Romasco, *The Poverty of Abundance: Hoover, the Nation, the Depression* (1965); Gene Smith, *The Shattered Dream: Herbert Hoover and the Great Depression* (1970); and Jordan A. Schwarz, *The Interregnum of Despair: Hoover, Congress, and the Depression* (1970). Herbert Hoover, *Memoirs* (3 vols., 1951-1952), Vol. III, concedes nothing to his critics.

For vivid accounts of the impact of the depression on American life, thought, and politics, see Clarence J. Enzler, *Some Social Aspects of the Depression* (1939); Dixon Wecter, *The Age of the Great Depression, 1920-1941* (1948); Frederick Lewis Allen, *Since Yesterday: The Nineteen-Thirties in America* (1940); Bernard Sternsher (ed.), *Hitting Home: The Great Depression in Town and Country* (1970); and Roger Daniels, *The Bonus March: An Episode of the Great Depression* (1971). Broadus Mitchell, *Depression Decade* (1947), analyzes the causes and problems of the depression in a general way, but the following are useful for specific aspects: Elmus R. Wicker, *Federal Reserve Monetary Policies, 1917-1933* (1966); Milton Friedman and Anna J. Schwartz, *A Monetary History of the United States, 1867-1960* (1963); John Kenneth Galbraith, *The Great Crash* (1955); Brookings Institution, *The Recovery Problem in the United States* (1936); Charles S. Johnson et al., *The Collapse of Cotton Tenancy* (1935); Maurice Levin et al., *America's Capacity to Consume* (1934); and Edwin G. Nourse et al., *America's Capacity to Produce* (1934). Josephine C. Brown, *Public Relief, 1929-1939* (1940), is good for Hoover's relief policies.

G. *Franklin D. Roosevelt and American Politics*

The literature on the era of Franklin Roosevelt, already richer than that dealing with any other comparable period in American history since 1865, is constantly growing. A basic source for the entire New Deal period is Samuel I. Rosenman (ed.), *The Public Papers and Addresses of Franklin D. Roosevelt* (13 vols., 1938-1950). The best introduction is Dr. Schlesinger's multivolume *The Age of Roosevelt*, which is both excellent history and great literature. He has published *The Crisis of the Old Order, 1919-1933* (1957), *The Coming of the New Deal* (1958), and *The Politics of Upheaval* (1960). William E. Leuchtenberg, *Franklin D. Roosevelt and the New Deal, 1932-1940* (1963), is a superb brief survey. Much more critical of Roosevelt is Paul K. Conkin, *The New Deal* (1967). Dixon Wecter, *The Age of the Great Depression, 1920-1941* (1948), is good for the social impact of New Deal policies, but Broadus Mitchell, *Depression Decade* (1947), sometimes sounds as if the author was lecturing from a Socialist soapbox. Samuel Lubell, *The Future of American Politics* (1952), and John M. Allswang, *The New Deal and American Politics: A Study in Political Change* (1978), shrewdly analyze the impact of the New Deal on party loyalties and the party structure, while Matthew Josephson, *Sidney Hillman: Stateman of American Labor* (1952), is useful for understanding the New Deal's impact on labor politics. J. Joseph Huthmacher, *Senator Robert F. Wagner and the Rise of Urban Liberalism* (1968), is significant for the entire New Deal period.

Useful specialized studies are Harold F. Gosnell, *Champion Campaigner* (1952); Thomas H. Greer, *What Roosevelt Thought* (1958); Daniel R. Fusfield, *The Economic Thought of Franklin D. Roosevelt* (1956); Bernard Bellush, *Franklin D. Roosevelt as Governor of New York* (1955); A. J. Wann, *The President as Chief Administrator: A Study of Franklin D. Roosevelt* (1968); George Q. Flynn, *American Catholics and the Roosevelt Presidency, 1932-1936* (1968); Max Freedman (ed.), *Roosevelt and Frankfurter: Their Correspondence, 1928-1945* (1968); and Richard Polenberg, *Reorganizing Roosevelt's Government: The Controversy over Executive Reorganization, 1936-1939* (1966). No thoughtful student should ignore

Edgar E. Robinson, *The Roosevelt Leadership, 1933-1945* (1955), for it is the only responsible conservative critique. For Roosevelt's third-term nomination and campaign, see Bernard F. Donahoe, *Private Plans and Public Dangers: The Story of FDR's Third Nomination* (1965), and Herbert S. Parmet and Marie B. Hecht, *Never Again: A President Runs for a Third Term* (1968).

Biographies of Roosevelt are numerous enough to fill a special volume, and we will mention only the most important of them. Frank Freidel's objective biography has reached the first months of the New Deal. The volumes that have been published include *Franklin D. Roosevelt: The Apprenticeship* (1952); *Franklin D. Roosevelt: The Ordeal* (1954); *Franklin D. Roosevelt: The Triumph* (1956); and *Franklin D. Roosevelt: Launching the New Deal* (1973). Robert E. Sherwood, *Roosevelt and Hopkins* (1948), is a fascinating biography of Harry L. Hopkins, Roosevelt's closest adviser from 1935 to 1945. Rexford G. Tugwell, *The Democratic Roosevelt* (1957) and *FDR: Architect of an Era* (1967), are important studies by a contemporary, while James M. Burns, *Roosevelt: The Lion and the Fox* (1956), is a superb study of Roosevelt the political leader. Joseph P. Lash, *Eleanor and Franklin* (1971) and *Eleanor: The Years Alone* (1972), constitute the definitive life of Mrs. Roosevelt.

Some of our best sources for the New Deal era are the memoirs of Roosevelt's contemporaries. Among the best of these are Samuel I. Rosenman, *Working with Roosevelt* (1952); Frances Perkins, *The Roosevelt I Knew* (1946); Eleanor Roosevelt, *This Is My Story* (1937) and *This I Remember* (1949); Raymond Moley, *After Seven Years* (1939) and *The First New Deal* (1966); Cordell Hull, *Memoirs* (2 vols., 1948); and Harold L. Ickes, *Secret Diary* (3 vols., 1953-1954).

H. *Aspects of the New Deal*

There are many very good volumes dealing with financial reform, fiscal policies, and the problem of recovery. Of major significance, because they cut across all the New Deal period, are John M. Blum (ed.), *From the Morgenthau Diaries: Years of Crisis, 1928-1938* (1959), *From the Morgenthau Diaries: Years of Urgency, 1938-1941* (1965), and *From the Morgenthau Diaries: Years of War, 1941-1945* (1967). For those who want a briefer version, there is John M. Blum, *Roosevelt and Morgenthau: A Revision and Condensation of From the Morgenthau Diaries* (1970). For another major work, see Beatrice Bishop Berle and Travis Beal Jacobs (eds.), *Navigating the Rapids, 1918-1971: From the Papers of Adolf A. Berle* (1973). Also useful is Patrick J. Mancy, *"Young Bob" La Follette: A Biography of Robert M. La Follette, Jr., 1895-1953* (1978). Norman D. Markowitz, *The Rise and Fall of the People's Century: Henry A. Wallace and American Liberalism, 1941-1948* (1973), is overly partial to its subject, so one should also see John M. Blum (ed.), *The Price of Vision: The Diary of Henry A. Wallace, 1942-1946* (1973).

Ferdinand Pecora, *Wall Street Under Oath* (1939), and J. T. Flynn, *Security Speculation* (1934), demonstrate the need for financial reform. Marriner S. Eccles, *Beckoning Frontiers: Public and Personal Recollections* (1951), tells the story of the writing of the Banking Act of 1935, while Marion L. Ramsay, *Pyramids of Power: The Story of Roosevelt, Insull and the Utility Wars* (1937); Michael E. Parrish, *Securities Regulation and the New Deal* (1970); and Ralph F. de Bedts, *The New*

Deal's SEC: The Formative Years (1964), cover the Public Utility Holding Company Act of 1935 and the effort to regulate the securities exchanges.

Milton Friedman and Anna J. Schwartz, *A Monetary History of the United States, 1867-1960* (1963), is the best source for New Deal fiscal policies, but see also G. Griffith Johnson, Jr., *Treasury and Monetary Policy* (1939); John Kenneth Galbraith and G. Griffith Johnson, Jr., *The Economic Effects of the Federal Public Works Expenditure, 1933-1938* (1940); John A. Brennan, *Silver and the First New Deal* (1969); Robert Lekachman, *The Age of Keynes* (1966); and Herbert Stein, *The Fiscal Revolution in America* (1969).

Ellis W. Hawley, *The New Deal and the Problem of Monopoly: A Study in Economic Ambivalence* (1966), is the best analysis of the NRA, but also useful are Leverett S. Lyon et al., *The National Recovery Administration* (1935); Merle Fainsod and L. Gordon, *Government and the American Economy* (1959); and Thomas E. Vadney, *The Wayward Liberal: A Political Biography of Donald Richberg* (1971). For the work of the RFC, see Jesse H. Jones, *Fifty Billion Dollars: My Thirteen Years with the RFC, 1932-1945* (1951). Otis L. Graham, Jr., *Toward a Planned Society: From Roosevelt to Nixon* (1976), is the best general study of that subject.

For general surveys, see Broadus Mitchell, *Depression Decade* (1947); Josephine C. Brown, *Public Relief, 1929-1939* (1940); and Robert E. Sherwood, *Roosevelt and Hopkins* (1948). Searle F. Charles, *Minister of Relief: Harry Hopkins and the Depression* (1963), is more detailed. For various aspects of the New Deal relief program, see John A. Salmond, *The Civilian Conservation Corps, 1933-1942: A New Deal Case Study* (1967); Jane De Hart Mathews, *The Federal Theatre, 1935-1939: Plays, Relief, and Politics* (1967); William F. McDonald, *Federal Relief Administration and the Arts* (1969); Paul K. Conkin, *Tomorrow a New World: The New Deal Community Program* (1959); and Bernard Sternsher, *Rexford G. Tugwell and the New Deal* (1964), which covers relief and many other matters.

For the background of the Social Security Act, see Roy Lubove, *The Struggle for Social Security, 1900-1935* (1968), and David Nelson, *Unemployment Insurance: The American Experience, 1915-1935* (1969). The writing of the Social Security Act and subsequent developments are well recounted in Frances Perkins, *The Roosevelt I Knew* (1962); Edwin E. Witte, *Development of the Social Security Act* (1962); Arthur J. Altmeyer, *The Formative Years of Social Security* (1966); Theron F. Schlabach, *Edwin E. Witte: Cautious Reformer* (1969); and Charles McKinley and R. W. Frase, *Launching Social Security: A Capture-and-Record Account, 1935-1937* (1971). Daniel S. Hirshfield, *The Lost Reform: The Campaign for Compulsory Health Insurance in the United States from 1932 to 1943* (1970); and Charles O. Jackson, *Food and Drug Legislation in the New Deal* (1970), deal with related subjects. A radical approach to New Deal legislation is Francis Fox Piven and Richard A. Cloward, *Regulating the Poor: The Functions of Public Welfare* (1972), which views the various initiatives as instruments used to assuage a disgruntled populace.

For the entire New Deal period, we have the largest and best literature on agrarian problems and policies. Theodore Saloutos and John D. Hicks, *Agrarian Discontent in the Middle West, 1900-1939* (1951), Gilbert C. Fite, *George N. Peek and the Fight for Farm Parity* (1954); and Broadus Mitchell, *Depression Decade* (1947), should be supplemented for general coverage by Murray R. Benedict,

Farm Policies of the United States, 1790-1950 (1953); Frederick H. and Edward L. Schapsmeier, *Henry A. Wallace of Iowa: The Agrarian Years, 1910-1940* (1968); Richard S. Kirkendall, *Social Scientists and Farm Politics in the Age of Roosevelt* (1966); and Robert J. Morgan, *Governing Soil Conservation: Thirty Years of the New Decentralization* (1966).

John L. Shover, *Cornbelt Rebellion: The Farmers' Holiday Association* (1965), is excellent for the general farm crisis. The writing of the AAA and subsequent policies are well covered by William D. Rowley, *M. L. Wilson and the Campaign for the Domestic Allotment* (1970); Van L. Perkins, *Crisis in Agriculture: The Agricultural Adjustment Administration and the New Deal, 1933* (1969); David E. Conrad, *The Forgotten Farmers: The Story of Sharecroppers in the New Deal* (1965); Donald H. Grubbs, *Cry from the Cotton: The Southern Tenant Farmers' Union and the New Deal* (1971); and Louis Cantor, *A Prologue to the Protest Movement: The Missouri Sharecropper Roadside Demonstration of 1939* (1968). Sidney Baldwin, *Poverty and Politics: The Rise and Decline of the Farm Security Administration* (1968), is excellent. Clyde T. Ellis, *A Giant Step* (1966), tells the story of the REA, while Dean Albertson, *Roosevelt's Farmer: Claude R. Wickard in the New Deal* (1961), is useful for the later stages of New Deal farm policy. Nathan Straus, *Seven Myths of Housing* (1944), surveys the New Deal's housing program.

On the South, the regions and states, and the TVA, Rupert B. Vance, *All These People, the Nation's Human Resources in the South* (1945), is comprehensive, as is V. O. Key, Jr., *Southern Politics in State and Nation* (1949). George B. Tindall, *The Emergence of the New South, 1913-1945* (1967), is excellent for the impact of the New Deal on the South. See also Frank Freidel, *F. D. R. and the South* (1965); Thomas A. Krueger, *And Promises to Keep: The Southern Conference for Human Welfare, 1938-1948* (1967); Wilma Dykeman and James Stokely, *Seeds of Southern Change: The Life of Will Alexander* (1962); and Wilma Dykeman, *Prophet of Plenty: The First Ninety Years of W. D. Weatherford* (1966). Howard W. Odum and H. E. Moore, *American Regionalism* (1938), is the pioneer work in developing the concept of the region. For the impact of the New Deal on the cities and states, see James T. Patterson, *The New Deal and the States: Federalism in Transition* (1969); Robert E. Burke, *Olson's New Deal for California* (1953); Francis W. Schruben, *Kansas in Turmoil, 1930-1936* (1969); and Bruce M. Stave, *The New Deal and the Last Hurrah: Pittsburgh Machine Politics* (1970).

For the TVA, see C. Herman Pritchett, *The Tennessee Valley Authority: A Study in Public Administration* (1943); David E. Lilienthal, *TVA: Democracy on the March* (1953) and *The Journals of David E. Lilienthal: The TVA Years, 1939-1945* (1965); Thomas K. McCraw, *TVA and the Power Fight, 1933-1939* (1970); Wilmon H. Droze, *High Dams and Slack Waters: TVA Rebuilds a River* (1965); and John R. Moore (ed.), *The Economic Impact of the TVA* (1967). Richard Lowitt, *George W. Norris: the Triumph of a Progressive* (1978), is the third and final volume in the biography of the father of the TVA.

The following discuss opposition to the New Deal. There is still no general study of Republican politics in the 1930s, but Donald R. McCoy, *Landon of Kansas* (1966); Donald B. Johnson, *The Republican Party and Wendell Willkie* (1960); Warren Moscow, *Roosevelt and Willkie* (1968); and Ellsworth Barnard, *Wendell Willkie: Fighter for Freedom* (1966), fill in many gaps, while Samuel Lubell, *The Future of American Politics* (1952), analyzes the causes of the GOP's weakness during this period. Morton Keller, *In Defense of Yesterday: James M. Beck and the Politics of Conservatism, 1861-1936* (1959), reflects the conservative Republican reaction to the New Deal, while Otis L. Graham, Jr., *An Encore for Reform: The Old Progressives and the New Deal* (1967), tells about widespread disenchantment. Even more revealing are George Wolfskill, *Revolt of the Conservatives, a History of the American Liberty League, 1934-1940* (1962), and George Wolfskill and John A. Hudson, *All but the People: Franklin D. Roosevelt and His Critics, 1933-1939* (1969). For the beginnings of effective congressional opposition, see James T. Patterson, *Congressional Conservatism and the New Deal: The Growth of the Conservative Coalition in Congress, 1933-1939* (1967), and John Robert Moore, *Senator Josiah William Bailey of North Carolina* (1968).

We now have a number of excellent studies of non-Communist left wing opposition to the New Deal: T. Harry Williams, *Huey Long* (1969); Allan P. Sindler, *Huey Long's Louisiana* (1956); Donald R. McCoy, *Angry Voices: Left-of-Center Politics in the New Deal Era* (1958); David H. Bennett, *Demagogues in the Depression: American Radicals and the Union Party, 1932-1936* (1969); and Charles J. Tull, *Father Coughlin and the New Deal* (1965).

Donald D. Egbert and S. Persons (eds.), *Socialism and American Life* (2 vols., 1952), contains the best brief survey of the rise and decline of communism in the United States in the 1930s. But see also John P. Diggins, *Up from Communism: Conservative Odysseys in American Intellectual History* (1975); Vivian Gornick, *The Romance of American Communism* (1977); Earl Latham, *The Communist Controversy in Washington: From the New Deal to McCarthy* (1966); Frank A. Warren III, *Liberals and Communism: The "Red Decade" Revisited* (1966); Wilson Record, *The Negro and the Communist Party* (1951); Ralph L. Roy, *Communism and the Churches* (1960); Robert W. Iverson, *The Communists and the Schools* (1959); Daniel Aaron, *Writers on the Left* (1961); and Richard H. Pells, *Radical Visions and American Dreams: Culture and Social Thought in the Depression Years* (1973). For the decline of the Socialist party during the New Deal period, see David A. Shannon, *The Socialist Party of America: A History* (1955); Murray B. Seidler, *Norman Thomas: Respectable Rebel* (1967); Bernard K. Johnpoll, *Pacifist's Progress: Norman Thomas and the Decline of American Socialism* (1970); and W. A. Swanberg, *Norman Thomas: The Last Idealist* (1976).

The best study of the Supreme Court controversy and the New Deal court is Leonard Baker, *Back to Back: The Duel Between FDR and the Supreme Court* (1967); but see also Samuel Hendel, *Charles Evans Hughes and the Supreme Court* (1951); Merlo J. Pusey, *Charles Evans Hughes* (2 vols., 1951); Alpheus T. Mason, *Brandeis: A Free Man's Life* (1946) and *Harlan Fiske Stone* (1956); and Paul L. Murphy, *The Constitution in Crisis Times, 1918-1969* (1972). For the New Deal Court, see C. Herman Pritchett, *The Roosevelt Court* (1948); Alpheus T. Mason, *Harlan Fiske Stone* (1956); J. Woodford Howard, *Mr. Justice Murphy: A Political Biography* (1968); and Gerald T. Dunne, *Hugo Black and the Judicial Revolution* (1977).

I. *The Home Front During the Second World War*

We now have an excellent general study of domestic politics during this period: John M. Blum, *V Was for Victory: Politics and American Culture During World War II* (1976). Geoffrey Perrett, *Days of Sadness, Years of Triumph: The American People, 1939-1945* (1973), is another interesting survey. Jack Goodman (ed.), *While You Were Gone: A Report on Wartime Life in the United States* (1946), contains some good essays. Alan S. Milward, *War, Economy and Society, 1939-1945* (1977), surveys the impact of the war on the American economy in a worldwide setting.

Donald M. Nelson, *Arsenal of Democracy* (1946), is an "official" history of industrial mobilization, while Eliot Janeway, *The Struggle for Survival* (1951), is extremely critical of the administration. Frederick C. Lane et al., *Ships for Victory* (1951), is excellent for the shipbuilding program; E. R. Stettinius, Jr., *Lend-Lease, Weapon of Victory* (1944), is good for the export of war materials; James P. Baxter III, *Scientists Against Time* (1946), is a superb account of American scientific achievement during wartime; and Leslie R. Groves, *Now It Can Be Told* (1962), is the story of the Manhattan Project by its director. Walter W. Wilcox, *The Farmer in the Second World War* (1947), is excellent, while Randolph E. Paul, *Taxation for Prosperity* (1947), recounts wartime tax struggles with commendable objectivity. Herman M. Sowers, *Presidential Agency OWMR* (1950), is especially good on plans for reconversion of the wartime economy. Davis R. B. Ross, *Preparing for Ulysses: Politics and Veterans During World War II* (1969), is a significant contribution. Dorothy S. Thomas et al., *The Spoilage* (1946), and Roger Daniels, *Concentration Camps, U. S. A., Japanese Americans and World War II* (1972), are scholarly studies of the treatment of Japanese Americans.

2. THE UNITED STATES AND ITS WORLD RELATIONS, 1900-1945

A. *General*

Samuel F. Bemis and Robert H. Ferrell (eds.), *The American Secretaries of State and Their Diplomacy* (17 vols., 1927-1967); Foster R. Dulles, *America's Rise to World Power, 1898-1954* (1955); George F. Kennan, *American Diplomacy, 1900-1950* (1951); Norman A. Graebner (ed.), *An Uncertain Tradition, American Secretaries of State in the Twentieth Century* (1961); Robert E. Osgood, *Ideals and Self-Interest in America's Foreign Relations* (1953); Selig Adler, *The Isolationist Impulse* (1959); H. C. Allen, *Great Britain and the United States* (1955); William Appleman Williams, *The Roots of the Modern American Empire* (1969); Julius W. Pratt, *Challenge and Rejection: The United States and World Leadership, 1900-1921* (1967); E. Berkeley Tompkins, *Anti-Imperialism in the United States, 1890-1920* (1970); Sondra R. Herman, *Eleven Aginst War: Studies in American Internationalist Thought, 1898-1921* (1969); and Warren F. Kuehl, *Seeking World Order: The United States and International Organization to 1920* (1969), are good surveys for readers deficient in background. Charles Chatfield, *For Peace and Justice: Pacifism in America, 1914-1941* (1971), is excellent on the peace movement in the twentieth century. However, the best general work is Richard W. Leopold, *The Growth of American Foreign Policy* (1962).

B. *Colonial Administration and the United States and Europe and Asia, 1900-1914*

Julius W. Pratt, *America's Colonial Experiment* (1950), is a splendid survey of the rise, governing, and decline of the American colonial empire. It may be supplemented by Edward J. Berbusse, *The United States in Puerto Rico, 1898–1900* (1966); David A. Lockmiller, *Magoon in Cuba: A History of the Second Intervention, 1906–1909* (1938); Allan Reed Millett, *The Politics of Intervention: The Military Occupation of Cuba, 1906–1909* (1968); W. Cameron Forbes, *The Philippine Islands* (2 vols., 1928); and Charles C. Tansill, *The Purchase of the Danish West Indies* (1932).

We lack any good general study of American relations with Europe from 1900 to 1914. Howard K. Beale, *Theodore Roosevelt and the Rise of America to World Power* (1956); Walter V. and Marie V. Scholes, *The Foreign Policies of the Taft Administration* (1970); John A. Garraty, *Henry Cabot Lodge* (1953); Richard W. Leopold, *Elihu Root and the Conservative Tradition* (1954); Philip C. Jessup, *Elihu Root* (2 vols., 1938); Henry F. Pringle, *Theodore Roosevelt, a Biography* (1931) and *The Life and Times of William Howard Taft* (2 vols., 1939); William H. Harbaugh, *Power and Responsibility: The Life and Times of Theodore Roosevelt* (1961); Tyler Dennett, *John Hay* (1933); and Allan Nevins, *Henry White: Thirty Years of American Diplomacy* (1930), are all valuable for the diplomacy of the Roosevelt-Taft period. Bradford Perkins, *The Great Rapprochement: England and the United States, 1895–1914* (1968); Richard R. Heindel, *The American Impact on Great Britain, 1898–1914* (1940); Charles S. Campbell, Jr., *Anglo-American Understanding, 1898–1903* (1957); Alexander E. Campbell, *Great Britain and the United States, 1895–1903* (1961); Clara E. Schieber, *The Transformation of American Sentiment Toward Germany, 1870–1914* (1923); and H. G. Nicholas, *The United States and Britain* (1975), are excellent particular studies.

In contrast to the paucity of general works on American-European relations from 1900 to 1914 stands a large body of general literature dealing with the United States and the Far East during the same period. A. Whitney Griswold, *The Far Eastern Policy of the United States* (1938); Edwin O. Reischauer, *The United States and Japan* (1965); and John K. Fairbank, *The United States and China* (1958), are the best surveys, but George F. Kennan, *American Diplomacy, 1908–1950* (1951), and Louis J. Halle, *Dream and Reality: Aspects of American Foreign Policy* (1958), make some provocative observations. For important monographs on Japanese-American relations, see Raymond A. Esthus, *Theodore Roosevelt and Japan* (1966); Tyler Dennett, *Roosevelt and the Russo-Japanese War* (1925); John A. White, *The Diplomacy of the Russo-Japanese War* (1964); Eugene P. Trani, *The Treaty of Portsmouth: An Adventure in American Diplomacy* (1969); Thomas A. Bailey, *Theodore Roosevelt and the Japanese-American Crises* (1934); and Charles E. Neu, *An Uncertain Friendship: Theodore Roosevelt and Japan, 1906–1909* (1967). For special studies on Chinese-American relations, see Herbert Croly, *Willard Straight* (1924); Paul A. Varg, *Missionaries, Chinese, and Diplomats* (1954) and *The Making of a Myth: The United States and China, 1897–1912* (1968); Jerry Israel, *Progressivism and the Open Door: America and China, 1905–1921* (1971); Thomas J. McCormick, *China Market: America's Quest for Informal Empire* (1967); Charles Vevier, *The United States and China, 1906–1913* (1955); and Nemai S. Bose, *American Attitude and Policy to the Nationalist Movement in China (1911–1921)* (1970). L. Ethan Ellis, *Reciprocity, 1911* (1939), relates Taft's ill-fated effort to win a reciprocal trade agreement with Canada. The most concise survey of Wilson's Far Eastern policy before 1917 is in Arthur S. Link,

Woodrow Wilson and the Progressive Era (1954), but see also his *Wilson: The New Freedom* (1956) and *Wilson: The Struggle for Neutrality, 1914-1915* (1960).

C. The United States and Latin America, 1900-1920

Samuel F. Bemis, *The Latin American Policy of the United States* (1943), covers the entire period and is the best general survey. For general works on the United States and the Caribbean, see Wilfrid H. Callcott, *The Caribbean Policy of the United States, 1890-1920* (1942); Dexter Perkins, *Hands Off: A History of the Monroe Doctrine* (1941), *The Monroe Doctrine, 1867-1907* (1937), and *The United States and the Caribbean* (1947); Howard C. Hill, *Roosevelt and the Caribbean* (1927); Dana G. Munro, *Intervention and Dollar Diplomacy in the Caribbean, 1900-1921* (1964); Dwight C. Miner, *The Fight for the Panama Route* (1940), and William D. McCain, *The United States and the Republic of Panama* (1937), are good for the Panama incident. Arthur S. Link, *Woodrow Wilson and the Progressive Era* (1954), *Wilson: The New Freedom* (1956), *Wilson: The Struggle for Neutrality, 1914-1915* (1960), *Wilson: Confusions and Crises, 1915-1916* (1964), and *Wilson: Campaigns for Progressivism and Peace, 1916-1917* (1965), have the best accounts of Wilson's Caribbean and Mexican policies, but for specialized works on the United States and Mexico, see Howard F. Cline, *The United States and Mexico* (1953); Peter Calvert, *The Mexican Revolution, 1910-1914: The Diplomacy of Anglo-American Conflict* (1968); Kenneth J. Grieb, *The United States and Huerta* (1969); Robert E. Quirk, *An Affair of Honor: Woodrow Wilson and the Occupation of Veracruz* (1962) and *The Mexican Revolution, 1914-1915: The Convention of Aguascalientes* (1960); and Clarence E. Clendenen, *The United States and Pancho Villa* (1961).

D. The First Road to War, 1914-1917

Among the general studies, Charles Seymour, *American Diplomacy During the World War* (1934) and *American Neutrality, 1914-1917* (1935); Ernest R. May, *The World War and American Isolation* (1959); Patrick Devlin, *Too Proud to Fight: Woodrow Wilson's Neutrality* (1974); and Edward H. Buehrig, *Woodrow Wilson and the Balance of Power* (1955), are the best. Charles Seymour (ed.), *The Intimate Papers of Colonel House* (4 vols., 1926-1928), includes materials indispensable to understanding Wilson's policies. Arthur S. Link, *Woodrow Wilson and the Progressive Era* (1954), is a useful summary, but see particularly Link's much fuller account in *Wilson: The Struggle for Neutrality, 1914-1915* (1960), *Wilson: Confusions and Crises, 1915-1916* (1964), and *Wilson: Campaigns for Progressivism and Peace, 1916-1917* (1965), and the same author's *Wilson the Diplomatist* (1957 and 1963) and *Woodrow Wilson: Revolution, War, and Peace* (1979).

Special studies on this subject abound, and we will mention only a few of them: Karl E. Birnbaum, *Peace Moves and U-Boat Warfare* (1958), is one of the best monographs in modern diplomatic history; Joseph P. O'Grady (ed.), *The Immigrants' Influence on Wilson's Peace Policies* (1967), begins in the period 1914-1917; Laurence W. Martin, *Peace Without Victory: Woodrow Wilson and the British Liberals* (1958), is useful for the entire period 1914-1919; H. C. Peterson, *Propaganda for War* (1939), overrates the influence of Allied propaganda;

George S. Viereck, *Spreading Germs of Hate* (1930), is excellent for German propaganda in the United States; and Carl Wittke, *German-Americans and the World War* (1936), is the standard work on that subject.

Robert E. Osgood, *Ideals and Self-Interest in America's Foreign Relations* (1953), and John Milton Cooper, Jr., *The Vanity of Power: American Isolationism and the First World War* (1969), present incisive analyses of American reactions to the challenges of the war. For the preparedness controversy and the peace movements from 1914 to 1917, see Hermann Hagedorn, *The Bugle That Woke America* (1940), a study of Theodore Roosevelt and the preparedness crisis; Elting E. Morison, *Admiral Sims and the Modern American Navy* (1942); Hermann Hagedorn, *Leonard Wood* (2 vols., 1931); Peter Brock, *Pacifism in the United States* (1968); Charles Chatfield, *For Peace and Justice: Pacifism in America, 1914-1921* (1971); and Arthur S. Link, *Wilson: Confusions and Crises, 1915-1916* (1964).

Almost all the biographies and memoirs cited in preceding sections have chapters on the background of America's first intervention in Europe. To these should be added Robert Lansing, *War Memoirs of Robert Lansing* (1935); Burton J. Hendrick, *The Life and Letters of Walter H. Page* (3 vols., 1922-1926); John Milton Cooper, *Walter Hines Page: The Southerner as American, 1855-1918* (1977); Ross Gregory, *Walter Hines Page: Ambassador to the Court of St. James* (1970); and Stephen Gwynn (ed.), *Letters and Friendships of Sir Cecil Spring Rice* (2 vols., 1929).

E. *American Participation in the First World War*

Two recent general works are Edward M. Coffman, *The War to End All Wars: The American Military Experience in World War I* (1968), and Harvey A. De-Weerd, *President Wilson Fights His War: World War I and the American Intervention* (1968). The best summaries of military operations are John J. Pershing, *Final Report* (1919), and Leonard P. Ayres, *The War with Germany* (1919). John J. Pershing, *My Experiences in the World War* (2 vols., 1931), and James G. Harbord, *The American Army in France, 1917-1919* (1936), are candid memoirs by two American commanders. On the American naval contribution, see Thomas G. Frothingham, *The Naval History of the World War* (3 vols., 1924-1926), and Elting E. Morison, *Admiral Sims and the Modern American Navy* (1942). The definitive biography of General Pershing is Frank E. Vandiver, *Black Jack: The Life and Times of John J. Pershing* (2 vols., 1977).

F. *The War, the Paris Peace Conference, and the Treaty Fight*

We are now beginning to have an excellent literature on American diplomacy during the First World War. Among the general works, Charles Seymour, *American Diplomacy During the World War* (1934), is strongly supplemented by W. B. Fowler, *British-American Relations 1917-1918: The Role of Sir William Wiseman* (1969); Arno J. Mayer, *Political Origins of the New Diplomacy, 1917-1918* (1959); Harry R. Rudin, *Armistice, 1918* (1944); Louis L. Gerson, *Wilson and the Rebirth of Poland* (1953); Victor S. Mamatey, *The United States and East Central Europe, 1914-1918* (1957); George F. Kennan, *Russia Leaves the War* (1956), *The Decision to Intervene* (1958), and *Russia and the West Under Lenin and Stalin* (1961);

Betty Miller Unterberger, *America's Siberian Expedition, 1918-1920* (1956); Carl P. Parrini, *Heir to Empire: United States Economic Diplomacy, 1916-1923* (1969); and David F. Trask, *The United States in the Supreme War Council* (1961).

The early American movement for a League of Nations is related by Ruhl J. Bartlett, *The League to Enforce Peace* (1944). For background on the Paris Peace Conference, see Charles Seymour, *American Diplomacy During the World War* (1934), and Lawrence E. Gelfand, *The Inquiry: American Preparations for Peace, 1917-1919* (1963). The best single volume on the Paris Conference is Inga Floto, *Colonel House at Paris* (1980). R. S. Baker, *Woodrow Wilson and World Settlement* (3 vols., 1922), is a friendly account rich in source materials. Also sympathetic to Wilson are N. Gordon Levin, Jr., *Woodrow Wilson and World Politics: America's Response to War and Revolution* (1968); Paul Birdsall, *Versailles Twenty Years After* (1941); Herbert Hoover, *The Ordeal of Woodrow Wilson* (1958); and Seth P. Tillman, *Anglo-American Relations at the Paris Peace Conference* (1961). Thomas A. Bailey, *Woodrow Wilson and the Lost Peace* (1944), is more critical of Wilson. Arno J. Mayer, *The Politics and Diplomacy of Peacemaking: Containment and Counterrevolution at Versailles, 1918-1919* (1967), and John M. Thompson, *Russia, Bolshevism, and the Versailles Peace* (1966), highlight the Russian problem. Russell H. Fifield, *Woodrow Wilson and the Far East* (1952), relates Wilson's struggles with the Japanese at Paris.

The best accounts of the treaty fight in the United States are Ralph Stone, *The Irreconcilables: The Fight Against the League of Nations* (1970); Thomas A. Bailey, *Woodrow Wilson and the Great Betrayal* (1945); and Denna F. Fleming, *The United States and the League of Nations, 1918-1920* (1932). John M. Blum, *Joe Tumulty and the Wilson Era* (1957 and 1963); Richard W. Leopold, *Elihu Root and the Conservative Tradition* (1954); and Charles Seymour (ed.), *The Intimate Papers of Colonel House* (4 vols., 1926-1928), have significant chapters on the treaty fight.

G. *The Search for Isolation, 1921-1932*

The most comprehensive general histories of American foreign policy during this period are Denna F. Fleming, *The United States and World Organization, 1920-1933* (1938), and L. Ethan Ellis, *Republican Foreign Policy, 1921-1933* (1968), but see also the briefer Selig Adler, *The Uncertain Giant: 1921-1941, American Foreign Policy Between the Wars* (1965). Studies of secretaries of state include Merlo J. Pusey, *Charles Evans Hughes* (2 vols., 1951); L. Ethan Ellis, *Frank B. Kellogg and American Foreign Relations, 1925-1929* (1961), which is also the best general work on the foreign policies of the second Coolidge administration; Robert H. Ferrell, *Frank B. Kellogg-Henry L. Stimson* (1963); Richard N. Current, *Secretary Stimson* (1954); and Elting E. Morison, *Turmoil and Tradition: A Study of the Life and Times of Henry L. Stimson* (1960).

The postwar naval race, the Washington Naval Conference, Japanese-American tension, and Russian-American relations from 1920 to 1933 are discussed by Thomas H. Buckley, *The United States and the Washington Conference* (1970); Harold and Margaret Sprout, *Toward a New Order of Sea Power* (1940); A. Whitney Griswold, *The Far Eastern Policy of the United States* (1938); Akira Iriye, *After Imperialism: The Search for a New Order in the Far East, 1921-1931* (1965); Merze Tate, *The United States and Armaments* (1948); Rodman W. Paul, *Abroga-*

tion of the Gentlemen's Agreement (1936); Robert P. Browder, *The Origins of Soviet-American Diplomacy* (1953); William A. Williams, *American-Russian Relations, 1781-1947* (1952); and Peter G. Filene, *Americans and the Soviet Experiment, 1917-1933* (1967). Robert H. Ferrell, *Peace in Their Time* (1952), is a fine account of the American peace crusade of the 1920s and the negotiation of the Kellogg-Briand Pact. For American international economic policy during the 1920s, see Herbert Feis, *The Diplomacy of the Dollar, First Era, 1919-1932* (1950); Carl P. Parrini, *Heir to Empire: United States Economic Diplomacy, 1916-1923* (1969); and Joan Hoff Wilson, *American Business and Foreign Policy* (1971). The best general work on the foreign policy of the Hoover administration is Robert H. Ferrell, *American Diplomacy in the Great Depression* (1957). Works on the Manchurian crisis are cited in the following section.

H. *The United States and the Collapse of the International Order, 1931-1936*

One of the basic sources is Edgar B. Nixon (ed.), *Franklin D. Roosevelt and Foreign Affairs* (3 vols., 1969), which covers the period 1933-1937. The best general survey for the Roosevelt era is Robert Dallek, *Franklin D. Roosevelt and American Foreign Policy, 1932-1945* (1979). The literature on the first important challenge to the postwar treaty structure—Japan's invasion of Manchuria in 1931—is voluminous and many-sided in interpretation. Among the general works, Richard W. Leopold, *The Growth of American Foreign Policy* (1962); Robert H. Ferrell, *American Diplomacy in the Great Depression* (1957); A. Whitney Griswold, *The Far Eastern Policy of the United States* (1938); Denna F. Fleming, *The United States and World Organization, 1920-1933* (1938); and Council on Foreign Relations, *The United States in World Affairs, 1931-1933* (3 vols., 1932-1934), are most useful. Hoover defends his failure to take stern action in his *Memoirs* (3 vols., 1951-1952), Vol. III, while Stimson explains his differences with Hoover frankly in Henry L. Stimson and M. Bundy, *On Active Service in Peace and War* (1948).

Specialized studies of the Manchurian crisis are Robert Langer, *Seizure of Territory: The Stimson Doctrine* (1947); Sara R. Smith, *The Manchurian Crisis, 1931-1932* (1948); Reginald Bassett, *Democracy and Foreign Policy, the Sino-Japanese Dispute, 1931-1933* (1952); and Armin Rappaport, *Henry L. Stimson and Japan, 1931-33* (1963).

The shifting pattern of Roosevelt's international economic policies comes out clearly in Raymond Moley, *After Seven Years* (1939), and Cordell Hull, *Memoirs* (2 vols., 1948). But see also Lloyd C. Gardner, *Economic Aspects of New Deal Diplomacy* (1964); R. L. Buell, *The Hull Trade Program* (1938); Herbert Feis, *The Changing Pattern of International Economic Affairs* (1940); Richard N. Kottman, *Reciprocity and the North Atlantic Triangle, 1932-1938* (1968); and Julius W. Pratt, *Cordell Hull, 1933-1944* (2 vols., (1964), which is, of course, useful for the entire period.

Cordell Hull, *Memoirs* (2 vols., 1948), and Sumner Welles, *The Time for Decision* (1944), are basic sources for the Good Neighbor policy. Edward O. Guerrant, *Roosevelt's Good Neighbor Policy* (1950), is a brief analysis, but see also Bryce Wood, *The Making of the Good Neighbor Policy* (1961), and Samuel F. Bemis, *The Latin American Policy of the United States* (1943). E. David Cronon, *Josephus Daniels in Mexico* (1960), is excellent for Mexican-American relations in the 1930s.

Other important works for this period are Arnold A. Offner, *American Appease-ment: United States Foreign Policy and Germany, 1933-1938* (1969); Brice Harris, Jr., *The United States and the Italo-Ethiopian Crisis* (1964); John P. Diggins, *Mussolini and Fascism: The View from America* (1972); and Richard P. Traina, *American Diplomacy and the Spanish Civil War* (1968). Robert Dallek, *Democrat and Diplomat: The Life of William E. Dodd* (1968), is particularly good on Ger-man-American relations during the early years of the Roosevelt administration. See also Beatrice Farnsworth, *William C. Bullitt and the Soviet Union* (1967), on Roosevelt's early relations with Russia, and Joan Hoff Wilson, *Ideology and Eco-nomics: U. S. Relations with the Soviet Union, 1918-1933* (1974).

There is no general history of the antiwar crusade of the 1930s, but the volumes of *The United States in World Affairs* for the years 1934 to 1939 contain a wealth of information on public opinion, while Selig Adler, *The Isolationist Impulse* (1959), and Thomas A. Bailey, *The Man in the Street* (1948), have relevant chap-ters. More specialized are Ralph B. Levering, *American Opinion and the Russian Alliance, 1939-1945* (1976); Warren I. Cohen, *The American Revisionists: The Lessons of Intervention in World War I* (1967); John K. Nelson, *The Peace Proph-ets: American Pacifist Thought, 1919-1941* (1967); and Manfred Jonas, *Isolation-ism in America, 1935-1941* (1966). For the enactment of the neutrality legislation, see James M. Seavey, *Neutrality Legislation* (1939), and Elton Atwater, *American Regulation of Arms Exports* (1941).

I. *The Second Road to War, 1937-1941*

The body of literature on the background of American participation in the Second World War is immense. The two outstanding works on the subject are William L. Langer and S. E. Gleason, *The Challenge to Isolation, 1937-1940* (1952) and *The Undeclared War, 1940-1941* (1953), which rank among the finest products of American historical scholarship. Other fine general works are Robert Dallek, *Franklin D. Roosevelt and American Foreign Policy, 1932-1945* (1979); James M. Burns, *Roosevelt: The Soldier of Freedom* (1970); Robert A. Divine, *The Reluctant Belligerent: American Entry into World War II* (1965); T. R. Fehrenbach, *F. D. R.'s Undeclared War, 1939 to 1941* (1967); and James V. Compton, *The Swastika and the Eagle: Hitler, the United States, and the Origins of World War II* (1967). Robert E. Sherwood, *Roosevelt and Hopkins* (1948); and Winston S. Churchill, *The Gathering Storm* (1948) and *Their Finest Hour* (1949), are invaluable sources. See also Charles A. Beard, *American Foreign Policy in the Making, 1932-1940* (1946) and *President Roosevelt and the Coming of the War, 1941* (1948), critical studies deserving of serious consideration. Particular works relating to the United States and Europe from 1938 to 1941 are Alton Frye, *Germany and the American Hemisphere, 1933-1941* (1967); John M. Haight, *American Aid to France, 1938-1941* (1970); Philip Goodhart, *Fifty Ships That Saved the World* (1965); Warren F. Kimball, *The Most Unsordid Act: Lend-Lease, 1930-1941* (1969); and Theodore A. Wilson, *The First Summit: Roosevelt and Churchill at Placentia Bay, 1941* (1969).

Relations with Japan during the 1930s to 1941 are traced by A. Whitney Gris-wold, *The Far Eastern Policy of the United States* (1938); Dorothy Borg, *The United States and the Far Eastern Crisis of 1933-1938* (1964); Waldo H. Hein-richs, Jr., *American Ambassador: Joseph C. Grew and the Development of the*

United States Diplomatic Tradition (1966); and Joseph C. Grew, *Turbulent Era, a Diplomatic Record of Forty Years, 1904-1945* (2 vols., 1952). The Langer and Gleason volumes contain the best account of events leading to the rupture in Japanese-American relations, but see also Manny T. Koginos, *The Panay Incident: Prelude to War* (1967); John Toland, *The Rising Sun: The Decline and Fall of the Japanese Empire, 1936-1945* (1970); Herbert Feis, *The Road to Pearl Harbor* (1950); Paul W. Schroeder, *The Axis Alliance and Japanese-American Relations, 1941* (1958); Robert J. C. Butow, *Tojo and the Coming of the War* (1961); and Roberta Wohlstetter, *Pearl Harbor: Warning and Decision* (1962). Insightful essays on various aspects of Japanese and American foreign policies are contained in Dorothy Borg and Shumpei Okamoto (eds.), *Pearl Harbor as History* (1973).

For the great debate over American policies toward the belligerents, we now have adequate studies for both the internationalists and the isolationists: Walter Johnson, *The Battle Against Isolation* (1944); Mark L. Chadwin, *The Hawks of World War II* (1968); Donald J. Friedman, *The Road from Isolation: The Campaign of the American Committee for Non-Participation in Japanese Aggression, 1938-1941* (1968); Wayne S. Cole, *America First, the Battle Against Intervention, 1940-1941* (1953); and Manfred Jonas, *Isolationism in America, 1935-1941* (1966).

J. The Diplomacy and Conduct of the Second World War

Robert Dallek, *Franklin D. Roosevelt and American Foreign Policy, 1932-1945* (1979); James M. Burns, *Roosevelt: Soldier of Freedom* (1970); and Herbert Feis, *Churchill, Roosevelt, Stalin* (1957), are the best one-volume accounts, but see also Churchill's magisterial *The Grand Alliance* (1950), *The Hinge of Fate* (1950), *Closing the Ring* (1951), and *Triumph and Tragedy* (1953); Robert E. Sherwood, *Roosevelt and Hopkins* (1948); and W. Averell Harriman and Elie Abel, *Special Envoy to Churchill and Stalin, 1941-1946* (1975). Other general studies are Robert A. Divine, *Roosevelt and World War II* (1969); Gaddis Smith, *American Diplomacy During the Second World War* (1965); Christopher Thorne, *Allies of a Kind: The United States, Britain, and the War Against Japan* (1978); and William Roger Louis, *Imperialism at Bay: The United States and the Decolonization of the British Empire, 1941-1945* (1978), a monumental study. For particular works, see Mark A. Stoler, *The Politics of the Second Front: American Military Planning and Diplomacy in Coalition Warfare, 1941-1943* (1977); Herbert Feis, *The China Triangle* (1953); Paul A. Varg, *The Closing of the Door: Sino-American Relations, 1936-1946* (1973); E. J. Kahn, Jr., *The China Hands: America's Foreign Service Officers and What Befell Them* (1975); John L. Snell (ed.), *The Meaning of Yalta* (1956); Diane S. Clemens, *Yalta* (1970); Stephen E. Ambrose, *Eisenhower and Berlin: The Decision to Halt at the Elbe* (1967); Robert A. Divine, *Second Chance: The Triumph of Internationalism in America During World War II* (1967); Herbert Feis, *Between War and Peace: The Potsdam Conference* (1960), *Japan Subdued* (1961), and *From Trust to Terror: The Onset of the Cold War, 1945-1950* (1971); Frank D. McCann, Jr., *The Brazilian-American Alliance, 1937-1945* (1973); Robert J. C. Butow, *Japan's Decision to Surrender* (1954); and William L. Neumann, *After Victory: Churchill, Roosevelt, Stalin and the Making of the Peace* (1969). Gabriel Kolko, *The Politics of War: The World and United States Foreign Policy, 1943-1945* (1969), challenges, not always successfully and rarely without bias in favor of Russia, many traditional assumptions about relations between the Western Allies and the Soviet Union and about Russian policies.

The sad story of the Roosevelt administration's failure to do much to help European Jews in danger of extermination is related in David S. Wyman, *Paper Walls: America and the Refugee Crisis, 1938-1941* (1968); Henry L. Feingold, *The Politics of Rescue: The Roosevelt Administration and the Holocaust, 1938-1945* (1970); Arthur D. Morse, *While Six Million Died* (1968); and Saul S. Friedman, *No Haven for the Oppressed: United States Policy Toward Jewish Refugees, 1938-1945* (1973).

Winston S. Churchill, *The Grand Alliance* (1950), *The Hinge of Fate* (1950), *Closing the Ring* (1951), and *Triumph and Tragedy* (1953), include brilliant summaries of all major military operations. The best single-volume history is Martha Byrd Hoyle, *A World in Flames: The History of World War II* (1970), but see also A. Russell Buchanan, *The United States and World War II* (2 vols., 1964); Chester Wilmot, *The Struggle for Europe* (1952); and Charles B. MacDonald, *The Mighty Endeavor: American Armed Forces in the European Theater in World War II* (1969). The Department of the Army's Office of Military History has published numerous volumes in its large and generally excellent series, *U. S. Army in World War II*. Samuel E. Morison, *History of United States Naval Operations in World War II* (15 vols., 1947-1962), is definitive, but see Walter Lord, *Incredible Victory* (1967), on the Battle of Midway. Kent Roberts Greenfield (ed.), *Command Decisions* (1959), contains a number of brilliant analyses of crucial military events and also reveals how considerations of military strategy affected diplomacy. Kent Roberts Greenfield, *American Strategy in World War II: A Reconsideration* (1963), is a provocative assessment. For a British perspective on Anglo-American strategic planning, see Michael Howard, *The Mediterranean Strategy in the Second World War* (1966).

For American military and naval leaders, see Alfred D. Chandler, Jr., Stephen E. Ambrose, and Louis Galambos (eds.), *The Papers of Dwight David Eisenhower: The War Years* (9 vols., 1970, 1978); Stephen E. Ambrose, *The Supreme Commander: The War Years of General Dwight D. Eisenhower* (1970); Dwight D. Eisenhower, *Crusade in Europe* (1948); Forrest C. Pogue, *George C. Marshall* (3 vols., 1962-1973); William Raymond Manchester, *American Caesar, Douglas MacArthur, 1880-1964* (1978); Gavin Long, *MacArthur as Military Commander* (1969); D. Clayton James, *The Years of MacArthur*, Vol. I (1970); Douglas MacArthur, *Reminiscences* (1964); H. Essame, *Patton: A Study in Command* (1976); E. B. Potter, *Nimitz* (1976); Henry H. Arnold, *Global Mission* (1949); Omar N. Bradley, *A Soldier's Story* (1951); Ernest J. King and W. M. Whitehill, *Fleet Admiral King* (1952); and William D. Leahy, *I Was There* (1950). Richard F. Haynes, *The Awesome Power: Harry S. Truman as Commander in Chief* (1973), is a significant study of the military power inherent in the office of the presidency.

3. THE AMERICAN PEOPLE AND THEIR ECONOMIC INSTITUTIONS, 1900-1945

A. *The American People: Demographic Changes and Wealth*

The handiest references for general economic and social data are Bureau of the Census, *Historical Statistics of the United States* (1960), and *Statistical Abstract of the United States* (published annually). Warren S. Thompson, *Population Problems*

(1953), is an excellent survey. The best sources for decennial demographic changes are the summary volumes of the Census.

There are a number of excellent studies of wealth, income, and income distribution in the United States in the twentieth century. For discussions in the broad context of economic development, see Harold U. Faulkner, *The Decline of Laissez Faire, 1897-1917* (1951); George Soule, *Prosperity Decade: From War to Depression, 1917-1929* (1947); and Broadus Mitchell, *Depression Decade* (1947). Milton Friedman and Anna J. Schwartz, *A Monetary History of the United States, 1867-1960* (1963), is a monumental study. Robert F. Martin, *National Income in the United States, 1799-1938* (1939), is an excellent statistical summary. Charles B. Spahr, *An Essay on the Present Distribution of Wealth* (1896); Wilford I. King, *The Wealth and Income of the People of the United States* (1915); and Wesley C. Mitchell et al., *Income in the United States . . . 1909-1919* (2 vols., 1921-1922); President's Conference on Unemployment, *Recent Economic Changes in the United States* (2 vols., 1929); and Robert J. Lampman, *The Share of Top Wealthholders in National Wealth, 1922-1956* (1962), discuss income distribution from the late 1890s to 1960. Simon Kuznets, *Capital in the American Economy* (1961), and Raymond W. Goldsmith, *The National Wealth of the United States* (1962), are general studies. Louis Galambos and Barbara Barrow Spence, *The Public Image of Big Business in America, 1880-1940* (1975), is an excellent study of the popular esteem in which the major economic conglomerations were held.

B. *American Industry, Financial Institutions, and the Economy, 1900-1945*

W. Elliot Brownlee, *Dynamics of Ascent: A History of the American Economy* (1979); Stuart Bruchey, *Growth of the Modern American Economy* (1975); Harold U. Faulkner, *Decline of Laissez Faire, 1897-1917* (1951); George Soule, *Prosperity Decade: From War to Depression, 1917-1929* (1947); Broadus Mitchell, *Depression Decade* (1947); and Harold F. Williamson (ed.), *The Growth of the American Economy* (1957), include chapters on the growth of industry from 1900 to 1920. Thomas C. Cochran, *The American Business System, 1900-1950* (1957), is a thoughtful analysis. Interesting also among the general studies are Alan R. Raucher, *Public Relations and Business, 1900-1929* (1968), and Morrell Heald, *The Social Responsibilities of Business: Company and Community, 1900-1960* (1970). The government's influence upon the economy is surveyed by Merle Fainsod and L. Gordon, *Government and the American Economy* (1959); Gerald D. Nash, *United States Oil Policy, 1894-1964* (1968); Ari and Olive Hoogenboom, *A History of the ICC* (1976); and Albro Martin, *Enterprise Denied: Origins of the Decline of American Railroads, 1897-1917* (1971).

For general developments in the late nineteenth century and from 1900 to 1920, see also Thomas C. Cochran and W. Miller, *The Age of Enterprise* (1942); Edmund E. Day and W. Thomas, *The Growth of Manufacturers, 1899 to 1923* (1928); Solomon Fabricant, *The Output of Manufacturing Industries, 1899-1937* (1940); and John W. Kendrick, *Productivity Trends in the United States* (1961).

For the growth of particular industries, see Harold F. Williamson and Arnold R. Daum, *The American Petroleum Industry, 1850-1899: The Age of Illumination* (1959); Harold F. Williamson et al., *The American Petroleum Industry: The Age of Energy, 1899-1959* (1963); Harless D. Wagoner, *The U. S. Machine Tool Industry from 1900 to 1950* (1968); Arthur M. Johnson, *The Development of American Petroleum Pipelines . . . 1862-1906* (1956) and *Petroleum Pipelines and Public Policy, 1906-1959* (1967); Alfred S. Eichner, *The Emergence of Oligopoly: Sugar Refining as a Case Study* (1969); Erik Barnouw, *A Tower in Babel: A History of Broadcasting in the United States. Volume I: to 1933* (1966) and *The Golden Web: A History of Broadcasting in the United States. Volume II: 1933-1953* (1968); and John B. Rae, *Climb to Greatness: The American Aircraft Industry, 1920-1960* (1968).

The great work on the rise of the modern supercorporation is Alfred D. Chandler, *The Visible Hand: The Managerial Revolution in American Business* (1977), but Henry R. Seager and C. A. Gulick, Jr., *Trust and Corporation Problems* (1929), is still useful. See also Arthur F. Burns, *The Decline of Competition* (1936); Ralph L. Nelson, *Merger Movements in American Industry, 1895-1956* (1959); Adolf A. Berle, Jr., and G. C. Means, *The Modern Corporation and Private Property* (1932); G. Warren Nutter, *The Extent of Enterprise Monopoly in the United States, 1899-1939* (1951); Louis Galambos, *Competition and Cooperation: The Emergence of a National Trade Association* (1966); Federal Trade Commission, *The Merger Movement* (1948); Thurman W. Arnold, *The Bottlenecks of Business* (1940); Walton H. Hamilton, *Antitrust in Action* (1940); and Corwin D. Edwards, *Maintaining Competition* (1949).

Frederick Lewis Allen's racy *The Lords of Creation* (1935) gives special attention to the financial leaders during this period. Indispensable general works for the serious student are George W. Edwards, *The Evolution of Finance Capitalism* (1938); Margaret G. Myers, *A Financial History of the United States* (1970); and Vincent P. Carosso, *Investment Banking in America: A History* (1970). For specialized studies, see C. A. E. Goodhart, *The New York Money Market and the Finance of Trade, 1900-1913* (1969); Cedric B. Cowing, *Populists, Plungers, and Progressives: A Social History of Stock and Commodity Speculation, 1890-1913* (1965); Louis D. Brandeis, *Other People's Money, and How the Bankers Use It* (1914), which summarizes the findings of the Pujo committee in 1913; Henry L. Staples and Alpheus T. Mason, *The Fall of a Railroad Empire* (1947), the story of J. P. Morgan and the New Haven Railroad; William Z. Ripley, *Main Street and Wall Street* (1927); Ferdinand Pecora, *Wall Street Under Oath* (1939); J. T. Flynn, *Security Speculation* (1934); S. E. Harris, *Twenty Years of Federal Reserve Policy* (2 vols., 1933); and Elmus R. Wicker, *Federal Reserve Monetary Policy, 1917-1933* (1966).

Excellent surveys and special studies of the technological revolution are Elting E. Morison, *From Know-How to Nowhere: The Development of American Technology* (1974); John W. Oliver, *History of American Technology* (1956); Leonard S. Silk, *The Research Revolution* (1960); and Harry Jerome, *Mechanization in Industry* (1934).

Biographies are often the most palatable form of economic history for the general reader. Frederick Lewis Allen, *The Great Pierpont Morgan* (1949), and Lewis Corey, *The House of Morgan* (1930), reveal different points of view about the great financier. Allan Nevins, *Study in Power: John D. Rockefeller, Industrialist and Philanthropist* (2 vols., 1953), is as much a history of the American oil industry as a biography of its master builder, just as his *Ford, the Times, the Man, the Company* (1954) tells the saga of the automobile industry. For the leaders in iron, steel, and tobacco, see Joseph Frazier Wall, *Andrew Carnegie* (1970); Ida M.

Tarbell, *The Life of Elbert H. Gary* (1925); and Robert F. Durden, *The Dukes of Durham, 1865-1929* (1975).

C. *Labor from Roosevelt to Roosevelt*

There are brief discussions in Harold U. Faulkner, *Decline of Laissez Faire, 1897-1917* (1951); George Soule, *Prosperity Decade: From War to Depression, 1917-1929* (1947); Philip Taft, *Organized Labor in American History* (1964); and Henry Pelling, *American Labor* (1960). However, the third and fourth volumes of John R. Commons et al., *History of Labour in the United States* (4 vols., 1918-1935), and Philip Taft, *The A. F. of L. in the Time of Gompers* (1957), are the best general works for the period.

Daniel T. Rodgers, *The Work Ethic in Industrial America, 1850-1920* (1978), is a magnificent study which explains why American labor did not take the road of socialism. For detailed and specialized studies of unionization, union politics, and labor struggles, see Melvyn Dubofsky, *When Workers Organize: New York City in the Progressive Era* (1968); Lewis L. Lorwin, *The American Federation of Labor* (1933); Leo Wolman, *The Growth of American Trade Unions, 1880-1923* (1924); Marguerite Green, *The National Civic Federation and the American Labor Movement, 1900-1925* (1956); David Brody, *Steelworkers in America: The Nonunion Era* (1960); and Marc Karson, *American Labor Unions and Politics, 1900-1918* (1958). See also Louis Adamic, *Dynamite, the Story of Class Violence in America* (1934); Samuel Yellen, *American Labor Struggles* (1936); Stanley Buder, *Pullman: An Experiment in Industrial Order and Community Planning, 1880-1930* (1967); and George S. McGovern and Leonard F. Guttridge, *The Great Coalfield War* (1972), on the Colorado coal strike of 1913-1914.

Excellent for labor during the 1920s, the Great Depression, and the New Deal era are Irving Bernstein, *The Lean Years: A History of the American Worker, 1920-1933* (1960) and *Turbulent Years: A History of the American Worker, 1933-1941* (1970), but see also James O. Morris, *Conflict Within the AFL: A Study of Craft Versus Industrial Unionism, 1901-1938* (1958); Walter Galenson, *The CIO Challenge to the AFL: A History of the American Labor Movement, 1935-1941* (1960); Sidney Fine, *The Automobile Under the Blue Eagle: Labor, Management, and the Automobile Manufacturing Code* (1963) and *Sit Down: The General Motors Strike of 1936-1937* (1969); Jerold S. Auerbach, *Labor and Liberty: The La Follette Committee and the New Deal* (1966); David Brody, *The Butcher Workmen: A Study of Unionization* (1964); and Joel I. Seidman, *American Labor from Defense to Reconversion* (1953).

For specialized studies on hours and working conditions, see Albert Rees, *Real Wages in Manufacturing, 1890-1914* (1961); Solomon Fabricant, *Employment in Manufacturing, 1899-1939* (1942); and Robert M. Woodbury, *Workers' Health and Safety* (1927).

All the general and many of the special studies cited above include discussions of the development of public policy and judicial interpretation concerning labor unions. For judicial interpretation, the following monographs are excellent: Felix Frankfurter and N. Greene, *The Labor Injunction* (1930); Edward Berman, *Labor and the Sherman Act* (1930); Charles O. Gregory, *Labor and the Law* (1946); and Elias Lieberman, *Unions Before the Bar* (1950). Arthur S. Link, *Woodrow Wilson and the Progressive Era* (1954) and *Wilson: The New Freedom* (1956), discuss the labor policies of the Wilson administration, but for labor during the First World War, see Henry F. Pringle, *The Life and Times of William Howard Taft* (2 vols., 1939), and Alexander M. Bing, *War-Time Strikes and Their Adjustment* (1921). Concerning public policy during the New Deal, Carroll R. Daugherty, *Labor Under the N.R.A.* (1934), is a contemporary survey, while Robert R. R. Brooks, *When Labor Organizes* (1937) and *Unions of Their Own Choosing* (1939), survey the impact of the Wagner Act. J. Joseph Huthmacher, *Senator Robert F. Wagner and the Rise of Urban Liberalism* (1968), is excellent for the writing of labor's charter of liberties.

The history of the labor movement since 1900 is writ large in the memoirs and biographies of its leaders. Samuel Gompers, *Seventy Years of Life and Labor* (2 vols., 1925), is one of the great autobiographies in American literature. See also Bernard Mandel, *Samuel Gompers: A Biography* (1963). Elsie Glück, *John Mitchell, Miner* (1929), and Hyman Weintraub, *Andrew Furuseth: Emancipator of the Seamen* (1959), illuminate the careers of two wise leaders. James A. Wechsler, *Labor Baron: A Portrait of John L. Lewis* (1944), and Saul D. Alinsky, *John L. Lewis: An Unauthorized Biography* (1949), present radically different portraits of the stormy petrel of the twentieth-century labor movement. Matthew Josephson, *Sidney Hillman: Statesman of American Labor* (1952), is an important if uncritical contribution, while Charles A. Madison, *American Labor Leaders* (1950), is also useful. Robert L. Tyler, *Walter Reuther* (1973), is a fine biography of the most important American labor leader since John L. Lewis. David Dubinsky and A. H. Raskin, *David Dubinsky: A Life with Labor* (1977), provides another interesting portrait of the labor movement in the interwar years through the eyes of one of its leaders.

D. *Immigration and Its Impact on American Society*

Carl Wittke, *We Who Built America* (1939); George M. Stephenson, *History of American Immigration, 1820-1924* (1926); Oscar Handlin, *The American People in the Twentieth Century* (1954); and Leonard Dinnerstein and David M. Reimers, *Ethnic Americans: A History of Immigration and Assimilation* (1975), are the standard surveys, but John R. Commons, *Races and Immigrants in America* (1907), is still useful. Louis Adamic, *From Many Lands* (1940), and Oscar Handlin, *The Uprooted* (1951), highlight the impact of the uprooting upon the immigrants and their contributions to American life. Good specialized studies are Humbert S. Nelli, *The Italians in Chicago, 1880-1930* (1970); John M. Allswang, *A House for All Peoples: Ethnic Politics in Chicago, 1890-1936* (1970); Rowland T. Berthoff, *British Immigrants in Industrial America, 1790-1950* (1953); Theodore Saloutos, *They Remember America: The Story of the Repatriated Greek-American* (1956); Carl Wittke, *The Irish in America* (1956); and William I. Thomas and Florian Znaniecki, *The Polish Peasant in Europe and America* (2 vols., 1927). John Higham, *Send These to Me: Jews and Other Immigrants in Urban America* (1975), is the authoritative work on this subject.

Most of the works on immigration policy reflect the controversial aspects of the issue, but Roy L. Garis, *Immigration Restriction* (1927), and William S. Bernard, *American Immigration Policy* (1950), are thorough and objective. John Higham,

Strangers in the Land, Patterns of American Nativism, 1860-1925 (1955), concentrates on nativism in the twentieth century. A pioneer study of anti-Semitism in higher education is Marcia G. Synnott, *The Half-Opened Door: Discrimination and Admissions at Harvard, Yale, and Princeton, 1900-1970* (1979). Roger Daniels, *The Politics of Prejudice: The Anti-Japanese Movement in California and the Struggle for Japanese Exclusion* (1962), is excellent.

4. SOCIAL AND INTELLECTUAL MAIN CURRENTS IN AMERICAN LIFE, 1900-1945

A. Social Trends and Changes

Daniel J. Boorstin, *The Americans: The Democratic Experience* (1973), is a fascinating discussion of many recent social changes placed within the larger context of the period since the Civil War. Harold U. Faulkner, *The Quest for Social Justice, 1898-1914* (1931); Preston W. Slosson, *The Great Crusade and After, 1914-1928* (1930); Lloyd R. Morris, *Postscript to Yesterday* (1947); and Frederick Lewis Allen, *The Big Change: America Transforms Itself, 1900-1950* (1952), are excellent general surveys emphasizing manners and ideas. Mark Sullivan, *Our Times: The United States, 1900-1925* (6 vols., 1926-1935), contains a wealth of social history, as does Walter Lord, *The Good Years: From 1900 to the First World War* (1960). Most helpful for understanding prewar social and intellectual currents is Henry F. May, *The End of American Innocence: A Study of the First Years of Our Own Time, 1912-1917* (1959). See also Nathan G. Hale, Jr., *Freud Comes to America* (1971); John C. Burnham, *Psychoanalysis and American Medicine, 1894-1918* (1967); Dorothy Ross, *G. Stanley Hall: The Psychologist as Prophet* (1972); Richard Weiss, *The American Myth of Success: From Horatio Alger to Norman Vincent Peale* (1969); and James Harvey Young, *The Medical Messiahs: A Social History of Health Quackery in Twentieth-Century America* (1967). The best general survey of urbanization is Charles N. Glaab and A. Theodore Brown, *A History of Urban America* (1976), but see also Zane L. Miller, *The Urbanization of Modern America* (1973). The subject of childhood in American history is at an incipient stage. Joseph F. Kett, *Rites of Passage: Adolescence in America 1790 to the Present* (1977), is the best and most comprehensive study, but also useful are Fred M. Hechinger and Grace Hechinger, *Growing Up in America* (1975), and Robert H. Bremner et al., *Children and Youth in America* (4 vols., 1974).

The following works illuminate social and intellectual main currents of the 1920s and 1930s: President's Committee, *Recent Social Trends in the United States* (2 vols., 1933); Dixon Wecter, *The Age of the Great Depression, 1929-1941* (1948); Frederick Lewis Allen, *Only Yesterday, an Informal History of the Nineteen-Twenties* (1931) and *Since Yesterday: The Nineteen-Thirties in America* (1940); Robert S. and Helen M. Lynd, *Middletown* (1929) and *Middletown in Transition* (1937); James W. Prothro, *The Dollar Decade: Business Ideas in the 1920's* (1954); Sigmund Diamond, *The Reputation of the American Businessman* (1955); Harold E. Stearns, *America Now* (1938); Ruth Lindquist, *The Family in the Present Social Order* (1931); Foster R. Dulles, *America Learns to Play* (1940); G. J. Stigler, *Domestic Servants in the United States, 1900-1940* (1946); and David

L. Cohn, *Combustion on Wheels, an Informal History of the Automobile Age* (1944).

B. *Currents of American Thought*

Herbert W. Schneider, *A History of American Philosophy* (1946); Merle Curti, *The Growth of American Thought* (1964); and Ralph H. Gabriel, *The Course of American Democratic Thought* (1956), discuss important developments since the 1890s. Henry S. Commager, *The American Mind* (1950), is also general in scope.

For specialized studies, see Morton White, *Social Thought in America* (1949); Joseph Dorfman, *The Economic Mind in American Civilization* (5 vols., 1946-1959); Sidney Hook, *John Dewey* (1939); Donald B. Meyer, *The Positive Thinkers* (1966); R. Wilson Jackson, *In Quest of Community: Social Philosophy in the United States, 1860-1920* (1968); John Tipple, *The Capitalist Revolution: A History of American Social Thought 1890-1919* (1970); John P. Diggins, *The Bard of Savagery: Thorstein Veblen and Modern Social Theory* (1978); and Arthur A. Ekirch, Jr., *Ideologies and Utopias: The Impact of the New Deal on American Thought* (1969). Harold E. Stearns (ed.), *Civilization in the United States* (1922); Joseph Wood Krutch, *The Modern Temper* (1929); and Walter Lippmann, *A Preface to Morals* (1929), summarize the intellectual discontent of the 1920s.

C. *American Education*

Of all the major fields of American history, the history of education is most neglected. Among the general surveys, Ellwood P. Cubberly, *Public Education in the United States* (1934); Stuart G. Noble, *A History of American Education* (1938); and Edgar W. Knight, *Education in the United States* (1951), are the best. Isaac L. Kandel (ed.), *Twenty-Five Years of American Education* (1924), has excellent chapters on developments during the first two decades of this century, but see especially his thoughtful *American Education in the Twentieth Century* (1957). Lawrence A. Cremin, *The Transformation of the School: Progressivism in American Education, 1876-1957* (1961), is excellent social history, while Laurence R. Vesey, *The Emergence of the American University* (1965), is superb.

Among the specialized studies, President's Committee, *Recent Social Trends in the United States* (2 vols., 1933), is very informative about developments in the twenties. Malcolm W. Willey (ed.), *Depression, Recovery, and Higher Education* (1933); Isaac L. Kandel, *The End of an Era* (1941); and Hollis P. Allen, *The Federal Government and Education* (1950), are useful for the depression and the impact of federal aid in the 1930s. Isaac L. Kandel, *The Impact of the War upon American Education* (1948), is a good source for the period of the Second World War.

D. *American Religious Institutions and Thought*

Sydney E. Ahlstrom, *A Religious History of the American People* (1972), and James W. Smith and A. Leland Jamison (eds.), *Relgion in American Life* (4 vols., 1961), are the best introductions. The two bibliographical volumes in the latter are particularly helpful. William W. Sweet, *The Story of Religion in America* (1939); Winthrop S. Hudson, *Religion in America* (1973); Robert T. Handy, *A Christian*

America: Protestant Hopes and Historical Realities (1971); Martin E. Marty, *Righteous Empire: The Protestant Experience in America* (1970); Jerald C. Brauer, *Protestantism in America* (1953); and Clifton E. Olmstead, *History of Religion in the United States* (1960), cover the period, but more detailed are Herbert W. Schneider, *Religion in Twentieth Century America* (1952), and Willard Sperry, *Religion in America* (1945). Other useful special works are Thomas T. McAvoy, *A History of the Catholic Church in the United States* (1969); John T. Ellis, *American Catholicism* (1956); Will Herberg, *Protestant, Catholic, Jew* (1955); Nathan Glazer, *American Judaism* (1957); Joseph L. Blau, *Judaism in America* (1976); Melvin L. Urofsky, *American Zionism from Herzl to the Holocaust* (1976); Naomi W. Cohen, *American Jews and the Zionist Idea* (1975); Winthrop S. Hudson, *American Protestantism* (1961); and Kenneth K. Bailey, *Southern White Protestantism in the Twentieth Century* (1964). William G. McLoughlin, Jr., *Modern Revivalism* (1959) and *Billy Sunday Was His Real Name* (1955), are superb on twentieth-century revivalism. Gerald B. Smith (ed.), *Religious Thought in the Last Quarter-Century* (1927), and Arnold S. Nash (ed.), *Protestant Thought in the Twentieth Century* (1951), are both very useful. Charles A. Braden, *These Also Believe* (1949), is an account of the sects along the frontier of Protestantism. Norman F. Furniss, *The Fundamentalist Controversy, 1918-1931* (1954), should be supplemented by Ernest R. Sandeen, *The Roots of Fundamentalism: British and American Millenarianism, 1800-1930* (1970).

Excellent for the awakening of the church's social conscience in the progressive era are Charles H. Hopkins, *The Rise of the Social Gospel in American Protestantism, 1865-1915* (1940); Aaron I. Abell, *The Urban Impact on American Protestantism, 1865-1900* (1943); Henry F. May, *Protestant Churches and Industrial America* (1949); Aaron I. Abell, *American Catholicism and Social Action* (1960); Herbert A. Wisbey, Jr., *Soldiers Without Swords: A History of the Salvation Army in the United States* (1955); Charles H. Hopkins, *History of the Y. M. C. A. in North America* (1951); Jacob Henry Dorn, *Washington Gladden: Prophet of the Social Gospel* (1967); Dores R. Sharpe, *Walter Rauschenbusch* (1942); and Ronald C. White, Jr., and C. Howard Hopkins, *The Social Gospel: Religion and Reform in Changing America* (1976).

Robert M. Miller, *American Protestantism and Social Issues, 1919-1939* (1958); Paul A. Carter, *The Decline and Revival of the Social Gospel, 1920-1940* (1956); and David J. O'Brien, *American Catholics and Social Reform: The New Deal Years* (1968), are excellent for the Social Gospel during the 1920s and beyond. For American religious thought during this period, see Donald B. Meyer, *The Protestant Search for Political Realism, 1919-1941* (1960).

E. American Writing

For significant work in fiction, poetry, and drama, see the relevant sections in this volume. The following list includes only general works and omits critical studies of individual writers.

The basic general history is Robert E. Spiller et al., *Literary History of the United States* (1963), which contains discussions of virtually every American writer worthy of mention, lengthy essays on major writers, and a good bibliography. For general works on fictional writing, see Leon Howard, *Literature and the American Tradition* (1960); Willard Thorp, *American Writing in the Twentieth*

Century (1960); and Frederick J. Hoffman, *The Modern Novel in America, 1900-1950* (1951), all brief but incisive surveys. For more specialized studies, see Walter F. Taylor, *The Economic Novel in America* (1942); Walter B. Rideout, *The Radical Novel in the United States, 1900-1954* (1956); Alfred Kazin, *On Native Grounds* (1942); Malcolm Cowley, *Exile's Return: A Literary Odyssey of the 1920's* (1951); John W. Aldridge, *After the Lost Generation* (1951); Leo Gurko, *The Angry Decade* (1947); and F. Garvin Davenport, Jr., *The Myth of Southern History: Historical Consciousness in Twentieth-Century Southern Literature* (1970). Alan S. Downer, *Fifty Years of American Drama, 1900-1950* (1951), and Louise Bogan, *Achievement in American Poetry, 1900-1950* (1951), cover the main currents in their respective fields. James O. Young, *Black Writers of the Thirties* (1973), is excellent on that subject.

F. American Blacks, 1900-1920

There is a rewarding, rich, and fast-growing literature in this field. The best guide is James W. McPherson et al., *Blacks in America: Bibliographical Essays* (1971). Rayford W. Logan, *The Negro in American Life and Thought: The Nadir, 1877-1901* (1954) and *The Betrayal of the Negro from Rutherford B. Hayes to Woodrow Wilson* (1965), and C. Vann Woodward, *The Strange Career of Jim Crow* (1974), provide background discussions for twentieth-century developments. General histories abound, but the best are John Hope Franklin, *From Slavery to Freedom: A History of American Negroes* (1974); August Meier and E. M. Rudwick, *From Plantation to Ghetto: An Interpretive History of American Negroes* (1976); and Lawrence W. Levine, *Black Culture and Black Consciousness: Afro-American Folk Thought from Slavery to Freedom* (1977). Other useful general volumes are Gunnar Myrdal, *An American Dilemma* (2 vols., 1944), a massive, penetrating study; Arnold M. Rose, *The Negro in America* (1948), an abridgment of Myrdal's volumes; E. Franklin Frazier, *The Negro Family in the United States* (1939) and *The Negro Church in America* (1973); Charles S. Johnson, *Patterns of Negro Segregation* (1943); John Hope Franklin and Isidore Starr, *The Negro in Twentieth Century America: A Reader on the Struggle for Civil Rights* (1967); S. P. Fullinwider, *The Mind and Mood of Black America: 20th Century Thought* (1969); August Meier and E. M. Rudwick (eds.), *The Making of Black America* (2 vols., 1969); August Meier and E. M. Rudwick, *Along the Color Line: Explorations in the Black Experience* (1976); August Meier, *Negro Thought in America, 1880-1915* (1963); Francis L. Broderick and August Meier (eds.), *Negro Protest Thought in the Twentieth Century* (1970); and Talcott Parsons and Kenneth B. Clark (eds.), *The Negro American* (1966).

For black movements and militancy and the Negro in politics during the first two decades of the twentieth century, see Samuel R. Spencer, Jr., *Booker T. Washington* (1955); Charles F. Kellogg, *NAACP: A History, Volume I: 1909-1920* (1967); Nancy J. Weiss, *The National Urban League, 1910-1940* (1974); Robert L. Jack, *History of the National Association for the Advancement of Colored People* (1943); Walter White, *A Man Called White* (1948); Arvarh E. Strickland, *History of the Chicago Urban League* (1966); E. David Cronon, *Black Moses: The Story of Marcus Garvey* (1955); W. E. B. Du Bois, *Dusk of Dawn* (1940) and *The Autobiography of W. E. B. Du Bois* (1968); Francis L. Broderick, *W. E. B. Du Bois: Negro Leader in a Time of Crisis* (1959); Shirley Graham, *Du Bois, His Day Is*

Marching On: A Memoir of W. E. B. Du Bois (1971); Andrew Buni, *Robert L. Vann of the Pittsburgh Courier: Politics and Black Journalism* (1974); Stephen R. Fox, *The Guardian of Boston: William Monroe Trotter* (1970); Jervis Anderson, *A. Philip Randolph* (1973); Margaret L. Callcott, *The Negro in Maryland Politics, 1870-1912* (1969); and Henry L. Moon, *Balance of Power: The Negro Vote* (1948). William B. Hixson, Jr., *Moorefield Storey and the Abolitionist Tradition* (1972), is excellent on a white leader of the early civil rights movement.

The following is an incomplete list of specialized studies: Edwin S. Redkey, *Black Exodus: Black Nationalist and Back-to-Africa Movements, 1890-1910* (1969); John D. Weaver, *The Brownsville Raid* (1970); Gilbert Osofsky, *Harlem: The Making of a Ghetto* (1966); Seth M. Scheiner, *Negro Mecca: A History of the Negro in New York City, 1865-1920* (1965); Allan H. Spear, *Black Chicago: The Making of a Negro Ghetto, 1890-1920* (1967); Louis R. Harlan, *Separate and Unequal: Public School Campaigns and Racism in the Southern Seaboard States, 1901-1915* (1958); John Dittmer, *Black Georgia in the Progressive Era, 1900-1920* (1977); Thomas Cripps, *Slow Fade to Black: The Negro in American Film, 1900-1942* (1977); Daniel J. Leab, *From Sambo to Superspade: The Black Experience in Motion Pictures* (1975); Claude H. Nolen, *The Negro's Image in the South: The Anatomy of White Supremacy* (1967); Thomas F. Gossett, *Race: The History of an Idea in America* (1963); I. A. Newby, *The Development of Segregationist Thought* (1969) and *Jim Crow's Defense: Anti-Negro Thought in America, 1900-1930* (1965); and David M. Reimers, *White Protestantism and the Negro* (1965). Louise V. Kennedy, *The Negro Peasant Turns Cityward* (1930), and Ira DeA. Reid, *The Negro Immigrant* (1939), are both excellent for the black migration from the South during and after the First World War. Walter White, *Rope and Faggot* (1929), and Arthur F. Raper, *The Tragedy of Lynching* (1933), are both good on lynching in the twentieth century. Morton Sosna, *In Search of the Silent South: Southern Liberals and the Race Issue* (1977), is excellent for the beginnings of southern white liberal attitudes toward race.

Excellent specialized studies for the more recent period are Nathan I. Huggins, *Harlem Renaissance* (1972) and *Voices from the Harlem Renaissance* (1976); Wayne Cooper (ed.), *The Passion of Claude McKay* (1973); Dan Carter, *Scottsboro: A Tragedy of the American South* (1969); Raymond Wolters, *Negroes and the Great Depression* (1970); Horace R. Cayton and G. S. Mitchell, *Black Workers and the New Unions* (1939); Walter B. Weare, *Black Business in the New South: A Social History of the North Carolina Mutual Life Insurance Company* (1973); and Herbert R. Northrup, *Organized Labor and the Negro* (1944).

Index

About the Authors

ARTHUR S. LINK, who received his B.A. and Ph.D. from the University of North Carolina, is the George Henry Davis '86 Professor of American History at Princeton University and Director and Editor of *The Papers of Woodrow Wilson*. He has held Rockefeller, Guggenheim, and Rosenwald fellowships, in addition to memberships at the Institute for Advanced Study. He has been the Harmsworth Professor of American History at Oxford University and has lectured in South America, Japan, Western Europe, and Poland. Two of his many books have been awarded The Bancroft Prize, and he has received six honorary degrees. He is a member of and has been an officer of many professional societies and is a past president of the Southern Historical Association and the Association for Documentary Editing.

WILLIAM B. CATTON received his A.B. and M.A. from the University of Maryland and his Ph.D. from Northwestern University. He has taught at Northwestern University, the University of Maryland, Princeton University, and since 1964, at Middlebury College, where he has been Charles A. Dana Professor of American History and Chairman of the Division of the Social Sciences. Currently he is Professor Emeritus and Historian in Residence. He is coauthor, with Bruce Catton, of *Two Roads to Sumter* and *The Bold and Magnificent Dream: America's Founding Years 1492–1815*.

A Note on the Type

The text of this book is set in CALEDONIA, a Linotype face designed by W. A. Dwiggins. It belongs to the family of printing types called "modern face" by printers—a term used to mark the change in style of typeletters that occurred about 1800. Caledonia borders on the general design of Scotch Modern, but is more freely drawn than that letter.

This version of Caledonia was set by a computer-driven cathode ray tube by Lehigh/Rocappi from input provided by Random House/Alfred A. Knopf, Inc.

Printed and bound by R. R. Donnelley & Sons, Crawfordsville, Ind.